A
QUESTION
OF
MANHOOD

BLACKS IN THE DIASPORA
Darlene Clark Hine, John McCluskey, Jr.,
and David Barry Gaspar

GENERAL EDITORS

A
QUESTION
OF
MANHOOD

A Reader in U.S.

Black Men's

History and Masculinity

VOLUME 1

"Manhood Rights": The Construction of
Black Male History and Manhood, 1750–1870

Edited by
Darlene Clark Hine and Earnestine Jenkins

INDIANA UNIVERSITY PRESS   BLOOMINGTON & INDIANAPOLIS

This book is a publication of

Indiana University Press
601 North Morton Street
Bloomington, IN 47404-3797 USA
http://www.indiana.edu/~iupress

Telephone orders   800-842-6796
Fax orders   812-855-7931
Orders by e-mail   iuporder@indiana.edu

Library of Congress Cataloging-in-Publication Data

A question of manhood : a reader in U.S. Black men's history and
masculinity / edited by Darlene Clark Hine and Earnestine Jenkins.
        p.   cm. — (Blacks in the diaspora)
Includes bibliographical references and index.
Contents: v. 1. Manhood rights —
ISBN 0-253-33639-2 (v. 1 : alk. paper). — ISBN 0-253-21343-6
(v. 1 : pbk. : alk. paper)
1. Afro-American men—History. 2. Masculinity—United States—
History.   I. Hine, Darlene Clark.   II. Jenkins, Earnestine.
III. Series.
E185.86.Q46   1999
305.38'896073—dc21   99-24464

1 2 3 4 5   04 03 02 01 00 99

IN MEMORY OF OUR FATHERS

CONTENTS

FOREWORD

The time has arrived for a more balanced view of African American men. The explosion of gender studies over the last two decades has played a crucial role in changing how we conceive of women and gender relations. The resulting body of literature, in conjunction with the great social movements of the 1960s and 1970s, has torn asunder the antiquated views of women that were routinely produced by long-standing patriarchal structures and practices. Moreover, we are beginning to understand that the beliefs and actions of human beings are shaped and influenced at a deep level by gender, class, and race dynamics. This view is now so entrenched that the trilogy of race, class, and gender has become the touchstone of modern social scientific discourse. This new conceptual lens has enabled us to produce far more complex and nuanced accounts of human behavior.

Nevertheless, this conceptual trilogy is often applied in such a faddish and mechanical fashion that it renders obscure the very dynamics that analysts seek to illuminate. There can be little doubt that the concept of "gender" usually invokes images of femaleness, and of women's influence on social behavior and the major contributions they have made. It is as if women have "gender" while men are simply men.

To be sure, some accounts imply that men are gendered beings, and a few even address the issue explicitly. But if substantial progress is to be made analytically, the idea that men and their behavior are gendered must take center stage. This is especially true if we are to advance our understanding of the African American male. If the goal is to shed light on Black manhood, we need to take up the challenge presented by this volume and develop a gendered perspective of Black men through history.

In America, the word "man" conjures up dual images. On the one hand, a man is a conqueror, a protector of turf, tough, physically strong, selfish, emotionally cold, and possessed of a strong need to be in control. This conception can be labeled the negative male image. On the other hand, a man is brave, courageous, bound by noble principles, a provider, someone who is governed by reason and intellect and who possesses a tender heart underneath a rugged exterior. This conception can be labeled the positive, enno-

bling male image. In the popular imagination, any given male may personi-
fy either set of these characteristics, or he may combine them or alternate
between them, depending on the situation. The important point is that these
"male" characteristics are derived from a gendering process that determines
what it means to be a man.

The editors of this volume are well aware that the negative male image
is the one most often associated with African American men. Indeed, the
popular imagination, the media, and social science literature have focused
on the Black male as criminal, violent, family deserter, lazy and shiftless
predator, and extremely self-centered. Typically he is thought to be a crea-
ture of emotion and impulse rather than intellect. In short, African American males emerge from these venues as dangerous, menacing, and a drain
on the resources of the larger society. Their rates of incarceration and homicide appear to confirm the validity of the negative Black male image. In the
words of the editors, academia has been obsessed with portraying Black men
as a sociological ill.

However, the fact that most Black men are hard workers and are committed to the preservation of their families at any cost is obvious to any serious
observer of the Black community. Black men are widely committed to religious values, and many of them care about the well-being of their neighborhoods and embrace self-help strategies designed to stabilize and advance
their communities. A large proportion of Black men, like Black women,
have always been strong advocates of education, seeing it as the most important means of attaining social mobility and respectability. Black men value
their roles as fathers, sons, husbands, brothers, lovers, and loyal friends.
Similarly, the historical record is clear that throughout the Black American
experience, large numbers of Black males have pursued freedom and equality as their most precious goals, and have not hesitated to resist white domination even at the risk of death. Clearly, Black men have also embraced the
noble side of the notion of what it means to be a man.

Scholarship on the Black community, whether radical or conservative,
feminist or gender-neutral, has largely ignored this side of the Black male
experience. The cost has been enormous, for this vacuum has led to the
ongoing false portrayal of Black men as the lesser side of humanity, while
simultaneously elevating white men, perhaps unwittingly, to a lofty perch
where they are depicted as complex beings who are equally capable of being
brutish and noble.

Darlene Clark Hine and Earnestine Jenkins, as well as the numerous
contributors to this volume, have begun to address this lacuna. They have
chosen to present the ennobling side of the Black male experience. They do
so because this aspect of Black manhood exists as a social fact, and because
this approach helps to discredit the overall conception of the Black man as
sociological ill.

The essays herein examine the noble behavior and values of Black males
in the eighteenth century and the decades surrounding the Civil War. By

presenting essays that reveal the gendered dimensions of Black males, Hine and Jenkins provide valuable insights into what it meant to be a Black man during a terrible time in our nation's history. An important goal of slavery was to prevent the emergence of a sense of Black manhood. The slaveholders realized that the solidification of a robust Black masculinity could prove detrimental to the institution of slavery.

This volume makes it clear that despite the aims of the slaveholders, a strong and noble sense of what it meant to be a Black male developed in the eighteenth century among both slaves and free Blacks. While this conception of manliness had in some instances been transported from Africa, it was during the regime of slavery that it took deep root and flourished. The driving force behind this manhood was the idea that freedom, equality, and masculine pride were the ultimate values for a man to pursue.

The essays that Hine and Jenkins have chosen to include show how Black males of the period pursued these values in the context of work, culture, military action, and resistance, including slave revolts. In these public spheres the challenge for the Black male was to perform superbly and eventually emerge victorious. Black men believed that such triumphs would hasten the day when they and their families and the larger slave community would achieve emancipation. Thus active resistance to slavery became a central activity for them and the defining characteristic of their manhood.

This volume teaches us that the Black experience—indeed, the human experience—cannot be fully comprehended outside the gendered context in which it is embedded. Human ideals have always served as a springboard for action, and such ideals are deeply influenced by a gendering process. A deeper understanding of how Black men in earlier centuries conceived of their gender-related responsibilities enables us to understand the true motivation for so many of their activities as workers and freedom fighters—the belief that to do less meant to be less than men.

A *Question of Manhood* reveals that gendering is a social process. Gendered roles and identities contain both noble and retrogressive ideals. By examining these dimensions of the human experience, we can begin to probe the social conditions that favor the enactment of noble ideals and that minimize the realization of factors that lead to human misery. By utilizing a gendered perspective, this volume shows that Black men have embraced ennobling gender ideals, and in doing so have elevated humanity. This realization alone is a major step forward.

—ALDON D. MORRIS

PREFACE

DARLENE CLARK HINE AND EARNESTINE JENKINS

Class, race, and gender. These pivotal categories of analysis have come to permeate our view of the world in the second half of the twentieth century. Now, as the century comes to an end, the last of them is finally being applied to our view of the past. In the past few decades, the field of women's studies has caused a conceptual shift in scholarly thought, focusing for the first time on gender as a crucial category of historical analysis. Women's historians have shown that gender is as important as race and class in understanding the past and comprehending modern society, and historians in all fields have been forced to acknowledge that men not only are as influenced by their gender as women, but have actively participated in a history of gender construction, shaped by certain prevailing notions about what it means to be a man in American society and culture.

However, although there is no dearth of historical studies concerning individual "great" men—and/or the world viewed from a generic male perspective—few have examined men as gendered beings, whose lives and actions have been shaped by specific constructs of masculine identity and manhood. Historian Bruce Dorsey declares in the journal *Radical History Review* (1996) that the main task lying before historians of gender is the "intellectual quest to engender all of American history," and men's studies has only recently begun that task. Most of men's studies is situated in the present and, having been very much influenced by the feminist movement, is concerned with modern-day male behavior, in particular the ramifications of white male dominance and its legacy. It is necessary now for historians to demonstrate how concepts of manhood have been subject to change over time. Throughout American history, social, economic, and political changes—along with race, class, and even sexuality and region of birth—have all influenced the development of gender systems.

At present, there still exist only a few dozen monographs that have attempted to add a historical context to men's studies. Among the representative and innovative works are Peter Stearns's *Be a Man! Males in Modern*

Society (1979); *Him/Her/Self: Sex Roles in Modern America* by Peter Filene (1986); *The American Man*, edited by Joseph and Elizabeth Pleck (1980); and *Manhood in America* by Michael Kimmel (1996). Stearns deals with how the roles of middle- and lower-class men have changed since the eighteenth century, concluding that industrialization created more rigid gender roles for men and women. Filene analyzes masculine behavior from the late nineteenth century to the present in the context of the family, work, war, sexuality, and social reform movements. *The American Man* offers a new periodization, dividing men's history into Agrarian Patriarchy (1630–1820), the Commercial Age (1820–1860), the Strenuous Life (1861–1919), and Compassionate Providing (1920–1965). Kimmel's work examines the changing culture of masculinity, suggesting that being required to "prove" manhood eventually became a dominant theme in American history. He goes on to describe how this particular idea paralleled the rise of capitalism in U.S. society, leading to the construction of a hegemonic manhood bereft of a strong inner self and making manhood into a "possession" that males are forced to "acquire."

The methodologies and topics covered in these texts are indicative of the direction in which historical men's studies are headed, influenced significantly by social history. In the past, traditional historical scholarship focused on the public accomplishments of great men, a perspective that marginalized or even completely obscured certain groups of men and women. This view also negated the importance of collective identities and group action on the part of those who were considered minor players in American history. Contemporary men's studies have begun to investigate the experiences of working-class men, as well as the middle class and the elite. This social historical approach has highlighted the role of gender in class formation and the politics of power. It has revealed the existence of hegemonic masculinities lying at the heart of social distinctions that are divisive within groups of men and groups of women, even as they divide men from women.

Social history has also focused our attention on race. As a result, the field of men's studies has begun serious research into the life experiences of African American men. Actually, few groups have received as much public scrutiny as black men. This is understandable, given that being black and male in America has always been, as social philosopher Kenneth Clatterbaugh says in *Contemporary Perspectives on Masculinity* (1997), a "sociopolitical issue." Unfortunately, however, past and present scholarship has been obsessed with black men as a sociological ill. Since the early twentieth century, academe has been influenced by schools of thought that portrayed black people as America's great social problem, drawing attention away from the real culprit, racial oppression. Within that theoretical framework, the few contemporary academic studies on black men have for the most part been written by those outside their experience, who see only the impact of historical oppression, drugs, imprisonment, fatherlessness, or unemploy-

ment. It is no surprise, then, that black manhood has been stereotyped as a
negative and dismal experience.

In *Slim's Table: Race, Respectability, and Masculinity*, sociologist Mitchell
Duneier admits that sociological research has produced invaluable insights
into the lives of black men. But he describes how the discipline has also
contributed to one-dimensional images of the black man as hustler and
criminal, navigating his way through the mire of the urban ghetto. These
contemporary images of a negative, self-destructive black masculinity tend
to validate historical assumptions about black men as violent, oversexed,
ignorant, and immoral beings. Certainly there should be serious concern
about the status of all groups of black men and women in American society,
but to present only the negative is simply not historically accurate. What it
means to be a black man in America cannot be reduced to the sum total of
negative experiences and stereotypes.

*A Question of Manhood: A Reader in U.S. Black Men's History and
Masculinity* is a wide-ranging exploration of the history of African American
men from a gendered perspective. We need to examine black male behavior
in response to the dynamics of slavery and racial oppression across regions
and centuries. The essays in this anthology analyze how black masculinities
were constructed to resist the dominance of white middle-class male identity. However, it is well to underscore that the evolution of black manhood is
more than a history of public contests between white men and black men.
Clearly, by the early National era black men were born into existing slave
and free communities and cultures, where they first learned about manhood
from other black men and women, family members, friends, and community. Finally, just as the examination of black women's history and womanhood proved to be of transformative significance, the study of black men's
history and manhood is enormously instructive and will greatly facilitate the
ongoing project of reconstructing American history.

ACKNOWLEDGMENTS

It is exhilarating to complete a project and send a book out into the world to make its own way. Our pleasure is doubled by the opportunity now afforded to express, at last, our deep appreciation to a wonderful cadre of friends and colleagues for invaluable assistance with the preparation of *A Question of Manhood*.

We are especially appreciative of the many essential contributions made by Linda Werbish, Assistant to Darlene Clark Hine, that so effectively kept this project on track during the past four years. At Indiana University Press, Joan Catapano provided expert editorial guidance and words of encouragement at every stage in the process. We owe special praise and thanks to the talented graduate students in the Comparative Black History Ph.D. program at Michigan State University who helped with the research, photocopying, and critical readings of our essay: Kenneth Marshall, Julia Robinson-Harmon, Jacqueline McLeod, Hilary Jones, and Matthew Whitaker. We are grateful to Christopher Reed for generously allowing us to use the Civil War photograph and discharge papers of his great-grandfather. We appreciate the insightful comments that Kathleen Thompson, Joe Trotter, Robert L. Harris, Bill Lawson, and Aldon D. Morris made on early drafts of our essay. We treasure the support of our families.

INTRODUCTION

Black Men's History:
Toward a Gendered Perspective

DARLENE CLARK HINE AND EARNESTINE JENKINS

How do we determine how black men construct manhood and express masculinity? Specifically, what social, economic, political, and cultural forces have helped shape black male identity, and what has been the male-gendered response of black men to historical events and change? Answering these questions requires a historical approach to contemporary studies on black men. *A Question of Manhood: A Reader in U.S. Black Men's History and Masculinity* addresses a lacuna in gender studies. This reader is grounded in a sociohistorical approach. Major historical events and social phenomena are of course recognized as important influences on masculine and feminine behavior. Taking a cue from women's studies, historians of gender have learned that the private sphere—the realm of courtship and marriage, the home and family, men's relationship to women and to each other, sexuality, religious beliefs, and cultural expression—plays an equally important role in creating masculinities. *A Question of Manhood* provides a structure for the study of black men's history and manhood by examining themes in both these realms.

The simple fact is that enslavement and oppression have not kept black men from grappling with most of the same issues of manhood faced by other males in American society. The essays in this book acknowledge that black manhood in the United States is rooted in the slave experience, but they do not view the life that African Americans constructed under slavery as entirely delimiting or as entirely negative. Slavery generated a response in black men that can best be described as "resistant masculinity." American manhood has always been contested ground, and the ground on which black men were forced to assert their masculine identity was slavery.

THEMES IN THE HISTORY OF BLACK MASCULINITIES

Although few academics have studied black men from a clearly defined gender perspective, a significant number of scholars have evidenced a general historical interest in black men. This reader is the result of wide-ranging research through more than two hundred scholarly journals on all topics. It includes essays that range from the colonial era to the Civil War. These essays reveal that black men's history and manhood has been a diverse experience, multi-faceted and complex. Our initial exploration into the history of black masculinities has presented certain themes in the lives of black men that require further study. They include recognition of pre-existing notions about masculinity among the first Africans; the concept of gendered resistance and its influence on masculine behavior; the evolving role of American wars and the military as an important means of achieving freedom specific to black men; black men's complicated relationship to work and not owning their own labor; the impact of family and community on black male survival.

First, we cannot begin to understand what it means to be black and male in modern America without addressing the fact that, in spite of their status as an oppressed group, the first generations of African men and women arrived on these shores with certain established notions about gender roles and identity. These values and beliefs were the basis for constructing models of manhood that echoed hegemonic masculinities in America but were unique to the experiences of African Americans.

Then we must look at the ways black men resisted attempts by the white hegemony to negate their manhood from the very beginnings of their peculiarly American experience. Resistance is a dominant theme in the everyday experiences of eighteenth-century black men, slave or free. In the past, resistance was defined only as bloody revolt. Current scholarship, however, defines resistance as the myriad ways in which slaves and free people in the Americas, against all odds, kept alive the will to survive, for themselves and their descendants, with their humanity intact. It includes slave flight and revolt, sabotage and the destruction of property, the feigning of illness, manipulation and refusal to work, self-mutilation, suicide and even the killing of one's children, poisoning, physical and violent confrontation. Resistance is part of the complex dynamic between dominant and subordinate groups in society, and gender influenced both the decision to resist and the manner of resistance. In other words, black people did not let centuries of enslavement kill their hopes for freedom. Neither did slavery destroy black men and women's inherent identities as gendered human beings, with certain ideas, values, and beliefs that influenced how they responded to specific social/historical events.

AFRICAN MANHOOD

We can illustrate the theme of resistance for black men in early America by looking at one case study. "'Not Fade Away': The Narrative of Venture Smith, an African American in the Early Republic," by Robert E. Desrochers, Jr., is an insightful examination of the slave narrative as a means of investigating early African American consciousness and identity. It is equally useful for what it reveals about black manhood in this era. In addition, this representative look at one black man's life in the New Republic speaks to the continuing influence of an egalitarian ideal.

As Desrochers points out, Venture's autobiography actually predates the appearance of what literary specialists and historians call the slave narrative. Most of the nineteenth-century examples were antebellum works, published in the three decades before the Civil War and meant to further the abolitionist cause. The nineteenth-century slave narratives, written by formerly enslaved men and women like Frederick Douglass and Harriet Jacobs, have always incorporated resistance as a major theme, and freedom for all black people still enslaved as their ambitious goal. For this reason Desrochers points out what appears to be the absence of a strong resistance theme in Venture's narrative and suggests that the open expression of resistance or protest was too dangerous for the first black writers.

However, when one provides a gender framework for the Venture Smith narrative, it emerges as an open expression of the qualities that the author associates with his own manliness. Smith's narrative becomes not only a work of resistance, but a powerful use of his culture. It is a protest against America's attempts to destroy his manhood and humanity. His story is rich in information about conceptions of West African manhood that he brought with him as a youth, at the time of his capture and sale into slavery. Two elements stand out as major influences shaping Smith's understanding of manhood: his memories of his father as a male role model, and the existence of a strong, elite male culture among his people.

Smith's African name was Broteer. He was native to a small country in the kingdom of Bambara and an elite member of an ethnic group called the Mande. According to Venture, his father, Prince Saungm Furro, was an ideal man and an exemplary father who died in defense of his and his people's freedom. Saungm Furro was a man who valued freedom more than land, houses, or money. And he was known to be a man of integrity, truth, and good character. Smith's father taught him that it was important that a ruler, or a man who was to have power over other men, should first of all be an honorable man himself. He could then rule justly and well. A good ruler governed with reason and was not swayed by whim. He abused no one's rights, and he took the advice of old men. In short, the leader who wisely used power and authority and conducted himself with honor would be well respected in life by his subjects.

Oral tradition seems to have played a fundamental role in conveying societal concepts about great men and heroic deeds in Mande society. Mande was one of the eighteenth-century Savannah cultures descended from the great Mali empire in Senegal, founded by King Sundiata in the thirteenth century. A cultural institution of praise singers known as bards or griots occupied a key role in the preservation of memory, the reinterpretation of historical events, and the popularizing of ideas about heroic male behavior. A male child born into Mande society was expected to create his own reputation by surpassing the deeds of outstanding male heroes, especially his father. Mande men admired the rebel, or man of action, the type of man who was sung about in praise songs. In Mande culture, praise singing was itself a specifically male expression, wherein men sang about and honored the deeds of great men. From the way that Smith outlined his "masculinist" narrative, we might suggest that his story is equivalent to a Mande praise song. Smith shaped an acceptable and honorable male identity for himself by confronting his singular American experience with strength and resolve. The American slave experience certainly fit the requirements for a story of great trials and deeds.

For instance, Smith survived the Middle Passage and confronted whites when he thought they had exceeded their bounds in abusing their authority over him. He took up arms and defended himself when a young white man attacked him with a pitchfork and his second owner hit him with a bat. In the latter incident, Smith did not return the blows of his owner but dispossessed him of his weapon. He then took the weapon to white authorities, related the incident, and appealed to them for help in his defense. He did not receive it, but the important issue here is Smith's judicious handling of the situation as an enslaved man. On the surface, it may have looked as though he had no recourse at his disposal. But Smith still carried in his heart certain beliefs about manhood and the correct way to treat people. The message we get from his story is that he continued to hold these values dear because they provided him with the strength to keep believing in himself as a worthy man.

Smith conducted himself with equal honor in the defense of his wife. When his second owner's wife beat Meg with a whip, Smith once again did not meet violence with violence, but placed himself between his wife and the mistress. When she then began to flail him in turn, Smith snatched the whip and threw it into the fire. Each confrontational episode in Smith's life did much to bolster his self-esteem, thereby reinforcing the positive conception that he strove to hold on to of himself as a man.

Venture Smith's narrative also reveals much about the status of women and about relations between men and women in Mande society. Smith briefly informs us that his people practiced polygamy and that his father had two wives. Smith's mother once left Saungm Furro, taking the children back to her parents' household, when he took a third wife without her consent. She did not return until a year later, after Saungm Furro agreed to the terms of the original bridewealth. It seems that Smith's mother was exercising the autonomy and rights to property common to women in many West African societies.

In the past, scholars lacking a background in African history have surmised that such incidents were evidence that African women exercised power and autonomy in their societies uncommon among women in European cultures. However, even though some African women had the right to own property and were traditionally heavily involved in trade, few occupied positions of power that placed them in control of political and economic institutions. For the most part, all major positions of authority were reserved for and controlled by African men.

The visible presence of African women in the marketplace economy has also encouraged foreign scholars to exaggerate female power, or dominance, in African societies. If African women seemed to exercise a significant degree of autonomy working as traders, it is because women in the culture are expected to take on the major responsibility for their family's immediate needs. Smith's mother may have acted within certain inherent rights in Mande culture and society, but her rights extended only insofar as she was a member of a particular family lineage. She held no individual authority outside the extended African family structure. Smith does not even record his mother's name, which seems to reinforce the reality of her lower status as a female. In "Africa into the Americas?" in *More Than Chattel: Black Women and Slavery in the Americas* (1996), historian Claire Robertson clarifies women's status in Africa by explaining that while many West African societies are matrifocal, readily acknowledging a woman's spiritual powers, her ability to pass down culture, and her great influence upon children, few granted to women significant social, economic, or political power.

It should be understood, then, that patriarchal authority was the norm in Africa, and Venture Smith's narrative is very much centered upon the father figure as the locus of his male identity and ideas about manhood. He arrived in the Americas with certain notions about male and female roles that had much in common with European values and beliefs. Hence, at some level of his experience as a male slave and a free black man in the New Republic, he was able to find common ground with white men, and when he judged them in comparison with himself, Smith emerged the triumphant male. He not only created his own praise song, in which he surpassed his own father, but in a decidedly American way he became his own griot, or storyteller, in the process.

REBELS AND MAROON COMMUNITIES

Throughout the colonial era, black men openly expressed their anger and resentment toward the institution of slavery by establishing maroon communities, plotting rebellion, running away, and fighting in American wars. Jane Landers examines one of the earliest black male revolts and maroon communities in her essay "Gracia Real de Santa Teresa de Mose: A Free Black Town in Spanish Colonial Florida." Mose was the only free black town founded in the colonial South, and was a unique example of a frontier society.

Mose was started by runaway black men from South Carolina, many of them West Africans only recently arrived in the Americas. As enslaved men, they had fought in the Yamassee Indian War of 1715 against the British. When the Yamassee were defeated, their slave allies escaped to St. Augustine, Florida. Over a period of ten years or so, more runaways escaped to Florida. Recognizing their military potential, Florida's governor organized them into a slave militia to aid in the continuing conflicts with the British. The slave militia would fight in the defense of what was then Spanish territory throughout the 1720s and 1730s.

The slave men, under the leadership of a Captain Menendez, soon began to solicit the Spanish government for their freedom. They cited their royal service, bravery, and loyalty, along with their previous service as warriors in the Yamassee War. In 1738, the governor finally granted the men unconditional freedom and the right to set up a town north of St. Augustine. Mose operated as a successful military outpost, serving as protection against the British until the 1760s, when the Spanish lost St. Augustine.

The hard-won respect that the formerly enslaved men gained from the Spanish rulers and the Yamassee Indians was due in no small measure to their military experiences. Landers points out that the African, Indian, and Spanish cultures in this frontier territory shared some important characteristics. Among these was a strong respect for military skills and leadership. The Spanish authorities and the Yamassee leadership judged the Africans to be estimable men, worthy of freedom, because of their skills in battle. When the Spanish governor finally granted their petition for freedom, he described the formerly enslaved Menendez, their chosen leader, as the exemplification of military skill, knowledge, and courage, as well as a model for his men as an individual who valued hard work. Thus, in addition to his military skills and courage, Menendez possessed the virtue of industry —all qualities that the Spanish leaders valued as essential for promoting the settlement of towns.

Landers's study also opens a window onto how black men sought to construct families and build communities in their new society, where everyday existence was very difficult. Mose was a predominantly male, frontier society. The number of women available for marriage always remained small. Initially, the men formed unions with Native American women from adjacent villages. Soon after the town was established, however, the men, apparently desiring marriage within their own ethnic group, began to seek partners among the enslaved and free black women from nearby St. Augustine. Some households consisted only of males, but such cases included black men married to enslaved women from St. Augustine, forced to accept living arrangements separate from their wives.

Culturally, Mose was an interesting mix of the African and the Hispanic, blending customs from both cultures. For instance, Landers found that the Africans and the Spanish shared compatible ideas about family life and men's role. Both cultures had strong patriarchal structures in place that viewed society as an extension of family, or kinship, ties. Men headed the households, families, and political institutions. In both societies, a male was deemed a responsible adult member of his community when he married, established a household, and produced children.

In the colonies, as opposed to frontier territory, there were fewer chances for black men to establish maroon communities, so resistance often took the form of revolt. John K. Thornton's "African Dimensions of the Stono Rebellion" takes a look at the most famous slave uprising in colonial America. The Stono Rebellion took place in South Carolina in 1739, a year after Mose was established in Spanish territory, but the circumstances were very different. Thornton focuses on possible African influences in the Stono Rebellion, highlighting the effects of West African military experience and religious belief on slave uprisings in the New World.

Thornton suggests that the rebellious slaves did not originate from Angola, as eyewitness accounts claim, but probably from the Kongo. He describes their strongly professed Christian and Catholic heritage as characteristic of Africans from that region. The Kongo kingdom was not a Portuguese colony like Angola, but an independent African state that had adopted Christianity as the national religion when King Nzinga Nkuwu voluntarily converted in 1491. By the eighteenth century, the Kongolese regarded Christianity as an integral part of their national and cultural identity. They were practicing Catholics who sent their children to mission schools, built chapels for worship, and recited prayers and hymns as part of their religious faith and practice. Hence, the African males involved in the Stono Rebellion brought with them a history of European acculturation several centuries old, long predating their forced migration to the Americas.

Thornton's essay provides additional insight into the role of previous military experience in West African societies, and how earlier engagement in such activities may have directly influenced black men's attitudes toward the use of violence and direct confrontation in the colonies. For example, he draws parallels between the Stono Rebellion and Kongo war history, based on the fact that the eighteenth-century Kongo state was the site of several civil wars. Male war captives from the Kongo were already skilled in the use of firearms and experienced in the traditional skirmishing tactics characteristic of Kongo warfare. The men played drums, performed warrior dances, and carried banners into battle, all in an effort to arouse the fighting spirit. Thornton notes that, according to witnesses, the Stono rebels exhibited the same military skills and cultural traits.

RUNAWAYS AND THE LOGISTICS OF FLIGHT

After the unsuccessful Stono Rebellion, revolt in the mainland colonies as an expression of black manhood took on more problematic and complex dimensions. "Slave Runaways in Colonial North Carolina, 1748–1775," by Marvin L. Michael Kay and Lorin Lee Cary, explains some of the reasons. Revolts such as the Stono Rebellion were led by the first generations of West African men, who were generally less successful as runaways in British North America. Like Kunte Kinte, the recently arrived young male hero in Alex Haley's novel *Roots*, both African men and women tended to run away quite soon after their arrival in the colonies. However, unlike Kunte Kinte, who struck out alone, the first Africans usually ran away in groups. Their actions were an immediate response to the recent trauma of capture and enslavement, separation from spouses, family members, and community, the horror of the Middle Passage, and the culture shock of being thrown into a new environment. Little planning went into early escape attempts, and new Africans often lacked the language, let alone writing, skills necessary to steal or negotiate freedom in their new North American context.

Kay and Cary, however, found that this situation changed in the second generation, and by the mid-eighteenth century, running away had become widespread in the North American colonies. On the other hand, it was accepted that violent group insurrection leading to escape and the establishment of maroon communities was nearly impossible to achieve. Although open rebellions would continue, the majority of enslaved people seemed to opt for individual flight as a means of resistance. Most important, in terms of gender analysis, slave flight soon became a gendered phenomenon, an action attempted predominantly by black males.

Slave flight evolved into a complex and arduous maneuver for freedom and manhood. It involved scheming, evasive actions, shifting tactics, and a well-thought-out consideration of all the gains and losses involved, as complex as any military procedure. In other words, running away was not easy. Therefore, calculated decision making and planning were essential. Furthermore, slave flight was a considerable risk for black men. It separated them from loved ones, community, and place. Much thought went into evaluating the likelihood of success. When to run, under what circumstances, and with what goals in mind were crucial questions. Running off was also "contagious." Enslaved men who ran away inspired others to try.

Kay and Cary identify several crucial factors that determined the logistics of slave flight. Enslaved men ran away for a variety of reasons, including the strong pull of freedom, economic incentives, reunification with family, and extreme acts of brutality on the part of slaveowners. A number of the male runaways in North Carolina were skilled craftsmen who wanted to make use of their occupational skills. White owners commonly hired out their skilled slave carpenters, blacksmiths, and other artisans in order to maximize their profits. They also hired out some unskilled workers to work on road gangs.

Large numbers of slaves worked as skilled watermen as well. They labored as boatmen, sailors, ferrymen, and guides on the Carolina waterways. Enslaved men generally had a better chance than female slaves of working in the sorts of occupations that brought them into wider contact with the larger society. As a result, they amassed more knowledge about their geographical surroundings.

By the mid-1700s, most enslaved men were native-born, with the acculturation and familiarity with American culture needed for a successful escape. They could enhance their chances of staying free by going to southern towns, where the growing free black populations and urban enslaved communities safeguarded their anonymity. Some enslaved men from North Carolina managed to travel long distances, attempting to leave the colony altogether. It seems, then, that the odds for escape favored enslaved men over enslaved women.

Kay and Cary, however, present an even more complicated picture of slave flight, especially when they apply what they call a "sex-specific analysis." They emphasize that by the mid-1700s, the single most important factor in enslaved men's decision to take flight was the same thing that made enslaved women determined to remain in place: the existence and growing strength of the slave family, the most significant psychological, social, and spiritual reality for slaves. This study found that family ties in the Carolinas and Virginia were the reason that men ran away in greater numbers than women. Slave owners in the southeast generally sold men away from their kin more often than women, who were more likely to remain behind with members of the family who had not been sold. As a result, most of the enslaved men in the region ran away in order to reestablish family ties. Others, however, ended up in the same situation as black women, having to choose family over freedom. Most opted to remain and endure, resisting the institution from within. Either way, enslaved women's and men's attempts to construct and maintain their families were a strong determining factor in the practice of resistance activity.

Kay and Cary conclude that slave flight from the mid-colonial era up until the eve of the revolution remained an extremely dangerous activity. Slaves were usually recaptured and subjected to physical abuse in the form of whipping, branding, and other tortures, and sometimes death. Given that this particular form of resistance did not usually result in freedom, American-born enslaved men's persistence in running away and plotting revolts suggests that such activity was probably an important expression of their manhood. Perhaps resistance of this type provided some black men with the psychic or emotional release they required for their inner survival.

MILITARY SERVICE AND THE QUEST FOR FREEDOM: THE AMERICAN REVOLUTION

Conspiracies, revolt, and flight were not the only means of resistance that enslaved men used to assert their manhood and possibly achieve freedom.

Despite the obstacles and the reality that black men were not regarded as citizens for most of American history, it can be argued that military service in American wars actually freed more black men during the slave era than all the plots, insurrections, and slave flight put together. War offered enslaved men at least the chance for achieving freedom, and it left the door ajar for freedmen to struggle for citizenship rights.

The culture and history of war are not the subject of this introduction, but a few relevant points should be made in reference to the subject at hand. First, it is apparent that military service was not an option for enslaved women, or for women in general, particularly when it came to the reality of combat. The making of war is an ancient male institution, with values, beliefs, and practices common to human societies around the world. Patriarchal culture has traditionally sanctioned violence in the context of war, asserting that it gives men an opportunity to prove manhood through willing sacrifice for the society and way of life into which they were born. The reward for this sacrifice has been certain rights and privileges, in addition to the glory gained from heroic deeds. These may include the right to vote, access to land or education, pensions, and symbolic rewards such as medals. Women have traditionally benefited from these rights only indirectly, through their associations with men as mothers, wives, daughters, or other close kin.

In interpreting the meaning of resistance for enslaved or free men, we must acknowledge that certain traditional notions about manhood and military action made it possible for significant numbers of enslaved men to negotiate, and win, their freedom as a result of the War of Independence. However, white men repeatedly denied black men the specific male rights associated with war. Our analysis, therefore, must deal with how slave status and oppression, race, and class figured into black men's attempts to make these age-old beliefs about war and manhood apply to them.

Sidney Kaplan and Emma Nogrady Kaplan investigate these very issues in their book *The Black Presence in the Era of the American Revolution*. Their work is not a recounting of the history of black men in the Revolutionary War, which is already generally well known, but focuses in part upon the meaning of the revolution to black men, the documentation of important visual resources pertaining to their war experience, and the identification of these men, where possible. This study uses a chapter from that text entitled "Bearers of Arms: Patriot and Tory," which presents a multilayered perspective, focusing on the diverse ways in which black men were active during the war.

Kaplan and Nogrady Kaplan point out that, generally, enslaved men did not care one whit about tea and taxes. Instead, the evidence the authors collected indicates that black men weighed the advantages of participating in the rebellion, whether for or against independence from England, with admirable forethought and deliberation. This perspective is far removed from the language of protest, generally referred to as the "rights of man" rhetoric, so popular with white patriots. To them, the rebellion was a matter of the young and vigorous white male colony rising up to overthrow its "Old World" patriarchs. Black men had no "old fathers" to rise up against in order to prove their manhood. Be they slave or free, their eyes were uplifted instead toward individual freedom and equality. These were the two pre-eminent ideals that black men drew out of the "rights of man" rhetoric, and the immediate goal of most was escape from slavery.

Garshom Prince, Saul Matthews, and Austin Dabney are just a few of the black revolutionary soldiers who have been identified and whose varied efforts to achieve freedom through war have come to light. We know about Garshom Prince only because of the beautiful powderhorn he fashioned for himself. Though born a slave, he had already previously fought in the French and Indian Wars. During the Revolutionary War, Prince commemorated his own service by carving a horn, which he then engraved with images of ships and inscribed "Prince Negro His Hornn." The expertise that went into the making of the horn suggests that Prince was a skilled artisan—a woodcarver, to be exact—of some merit. Unfortunately, his military service and the craftsmanship he left behind are all that remain of this black soldier's life experience.

Matthews and Dabney were among the numbers of black men who actually acquired their freedom as a result of the war. Matthews had been a slave in Virginia before he worked as a spy and soldier around Portsmouth and Norfolk. Like too many other black men who had served, he was re-enslaved after the war. But acting under his own volition, Saul petitioned the Virginia legislature for his freedom. In 1792, almost ten years after the war's end, the legislature finally granted Saul his request because of his military service.

Austin Dabney was emancipated as a result of his service in Georgia. Dabney had fought in his white owner's place, so there was no question about his soldierly contributions. In fact, he even received his pension, which was denied many black veterans, but that was the extent of his equal treatment under the law as a free black man in the New Republic. Dabney took part in the land lottery that Georgia held for veterans of the Revolutionary War and was allotted 112 acres for exemplary services "rendered in the war for liberty." White citizens protested his reward, however, and Dabney never gained access to his land. The existing records state that Dabney's opponents claimed it was "an indignity to white men, for a mulatto to be put upon equally with them in the distribution of the public land."

Kaplan and Nogrady Kaplan give equal time to those slaves and free men who cast their lot with the British. In the South, for instance, Lord Dunmore, the royal governor of colonial Virginia, issued a proclamation for slaves and free men to join His Majesty's troops in November of 1775, in return for their freedom. In the North, on the other hand, the enlistment of freedmen would not be authorized until December of the same year. And not until the success of the revolution was in question did the Continental Army authorize enslaved men to enlist on the American side. The reality of several major defeats at the hands of the British, along with low morale and difficulties in meeting the white male quota, was the reason for enslaved men's finally being promised freedom in exchange for military service. Even so, the army guaranteed the white planter class compensation for their economic loss, in order to encourage them to support slave enlistment.

Some enslaved men chose neither patriot nor Tory alliances. Throughout the war, slave flight, revolt, and individual confrontations with white men increased. Southern enslaved men ran away in great numbers, irrespective of whether they could reach the British. Southern white men feared, and therefore resisted, enlisting and arming their slaves, so most enslaved men in the South chose the British side or slave flight and revolt. In the end, it was primarily northern enslaved and free men who made up the five thousand black soldiers who served in the Continental Army.

At the end of the War of Independence, black men were quickly made to understand the limits of liberty and freedom for them in their everyday lives. Revolutionary philosophy lasted long enough, however, to ensure that most of the states that enlisted enslaved men freed them at the outset of their service in the war, or promised manumission afterwards. Some states, including Virginia in 1783, passed laws that granted freedom to all slaves who could prove they had served in the conflict. Possibly thousands of black men did acquire their hard-won freedom in this way. On the other hand, state records are full of manumission petitions filed by enslaved men and their families, still seeking freedom decades after the war.

Service for the British was another road to freedom, but it too was rocky and uncertain. The British troops who left America between 1782 and 1783 took with them about twenty thousand African Americans, a number that dwarfs the enlistment figures of black soldiers in the Continental Army. About three thousand of these people, both men and women, were granted the right to settle in Nova Scotia but were denied the land they had been promised. Others, sponsored by English abolitionists, relocated to Africa to settle in Sierra Leone. The British took many of their black supporters back to their colonies in the West Indies, where most landed as freedmen, but almost a thousand were sold back into slavery to British plantation owners. Thus the freedom sought by black men through military service was often contested after the war.

Most of the enslaved men who were granted freedom by the new nation as a direct result of their military service were manumitted in the North and in the South's Chesapeake region. Spurred on even further by egalitarian ideals, black and white abolitionists in the North would end the existence of slavery through the passage of gradual emancipation laws. Pennsylvania passed such a law in 1780. Massachusetts abolished slavery by judicial decision in 1783. In 1784, both Rhode Island and Connecticut passed gradual emancipation laws. Manumission acts were passed in New York in 1785 and in New Jersey in 1786. In addition, large numbers of southern slaves were freed during the post-revolutionary era. Just as the American Revolution was the crucible out of which the United States of America was born, so too did it transform blacks, giving birth to the people we now call African Americans. Even though freedom and equality were still largely denied them, no people better understood, and took to heart, the revolutionary principles over which the war had been fought. For black people, the War of Independence reinforced their belief that freedom was the inherent right of all humanity.

BLACK MANHOOD AND WORK CULTURE

The next important consideration in our gendering of the African American experience is work. During the nineteenth century, a complex relationship emerged between African American men, work, and masculinity. In the New Republic, the dominant ideal equated manhood with the state of being free and powerful, power being understood as authority over other men, as well as women and children. As James and Lois Horton assert in *Free People of Color: Inside the African American Community* (1993), early white male conceptions of manhood were influenced by the ideal known as the "Masculine Achiever." America's fast-growing market economy encouraged the development of the upwardly mobile, white, middle-class American male who was obsessed with competition and proving his manhood in the world arena of commercial capitalism. Some other scholars, such as Michael Kimmel in *Manhood in America: A Cultural History* (1996), refer to this same theoretical model as the "Self Made Man." The phenomenon arose out of the economic, political, and social changes that occurred from the post-revolutionary period throughout the antebellum era. These included the expansion of democracy, the emerging capitalist market, industrial growth, high levels of immigration, the spread of slavery, and territorial expansion that engendered a series of wars with Native Americans, Mexicans, and Europeans.

The idea of the "Self Made Man" was a very "freeing" notion, in that it encouraged the individual male to fashion himself in his own image. This new man was no longer tied to Old World ideas about manhood, based upon membership in craft guilds and life in a small town. Modern American men could experience the ultimate freedom, creating their own destinies and rising as high as their talents, competition, and luck would take them. Success now could be earned, and manhood had to be proven. Kimmel argues, however, that the average native-born white male responded to these turbulent changes with feelings of insecurity and displacement about his position in the new society and the belief that America was a world out of control. The negative aspects of the "new man" ideal were expressed in the desperate need the American male experienced for control over himself and others.

Kimmel claims that the Self Made Man paradigm soon became the dominant expression of masculinity in America. Two important components of the ideology were especially influential for American men who were perceived as "other," incapable of fitting into this new mold. These were what Kimmel calls the practice of exclusion and the emphasis placed upon the workplace as the most important public space for proving manhood.

Kimmel writes that white men's sense of themselves as men depended upon the exclusion of others. America as a political entity has been a multicultural society from its very beginning, but authentic membership in the dominant group was increasingly limited to white, Anglo-Saxon, Protestant males. The "Self Made Man" model excluded non-white males and certain ethnic whites by denying equal opportunities for employment, education, and political empowerment. Such discriminatory practices were meant to control "other" males' access to freedom and equal rights. In this way, white men sought to limit the extent to which they were forced to deal with competition from the diverse masculinities that were actually the norm in America. They also bolstered their own sense of importance as men through the time-honored method of denying the importance of others.

The second aspect of this model of masculinity that strongly affected black men was that the public sphere was the central proving ground for the Self Made Man, with the workplace being the most important site for masculine competition. Every individual white male was pressured to prove his manhood by achieving maximum success in procuring his part of the "American Dream." The ability to secure enough worldly goods for the survival of himself, his family, and his community would translate into economic independence, social morality, and political power.

From the beginning, white working-class men regarded black men's slave status as the antithesis of the Self Made Man, denying the existence of a different and authentic American male experience. Slave labor, upon which an entire region and elite class of white males actually depended, was equated not with virtue and manhood but with economic dependency and emasculation. Black men, however, although enslaved or problematically free, managed to come up with their own ideas about the connections between their work and masculinity. By the early nineteenth century, they were selectively blending certain African, Euro-American, and Native American ideas into their own complex socialization into adult men.

ENSLAVED LABOR AND THE KINGDOM OF COTTON

Nineteenth-century black men had a very different experience with slavery from that of their colonial predecessors. The new cotton-based economy dominated southern antebellum culture, and slavery was stabilized as labor-intensive agricultural work. Before the American Revolution, few North American slaves were involved in cotton production, but the Industrial Revolution's growing demand for fiber, as well as technological advancement in the form of Eli Whitney's cotton gin, changed that. The gin made the production of tough, short-staple cotton profitable by making it easier to separate its coarse fibers. Where it once had taken a slave a full workday to clean one pound of cotton, that same worker was now expected to clean fifty pounds a day. The South made cotton its number one cash crop, and North American slavery was given a new lease on life.

For black people, the cotton phenomenon struck hard. The first and immediate impact was a second forced migration, this time across land. Selling and transporting enslaved people across the United States was suddenly hugely profitable. In 1800, more than 80 percent of the enslaved population had lived for several generations in the states of Delaware, Virginia, Maryland, and the Carolinas. By the time the Civil War rumbled around, only one-third of the slave population resided in these areas. Most had been removed to the lower southern states of Alabama, Georgia, Mississippi, and Louisiana, and to Arkansas and Texas on the western frontier. Within the Lower South, slaves were concentrated in two areas: that ribbon of dark soil stretching from Georgia to Mississippi called the black belt, and the area bordering the Mississippi River system between New Orleans and Memphis.

Approximately one million slaves left their two-hundred-year-old seaboard homes during the forced exodus to the southern interior. Enslaved men and women had created societies based on kinship and friendship ties, with shared values and beliefs. But the new frontier demanded these young black men and women, who left in equal numbers. This first generation of migrant slaves laid the foundation for the emergent cotton kingdom.

The second great impact upon enslaved men and women was the fundamental way in which cotton altered slave labor. As the crop spread throughout the South, the majority of enslaved people became tied to its cultivation. Cotton production was less refined than the production of sugar, tobacco, or rice. Whereas sugar production is industrial as well as agricultural, and the tobacco and rice production common to the seaboard states had required the skills of craftsmen such as blacksmiths or tanners, cotton was produced simply. After cotton was picked, the cotton gin removed the seeds from its fibers, which was the only major technological refinement required in its production. The cotton was then squeezed into bales, where it could sit, as long as it remained dry, from months to years before it was exported.

The vast majority of enslaved men and women in cotton cultivation were field workers performing identical work. Thus, the new agricultural economy reduced the number of slaves, primarily male, who might be elevated into managerial positions. The black slave driver, or foreman, common to the eighteenth century and the Chesapeake region, was almost unknown in the land of cotton. The white overseer assumed this traditional post.

Even the number of enslaved people tied to domestic work in the "Big House" declined. The few adults, male or female, who had special duties in the house were usually inside only part of the time, remaining responsible for field work. Moreover, permanent occupations in or around the house, such as cook, gardener, or carriage driver, were no longer passed down in families, as they might have been in the Old South. Most house slaves, therefore, had kin or friends who were field workers. There was an extensive interaction between house and field, which formed the basis for a cultural cohesiveness among nineteenth-century North American slaves that was uncommon to enslaved populations in the Western Hemisphere.

SKILLED TRADESMEN:
CHIMNEY SWEEPS AND IRONWORKERS

Although the majority of slaves lived out their lives as field workers, a significant number of southern enslaved men participated in the trade and industrial sector, in occupations open only to men. Males in domestic work might be coachmen, cooks, valets, butlers, gardeners, and horse breeders. In a place such as Richmond, young slaves were hired out as errand boys or porters for white businessmen, while adult men were often hired out to work at common labor such as ditch digging. Throughout the South, white owners hired out enslaved men with more highly developed skills to build ships, operate lumber mills, or serve as printers' assistants. The most skilled artisans were blacksmiths, carpenters, coopers, and silversmiths. Enslaved men also forged iron, made ropes, and worked as tailors, alcohol distillers, and bakers.

Enslaved men were an integral part of southern industries and trade, to a degree uncommon for free black men in the North. On Mississippi river-boats they were the boiler stokers and deck hands. In Georgia and Louisiana they labored in the textile industry. They were the lumberjacks and producers of turpentine in the Carolina and Georgia forests. And in Virginia, Kentucky, Tennessee, North and South Carolina, Georgia, and Alabama they worked the salt and coal mines and labored on the railroads. Charles B. Dew and Bayly E. Marks speak to work and the enslaved male experience in specialized occupations in, respectively, "Disciplining Slave Ironworkers in the Antebellum South: Coercion, Conciliation, and Accommodation" and "Skilled Blacks in Antebellum St. Mary's County, Maryland."

Dew's title suggests that enslaved men responded in a variety of ways to industrial slavery. Although scholars have long considered this form of slavery to be the most brutal, Dew shows that enslaved men actually preferred hiring out in the industrial sector because of the freedom, albeit limited, that it allowed them, along with the accompanying monetary rewards and social opportunities. Dew's gender-centered study describes an arena in which the white ironmasters and the enslaved hands at Buffalo Forge and Etna Furnaces in Virginia worked out a negotiated middle ground. The ironmasters received the benefit of a willing labor force in return for accommodating the workers' demands for more control over their families, working conditions, and daily lives. White men depended on a large labor force to operate their mining facilities. Recruiting enough enslaved men to work the Virginia mines was difficult, expensive, and competitive work. The ironmasters therefore sought to avoid excessive abuse of the people they employed, because complaints from enslaved men to their owners could sabotage their chances for hiring out the next year. Thus, enslaved men were in a position to maneuver, to some extent, for better treatment and wages. For example, they let their owners know at which mines they preferred to work. Normally, slave owners complied, in order to counteract confrontational resistance activity such as running away or refusing to work. Also, when black men suffered excessively brutal treatment at the mines, they protested by sabotaging the ironmasters' equipment, damaging property by setting fire to it, and abusing draft animals. An enslaved man named Anthony even struck a white manager when the man physically assaulted him, trying to force Anthony to work on Sunday.

It would appear, then, that physical abuse was an important issue in the workplace, around which black and white men contested the extent to which each could control the other. In an effort to lessen recourse to physical abuse, ironmasters offered enslaved men overwork pay to get them to produce beyond their standard quota of iron. Some used the overwork system to earn more money for themselves and their families; others chose not to participate in the system at all. Either way, it was a measure of choice in their everyday lives that made it possible for enslaved men to be "more their own men." The extra earnings improved the quality of life for men with families. Sam Williams bought sugar, coffee, and cloth for his wife, and opened a savings account in a Lexington, Virginia, bank. A large number of enslaved men who worked at the forge were married. The ability to buy small gifts for their wives enhanced their sense of pride, and having surplus cash to save empowered them economically. As Dew notes, this type of work environment turned enslaved men into disciplined, productive workers, even before the end of slavery.

Bayly Marks's essay presents a different aspect of the work life of black men in the South. It is a quantitative piece that uses county records, censuses, and private accounts to arrive at a statistical profile of skilled workers in Maryland between 1790 and 1864. The article's main contribution is the comparative analysis it offers between skilled black men and women, and between skilled enslaved and free black men. Bayly suggests some reasons why enslaved and free men were more likely than women to be involved in what has traditionally been considered "skilled" labor.

As Kay and Cary found in "Slave Runaways in Colonial North Carolina, 1748–1775," enslaved men in Maryland generally had more opportunities than black women to acquire skills in the trades. In discussing the origins of crafts skills among slaves, Bayly asserts that enslaved men first learned these skills from African forebears. Over time, white plantation owners, usually male, chose a few enslaved men for training in the trades as well. Whether these craftsmen learned their skills from African or European men, the knowledge was usually passed down through another male. Slave and master evidently found some common ground when it came to beliefs about the division of labor based on gender roles. Historically, men have passed down specialized knowledge to their sons and other male apprentices, while women have passed down certain domestic-based skills to young females. The male-related skills were more likely to be considered trades or professions, capable of being turned into an important means of earning a livelihood. Hence, enslaved women, more than enslaved men, were locked into the agrarian economy and way of life. The few enslaved women in occupations outside agriculture were cooks, laundresses, midwives, seamstresses, and spinners or weavers. Black women were able to work in only about half a dozen occupations, while there were at least three times that many skilled and semiskilled jobs available to black men.

Although Bayly notes that it was more difficult to uncover information about black women, the records do indicate class and racial biases between black and white women as well. Since black women had traditionally been cooks and laundresses, poor white women, perceiving this as slave or poor free black women's work, generally refused to take in laundry or hire themselves out as cooks. They preferred to weave and sew in order to earn a living. Black women sought these occupations as well but were not as successful at procuring them most of the time.

Carpenters were the most valued of all the enslaved black artisans, followed by blacksmiths and then sailors, who were owned primarily by mariners and pilots. They were sold for between three hundred and one thousand dollars, the high prices reflecting a carpenter's or blacksmith's potential earning power for the owner. They could be hired out to neighbors and any other whites demanding their skills for about one hundred dollars a year, in addition to room and board. Skilled enslaved men competed successfully with free black men and whites. Enslaved artisans not only saved an owner money because of all the work they performed on plantations, but they earned additional income for slave owners as well.

Bayly's study also indicates that among the small but growing population of free blacks in St. Mary's County, there seems to have been no economic advantage in a craftsman's becoming free. In fact, earning potential deteriorated after a slave was manumitted, and free black craftsmen were forced to work as common laborers as often as unskilled free men or slaves. Neither were freemen very successful in procuring land or other property. It may be, as the author suggests, that rural antebellum Maryland was still too dependent upon enslaved labor to accommodate free black men working and competing with white men for jobs and wages. Bayly also implies, though, that racism may have played a role in limiting the economic opportunities for free black men in the rural South.

BLACK MALE CRAFTSMEN IN THE NORTH:
EARNING A MANLY LIVING

Silvio Bedini, along with Paul A. Gilje and Howard B. Rock, continues this line of discussion by examining the lives of free black men in the North during the first half of the nineteenth century. As the ideals of liberty and equality pushed the northern states toward gradual emancipation and abolition, black men, women, and children strove to find wage-earning work in the New Republic. Ironically, the North's freedmen sometimes found it even more difficult to find skilled work than free black men in the South. This was because the strong commercial economy in the North's large cities, such as New York and Philadelphia, attracted greater numbers of immigrant workers, who, along with native-born white men, competed with black men for jobs. Most free black men in the Northeast, consequently, continued in the same common labor they had performed as urban slaves in the colonial era. They dug graves, cellars, and wells and labored as stevedores, construction workers, bootblacks, stable hands, porters, and street cleaners. There was, however, a significant minority of black men in the occupations that had been traditionally theirs in the North: barber, painter, domestic servant, waiter, caterer, oysterman, and mariner. There was even a small group of professional black men who became doctors, ministers, and teachers in the North's growing free black communities.

Bedini's case study of the first black clockmaker in America illuminates this transitional period between slavery and quasi-freedom for black men who were trying to work in the skilled trades. Peter Hill (1767–1820) was among the small number of black men and women who managed to open small businesses as barbers, restaurateurs and caterers, merchants, and tailors. To achieve the level of clockmaker was a rare accomplishment. To this date, Hill is the only known black clockmaker from early American history.

The significance of Hill's achievement is directly related to the existence of the Society of Friends. The group was representative of early abolitionist movements in the North. By 1759, it is known from the meticulous records the institution kept that Quaker slave owners in Burlington County, New Jersey, were no longer importing or purchasing slaves and were slowly manumitting those they had previously purchased. The Quakers were also providing educational and religious instruction for enslaved people and freedmen. By 1801, there was a school for poor children in Burlington Township that was attended by both blacks and whites.

Free black men in this area occupied a tenuous and hazardous position between slave and free white men. They had the right to keep their wages, as well as a certain prescribed amount of physical freedom. However, if a male slave wished to leave the New Jersey county in which he had been freed, he was required by law to obtain two permission certificates from two different justices of the peace. A black man who was manumitted in another state was not allowed to travel through, or reside in, New Jersey. And even though adult black men who owned property worth at least fifty pounds received permission to vote under the 1776 Constitution, an 1807 law denied freedmen the vote, restricting the right to free white adult male citizens. Such was the context in which Peter Hill became a clockmaker and opened his own business.

While Hill was a slave, his owner trained him in the highly skilled craft of clockmaking, starting him out as shop assistant. Then Hill's owner assisted him in opening up his own shop while he was still a slave. It was the earnings from this business that made it possible for Hill to purchase himself. Burlington Township property records show that Hill's certificate of freedom was filed in 1795, when he was twenty-seven years of age. For the rest of his life, Hill plied his trade, working at cleaning, repairing, and making clocks, in addition to selling watches, for at least twenty-three years. He was a traditional craftsman. He made no innovations in the artistry of his craft, but he was excellently trained and was regarded as one of the best clockmakers in the county.

In "'Sweep O! Sweep O!': African-American Chimney Sweeps and Citizenship in the New Nation," Paul Gilje and Howard Rock describe the hard and dangerous lives of black male youth and adults who labored cleaning chimneys. Poor white men and boys had at one time worked as chimney sweeps, but even before 1800, slave owners had begun to hire out enslaved males for this work. In 1817, New York revived a 1719 gradual emancipation law, which finally resulted in freedom for all enslaved people in New York State by 1827. Earning a living in the free labor market during this transitional period became a serious scramble for black people. Some freedmen saw chimney sweeping as an occupation that would allow them to earn an independent income and a certain level of respect in their communities. Hence, they were willing to take despised, low-level work, and turn it into a respectable trade.

Chimney sweeping was an extremely hazardous job. Besides the physical difficulties and dangerous nature of the work, the occupation was unhealthy. Cancer, lung disease, tuberculosis, and broken bones were common. By the early nineteenth century, black men dominated the trade. In 1810, there were 60 black masters, along with 150 young black males identified as apprentices. Like most trades, chimney sweeping was male-dominated, but a few black women achieved success. At least 3 were listed among the 60 masters working in 1810.

What is most interesting, though, is how chimney sweepers sought the same citizenship rights as other working-class men in New York City, and how they started self-help organizations in their communities. This early political activity was first expressed between 1816 and 1818, when master sweeps began petitioning the city for the same municipal regulation and protection given white tradesmen. They called for set rates, limited licenses, and the appointment of an "Inspector of Chimney Sweeps." The sweeps also established a trade association, the United Society of Chimney Sweeps. The USCS provided funds for disabled and sick members, took care of group burial needs, and assisted its members' widows and children. The formation of the USCS was typical of the general self-help movement in American cities during the early nineteenth century. Recently freed blacks in northern settings were thrown into competition with many other new immigrant groups and, like them, tended to organize their own institutions and communities for their very survival. The black men and women who organized political and benevolent societies such as the USCS intended for such activity to raise their level of social and financial parity with whites.

We can glean some additional information about the unique manner in which black men linked work and survival, manhood and honor in the New Republic. When city officials attacked the abilities of master sweeps to adequately protect and provide for their apprentices, black men responded with vigor. As the authors describe them, the "city fathers" were not so much concerned about the lives of poor black male children as they were caught up in the reform movements of the day. Influenced by the British social reform movement centered on chimney sweeping and the issue of child labor and abuse, American reformers tried to revamp the "despised" trade in the same manner. However, instead of focusing on the white male youth still involved in chimney sweeping, they made the "welfare" of black male children — the "little sufferers," as they categorized them — the primary issue.

Thus when the white male elected officials of New York City claimed that master sweeps were incapable of acting in the role of paternal caregivers like other master craftsmen, they were attacking the manhood of the newly freed blacks in the city by accusing them of being not only bad fathers, but of the lowest class. However, the master sweeps asserted the value of their work and their manhood on several fronts.

First, they explained that chimney sweeping was valid work that made it possible for freedmen to take care of themselves and their families and to aid the disabled, widowed, and orphaned members of their communities. Then, the master sweeps reminded city officials that they might be colored people, a class once very much "despised," but that the post-revolutionary era was an "enlightened period" in which every free man, regardless of race, should be treated as a working member of a civil society. They reminded the city that several of their workers were Revolutionary War veterans, deserving of the right to employment. With regard to their apprentices, the master sweepers admitted that there was much room for upgrade and improvement. They agreed that apprentices should be treated with humanity and provided with decent food, clothing, some education, and religious and moral guidance. But they also revealed awareness of the discriminatory practices city officials were engaging in, saying that master sweepers generally provided these things for the youth in their employ on a level comparable to that of white tradesmen in other occupations. And although there were certainly "disreputable masters," they should be distinguished from honorable workers. The master sweepers asked city officials not to stigmatize the whole lot of free, working-class black men because of an unworthy few.

As for the boys at the center of this controversy, they certainly were mistreated, suffered ill health and poverty, and received little education. But like the adult men in the trade, black male youth relished the independence the job allowed them, and in their own way they resisted the efforts of white city officials to play the part of patronizing white "fathers" offering "guidance and control" to the "little sufferers." It seems that they resisted the efforts of black men to control them as well. The importance placed on being an independent free wage earner, even for young males, was pointed out by the master sweeps themselves. They reminded city officials that these were "free" young black males who "earned" a weekly salary. Consequently, it was difficult to control them beyond making sure that they received the bare necessities that the trade regulations required master sweeps to provide. It is interesting that white youth in the same trade were in very similar social circumstances and also resisted the efforts of city officials to provide paternal control and guidance.

It would seem, then, that in the urban industrialized North, newly freed black men thrown into the free labor market regarded wage-earning work and independence as important aspects of manhood. They did not, however, see themselves *as* their work, or evaluate the quality of their manhood based upon the status of the work. Given that racism and oppression relegated them to the lowest-status jobs, it may be that black men learned to place more value on other aspects of being an adult male. These seem to have included honor and integrity, performing one's work well regardless of the status of the job, and being responsible for oneself, one's family, and the community. It may be that enslaved and free men came to interpret work largely as a means toward achieving these goals and rejected the obsession with the nature and status of work that was so prevalent in class-driven white American society.

CULTURE WORKERS:
MUSICIANS, BARBERS, AND PREACHERS

By the nineteenth century, what we now identify as African American culture had emerged with its characteristic vitality, its blending of African, Native American, and European cultures, and its progressive outlook. Black American culture, with two centuries of experience behind it, had already laid a solid foundation in two of its most distinctive creative expressions, music and religion.

Making Music

Scholars have now acknowledged that music was not mere entertainment, nor religion only ecstatic release. These were, above all, creative and spiritual necessities for black American survival. Moreover, music and religious culture (the black church) operated on several complex levels in nineteenth-century black communities, and participation by men and women was often greatly influenced by their gender. By the antebellum period, for example, the making of music had come to be divided along gender lines, with women playing a major role in spiritual music and in music enjoyed solely within the black community, while men were more heavily involved in musical entertainment for both black and white audiences.

In the earliest reports of slave festivals and other sites of African American singing and dancing, such as the Sunday afternoon gatherings in Congo Square in New Orleans of the 1700s, women were reported to be instrumentalists as frequently as men. On plantations, when enslaved people performed for themselves and each other, women were among the drummers as well as the juber rhymers. However, when a slave was chosen by an owner to serve in the occupation of musician, that person was inevitably a man. The result was that, while women continued to participate in music as a community activity, both as singers and as instrumentalists, professional musicians were increasingly men.

Paul A. Cimbala elaborates on the importance of the black male instrumentalist in "Black Musicians from Slavery to Freedom: An Exploration of an African-American Folk Elite and Cultural Continuity in the Nineteenth-Century Rural South." He writes that enslaved musicians were regarded as craftsmen, and that in the South the musician's occupation was low-class work that white men refused to perform. As a result, black men ended up as the primary musicians and skilled instrumentalists in black and white rural southern society.

The image of the enslaved black man as a great fiddler or banjo player has indelibly marked American musical history. The influence, of course, begins even earlier, when Africans first transported the banjo to the colonies. Most important, many African musicians/craftsmen were certainly among the hundreds of thousands of enslaved people who survived the Middle Passage to reach North America. Stringed instruments from southern plantations have survived as well, along with visual sources that depict the black fiddler as entertainer. White artists sometimes painted the black fiddler as an old man playing for the amusement of white children. At other times, the fiddler is a young man, or a group of male musicians, playing for the enjoyment of adult whites at leisurely social functions. By the nineteenth century, then, it would appear that white Americans had come to associate the black male musician solely with pleasure, revelry, and entertainment.

Cimbala comes to a different conclusion about the role and meaning of musicians in nineteenth-century black American life when he examines this historical question from the perspective of enslaved communities. He points out that musicians were highly regarded in southern slave society because they had succeeded in learning a technical skill and achieving a musical expertise that most slaves, men or women, would never have the opportunity to acquire. The enslaved community distinguished a talented artist by calling him a "musicianer," even though he was most likely to be a field hand like the rest of them. Along with their creative gifts and technical skills, enslaved musicians were admired for their role as culture-bearers. These men were teachers, laying the foundation for a tradition of apprenticeship in American musical history. They passed their skills and songs on to younger men. In fact, such individual, personal instruction was the only way a young black male would have learned the craft.

Last but not least, enslaved musicians became culturally essential to the soul of slave communities. Cimbala suggests that their talent and expertise made them an important example of resistance to negative white stereotypes and a symbol of pride in black American culture. In this way, enslaved musicians contributed to the social, cultural, and spiritual health of their community. After emancipation, ex-slave musicians passed their cultural legacy on to succeeding generations of freed black men. Black men went on to give up the fiddle, possibly because it was synonymous with the slave experience; bluesmen then adopted the guitar in the early twentieth century as their instrument of preference. Most female blues performers were vocalists, but some also played the guitar. Much more frequently, female instrumentalists were piano players or, interestingly, horn players in the popular brass bands and marching bands that were part of the beginnings of jazz. Gender roles began to reassert themselves, however, as jazz gained popularity and became the province of professional musicians. Women were again excluded as instrumentalists, except on the piano, with the result that most of the great women jazz musicians from the turn of the century until the last decade or so were vocalists or piano players. It was primarily men, then, who created the jazz sound, that remarkable interpretation of the black American experience which revolutionized music around the world. They also continued the tradition of black musical craftsmanship, artistic creativity, and the tradition of apprenticeship on a variety of instruments that harked back to the slave musicianer.

The Art of Oratory

The art of oratory evolved as the other most important avenue for creativity and leadership among nineteenth-century enslaved black men in the South. The rise of the slave preacher as a dominant force in southern slave societies accompanied developments in nineteenth-century African American Christianity, when tens of thousands of enslaved people either converted to or were born into the new faith. Black Americans grafted Christianity onto

African practices and beliefs, and the black church became an amalgam-
ation of traditional African religions, Islam, and European Christianity. It
also became institutionally independent from the Methodist, Baptist, and
Presbyterian denominations in which most African American Christians
had begun. Independence allowed for the creation of important leadership
roles for black people. In a patriarchal society and religion, men emerged as
the most visible leaders in the black church hierarchy, while women made
up the bulk of the congregation, fulfilling equally crucial roles in the areas
of music, testimony, and outreach to the community.

Black male authority was centered in the roles of preacher and deacon.
Some scholars have suggested that leadership roles in the black church
became such an important avenue for black men's ambition, leadership, and
expression because the onset of cotton culture in the early nineteenth
century in the lower southern states eliminated some of the traditional craft
and managerial positions that had been common on the old plantations
along the southeastern coast. By the antebellum era, then, the male preacher
had stepped forward to claim the premier black leadership role in the "new"
plantation South. William H. Becker, in "The Black Church: Manhood and
Mission," argues that the black preacher symbolized assertive masculinity,
and that the role of charismatic religious leader and healer can be linked to
African patterns of social organization that frequently place the priest/healer
male at the pinnacle of power.

Aside from being a leader, the preacher, like the musician, was an important culture-bearer. Slave preachers cultivated exceptional oratorical skills.
They were literally folk poets, schooled in call and response, the dramatic
phrase, visually descriptive speech, and exhortation. Above all, they were
master storytellers, and often gifted songsters. Ultimately, the nineteenth-
century southern rural black male preacher succeeded in creating a singular performance art tradition that has been directly passed down to succeeding generations of black orators, both male and female.

The Barbering Trade: Color, Class, and Caste

Loren Schweninger builds an interesting case study around Nashville's
urban class of nominal slaves in "The Free-Slave Phenomenon: James P.
Thomas and the Black Community in Ante-Bellum Nashville." Because of
laws requiring freed slaves to leave Tennessee immediately, many remained
slaves in name after attaining their freedom in order to remain with their
families and in their homes. In Schweninger's examination of what he calls
the city's "free-slaves," several themes stand out. According to the author, the
urban setting, the possibility of learning a trade, and the significant number
of African Americans of mixed heritage all factored into the economic independence and maintenance of some distinctive African American cultures and communities.

Schweninger's study focuses on the family of James P. Thomas, who became a "free-slave" and one of the city's premier barbers. His story is representative of those individuals who succeeded in manipulating their ties to the white community, acquiring knowledge of a skilled trade, and turning the opportunities city life offered into a privileged status. However, James Thomas did not attain this status on his own. Schweninger points out that the most important elements in the achievement of such goals for former slaves in this region were probably the existence of strong family bonds and a large, free antebellum community in Nashville with a substantive African American culture.

It was Thomas's mother who purchased her youngest son's "freedom" with her earnings as a cleaning woman and eventually opened her own cleaning business. Thomas was the third of Sally's mulatto male children to attain freedom when they were threatened with sale by their owners. Her first son, John, found his path to freedom when he hired out to a barge captain named Richard Rapier, at his mother's suggestion. After several years of service, John took the captain's surname, became a barber, and was emancipated by Rapier. When Henry was to be sold, Sally Thomas told him to escape. Although he was recaptured in Louisville, Kentucky, he eventually escaped across the Ohio River to reach freedom in New York in 1833. James was just eight years old when his sale was proposed; with the help of a white lawyer, Sally purchased his freedom papers for $400, although he remained nominally a slave until 1851, when he was twenty-four. Ultimately, it was hard work, strong family loyalty, and ties to whites who could vouch for the good character of the family that resulted in freedom for these young men of color.

The most fascinating feature of this story, though, as it relates to the history of black male culture and community, is the economic and cultural significance of the barbering trade. In the mid-nineteenth century, black men had long dominated the trade in both the South and the North. In fact, it can be said that barbering was perceived as a black man's occupation to such an extent that, like the trade of musician, it was a job many white men refused to perform, especially in the South. During the antebellum era, although white immigrants had begun to compete with black men for control of the trade in the North, black men continued to dominate the trade in the South.

It is no surprise, then, that it was barbering that enabled Sally's three sons to achieve economic independence and status in Nashville's freed community. John Rapier, Sally's oldest son, and the first to acquire his freedom, earned his living as a barber in Florence, Alabama, while the second son, Henry Thomas, established a barbershop in Buffalo, New York. The youngest, James Thomas, who is the main subject of Schweninger's case study, started out as apprentice to another freed slave and barber named Frank Parrish. At the age of nineteen, he was able to open his own barbershop in his mother's house, which was also the site of Sally's cleaning business. Thomas would eventually oversee one of the largest barbering establishments in Nashville. Furthermore, the city's pre-eminent barbershop was owned by Henry's former trainer, Frank Parrish. Parrish managed a deluxe barbershop and bathhouse considered the most elegant in Nashville. In the 1853 Nashville business directory, six of the eight barbers advertised were black.

Schweninger's essay opens an interesting door into the world of barbering and the working environment for free black men. It touches on the influence of class and color on barbering as an economic and cultural institution in the history of African Americans as well. Thomas and Parrish both owned shops located in the downtown business district, where they were patronized by white politicians, lawyers, merchants, bankers, and other professional white men. Schweninger suggests that being mulatto may have affected the type of clientele that a former slave and free entrepreneur could expect to attract. In fact, the physical appearance of the men was cited as an important aspect of their work. In an age when white men of a certain class and standing in southern society paid particular attention to good clothes and grooming, it appears that the male servants who took care of such personal details for them also took considerable care with their own appearance.

Schweninger describes both Thomas and Parrish as mulatto men, Parrish possibly being light enough to pass for white. When they traveled within the United States and to Europe, their appearance caused confusion about their racial identity, which white Americans sought to clear up with direct interrogations, while Europeans readily assumed that their handsome, well-groomed looks indicated men of status and wealth, not slaves. Although Schweninger's article lacks visual documentation, his written text presents an image of Thomas and Parrish as, essentially, differing little in appearance, fashionable style of dress, or social status from their white patrons.

It is possible that the barbering trade in Nashville was not only a free black man's occupation, but one dominated by blacks who were specifically recognized as mulattoes. For, in addition to indicating connections between color and caste in Nashville's free black economy and community, Schweninger also notes the general similarities to other, better known examples of antebellum southern cities with significant mulatto populations, such as Mobile, Alabama, and New Orleans, Louisiana. When examining the complex history of black American work, culture, and community, scholars need to be aware of the complicated dimensions that not only race and class but also intraracial dynamics bring to the picture.

Traditionally, barbershops in African American communities have been described as single-sex environments where black men have enjoyed the company of other men and have been socialized in black male culture. This is an accurate appraisal, for black barbershops provided a haven where everything from work and politics, health and community, to women, marriage, and family could be discussed. A boy's first haircut has for generations been a rite of passage. (Black women have long valued the beauty shop for exactly the same reasons.) In addition, black barbershops have historically played a crucial economic and civic role in their communities. Particularly during the era of emancipation and reconstruction and into the twentieth century with the Great Migration and the civil rights movement, black barbers were members of the growing middle class and among the most influential and prominent black men in a community. Barbers started other black businesses, such as the first insurance companies, and black-owned barbershops were often the site of political and community organizing. Thus, black barbers forged strong ties in black communities, and the black barbershop remains important in the construction of black male culture and identity.

However, Schweninger pictures a setting where the social and community dimensions so important to barbershops in black communities seem to have been absent. It is apparent that men such as Thomas and Parrish actively sought the white male market and were, in turn, patronized by white men of standing. Given the racialist class structure characteristic of the slaveholding South, it is likely that a prominent white male clientele would not have taken their business to black barbers who provided services to non-white men. If Thomas and Parrish cut the hair, shaved the faces, and extracted the teeth of other black men in Nashville, that fact does not surface in the written documents.

So, although Thomas and Parrish built up economically solvent businesses, they practiced their craft in an arena where they were always on guard. They were constantly mindful of the deference they were forced to accord to whites and must have always been aware that they were former slaves, whose freedom was insecure. Although "free-slaves" were unlikely to engage in overt political or social activism that would threaten their hard-won and precarious liberty, the degree to which they pursued legal freedom for themselves should be regarded as political activity. Through their barbershop network, entrepreneurs such as Parrish and Thomas were privy to important social and political discussions, filtered through the conversations of prominent white men, that affected the free community in Nashville. And they were quite aggressive in calling upon these very same class associations when opportunities arose to negotiate their own freedom and to buy other members of their families out of bondage. When James Thomas petitioned the court for immunity from the 1831 law which said he must leave Tennessee unless he was nominally a slave, he was assisted by a prominent liberal United States senator. With support from the senator and some of Thomas's faithful white customers, Thomas was probably the first former slave to achieve both freedom *and* legal residency in Tennessee during the antebellum era.

CONSTRUCTING MASCULINITY:
FINDING FREE SPACES ON THE SEAS

Three of the essays in this book examine black manhood in northern settings. Along the northern seaboard, one of the more common occupations open to black men in the late eighteenth and early nineteenth centuries was seafaring. In "'To Feel Like a Man'": Black Seamen in the Northern States, 1800–1860," W. Jeffrey Bolster describes how black men were attracted to the maritime trade because of economics and the alluring link between seafaring and masculinity. The six thousand black men involved in the maritime trade by the 1850s were a fascinating lot. The typical black male in the trade was a sailor, steward, or cook. Some black seafarers were slaves forced by their owners to hire out at sea, working on the ships of masters. Others were successful runaways. Freedmen in the North often sought out jobs in seafaring as dignified work that offered wages and skills equal to those of white men. Black men were rarely officers, but a few, such as shipmaster Paul Cuffe and sailmaker James Forten, did acquire substantial fortunes.

Seafaring had certain specialized psychological, social, and cultural aspects that allowed for the growth of a relatively independent black male culture. The American maritime tradition common to the North was very much influenced by the British example, which encouraged a strong, independent, egalitarian male culture and identity. The trade had its own laws and institutions aboard ship, largely characterized by the concepts of order, hierarchy, and status. Bolster acknowledges that racism certainly existed in shipboard life, but it was sometimes "subverted" under the seafaring ideals and principles.

For many men, seafaring was a thrilling occupation with an international flavor. There was a strong romantic tradition, tempered by a pragmatic outlook on life, associated with the trade. Seafarers traveled around the world, possessed specialized technical knowledge, and frequently encountered dangerous situations. Thus, the culture valued and demanded courage in the face of fear, stoicism in order to bear up under the strenuous life aboard ship, and the pugilistic skills required for taking care of oneself in the company of other men. During the first half of the nineteenth century, seafaring was particularly admired as an occupation thought to provide exactly the sort of life situation that transformed youth into men. It was decidedly a "man's" job.

Black men were not immune to the lure of the sea; Bolster suggests that, along with its economic promise, they were attracted to its romance and its possibilities as a setting in which to affirm black manhood. For instance, in the early 1800s there were even all-black crews, although the officers were still white. Over one-quarter of the black sailors in Providence, Rhode Island, worked on ships sailing to New York, Philadelphia, the Caribbean, Europe, and the African coast with majority black crews. In such instances, a black male social life was fashioned based on shared labor, seafaring ideals, and early-nineteenth-century black urban culture.

BLACK MALE POLITICAL CULTURE

In their investigations of black urban life and free men in the North, James Oliver Horton and Lois E. Horton, in "Violence, Protest, and Identity: Black

Manhood in Antebellum America," and Emma Jones Lapsansky, in "'Discipline to the Mind': Philadelphia's Banneker Institute, 1854–1872," find that class played a part in how black men constructed manhood. During the early republic, free blacks began to actively engage in American social, cultural, economic, and political affairs in spite of the barriers obstructing their opportunities for advancement and a better life. This urban class of free black activist leaders consisted primarily of ministers, businessmen, and teachers. They usually based their activities in small groups of black businesspeople — restaurants owners, barbers, tailors, funeral directors, and so forth. Some had a private education, and some had attended colleges or seminaries.

The Hortons find that by the 1820s, there was a free black middle class emerging in the North that was the basis for a lively political culture focused on the struggle for equal rights and the abolition of slavery. Its leaders included men such as David Walker, Frederick Douglass, Henry Highland Garnet, and Martin Delany, and women such as Sojourner Truth and Maria Stewart. Their literary contributions, newspaper editorials, pamphlets, slave narratives, lectures, and convention programs are preservable resources that continue to illuminate our understanding of early black protest activities.

As the Hortons point out, antebellum middle-class black activists were also influenced by the issues of gender identity current in nineteenth-century America. Specifically, they carried on an energetic public debate about the relationship between black manhood and the pursuit of freedom. Some, such as David Walker and newspaperman John Russwurm, advocated open confrontation and violence as the only path to freedom and manhood for black men in American society. The call to "be a man" was often used to counter arguments about the dangers of open rebellion for those still enslaved. The emotional appeal of this position is so powerful that it is difficult to follow the debate without becoming ensnared in the trap of equating manhood with violence. However, an alternative definition of manhood in the abolitionist movement was inspired by Quakerism, one that emphasized strength of character and principled action. And there were black leaders prepared to assert still other definitions of manhood, including Frederick Douglass and Maria Stewart.

Douglass was against violence, unless it was a sanctioned form such as military service. Such action he perceived as a way for black men to prove their manhood through fighting for their own freedom, while at the same time upholding and safeguarding the treasured American ideals of freedom and equality. He was not a pacifist, and he certainly had sympathy for the idea of expressing manhood through violent resistance. His autobiography recounted his own refusal to be beaten by the slavemaster Covey and the resultant two-hour fight. However, Douglass believed that violent rebellion was doomed to failure in the face of overwhelming force. And he most assuredly did not equate violence with manhood.

Maria Stewart was another who called for black men to affirm their manhood through means other than violence. James and Lois Horton note that Stewart espoused a "Masculine Achiever" or Self Made Man framework for black men. First, it was paramount that black men assert their equality to white men. Stewart then encouraged competition in the capitalist market-place, along with striving for achievement and economic independence. She also admonished successful free black men to remain committed to the black community and to be involved in the struggle for freedom. Like Douglass, Stewart did not generally support violence, but she was in favor of black men fighting as soldiers for their freedom, as they had done in the American Revolution and the War of 1812.

It could be said that the leaders of the new black urban middle class in the North generally equated the ongoing struggle for freedom and equality, however it was carried out, with black manhood. Freedom and equality for black people in the nineteenth century came to be understood and expressed in masculine terms. One of the consequences of this equation would be seen in the demand that women accept a position of inferiority in black society in order to uphold the "manhood" of black men, which was equivalent to the salvation of the race. This demand has had ramifications throughout the nineteenth and twentieth centuries, for both men and women.

The same emphasis on manhood as emblematic of the pride of the race is made in William Becker's "The Black Church: Manhood and Mission." In this essay, we see how the black preacher in the rural South evolved as a significant spiritual, cultural, and community leader. However, Becker also examines aspects of the black church and male leadership that seem to be specific to developments in the North.

For free blacks in the North, the separate black church became the most important center for black political culture and leadership. Individuals such as Richard Allen and Daniel Coker, founders of the African Methodist Episcopal Church in Philadelphia in 1816; Samuel Cornish, who estab-lished the Colored Presbyterian Church in New York; and Thomas Paul, who built the African Baptist Church in Boston, all used their establish-ments as bases for political activism. The emergence of these official reli-gious institutions independent of their white counterparts in the slave-free North encouraged the internal growth of a political activism not yet possi-ble for blacks in the South. Such activity among middle-class free blacks in the South would surely have resulted in the loss of an already shaky freedom.

Becker points out that the independent black church movement in the North coincided with the birth of the American Colonization Society in 1816, an organization founded by whites who favored the settlement of free black Americans in Africa. Some influential white Americans believed that colonization in Liberia was the answer to the problem of the growing free black population, which they perceived as a threat. The ACS framed its movement as an opportunity for free, educated, Christian black men and women to emigrate to Africa as missionaries. Some black men who were prominent in free black communities in the North—for example, Captain

Paul Cuffe and John Russwurm, founder of the first black newspaper, *Freedom's Journal*—lent their support to colonization in Liberia because they were convinced that black people would never be treated as equal citizens on American shores. This particular expression of black male identity seems to have been most characteristic among leaders in independent churches in free northern black communities, the new class of black entrepreneurs, and African-born blacks. The masses of American blacks expressed vehement opposition to colonization in Africa, and they soon forced the black male leadership to reject their initial support for the enterprise. At the same time, they rejected African missions, preferring the abolition of slavery as a political focus.

After emancipation, however, black manhood became characterized by a strong Christian missionary outlook in some northern cities. (Women were again relegated to support roles, usually as missionary wives, although black women would continue to fight for the opportunity to serve as missionaries until 1888, when Sarah E. Gorham became the first woman granted this right by the AME.) This view appears to have been particularly strong in the AME church, where Becker notes that, generally, black Christian manhood was equated with four identifying characteristics: leadership and self-assertion, black identity, independence, and Christian vocation. Individuals such as Allen and Bishop Payne wrote that the AME church had a crucial role in the creation of what they called a "heaven-created manhood." They described black manliness as the cultivation of dignity, integrity, and independence of character, thought, and action. Personal courage and commitment were also important character traits. And especially in reference to leadership potential, black male Christians were perceived as "militant soldiers for the cross," who were daring, exhibited an indomitable will, and displayed a relentless pioneering spirit.

Some of the leaders in the independent black churches, then, combined nineteenth-century missionary zeal with aspirations for freedom and equality. They encouraged recently freed blacks to achieve a Christian education and emigrate to Africa, where they would be recognized as "men." It was an idea that appealed to some black males in leadership roles within independent churches, because it fulfilled their middle-class aspirations. They would be regarded favorably as independent, educated Christian leaders who had been chosen by God for the special missionary work of leading other men of color to Jesus.

Social, political, and religious organizations were not the only institutions created by African American men. In Philadelphia, a group of about sixty men organized an institution for the purpose of stimulating the minds of young black men through public programs. Inspired by the black American intellectual Benjamin Banneker (1731–1806), these men founded the Banneker Institute in 1853. Its success was based upon a strong network of black families and friendships influential in the intellectual, political, social, and economic life of black urban Philadelphians. The institute pursued its mission for almost two decades.

The Banneker story also reflects on the nature of class among the new, free black urban communities in the North by describing the lives of one very specific group. The Banneker Institute offered the middle-class black men who founded it a means of distinguishing themselves from the masses of unskilled, poor, illiterate free black men. Members were recruited only from among the middle-class and upper-middle-class blacks in Philadelphia. An individual young male had to be nominated, and membership was by invitation only. In addition, because the institute's main goals were educational, some degree of intellectual achievement was a prerequisite.

Although Lapsansky's essay focuses on one middle-class black male organization, it includes enough information to suggest interesting comparisons between black men's and women's clubs. Male and female benevolent and literary societies were parallel movements, existing in relationship to and not in isolation from each other, even though they grew out of differential sex roles and maintained gender-specific identities. The black women connected to the Banneker Institute as wives, teachers, or friends seem to have shared the same social positions, values, and beliefs as the men. They expressed their support in various ways, including attending public functions, donating books, and serving as lecturers, all while busily involved with their own organizations. Several prominent black female intellectuals of the day actually delivered some of the more fascinating lectures, dealing with topics normally handled by men. Sarah Mapps Douglass gave a science lecture on anatomy in 1855, and Mary Ann Shadd brought the group her powerful political message concerning Canadian emigration in the same year. And a young male member named Parker T. Smith actually gave a progressive lecture entitled "The History of Women" in 1855, which attracted a full house.

The young black men who came through the Banneker Institute made close friendships and lifelong business connections with other middle-class black men. They were encouraged to be active in public service and would become an important source of leadership in black communities. Many of the young members went on as adult men to become influential educators and activists in Philadelphia, establishing schools, newspapers, banks, and historical societies, and working for the free black citizen's right to vote. Many of the ideals and institutions that the founders of the Banneker Institute honored and initiated were passed on to their descendants, who preserved them into the twentieth century.

Clearly, the American experience was a diverse phenomenon for black men and women, whether they were slave or free. From the very beginning, African Americans resisted their enslavement and oppression, even while working as an unpaid labor force, raising families, and creating interesting cultural complexes and communities throughout the South, North, and the mid-Atlantic states. However, by the mid-nineteenth century, the slave experience defined the lives of all black Americans, and the ideology of race had become the dominant theme in the everyday lives of African Americans.

SLAVE CONSPIRATORS AND WARRIORS

The nineteenth century was the nadir. The American South made the transition to a society entirely dependent upon slavery as a central economic institution. The master–slave dynamic became entrenched and was most fully developed as the paradigm of black–white relations. Racism—the belief in the inherent inferiority of the black "race"—paralleled the entrenchment of slavery and was used to justify the increased exploitation of blacks as America's agricultural labor force. Black Americans were relegated to a subordinate position within the hierarchy of American society that appeared to be permanent.

Three different essays examine the specific evolving relations between black men and mainstream American society. These essays take varying approaches, but they all deal with some of the larger social forces that affected black men's lives throughout the first half of the nineteenth century: changes in slavery which triggered more radical response from black men, the growth of racism with its accompanying myths, and black men's role in the American wars for expansion.

Radical Resistance

Some black men took a quite radical approach to solving the dilemma of relentless bondage and oppression. Douglas R. Egerton's "'Fly across the River': The Easter Slave Conspiracy of 1802" looks at the nature of early-nineteenth-century black male revolt and how white men responded to what they perceived as black male insubordination. The Virginia–North Carolina plot discussed by Egerton is best understood as a transitional event that sheds light on black men's response to the implementation of harsh slave codes, as well as the complex implications of their own acculturation into American society. Such examples of early crisis effectively convey the grim nature of the "new slavery" and the near impossibility of escape for black men, women, and children. But we are likewise struck by the persistence of armed resistance on the part of black men up to and including the Civil War.

Egerton's essay is an examination of a largely unexplored conspiracy. The author presents a fascinating historical dimension to the plot, as well as attempts to trace the movements of the conspiracy as it wound its way among the black boatmen who worked the Virginia–North Carolina riverways. The historical angle is particularly useful in illuminating the black male response to early-nineteenth-century events. For example, Egerton's evidence reveals that black men devised, discussed, and planned this conspiracy on the basis of knowledge gleaned from previous insurrections. In fact, this 1802 conspiracy was linked to the 1800 rebellion led by the slave Gabriel Prosser. Located near Richmond, Virginia, and involving as many as a thousand slaves with plans to attack the city, the Prosser rebellion was representative of the unrest and insurrection prevalent along the eastern seaboard during the first decades of the nineteenth century. Because of the widespread nature of the Prosser conspiracy, Egerton thinks that Sancho, the slave leader of the 1802 conspiracy, was probably involved in the Petersburg, Virginia, wing of Gabriel's plot and adjusted his plans for insurrection accordingly. Consequently, Sancho enlisted far fewer men than the Gabriel plot, went to great pains to guard the secret date of the revolt, and did not stockpile arms.

The historical dimension that Egerton brings to the subject of radical resistance allows us to suggest a sort of profile for the charismatic leaders who instigated revolts and the black men who chose to follow this course of action. It also makes it possible to identify some of the effects of acculturation on radical resistance as an ongoing theme in the experiences of black American men. Both Sancho and Gabriel Prosser before him possessed knowledge of some type of skilled trade. Sancho was a ferryman, or skilled navigator, on the Roanoke River, while Prosser was by training a blacksmith. They were also literate men, married with families, and already regarded as leaders in their respective slave or free communities. In addition, the sixty or so identified followers whom Sancho recruited were also skilled slaves, comprising a dedicated lot of rivermen, ship artisans, sailmakers, pilots, riggers, dock workers, and caulkers.

Sancho and his men were accustomed to being hired out, thereby earning cash for themselves above the amount they were required to hand over to their masters. Egerton thinks that the introduction of a cash flow into the equation increased the impetus in these early-nineteenth-century enslaved men to plot rebellion. It seems certain that the occupations of these men are what first brought them together and served as a basis for collective radical action. In addition, most were married and were clearly devising a future for themselves that incorporated not merely escape, but support for themselves and their families in freedom. Egerton suggests that the possession of valuable skills led these men to believe that they would be able to find work and become self-sufficient and independent. Thus, in their trial depositions, Sancho and his chosen followers attested to their attempts to implement a well-thought-out plan in which they demanded freedom, the monies owed them from hiring out, and the distribution of property.

The nature of their demands also reinforces what twenty years of scholarly case studies have began to show: that significant acculturation had occurred by the nineteenth century, and that the process influenced black men and women's ideas about resistance and their place in American society. Unlike the earlier rebellious Africans who plotted the 1739 Stono Rebellion, the deadliest revolt in colonial history, or the many fugitives who escaped to form frontier societies in Florida, Sancho and his men did not seek to return to the land of their African ancestors or to create maroon communities. Nor did they call for the overthrow of the New Republic. Instead, they planned to fit into the American ideal of middle-class manhood by acquiring their freedom, working as free wage earners, and becoming owners of property. Furthermore, they were so rooted to their home places in the South that most would not even consider fleeing their respective states. In fact, they actually expressed their intentions to stay in their home counties in Virginia and North Carolina, living independently and working among the family, friends, and whites they already knew, after they had taken their freedom. No individual stated his ambitious goals with more certainty than the slave Salem, whom Sancho had recruited from the North Carolina shipyards. Salem declared that he was fighting to gain control over his own time, labor, and earnings. "United we can do anything," Salem told the other enslaved men, even "fly across the river." Clearly these men were fired up by recent revolutionary ideals. As Egerton suggests, these particular enslaved men expressed well-defined aspirations for equality, independence, and citizenship.

The white male response, though, was anything but egalitarian. Ultimately, twenty-five black men were executed as a result of the conspiracy, and scores of others were beaten, whipped, cropped, and branded. The North Carolina slave codes stipulated that slaves who committed crimes were to be punished and permanently scarred, "the punishment whereof shall extend to life, limb, or member." However, conspiracies and rebellions continued unabated throughout the South, which led to all manner of counter-activities in an attempt to fight this undeclared war. Southern states convened special sessions of their legislatures to deal with what they designated as states of emergency. They strengthened slave codes, restricting the movements and gatherings of blacks, slave and free, and making it a crime to teach enslaved people to read. White males who worked in state patrols closely watched blacks, and were always in a state of armed readiness to uncover the next planned insurrection or put down the next violent uprising.

The nation also made it increasingly difficult to free slaves, severely inhibiting the growth of the free black population in the South. By the mid-1830s, free black men could vote only in the four northern states of Maine, Massachusetts, Vermont, and New Hampshire. Free blacks were effectively segregated in all areas of daily life, while the masses of enslaved people were now tied to the cotton culture and the paternalistic structure that supported it.

However, the vicious attempts of free white men to convince enslaved black men of the futility of plots and insurrections were as unsuccessful as the plots themselves. In spite of the hopeless odds enslaved men faced, they refused to give up the belief that revolts might one day succeed. In 1810, a plot was discovered in Lexington, Kentucky. In 1811, slave Charles Deslondes led almost four hundred slaves to revolt in St. John the Baptist and St. Charles parishes in Louisiana; about seventy-five whites fled to New Orleans for safety, but the next year found them experiencing the same terror of black rebellion in the Crescent City. George Boxley tried to free the slaves in Virginia in 1815. When whites found out about his detailed plans, Boxley escaped, but six conspirators were hanged, and six others were banished from the state, a common punishment for insurrection under the slave codes. The most famous insurrection of the 1820s was engineered by a literate free carpenter named Denmark Vesey in Charleston, South Carolina, in 1822. Louisiana was again the site of several uprisings in 1829.

What white southerners feared most became a reality in 1831, when the bloodiest insurrection in U.S. history occurred in Southampton County, Virginia. The Nat Turner Revolt may also indicate a major shift in the nature and history of black male resistance. Egerton states that Turner was black America's first non-secular rebel leader. He describes Turner as a charismatic man with a messianic vision. As he notes, this was one man who did not give a damn about fighting his way into the social, economic, or political fabric of American society. Instead, Turner tried to tear it asunder by annihilating all whites and bringing on the day of final reckoning. It may be that by the 1830s, slave men were moving toward the conclusion that nothing but armed and bloody war, with mass destruction and loss of life, would ever end the evil that was slavery.

Black men plotted and planned till slavery's end. A conspiracy erupted in Monroe County in 1835. Several of the rebels were hanged, or whipped until they died. Insurrection followed the spread of slavery westward into the Deep South. Throughout the 1840s and 1850s, revolts were reported in Mississippi, Alabama, and Louisiana. The 1853 slave rebellion in New Orleans involved twenty-five hundred men. And in 1856, several North Carolina counties reported that unruly male slaves were again terrorizing the state.

It is clear, then, that the idea of the violent overthrow of slavery occupied an important psychic space in the lives of black men. It may be that black male revolt came to be associated with manhood and masculinity, for it was an unequivocal challenge to white male authority. Armed rebellion was direct confrontation, a decision, once made, from which there was no turning back. Most nineteenth-century black men who participated in what whites saw as equivalent to a type of guerilla warfare against the state were killed in an effort that would ultimately fail. But other enslaved people remembered, and they passed down the names of the rebellious slave leaders, who came to be regarded as symbols of heroic black male behavior. African American men would not get a chance to participate in the sanctioned, militant abolition of slavery until the institution's very existence threatened the integrity of the United States. But until then, they sacrificed life and limb and willingly shed the blood of whites in the name of freedom.

SEXUAL STEREOTYPES AND RAPE MYTHOLOGIES

Black men's response to the larger world outside their slave and free communities involved more than the hostile relations they endured with white men on a daily basis. They were forced to adhere to certain racial codes pertaining to white women as well. As racism grew in the nineteenth century, it was accompanied by the development of stereotypes and racial myths. Among the most pervasive and deeply embedded stereotypes is the black man as the rapist of white women, a negative symbol of iconic proportions. Scholars, particularly those reconstructing the history of the South and the history of sexualities, have only recently begun the serious study of such phenomena. They are tracing the historical evolution of racial mythologies, in an attempt to understand their origins, their development, and the role they play in race ideology. "The Rape Myth in the Old South Reconsidered," by Diane Miller Sommerville, is an example of the new research in this area.

Sommerville's case study investigates the combined influence of gender conventions, race, and class in relation to black men and rape in rural Southampton County, Virginia. Southampton reported more than two hundred cases of black men, slave and free, accused of sexually assaulting white women between 1800 and 1865. In about half of these cases, the local white citizenry actually suspended sentences of execution. Sommerville's research is strong reinforcement for the theoretical goals of this reader, for her work indicates that historians have too quickly assumed that late-nineteenth-century fears about black male sexuality were present in the antebellum period and earlier. In reality, according to the author, the most pervasive racial fear in the antebellum South was of slave violence, not the black rapist. White Americans perceived the rebellion—in our view, justified resistance—as slave violence expressly directed toward them. As Sommerville notes, whites included acts of poisoning, arson, and murder among their complaints, but their greatest fear was the chilling possibility of black men in armed rebellion. The rape of white women by black men was simply not among the dominant fears in the antebellum South. Blacks, however, were given the death penalty for rape more frequently than white men convicted of the same crime.

Sommerville focuses on class and its role in relationships between black men and white women, and among whites, showing that the taboo against interracial sex we have so long assumed to have existed is actually part of the myth of race and sex in America. There is a history of sexual relations between black men and white women that dates back to the colonial era. They married in the colonies and carried on overt relationships until the implementation of laws that prohibited such unions beginning in the mid- to late eighteenth century. White male leaders in the colonies sought to control the sexual behavior of white women by passing laws that penalized their associations with black men with monetary fines, jail time, public humiliation, increased indentured servitude, and other punitive practices. By the nineteenth century, relationships between the two groups were deemed illegal, but they certainly continued, mainly with white women of marginal class status.

When Sommerville looked at Southampton in the nineteenth century, she found that in a number of cases, elite whites moved to protect their economic investments in slavery by successfully preventing the executions of black men convicted of raping poor white women and girls. In other words, white women who continued to conduct illicit unions with black men were still being punished. In fact, the racial ideology of the day had come to label all white women who had relations and children with black men as whores. Poor white women in southern society fell outside the perimeters of respectable white womanhood, and if they chose to consort with black men, in any way and at any time, their actions effectively negated their right to expect protection from white men. These exclusionary practices did not change until after emancipation, when racial ideology evolved in such a way that all whites, irrespective of class or other divisions, benefited from the privilege of their skin color.

Ironically, it does not appear that there was ever any special abhorrence of rape by black men, in comparison to any other criminal activity. Moreover, it seems that neither the white nor the black men involved regarded rape as a serious crime, unless the victim was a white woman of a certain elevated class. Black women did not enter into the equation. Therefore, it is understandable that leniency toward rapists did not extend to cases in which white women who were members of the planter class were assaulted. Black men rarely raped women from the upper classes, but when it happened, death by execution was carried out, and mob rule was likely. Some leniency toward black men prevailed in Southampton County, even in the aftermath of the Nat Turner Revolt in 1831. And as the nation moved closer to civil war, the trend toward avoiding the imposition of capital punishment for black men found guilty of rape actually increased.

In the final analysis, then, Sommerville asks us to consider the dimensions of class and gender to be as important as race in southern history. In the social history of the South, especially among whites, class sometimes superseded race and, when combined with gender, worked to the detriment of marginal groups such as poor white and black women. Furthermore, the combined effects of race, class, gender, and economic issues appear to have made strange bedfellows out of elite whites and enslaved men. Arguably, these groups may have found common ground in their devaluation of a certain class of women. Still, white males were at all times clearly in charge of the punishment of black men and of white women for sexual transgression.

Fears about black male sexual assault require a historical context. Black rape myths began to appear during emancipation and exploded during Reconstruction, when whites expressed their fears of unprecedented black political power by creating the appearance of a solid white racial front. Only then did poor white women eventually become southern ladies, while every black man became a potential rapist. As Sommerville asserts, nineteenth-century race ideology was an incredibly fluid concept.

BLACK SOLDIERS IN THE WARS OF EXPANSION

The nineteenth century was also the most important era for territorial expansion. Major American wars of expansion were fought, which involved black men's involuntary participation. Thus examination of the black male role in the U.S. military conflicts in the decades preceding the Civil War can add to our understanding of how black men have historically responded to American aggression.

The Revolutionary War had established two important precedents for black and white men, in terms of the history of war and military service in the States. Black men had served in all divisions of the army during the war, including the Continental Army, the state militias, units made up of U.S. allies, and the navy. Given that several thousand achieved freedom in this manner, some black men began to view military service as a means of liberation. The Revolutionary War was a fight for freedom, whether one was fighting for American independence or the British Crown. An interesting pattern became apparent after the Revolution, however, and it was obviously based on the growing racism and the practice of exclusion. Whenever the country was at peace, and the need for combat soldiers was at a low level, the military excluded black men. Thus, toward the end of the post-revolutionary period, and during the first half of the nineteenth century, black men were hampered in their attempts to participate in the newly formed military apparatus as a means of achieving freedom and equality.

Legal measures went into effect that strongly limited black men's participation in the American military and cemented segregation in the armed forces. Congress passed the Militia Act in 1792, making it possible for every healthy white male citizen between the ages of eighteen and forty-five to enroll in the army. Although the act did not directly mention restrictions on enslaved or free black males, blacks were discouraged and excluded from joining, especially in the North. In keeping with the southern practice of employing blacks in more diverse occupations, white southerners still hired out enslaved men to military units for service duties, while some free blacks served in various military capacities. According to a 1798 law, black men could not enlist in the Marine Corps, and neither could "Indians" or Mulattoes." The navy was the only branch of the military that could not afford discrimination. Black men worked on the majority of navy crews, including warships.

The War of 1812

The wars for expansion were problematic, irrespective of the limitations black men experienced. The War of 1812, for instance, was a mass of contradictions. Throughout its duration, there was never a clear-cut issue over which to risk one's life, so it was difficult to whip up any patriotic fervor, even among white males. The United States claimed that the war was a result of interference with their shipping rights. But the New England and Middle Atlantic states most affected by shipping opposed the war, since many sympathized with Great Britain's struggle against Napoleon. Ironically, the South and West screamed loudest for war because they favored expansion. They demanded that the British leave Canada, which had supported Indian opposition, thereby hampering American efforts to seize more lands. Thus, the War of 1812 was one in which neither the British nor the Americans made much of an effort. Generally, it was regarded as an unjustified and self-serving war, fueled mainly by the expansionist goals of the South and West.

Clearly, the War of 1812 involved no strong principles that might have drawn black men into it if they had not already been barred. But after two disastrous years on land and sea, and after the British burned the capital of Washington, D.C., in 1814, the military again opened its doors to black men. White New Yorkers passed legislation to raise two black regiments. Each was made up over a thousand men, and they were to be paid the same as white soldiers. Service was open to enslaved and freedmen, but slaves served only if their owners hired them out. To add to the indignity, the owners were paid their enlistment bonuses and wages. Enslaved men were promised their freedom only if they hired out for three years in the military.

Philadelphia also organized black battalions, specifically from among its free community. Three of the city's most prominent black male leaders, Bishop Richard Allen, Absalom Jones, and James Forten, were asked to encourage black men to aid in protecting the city. More than twenty-five hundred free black men worked nonstop for two days constructing defenses. The New York and Philadelphia regiments, though, never were trained or went into combat, because the British soon agreed to the Treaty of Ghent, which ended the war. Black men met with more success enlisting in the navy, which authorized the employment of free blacks. Blacks made up 10 to 20 percent of American sailors and took part in the naval battles on the Great Lakes that finally ended the war.

Black soldiers' most important land engagements occurred in New Orleans under General Andrew Jackson. Jackson issued a strong appeal to Louisiana's Battalion of Free Men of Color, promising them equal pay ($24), land (160 acres), and treatment. More than six hundred black men responded, and at the Battle of New Orleans they helped Jackson and his forces mow down more than fifteen hundred British soldiers, while the Americans lost only sixty men. Since that battle was fought after the Treaty of Ghent was signed, some scholars have stated that it had no effect on the war and was more significant for the political standing it gave the U.S. in Europe, as well as for bestowing military fame upon Andrew Jackson and influencing his presidential election. But to the freedmen who fought with him, Jackson kept his promises of equal pay, land, and the respect that men allot other men for honorable service in war.

It is likely that this was the most significant group of black men to benefit from participation in the War of 1812, and they were already free. Enslaved men did run off to the British lines seeking freedom, as they had done during the War of Independence. But it is not known exactly how many reached freedom. In fact, the British returned many to slavery after the war, since the Treaty of Ghent required them to restore all personal property to its American owners, including territory and slaves.

The U.S. government continued its racist policies after the War of 1812, finally passing legislation that expressly stated that black men were not to be treated as citizens equal to white men. When Congress authorized the formation of a postwar American army of ten thousand soldiers, black men were not actively recruited. The army issued orders with a specific racial bias in 1820 and 1821, formally stating that blacks and mulattoes would be rejected as army recruits, and that military service was restricted to free white males. This policy was widely adopted by state militias.

Again the navy proved to be a different case. Black men, including runaway slaves, had continued to enlist in the U.S. Navy until an 1816 act prohibited slaves from working on ships. Despite the new law, some owners still hired enslaved men out in order to claim their wages. Gradually, though, even the navy came into line with the strengthening of racist attitudes in the country. After the War of 1812, black men were still 10 percent of navy enlisted personnel, but increasing complaints from white men about competition in the job force finally caused the navy to pass restrictions affecting black men's ability to get work. In 1839, the navy ordered that black men were to make up no more than 5 percent of personnel. By the 1830s, then, the U.S. Army was an exclusively white male institution, and the navy practiced a quota system with respect to black men.

Given that racism was becoming part of U.S. military institutions, it is small wonder that black men continued to find other ways to express their need to fight for their freedom. Like those who took part in rebellions on behalf of their own people, many chose to collaborate with Native Americans in rebellious action against the U.S. military and government. Once again, this activity on the part of America's non-white males grew out of the country's expansionist policies during the early decades of the nineteenth century.

War against the Seminoles

The U.S. purchased Florida early in 1819. This was a pivotal event, which unleashed a tremendously rebellious response on the part of the Indian and black allied forces in that territory that did not end until the 1840s. The Seminoles fought two wars with the U.S. government. The first began in 1816, when Andrew Jackson was assigned the duty of destroying an independent black frontier community based at an abandoned British outpost called Negro Fort. Negro Fort had been established by slaves who escaped to Florida after the War of 1812. Jackson and his men first killed most of the fort's three hundred defenders. They then carried on their military campaign against the village by recapturing the male escapees and returning them to their owners. The Seminoles and their African American allies were finally defeated in 1819.

The incorporation of Florida territory into a state in 1822 aggravated the rebellions by Indians and blacks. The Indians, fighting for their lands and their way of life, raided white settlements as far away as Georgia, stealing slaves and killing whites. Thus the second war began in 1835, when American troops were sent in to put down the rebellions, destroy the independent black and Indian communities, and forcibly take all Indian lands. The war involved state militias from Florida, Georgia, and Tennessee.

These were probably the only armed conflicts in the first half of the nineteenth century that aroused a passion for freedom in black men similar to the passion they felt toward their own struggles. Hence, those involved participated of their own free will. They fought not only for their freedom, but to preserve the culture and communities they had built with their Seminole comrades in arms. So many black men took part in the Seminole Wars, and they fought with such skill, bravery, and endurance, that white American soldiers often described it as a black man's war. At any rate, Osceola, a brilliant warrior of the Seminole people, led his men and their black allies so successfully that they were able to repel force after force sent against them. The black and Indian wars were not concluded until 1842, with the loss of about eighteen hundred men, and a cost to the U.S. government of $40 million.

The Mexican War

By the time of the Mexican War, the last major conflict of the antebellum era, participation in the U.S. military was perceived as a white male preserve. Technically, the army was, on the basis of its own legislation, all white by the time of the Seminole Wars, and it remained so. The navy's quota system allowed for the presence of at least 1,000 black sailors during this conflict. About 160,000 white Americans served in the Mexican War, while 1,300 perished from disease or in battle. Official military records have traditionally claimed that no black men served in the Mexican War because they were prohibited from doing so. Historians had likewise conceded that there was no work to be done regarding black men's involvement in what was essentially America's first foreign war.

However, Robert E. May's essay "Invisible Men: Blacks and the U.S. Army in the Mexican War" investigates a number of black men who actually served with the American forces after they reached Mexico. Until now, little attention has been given to discovering the identities of these men or citing their accomplishments. In discussing the reasons for this, May suggests that, given the fact that black men were now excluded from the U.S. Army, the only role open to them was that of "service duty," a far less dramatic or heroic role than that of combat soldier or leader. Still, examining even the previously ignored experience of black men's voluntary and involuntary "service duty" can inform us about the evolving connections between race, class, and gender in the American military. Furthermore, the experiences of those who were part of America's first foreign war predicted much of the official racist and inhumane treatment that black men would receive at the hands of the U.S. military in successive wars on foreign soil.

White American men entered the Mexican War carrying traditional notions about war, leadership, and status attached to military service. They expected, and demanded, servants to take care of their personal needs. The practice was sanctioned by the U.S. government in federal regulations that not only allowed major generals up to four servants, but reimbursed officers when they hired servants. Therefore, May points out, male servants were dispersed throughout the American troops that went to war. Most were enslaved or free black men, although a few seem to have been Mexican, Indian, and ethnic whites such as the Irish.

Some black men did actually enlist as soldiers, seizing the opportunity to fight in battle after reaching Mexico. John Taylor, for example, managed to enlist by passing for white, but he was dishonorably discharged when found out. And since black servants routinely followed their owners into battle, many found themselves in the thick of combat even though they were not soldiers. Dick Green, who shouldered arms after his owner, Charles Brent, was killed, was wounded at the Battle of El Embudo. Most black men, though, performed routine camp duty, while they struggled to stay alive and take care of their owners.

Performance of the services required of them, however, did not result in a reprieve from the racial attitudes typical of white male behavior back home. American troops elevated their egos and safely indulged their racial hostilities toward black men through verbal abuse, encouraging the spread of racial stereotypes in Mexico, and violent assaults. The word "nigger" was in common use, and white men frequently entertained themselves telling stories about the supposed cowardice of black men in combat. White males participated in such group behavior in order to instill fear in black men and to maintain blacks' subordinate status in a highly charged military environment. Racial threats of this sort, though, could easily take a violent turn. There were reported incidents involving the outright murder of black men, along with several instances in which black men were convicted of crimes and executed. A free black servant from Kentucky, whose sentence was later acknowledged as unjustified, was hanged for allegedly raping a Mexican woman. On the other hand, a white man who shot a free mulatto servant named Samuel was sentenced to just one year in prison. May suggests that there were probably other unprovoked murders of black servants that went unreported. And in general, the racial hostility that black men experienced was compounded by the ill effects, and deaths in disproportionate numbers, that resulted from the everyday hardships of military life and war. Disease, lack of food, shelter, and medical care, accidents, and horrific weather all contributed to a high mortality rate.

May's essay shows how racial discrimination increasingly characterized the U.S. armed forces' relationship to black men. Nineteenth-century racial policies ultimately resulted in black men's being able to participate in the Mexican War only in subservient roles. When that war is compared to black men's previous American military engagements, alongside their long history of slave flight, conspiracy, and rebellion, it is possible to make a few assessments about how black men perceived the Mexican War and their role in it.

The Mexican War and the War of 1812 are significant for the lack of interest they generated among black men as vehicles for achieving freedom. Certainly the growing racism in the military limited opportunities to exchange freedom for military service. Moreover, the self-serving nature of these wars did not motivate black men to fight. The Revolutionary War had been fought over the higher principles of equality, independence, and freedom, ideals that enslaved black men could extend to themselves through active participation. At the same time, whites in the revolutionary era had initially been more influenced by its ideals and had freed large numbers of black men who fought in the war. Even those who fought on the British side found freedom in other lands.

CONNECTING RADICAL RESISTANCE
TO MILITARY SERVICE

The same motivating factor was involved in armed rebellion, conspiracies, and slave flight. From the Stono Rebellion (1739) to the Nat Turner Revolt (1831), from King William's War (1689) to the Mexican War (1846), whether as rebel warriors against the state or as part of a sanctioned military apparatus, black men were fighting for freedom. Whereas white males may have seen one action as rebellion and the other as patriotism, the goal was the same for black men. Black men who may have disagreed over whether to rebel against the worst that was America (slavery) or to fight to preserve the best that was America (its democratic ideals) were all reaching for freedom and equality.

Thus, by the antebellum era, we can speak of an evolving black male consciousness that linked freedom to black men's radical resistance, on the one hand, and to military service, on the other, in a way heretofore unacknowledged. From this perspective, it is understandable why the wars for expansion attracted the involvement of so few black men or held so little symbolic importance for them. It may also further explain the persistence of conspiracies and armed rebellion as important alternative outlets for resistance in an era of increased slave vigilance and restrictions. At any rate, the long history of combined rebel and military activity as a decidedly male response to slavery and racism had much to do with black men's phenomenal response to the American Civil War.

According to sociologist Michael Kimmel, all wars are "meditations on masculinity." In *Manhood in America* (1996), Kimmel claims that the Civil War was as much about contesting masculinities and an alternative model of manhood as it was about the "morality of slavery," the politics of states' rights, or the conflict between a southern agrarian economy and northern industrial capitalism. The author argues that when we examine the War Between the States as a "gendered war," it reveals itself as an embittered conflict to settle which version of manhood should dominate America.

The years leading up to the Civil War saw the furor surrounding slave abolition fuel debates about manhood. There was, for instance, the model of the Self Made Man, prevalent in the North among the upper classes and "urban industrial entrepreneurs." The North and the eastern regions of the country were often described as the domain of weak, over-civilized, over-educated, elite white males. Kimmel suggests that this group of men saw the war as a means of proving their manhood.

The southern elite saw themselves as authentic aristocrats whose genteel way of life was based on the idea of the white patriarch, authoritarian father over all he owned and ruled. Even though the majority of southern white males were not members of this class, they participated in an agrarian ideology that believed in the male as supreme authority and presented a picture of southern white men as honorable, chivalrous toward women, and more community-oriented than their moneygrubbing, commerce-driven northern brothers.

CIVIL WAR AND THE MEANING OF BLACK MANHOOD

This reader, of course, is especially concerned with how black men responded to the "question of manhood." The ramifications of how the question was settled were far more intense and important for enslaved men and women than for anyone else. For out of the horrendous conflict of the Civil War, the meaning of black manhood in America became inseparable from freedom and equality. This particular worldview allowed black men to eventually see their role in the Civil War as one of duty and responsibility. By the time the Union made it legal for black men to enlist to fight in the war, they had come to believe that emancipation and the birthright of citizenship depended upon how well they conducted themselves in military service. Whereas native-born white American men, irrespective of their position on the "question of manhood," were already in possession of citizenship, and hence the right to soldier, former slaves believed that they had to prove their manhood as soldiers first. Only then would the country reward them with freedom and citizenship for all African Americans.

Five essays were chosen for this reader because they all deal in some way with the Civil War as social revolution, and the meaning of black manhood, freedom, and citizenship. "'I's a Man Now': Gender and African American Men" by Jim Cullen looks at the impact of national discussions of manhood rights in the mid-nineteenth century. What Cullen calls the "manly rhetoric of action" was a core of conservative ideas in which the willingness to fight in order to protect one's freedom, rights, and way of life was seen as indicative of an individual man's sense of duty to his nation. Manhood was obviously equated with duty and responsibility. Cullen notes that these ideas were mostly discussed and openly debated among white males, and in reference to black men, among those who were already free. Many free men expressed agreement with these general ideas about manhood. Hence, they were willing to fight because they believed they would not be regarded as men in the eyes of others until they proved their manhood by their willingness to go into battle and fight for their principles. Even though they were not regarded as citizens, they believed that their sacrifice would force the nation to recognize them as such.

Cullen also points out some of the different opinions and ambiguous feelings that free black men expressed at the beginning of the war. In the North, the consequences of war, and the particular issues black men would face in trying to enlist as soldiers, were openly debated in black newspapers. Some said the conflict was a white man's war, from which black men had nothing to gain in supporting a Republican government. Many freedmen stated that they would never volunteer for military service unless they could serve on an equal basis with white men. It would appear, then, that free black men in the North, who already regarded themselves as citizens, although unequal, did not fool themselves regarding the racism and exclusionary practices of whites. But most still felt compelled to struggle for the right to fight, in order to protect what rights they had attained and attempt to gain others.

At the beginning of the war, however, being willing to take up arms in defense of country and actually possessing the right to do so were not the same. All white men had the right to enlist and were encouraged to do so, but securing the right to participate was a protracted struggle for blacks. Michael O. Smith relates the story of black enlistment in Detroit in "Raising a Black Regiment in Michigan: Adversity and Triumph." His case study provides a much-needed look at local history and the logistics of black recruitment. Michigan's black regiments were organized only after much public debate, the efforts of a few influential white men, and the support of Detroit's black community. From the beginning, black men in Michigan were eager to join, seeing the war as the means to equality and the end to all slavery. They had even already organized themselves into the Detroit Liberty Guards, pledging to sacrifice their lives for freedom. But for two years they confronted numerous obstacles.

First, the incentives encouraging black men to enlist were very poor. The most important roadblock was economic discrimination. Black men were offered lower pay than white soldiers, and recruiters would not pay them the enlistment bounty of $150 that was allotted to white males. Black men also knew that "colored troops" were housed in dilapidated winter barracks with insufficient supplies. The economic difficulties were compounded by the fact that black men were being asked to enlist at the same time that the state economy was improving and more job opportunities had become available. Probably the most damaging impediment to recruitment, though, was the very public race-mongering carried out in Michigan newspapers. Racial stereotypes ridiculed black men as poor soldiers and cowards in battle. Despite all these difficulties, Michigan's black regiment was mustered into the Union Army with 895 men. They were attached to the Union's Department of the South and fought honorably in numerous battles and skirmishes with the Confederate forces in South Carolina.

Even more interesting was the large number of blacks in the First Michigan Colored Infantry who enlisted as substitutes for white men. As the war progressed, it became more difficult for states to meet their quotas for white enlistment, and passage of the Enrollment Act of March 1863 actually removed one white male from a state's draft quota for every black male who joined the army. This official act made substitution a legal escape route for white male citizens who could afford to buy their way out of the draft. Ultimately, more than 254 of the black men who made up the First Michigan Colored Infantry gained entry into the Civil War as substitutes, motivated by the fact that they were paid the three-hundred-dollar fee that the federal government required for escaping military service. Michigan records show that black substitutes not only fulfilled their obligations but, as a group, came through the war with very low desertion rates. It seems that free black men in Michigan were determined to conduct themselves honorably and with distinction.

The experiences of blacks in Louisiana offer another perspective on free black men, this time in one of the South's old, established communities of color. In "'To Come Forward and Aid in Putting Down This Unholy Rebellion': The Officers of Louisiana's Free Black Native Guard during the Civil War Era," Manoj K. Joshi and Joseph P. Reidy deal with the complicated issue of intra-racial division and its influence on the black military experience. Free blacks in Louisiana, most of them considered mulatto, were pulled in two directions by the Civil War. Their particular experience of the war, though, foreshadowed the struggle for political and civil rights that would distinguish the lives of American blacks in the post–Civil War era. It likewise provides a look at the evolution of black male leadership and how it was affected by the larger changes set in motion by the Civil War.

During the nineteenth century, free people of color had worked as professionals, artisans, and entrepreneurs, which enabled them to build a free black community where they enjoyed uncommon social, cultural, and economic privileges. In this French-dominated setting, a class system was encouraged to flourish among free blacks that inhibited any feelings of solidarity with enslaved blacks. Historically, free people of color in Louisiana maintained their position by distancing themselves from enslaved people and cultivating relations with white relatives, patrons, and allies.

The Louisiana example fits into what historical studies have generally discerned about the lives of some free black communities in the Lower South that have been identified as mulatto. Because these communities arose in the deep slave South, theirs was a limited freedom, an even more precarious situation than that of free blacks in the North. They tended to maintain connections with the whites who had freed them and had first provided the money, land, and education with which they had established themselves, their businesses, and their communities. Unlike free blacks in the North, who were somewhat freer to participate in the abolitionist movement and generally agitate for equality, free people in the South were less likely to be public activists. Identification with, and loyalty to, family and class seem to have come before any similar feelings about race.

Free men of color in Louisiana had a long history of using military service to protect their position. They fought with the French, the Spanish, and the United States. We have already discussed how they were among the limited number of blacks to benefit from fighting in the War of 1812. Unlike most black men, though, free people of color in Louisiana had a long history of freedom as well. Hence, they usually fought to protect their privileges and position, not to secure the freedom of black people as a whole. Such was the dilemma in which free black men in Louisiana found themselves at the outbreak of the Civil War.

Given their long history with the military, Louisiana's Free Black Native Guard were among the first free black regiments mustered into the war, and they fought the first important battles involving black soldiers. In May 1863, they conducted themselves in a ferocious battle to take Port Hudson with such bravery, skill, and loss of life that even the white officers proclaimed them superior to white troops. The Battle for Port Hudson became early evidence of the black soldier's stalwart character and fighting ability, and was commonly used as the standard by which other black men would be judged.

The Free Native Guard, originally organized to fight for the Confederacy, was designated a regiment of the state militia in order to circumvent regulations against blacks' participation in the Army of the Confederacy. The unit never fought for the South, however, and when their white counterparts fled New Orleans, leaving it to Union occupation, the Free Native Guard remained to offer their services to the North. They became the First Louisiana Native Guard and were joined by two other Native Guard units. Influenced by their deeply held notions about class and position in New Orleans society, they struggled mightily with the War Department over the issue of black officers. In the end, however, white male exclusionary practices successfully prevented free mulattoes in the Native Guard from serving in the Civil War as commissioned officers.

Still, the authors stress that, when defeated on one level, members of the

Native Guard, particularly its officers, began to broaden their approach to the struggle for equal rights and led the attack from other vantage points. The New Orleans free community was being influenced here by an unprecedented political activism that had begun during the Civil War. Free men around the country, anticipating the coming freedom of more than four million ex-slaves, had started to organize state conventions to deal with the political, economic, and social issues significant to the race. Joshi and Reidy point out that Native Guard officers attended the National Convention of Colored Men, which held its meeting in Syracuse, New York, in October of 1864. During that meeting, African Americans formed the National Equal Rights League, which urged black men to organize branches across the country. There were state conventions in South Carolina and Alabama the next year as well. At all of these conventions, the demands were the same: free black men claimed the same rights as white men to carry arms, hold public office, ride public transportation, act as jurists, educate themselves and their children, exercise free speech, and possess the right to vote. Most important, they claimed these rights for all black people irrespective of class or color.

Inspired and motivated by renewed political aspirations, officers from the Native Guard returned to Louisiana and organized their own state equal rights convention in 1865, out of which was formed their own chapter of the National Equal Rights League. They first turned their attention toward abolishing segregation on public transportation. In demanding first-class accommodations, they did everything from drawing their pistols to remind whites of their status as soldiers to organizing a public campaign followed by petitions to military authorities. Their activism actually achieved integration aboard streetcars in New Orleans for the most of the nineteenth century, until the implementation of Jim Crow laws.

They next turned their considerable energies toward the issue of black male suffrage. They had long pushed for voting rights, but only for free blacks. However, impending freedom for the masses of blacks forced upper-middle-class and elite free blacks around the country to recognize that they would have to share leadership and control with black men who only recently had been slaves. This explains why, shortly before their 1864 convention, free blacks in Louisiana still continued to demand the right to vote as the privilege of "intelligent free men." It was only after meeting with congressional Radicals that the free community in New Orleans saw their destiny as inseparable from that of those born slave, and their emancipation. As Joshi and Reidy describe it, free men now agitated in terms of "universal black suffrage." Their new political savvy was also probably the result of having attended the New York convention.

Unfortunately, the alliance was short-lived. Joshi and Reidy explain how differences in history and culture specific to the region made it nearly impossible to bridge the gap between those "born free and those born slave." The larger, national movement toward building alliances between the two groups, using a racial ideology whose fundamental belief was in a solidarity based upon the shared experience of African descent, slavery, and racial oppression in the New World, may have been the new rallying cry for freedom and equality in the years to come, but the old vanguard of free black male leaders in Louisiana allowed intra-racial and class conflicts to undermine the common struggle for freedom and civil rights for all. Their problematic response helped determine postwar conditions for all Louisiana blacks for decades to come.

The average black soldier in the Civil War was a former slave. From the moment that President Lincoln publicly proclaimed to the nation that the Civil War was about slavery, and at the same time legalized the widespread enlistment of former slaves, blacks began to see their future in America as tied to a complex relationship between nation and federal government, the military, and the struggle for human rights. All that America had promised in terms of democracy, liberty, and equality to its free citizens, but denied to those it held in bondage, would forevermore depend upon this intricate balance of principles and ideas, legislation, and military service. In essence, the Civil War turned the former slaves and free black men into soldier-citizens.

The Civil War experience, then, politicized black men, whether they fought as soldiers or rendered service as laborers for freedom. The war was the catalyst for much of the political, social, and economic change that was to come, a wide-ranging experiment that would test whether black people and human rights could coexist in the United States. It was during the Civil War that agencies were first introduced to deal with the reality of blacks' becoming members of civil society. Thus the war marked the transition for blacks between the struggle for emancipation and the upcoming lengthy battle for civil and human rights. At the same time, it further strengthened the belief that military service would continue to be an important public space where black men and women could wage the struggle for freedom. From now on, once black men became soldier-citizens, the main line of resistance was from within their native country's system of government, using its own laws and regulations to battle slavery's legacy, racism.

SOLDIER-CITIZENS AND THE
SECOND AMERICAN REVOLUTION

The last two essays in this section examine black men's role in the war from this perspective. Edward G. Longacre first discusses the Civil War as military revolution and social experiment in "Black Troops in the Army of the James, 1863–65." He draws attention to the Union Army, its contraband camps, and its military agencies as crucial transition sites into freed people's initiation into the struggle for not only liberty, but equal rights, free labor, and education.

At the same time that the fleeing slaves were forcing the Union to grapple with their status, they presented the Union Army with a monumental problem: What was to be done with all of them? The army began to set up contraband camps for the escaped slaves near Union encampments. The experiences of former slaves, first as laborers and then as triumphant black troops in the Army of the James, were unique. United States Colored Troops made up approximately 40 percent of the 40,000 enlisted men and officers in the Army of the James, the largest percentage of black troops under any Civil War command. As the author describes it, the Army of the James was for several reasons probably the "most highly politicized fighting force in American history," and certainly, greatly influenced by the politics of race.

The Army of the James was under the command of Major General Benjamin Butler from 1862 to 1865. Butler's work with black troops has not received as much attention as the justly famous 54th Massachusetts regiment, made up mostly of free men, and its white commander, Captain Shaw, but Butler was already known for his progressive—some said radical— ideas about black men and the military. He thought the former slaves should have the right to participate in winning their own freedom. Thus Butler was one of the growing number of whites who favored the use of black men. Confederate victories and growing Union casualties were forcing the North to support the widespread enlistment of blacks, and white men were beginning to resist volunteering for service in a war increasingly perceived as being fought over the issue of slavery. Hence, the War Department established the Bureau of Colored Troops in May 1863. From then on, the goal was competitive recruitment, intended to enlist as many former slaves throughout the South as possible. It was now understood that the widespread enlistment of black men as soldiers was a direct attack on slavery, guaranteed to undermine the institution and finally destroy it.

When Butler assumed command of the Department of Virginia and North Carolina, the region was already crowded with refugees settled in contraband camps near captured southern towns with Union garrisons, such as Norfolk, Hampton, and Williamsburg. Most former slaves lived in squalid conditions in a contraband camp called Sabletown, run by incompetent Union Army officers. However, Butler had been sent to recruit and train blacks as soldiers, and he proceeded with a vengeance, freeing former slaves and enlisting them in the "African Brigade," the first command recruited under his administration. Recruitment posters directed at black men claimed that joining the military would prove loyalty to the country and the manhood of the former slaves. They also told black men that, as soldiers, they would be fighting the Slaveholders' Rebellion, that to strike against the rebels meant freedom for themselves and their kin.

By May of 1864, Butler had raised black regiments, artillery, and cavalry made up of 8,000 former slaves and freedmen, and he soon amassed the United States Colored Troops into a single unified corps of 16,000 black men. When it came to combat and battle, the USCT met every demand made upon them, as Butler placed them in the line of fire with the same strategic duties and fighting engagements as white soldiers. As Butler had reasoned, he gave the blacks "heavy responsibilities" because they would fight harder than white men in order to prevent their capture and return to slavery.

In looking at the military as a political-social force for change, Longacre draws attention to the value and influence of military agencies. The Army of the James was unique in the number of support and social institutions that operated under its auspices. Major Butler encouraged benevolent societies and government institutions such as the Freedman's Aid Society, the United States Christian Commission, the Freedman's Savings Bank, and the Office of Negro Affairs to play an early role in the changeover from slavery to freedom among the USCT. Longacre states that the practice was in keeping with Butler's idea of the "military equality of the races," and a belief that the act of soldiering could improve the "physical, intellectual, and moral lives of men."

For instance, every USCT regiment operated a schoolhouse, as illiteracy and ignorance were regarded as impediments in military service and civilian life. Black soldiers proved to be such enthusiastic students that the missionaries brought in to educate them were as eager to teach as the black men were committed to learning to read, write, and spell. The USCT could boast that when many of its regiments were mustered out of the service, the majority of former slave men could read, and many could write fairly well. Most important, the rudiments of education they achieved for themselves in the military strengthened their "self-reliance and self-respect" as men.

Economic issues and the extension of social services to the dependents of black military personnel were other concerns that the Butler administration addressed. Butler established a Freedman's Savings Bank at Norfolk, Virginia, where USCT members deposited their bounties and wages. One regiment alone deposited $90,000 in assets. Butler organized the Office of Negro Affairs to extend social services to women and children. As the war progressed, many women accompanied their husbands to camps. Some went along with the troops when they departed for campaigns, working as nurses, cooks, and laundresses. Many were left behind, far from home and with no means of support. Assistance came in the form of employing women, along with elderly men and children, on former slave plantations as wage laborers. This placed black women at the forefront of the military's first experiments with a free labor force in the South. During Butler's command, black women also found jobs in northern factories and, like the black soldiers, were encouraged to take advantage of the opportunities to educate themselves.

Bobby L. Lovett further investigates the politicization of black men and women and the military as a force for social and economic change. In

"Nashville's Fort Negley: A Symbol of Blacks' Involvement with the Union Army," he examines the complex relationship between empowerment and black labor and its far-reaching effects, all set in motion by the Union Army's invasion of the South. Tens of thousands of black men first entered the war as impressed labor for the Confederacy, working in army camps and constructing fortifications. As the Union armies advanced south, those same men seized the opportunity to escape. Thousands ended up working for the Union as construction workers, wagon masters, cooks, and even spies. As black women and children joined the men who had escaped and followed the Union armies throughout the South, contraband camps became blacks' initial entry into American society as freedpeople. Lovett's essay on Fort Negley is a case study of black men and women's involvement with the Union Army, as one of its first experiments in hiring local blacks to build fortifications, and to provide support duty in Nashville. According to Lovett, the Fort Negley program set the standard and guidelines for the use of extensive local labor and the introduction of free labor practices in the Union Army's military projects in Middle Tennessee.

The project began in August 1862. Fort Negley was one of the twenty-three forts and bridges encircling Nashville that were erected by black artisans and laborers native to the region, under the direction of white Union engineers. It was the "pivot point" for the city's well-built defense system of garrison and forts. Interestingly, the planning for this fort early on involved blacks and whites in negotiations over black labor. By 1862, slaves were certainly beginning to think of the war as being about them. Evidence of this perspective surfaced over the issue of wages. Captain Morton, who commanded the Pioneer Brigade, the engineering unit of the Union branch of the military in Nashville, had initially informed "rebel slaveholders" that they were required to turn over one thousand slaves to build Fort Negley. Soon, though, Captain Morton had to deal more directly with the slaves. After the last Confiscation Acts had been passed, the Union Army's policy was to "employ" and "pay" the former slaves for their labor. However, the army's actual performance record on this issue was marred by the fact that slaves were often not compensated for their work, and the contraband camps in which the former slaves now chose to live were notorious for their inhumane living conditions. In the Fort Negley case, Captain Morton promised the slaves "Certificates of Labor" in lieu of payment, which they would not even receive until after services were rendered. Slave men and women, now negotiating for themselves, would have none of it. Slaves who had worked for nothing before now demanded daily wages. In order to keep them on the job, Captain Morton issued "Special Orders No. 17," which forced a known rebel sympathizer to advance the captain the money needed to pay the former slaves.

The Fort Negley project is likewise representative of the diverse responses that black men exhibited to the war, ranging from resistance to caution and finally to voluntary action. Although most of those employed as laborers were escaped slaves, the Union Army was also guilty of impressing free black men and women and children into service. They even raided the First Colored Baptist Church during services at which free blacks and slaves worshiped, causing some of the men to elude capture by leaping out the windows. Fort Negley also presents a rather unusual working situation because of the large numbers of artisans employed on the project. Nashville was home to Tennessee's largest free black population, a predominantly skilled group. Among them were black men trained as stonemasons, blacksmiths, carpenters, and wagon masters, some of the very occupations in demand by the Union Army engineers.

Ultimately, a workforce made up primarily of former slaves performed every imaginable type of construction in the building of the fort. Black men first chopped trees and completely cleared the site in order to leave no place where enemy rebels could hide. Black stonemasons "blasted the rock, fashioned the stone, laid the walls, and dug the underground magazines." Black women and youth worked as teamsters, driving long lines of wagons back and forth, piled with fallen trees and blasted rock. Black women also took care of children and did the washing, cooking, and other domestic duties for their people and the Union Army. For the duration of the war, they lived in a contraband camp called St. Cloud Hill near the rising fort. This contraband camp essentially became a black working community made up of laborers and craftspeople.

Over time, it seemed that even though some blacks had been forced to work for the Union and there was a cautious attitude toward the Union soldiers, blacks living in the contraband camp came to openly sympathize with the Union forces, reflecting the growing trend toward seeing the war as the final struggle for liberty. These sentiments surfaced in their response to the first Confederate attacks on Nashville. When General Nathan Bedford Forrest attacked Nashville on November 2, 1862, the former slaves requested arms to protect themselves and Fort Negley. The Union Army in Nashville had come to rely so heavily upon local black labor to build the army's infrastructure that they began issuing orders to protect their labor source. Whereas white owners had once been allowed to search the contraband camp on St. Cloud Hill for escaped slaves, the Nashville army implemented orders prohibiting them from doing so by making it illegal for Union soldiers to return escaped slaves. An officer could even be arrested for selling or returning an escaped slave. For each male slave recruited for labor in the Union Army, a white male could be released from labor and support responsibilities and transferred to combat duty. Overall, by 1864, the Union Army had established three contraband camps in and around Nashville alone, where several thousand escaped men, women, and children first settled and initiated the transition from slave to free blacks.

Besides operating as the army's base for labor recruitment, the Union's

Nashville command became a site for the recruitment and training of local black soldiers in Middle Tennessee. In fact, most of the able-bodied escaped slaves and free men in the region were mustered into military service via contraband camps. Local bureaus for the recruitment of United States Colored Troops were set up in Nashville, Clarksville, Lynneville, Columbia, Pulaski, Murfreesboro, Shelbyville, Wartrace, and Tullahoma. The Union Army in Nashville even took in escaped males; they first employed them as laborers, then swore them into the military to arm and train them as soldiers, because the military's need for manpower was so great.

The contraband camps and local recruitment bureaus in Middle Tennessee raised a total of twelve black regiments and two artillery units made up of former slaves and free men. The existence of these military agencies seems to have made the region an attractive destination point for escaped slaves and free men from neighboring states. Free blacks from Ohio and runaway slaves from Kentucky and Alabama were mustered into the army as black soldiers in these regiments. So many escaped slaves from Alabama made their way to contraband camps in Middle Tennessee and ended up joining the army as soldiers that they were at first named the 1st, 2nd, 3rd, and 4th Alabama Infantry Regiments of African Descent. Black soldiers from these regiments fought in Fort Negley's first military involvement, the Battle of Nashville, December 17–18, 1864, one of the last major engagements of a defeated Confederacy. The fifty thousand Union troops included seven black regiments consisting of thirteen thousand black soldiers, who aided in the defense against the Confederate Army of Tennessee.

The Civil War was, without a doubt, epic history, full of drama with many themes and meanings for Americans. Those most recently freed, however, certainly saw black soldiers as the war's main protagonists for freedom. The entry of former slaves into what some historians now call the Second American Revolution made clear an anti-slavery direction for the country. The Civil War politicized black men, leaving them with a sense of character, dignity, resolve, and manhood that would have been almost impossible to achieve in any way other than through the shedding of blood in war and the sanction of military service. As sociologist Michael Kimmel writes, the Civil War "formally established" black manhood through emancipation, but "asserting their manhood would continue to be a central struggle for black American men throughout American history."

We began with two questions: How do we determine how black men construct manhood and express masculinity? And, what social, economic, political, and cultural forces have helped shape black male identity, and what has been the male-gendered response of black men to historical events and change? The essays in this volume demonstrate that enslavement and oppression did not prevent black men in the United States from grappling with the same issues and questions of manhood and masculinity facing every other group of men in the nation. Black men differ, however, in that their sense of masculinity is specifically rooted in the slave experience and reflected in the "resistant masculinity" that it provoked.

Like Broateer, who became Venture Smith, the first generations of African men to arrive on American shores brought with them strong ideas and feelings regarding the relationship between manhood and freedom. How could it have been otherwise? For enslaved Africans, freedom was worth fighting for, and even death could be preferable to slavery. But like black women, black men practiced the art of daily survival, ensuring that future generations would be prepared for freedom, and fortified enough to continue in the ongoing struggle for civil rights and human dignity. We need only recall that the runaway slaves who escaped to Spanish territory and founded the maroon community of Mose married and established households and families. Over time, as families and community networks developed into important survival institutions, black men in antebellum North Carolina were inspired to run away in large numbers, expressly to reunite with their families.

Black men constructed a variety of work cultures and environments to meet their needs, as both ostensibly free and enslaved men in the North and South. They acquired skills as trained artisans, carpenters, blacksmiths, chimney sweeps, sailors, and ironworkers; one even became a clockmaker. To be sure, slavery in the coal mines of West Virginia was brutally exploitative, but here again, black men preferred this work, because it allowed them more freedom, as well as a bit of extra money with which to support themselves and their families. A gendered perspective on the experiences of black males as creators of culture, music, preaching, and writing illuminates how they connected black communities throughout America. Free black men developed and nurtured a vibrant political culture in the free black communities in the North, forming the essential organizations that allowed them to develop the leadership skills needed to meaningfully engage in the struggle for freedom. At virtually every juncture, black men interpreted the struggle for freedom and resistance to oppression as the central tenet of manhood.

Black men's radical resistance parallels their daily survival struggles. From the newly arrived Kongo warriors who orchestrated the Stono Rebellion of 1739 to the African Americans who joined Nat Turner's 1831 revolt, radical resistance remained a persistent threat to white rule. At times, black men linked their struggle for freedom with that of Native American men. Indeed, black male participation in the Seminole Wars held the United States Army at bay until 1842. Ironically, black men fought, heroically and with great determination, in every American war, hoping that their service would result in personal freedom and freedom for their families. Only in the aftermath of the Civil War, however, did they wrest emancipation from slavery. But the struggle for civil and political rights, for social justice and economic opportunity, was only just beginning for men whose manhood remained contested ground through Reconstruction and the age of Jim Crow. Black manhood in America has always been inextricably connected to freedom.

PART ONE

ANCESTRAL
BLACK
MALE
LEGACIES

ONE

"Not Fade Away": The Narrative of Venture Smith, an African American in the Early Republic

ROBERT E. DESROCHERS JR.

Identity! My God! Who has any identity
anymore anyway? It isn't so perfectly simple.

—RALPH ELLISON, *Invisible Man*, 1952

It was a scene replayed countless times in the annals of the Atlantic slave trade. Only about six years old in 1735, when slave raiders ambushed his tribe and killed his father, a West African prince known as Broteer was captured and marched hundreds of miles to Anamaboe on the Gold Coast. There, told to "appear to the best possible advantage for sale," the boy and some two hundred and sixty fellow Africans became cargo on a slaver bound for Rhode Island. Before hauling anchor, the ship's steward Robertson Mumford traded "four gallons of rum and a piece of calico" for young Broteer, changing his name to Venture on account of "having purchased me with his own private venture."[1]

Venture touched Narragansett soil in 1737, having survived an "ordinary voyage" that included shipboard smallpox and a stopover in Barbados, where what was left of the ship's human freight had been sold. Over the next three decades Venture Smith—he added the surname of the master who let him purchase his freedom—met northern slavery head on, commanding respect with physical strength he deemed "equal if not superior to [that of] any man whom I have ever seen." As it had in Africa, slavery rent Smith from relatives in southern New England, where he spent his first years of freedom cleaving wood tirelessly to reunite his cloven family. Against the odds, Smith forged an independent livelihood in late colonial and early republican America. Remarkable achievements earned Smith immortality in a thirty-two-page memoir, *"Related by Himself"* and published late in 1798 by the printer Charles Holt of New London, Connecticut.[2]

In three chronological chapters, sandwiched between an editorial preface by Smith's white amanuensis and an authenticating certificate signed by prominent local white men, A *Narrative of the Life and Adventures of Venture, a Native of Africa: But resident above sixty years in the United States of America*, paints Smith's life in broad strokes. Chapter 1, eight pages long, outlines his early memories of Africa; the book's remaining sections recount selected events from Smith's life in slavery and, ultimately, in freedom. An advertisement for the *Narrative* ran for six weeks in Holt's newspaper, the *New London Bee*, beginning on December 26, 1798. It described Smith as "a negro remarkable for size, strength, industry, fidelity and frugality, and well known in the state of Rhode Island, on Long Island, and in Stonington, East Haddam, and several other parts of" Connecticut. Smith was already something of a legend, as these remarks attest; the *Narrative's* publication helped to ensure that his fame would not be fleeting. A family member reprinted his account in New London in 1835; burgeoning local folklore surrounding the tale and its memorable teller led to its republication at Middletown, Connecticut, in 1897, augmented by the "Traditions of Venture!," a nine-page folk history included, its compiler wrote, "to meet the demand." Venture Smith had been dead for ninety-two years.[3]

Just seven years from the grave when he dictated his plain-style *Narrative*, Smith summoned the bittersweet wisdom gained from sixty-nine years of slavery and freedom in Africa and America. By 1798 the man who had once stood well over six feet tall barefooted and, tradition has it, as much around, now stooped over a cane. But long after legendary brawn and eyesight faded, Smith kept his pride, recounting at tale's end his "many consolations" against old age. Ever the businessman, Smith made a list that reads like an inventory: one devoted and loving wife, "three habitable dwelling houses," and some fivescore acres of land. Further memorializing Smith left to posterity, maintaining only, "It gives me joy to think that I have and that I deserve so good a character, especially for truth and integrity."[4]

He was being modest. Within ten years of buying his way out of bondage, Smith had purchased freedom for his wife, three of their children, and three other male slaves. Despite the chicanery of "false-hearted friends," by 1770 Smith had bought and sold a house in Stonington, Connecticut; in 1774 he held sizable cash savings, a considerable farm, and a second dwelling on far eastern Long Island. During the American Revolution, Smith employed his own fleet of more than twenty sailing vessels in the lucrative coasting trade around Long Island Sound, selling fish, cordwood, and homegrown produce. But beyond material success, Smith affirmed, "My freedom is a privilege which nothing else can equal." Armed with heady rhetoric that bore the mark of a revolutionary generation and emblazoned with its author's proud recollection of things African, Venture Smith's freedom tale boldly proclaimed one former slave's perseverance and prosperity in the new republic. It also demonstrated how Euro-American and African cultures could mingle in the storytelling of the life of one exceptional man.[5]

LANGUAGE, IDENTITY, AND SLAVE NARRATIVES

When they consider them at all, historians and literary critics too often stress the limitations of eighteenth-century slave narratives. Emphasizing the authors' dependence on the assistance of white amanuenses and on the patronage of Anglo-American society, scholars have undervalued these potential sources of vestigial African American identity and consciousness. Editors, the literary historian William L. Andrews wrote, ultimately not only controlled the context in which a black subject's "brute facts" were presented but also decided whether those facts were presented at all. For many scholars, the power of whites to omit, arrange, correct, and otherwise manipulate the dictated stories of slaves and former bondsmen sabotaged the unique black perspectives that texts such as Smith's might otherwise have illuminated.[6]

Andrews and others are rightly skeptical of early narratives that celebrated mainly "the acculturation of the black man into established categories of the white social and literary order." Manipulation undoubtedly bore upon these first slave testimonies, especially when white editors and printers sponsored them as weapons in the battle to end slavery. But in assuming that whites consciously and effectively silenced the voices of the first black narrators, scholars too often limit themselves in search of a "true" black voice of irreconcilable and discernible difference. It is only by assuming black difference—and being dismayed when evidence of it does not gush from the page—that the literary historian Blyden Jackson can write that the first black American authors were "so overwhelmingly conditioned by an American environment that, behaviorally, they might as well have been [Anglo-Americans]." But to presume that whites exerted arbitrary control over the first African American narratives is to belittle the capacity of black literary pioneers to adapt so-called white language and culture and exploit it according to their own needs or, borrowing a phrase from Ralph Ellison, their ability to "change the joke and slip the yoke." We do not have to disavow real differences between black author and white editor to suppose that both could share and employ similar ideas, rhetorical strategies, and, above all, language that often allowed them to convey mixed, multiple, and contradictory messages.[7]

Likewise, it is not sufficient to fasten the African American literary canon to a paradigm of naked protest against racial caste. Such a model implies a transhistorical conceptualization of race. Notions of race and radicalism in any age must be understood as socially and culturally specific constructs and explored on their own terms.[8] Similarly, conceptions of racial protest must take account of changing historical notions of race and freedom. To impose modern, and narrowly defined, views of racial protest on African Americans who lived and died two centuries ago is to seek disappointment. Should we disfranchise Venture Smith for not being Frederick Douglass or Richard Wright? It seems absurd to ostracize eighteenth-century African American authors became they did not, or could not, or thought better not to, display the open protest evident in much later black literature. To do so is to misunderstand or, at least, to underestimate the temporal exigencies faced by the first black Americans setting pen to paper.

This essay seeks to establish some of the ways in which Venture Smith worked within and around Anglo-American cultural and literary restrictions, capitalizing on the malleability of the words and language that supposedly bound him, to forge a narrative persona that drew on the African and New World materials available to him. If white institutional power constantly pushed slave narrators' individuality to the periphery, this essay scours that periphery in a historically sensitive attempt to extract Smith's black message from its white envelope. It seeks to recover the self-perception and world view of one African American coming to terms with life in postrevolutionary New England. As this reconsideration exposes previously overlooked nuances in his rich *Narrative*, the portrait of Smith that emerges reminds us how limited our own approaches to issues of consciousness and identity have been. Smith's represented *one*, rather than *the*, black voice of early republican America. And if anecdotal themes of rugged, self-sufficient individualism have made Smith seem at first glance much like his white neighbors, close reading reveals the complex story of a man with intertwining African and Yankee sensibilities, reconcilable in ways largely unimagined by scholars in our multicultural age.[9]

REVOLUTION AND THE WORD IN BLACK AND WHITE

Smith's *Narrative* began with an editorial preface by Elisha Niles—Yale man, Connecticut schoolteacher, Revolutionary War veteran, and son of a Patriot minister whose sermons in the 1770s prominently linked successful resistance to Britain with antislavery and millennial aspirations. Besides demonstrating that Niles's intellectual apple did not fall far from his father's democratic Calvinist tree, this brief proem merits sustained attention on two fronts. First, it reveals Niles's utilitarian view of the *Narrative* as a jeremiad on American education and moral habits and the relation of both to slavery, bondsmen, and free blacks. Equally important, prefatory ruminations on slavery and persons of African descent speak directly to the slippery and often contradictory nature of late-eighteenth-century American racial thought. Historicizing Niles's editorial notions of race and slavery, reform and regeneration, in turn situates Smith's text in the context of political culture in early federal New England.[10]

Niles's opening remarks alert scholars to areas in which shared cultural assumptions—about American morality, for instance—may have enabled language to address the rhetorical agenda of black author and white amanuensis alike. Not that Smith and Niles invariably agreed, or that Smith's voice found expression only when it jibed perfectly with his editor's. Rather, acknowledging that these two men held certain social values in common renders less vital the self-defeating task of separating authorial from editorial expression in search of a universal voice of black difference.

Like many Americans of the 1790s, Niles believed that backsliding heirs of the Revolution—including many lately freed slaves—had enervated the spirit of their age. Niles offered Smith's rags-to-riches story as blueprint for regeneration. Inverting racialized behavioral roles, Niles jabbed especially hard at incorrigible whites: "This narrative exhibits a pattern of honesty, prudence, and industry to people of [Smith's] own color; and perhaps some white people would not find themselves degraded by imitating such an example." Following the moral gospel according to Venture, all Americans could step toward an uncertain future while training an eagle eye on the mores of an idealized revolutionary past.[11]

Niles, though, was not merely pouring anxious new wine from an old bottle of Puritan declension. More secular that the outlook of his own father and many of the nation's founders, Niles's millennial vision and his abolitionism merged Calvinism and republican principles in ways that beckon toward what the historian Nathan O. Hatch has described as the democratization of American Christianity. The Smith *Narrative* appeared on the heels of a sweeping emancipation bill, rejected in the Connecticut legislature in 1794, that would have made Connecticut only the third state to provide mandatory education for slaves and free blacks. The preface, and indeed Smith's text, must be read as a salvo in an ongoing debate over black instruction and, more generally, over the status of African Americans in postrevolutionary Connecticut and the new nation. For slaves and free black such as Smith, the stakes of this republicanized morality play were especially high, as hopes for freedom often became entangled with white estimations of their moral capacity.[12]

To Niles, who had been a teacher since age fifteen, educating blacks seemed the best way to inculcate industry and probity among them and thus to stifle whites (including his father) who questioned slaves' moral fitness for freedom. A virtuous free black population would also give the lie to colonizationist arguments holding that freed Negroes—crippled by their bondage—were reformable only where they could no longer count on whites for support. Despite being "an untutored African slave . . . destitute of all education" except that received by "other domesticated animals," Smith bolstered Niles's case; he exhibited "striking traces of native ingenuity and good sense" that only augured further advancement had he "a common education" to match. And if an "uncultivated" African could aspire so well,

Niles hoped that suitably instructed blacks would strike deeper at slavery's roots and thereby rechart America's millennial course.[13]

All of this would have sounded quite familiar to moral watchdogs and anti-slavery advocates throughout the early republican North. Just two years prior, in 1796, the American Convention of Delegates from Abolition Societies, meeting in Philadelphia, assumed that the future of abolition depended in large part upon how black Americans utilized their newly won freedom. The convention issued a lengthy moral and social guide for ex-slaves that Niles could have lifted word for word. Closer to home, expressions of public anxiety over such sweeping social issues as education, morality, industry, temperance, frugality, and filial relations flew from Connecticut printing presses and filled the pages of local newspapers. Indicative of these concerns, in 1796 a new edition of Joseph Priestly's *Miscellaneous Observations Relating to Education* went to press in New London; in nearby Middletown the *Middlesex Gazette* of December 20, 1798, promised that "Advice of a Father to his Son" would appear in the next issue. A cursory glance at contemporary lists of titles sold by Connecticut booksellers, often printed in newspapers, further confirms the point. With African Americans clearly in mind, offerings bearing such titles as "Baybay, A true Story of a good Negro Woman," and "The Pious Negro" took aim at a moral target hard to miss.[14]

Much in Nile's preface agreed with the unmistakable sociomoral agenda of Charles Holt, printer of the *Narrative*. Holt concluded a published account of the yellow fever that gripped New London in late summer 1798 with two pages of "Moral Reflections" that veered sharply from what had been a simple chronicle of who died and who helped. Holt's quasi-literary (and mildly anti-Federalist) weekly, the *New London Bee*, likewise leaned toward the instructive and the moral. An issue from September 1797 told of a man from Elizabeth, New Jersey, who drank "two quarts of wine, a pint of brandy, and a gill of rum" and then died. Another article from 1797 taught readers the lessons of proper—and improper—modes of "Family Government." But perhaps most relevant to our discussion of Smith's *Narrative*, early in 1798 Holt undertook to reprint the *Life of Dr. Benjamin Franklin*, the leading American man of letters and of business. In an advertisement for the *Life* that ran in the *Bee* on November 7, 1798, Holt explained to potential buyers that "all orders of men" could behold, in Franklin's rise from "errand-boy" to "ambassador of nations," "lessons of the purest morality and laudable economy." Noting the way Franklin's book combined "the happy effects of industry, temperance, and integrity" to produce "independence, health, and integrity," Holt urged "PARENTS!" not only to buy it for their children but also to "bid them study the virtues, observe the precepts, and endeavor to imitate" the worthy example of Franklin. With less fanfare and an emphasis more on the race than on the age of prospective readers, the preface to Smith's *Narrative* echoed this appeal.[15]

Niles's preface made explicit the similarities between Smith's tale and Franklin's, likening the former bondsman to "a Franklin and a Washington in a state of nature, or rather a state of slavery." But the resemblance extended only so far, and Niles's roundabout faith in blacks' improvability had limits that reveal his own racialist thinking, distinct from but as synthetic, contradictory, and stubborn as that of the skeptics and colonizationists with whom he quibbled. Niles's own moral criteria certified Smith's superiority to most whites. Yet even as he called for universal emulation of Smith, Niles wrote without apparent irony that Smith "*might have been* a man of high respectability and usefulness," and that he *might have been* an ornament and an honor to human nature."[16] Though Niles was a disciple of black assimilation and advancement, his inability to accept Smith's preeminence at face value led him toward a contradictory stance that seemed at the same time to assume Smith's moral superiority and social inferiority.

The passage comparing Smith to "a Franklin and a Washington" suggests that Niles's conflicted view owed a debt to murky notions of racial hierarchy, that educational disadvantages alone did not account in his mind for Smith's "might-have-been" status. Here Niles juxtaposed two social states—nature and slavery—that were not as easily interchangeable as his pithy wit made them seem. The editor may have meant merely to imply that Smith's supposed shortcomings resulted from his servitude. In other words, Smith had been "enfeebled and depressed by slavery," indeed "broken," and bondage, flying as it did in the face of reason and nature, had limited his natural ability to evolve into a Franklin or Washington. But such a typically environmentalist explanation of black inferiority begins to smack of racial permanence —if not inherence—when clear evidence to the contrary could not shake what Niles apparently saw as slavery's decisive arrest of Smith's development. Ultimately, it seems that in the editor's mind, no amount of remedial education could erase the stain of slavery.[17]

Niles's own confusion and the general debate among Americans attest to the unsettled nature of race in the late eighteenth century. Smith's supposed debasement resulted, albeit not equally, from poor education and years spent in slavery—not blackness as such. If time proved such logic to be only a step away from more decisive statements of innate black inferiority, Elisha Niles made no such racial leap in 1798. While hardly immaterial to his argument, neither was the black image in his white mind systematic. To explain Afro-American literature generally and Smith's *Narrative* specifically as a protest against immutable color caste is thus to disparage the complexity of Smith and his age by lending ahistorical weight to race. What is more, the unexceptionality of Niles's contradictory racial views underlines the perfidious nature of race as culturally constructed ideology in any age. Niles was hardly the only American in whom convoluted racial *attitudes* cohabited with observably contrary *reality*. Nor was he alone in nonetheless maintaining a dangerously incompatible position.[18]

POWER AND AUTHORITY, MORALITY AND JUSTICE
ON TWO CONTINENTS

This revealing preface may be of great value to the historian, but Venture Smith needed no editor's sermon to convince him of the urgent need for American reformation. Time and again, Smith's entrepreneurial energy ran up against "the injustice of knaves" who preyed upon his "ignorance of numbers" and disfranchised status, while the handful of slaves Smith redeemed from bondage proved a succession of thieving runaways. And Smith's own sons dramatized the tragic fate of children who mocked the guidance of virtuous ancestry. Ignoring his father's advice and spartan example, eldest son Solomon shipped out around 1773 aboard a whaler, enticed by a promised "pair of silver buckles." He died of scurvy at sea. While younger son Cuff's lot is unclear, his father's opprobrium is not: "If Cuff and Solomon—O! that they had walked in the way of their father," Smith lamented.[19]

In reality few Americans had filled (and, quite literally, even fewer could have filled) the shoes of a man who has been likened by the historians Sidney Kaplan and Emma Nogrady Kaplan to a black Paul Bunyan "who swung his axe to break his chains." Eschewing Niles's might-have-beens, Smith held himself up as the true revolutionary son—an African son at that. Pairing prosperity and frugality, diligence and self-control, Smith had avoided the trap of ease and luxury and thereby solved a social dilemma as old as the Puritans. "A good supply of money and prudence" went hand in hand over the many years that Smith served masters by day while fishing, trapping, and planting at night. He invariably chose "decent homespun dresses" over "superfluous finery," avoided the "expensive gatherings" of frivolous blacks, and was never "at the expense of sixpence worth" of liquor. An entire Long Island winter Smith slept on the floor with only a "coverlet over and another under me" in order to conserve his meager wages. Using language typical of Federalist-era attempts to perfect the hearts and minds of Americans increasingly devoted to the main chance, Smith embodied republican virtue as many whites had not, at the same time distinguishing himself from those blacks who, he felt, frittered away their freedom on song, spirits, and silver buckles.[20]

Smith may have been implicitly criticizing the long-standing New England tradition of black elections—costly annual festivals that coincided with white election day and brought African Americans together for as long as a week of song, dance, drinking, and often the election of a governor. Indeed, disdain for the extravagant may explain why Smith never was chosen black governor by his peers. He boasted most of the qualifications for election: ties to the old country, an impeccable record of achievement, and imposing physical stature. Governor Eben Tobias of Massachusetts was described as "over six feet tall and admirably proportioned," while tradition held Quash Freeman of Derby, Connecticut, to have been "a man of herculean strength, a giant six-footer." Though something of an eighteenth-century Stagolee, Smith was not "ready to pay freely for diversion," to quote a nineteenth-century local historian's description of another prerequisite for the office. Of course, Smith's putative derision of an important aspect of black folk life in New England might have reflected sour grapes over the unwillingness of "superficial" blacks to recognize him as their true leader.[21]

No parsimonious Yankee, white or black, guarded his freedom or his money more vigilantly than Smith. He timed the purchase of his pregnant wife, Meg, in order to avoid, "having another child to buy" later on. Even family tragedies could be translated to the bottom line. After Solomon's death, remorse mingled with indignation when Smith recalled that "besides the loss of [my son's] life, I lost equal to seventy-five pounds" in back wages owed by the white ship captain who had hired Solomon from Smith. And when daughter Hannah "fell sick of a mortal disease," Smith reckoned her medical bills to have cost him another fifty pounds.[22]

It is perhaps not surprising that a man who had to buy himself in 1765 for "seventy-two pounds, two shillings" came to affix price tags to human worth. Smith's commercial mentality and experience only increased his tendency to register ultimate value in dollars and pounds. But if Smith was, as Andrews claims, the "prototype of the black bourgeois autobiographer," Andrew's further claim that he did not draw "on his African origins for values and 'terms for order'" seems to forget that as an African prince, Smith was a stranger neither to wealth nor, probably, to the language of hard work. West African proverbial wisdom holds that "poverty is the eldest daughter of laziness" and that "dust on the feet is better than dust on the behind." Grasping materialism clearly formed part of Smith's narrative persona. It is less clear that his appetite for material success—comfortably associated with moneygrubbing early capitalist New England—grew solely out of an American context. We learn early in the Narrative that Smith's African father, Saungm Furro, died rather than inform "his enemies of the place where his money lay." Though simple, the point needs emphasis: By too readily applying "African" and "American" tags to human activities, scholars may falsely dichotomize "African American" experience.[23]

Smith *and* Niles rang notes of dismay over wanton youth and the moral delinquency of American Christians, agreeing that Smith came closer than most to actualizing revolutionary promise (with Niles's uncertainties duly noted). But the didacticism that structured Smith's Narrative, while clearly attuned to utilitarian and functional views of literature in the early republic, characterized as well the folk narratives slaves told in New England and throughout the Americas. Making subtle use of satire, metaphor, and self-deprecating humor, black storytellers captivated multiracial audiences with tales of bondage and the African homeland that inculcated, among other things, a view of ethics from the bottom up. Smith perhaps drew on this vibrant Afro–New England anecdotal culture—with oral roots that stretched to the griot castes of Africa—in ways that neither Niles nor modern scholars have fully appreciated. Traditional storytelling modes enabled black Yankees like Smith to question the basic assumptions of white society, utilizing an oral style that adapted well to the page and a language that addressed the specific concerns of African Americans even as it spoke to larger American concerns.[24]

Afro–New England folk narratives often featured the power and prestige of the teller's African, and usually royal, ancestry. Thus African-born Senegambia, a slave in the colonial Narragansett, earned renown with stories about his father, the Gambian king, who, Senegambia bragged, maintained a fleet of ships bigger than any the English could boast and dressed in clothes given him by supplicant British sea captains. In his *Narrative* Smith proudly recalled African names and customs along with anecdotes about his native land and peoples—facts seemingly overlooked by scholars theorizing with John Sekora that he could "imagine no existence outside [white American institutional] confines." We learn that Venture's African name was Broteer; that his father, Saungm Furro, was "Prince of the Tribe of Dukandarra"; and that Broteer had two siblings by his father's first wife (Smith's mother) named Cundazo and Soozaduka. Smith's portrait of his kinsmen as "very large, tall, and stout . . . commonly above six feet in height, and every way well proportioned" in no way rationalized African inferiority. To the contrary, Dukandarran size availed in Smith's often physical struggle for leverage against oppression in the New World.[25]

Smith affirmed other aspects of his African heritage. Smith made no apologies for Dukandarran polygamy, practiced "especially among the rich" families like his own. When Saungm Furro, "contrary to the custom generally observed among my countrymen," married a third wife "without the consent of his first and eldest," Broteer's mother—whose name we never learn—took her three children and left the country in protest. The two eventually resolved their differences, and after a year's absence Broteer returned to his "paternal dwelling place in peace and happiness." Polygamy created occasional friction between husband and wives, but Smith's remembrance of it hardly corroborated white linkages between multiple marriage and Africans' libidinous nature. In fact, measured against its authoritarian Euro-American counterpart, African marriage as presented by Smith could as easily have seemed a just model of mutuality and spousal recourse.[26]

It would be naïve to place undue faith in the accuracy of memories sixty-odd years old. Smith may have misremembered or exaggerated these and other African recollections. No less is true of any retelling of the past. Smith certainly reconstructed Africa to suit his needs and those of his much-abbreviated life story. For our purposes, however, the greater significance of Smith's African memories does not lie in their ultimate veracity —though his memory apparently served better than might be expected. Rather, they are meaningful because they provided Smith with a supplementary means of understanding himself and his relation to his world, acting as a counterpoint to American hypocrisy and injustice. Smith went out of his way to inform white New Englanders that many of the values and ideals to which he clung were like theirs, but not necessarily *of* them.

The work of such scholars as Melville J. Herskovits and the African theologian John Mbiti brings West African marriage, as Smith sketched it, into sharper relief, illuminating its consensual basis and the relative freedom of separation and divorce it afforded to women. According to Herskovits, men in patrilineal societies of western and central Africa presented prospective wives and their families with "bridewealths" that preceded matrimonial assent and, perhaps most significant, acted as symbolic assurance of a wife's equitable treatment in the future since violation of the bridewealth agreement nullified the marriage pact. Children remained under the control of their mothers until the bridewealth was honored by the husband; control could revert back to the wife if at any time a husband failed to uphold his prenuptial pledge. A husband's authority over wife and offspring remained contingent upon his good behavior. Saungm Furro apparently contravened the bridewealth agreement with Broteer's mother by marrying again without prior approval. Her rights as a lesser but not servile partner thus violated, Broteer's mother cut the marriage tie and reclaimed authority over her children until Saungm Furro made good.[27]

In New England, Smith confronted similar issues of power and authority as slave, free laborer, and employer, as husband and father. If nothing else, Smith's brief discussion of Dukandarran marriage offered an alternative to American relations of power that must have made blacks who became acquainted with his tale prick up their ears: Existing power relationships were not necessarily natural ones. More than that, this passage hints that Smith's introduction to the quasi-contractual limits of patriarchal domination—and the conditions that made resistance to authority justifiable—predated his arrival on American shores. Specifically, Smith's talk of power and authority in the homeland, though referring explicitly to marital relations, set a logical if metaphorical African precedent for overt resistance to slavery. Africans who had never consented to their bondage owed no allegiance to American slaveholders who held undue authority over them. Smith's metaphorical usage of language here would have been of a piece with African and Afro–New England oral traditions steeped in indirection and symbolism. African-born Chloe Spear of Boston was one New England slave who garnered whites' praise for what they deemed her remarkable skill for originating and "conveying ideas in metaphor."[28]

Finally, shared contractual language clearly likened Smith's passage on African marriage to representations of America's colonial connection with Britain and to the justifications used by American patriots in their opposition to imperial "slavery." Though parent-child allusions more commonly described the imperial bond, the rationale behind familial and conjugal metaphors was comparable: Parental Britain—like Saungm Furro when he overstepped the bounds of legitimate authority over Broteer's mother—

could no longer expect compliance from colonial children who had come of age. Shifting a familiar Anglo-American metaphor to a Dukandarran context, Smith's "black voice" could confound white manipulation, at the same time suggesting an area in which the two cultures may have been reconcilable. Smith could layer meaning on an idiom that whites clearly understood precisely because that language was adaptable enough to span real but not insurmountable cross-cultural gaps. We gain a deeper appreciation for the intertwining forces that constituted Smith's dynamic African American identity by understanding that "terms for order," even those that seem quite Lockean and American, as Smith's parental and paternal values do, may have derived as well from African models that were neither necessarily incompatible nor beyond the representative power of words.[29]

Chronicling the plight of rival Africans overrun by white-assisted African slave traders, Smith further revealed ancestral pride. The imperiled tribe beseeched Saungm Furro for military assistance, as Dukandarra stood literally and symbolically as the last African bastion against white-led tyranny. "A kind and merciful prince," Saungm Furro allied with a traditional enemy in Pan-African resistance of sorts against a European-backed army. Numbers still favored the Euro-African force, though, and Saungm Furro forfeited gold and livestock "rather than that his subjects should be deprived of their rights and privileges" in a probable bloodbath. When enemy promises to accept tribute in lieu of aggression "proved no better" than "pledges of faith and honor" made by "other unprincipled hostile nations," Saungm Furro refused demands for further recompense, enduring a torturous death as his family looked on.[30]

It is indicative of Smith's attempt to reconcile African pride with fierce determination to claim dignity as an American that he here referred to African traits and African resistance by way of a uniquely American late-eighteenth-century rhetoric of "rights and privileges." This time, though, the injustice defied looked much more like that a slave might expect to encounter in Smith's New England, and metaphorical leaps between the two thus became easier: Saungm Furro complied with enemy demands in order to protect the "liberties and rights" of his people. Applying recognizably republican terminology to Africans like himself, Smith pointed out who the *real* American was, at the same time boldly refuting white attitudes about African barbarism. Personified by the "affable, kind and gentle" figure of Smith's father, Dukandarrans appear conspicuously humane, ready to endure hardship and even death in the name of justice. By way of contrast, white invaders formed the "unprincipled hostile nations" Smith spoke of, aided only by those Africans who dishonored themselves with European depravity. Even in America, Smith never so corrupted himself, clinging instead to the highest African and American standards of nobility.[31]

Unlike most contemporary Americans and many African sons (Smith's own most literally), Smith followed in the footsteps of a good father. When

Smith talked of Saungm Furro he could as easily have been describing himself. Both were men "of remarkable stature . . . strength, and resolution" who ruled "with equity and moderation." To secure the "rights and privileges" of family and followers, Saungm Furro readily relinquished worldly possessions. Smith, too, valued freedom more than land, houses, and money, surrendering material wealth so that "his people" might live at liberty. Like Saungm Furro, Smith had found freedom promises to be half-truths at best: Upon becoming Smith's third owner, Hempstead Miner of Stonington, Connecticut, promised to give the slave "a good chance to gain my freedom"; Miner instead resold Smith for a quick profit. And not just whites but what Smith called "the perfidy of my own countrymen" betrayed father and son. Indeed, much as the "continued exercise and increase of" Euro-African "torment" had killed Saungm Furro, Smith's closing—where, as one "looking to the grave," he spoke of white oppression, filial recalcitrance, and the dishonesty of those he redeemed from bondage—implied that others' immorality had sped his arrival at death's door.[32]

This rich passage on the death of Saungm Furro suggests that Smith's *Narrative* established the crucial relationship in his mind between the African world he left at such a young age and the virtuous man he became. If Smith's uneducated integrity surprised Elisha Niles, Smith seemed to imply that he had learned all he needed from Saungm Furro, who can be taken to represent Smith's more perfect—and African—version of Niles's ideal American forefathers, Franklin and Washington. Thus what appeared in Smith as archetypical traits of American moral republicanism, he seemed to claim, actually originated in Africa.

Smith's text provides clues as to the specific region of West Africa from which he came—clues important in uncovering the meanings layered in the *Narrative*, in particular the consistency of certain African and "republican" values and metaphors. While no place called "Dukandarra" seems to have existed in the broad area of "Guinea" from which Smith claimed to have been taken, it appears that Smith's childhood home lay between the Bakoy and Bafing rivers in the region of modern-day western Mali known as Gangara. Historians of Africa know well the pitfalls of locating the historical sources of place names passed down for centuries by oral cultures and transmitted with frustrating inconsistency by Europeans of assorted tongues, to whom standardized spelling mattered little and whose phonetical skill ran up against at best rudimentary knowledge of the African language groups with which they dealt. All the problems associated with such an undertaking apply here. It is intriguing, though, that the place name rendered "Dukandarra" by Elisha Niles resonates with the construction of place names among speakers of Mandinkan—a language group that included the inhabitants of Gangara. In Mandinkan dialects, the root *du* (land) added to a clan name (in this case Gangara) yields Dugangara: "land of the Gangara."

While far from conclusive, such evidence is suggestive, especially when one notes that there remains little agreement among orthographers regarding the systematization of African languages—Gangara is known to modern scholars alternately as Gangaran, Gagara, Wangara, and Ungara, to name but a few variations.[33]

We know from the *Narrative* that Saungm Furro had gold at his disposal. The Gangara of the early eighteenth century lived in an area whose significant goldfields were coveted by the French Company of the Indies, looking to extend into the interior their foothold downriver on the Senegal. Indeed, the French probably were the "white nation who equipped and sent" the raiders who killed Smith's father: More than the English based on the Gambia River, they regarded the gold of Gangara as central to their expansionist ambitions in the early 1730s.[34]

More certain is the contention that the Africans who enslaved Smith were soldiers from the Bambara kingdom of Segu, located 250 miles east of Gangara on the middle Niger. Under the leadership of Biton Mamari Kulibali, the Segu Bambara state rose to dominate the western Sudan in the early decades of the eighteenth century. Segu political power depended on warfare and the constant acquisition of slaves both for sale and to replenish its warrior ranks. Since the Bambara had long acted as guides, boatmen, interpreters, and military reinforcements to the French on the Senegal, it is hardly surprising that the bulk of French slave exports from Senegambia during the 1720s and 1730s derived from Segu war captives. Nor would it be surprising to learn that the Segu Bambara allied with the French to subdue Gangara: The French coveted Gangaran gold and needed slaves for their American colony of Louisiana; Segu consolidated regional power in the 1730s by overpowering its rivals and reducing prisoners of war to military and agricultural slavery. But Smith offers better evidence of Bambara involvement in Saugnm Furro's death and his enslavement. The *Narrative* identifies the leader of the enemy army as "Baukurre," a name that looks and sounds remarkably similar to that of Biton Kulibali's warrior son, known alternately as Bakari, Bookari, and Bakiri.[35]

As a Mande-descended people, the Gangara share a common historical culture and Mandinkan dialect with others (including the Segu Bambara) dispersed throughout the West African savannah who trace their ancestry to the great Mali empire established by Sunjata in the thirteenth century. According to Charles S. Bird and Martha B. Kendall, it is this system of commonly held beliefs—largely functional, communicated by the *djeli* (bards or griots), and designed to travel well-that "defines appropriate behavior for individual [Mande] actors and allows in turn the interpretation of the behavior of others." Oral tradition plays a key role in preserving the cultural focus and collective wisdom of this scattered people, for whom the power of language is paramount and partly accounted for by the subtle ways in which it is often used.[36]

Legends, myths, and proverbs inculcate Mande values in Gangara children beginning at a very early age—a practice that, along with the memory
training through which oral cultures retain their vitality, may in part vindicate Smith's remarkably long and vivid boyhood recollections. According to
one scholar, the Mande cannot utter two or three sentences without retelling
a proverb. Celebrations of heroic behavior, expressed in poems and songs
that are still heard over the radio daily, are central to Mande culture, which
lavishes esteem and adulation on its rebels, and they are important to our
reconsideration of Smith's *Narrative*. Mande ideology holds that a child is
born with a reputation deriving primarily from that of his father and that
individuals gain reputations of their own, according to Bird and Kendall,
only by "surpassing the collective deeds of their predecessors and placing
their own names firmly in their clans' historical records." If nothing else,
then, Smith's paean to his father echoed the *djeli* practice of singing praise
songs that guaranteed the renown and immortality of Mande heroes, who
had to embody both courage in battle and laudable civic virtues of generosity, moderation, and reason. But Smith's heroic deeds in America, immortal-
ized in print and through the grapevine, can also be construed as his own
ultimately successful attempt to surpass the gallantry of his father and thus
establish his good character on two continents: in the Mande world, Bird
and Kendall continue, "a [heroic] name must be won not only in the arena
provided by one's peers, but also in that abstract arena created by one's
ancestors." If, as a Mande proverb maintains, "the hero is but welcome
on troubled days," certainly late-eighteenth-century Afro–New Englanders
should have welcomed one with open arms. And if, as Shane White recently
observed, much surviving northern black folklore concerns the black kings
and governors, any reaction by Smith to his non-election would make sense
coming from a man out to secure enduring fame—in the Mande sense or
any other.[37]

Heroic songs of the *djeli* bard-historians imparted notions of what was
honorable and dishonorable, just and unjust. They also touched on the
themes of filial disobedience and abusive authority that constituted the
thematic core of the *Narrative;* like Smith, the Mande knew a good son and
a good ruler when they saw one. In the early eighteenth century, legends
grew regarding the dawning of Segu, a Mande-descended kingdom (and the
probable attackers of Gangara). As one tale has it, before the time of Biton
Kulibali the original village of Segu was ruled by a young chief named
Trokomari, who assumed power following the death of his universally
praised father. Epitomizing everything that Smith (and Smith's father and—
at least according to Elisha Niles—America's revolutionary forefathers) did
not, Trokomari "ruled by whim rather than by reason," trifling "with the
chieftainship as if he were playing with a toy." Refusing "the advice of the old
men" whose wisdom he sorely lacked, Trokomari instead ruled with an iron
fist. "His justice was unpredictable," and "because he had the power to do so,

he abused people's rights." When Trokomari died, the *djeli* proclaimed simply that "sometimes it happens that a child does not have the good character of his father."[38]

Whether or not Smith referred so specifically in the *Narrative* to such Mande-inspired sensibilities regarding power, authority, and honor, he did make explicit the superiority of his African-informed sense of justice—though references to the homeland remained partially veiled, rooted in black oral traditions that counteracted white power safely with metaphors and barbs of wry wit. Protesting the actions of Captain Elisha Hart, a prominent local merchant who allegedly sued Smith under false pretense and then "insultingly taunted me with my unmerited misfortune," Smith said:

> Such a proceeding as this, committed on a defenseless stranger . . . without any foundation in reason or justice, whatever it may be called in a Christian land, would in my native country have been branded as a crime equal to highway robbery. But Captain Hart was a white gentleman, and I a poor African, therefore it was all right, and good enough for the black dog.

Tongue planted firmly in cheek, a vituperative Smith railed against a system that dispensed justice along lines of race and class. He also ensured that Hart's abuse would not go unnoticed. Talking about satirical songs that served functions similar to Smith's printed invective, a white writer in the West Indies noted that "the victim of a carnival song need never hope that his failings or his wrong will be forgotten; it will be sung long after he is in his grave." Like the rhymes and rhythms of such a song, Smith's manipulation of "white" language in this passage allowed him to reject hypocritical Christian notions of fair play while alluding to a positive African alternative. Attacking Hart's abuse of a "defenseless stranger," Smith asserts that, in Africa, the Yankee would have been convicted of "highway robbery"—a distinctly British term that Smith appropriated in the name of Africans who, it seemed, alone understood the true meaning. Hart may have won in court, but Smith avenged his enemy's dirty deed by immortalizing it—and Hart—on the page, turning "white" logic and language against itself and thus snatching moral victory from legal and pecuniary defeat.[39]

Early in the *Narrative*, Smith submitted—with due subtlety—a specific African substitute for New England's treatment of strangers, describing the year he spent tending sheep "at the house of a very rich farmer" as his parents' marital rift dragged on. "Although I was an entire stranger," Smith remembered, "during my stay with [the farmer] I was kindly used, and with as much tenderness . . . as his only son." Thus using the word "stranger" once each in African and American contexts, Smith may have been alluding to and condemning the biblical and Puritan tradition of identifying strangers (and non-Christians) as potential slaves. He may also have been referring to Mande praise songs that equated strangers with heroes. At any rate, though a stranger and literal servant, Smith received better treatment from a "heathen" master in Africa than he did from the Christian Hart, who lorded it over him in Connecticut.[40]

CROSSING THE WATERS:
PHYSICALITY AND RESISTANCE

In his own life, Smith, like the American colonists of the 1760s and 1770s, resisted tyranny with a mixture of force and appeals to rights. Had Hart, in fact, attempted to gouge him twenty-five years earlier, when he was in his physical prime, Smith's assertions of equality might not have been merely rhetorical. Time and again, a younger Smith served notice that all who crossed him did so at great personal risk. Scorned by American institutional justice and armed with strength that became the stuff of folk legend, Smith established physical and visible symbols of black equality and superiority.

Physical resistance first transpired after Smith questioned orders given by his first master's son. James Mumford (yet another bad son) oft grew "big with authority" in his father's absence, commanding Smith to perform "this and that business different from what my master directed me." When Smith finally refused on account of a heavy workload, young Mumford flew "into a great rage, snatched a pitchfork and went to lay me over the head therewith." Smith grabbed one too and defended himself, "or otherwise he might have murdered me in his outrage." Mumford, faced with an armed and larger opponent, called for help. Subdued by four assailants only after he "voluntarily caused [himself] to be bound," Smith hung on the cattle gallows (where beasts were hung to be slaughtered) an hour before a servant fetched three dozen peach tree whips intended for his back. But "that was all that was done with them," as Mumford declined another showdown with his headstrong slave. Smith recalled that whole affair left Mumford so shaken that he "put his pocket handkerchief before his eyes and went home . . . to tell his mother." Smith then returned to his original work, having successfully thwarted the junior Mumford's attempt to usurp authority that Smith felt did not belong to him.[41]

The Mumfords peddled their "stubborn" slave to Thomas Stanton after Smith and an Irish indentured servant made an aborted escape around Montauk Point headed for the Mississippi River. Violence followed. "Hearing a racket in the house," Smith rushed in to find Mrs. Stanton "in a violent passion" with his wife, Meg. Meg claimed to have "given no just occasion" for such harsh treatment; Smith urged her to apologize anyway "for the sake of peace." "But whilst I was thus saying," Smith recounted, "my mistress turned the blows which she was repeating on my wife to me." Like his father's efforts in Africa, Smith's attempt at pacification had been met with unwarranted white violence. Enough was enough: Mrs. Stanton "took down her horsewhip, and while she was glutting her fury with it, I reached out my great black hand, raised it up and received the blows of the whip on it which were designed for my head. Then I immediately committed the whip to the devouring fire."[42]

Retaliation came days later, when Thomas Stanton used "a club two feet long and as large round as a chairpost" to knock an unsuspecting Smith on the head as he stoked the fire. Anticipating a second blow, Smith snatched Stanton's weapon, "dragged him out of the door," took the club to a local justice of the peace, and demanded action—appealing once more to whites' standards to convict them. After advising Smith to return home, there to "wait till [Stanton] abused me again, and then complain," the judge chastised Stanton for treating his slave "hastily and unjustly, and told him what would be the consequence if he continued the same treatment." On the road home Stanton (who this time brought his brother along) waylaid Smith again. Smith, realizing Yankee law had done as much—or as little—for him as it would, now took justice unto himself. "I became enraged," he related, "turned them both under me, laid one of them across the other, and stamped both with my feet what I would."[43]

His recalcitrance rewarded with ankle and wrist cuffs, Smith needled his persecutors with saucy quips. Confronting Mrs. Stanton, who had been overjoyed to see him prostrated, Smith beamed, showing off his chains, and thanked the mistress for the "gold rings." And when Thomas Stanton announced that he had a good mind to send Smith to the West Indies, Smith answered that "I crossed the waters to come here, and I am willing to cross them to return."[44]

Smith's elliptical response to Stanton's threat may reveal an African, or at least African American, aspect of his complex identity. West Africans of various ethnic and regional origins brought with them to the New World a strong faith in transmigration of souls. Many slaves believed that, after death, their spirits returned to ancestral Africa. Thus for the aging Smith who created the Narrative, having one foot in the grave may have meant being one step closer to an African return. In his travels among the African-born residents of Connecticut, Long Island, and Rhode Island, Smith probably became acquainted with certain beliefs imported from central Africa. His reply to Stanton may have been a transmutation of the broadly shared central African concept of Kalunga, literally "the sea" or "God's ocean."[45] In many Kongo cultures the Kalunga line marked a division between one world and the next: a link to one's ancestors or between the living and the dead. According to the Africanist Robert Farris Thompson, ritual experts known in the northern Kongo as Banganga nkodi—specialists who use words to communicate with the dead—cut signs "into the shell of a tortoise so that the reptile, diving back into the water, will carry them across the Kalunga line into the world beyond." There "the ancestors will receive the encoded messages and act upon them on behalf of their descendants." Perhaps Smith, himself something of a specialist in the use of words, referred here to a distant but not forgotten African cosmogram, rousing ancestral spirits in what Thompson has called "an unseen court of last appeal." We can only speculate what Smith or, more properly, Broteer might have communicated to his ancestors. Were it committed to the sea, Smith's body, like that of the symbolic tortoise, would have borne some markings of its own. In addition to any "country marks"—ritual scars that, according to John Mbiti, united the initiated with African kin both living and dead—that he may have had, we read that Stanton's fireside ambush left a nasty scar on Smith's head. For that, African reprisal might have been appropriate.[46]

Closely complementing *Kalunga* and soul migration, many Africans held that the souls of their departed lived on by passing into surviving family members. This reincarnation of ancestral souls forged important cultural links that sustained community and carried African traditions through time and space. Viewed in this light, Smith's suggestive response to Stanton may again distinguish his vehement identification with his dead father from Niles's call to recapture the spirit of a nation's revolutionary forefathers. When Smith revealed myriad similarities between himself and Saungm Furro, he not only affirmed the need felt by Niles and many Americans to return to the days of a virtuous past but may also have invoked an African cosmogram whose significance remained lost on both his white editor and subsequent scholars. Smith may have believed that he was not merely like Saungm Furro, but that in real ways his father's soul lived on in him. To paraphrase Igor Kopytoff, Smith did not merely long to make the spirits of the dead active in worldly affairs. He perhaps knew that they already were.[47]

A MULTICULTURAL MAN

Though Smith had roots planted firmly in southern New England, the *Narrative* makes it clear that his thoughts wandered across the Atlantic to his childhood home. He probably listened with interest to late-1780s dockside gossip about African emigration plans emanating from urban ports like Boston and Newport. The Atlantic rumor mill no doubt also brought news of the black Tories who had literally crossed the waters, leaving Nova Scotia for Sierra Leone beginning around 1790. But if Americans had exposed the hypocrisy of their liberty-loving bluster, Smith apparently felt unsure about an African return. A transatlantic voyage would have been long indeed for a hobbled and almost blind old man. Assuming he survived the trip, what then? Smith had spent the major part of his life in Connecticut; his livelihood and two generations of descendants who had never glimpsed Africa were there. Besides, those recently emigrated black Loyalists had met with far from convincing success. Many who left felt frustrated by their precarious position in Anglo-American society. Smith's greater identification with that society, coupled with his ability to envisage an alternative African existence—and make it a big part of his tale—made his act of self-fashioning that much more complex. Smith could not easily resolve feelings of being tugged simultaneously between Africa and America, between proto–black nationalism and racial integration. Indeed, it may be just such a paradoxical swaying between seemingly antithetical goals, not some fixed voice of protest, that unites heterogeneous African American literature.[48]

The last slave narrative of the eighteenth century, Smith's tale, like his narrative persona in it, differed markedly from those of his few predecessors—notably Briton Hammon, who in 1760 published the first extant American slave narrative. Unlike Hammon, a prodigal slave mariner who willingly sailed from London back to Massachusetts slavery with his "good old Master," Smith sought no such happy reunion, no providential return to the anonymous certitude of slave life. As a self-made American individualist, fashioning identity in New England after the Revolution, Smith enjoyed no freedom where any yoke—political, religious, or familial—constricted his ability to chart his own destiny. The filial disobedience of Smith's sons proved fateful, not because they ignored imperious authority, but because they neglected their father's virtuous example. Doing his part by preparing his children to live in a corrupt world—as had Saungm Furro and America's republican forefathers—Smith then loosened the reins and allowed Solomon and Cuff to act as they would.[49]

Indeed, Smith's republican references to liberties, rights, and privileges hinted at a gradual shift in African American literature—and American culture generally—away from the language of providential deliverance and toward more secularized, self-reliant narrative personae. Smith's lone reference to the religion of his masters came via the stinging denunciation of the infamous Captain Hart. Emerging in a postrevolutionary milieu, Smith could draw upon not only politically charged rhetoric of liberty and equality but also nominal freedom and experience as an individualistic merchant capitalist. The self-dependence that would have been less acceptable to a pious public earlier in the century (from black author or white) became the dominant virtue of his *Narrative*. Smith—not God—became the heroic liberator.

Significantly, Smith claimed to have learned in Africa the limits of subjugation and when resistance was just. No mere black Poor Richard, Smith was every bit the bicultural man most consider his more celebrated contemporary, Olaudah Equiano, to have been. Since he was a proud African, many of Smith's New World actions and beliefs beckoned toward his ancestral past. When African values and ideals resonated with ideals of American republicanism, instances of cross-cultural overlap enabled Smith to make better sense of duality. Too, Smith had at hand an Afro–New England folk culture that provided an oral storytelling model rooted in satire and metaphor. Perfect for subtly lampooning whites, this style allowed Smith's language to speak on many levels and in ways that often eluded editorial manipulation.[50]

Venture Smith met an unsettling world head on, fighting whites with their own laws, language, and way of life. Rather than letting acrimony undermine the pride he took in his American accomplishments or making a restrictive choice "between the world and the self," as Andrews claims, a resolute Smith made a world *for* himself. His tale boldly punctuated the ways in which one African American beat the odds and the white man at his own game. Smith, wise to the myth of black integration into late-eighteenth-century white society, persevered by never abrogating his African heritage for the sake of acceptance. Ironically, then, in this way Smith's *Narrative* may be more "African" than most later ones, which tended—especially after 1816 and for reasons as political as cultural—to downplay Africa in favor of claims to American citizenship.[51] Fashioning self by drawing heavily upon an appropriately murky double vision, often too complex to be neatly dichotomized into constituent parts, Smith played an important early role in charting the trajectory of black assertions of freedom in an evolving America.

It was no accident that Frederick Douglass's *Narrative* (1845) and *My Bondage and My Freedom* (1855), arguably the most influential slave narratives of all, bore striking resemblances to Smith's, most generally through Douglass's refusal to resign himself to being "a slave for life!" or settling for emancipation in the hereafter; in Douglass's skeptical view of a religion whereby slaveholding whites "go to heaven with our blood on their shirts"; and finally, by way of Douglass's physical retaliation when pushed to the brink by the brutal Mr. Covey. Smith's persona as a black freedom fighter, the culmination of eighteenth-century attempts by American blacks to assert and define self through narrative forms, provided a signifying text—a resource both drawn on and transformed—for African American narratives of the antebellum period and beyond.[52] To be sure, concepts of race and freedom changed over time, as did the language with which black authors carved narrative identities that reflected the complexity of being African American. As the new century began, though, the foundations for vehement written denunciations of slavery and racism had been firmly laid by black literary pioneers like Venture Smith.

NOTES

1. Venture Smith, *A Narrative of the Life and Adventures of Venture, a Native of Africa: But resident above sixty years in the United States of America. Related by Himself* (New London, 1798), 13. The 1798 edition has been reprinted in Dorothy Porter, ed. *Early Negro Writing, 1760–1837* (Boston, 1971), 538–58.

2. Smith, *Narrative*, 13, 31.

3. *New London Bee*, Dec. 26, 1798, Jan. 2, 9, 16, 23, 30, 1799. No advertisements for the *Narrative* appeared in the *New London Connecticut Gazette*, the *Middlesex Gazette*, or the *Hartford Connecticut Courant*, from November 1798 through March 1799. Probably for sound financial reasons, Charles Holt rarely advertised his imprints in papers other than his own. On October 29, 1798, he publicized for sale his *Short Account of the Yellow Fever, as it Appeared in New-London, in August, September, and October, 1798: With an Accurate List of Those who Died of the Disease, the Donations, &c. &c. &c.* in Samuel Greene's *New London Connecticut Gazette*. Arna Bontemps, ed., *Five Black Lives: The Autobiographies of Venture Smith, James Mars, William Grimes, the Rev. G. W. Offley, and James L. Smith* (Middletown, 1971), 26. I have been unable to locate a copy of the 1835 publication of Smith's *Narrative*; Arna Bontemps provides a reprint of the 1897 edition.

4. On the Smith legend, see H. M. Selden, comp., "Traditions of Venture! Known as Venture Smith," in *Five Black Lives*, ed., Bontemps, 26–34. Smith, *Narrative*, 31.

5. Smith, *Narrative*, 31. Smith's prosperity in the new nation was exceptional but not

unprecedented. See, for example, William C. Nell, *The Colored Patriots of the American Revolution* (Boston, 1855); Sidney Kaplan and Emma Nogrady Kaplan, *The Black Presence in the Era of the American Revolution* (Amherst, 1989); Juliet E. K. Walker, *Free Frank: A Black Pioneer on the Antebellum Frontier* (Lexington, Ky., 1983); and two profiles of the North's wealthiest man of color: Sheldon H. Harris, *Paul Cuffe: Black America and the African Return* (New York, 1972); and Lamont D. Thomas, *Rise to Be a People: A Biography of Paul Cuffe* (Urbana, 1986). Smith probably knew Paul Cuffe. The two lived near each other, and both were free black maritime entrepreneurs. In any case, they surely knew *of* each other. Though few achieved Cuffe's level of subsistence, Smith was one of many northern black men who, like Cuffe, parlayed seafaring work into freedom. See W. Jeffrey Bolster, "'To Feel like a Man': Black Seamen in the Northern States, 1800–1860," *Journal of American History*, 76 (March 1990), 1173–99; and William Jeffrey Bolster, "African-American Seamen: Race, Seafaring Work, and Atlantic Maritime Culture, 1750–1860" (Ph. D. diss., John Hopkins University, 1991).

6. William L. Andrews, "The First Fifty Years of the Slave Narrative, 1760–1810," in *The Art of Slave Narrative: Original Essays in Criticism and Theory*, ed. John Sekora and Darwin T. Turner (Macomb, 1982), 7. See also John Sekora, "Black Message / White Envelope: Genre, Authenticity, and Authority in the Antebellum Slave Narrative," *Callaloo*, 10 (Summer 1987), 482–515; Charles Nichols, *Many Thousand Gone: The Ex-Slaves' Account of Their Bondage and Freedom* (Leiden, 1963); Marion Wilson Starling, *The Slave Narrative: Its Place in American History* (Boston, 1982); William L. Andrews, *To Tell a Free Story: The First Century of Afro-American Autobiography, 1760–1865* (Urbana, 1986), esp. 1–60; and Frances Smith Foster, *Witnessing Slavery: The Development of Antebellum Slave Narratives* (Madison, 1994). While the grounds for debates over "authenticity" have shifted, the discussion itself is not new. Nearly seventy years ago Ulrich B. Phillips wore that most slave narratives "were issued with so much abolitionist editing that as a class their authenticity is doubtful." Ulrich B. Phillips, *Life and Labor in the Old South* (Boston, 1929), 219.

7. Andrews, "First Fifty Years of the Slave Narrative," 8. Blyden Jackson writes that "all of the earliest black American writers, are black Anglo-Americans. Black preserving cultural distinctions which separate them . . . and proclaim their African identities and past emphatically they, as a group, are not." Blyden Jackson, *A History of Afro-American Literature*, vol. I: *The Long Beginning, 1746–1895* (Baton Rouge, 1989), 50, 52. Ralph Ellison, *Shadow and Act* (1953; New York, 1995), 45–59. On the "openness" of popular texts that use language creatively to "pack a multiplicity of meanings into a small space," see John Fiske, *Understanding Popular Culture* (Boston, 1989), 103–27.

8. For the paradigm of black writing as protest against racism, see Jackson, *History of Afro-American Literature*, I, 8. Other scholars and critics regard that paradigm as too restrictive. Charles Johnson notes that "a myopic emphasis on issues of race and sex" too often masquerades as "a truly sophisticated understanding of the integrative dimensions of the creative process [of writing]." Charles Johnson, "Keeping the Blues at Bay," *New York Times Book Review*, March 10, 1996, p. 4. Likewise, for all his polemical moralizing, Stanley Crouch maintains deep distrust of both separatism and assertions of black difference. He bemoans the "hand-me-down protest" that often springs from such an ideological bent, and he insists that "American life is far from the closed book of atrocities . . . stern critics seem to imagine." Stanley Crouch, "The One out of Many Blues," *American Enterprise*, 6 (March/April 1995), 53, 54. Elsewhere, he links acceptance of the protest mode with "a very circumscribed notion of African-American writing," opining with typical bravado that "any black writer who chooses human nature over platitudes, opportunism, or trends faces probably rejection." Stanley Crouch, *Notes of a Hanging Judge: Essays and Reviews, 1979–1989* (New York, 1990), 143. See also Nathaniel Mackey, "Other: From Noun to Verb," *Representations*, 39 (Summer 1992), 51–70; and Chinosole, "Tryin' to Get Over: Narrative Posture in Equiano's Autobiography," in *Art of Slave Narrative*, ed. Sekora and Turner, 45–54. On the construction of race, see Barbara J. Fields, "Ideology and Race in American History," in *Region, Race*

and *Reconstruction: Essays in Honor of C. Vann Woodward,* ed. J. Morgan Kousser and James M. McPherson (New York, 1982), 143–77.

9. Sekora, "Black Message / White Envelope," 503. Many scholars have written on the limits of current multiculturalism, stressing as I have the need to appreciate multiple cross-cultural affiliations based on individuals' ability to emphasize or de-emphasize the significance of prescribed ethnoracial descent. See John Higham, "Multiculturalism and Universalism: A History and Critique," *American Quarterly,* 45 (June 1993), 195–219; David A. Hollinger, *Postethnic America: Beyond Multiculturalism* (New York, 1995); Gary B. Nash, "The Hidden History of Mestizo America," *Journal of American History,* 82 (Dec. 1995), 941–62; and Ira Berlin, "From Creole to African: Atlantic Creoles and the Origins of African-American Society in Mainland North America," *William and Mary Quarterly,* 53 (April 1996), 251–88. Also important are the critical essays in Kwame Anthony Appiah and Henry Louis Gates, Jr., eds., *Identities* (Chicago, 1995), esp. Walter Benn Michaels, "Race into Culture: A Critical Genealogy of Cultural Identity," *ibid.,* 32–62.

10. On Elisha Niles's background, see J. William Frost, *Connecticut Education in the Revolutionary Era: "For God and Country"* (Chester, Conn., 1974), 32, 36. On Niles's father, Nathaniel, see David Brion Davis, *The Problem of Slavery in the Age of Revolution, 1770–1823* (Ithaca, 1975), 290–93, 296–97, 393; and Nathaniel Niles, *Two Discourses on Liberty* (Newburyport, 1774). Connecticut folk tradition tells us that Elisha Niles acted as Smith's amanuensis. See Selden, comp., "Traditions of Venture!," 26; and Kaplan and Kaplan, *Black Presence in the Era of the American Revolution,* 255. Although folk sources are obviously fallible, in the absence of better documentation, they are the best evidence we have. As many scholars point out, the silences in slave sources necessitate special, though not naïve, dependence on oral testimony when no written corroboration can be found. See Gilbet Osofsky, *Puttin' On Ole Massa* (New York, 1969), 45–48; and John W. Blassingame, ed., *Slave Testimony: Two Centuries of Letters, Speeches, Interviews, and Autobiographies* (Baton Rouge, 1977), xvii–lxv. More important, Smith's tale and my argument would look very much the same even if the *Narrative* had been edited, not by Niles, but by the next-most-likely candidate, the printer Charles Holt himself.

On education in the early republic, see Jay Fliegelman, *Prodigals and Pilgrims: The American Revolution against Patriarchal Authority, 1750–1800* (Cambridge, Eng., 1982); Gordon S. Wood, *The Creation of the American Republic, 1776–1787* (Chapel Hill, 1969), 393–429; and Cathy N. Davidson, *Revolution and the Word: The Rise of the Novel in America* (New York, 1986). On the education of slaves and free blacks more specifically, see Carter G. Woodson, *The Education of the Negro Prior to 1861* (1919; Salem, N.H., 1991), 1–121; Lorenzo Johnston Greene, *The Negro in Colonial New England* (1942; New York, 1974), 237–42; Gary B. Nash, *Forging Freedom: The Formation of Philadelphia's Black Community, 1720–1840* (Cambridge, Mass., 1988), 202–10; Robert J. Cottrol, *The Afro-Yankees: Providence's Black Community in the Antebellum Era* (Westport, 1982), 50; and Winthrop Jordan, *White over Black: American Attitudes toward the Negro, 1550–1812* (Chapel Hill, 1968), 352–56, 362–65.

11. Elisha Niles, "Preface," in Smith, *Narrative,* 3–4. On political culture in the new nation, see Gordon S. Wood, ed., *The Rising Glory in America, 1760–1820* (New York, 1971); Neil Harris, *The Artist in American Society: The Formative Years, 1790–1860* (Chicago, 1982), esp. x–xii, 2–53; Joseph J. Ellis, *After the Revolution: Profiles of Early American Culture* (New York, 1979); and Fliegelman, *Prodigals and Pilgrims.* On relationships between culture and literature in the early republic, see Davidson, *Revolution and the Word;* Michael Warner, *Letters of the Republic: Publication and the Public Sphere in Eighteenth-Century America* (Cambridge, Mass., 1990), 118–50; and Steven Watts, "Masks, Morals, and the Market: American Literature and Early Capitalist Culture, 1790–1820," *Journal of the Early Republic,* 6 (Summer 1986), 127–49.

12. Nathan O. Hatch, *The Democratization of American Christianity* (New Haven, 1989). To further situate Niles's idealism in time and place, see Nathan O. Hatch, *The*

Sacred Cause of Liberty: Republican Thought and the Millennium in Revolutionary New England (New Haven, 1977); Ruth H. Bloch, *Visionary Republic: Millennial Themes in American Thought, 1756–1800* (Cambridge, Eng., 1985); and Henry F. May, *The Enlightenment in America* (New York, 1976). On the Connecticut education bill, see Jordan, *White over Black*, 355. Noah Webster, fellow educator and classmate of Niles's at Yale in the late 1770s, struck the keynote in the failed ratification drive. More than cultural coincidence probably accounts for the fact that many of Webster's themes resurfaced virtually intact in Niles's preface. See Noah Webster, *Effects of Slavery, on Morals and Industry* (Hartford, 1793).

13. Niles, "Preface," 3–4. On colonization, see Gary B. Nash, *Race and Revolution* (Madison, 1990), 146–58; Floyd J. Miller, *The Search for a Black Nationality: Black Emigration and Colonization, 1787–1863* (Urbana, 1975), 3–53; and Jordan, *White over Black*, 546–69. Niles was one of many abolitionists of his day to link antislavery and self-purification. See Davis, *Problem of Slavery in the Age of Revolution*, 285–99.

14. On the minutes of the American Convention of Delegates from Abolition Societies, see Leon F. Litwack, *North of Slavery: The Negro in the Free States, 1790–1860* (Chicago, 1961), 18–19. Joseph Priestly, *Miscellaneous observations relating to education: More specifically as it respects the conduct of the mind* (New London, 1796). For Connecticut booksellers' lists, see "Lists of Books and Phamplets For Sale by Samuel Green," *New London Connecticut Gazette*, Feb. 7, 1798; and "Books For Sale at C[harles]. Holt's Printing-Office," *New London Bee*, Aug. 23, 1797. For "Baybay, a true Story of a good Negro Woman," and "The Pious Negro," see *The Entertaining, Moral, and Religious Repository; Written in a Simple yet Pleasing Stile, Eminently Calculated for the Amusement and Instruction of the Youth of Both Sexes* (Elizabethtown, N.J., 1798), 298–304. An advertisement for *The Entertaining, Moral, and Religious Repository* ran in the *Middlesex Gazette*, Nov. 9, 1798.

15. Holt, *Short Account of the Yellow Fever*, 18–19; *New London Bee*, Sept. 6, 13, 1797, Nov. 7, 1798; *The Life of Doctor Benjamin Franklin; Written by Himself: Together With Essays, Humorous, Moral and Literary, Chiefly in the Manner of the Spectator* (New London, 1798). My thanks to Robert A. Gross for calling my attention to Holt's edition of the *Life of Franklin*.

16. Niles, "Preface," 3–4. Emphasis added.

17. *Ibid.* Most white philanthropists cared less than Niles about instructing bondsmen and ex-slaves. The few who did share his concern tended to agree that education of blacks did not render (and often was not intended to render) them equal to whites. See, for example, James Sullivan, "To Jeremy Belknap, Boston, July 30, 1795," in Jordan, *White over Black*, 355–56. On eighteenth-century ambivalence about racial hierarchy, see George W. Stocking, Jr., *Race, Culture, and Evolution: Essays in the History of Anthropology* (New York, 1968), esp. 16–40. Samuel Stanhope Smith, a celebrated educator who received an honorary degree from Yale in 1783, may have influenced Niles's environmentalism. See Samuel Stanhope Smith, *Essay on the Causes of the Variety of Complexion and Figure in the Human Species* (Philadelphia, 1787).

18. On the hardening of ideas of race in the nineteenth century, see George M. Fredrickson, *The Black Image in the White Mind: The Debate on Afro-American Character and Destiny, 1817–1914* (New York, 1971). My thinking about race as historical construct owes much to Fields, "Ideology and Race in American History"; see also T. H. Breen, "Creative Adaptions: People and Cultures," in *Colonial British America: Essays in the New History of the Early Modern Era*, ed. Jack P. Greene and J. R. Pole (Baltimore, 1984), esp. 203.

19. Smith, *Narrative*, 31, 29, 26. On the preoccupation with familial relations evident in American literature of the last half of the eighteenth century, see Fliegelman, *Prodigals and Pilgrims*.

20. Kaplan and Kaplan, *Black Presence in the Era of the American Revolution*, 255; Edmund S. Morgan, *The Puritan Dilemma: The Story of John Winthrop* (Boston, 1958); Watts, "Masks, Morals, and the Market," 129; Smith, *Narrative*, 25–26, 24. On the cultural meaning of clothing and physical appearance to northern blacks, see Shane

White, "A Question of Style: Blacks in and around New York City in the Late 18th Century," *Journal of American Folklore*, 102 (Jan.–March 1989), 24–45.

21. William D. Piersen, *Black Yankees: The Development of an Afro-American Subculture in Eighteenth-Century New England* (Amherst, 1988), 129, 130–31. For the local historian Isaac W. Stuart's statement, see *ibid.*, 135. On black election festivals in the North, see Orville H. Platt, "Negro Governors," *New Haven Colony Historical Society Papers*, 6 (1900), 315–35; Greene, *Negro in Colonial New England*, 249–55; Joseph P. Reidy, "'Negro Election Day' and Black Community Life in New England, 1750–1860," *Marxist Perspectives*, 1 (Fall 1978), 102–17; Melvin Wade, "'Shining in Borrowed Plumage': Affirmation of Community in the Black Coronation Festivals of New England, ca. 1750–1850," in *Material Life in America, 1600–1860*, ed. Robert Blair St. George (Boston, 1988), 171–82; Piersen, *Black Yankees*, 117–40; and Shane White, "'It Was a Proud Day': African Americans, Festivals, and Parades in the North, 1741–1834," *Journal of American History*, 81 (June 1994), 13–50.

22. Smith, *Narrative*, 26–28. Smith's perspective is similar to that of David Hall, a white man who wrote in his diary that his slave "died like a saint but is thought that I have lost . . . near 200 old Tenor . . . by his death." Piersen, *Black Yankees*, 32.

23. Smith, *Narrative*, 24, 11; Andrews, "First Fifty Years of the Slave Narrative," 16, 21. For West African aphorisms, see Melville J. Herskovits, *Economic Anthropology: A Study in Comparative Economics* (New York, 1952), 118. See also Melville J. Herskovits, *Dahomey: An Ancient West African Kingdom* (2 vols., New York, 1938).

24. See William D. Piersen, "Puttin' Down Ole Massa: African Satire in the New World," *Research in African Literatures*, 7 (Summer 1976), 166–80; and Piersen, *Black Yankees*, 106–13, 137–40, 156–60. On the ubiquitous educational function of slave folk tales in the New World, see also Lawrence W. Levine, *Black Culture and Black Consciousness: Afro-American Folk Thought from Slavery to Freedom* (New York, 1977), 81–135; and Charles Joyner, *Down by the Riverside: A South Carolina Slave Community* (Urbana, 1984), 172–95.

25. Esther B. Carpenter, *South County Studies* (1887; Boston, 1924), 222–26; Sekora, "Black Message / White Envelope," 491; Smith, *Narrative*, 5.

26. Smith, *Narrative*, 5, 8. Smith's omission of his mother's name is indicative of the gender-specific content of most slave narratives. See Foster, *Witnessing Slavery*, xxix–xli. Smith's positive picture of Africa and the pride undergirding it become more striking when viewed alongside the overwhelmingly negative sketch offered by James Albert Ukawsaw Gronniosaw, *A Narrative of the Most Remarkable Particulars in the Life of James Albert Ukawsaw Gronniosaw, An African Prince, Written by Himself* (Newport, 1774); see also Henry Louis Gates Jr., "James Gronniosaw and the Trope of the Talking Book," *Southern Review*, 22 (Spring 1986), 252–72.

27. Melville J. Herskovits, *The Myth of the Negro Past* (Boston, 1941), 172–73, 64–65; Melville J. Herskovits, *Trinidad Village* (New York, 1964), 293; John S. Mbiti, *African Religions and Philosophy* (New York, 1970), 191. Newer scholarship has augmented the picture of African marriage provided by Herskovits and Mbiti without overturning the basic ideas cited here. On the historical range of gender and familial relations in West and central Africa, see Claire Robertson and Iris Berger, eds., *Women and Class in Africa* (New York, 1986); and Ifi Amadiume, *Male Daughters, Female Sons: Gender and Sex in African Society* (London, 1987).

28. Joyner, *Down by the Riverside*, 180; for Spear's statement, see Piersen, *Black Yankees*, 108. Mechal Sobel alludes to the "totally unexplored" issue of Africans bringing with them to the New World attitudes about "'proper' slave behavior and the 'rights' of slaves." See Mechal Sobel, *The World They Made Together: Black and White Values in Eighteenth-Century Virginia* (Princeton, 1987), 29. Scholars of Latin America, South America, and the Caribbean have done more than North American specialists to chart the existence in West and central Africa of such ideas and related notions of thrift, property, authority, and veneration of strength. See, for example, John Thornton, *Africa and Africans in the Making of the Atlantic World, 1440–1680* (Cambridge, Eng., 1992); João José Reis, *Slave Rebellion in Brazil: The Muslim Uprising of 1835 in Bahia*, trans.

Arthur Brakel (Baltimore, 1993); and Carolyn E. Fick, *The Making of Haiti: The Saint Domingue Revolution from Below* (Knoxville, 1990). On language styles, see Piersen, "Puttin' Down Ole Massa."

29. See Edwin Burrows and Michael Wallace, "The American Revolution: The Ideology and Psychology of National Liberation," *Perspective in American History*, 6 (1972), 167–89.

30. Smith, *Narrative*, 8–9.

31. *Ibid.*, 9.

32. *Ibid.*, 11, 9, 20, 31, 10, 31.

33. No scholar has maximized the chance to trace Smith's African ancestry. Many have found in Smith's language evidence of his total acculturation or the obliteration of his black voice by a manipulative amanuensis. To these scholars, there seems little "African" about Smith to warrant the effort. Skeptics also could claim that whatever Smith retained culturally was subject to six decades of dilution and distortion. Finally, limited evidence has made the odds of establishing Smith's birthplace seem long indeed. See Stephan Buhnen, "Place Names as an Historical Source: An Introduction with Examples from Southern Senegambia and Germany," *History in Africa*, 19 (1992), 45–101.

34. Smith, *Narrative*, 8. See Gwendolyn Midlo Hall, *Africans in Colonial Louisiana: The Development of Afro-Creole Culture in the Eighteenth Century* (Baton Rouge, 1992), 34; and Philip D. Curtin, *Economic Change in Precolonial Africa: Senegambia in the Era of the Slave Trade* (Madison, 1975), 199.

35. On the Segu Bambara state, see Richard L. Roberts, *Warriors, Merchants, and Slaves: The State and the Economy in the Middle Niger Valley, 1700–1914* (Stanford, 1987), esp. 1–43, 71, 102; and David C. Conrad, "Slavery in Bambara Society: Segou 1712–1861," *Slavery and Abolition* (London), 2 (May 1981), 69–80. On its relationship with the French, see Hall, *Africans in Colonial Louisiana*, 28–55. For a late-eighteenth-century European perspective, see Mungo Park, *Travels in the Interior Districts of Africa: Performed under the Direction and Patronage of the African Association, in the Years 1795, 1796, and 1797* (London, 1799). The French-Bambara slave trade on the Senegal flourished in the years around 1735—the approximate date given by Smith for his capture. Yet Smith did not leave Africa via a French post on the nearby Senegambian coast; in the *Narrative* he claims to have been marched instead "four hundred miles" to Anamaboe, an English fort on the Gold Coast (which is actually closer to six hundred miles from Gangara). Smith may have been sold by his Bambara captors to Dyula (also Juula or Diula) traders from the Asante hinterland below Segu, who often served as middlemen in Bambara commerce with the Ivory and Gold Coasts. In 1735 the Newport, Rhode Island, customhouse cleared a vessel for Africa registered to a shipmaster named Mumford. The Mumfords were prominent slave traders in eighteenth-century southern New England, and they traded almost exclusively on the Gold Coast at Anamaboe and at the adjacent fort, which sported their family name. Smith writes that the master of the Rhode Island slaver who bought him was Thomas Mumford and that the ship's steward, Robertson Mumford, then purchased him. Only one slave-trading vessel registered to the Mumfords left Rhode Island in 1735, and according to custom-house records it returned to Newport in July 1737; Smith claimed to have been born in 1729 and to have "completed [his] eighth year" upon arriving in Rhode Island: Thus it would appear that Smith had his dates right and indeed left Africa from the Gold Coast, as he contended. Curtin, *Economic Change in Precolonial Africa*, 162, 179, 70, 75–76; Smith, *Narrative*, 11, 14. See Elizabeth Donnan, *Documents Illustrative of the History of the Slave Trade to America*, vol. III: *New England and the Middle Colonies* (New York, 1969), 121; and Jay Coughtry, *The Notorious Triangle: Rhode Island and the African Slave Trade, 1700–1807* (Philadelphia, 1981), esp. 242.

36. Charles S. Bird and Martha B. Kendall, "The Mande Hero: Text and Context," in *Explorations in African Systems of Thought*, ed. Ivan Karp and Charles S. Bird (Bloomington, 1980), 13; David C. Conrad, "Searching for History in the Sunjata Epic: The Case of Fakoli," *History in Africa*, 19 (1992), 147–200, esp. 157.

37. For the statement of Moussa Travele (Traore) on the cultural importance of Mande proverbs, see Hall, *Africans in Colonial Louisiana*, 45. Bird and Kendall, "Mande Hero," 14, 15. See also Harold Courlander with Ousmane Sako, *The Heart of the Ngoni: Heroes of the African Kingdom of Segu* (New York, 1982); and White, "'It Was a Proud Day,'" 24.

38. Courlander with Sako, *Heart of the Ngoni*, 17, 19.

39. Smith, *Narrative*, 30. See Piersen, "Puttin' Down Ole Massa," 171–72; and John Lovell Jr., *Black Song: The Forge and the Flame* (New York, 1972).

40. Smith, *Narrative*, 7. On biblical justifications of slavery, see Jordan, *White over Black*, 55, 67–79; and Greene, *Negro in Colonial New England*, 167–68. The Massachusetts "Body of Liberties" of 1641 made legal the enslavement of "captives taken in just wars, and such strangers as willingly sell themselves or are sold to us." Edgar J. McManus, *Black Bondage in the North* (Syracuse, 1973), 59. On Mande beliefs, see Bird and Kendall, "Mande Hero," 18.

41. Smith, *Narrative*, 15–16.

42. Smith, *Narrative*, 18–19. Prominent among the earliest settlers of southern Rhode Island, in the eighteenth century the Stantons ranked with the wealthiest—and largest slave-holding—planter families in the fertile farming, dairy, and cattle-raising region of the Narragansett. As with the neighboring Mumfords, substantial Stanton involvement in the Atlantic slave trade can be documented. See Greene, *Negro in Colonial New England*, 104–6; William Davis Miller, "The Narragansett Planters," *American Antiquarian Society Proceedings*, 43 (1933), 49–115; Virginia B. Anderson, *Maritime Mystic* (Mystic, 1962); Donnan, *Documents Illustrative of the History of the Slave Trade to America*, III, 338, 339, 348–50; Coughtry, *Notorious Triangle*, 47, 50, 207, 209, 239–85; and Tommy Dodd Hamm, "The American Slave Trade with Africa, 1620–1807" (Ph.D. diss., Indiana University, 1975), 291–444.

43. Smith, *Narrative*, 19–20.

44. *Ibid.*, 20.

45. Based on the work of scholars of the African slave trade and the earlier estimates of Lorenzo J. Greene, William D. Piersen estimates that "more than three quarters of New England's black immigrants were African by birth." Thus, even if Smith did not recall much from his own youth about African beliefs in soul transmigration, he probably knew African Americans who did. Population figures bolster this claim and might explain how Smith, a West African, could have learned about *Kalunga*. New London County, where Smith spent most of his life, consistently contained Connecticut's largest black population, both numerically and as a percentage of the total number of inhabitants: 829 (3.8%) in 1756; 2,036 (6.1%) in 1774; 1,920 (6.4%) in 1782; and 1,445 (4.1%) in 1800. In 1798, Smith resided in East Haddam, a town of 2,805, including 47 free blacks and 11 slaves, in 1800. Smith's business dealings no doubt brought him into contact with slaves and free blacks in southern Rhode Island, where, as a result of plantation-style agricultural production, one out of every three persons was black and, in 1755, probably African-born. Although most New England slaves came from West African societies and cultures, a small number of central Africans surely entered the region as well. Piersen, *Black Yankees*, 6–7, 179; U.S. Department of Commerce and Labor, Bureau of the Census, *A Century of Population Growth: From the First Census of the United States to the Twelfth, 1790–1900* (Washington, 1909), 164, 167; [State of Connecticut], *A Return of the Number of Inhabitants in the State of Connecticut, February 1, 1782; and also of the Indians and Negroes*; U.S. Department of State, *Return of the Whole Number of Persons within the Several Districts of the United States or Second Census of the United States* (Washington, 1801), 18–20. On Rhode Island, see Rhett S. Jones, "Plantation Slavery in the Narragansett Country of Rhode Island, 1690–1790: A Preliminary Study," *Plantation Society*, 2 (Dec. 1986), 157; Louis P. Masur, "Slavery in Eighteenth-Century Rhode Island: Evidence from the Census of 1774," *Slavery and Abolition* (London), 6 (1985), 139–50; and Carl R. Woodward, *Plantation in Yankeeland: The Story of Cocumscussoc, Mirror of Colonial Rhode Island* (Chester, Conn., 1971).

46. Robert Farris Thompson and Joseph Cornet, *The Four Moments of the Sun: Kongo Art in Two Worlds* (Washington, 1981), 186; Mbiti, *African Religions and Philosophy*, 117. On African beliefs in transmigration, see Robert Farris Thompson, *Flash of the Spirit: African and Afro-American Art and Philosophy* (New York, 1983); Piersen, *Black Yankees*; Sylvia R. Frey, *Water from the Rock: Black Resistance in a Revolutionary Age* (Princeton, 1991); Michael Mullin, *Africa in America: Slave Acculturation and Resistance in the American South and British Caribbean, 1736–1831* (Urbana, 1992); and Hall, *Africans in Colonial Louisiana*. On *Kalunga*, see Robert Farris Thompson, "Kongo Influences on African-American Artistic Culture," in *Africanisms in American Culture*, ed. Joseph E. Holloway (Bloomington, 1990), esp. 148–57. On ritual scarring, see Samuel Johnson, *The History of the Yorubas: From the Earliest Times to the Beginning of the British Protectorate* (1921; London, 1966), 104–9; Gerald W. Mullin, *Flight and Rebellion: Slave Resistance in Eighteenth-Century Virginia* (New York, 1972); and Mullin, *Africa in America*, 28–29.

47. Mullin, *Africa in America*, 68–69; for Igor Kopytoff's statement, see *ibid.*, 73.

48. See Julius D. Scott, "The Common Wind: Currents of Afro-American Communication in the Era of the Haitian Revolution" (Ph.D. diss., Duke University, 1986). Boston King was one American-born ex-slave who fled to the British during the Revolution, took refuge in Nova Scotia at war's end, and emigrated to Sierra Leone in 1792, where he was educating and proselytizing the natives when his memoirs—like Smith's—were published in 1798. See "Memoirs in the Life of Boston King, a Black Preacher, Written by Himself," *Methodist Magazine* (London), 21 (1798), 105–10, 157–61, 209–13, 261–65.

49. *A Narrative of the Uncommon Sufferings and Surprising Deliverance of Briton Hammon* (Boston, 1760). On the transformative effect of the American Revolution, see Gordon S. Wood, *The Radicalism of the American Revolution* (New York, 1992). On the African American experience more specifically, see Benjamin Quarles, *The Negro in the American Revolution* (Chapel Hill, 1961); Ira Berlin and Ronald Hoffman, eds., *Slavery and Freedom in the Age of the American Revolution* (Charlottesville, 1983); Nash, *Forging Freedom*; Nash, *Race and Revolution*; Shane White, *Somewhat More Independent: The End of Slavery in New York City, 1770–1810* (Athens, 1991); Clement Alexander Price, ed., *Freedom Not Far Distant: A Documentary History of Afro-Americans in New Jersey* (Newark, 1980), 51–86; Graham Hodges, *Slavery and Freedom in the Rural North: African Americans in Monmouth County, New Jersey, 1665–1865* (Madison, 1996), 89–141; and Peter H. Wood, "'The Dream Deferred': Black Freedom Struggles on the Eve of White Independence," in *In Resistance*, ed. Gary Okihiro (Amherst, 1986), 166–87.

50. *The Interesting Narrative of the Life of Olauhdah Equiano, or Gustavus Vassa, the African, Written By Himself* (2 vols., London, 1789); Angelo Costanzo, *Surprising Narrative: Olaudah Equiano and the Beginnings of Black Autobiography* (New York, 1987). Denying that the same could have been true for Smith, Andrews writes that Equiano "imagine[d] his relationship to the world in terms that did not require his becoming either totally coopted by or totally alienated from the Western socio-cultural order." Andrews, "First Fifty Years of the Slave Narrative," 22.

51. Andrews, "First Fifty Years of the Slave Narrative," 21. Many African Americans responded to the formation of the American Colonization Society in 1817 with a renewed thrust for American citizenship. After 1830 and the rise of Garrisonian abolitionism in the North, slave narrators—and African American institutions—increasingly stressed their American roots: In 1837, Boston's African Baptist Church became the First Independent Baptist Church of People of Color of Boston "for the very good reason," wrote a member, "that the name African is ill applied to a church composed of American citizens"; also in 1837, New York's black paper, the *Weekly Advocate*, became Samuel E. Cornish's *Colored American*; and Providence's African Union Meeting House changed its name to the Meeting Street Baptist Church in the 1830s. James Oliver Horton and Lois E. Horton, *Black Bostonians: Family Life and Community Struggle in the Antebellum North* (New York, 1979), 91; C. Peter Ripley et al., eds., *Witness for Freedom: African American Voices on Race, Slavery, and Emancipation*

(Chapel Hill, 1993), 14, 266; Cottrol, *Afro-Yankees,* 67; Miller, *Search for a Black Nationality,* esp. 54–90; Ira Berlin, *Slaves without Masters: The Free Negro in the Antebellum South* (New York, 1974), 168, 204–7, 356, 358–60.

52. "Narrative of the Life of Frederick Douglass, an American Slave. Written by Himself," in *The Classic Slave Narratives,* ed., Henry Louis Gates Jr. (New York, 1987), 278, 295–99; Frederick Douglass, *My Bondage and My Freedom* (1855; New York, 1969), 195. It may be running the risk of intertextual presentism to observe that Richard Wright sounded a similar note of ambivalent disillusionment in his essay on American communism (Wright's idealistic equivalent to earlier republicanism?). See Richard Crossman, ed., *The God That Failed* (New York, 1949), 115–62. On "signifyin[g]," defined as the "repetition and revision [of a trope or metaphor] with a signal difference," see Henry Louis Gates Jr., *The Signifying Monkey* (New York, 1988), xxiv.

TWO

Gracia Real de Santa Teresa de Mose: A Free Black Town in Spanish Colonial Florida

JANE LANDERS

For too long, historians have paid little attention to Spain's lengthy tenure in the South.[1] As a result, important spatial and temporal components of the American past have been overlooked. Recent historical and archaeological research on the free black town of Gracia Real de Santa Teresa de Mose, located in northeast Spanish Florida, suggests ways in which Spanish colonial records might illuminate these neglected aspects of the Southern past.[2] Because of this black town's unusual origins and political and military significance, Spanish bureaucrats documented its history with much care.

Gracia Real de Santa Teresa de Mose, hereafter referred to as Mose, was born of the initiative and determination of blacks who, at great risk, manipulated the Anglo-Spanish contest for control of the Southeast to their advantage and thereby won their freedom. The settlement was composed of former slaves, many of West African origin, who had escaped from British plantations and received religious sanctuary in Spanish Florida. Although relatively few in number (the community maintained a fairly stable size of about 100 people during the quarter-century between 1738 and 1763, while St. Augustine's population grew from approximately 1,500 people in the 1730s to approximately 3,000 by 1763), these freedmen and women were of great contemporary significance.[3] By their "theft of self," they were a financial loss to their former owners, often a serious one.[4] Moreover, their flight was a political action, sometimes effected through violence, that offered an example to other bondsmen and challenged the precarious political and social order of the British colonies. The runaways were also important to the

Spanish colony for the valuable knowledge and skills they brought with them and for the labor and military services they performed.[5] These free blacks are also historiographically significant; an exploration of their lives sheds light on questions long debated by scholars, such as the relative severity of slave systems, the varieties of slave experiences, slave resistance, the formation of a Creole culture, the nature of black family structures, the impact of Christianity and religious syncretism on African-American societies, and African-American influences in the "New World."[6]

Although a number of historians have alluded to the lure of Spanish Florida for runaway slaves from the British colonies of South Carolina and Georgia, few have examined what became of the fugitives in their new lives or the implications of their presence in the Spanish province.[7] The Spanish policy regarding fugitive slaves in Florida developed in an ad hoc fashion and changed over time to suit the shifting military, economic, and diplomatic interests of the colony as well as the metropolis. Although the Spanish crown preferred to emphasize religious and humane considerations for freeing slaves of the British, the political and military motives were equally, if not more, important. In harboring the runaways and eventually settling them in their own town, Spanish governors were following Caribbean precedents and helping the crown to populate and hold territory threatened by foreign encroachment.[8] The ex-slaves were also served by this policy. It offered them a refuge within which they could maintain family ties. In the highly politicized context of Spanish Florida, they struggled to maximize their leverage with the Spanish community and improve the conditions of their freedom. They made creative use of Spanish institutions to support their corporate identity and concomitant privileges.[9] They adapted to Spanish values where it served them to do so and thereby gained autonomy. They also reinforced ties within their original community though intermarriage and use of the Spanish mechanism of godparenthood (*compadrazgo*). Finally, they formed intricate new kin and friendship networks with slaves, free blacks, Indians, "new" Africans, and whites in nearby St. Augustine that served to stabilize their population and strengthen their connections to that Hispanic community.[10]

That runaways became free in Spanish Florida was not in itself unusual. Frank Tannenbaum's early comparative work shows that freedom had been a possibility for slaves in the Spanish world since the thirteenth century. Spanish law granted slaves a moral and juridical personality, as well as certain rights and protections not found in other slave systems. Among the most important were the right to own property, which in the Caribbean evolved into the right of self-purchase, the right to personal security, prohibitions against separating family members, and access to the courts. Moreover, slaves were incorporated into the Spanish church and received its sacraments, including marriage. Slaves in the Hispanic colonies were subject to codes based on this earlier body of law.[11] Eugene Genovese and others have persuasively argued that the ideals expressed in these slave codes should not be accepted as social realities, and it seems obvious that colonials observed these laws in their own fashion—some in the spirit in which they were written and others not at all.[12] Nevertheless, the acknowledgment of a slave's humanity and rights, and the lenient attitude toward manumission embodied in Spanish law and social practices, made it possible for a significant free black class to exist in the Spanish world.[13]

Although the Spanish legal system permitted freedom, the crown assumed that its beneficiaries would live among the Spaniards, under the supervision of white townspeople (*vecinos*). While the crown detailed its instructions regarding the physical layout, location, and function of white and Indian towns, it made no formal provisions for free black towns. But Spanish colonizers throughout the Americas were guided by an urban model. They depicted theirs as a civilizing mission and sought to create public order and righteous living by creating towns. Urban living was believed to facilitate religious conversion, but, beyond that, Spaniards attached a special value to living a *vida política,* believing that people of reason distinguished themselves from nomadic "barbarians" by living in stable urban situations.[14] Royal legislation reflected a continuing interest in reforming and settling so-called vagabonds of all races within the empire. The primary focus of reduction efforts was the Indians, but, as the black and mixed populations grew, so too did Spanish concerns about how these elements would be assimilated into "civilized" society. The "two republics" of Spaniards and Indians gave way to a society of castes, which increasingly viewed the unforeseen and unregulated groups with hostility. Spanish bureaucrats attempted to count these people and to limit their physical mobility through increasingly restrictive racial legislation. Officials prohibited blacks from living unsupervised or, worse, among the Indians. Curfews and pass systems developed, as did proposals to force unemployed blacks into fixed labor situations.[15] The crown also recognized with alarm the increased incidence of *cimmaronage,* slaves fleeing Spanish control. Communities of runaway blacks, mulattos, Indians, and their offspring were common to all slave-holding societies, but they challenged the Spanish concept of civilized living, as well as the hierarchical racial and social order the Spaniards were trying to impose. Despite repeated military efforts, the Spaniards were no more successful than other European powers at eradicating such settlements.[16]

Paradoxically, it was in this context of increasing racial animosity that Spanish officials legitimized free black towns. These towns appeared in the seventeenth and eighteenth centuries in a region described by one scholar as the "Negroid littoral"—the sparsely populated and inhospitable coastal areas of the Caribbean.[17] Faced with insurmountable problems and lacking the resources to "correct" them, the Spanish bureaucracy proved flexible and adaptable. When maroon communities such as those described by Colin Palmer and William Taylor in Mexico were too remote or intractable to destroy, the Spaniards granted them official sanction.[18] The Spanish governor of Venezuela once chartered a free black town to reward pacification of lands held by hostile Indians.[19] Mose was established as a buffer against foreign encroachment and provides a third model of free black town formation.[20]

The experience of the residents of Mose was in many ways shaped by Caribbean patterns. Declining Indian populations, a Spanish disdain for manual labor, and the defense requirements of an extended empire had created an early demand for additional workers. Blacks cleared land and planted crops, built fortifications and domestic structures, and provided a wide variety of skilled labor for Spanish colonists. By the sixteenth century, they had become the main labor force in Mexican mines and on Caribbean plantations. Also by that time, the Spanish had organized them into militia companies in Hispaniola, Cuba, Mexico, Cartagena, and Puerto Rico.[21] In Florida, too, Spaniards depended on Africans to be their laborers and to supplement their defenses. Black laborers and artisans helped establish St. Augustine, the first successful Spanish settlement in Florida, and a black and mulatto militia was formed there as early as 1683.[22]

Florida held great strategic significance for the Spanish: initially, for its location guarding the route of the treasure fleets, later, to safeguard the mines of Mexico from the French and British. The colony was a critical component in Spain's Caribbean defense, and, when British colonists established Charles Town in 1670, it represented a serious challenge to Spanish sovereignty.[23] No major response by the weakened Spanish empire was feasible, but, when the British incited their Indian allies to attack Spanish Indian missions along the Atlantic coast, the Spaniards initiated a campaign of harassment against the new British colony. In 1686, a Spanish raiding party including a force of fifty-three Indians and blacks attacked Port Royal and Edisto. From the plantation of Governor Joseph Morton, they carried away "money and plate and thirteen slaves to the value of [£]1500." In subsequent negotiations, the new governor of Carolina, James Collecton, demanded the return of the stolen slaves as well as those "who run dayly into your towns," but the Spaniards refused.[24] These contacts may have suggested the possibility of a refuge among the enemy and directed slaves to St. Augustine, for, the following year, the first recorded fugitive slaves from Carolina arrived there. Governor Diego de Quiroga dutifully reported to Spain that eight men, two women, and a three-year-old nursing child had escaped to his province in a boat. According to the governor, they requested baptism into the "True Faith," and on that basis he refused to return them to the British delegation that came to St. Augustine to reclaim them.[25] The Carolinians claimed that one of Samuel de Bordieu's runaways, Mingo, who escaped with is wife and daughter (the nursing child), had committed murder in the process. Governor Quiroga promised to make monetary restitution for the slaves he retained and to prosecute Mingo, should the charges be proven.[26] Quiroga housed these first runaways in the homes of

Spanish townspeople and saw to it that they were instructed in Catholic doctrine, baptized and married in the church. He put the men to work as ironsmiths and laborers on the new stone fort, the Castillo de San Marcos, and employed the women in his own household. All were reportedly paid wages: the men earned a peso a day, the wage paid to male Indian laborers, and the women half as much.[27]

Florida's governors enjoyed considerable autonomy. Their dual military and political appointments, the great distance from the metropolis, and an unwieldy bureaucracy contributed to their ability to make their own decisions. In unforeseen circumstances, they improvised. But, as fugitives continued to filter into the province, the governors and treasury officials repeatedly solicited the king's guidance. Eventually, the Council of the Indies reviewed the matter and recommended approving the sanctuary policy shaped by the governors. On November 7, 1693, Charles II issued the first official position on the runaways, "giving liberty to all . . . the men as well as the women . . . so that by their example and by my liberality others will do the same."[28]

The provocation inherent in this order increasingly threatened the white Carolinians. At least four other groups of runaways reached St. Augustine in the following decade, and, despite an early ambiguity about their legal status, the refugees were returned to their British masters only in one known example.[29] Carolina's changing racial balance further intensified the planters' concerns. By 1708, blacks outnumbered whites in the colony, and slave revolts erupted in 1711 and 1714. The following year, when many slaves joined the Yamassee Indian war against the British, they almost succeeded in exterminating the badly outnumbered whites. Indians loyal to the British helped defeat the Yamassee, who with their black allies headed for St. Augustine. Although the Carolina Assembly passed harsh legislation designed to prevent further insurrections and control the slaves, these actions and subsequent negotiations with St. Augustine failed to deter the escapes or effect the reciprocal return of slaves. British planters claimed that the Spanish policy, by drawing away their slaves, would ruin their plantation economy. Arthur Middleton, Carolina's acting governor, complained to London that the Spaniards not only harbored their runaways but sent them back in the company of Indians to plunder British plantations. The Carolinians set up patrol systems and placed scout boats on water routes to St. Augustine, but slaves still made good their escapes on stolen horses and in canoes and piraguas.[30]

In 1724, ten more runaway slaves reached St. Augustine, assisted by English-speaking Yamassee Indians. According to their statements, they were aware that the Spanish king had offered freedom to those seeking baptism and conversion.[31] The royal edict of 1693 was still in force, and Governor Antonio de Benavides initially seems to have honored it. In 1729, however, Benavides sold these newcomers at public auction to reimburse their owners, alleging that he feared the British might act on their threats to recover their losses by force. Some of the most important citizens of St. Augustine, including the royal accountant, the royal treasurer, several military officers, and even some religious officials, thus acquired valuable new slaves.[32] Others were sold to owners who took them to Havana. In justifying his actions, Benavides explained that these slaves had arrived during a time of peace with England and, further, that he interpreted the 1693 edict to apply only to the original runaways from the British colony.[33]

Several of the reenslaved men were veterans of the Yamassee war in Carolina, and one of these, Francisco Menéndez, was appointed by Governor Benavides to command a slave militia in 1726. This black militia helped defend St. Augustine against the British invasion led by Colonel John Palmer in 1728, but, despite their loyal service, the Carolina refugees still remained enslaved.[34] Meanwhile, the Spaniards continued to send canoes of Carolina refugees and Yamassee Indians north in search of British scalps and live slaves. Governor Middleton charged that Governor Benavides was profiting by the slaves' sale in Havana, a charge that seems well founded.[35]

Perhaps in response to continued reports and diplomatic complaints involving the fugitives, the crown issued two new edicts regarding their treatment. The first, on October 4, 1733, forbade any future compensation to the British, reiterated the offer of freedom, and specifically prohibited the sale of fugitives to private citizens. The second edict, on October 29, 1733, commended the blacks for their bravery against the British in 1728; however, it also stipulated that they would be required to complete four years of royal service prior to being freed. But the runaways had sought liberty, not indenture.[36] Led by Captain Menéndez of the slave militia, the blacks persisted in attempts to secure complete freedom. They presented petitions to the governor and to the auxiliary bishop of Cuba, who toured the province in 1735, but to no avail.[37] When Manuel de Montiano became governor in 1737, their fortunes changed. Captain Menéndez once more solicited his freedom, and this time his petition was supported by that of a Yamassee cacique named Jorge. Jorge related how Menéndez and three others had fought bravely for three years in the Yamassee rebellion, only to be sold back into slavery in Florida by a "heathen" named Mad Dog. Jorge condemned this betrayal of the blacks whom he stated had been patient and "more than loyal," but he did not blame Mad Dog, for he was an "infidel" who knew no better. Rather, he held culpable the Spaniards who had purchased these loyal allies.[38] Governor Montiano ordered an investigation and reviewed the case. On March 15, 1738, he granted unconditional freedom to the petitioners. Montiano also wrote the governor and captain general of Cuba, attempting to retrieve eight Carolinians who had been taken to Havana during the Benavides regime. At least one, Antonio Caravallo, was returned to St. Augustine, against all odds.[39]

Governor Montiano established the freedmen in a new town, about two miles north of St. Augustine, which he called Gracia Real de Santa Teresa de

Mose.[40] The freedmen built the settlement, a walled fort and shelters described by the Spaniards as resembling thatched Indian huts. Little more is known about it from Spanish sources, but later British reports add that the fort was constructed of stone, "four square with a flanker at each corner, banked with earth, having a ditch without on all sides lined round with prickly royal and had a well and house within, and a look-out." They also confirm Spanish reports that the freedmen planted fields nearby.[41] The town site was said to be surrounded by fertile lands and nearby woods that would yield building materials. A river of salt water "running through it" contained an abundance of shellfish and all types of fish.[42] Montiano hoped the people of Mose could cultivate the land to grow food for St. Augustine, but, until crops could be harvested, he provided the people with corn, biscuits, and beef from government stores.[43]

Mose was located at the head of Mose Creek, a tributary of the North River with access to St. Augustine, and lay directly north of St. Augustine, near trails north to San Nicholas and west to Apalache. For all these reasons, it was strategically significant. Governor Montiano surely considered the benefits of a northern outpost against anticipated British attacks. And who better to serve as an advanced warning system than grateful ex-slaves carrying Spanish arms? The freedmen understood their expected role, for, in a declaration to the king, they vowed to be "the most cruel enemies of the English" and to risk their lives and spill their "last drop of blood in defense of the Great Crown of Spain and the Holy Faith."[44] If the new homesteaders were diplomats, they were also pragmatists, and their own interests were clearly served by fighting those who would seek to return them to chattel slavery. Mose also served a vital objective of Spanish imperial policy, and, once Governor Montiano justified its establishment, the Council of the Indies and the king supported his actions.[45]

Since Spanish town settlements implied the extension of *justicia*, the governor assigned a white military officer and royal official to supervise the establishment of Mose. Mose was considered a village of new converts comparable to those of the Christian Indians, so Montiano also posted a student priest at the settlement to instruct the inhabitants in doctrine and "good customs."[46] Although the Franciscan lived at Mose, there is no evidence that the white officer did. It seems rather that Captain Menéndez was responsible for governing the settlement, for, in one document, Governor Montiano referred to the others as the "subjects" of Menéndez. The Spaniards regarded Menéndez as a sort of natural lord, and, like Indian caciques, he probably exercised considerable autonomy over his village.[47] Spanish titles and support may have also reinforced Menéndez's status and authority. Whatever the nature of his authority, Menéndez commanded the Mose militia for over forty years, and his career supports Price's contention that eighteenth-century maroon leaders were military figures well-versed in European ways and equipped to negotiate their followers' best interests.[48]

As new fugitives arrived, the governor placed these in Menéndez's charge as well. A group of twenty-three men, women, and children arrived from Port Royal on November 21, 1738, and were sent to join the others at the new town. Among the newcomers were the runaway slaves of Captain Caleb Davis of Port Royal. Davis was an English merchant who had been supplying St. Augustine for many years, and it is possible that some of the runaways had even traveled to St. Augustine in the course of Davis's business. Davis went to the Spanish city in December 1738 and spotted his former slaves, whom he reported laughed at his fruitless efforts to recover them.[49] The frustrated Davis eventually submitted a claim against the Spanish for twenty-seven of his slaves "detained" by Montiano, whom he valued at 7,600 pesos, as well as for the launch in which they escaped and supplies they had taken with them. He also listed debts incurred by the citizens of St. Augustine. Among those owing him money were Governors Antonio Benavides, Francisco Moral Sánchez, and Manuel de Montiano, various royal officials and army officers, and Mose townsmen Francisco Menéndez and Pedro de Leon.[50] There is no evidence Davis ever recouped his losses.

In March 1739, envoys from Carolina arrived in St. Augustine to press for the return of their runaway slaves. Governor Montiano treated them with hospitality but referred to the royal edict of 1733, which required that he grant religious sanctuary.[51] In August, an Indian ally in Apalache sent word to Montiano that the British had attempted to build a fort in the vicinity, but that the hundred black laborers had revolted, killed all the whites, and hamstrung their horses before escaping. Several days later, some of the blacks encountered the Indians in the woods and asked directions to reach the Spaniards.[52] The following month, a group of Angola slaves revolted near Stono, South Carolina, and killed more than twenty whites before heading for St. Augustine. They were apprehended before reaching their objective, and retribution was swift and bloody. But officials of South Carolina and Georgia blamed the sanctuary available in nearby St. Augustine for the rebellion, and relations between the colonies reached a breaking point.[53] With the outbreak of the War of Jenkins' Ear, international and local grievances merged. In January 1740, Governor James Oglethorpe of Georgia raided Florida and captured Forts Pupo and Picolata on the St. John's River west of St. Augustine. These initial victories enabled Oglethorpe to mount a major expeditionary force, including Georgia and South Carolina regiments, a vast Indian army, and seven warships for a major offensive against the Spaniards.[54]

The free black militia of Mose worked alongside the other citizenry to fortify provincial defenses. They also provided the Spaniards with critical intelligence reports.[55] In May, one of Oglethorpe's lieutenants happened across five houses occupied by the freedmen and was able to capture two of them.[56] Unable to protect the residents of Mose, Governor Montiano was forced to evacuate "all the Negroes who composed that town" to the safety of St. Augustine. Thereafter, the Mose militia continued to conduct dangerous sorties against the enemy and assisted in the surprise attack and recapture of their town in June.[57] The success at Mose was one of the few enjoyed by the Spaniards. It is generally acknowledged to have demoralized the combined British forces and to have been a significant factor in Oglethorpe's withdrawal. British accounts refer to the event as "Bloody Mose" or "Fatal Mose" and relate with horror the murder and mutilation (decapitation and castration) of two wounded prisoners who were unable to travel. They do not say whether Spaniards, Indians, or blacks did the deed. Although Spanish sources do not even mention this incident, atrocities took place on both sides. Both Spanish and British authorities routinely paid their Indian allies for enemy scalps, and at least one scalp was taken at "Moosa," according to British reports.[58]

Cuban reinforcements finally relieved St. Augustine in July. Shortly thereafter, Oglethorpe and his troops returned to Georgia and Carolina.[59] Governor Montiano commended all his troops to the king but made the rather unusual gesture of writing a special recommendation for Francisco Menéndez. Montiano extolled the exactitude with which Menéndez had carried out royal service and the valor he had displayed in the battle at Mose. He added that, on another occasion, Menéndez and his men had fired on the enemy until they withdrew from the castle walls and that Menéndez had displayed great zeal during the dangerous reconnaissance missions he undertook against the British and their Indians. Moreover, he acknowledged that Menéndez had "distinguished himself in the establishment, and cultivation of Mose, to improve that settlement, doing all he could so that the rest of his subjects, following his example, would apply themselves to work and learn good customs."[60]

Shortly thereafter, Menéndez petitioned for remuneration from his king for the "loyalty, zeal and love I have always demonstrated in the royal service, in the encounters with the enemies, as well as in the effort and care with which I have worked to repair two bastions on the defense line of this plaza, being pleased to do it, although it advanced my poverty, and I have been continually at arms, and assisted in the maintenance of the bastions, without the least royal expense, despite the scarcity in which this presidio always exists, especially in this occasion." He added, "my sole object was to defend the Holy Evangel and sovereignty of the Crown," and asked for the proprietorship of the free black militia and a salary to enable him to live decently (meaning in the style customary for an official of the militia). He concluded that he hoped to receive "all the consolation of the royal support . . . which Christianity requires and your vassals desire." Several months later, Menéndez filed a second, shorter petition.[61] It was customary for an illiterate person to sign official documents with an X, and for the notary or witnesses to write underneath, "for ——, who does not know how to write." Both these petitions, however, were written and signed in the same hand and with a flourish, so it would seem that at some point Menéndez learned how to write in Spanish—perhaps when he was the slave of the royal accountant whose name he took.[62] Despite his good services, appropriate behavior and rhetoric, there is no evidence of a response, and the noted royal parsimony made such payment unlikely.

Nevertheless, the runaways from Carolina had been successful in their most important appeal to Spanish justice—their quest for liberty. Over the many years, they persevered, and their leaders learned to use Spanish legal channels and social systems to advantage. They accurately assessed Spain's intensifying competition with England and exploited the political leverage it offered them. Once free, they understood and adapted to Spanish expectations of their new status. They vowed fealty and armed service, establishing themselves as vassals of the king and deserving of royal protection. Governor Montiano commended their bravery in battle and their industry as they worked to establish and cultivate Mose. They were clearly not the lazy vagabonds feared by Spanish administrators, and the adaptive behavior of Menéndez and his "subjects" gained them at least a limited autonomy.

Such autonomy is evident in both the black and Indian militias that operated on St. Augustine's frontiers. Their role in the defense of the Spanish colony has not yet been appreciated. They were cavalry units that served in frontier reconnaissance and as guerrilla fighters. They had their own officers and patrolled independently, although Spanish infantry officers also commanded mixed groups of Spanish, free blacks, and Indians on scouting missions.[63] The Florida garrison was never able to maintain a full contingent, and these militias constituted an important asset for the short-handed governors.[64] Because England and Spain were so often at war during his administration, Governor Montiano probably depended on the black troops more than did subsequent Florida governors.

When the Spaniards mounted a major retaliatory offensive against Georgia in 1742, Governor Montiano once again employed his Mose militia. Montiano's war plans called for sending English-speaking blacks of the Mose militia to range the countryside gathering and arming slave recruits, which suggests that he placed great trust in their loyalty and ability, as well, perhaps, as in their desire to punish their former masters.[65] Bad weather, mishaps, and confusion plagued the operation, and several hundred of the Spanish forces were killed at Bloody Marsh on Saint Simon's island. By August, the Spaniards had returned to St. Augustine. Oglethorpe mounted two more attacks on St. Augustine in 1742 and 1743, but neither did major damage. An uneasy stalemate developed, punctuated occasionally by Indian and corsair raids.[66]

Corsairing was practiced by both the British and the Spanish during the 1740s and 1750s, and St. Augustine became a convenient base of operations for privateers commissioned by Spain. The capture and sale of prizes provided badly needed species and supplies for war-torn Florida, which had not received government subsidies in 1739, 1740, 1741, and 1745 and which struggled under the additional burden of maintaining the large number of Cuban reinforcements that had arrived in 1740.[67] Corsairing ships were manned by volunteers, some of whom were drawn from the free black community, for, as Governor García noted, "without those of 'broken' color, blacks, and Indians, which abound in our towns in America, I do not know if we could arm a single corsair solely with Spaniards."[68] Unfortunately, when these men were captured, the British presupposed them by their color to be slaves and sold them for profit.

When the British ship *Revenge* captured a Spanish prize in July 1741, found aboard was a black named "Signior Capitano Francisco," who was "Capt. of a Comp'y of Indians, Mollattos, and Negroes that was att the Retaking of the Fort [Mose] att St. Augus'ne formerly taken Under the Command of that worthless G— O—pe who by his treachory suffered so many brave fellows to be mangled by those barbarians." His captors tied Francisco Menéndez to a gun and ordered the ship's doctor to pretend to castrate him (as Englishmen at Mose had been castrated), but while Menéndez "frankly owned" that he was Captain of the company that retook Mose, he denied ordering any atrocities, which he said the Florida Indians had committed. Menéndez stated that he had taken the commission as privateer in hopes of getting to Havana, and from there to Spain, to collect a reward for his bravery. Several other mulattoes on board were also interrogated and substantiated Menéndez's account, as did several of the whites, but "to make Sure and to make him remember that he bore such a Commission," the British gave him 200 lashes and then "pickled him and left him to the Doctor to take Care of his Sore A-se." The following month, the *Revenge* landed at New Providence, in the Bahamas, and her commander, Benjamin Norton, who was due the largest share of the prize, vehemently argued before the Admiralty Court that the blacks should be condemned as slaves. "Does not their Complexion and features tell all the world that they are of the blood of Negroes and have suckt Slavery and Cruelty from their Infancy?" He went on to describe Menéndez as "this Fransisco that Cursed Seed of Cain, Curst from the foundation of the world, who has the Impudence to Come into this Court and plead that he is free. Slavery is too Good for such a Savage, nay all the Cruelty invented by man . . . the torments of the World to Come will not suffice." No record of Francisco's testimony appears in this account, but the Court ordered him sold as a slave, "according to the Laws of the plantation."[69] However, as we have seen, Menéndez was a man of unusual abilities. Whether he successfully appealed for his freedom in British courts as he had in Spanish, was ransomed back by the Spanish in Florida, or escaped is unknown, but, by at least 1752, he was once again in command at Mose. This incident illustrates the extreme racial hatred some British felt for Spain's black allies, as well as the grave dangers the freedmen faced in taking up Spanish arms. Other blacks captured as privateers in the same period were never returned.[70]

Although unsuccessful, Governor Oglethorpe's invasion in 1740 had wreaked havoc in Spanish Florida. Mose and other outlying forts had been destroyed, along with many of the crops and animals on which the community subsisted. For the next twelve years, the townspeople of Mose lived among the Spanish in St. Augustine. This interlude was critical to the integration of the Carolina group into the larger and more diverse society in the city. Wage lists in treasury accounts and military reports from this period show that they performed a variety of valuable functions for the community. Free blacks labored on government projects, were sailors and privateers, tracked escaped prisoners, and helped forage food for the city. In the spring, they rounded up wild cattle for slaughter and wild horses for cavalry mounts.[71] They probably led lives much like those of free blacks in other Spanish colonial ports and may have engaged in craft production, artisanry, and the provision of services.[72] Although certain racial restrictions existed, they were rarely enforced in a small frontier settlement such as St. Augustine, where more relaxed personal relations were the norm. Everyone knew everyone else, and this familiarity could be a source of assistance and protection for the free blacks of Mose, who had acquired at least a measure of acceptability.[73]

Parish registers reflect the great ethnic and racial diversity in Spanish Florida in these years. Because there were always fewer female runaways, the males of that group were forced to look to the local possibilities for marriage partners—either Indian women from the two outlying villages of Nuestra Señora de la Leche and Nuestra Señora de Tholomato, or free and slave women from St. Augustine. Interracial relationships were common, and families were restructured frequently when death struck and widowed men and women remarried. The core group of Carolina fugitives formed intricate ties among themselves for at least two generations. They married from within their group and served as witnesses at each other's weddings and as godparents for each other's children, sometimes many times over. They also entered into the same relationships with Indians, free blacks, and slaves from other locations. Some of these slaves eventually became free, which might suggest mutual assistance efforts by the black community. The people of Mose also formed ties of reciprocal obligation with important members of both the white and black communities through the mechanism of ritual brotherhood (*compadrazgo*). A few examples should serve to illustrate the complex nature of these frontier relationships.

Francisco Garzía and his wife, Ana, fled together from Carolina and were among the original group freed by Governor Montiano. Francisco was black, and Ana, Indian. As slaves in St. Augustine, they had belonged to the royal treasurer, Don Salvador Garzía. Garzía observed the church requirement to have his slaves baptized and properly married, for the couple's children are listed as legitimate. Francisco and Ana's daughter, Francisca Xaviera, was born and baptized in St. Augustine in 1736, before her parents were freed by the governor. Her godfather was a free mulatto, Francisco Rexidor. This man also served as godfather for Francisco and Ana's son, Calisto, born free two years later. Garzía died sometime before 1759, for in that year his widow, Ana, married a black slave named Diego. Calisto disappeared from the record and presumably died, while Francisca Xaviera married Francisco Díaz, a free black from Carolina. Their two children, Miguel Francisco and María, were born at Mose and Francisco Díaz served in the Mose militia.[74]

Juan Jacinto Rodríguez and his wife, Ana María Menéndez, were also among the first Carolina homesteaders at Mose. Shortly after the town was founded, their son Juan married Cecilia, a Mandingo from Carolina who was the slave of Juan's former owner, cavalry Captain Don Pedro Lamberto Horruytiner. Cecilia's sister-in-law, María Francisca, had served as god-mother at Cecilia's baptism two years earlier. María Francisca married Marcos de Torres, a free and legitimate black from Cartagena, Colombia, during the time the Mose homesteaders lived in St. Augustine. Marcos de Torres and María Francisca had three children born while they lived in town, and María Francisca's brother, Juan, and his wife, Cecilia, served as the children's godparents. After Marcos de Torres died, María Francisca and her three orphaned children lived with her parents at Mose. In 1760, the widowed María Francisca married the widower, Thomas Chrisostomo.[75]

Thomas and his first wife were Congo slaves. Thomas belonged to Don Francisco Chrisostomo, and his wife, Ana María Ronquillo, to Juan Nicolás Ronquillo. The couple married in St. Augustine in 1745. Pedro Graxales, a Congo slave and his legitimate wife, María de la Concepción Hita, a Cara-valí slave, were the godparents at the wedding. By 1759, Thomas was a free widower living alone at Mose. The next year, he and María Francisca were wed. By that time, Thomas's godfather Pedro Graxales, was also living at Mose as a free man, but Pedro's wife and at least four children remained slaves in St. Augustine.[76]

A simple bicultural encounter model will not suffice to explain the extent of cultural adaptation at Mose and the formation of this African-Hispanic community.[77] Many of its members were both born on the western coast of Africa and then spent at least some time in a British slave society before risking their lives to escape. Some had intimate contact for several years with the Yamassee Indians and fought other non-Christian Indian groups before reaching Spanish Florida. At least thirty-one became slaves of the Spanish prior to achieving free status. Once free, they associated closely with the remnants of the seven different Indian nations aggregated into the two outlying Indian towns. From 1740 until 1752, the Mose group lived within the city of St. Augustine; after that time, they were forcibly removed to a rebuilt settlement. Meanwhile, new infusions of Africans continued to be incorporated into the original Mose community through ties with godpar-ents. Many historians now agree that, although the ex-slaves did not share a single culture, their common values and experiences in the Americas enabled them to form strong communities, as they did in Spanish Florida. Ira Berlin, Steven F. Miller, and Leslie S. Rowland have argued that British slaves understood their society "in the idiom of kinship" and that, for slaves, "familial and communal relations were one."[78] The Spaniards also viewed society as an extension of family structures. The institution of the extended kinship group (*parentela*), which included blood relations, fictive kin, and sometimes even household servants and slaves, and the institution of *clientela*, which bound powerful patrons and their personal dependents into a network of mutual obligations, were so deeply rooted in Spain that, according to one scholar, they might have been the "primary structure of Hispanic society." Thus African and Spanish views of family and society were highly compatible, and each group surely recognized the value that the other placed on kinship.[79]

Despite the relationships that developed between people of St. Augustine and the Mose settlers, there were objections to their presence in the Spanish city. Some complaints may have stemmed from racial prejudice or ethnocentrism. To some of the poorer Spanish, the free blacks represented competition in a ravaged economy. Indians allied to the British remained hostile to the Spaniards and raided the countryside with regularity. Plantations were neither safe nor productive. Havana could not provide its dependency with sufficient goods, and the few food shipments that reached St. Augustine were usually ruined. British goods were cheaper and better, and the governor was forced to depend on enemy suppliers for his needs. War and corsair raids on supplies shipped from Havana further strained the colony's ability to sustain its urban population. As new runaways continued to arrive, they only exacerbated the problem.[80] Finally, Melchor de Navarrete, who succeeded Montiano in 1749, decided to reestablish Mose. He reported his achievements in converting the newcomers, remarking that he withheld certificates of freedom until the supplicants had a satisfactory knowledge of doctrine. Navarrete also claimed to have resettled all the free blacks from Carolina at Mose.[81]

Governor Fulgencio García de Solís, who served from 1752 to 1755, refuted his predecessor's claims, stating that persistent illnesses among the blacks had prevented their relocation. When García attempted to remove the freedmen and women to Mose, he faced stubborn resistance. The governor complained that it was not fear of further Indian attacks but the "desire to live in complete liberty" that motivated the rebels. He "lightly" punished the two unnamed leaders of the resistance and threatened worse to those who continued to fight the resettlement. He fortified the town to allay their fears and finally effected the resettlement. In a familiar litany, he alluded to "bad customs," "spiritual backwardness," and "pernicious consequences" and condemned not only the original Mose settlers but also "those who have since fled the English colonies to join them." He was determined that they would have "no pretext which could excuse them" from living at Mose and sought to isolate them from "any dealings or communication with . . . the town within the walls."[82] The Spanish association of urbanization with the advance of civilization traditionally had as its corollary the idea that those living outside a city's boundaries were lacking in cultural and spiritual attainments. In his official papers, García evidenced a much lower opinion of the free blacks than had Governor Montiano, and by removing them "beyond the walls" he made a visible statement about their supposed inferiority.

García was no doubt angered by the rebellion he faced, and he was probably correct in contending that it actually arose from the free black desire to live in "complete liberty." The crown had many times reiterated its commitment to their freedom, and, after living in St. Augustine for thirteen years and repeatedly risking their lives in its defense, the free blacks surely recognized the eviction for the insult it represented. Possibly, after García's interim term ended, there was greater interaction between the peoples of St. Augustine and its satellite, as later governors did not display his antipathy toward the free blacks.[83] Governor García may also have been disturbed by the presence and influence of unacculturated Africans (*bozales*) among the latecomers. The "bad customs" that he alleged had so troubled his predecessors and himself might have been African cultural retentions. In 1744, Father Francisco Xavier Arturo baptized Domingo, a Caravalí slave, in extremis, with the comment that his "crudeness" prevented his understanding Christian doctrine.[84] Four years later, Miguel Domingo, a Congo slave, received a conditional baptism, because he told the priest that he had been baptized in his homeland, and continued to pray in his native language.[85]

Peter Wood's analysis of slave imports into South Carolina during the late 1730s determined that 70 percent of those arriving during this brief period came from the Congo-Angola region.[86] St. Augustine's church registers suggest a similar preponderance there but within a broader context of considerable ethnic diversity. The Spanish often recorded the nation of origin for the Africans among them, and, although these designations are troublesome and must be used with caution, they offer at least a general approximation of the origins of those recorded. One hundred and forty-seven black marriages were reported from 1735 to 1763, and fifty-two of those married were designated as Congos—twenty-six males and twenty-six females. The next largest group was the Caravalís, including nine males and nineteen females. The Mandingos constituted the third largest group and had nine males and four females. Also represented in the marriage registers were the Minas, Gambas, Lecumis, Sambas, Gangas, Araras, and Guineans.[87]

Governor García was required by royal policy to grant sanctuary to slave refugees, but he was not required by royal policy to accommodate them in St. Augustine, and he did not. The chastened freedmen built new structures at Mose, including a church and a house for the Franciscan priest within the enclosed fort, as well as twenty-two shelters outside the fort for their own households. A diagram of the new fort, which had one side open on Mose Creek, shows the interior buildings described by Father Juan Joseph de Solana but not the houses of the villagers.[88] The only known census of Mose, from 1759, recorded twenty-two households with a population of sixty-seven individuals. Mose had almost twice as many male as female occupants, and almost a quarter of its population consisted of children under the age of fifteen. Thirteen of the twenty-two households belonged to nuclear or nuclear extended families, and fifty villagers, or 75 percent of the total population, lived with immediate members of their families. There were no female-headed households at this outpost, and nine households were composed solely of males. At the time of the census, four men lived alone, Francisco Roso, Antonio Caravallo, Thomas Chrisostomo, and Antonio Blanco, but at least two of those men, Roso and Chrisostomo, had family members among the slaves in St. Augustine. A third all-male household consisted of a father, Francisco de Torres, and his son, Juan de Arranzate. Francisco's wife and Juan's mother, Ana María, was a slave in St. Augustine. Pedro Graxales was also separated from his slave wife and their children but had a younger man, Manuel Rivera, attached to his household. Three other all-male households included a total of eleven men living together, at least three of whom had slave wives in St. Augustine.[89] Although spouses lived separately, parish registers record that children continued to be born of these unions and attest that family ties were maintained. Father Solana reported that some members of the Mose community were permitted to live in St. Augustine even though they continued to serve in the Mose militia. Several of those men appear on 1763 evacuation lists for Mose.[90]

The people of Mose were remarkably adaptable. They spoke several European and Indian languages, in addition to their own, and were exposed to a variety of subsistence techniques, craft and artistic traditions, labor patterns, and food ways. We know that the freedmen and women of Mose adopted certain elements of Spanish culture. For example, since their sanctuary was based on religious conversion, it was incumbent on them to exhibit their Catholicism. Their baptisms, marriages, and deaths were faithfully recorded in parish registers. But studies of other Hispanic colonies show that religious syncretism was widespread and tolerated by the church. Following centuries-old patterns set in Spain, Cuba's blacks organized religious brotherhoods by nations. They celebrated Catholic feast days dressed in traditional African costumes and with African music and instruments.[91] Because St. Augustine had such intimate contact with Cuba and blacks circulated between the two locations, it would not be surprising to find that Africans in Florida also observed some of their former religious practices.

Kathleen Deagan, of the Florida Museum of Natural History, currently directs an interdisciplinary team investigating Mose. In addition to locating and excavating the site, this group is exploring the process of cultural adaptation at Mose to determine what mixture of customs and material culture its residents adopted and what in their own traditions might have influenced Spanish culture.[92] One suggestive find is a hand-made pewter medal that depicts St. Christopher on one side and a pattern resembling a Kongo star on the other.[93] Other recovered artifacts include military objects such as gunflints, a striker, and musket balls; and domestic articles such as metal buckles, a thimble, and pins, clay pipe bowls — of both local and European design — metal buttons, bone buttons — including one still in the process of manufacture — amber beads (perhaps from a rosary); and a variety of glass bottles and ceramic wares. Many of the latter are of English types, verifying documentary evidence of illicit, but necessary, trade with the enemy.

Preliminary analysis of faunal materials from the site indicates that the diet at Mose approximated that of indigenous villages and supports documentary evidence that the Indian and black villages resembled each other in many respects. Mose's villagers incorporated many estuarine resources and wild foods into their diet. The fish were net-caught, perhaps using African techniques. The people at Mose also caught and consumed deer, raccoon, opossum, and turtle to supplement the corn and beef occasionally provided them from government stores.[94]

Although noted for its poverty and the misery of its people, Mose survived as a free town and military outpost for St. Augustine until 1763, when, through the fortunes of war, Spain lost the province to the British. The Spanish evacuated St. Augustine and its dependent black and Indian towns, and the occupants were resettled in Cuba. The people of Mose left behind their meager homes and belongings and followed their hosts into exile to become homesteaders in Matanzas, Cuba—consigned once more to a rough frontier. The crown granted them new lands, a few tools, and a minimal subsidy, as well as an African slave to each of the leaders of the community; however, Spanish support was never sufficient, and the people from Mose suffered terrible privations at Matanzas. Some of them, including Francisco Menéndez, eventually relocated in Havana, which offered at least the possibility of a better life, and this last diaspora scattered the black community of Mose.[95]

Located on the periphery of St. Augustine, between the Spanish settlement and its aggressive neighbors, Mose's interstitial location paralleled the social position of its inhabitants—people who straddled cultures, pursued their own advantage, and in the process helped shape the colonial history of the Caribbean as well as an African-American culture. In 1784, Spain recovered Florida, and many Floridanos, or first-period colonists, returned from Cuba. It is possible that among these were some of the residents of Mose. During its second regime, however, the weakened Spanish government made no effort to reestablish either Indian missions or the free black town of Mose. Free blacks took pivotal roles on interethnic frontiers of Spanish America such as Florida, serving as interpreters, craftsmen, traders, scouts, cowboys, pilots, and militiamen. The towns they established made important contributions to Spanish settlement. They populated areas the Spaniards found too difficult or unpleasant, thereby extending or maintaining Spanish dominion. They buffered Spanish towns from the attacks of their enemies and provided them with effective military reserves.

Although there were other towns like Mose in Latin America, it was the only example of a free black town in the colonial South. It provides an important, and heretofore unstudied, variant in the experience of African-born peoples in what was to become the United States. Mose's inhabitants were able to parlay their initiative, determination, and military and economic skills into free status, an autonomy at least equivalent to that of Spain's Indian allies in Florida, and a town of their own. These gains were partially offset by the constant danger and deprivation to which the townspeople of Mose were subjected, but they remained in Mose, perhaps believing it their best possible option. Despite the adversities of slavery, flight, wars, and repeated displacements, the freedmen and women of Mose managed to maintain intricate family relationships over time and shape a viable community under extremely difficult conditions. They became an example and possibly a source of assistance to unfree blacks from neighboring British colonies, as well as those within Spanish Florida. The Spanish subsequently extended the religious sanctuary policy confirmed at Mose to other areas of the Caribbean and applied it to the disadvantage of Dutch and French slaveholders, as well as the British.[96] The lives and efforts of the people of Mose thus took on international significance. Moreover, their accomplishments outlived them. The second Spanish government recognized religious sanctuary from 1784 until it bowed to the pressure of the new U.S. government and its persuasive secretary of state, Thomas Jefferson, and abrogated the policy in 1790. Before that escape hatch closed, several hundred slaves belonging to British Loyalists followed the example of the people of Mose to achieve emancipation in Florida.[97] Thus the determined fugitives who struggled so hard to win their own freedom inadvertently furthered the cause of freedom for others whom they never knew.

NOTES

This research was funded by the Spain/Florida Alliance, the Florida Legislature, the Program for Cultural Cooperation between Spain's Ministry of Culture and United States' Universities, and the Department of History of the University of Florida.

1. An early classic that examined the triracial Southern frontier was Verner W. Crane, *The Southern Frontier, 1670–1732* (New York, 1981), but, as Peter Wood noted in his historiographic review, "'I Did the Best I Could for My Day': The Study of Early Black History during the Second Reconstruction, 1960–1976," *William and Mary Quarterly*, 3d ser., 35 (1978): 185–225, few scholars followed Crane's lead. The difficulty of the sources deterred some from crossing the cultural and linguistic frontier into Florida, but Latin Americanists have also neglected what were the northern boundaries of the Spanish empire. The "Borderlands" school pioneered by Herbert Bolton produced a number of important studies, but these focused primarily on the southwestern areas of the present-day United States. See Herbert E. Bolton, *The Spanish Borderlands, A Chronicle of Old Florida and the Southwest* (Toronto, 1921); and Herbert E. Bolton and Mary Ross, *The Debatable Land* (Berkeley, Calif., 1925). For a review of these borderland studies, see David Weber, "John Francis Bannon and the Historiography of the Spanish Borderlands," *Journal of the Southwest*, 29 (Winter 1987): 331–63.

2. Scholars who have attempted to explore the African experience in northern America through Spanish sources include John TePaske, "The Fugitive Slave: Intercolonial Rivalry and Spanish Slave Policy, 1687–1764," in Samuel Proctor, ed., *Eighteenth-Century Florida and Its Borderlands* (Gainesville, Fla., 1975), 1–12; Jack D. L.

Holmes, "The Role of Blacks in Spanish Alabama: The Mobile District, 1780–1813," *Alabama Historical Quarterly*, 37 (Spring 1975): 5–18; Gilbert Din, "Cimarrones and the San Malo Band in Spanish Louisiana," *Louisiana History*, 21 (Summer 1980): 237–62; Jack D. Forbes, "Black Pioneers: The Spanish-Speaking Afroamericans of the Southwest," *Phylon* 27 (1966): 233–46; Peter Stern, "Social Marginality and Accultur-ation on the Northern Frontier of New Spain" (Ph.D. dissertation, University of Cali-fornia, Berkeley, 1984); and Kimberly Hanger, "Free Blacks in Spanish New Orleans —The Transitional Decade, 1769–1779" (Masters thesis, University of Utah, 1985). Gwendolyn Midlo Hall has a detailed study of Africans in colonial Louisiana forthcom-ing that is drawn from Spanish as well as French sources.

3. Theodore G. Corbett, "Migration to a Spanish Imperial Frontier in the Seven-teenth and Eighteenth Centuries: St. Augustine," *Hispanic American Historical Review*, 54 (August 1974): 419–20. Corbett noted that St. Augustine, the largest of the borderland settlements, also had the most blacks, slave and free, in the Spanish borderlands. As late as 1763, St. Augustine was larger than any other town in the southern colonies except Charleston. See Theodore G. Corbett, "Population Structure in Hispanic St. Augustine, 1629–1763," *Florida Historical Quarterly*, 54 (July 1975–April 1976): 268.

4. Peter Wood, *Black Majority; Negroes in Colonial South Carolina from 1670 through the Stono Rebellion* (New York, 1974), 239–68; Philip D. Morgan, "Colonial South Carolina Runaways: Their Significance for Slave Culture," in *Slavery and Abolition*, 6 (December 1985): 57–78; Darrett Rutman and Anita Rutman, *A Place in Time: Middlesex County, Virginia, 1650–1750* (New York, 1984), 180–87.

5. The role of the Africans as cultural agents is discussed in Wood, *Black Majority*, 35–63, 95–130. Also see Daniel Littlefield, *Rice and Slaves, Ethnicity and the Slave Trade in Colonial South Carolina* (Baton Rouge, La., 1981), 98–99. Wood also pointed out that "in literally every conflict in eighteenth-century South Carolina there were Negroes engaged on both sides"; Wood, *Black Majority*, 128–29.

6. Frank Tannenbaum, *Slave and Citizen* (New York, 1946). Tannenbaum's early view that institutional protections benefited slaves in Hispanic areas was challenged by scholars who found economic determinants of slave treatment more significant. See Eugene Genovese, "The Treatment of Slaves in Different Countries: Problems in the Application of the Comparative Method," in Laura Foner and Eugene Genovese, eds., *Slavery in the New World* (Englewood Cliffs, N.J., 1969), 202–10; Marvin Harris, *Patterns of Race in the Americas* (New York, 1964). Historians who have reviewed Spanish racial prejudice and discriminatory regulations include Lyle McAlister, "Social Structure and Social Change in New Spain," *Hispanic American Historical Review*, 43 (April 1963): 349–70; Magnus Mörner, *Race Mixture in the History of the Americas* (Boston, 1967); and Leslie B. Rout, Jr., *The African Experience in Spanish America, 1502 to the Present* (Cambridge, 1976). On the varieties of slave experiences, see Sidney M. Mintz and Richard Price, *An Anthropological Approach to the Afro-American Past: A Caribbean Perspective* (Philadelphia, 1976). On resistance in Latin America, see Rich-ard Price, ed., *Maroon Societies, Rebel Slave Communities in the Americas* (Garden City, N.Y., 1973). On the formation of Creole cultures, see Charles Joyner, *Down by the Riverside, A South Carolina Slave Community* (Urbana, Ill., 1984). On black families, see Ira Berlin, "Time, Space and the Evolution of Afro-American Society on British Mainland North America," *AHR*, 85 (June 1980): 44–78. On black religion and African cultural retentions in the "New World," see Robert Farris Thompson, *Flash of the Spirit: African and Afro-American Art and Philosophy* (New York, 1984); and Margaret Wash-ington Creel, *"A Peculiar People": Slave Religion and Community-Culture among the Gullahs* (New York, 1988). For an interesting comparison of African and British world views and attitudes, see Mechal Sobel, *The World They Made Together: Black and White Values in Eighteenth-Century Virginia* (Princeton, N.J., 1987).

7. Irene Wright, "Dispatches of Spanish Officials Bearing on the Free Negro Settle-ment of Gracia Real de Santa Teresa de Mose," *Journal of Negro History*, 9 (1924): 144–93; TePaske, "Fugitive Slaves"; Luis Arana, "The Mose Site," *El Escribano*, 10 (April

1973): 50–62; Kenneth Wiggins Porter, *The Negro on the American Frontier* (New York, 1971); Jane Landers, "Spanish Sanctuary; Fugitive Slaves in Florida, 1687–1790," *Florida Historical Quarterly*, 62 (September 1984): 296–313; Larry W. Kruger and Robert Hall, "Fort Mose: A Black Fort in Spanish Florida," *The Griot*, 6 (Spring 1987): 39–48.

8. Lyle N. McAlister, *Spain and Portugal in the New World, 1492–1700* (Minneapolis, Minn., 1984), 133–52.

9. On corporate privileges of the Spanish militias, see Lyle N. McAlister, *The "Fuero Militar" in New Spain, 1764–1800* (Gainesville, Fla., 1957); Herbert S. Klein, "The Coloured Militia of Cuba: 1568–1868," *Caribbean Studies*, 6 (July 1966): 17–27; Allan J. Kuethe, "The Status of the Free Pardo in the Disciplined Militia of New Granada," *Journal of Negro History*, 56 (April 1971): 105–15; Roland C. McConnell, *Negro Troops of Antebellum Louisiana—A History of the Battalion of Free Men of Color* (Baton Rouge, La., 1968).

10. On the function and meaning of godparents, see George M. Foster, "Cofradía and Compadrazgo in Spain and Spanish America," *Southwestern Journal of Anthropology*, 9 (1953): 1–28; Sidney W. Mintz and Eric Wolf, "An Analysis of Ritual Co-Parenthood (Compadrazgo)," *Southwestern Journal of Anthropology*, 6 (1950): 341–67.

11. Tannenbaum, *Slave and Citizen.*

12. Genovese, "Treatment of Slaves"; Mörner, *Race Mixture*; Rout, *African Experience*. For a study of the law in practice, see Norman A. Meiklejohn, "The Observance of Negro Slave Legislation in Colonial Nueva Granada" (Masters thesis, Columbia University, 1968).

13. Hanger, "Free Blacks"; David W. Cohen and Jack P. Greene, eds., *Neither Slave nor Free, The Freedmen of African Descent in the Slave Societies of the New World* (Baltimore, Md., 1972); Landers, "Spanish Sanctuary"; Ira Berlin, *Slaves without Masters—The Free Negro in the Antebellum South* (New York, 1974), 108–32; Lyman L. Johnson, "Manumission in Colonial Buenos Aires," *Hispanic American Historical Review*, 59 (1979): 258–79; Frederick Bowser, "Free Persons of Color in Lima and Mexico City: Manumission and Opportunity, 1580–1650," in Stanley Engerman and Eugene D. Genovese, eds., *Slavery in the Western Hemisphere: Quantitative Studies* (Princeton, N.J., 1974), 331–68.

14. Richard Morse elegantly analyzed the concept of the *ciudad perfecta* and Spanish efforts to reproduce it in the New World in his chapter "A Framework for Latin American Urban History" in Jorge Hardoy, ed., *Urbanization in Latin America: Approaches and Issues* (Garden City, N.Y., 1975), 57–107.

15. Richard Konetzke, "Estado y sociedad en las Indias," *Estudios Americanos*, 3 (1951): 33–58; Rolando Mellafe, *Negro Slavery in Latin America* (Berkeley, Calif., 1975), 109–17.

16. Meiklejohn, "Observance of Negro Slave Legislation," 103–14, 295–306; Carlos Federico Guillot, *Negros rebeldes y negro cimarrones: Perfil afroamericano en la historia del Nuevo Mundo durante el siglo XVI* (Buenos Aires, 1961); Miguel Acosta Saignes, *Vida de los esclavos negros en Venezuela* (Caracas, 1967), 249–84; R. K. Kent, "Palmares: An African State in Brazil," *Journal of African History*, 6 (1965): 161–75; Carlos Larrazábal Blanco, *Los negros y la esclavitud en Santo Domingo* (Santo Domingo, 1967).

17. Leon Campbell used this term in his article, "The Changing Racial and Administrative Structure of the Peruvian Military under the Later Bourbons," *The Americas*, 32 (July 1975): 117–33.

18. Colin Palmer, *Slaves of the White God-Blacks in Mexico, 1570–1650* (Cambridge, 1976); William Taylor, "The Foundation of Nuestra Señora de Guadalupe de los Amapa," *The Americas*, 26 (April 1970): 442–46.

19. Richard Konetzke, *Colección de documentos para la historia de la formación social de Hispano-América, 1493–1810*, 3 vols. (Madrid, 1953–58), 2: 118–20.

20. For a later example of a buffer town, see John Hoyt Williams, "Trevegó on the Paraguayan Frontier: A Chapter in the Black History of the Americas," *Journal of Negro*

History, 56 (October 1971): 272–83; and Germán de Granda, "Origen, función y estructura de un pueblo de negros y mulatos libres en el Paraguay del siglo XVIII (San Agustin de la Emboscada)," *Revista de Indias*, 43 (enero–junio 1983): 229–64.

21. Klein, "Colored Militia"; Kuethe, "Status of the Free Pardo."

22. Roster of Black and Mulatto Militia for St. Augustine, September 20, 1683, Santo Domingo (hereafter cited as SD), 266, Archivo General de Indias: Seville (hereafter cited as AGI).

23. Crane, *Southern Frontier*, 3–17; John Jay TePaske, *The Governorship of Spanish Florida, 1700–1763* (Durham, N.C., 1964), 3–6; Verne E. Chatelain, *The Defenses of Spanish Florida, 1565–1763* (Washington, D.C., 1941).

24. Letter from Mr. Randolph to the Board, June 28, 1699, in A.S. Salley, *Records of the British Public Records Office Relating to South Carolina, 1698–1700* (Columbia, S.C., 1946), 4: 89; Crane, *Southern Frontier*, 31–33.

25. "William Dunlop's Mission to St. Augustine in 1688," *South Carolina Historical and Genealogical Magazine*, 34 (January 1933): 1–30; Diego de Quiroga to the king, February 2, 1688, cited in Wright, "Dispatches," 150. Morton's stolen male slaves included Peter, Scipio, Doctor (whose name suggests a specialized function or skill), Cushi, Arro, Emo, Caesar, and Sambo. The women included Frank, Bess, and Mammy. Sambo was the Hausa name for a second son, while in Mende or Vai it meant "disgrace." Cushi may have been "Quashee," the Twi day-name for Sunday, which also came to signify "foolish" or "stupid." For a discussion of slave naming, see Wood, *Black Majority*, 181–86, among others. The men who stole the canoe were named Conano, Jesse, Jacque, Gran Domingo (Big Sunday), Cambo, Mingo, Dicque, and Robi. Wood suggests that forms of the name Jack derived from the African day-name for Wednesday, Quaco. Names of the two women and the little girl were not given. The owners of the fugitives who escaped in the canoe were: Samuel de Bordieu, Mingo, his wife and daughter; John Bird, two men; Joab Howe, one man; John Berresford, one woman; Christopher Smith, one man; Robert Cuthbert, three men. "William Dunlop's Mission," 4, 26, 28.

26. "William Dunlop's Mission," 25.

27. Royal officials to the king, March 3, 1689, cited in Wright, "Dispatches," 151–52.

28. Royal edict, November 7, 1693, SD 58–1–26 in the John B. Stetson Collection (hereafter cited as ST), P. K. Yonge Library of Florida History, University of Florida, Gainesville (hereafter cited as PKY). Also see "William Dunlop's Mission," 1–30.

29. The various petitions of Carolina fugitives gathered together by Governor Manuel de Montiano are found in SD 844, fols. 521–46, microfilm reel 15, PKY. They mention groups arriving in 1688, 1689, 1690, 1697, 1724, and 1725. Governor Joseph de Zuñiga reported that his predecessor, Governor Laureano de Torres y Ayala, on August 8, 1697, returned six blacks and an Indian who had escaped from Charlestown that year, "to avoid conflicts and ruptures between the two governments." Joseph de Zuñiga to the king, October 10, 1699, SD 844, microfilm reel 15, fol. 542, PKY.

30. Wood, *Black Majority*, 304–05. For a new overview of the broader demographic context, see Peter H. Wood, "The Changing Population of the Colonial South: An Overview by Race and Region, 1685–1790," in Peter H. Wood, Gregory A. Waselkov, and M. Thomas Hatley, eds., *Powhatan's Mantle: Indians in the Colonial Southeast* (Lincoln, Neb., 1989), 35–103.

31. Memorial of the Fugitives, 1724, SD 844, fol. 530, microfilm reel 15, PKY.

32. Governor Antonio de Benavides to the king, November 11, 1725, cited in Wright, "Dispatches," 164–66. The noted citizens who acquired the slaves filed various memorials to record their concerns about British threats to come take the slaves and the fact that British forces outnumbered Spanish. Memorial, August 26, 1729, SD 844, fols. 550–62. Governor Benavides then authorized their auction and gave the proceeds to a British envoy, Arthur Hauk. Accord, June 27, 1730, SD 844, fols. 564–66, microfilm reel 15, PKY.

33. Consulta by the Council of the Indies, April 12, 1731, cited in Wright, "Dispatches," 166–72.

34. Petition of Francisco Menéndez, November 21, 1740, SD 2658, AGI. On the role of the black militia in 1728, see TePaske, *Fugitive Slave,* 7.

35. Governor Arthur Middleton, June 6, 1728, British Public Record Office Transcripts, 13: 61–67, cited in Wood, *Black Majority,* 305.

36. Royal edict, October 4, 1733, SD 58–1–24, ST; Royal edict, October 29, 1733, SD 58–1–24, ST.

37. Memorial of the Fugitives, SD 844, fols. 533–34, included in Manuel de Montiano to the king, March 3, 1738, SD, 844, microfilm reel 15, PKY.

38. Memorial of Chief Jorge, SD 844, fols. 536–37, *ibid.* Jorge claimed to be the chief who had led the Yamassee uprising against the British. Jorge stated that he and the rest of the Yamassee chiefs commonly made treaties with the slaves, and that he now wanted to help Menéndez and the three others who fought along with him become free. Mad Dog sold them into slavery for some casks of honey, corn, and liquor (*aguardiente*).

39. Decree of Manuel de Montiano, March 3, 1738, SD 844, fols. 566–75, microfilm reel 15, PKY. The eight slaves who were sold to Havana included "Antonio, an English slave from San Jorge [the Spanish name for Charlestown], another of the same name, Clemente, Andres, Bartholome Chino [the term for a mixed-blood], Juan Francisco Borne, Juan (English), Jose, who's other name is Mandingo, all of whom are from San Jorge."

40. Montiano to the king, February 16, 1739, SD 844, microfilm reel 15, PKY. The name is a composite of an existing Indian place name, Mose, the phrase that indicated that the new town was established by the king, Gracia Real, and the name of the town's patron saint, Teresa of Avilés, who was the patron saint of Spain.

41. *St. Augustine Expedition of 1740: A Report to the South Carolina General Assembly Reprinted from the Colonial Records of South Carolina with an introduction by John Tate Lanning* (Columbia, S.C., 1954), 25.

42. Report of Antonio de Benavides, SD 58–2–16/45, bundle 5725, ST.

43. Purchases and Payments for 1739, Cuba 446, AGI.

44. Manuel de Montiano to the king, February 16, 1739, SD 845, fol. 700, SD 845, microfilm reel 16, PKY. Fugitive Negroes of the English plantations to the king, June 10, 1738, SD 844, microfilm reel 15, PKY.

45. Council of the Indies, October 2, 1739, cited in Wright, "Dispatches," 178–80; Council of the Indies, September 28, 1740, SD 845, fol. 708, microfilm reel 16, PKY.

46. Manuel de Montiano to the king, February 16, 1739, SD 845, fol. 701, microfilm reel 16, PKY.

47. Manuel de Montiano to the king, September 16, 1740, SD 2658, AGI. Montiano's successor also stated that the townspeople of Mose were "under the dominion of their Captain and Lieutenant." Melchor de Navarrete to the Marqués de Ensenada, April 2, 1752, cited in Wright, "Dispatches," 185.

48. Evacuation report of Juan Joseph Eligio de la Puente, January 22, 1764, SD 2595, AGI; Price, *Maroon Societies,* 29–30.

49. Manuel de Montiano to the king, February 16, 1739, SD 845, fol. 700, microfilm reel 16, PKY; "Journal of William Stephens," cited in Wood, *Black Majority,* 307.

50. Claim of Captain Caleb Davis, September 17, 1751, SD 2584, AGI.

51. Manuel de Montiano to the king, March 13, 1739, Manuscript 19508, Biblioteca Nacional, Madrid.

52. Letter of Manuel de Montiano, August 19, 1739, "Letters of Montiano, Siege of St. Augustine," *Collections of the Georgia Historical Society* (Savannah, Ga., 1909), 7: 32.

53. "The Stono Rebellion and Its Consequences," in Wood, *Black Majority,* 308–26.

54. TePaske, *Governorship,* 140.

55. On January 8, 1740, Montiano sent Don Pedro Lamberto Horruytiner "with 25 horsemen from his company, 25 infantry and 30 Indians and free Negroes (of those who are fugitives from the English Colonies) to scout the country." Manuel de Montiano to the king, January 31, 1740, SD 2658, AGI. On January 27, 1740, Montiano sent Don Romualdo Ruiz del Moral out on a similar mission accompanied by "25 horsemen, 25 Indians, and 25 free Negroes." Montiano wrote, "The difficulty of getting information in

our numerous thickets, lagoons and swamps, is so great as to make the thing almost impossible." Manuel de Montiano to the king, January 31, 1740, "Letters of Montiano," 7: 36.

56. *St. Augustine Expedition*, 23. One was the escaped slave of Mrs. Parker, and the other claimed to have been carried away from Colonel Gibbs by the Indians.

57. Manuel de Montiano to the king, January 17, 1740, SD 2658, AGI. For Montiano's account of Oglethorpe's siege and the victory at Mose, see Manuel de Montiano to the king, August 9, 1740, SD 845, fols. 11–26, microfilm reel 16, PKY; and "Letters of Montiano," 7: 54–62.

58. Mills Lane, ed. *General Oglethorpe's Georgia: Colonial Letters, 1738–1743*, II (Savannah), 447. For more accounts of atrocities, see *St. Augustine Expedition of 1740*, 47; TePaske, *Governorship of Spanish Florida*, 143; Larry E. Ivers, *British Drums on the Southern Frontier, The Military Colonization of Georgia 1733–1749* (Chapel Hill, N.C., 1974). This account is written from British sources and therefore is inaccurate on many aspects of the Spanish history. Ivers seriously undercounts St. Augustine's population, glamorizes Oglethorpe's role, and fails to recognize the role of blacks at Mose and throughout the Anglo-Spanish conflict.

59. TePaske, *Governorship of Spanish Florida*, 144.

60. Manuel de Montiano to the king, January 31, 1740, SD 2658, AGI.

61. Memorial of Francisco Menéndez, November 21, 1740, SD 2658, AGI. Memorial of Francisco Menéndez, December 12, 1740, *ibid.*

62. The proprietary royal accountant for St. Augustine was Don Francisco Menéndez Márquez. The Menéndez Márquez family is the subject of several works by Amy Turner Bushnell. See "The Menéndez Márquez Cattle Barony at La Chua and the Determinants of Economic Expansion in Seventeenth-Century Florida," *Florida Historical Quarterly*, 56 (April 1978): 407–31; and *The King's Coffers, Proprietors of the Spanish Florida Treasury, 1565–1702* (Gainesville, Fla., 1981).

63. Manuel de Montiano to the king, January 22, 1740, "Letters of Montiano," 7: 32–42. Indian militias continued to serve Florida's governors, and in 1759 Cacique Bernardo Lachiche commanded a unit of twenty-eight men, by election of the other caciques. Report of Don Lucas de Palacio on the Spanish, Indian and Free Black Militias, April 30, 1759, SD 2604, AGI.

64. Although St. Augustine was allotted a troop complement of 350 men, Montiano had only 240 men fit for service in St. Augustine when the siege of 1740 ended. Manuel de Montiano to the king, August 9, 1740, SD 846, fol. 25 V, microfilm reel 16, PKY.

65. Manuel de Montiano to the captain general of Cuba, Don Juan Francisco de Güemes y Horcasitas, March 13, 1742, SD 2593, AGI; TePaske, *Governorship of Spanish Florida*, 146–52.

66. TePaske, *Governorship of Spanish Florida*, 152–55.

67. TePaske, *Governorship of Spanish Florida*, 100–05.

68. Fulgencio García de Solís to the king, August 25, 1752, SD 845, fols. 81–112, microfilm reel 17, PKY.

69. "Account of the Revenge," in John Franklin Jameson, ed., *Privateering and Piracy in the Colonial Period: Illustrative Documents* (New York, 1923), 402–11. My thanks to Charles Tingley for providing this source.

70. Report of Captain Fernando Laguna, October 7, 1752, SD 846, fols. 84–108, microfilm reel 17, PKY.

71. Michael C. Scardaville and Jesus María Belmonte, "Florida in the Late First Spanish Period: The Griñán Report," *El Escribano*, 16 (1979): 10.

72. Works that provide information on the life and labor of blacks in colonial Spanish America include: Jorge Juan and Antonio de Ulloa, "Eighteenth-Century Spanish American Towns—African and Afro-Hispanic Life and Labor in Cities and Suburbs," in Anne Pescatello, ed., *The African in Latin America* (New York, 1975): 106–11; Greene and Cohen, *Neither Slave nor Free*; and Louisa Schell Hoberman and Susan Migden Socolow, eds., *Cities and Society in Colonial America* (Albuquerque, N.Mex., 1986).

73. Michael P. Johnson and James L. Roark's work, *Black Masters: A Free Family of Color in the Old South* (New York, 1984), demonstrates how personalism might mediate race relations even in a more rigid caste society, but free blacks always had to balance carefully their legal rights against the social limits accepted in their community. For other examples of upwardly mobile slaves from Spanish Florida, see Jane Landers, "Black Society in Spanish St. Augustine, 1784–1821" (Ph.D. dissertation, University of Florida, Gainesville, 1988).

74. In 1738, Francisco and Ana were the slaves of Don Salvador Garzía, SD 844, fols. 593–94, microfilm reel 15, PKY. Baptism of Francisca Xaviera, August 30, 1736, and baptism of Calisto, October 23, 1738, Black Baptisms, Cathedral Parish Records, Diocese of St. Augustine Catholic Center, Jacksonville (hereafter cited as CPR), microfilm reel 284 F, PKY. Marriage of the widowed Ana García Pedroso to Diego, the slave of Don Juan Joseph Eligio de la Puente, January 14, 1759, Black Marriages, CPR, microfilm reel 284, C, PKY. Baptism of Miguel Francisco, January 29, 1753, Black Baptisms, CPR, microfilm reel 284 F, PKY. Mose militia list, included in evacuation report of Juan Joseph Eligio de la Puente, January 22, 1764, SD 2595, AGI.

75. In 1738, Juan Jacinto Rodríguez and Ana María Menéndez were the slaves of Petronila Pérez, SD 844, fol. 594, PKY. They were married as slaves on October 9, 1735, CPR, 284 C, PKY. After Juan Jacinto died, Ana María married the free black, Antonio de Urisa, of the Lara nation on April 26, 1740, *ibid.* Juan Jacinto and Ana María's daughter, María Francisca, was baptized on October 11, 1736, while she was still the slave of Petronila Pérez, CPR, 284 F, PKY. Juan Lamberto Horruytiner married Cecilia Horruytiner on July 12, 1739, CPR, 284 C, PKY. Baptism of Cecilia, September 9, 1737, CPR, 284 F, PKY. Marriage of María Francisca to Marcos de Torres, August 20, 1742, CPR, 284 C, PKY. Baptism of their daughter, María, May 20, 1743, and their son Nicholás de la Concepción, January 10, 1746, CPR, 284 F, PKY. María Francisca and the children were living in her parents' home at the time of the 1759 census. Census of Father Gines Sánchez, February 12, 1759, SD 2604, AGI. Marriage of Thomas Chrisostomo and María Francisca, December 15, 1760, CPR, 284 C, PKY.

76. Marriage of Thomas Chrisostomo and Ana María Ronquillo, February 28, 1745, *ibid.* Baptism of Pedro Graxales, December 9, 1738, CPR, 284 F, PKY. Marriage of Pedro Graxales, Congo slave of Don Francisco Graxales, and María de la Concepción Hita, Caravalí slave of Don Pedro de Hita, January 19, 1744, CPR, 284 C, PKY. Baptisms of their children, María, November 4, 1744; Manuela de los Angeles, January 1, 1747; Ysidora de los Angeles, December 22, 1748; Joseph Ynisario, April 4, 1755; and Juana Feliciana, July 13, 1757, CPR, 284 F, PKY.

77. Mintz and Price, "Anthropological Approach."

78. Licenses for Slaves Imported into St. Augustine, 1762–1763, Cuba 472, AGI. Ira Berlin, Steven F. Miller, and Leslie S. Rowland, "Afro-American Families in the Transition from Slavery to Freedom," *Radical History Review*, 42 (1988): 89.

79. For a concise description of the importance of the extended family, *parentela*, and the system of personal dependency, *clientela*, in Spain, see McAlister, *Spain and Portugal*, 39–40.

80. TePaske, *Governorship*, 227–29. TePaske described the chronic financial shortages of Florida, saying the "poverty and want characterized life in Florida and pervaded all aspects of life." Father Juan Joseph de Solana also described Florida as a destitute colony, impoverished, despite its natural resources, by the continual attack of Indians loyal to the British. Father Juan Joseph de Solana to Bishop Pedro Agustin Morel de Sánchez, April 22, 1759, SD 516, microfilm reel 28 K, PKY.

81. Melchor de Navarrete to the Marqués de Ensenada, April 2, 1752, cited in Wright, "Dispatches," 184–86.

82. Fulgencio García de Solís to the king, November 29, 1752, SD, microfilm reel 17, PKY. Also, Fulgencio García de Solís to the king, December 7, 1752, cited in Wright, "Dispatches," 187–89.

83. Governors Alonso Fernández de Heredia and Lucas de Palacio both requested

special financial assistance for the townspeople of Mose, citing their poverty. Alonso de Heredia to Julian de Arriaga, April 7, 1756, cited in Wright, "Dispatches," 193–94; the king to Lucas de Palacio, April 21, 1759, *ibid.*, 195.

84. Baptism of Miguel, 1744, CPR, 284 F, PKY.

85. Baptism of Miguel Domingo, January 26, 1748, CPR, 284 F, PKY.

86. Wood, *Black Majority*, 302.

87. Dr. Kathleen Deagan, Florida Museum of Natural History, University of Florida, Gainesville, provided these figures.

88. In a map drawn by Pablo Castello, 1763, 833 B, PKY.

89. Census of Gines Sánchez, February 12, 1759, SD 2604, AGI. Marriage of Francisco Roso, free Caravalí and María de la Cruz, Caravalí slave of Don Carlos Frison, January 8, 1743, CPR, 284 C, PKY; Baptism of Carlos Roso, November 4, 1743, CPR, 284 F, PKY. Marriage of Francisco Xavier de Torres, Mandingo, to Ana María, Mandinga slave to Josepha de Torres, February 1, 1752, CPR, 284 C, PKY. Others with slave wives in St. Augustine were Joseph de Peña, Caravalí, married to Ana María Ysquierdo, Conga slave of Don Juan Ysquierdo, January 29, 1743, *ibid.*; Juan Francisco de Torres, married to María Guillen slave of Joseph Guillen, January 21, 1743, *ibid.*; Joseph Fernández, Mandingo, married to Ana María, Caravalí slave, December 1, 1756, *ibid.*; Juan Baptista married to María de Jesus, August 17, 1757, *ibid.*

90. Report of Father Juan Joseph de Solana to Bishop Pedro Agustin Morel de Sánchez, April 22, 1759, SD 516, microfilm reel 28 K, PKY; Evacuation report of Juan Joseph Eligio de la Puente, January 22, 1764, SD 2595, AGI.

91. Fernando Ortiz, "La Fiesta Afro-Cubana del 'Dia de Reyes,'" *Revista Bimestre Cubana*, 15 (January–June 1920): 5–16.

92. Kathleen Deagan analyzes elements and patterns of cultural exchange and adaptation in several works. See *Artifacts of the Spanish Colonies of Florida and the Caribbean, 1500–1800* (Washington, D.C., 1987); *Spanish St. Augustine: The Archaeology of a Colonial Creole Community* (New York, 1983); *St. Augustine: First Urban Enclave in the United States* (Farmingdale, N.Y., 1982); and *Sex, Status and Role in the Mestizaje of Spanish Colonial Florida* (Gainesville, Fla., 1974). On African-American archaeology, see Theresa Singleton, *The Archeology of Slavery and Plantation Life* (Orlando, Fla., 1985); and Leland Ferguson, "Looking for the 'Afro' in Colono-Indian Pottery," in Robert L. Schuyler, ed., *Archaeological Perspectives on Ethnicity in America: Afro-American and Asian American Culture History* (Farmingdale, N.Y., 1980), 14–28.

93. On Kongo-American connections, see Thompson, *Flash of the Spirit*, 112–15.

94. Personal communication from Kathleen Deagan, October 1989. On African fishing techniques in the colonial southeast, see Peter H. Wood, "'It Was a Negro Taught Them': A New Look at African Labor in Early South Carolina," *Journal of Asian and African Studies*, 9 (July and October 1974): 167–68.

95. Evacuation Report of Juan Joseph Eligio de la Puente, January 22, 1764, SD 2595, AGI. Accounts of the royal treasury of Matanzas, 1761–82 SD 1882, AGI. At least one family attempted to recover the losses of the evacuation, but they were denied on the basis of their color. Petition of María Gertrudis Roso, September 25, 1792, SD 2577, AGI.

96. Slaves escaped from Guadaloupe to Puerto Rico in 1752, and the case was still before the Council of the Indies twenty years later; Consulta, July 19, 1772. Slaves from the Danish colonies of Santa Cruz and Santo Thomas also fled to Puerto Rico in 1767, and eventually the governments signed a convention; Consulta, July 21, 1777. Slaves from the Dutch settlement at Esquibo fled to Guyana, October 22, 1802; Documents relating to fugitive slaves, Indiferente General 2787, AGI.

97. See Landers, "Spanish Sanctuary." Upon registering themselves and obtaining work contracts, slaves escaped from British colonists were freed by the second Spanish government; Census Returns, 1784–1814, East Florida Papers, PKY, microfilm reel 323 A; Royal decree, included in Captain General Luis de las Casas to Governor Manuel Vicente de Zéspedes, July 21, 1790, East Florida Papers, PKY, microfilm reel 1.

THREE

African Dimensions of the Stono Rebellion

JOHN K. THORNTON

The Stono Rebellion of 1739 was one of the largest and costliest in the history of the United States. In studying it, historians have generally not appreciated the extent to which the African background of the participants may have shaped their decision to revolt or their subsequent actions. This essay addresses this upheaval in South Carolina in terms of its African background and attempts to show that understanding the history of the early eighteenth-century kingdom of Kongo can contribute to a fuller view of the slaves' motivations and actions.

In some ways, the failure to consider the African background of the revolt is surprising, since a number of historians have recently explored the possibility of African religions, cultures, and societies playing an important role in other aspects of South Carolina life. Peter Wood, author of the richest examination of Stono, was one of the pioneers in considering African competence at rice growing as important in shaping the decisions of slave buyers, a point followed up in great detail by Daniel Littlefield.[1] Wood also argued that the African origins of the slaves can do much to explain a range of behaviors, from health patterns to language.[2] Tom Shick showed that African concepts of health and healing influenced the development of folk medicine in South Carolina, and Margaret Washington Creel explained religious development in terms of African religion and religiosity.[3]

Historians have yet to apply the same sort of approach to the Stono Rebellion. Scholars of the United States interested in the African background of American history have usually sought general information about African culture by reading the accounts of modern anthropologists and ethnologists, which are not always helpful for understanding specific historical situations. Appreciating the African roots of the Stono Rebellion, for example, requires a specific understanding of the kingdom of Kongo between 1680 and 1740 rather than simply a broad understanding of African culture. Historians of Africa, who have access to this type of specific information, have, unfortunately, rarely used it in a way helpful to their colleagues in U.S. history.[4]

Although the Stono Rebellion was very important in the history of South Carolina, it was not well documented. Only one eyewitness account is extant, supplemented by several secondhand reports.[5] Many English residents of South Carolina, including the anonymous author of the best account, believed that the revolt was somehow precipitated by Spanish propaganda and was part of the larger set of tensions that led to war between England and Spain in 1740. English officials reported a number of Spanish vessels acting suspiciously in English waters, and some Spaniards, including priests, were reported to have made surreptitious visits to South Carolina.[6] Among other things, these Spaniards were believed to be stirring up the slaves, offering freedom to any who would run away, as indeed many did.[7]

The actual rebellion broke out on Sunday (normally a slaves' day off), September 9, 1739, led by a man named Jemmy and including a core of some twenty "Angolan" slaves. The Spanish were suspected in the uprising because, according to the account, the slaves were Catholics, and "the Jesuits have a mission and school in that Kingdom [Angola] and many Thousands of the Negroes profess the Roman Catholic Religion." In addition to the sentiments of a common religion, many slaves could speak Portuguese, which was "as near Spanish as Scotch is to English,"[8] thus increasing their receptivity to Spanish offers and propaganda.

The rebels seized a store of firearms and marched off on a trail of destruction and killing, with two drums and banners flying, which attracted a large crowd of slaves. Having reached over sixty in number, they paused at a large field and "set to dancing, Singing and beating Drums to draw more Negroes to them." Shortly afterward, now numbering ninety, they met a force of militia, and a battle resulted. The slaves were dispersed, though not without "acting boldly" and leaving some dead.[9] The slaves were not finished, however, for they re-formed and continued toward the Spanish possessions around St. Augustine, one body of about ten fleeing until caught by mounted troops the next day.[10] A week later, another group fought a pitched battle with pursuing militia about thirty miles south of the initial skirmish.[11]

While the immediate causes of the revolt clearly lay in the difficult conditions of slavery in South Carolina, detailed in Wood's analysis of the colony and the revolt,[12] several elements in the eyewitness account suggest that, along with English mistreatment and Spanish promises, the African background of the slaves contributed to the nature of the revolt. A study of the African background supports the following interpretation: first, South Carolina slaves were in all likelihood not drawn from the Portuguese colony of Angola (as the account implies) but from the kingdom of Kongo (in modern Angola), which was a Christian country and had a fairly extensive system of schools and churches in addition to a high degree of literacy (at least for the upper class) in Portuguese. In its creole form, Portuguese was also a widely used language of trade as well as the second language of educated Kongolese. The Kongolese were proud of their Christian and Catholic heritage, which they believed made them a distinctive people, and thus Kongolese slaves would have seen the Spanish offers in terms of freedom of religion (or rather, freedom of Catholic religion) as additionally attractive beyond promises of freedom in general.

Second, throughout the eighteenth century, Kongo was disturbed by sporadic and sometimes lengthy civil wars, which resulted in the capture and sale of many people, no small number of whom would have been soldiers with military training. Significant changes in the organization and training of armies that were occurring at the same time had increased the number of soldiers trained in the use of firearms, thus increasing the likelihood that such soldiers would be enslaved. These ex-soldiers might contrast with the untrained villagers often netted by slave raids, judicial enslavement, or other means by which slaves ended up being sold to the Americas. Former soldiers might have provided the military core of the rebels, who fought on after their first engagement and generally gave a good account of themselves.

From patterns of the English slave trade to central Africa, we know it is unlikely that the "Kingdom of Angola" to which the author of the main account of the Stono Rebellion referred was the Portuguese colony known as Angola, largely because the colony sent its slaves on Portuguese and Brazilian ships to Brazil and not to English shipping bound for North America.[13] Rather, the author surely meant the general stretch of central Africa known to English shippers as the Angola coast. This area included coastal parts of modern Zaire, Congo-Brazzaville, and Gabon as well as Angola. The English slave trade, conducted in this period by the Royal African Company, fixed its operations on the northern part of the coast, especially at the town of Kabinda, just north of the mouth of the Zaire River.[14] The importance of Kabinda is underscored by the fact that, according to company records, every central African voyage the company undertook in the 1720s gave Kabinda as its destination.[15] Kabinda was the capital of an independent state, which, lying as it did against a sparsely inhabited interior, did not procure many slaves itself but served as an export station for suppliers coming from the south. Since Kabinda's first line of supply was its southern neighbor across the Zaire, the "Angolans" of the Stono Rebellion most likely came from Kongo. Eighteenth-century visitors such as James Barbot often left from Kabinda to visit other ports along the Kongo coast to the south or up the Zaire River to the town of Nzari (Zaire).[16] Accounts of the 1760s refer to a brisk trade in Kongo's province of Mbula lying on the Zaire and upstream of Nzari, which supplied English, French, and Dutch merchants (probably based at Kabinda) as well.[17]

The possibility that people from other parts of central Africa were involved in the rebellion cannot be completely ruled out, however, since Kabinda was also served by the Vili trading network. Centered in the kingdom of Loango, farther north up the coast, Vili traders had built a series of towns since at least the mid-seventeenth century under a disciplined caravan system across Kongo that supplied many of their slaves,[18] but they also contacted suppliers outside Kongo. The Vili engaged in trade with Portuguese Angola despite colonial attempts to prohibit it, and they dealt extensively with Matamba, Angola's independent eastern neighbor.[19] In eastern Kongo, they contacted the merchants of Kongo's marquisate of Nzombo, whose operations extended to the east and included many non-Kongolese.[20] Nzombo merchants capitalized on the expansion of the Lunda empire in the second quarter of the eighteenth century to supply slaves to the Vili, although, before 1740, such slaves would not have been available in large numbers.[21] Likewise, Vili merchants operating to the east and north of Kongo could buy slaves at the busy markets around the Malebo Pool, which was served by merchants originating higher up the Zaire River.[22]

Thus merchants based at Kabinda would buy slaves from an extensive area of central Africa. Nevertheless, the majority enslaved in the period between about 1710 and 1740 were probably from Kongo. First of all, the kingdom was the principal supplier to Kabinda-based merchants and to Vili merchants as well. Second, the eastern regions served by merchants in Nzombo and the Malebo Pool were not as fully engaged in the slave trade in the early eighteenth century as they would become by mid-century, especially after the arrival of Lunda armies in the Kwango region around 1750. Third, the southern regions were jealously guarded by the Portuguese authorities, who sought to block trade northward with a fort at Nkoje built in 1759 specifically to stop Vili traders.[23] Even though the Portuguese could not stop northbound trade completely—it continued to reach Kabinda by overland or coastal routes and French, English, and Dutch merchants based on the north coast—they probably did limit it considerably.

The background of trade points strongly to a Kongo origin of the Stono slaves, but it is their adherence to Catholicism that confirms it. Only two countries in central Africa were Christian: Kongo and the Portuguese colony of Angola. Missionaries based in Angola did some work in eastern areas outside colonial control, such as Matamba, but they were limited by a shortage of missionaries in the eighteenth century.[24] Even in the best of times, these missions were typically of short duration and did not lead to the establishment of a long-lasting, permanent church organization.[25] In eastern Angola, moreover, admission of missionaries and acceptance of baptism was usually linked to surrender to Portugal, which slowed missionary work and restricted mass conversions.[26] The slaves from the east of Kongo, supplied by Nzombo or Vili merchants, were definitely not Christians according to the

Italian Capuchin missionary in Kongo Cherubino da Savona, who referred to them as "heathens."[27]

Of these two Christian countries, Angola was unlikely to export slaves to English ships, especially Christian slaves who would surely have been drawn from areas under direct Portuguese control, where Portuguese restrictions were strongest. That Christian slaves in English hands would be from Kongo is substantiated by complaints of the Spanish Governor Antonio de Salas of New Granada (Colombia) to the Spanish crown in 1735. He stated that English merchants representing the South Sea Company (drawing on the same sources as the English supplying South Carolina) were introducing "black Christians of the Congo" into Cartagena.[28]

These same "black Christians of the Congo" were the leading rebels of the Stono Rebellion, susceptible to Spanish and Catholic propaganda. They came from a culture well disposed toward Catholics. The Kongolese of the eighteenth century regarded their Christianity as a fundamental part of their national identity,[29] since the kingdom was voluntarily converted with the baptism of King Nzinga Nkuwu as João I in 1491, not linked to submission to Portugal as many of the eastern Angolan conversions were. It had independent relations with Rome and its own internally developed church and school system.[30]

The locally rooted Christian tradition is sometimes regarded as less than orthodox. Most modern scholars have pointed out that the Kongolese simply added Christian labels to their indigenous beliefs. Foreign clergy who worked in Kongo in the seventeenth and eighteenth centuries often regarded them as "Christians in name only," although some other accounts praise them as model Christians.[31] But, whatever modern scholars or some eighteenth-century priests thought, the Kongolese regarded themselves as Christians. The elite carefully maintained chapels and sent their children to schools, and the ordinary people learned their prayers and hymns, even in the eighteenth century, when ordained clergy were often absent.[32] Even those priests who doubted the orthodoxy of the Kongolese did not doubt their sincerity, since, as priests, they were often surrounded by crowds of people singing hymns or demanding their children be baptized. The high wooden crosses that marked Kongolese chapels could still be seen in the twentieth century.[33] These observations by travelers in Africa were seconded by occasional clerical observations in the Americas, where Kongolese slaves were well known to be Christians.[34] The same was true in Spanish Florida, for, in 1748, a free Kongolese, Miguel Domingo, told the priest at Gracia Real de Santa Teresa de Mose that he had been baptized and continued to pray in Kikongo, probably using prayers like those printed in the Kikongo catechism of 1624.[35]

In many ways, acceptance of the Portuguese language as the official language of the kingdom of Kongo paralleled the acceptance of Christianity. The author of the account of the Stono Rebellion believed that the slaves were especially open to Spanish propaganda because some could speak its Iberian sister language, and at least some Kongolese slaves could indeed do this. Almost from the start of European contacts, the Kongolese developed literacy in Portuguese: the first letter composed by a literate Kongolese dated from 1491.[36] Schools developed rapidly in Kongo, and by the seventeenth century there was a school in every major provincial capital.[37] Literacy was more or less restricted to the upper class, but the fact that Kongo's archives and official documents were written in Portuguese helped create a general familiarity with the language among the ordinary people.[38]

More important for the people, undoubtedly, was the dominance of Portuguese in the language of trade, not just in Kongo but in the whole of west-central Africa.[39] The status of Portuguese (or rather, creole Portuguese) as a trade language did not mean that all, or even most, Kongolese could speak Portuguese; in fact, governors of Angola complained that even citizens of the colony seemed to prefer African languages to Portuguese at home.[40] But it did mean that among any sizable group of Kongolese slaves there were likely to be bilingual speakers. During an earlier period, Jesuit missionaries in America had routinely used bilingual Kongolese as catechists.[41] Thus, in the context of colonial South Carolina, Spanish agents were quite likely to be able to communicate with at least some Kongolese slaves, who could in turn communicate with others who knew no Portuguese.

The slaves fought well in the various military engagements that made up the Stono Rebellion. This may have been a result of their bravery and despera-tion, or they may have acquired military skills as soldiers of the colonies. In the Americas, slaves did sometimes serve in the colonial militia, and they may have been trained there. Wood examined the issue, however, and pointed out that militia service for slaves, while common in the earlier periods, had been phased out by the 1720s. By that time, South Carolina had already passed strong restrictions against slaves possessing firearms, and slaves not longer served in the militia, although many probably still had access to guns for hunting.[42]

Military service in Africa may well have served a more important role than occasional militia service or hunting. Considering that many slaves were first captured in wars, it is reasonable to assume that some of the rebels had been soldiers.[43] Of course, not every person enslaved during military action in Kongo was a soldier. Often, armed forces raided villages, carrying off civilians who would then be sold into slavery. Luca da Caltanisetta, traveling in Kongo, noted one such example that took place on February 10, 1701: "The Mani Lumbo [a title] returned with 58 slaves captured by order of the king; he had destroyed a *libata* [village] of one of his vassals, accused of treason . . . [A]mong these slaves were many free people, some inhabitants of the *libata* . . . and others who were just there on business."[44] In another incident, da Caltanisetta recorded the poignant tale of a woman who was already a slave but whose master decided to sell her to a trader with connections to the Atlantic trade. Once the woman heard of his plans, she killed her baby and then herself rather than be deported.[45] Obviously, incidents like these could be multiplied. There were many other ways to become enslaved—kidnapping, judicial punishment, or indebtedness. Any of these methods might capture a civilian with no knowledge of military affairs at all. Soldiers were only captured in wars, wars that ranged armies against each other. However, eighteenth-century Kongo had plenty of wars.

Before 1665, Kongo was a centralized kingdom, one in which there was a great deal of internal order. If Kongolese were enslaved, it would be as a result of external attack, not internal disorder; consequently, relatively few Kongolese were enslaved before the mid-seventeenth century.[46] After 1665, all this changed, as civil wars raged almost constantly for the next forty-four years. While the causes and development of the wars need not concern us here,[47] it is enough to note that fairly large-scale engagements between Kongolese armies were commonplace. Some of the differences that lay behind the civil wars were patched up when most contenders recognized King Pedro IV between 1709 and 1716 and brought a formal restoration of the kingdom, but intermittent wars broke out after that.[48] Unfortunately, the documentary record that affords substantial information about Kongo in the late seventeenth and early eighteenth centuries dries up after about 1720. Nevertheless, several incidents in the 1730s are clearly indicative of major wars during that period. For example, a Capuchin priest, Angelo Maria da Polinago, visiting Kongo's coastal principality of Nsoyo in 1733, noted that he was prevented from traveling to the southern areas (in the duchy of Mbamba) because of a major war in that area.[49] Soldiers captured in this war, or others like it that are not documented, would certainly be exported, via Kabinda to Spanish Cartagena or to South Carolina by the English companies.

Some features of the account of the Stono Rebellion suggest that Kongolese soldiers taken as slaves in this and other, undocumented, wars of the 1730s were among the rebels at Stono. For example, the rebels quickly seized a supply of guns and apparently handled them well.[50] The utility of guns in a revolt is directly proportional to the skill with which the rebels are capable of using them, and this, in turn, is dependent on training. Presumably, those unfamiliar with guns might have sought other weapons, such as knives, axes, or agricultural tools, and passed up a raid on an armory. Because the colonial militia did not provide much in the way of firearms training, the possibility of an African source of training seems more likely.

Kongolese soldiers would certainly have had training with modern weapons. By the early eighteenth century, guns were becoming more and more common on African battlefields, and skill in their use was being passed on to a larger and larger group of soldiers. A military revolution was altering war in Kongo and other parts of Africa, increasing the size of armies, and replacing the hand-to-hand combat of lances, swords, and axes with the missile combat of muskets.

Good descriptions of war in seventeenth-century Kongo make clear that, in general, firearms were not important in Angolan wars before 1680.[51] Rather, the musketeers who served were fairly small in number and, moreover, tended to be drawn from an elite of *mestiços*, racially mixed Kongolese with some Portuguese ancestry. At the battle of Mbwila in 1665, Kongo assembled only 360 musketeers under a *mestiço* commander, out of an army of many thousands.[52] Donigio Carli da Piacenza, an Italian Capuchin traveler, likewise met only some twenty musketeers in the service of the powerful duke of Mbamba in 1668, all *mestiços*.[53] Then, such soldiers were not only rare but had social connections that made their enslavement and sale to the Atlantic world improbable.

But this situation changed during the late seventeenth and early eighteenth centuries. In all probability, African generals decided to include more musketeers because of improvements in technology, dating from the 1680s, which saw the replacement of the matchlock musket by the more reliable flintlock weapon. In Europe, armies were altered dramatically; the masses of pikemen who had dominated seventeenth-century wars exchanged their pikes for muskets with fixed bayonets to serve the same purpose. Soldiers armed in this way prevailed over the European battlefield until well into the nineteenth century.[54] Many African armies seem to have rearmed at about the same time. Ray Kea has shown how many armies on the Gold Coast rearmed and swiftly changed battlefield tactics during this period.[55] Unfortunately, the sources do not allow us to trace developments in Angola with the detail that can be shown in West Africa. Nevertheless, mid-eighteenth-century sources that describe battles fought by the Portuguese-led Angolan army, and its African opponents in southern Kongo, include the musketeer as a prominent force on the battlefield.[56] He was perhaps significant much earlier. The thousands of soldiers who fell in to greet a Capuchin visitor to Kongo's coastal province of Sonyo in 1694 were already equipped with muskets.[57] In 1701, Prince António Baretto da Silva of Sonyo felt a sufficient need for firearms that he wrote the pope, asking for a dispensation on the ruling that Prince António not sell slaves to English and Dutch "heretics" in order to arm his soldiers with the muskets they imported.[58]

During the 1730s, however, this military revolution was still incomplete, especially in areas such as south Kongo, where access to firearms imports was restricted by distance, price, and Portuguese policy. When Anton Felice Tomassi da Cortona visited the duke of Mbamba in Kongo's southern interior in 1734, he found the duke's military retinue still contained archers and lancers as well as numerous musketeers, more than Dionigio Carli had noted fifty years earlier.[59] Although muskets were not yet the only weapon used, muskets had passed from the prerogative of a small, racially mixed elite to the hands of more people, and the trend toward an increasing use of muskets was clear. By the 1780s, the musket was the most important weapon in use in warfare. In 1781, Father Raphael de Castello de Vide saw the royal army assemble for war, composed, he believed, of "more than thirty thousand men, armed with powder and ball,"[60] a phrase suggesting a virtually exclusive reliance on muskets. Indeed, other military units that the priest traveled with were armed with muskets as well.[61]

Not only were muskets used by a greater percentage of soldiers than before but the use of trained military forces had also spread to outlying areas and led to recruitment of more soldiers among the population. At its height, Kongo's army was centralized: the authorities in the capital (São Salvador) had most of the soldiers, while the provincial nobility possessed relatively small guard units.[62] But after the civil wars began in Kongo, armed retinues became essential in even small provinces and towns. Tomassi da Cortona noted that the duke of Mbamba had a fairly large standing army in 1734, and his contemporary, Angelo Maria da Polinago, observed that even the small marquisate of Kitombo mustered a considerable force of soldiers to greet him in 1733.[63] Thus, although the size of any given army probably fell during the period 1665 to 1740, as a result of the decentralization of power the total number of people under arms and receiving military training with firearms probably rose.[64]

In addition to handling firearms in a way that suggests military training, the Stono rebels also gave other indications of an African military background. For example, they marched under banners like the unit flags that African armies flew in their campaigns,[65] and they used drums to encourage the rebels. Of course, such behavior might simply have been imitative of colonial militias in which Africans may still have served or at the very least observed. Far more significant was the fact that the rebels danced.[66] Their dancing need not have been simply a reflection of the joy of the prospect of freedom or the result of drunkenness. Although European and Euro-American armies and militias marched, flew flags, and beat drums as they approached combat, they did not dance. Military dancing was a part of the African culture of war. In African war, dancing was as much a part of military preparation as drill was in Europe. Before 1680, when soldiers fought hand to hand, dancing was a form of training to quicken reflexes and develop parrying skills. Dancing in preparation for war was so common in Kongo that "dancing a war dance" (*sangamento*) was often used as a synonym for "to declare war" in seventeenth-century sources.[67]

Dancing was less useful in the period after 1680, since hand-to-hand combat was largely replaced by missile tactics with muskets. However, Africans did not use bayonets on their muskets; they needed swords and other hand-to-hand weapons for those times when close fighting was required. One Portuguese commander who fought in the late eighteenth century in southern Kongo, after praising his opponents' skill with muskets and their nearly universal use of the weapon, noted that they retained the "arma blanca" for hand-to-hand fighting.[68] Thus dancing may have been important even after guns became the principal weapons to ensure that soldiers still honed their skill in hand-to-hand fighting, or it may have survived just as close-order drill survives in modern armies, where it has little combat utility, as a distinctive element of military life. Luca da Caltanisetta still described the musketeer armies of the prince of Nsoyo in 1691 as dancing in preparation for war, and Castello de Vide noted dancing before battle in 1781.[69]

The African military background can also shed some light on the tactics of the Stono rebels. At first glance, they do not appear to have been very soldierly, standing in a disorderly group and dispersing after a brief engagement. Many rapidly fled to their masters' homes, and only a small determined core persisted, fighting several more encounters with the colonial militia in the days after the first battle.[70] It is most likely that, by the time the colonial forces met the rebels, their numbers had been swelled by a large number of slaves who had no military experience but hoped that the rebels would succeed and deliver them from slavery. When the real fighting began, these hangers-on might have been the ones who dispersed quickly, hoping to get back to their masters' farms before they were missed.[71]

But the tactics of the core of the rebels, perhaps those twenty Angolans who started the revolt and a few others, who had all the guns, disorderly as they seemed, are consistent with a central African model. Europeans' ideas of a proper military formation were based on the necessity, created by cavalry, of maintaining close order at all times. Indeed, the European musketeer of the eighteenth century was a converted pikeman, just as his musket with bayonet was a combination pike and missile weapon.[72] In central Africa, where there was never a large or effective cavalry, the musketeer was more likely to be a converted skirmisher. Central African musketeers in the seventeenth century often opened engagements with random fire from covered positions to weaken enemy infantry. This infantry was armed with swords and battle axes intended for hand-to-hand fighting that would resolve the battle.[73] But, unlike Europeans, who retained the hand-to-hand aspects of pike warfare, central Africans greatly reduced their close fighting in favor of skirmishing tactics, which replaced the shock encounters of heavily armed infantry. Eighteenth-century battles tended to be drawn-out affairs in which units attacked the enemy, withdrew, maneuvered, and in general avoided hand-to-hand combat.[74]

Thus the Stono rebels were not revealing their rude origins when they fought in the way they did. Instead, their tactical behavior was perfectly consistent with tactics of the battlefields of Kongo. They withdrew after a brief encounter, relocated, and fought several battles over a protracted period, a pattern typical of Angola.

We can see the Stono Rebellion from a new angle if we consider the African contribution as well as the American one. The combination of evidence certainly suggests that the slaves' Christianity and the religious appeal of Spanish propaganda may have played a role in the revolt. Likewise, though less certain, the slaves' probable military experience in Africa could also have influenced their behavior and their ultimate fate.

NOTES

I would like to thank the Carter Woodson Institute of the University of Virginia, whose support for the years 1984–1985 began the project from which this essay is drawn. I also benefited from a grant for additional research from the National Endowment for the Humanities, Summer Stipend (1988) on European military encounters with non-European Atlantic societies in the Columbian era.

1. Peter B. Wood, *Black Majority: Negroes in Colonial South Carolina from 1670 through the Stono Rebellion* (New York, 1974), 56–62; Daniel Littlefield, *Rice and Slaves: Ethnicity and the Slave Trade in Colonial South Carolina* (Baton Rouge, La., 1981).

2. Wood, *Black Majority*, 63–91, 167–91.

3. Tom W. Shick, "Healing and Race in the South Carolina Low Country," in Paul Lovejoy, ed., *Africans in Bondage: Studies in Slavery and the Slave Trade* (Madison, Wis., 1986), 107–24; Margaret Washington Creel, *A Peculiar People: Slave Religion and Community Culture among the Gullahs* (New York, 1988).

4. The problem is compounded by linguistic difficulties: to do historical studies of eighteenth-century Angola, the most important African source of slaves for South Carolina before Stono, one needs to consult sources written in Portuguese and Italian, very few of which are available in translation and many of which are unpublished or have only been published in recent years.

5. See "An Account of the Negroe Insurrection in South Carolina" (undated, *ca.* 1740), in Allen D. Candler and William J. Northern, eds., *Colonial Records of the State of Georgia* (1904–16; rpt. Edn., New York, 1870), 22/2: 232–36. The most useful secondhand accounts are "A Ranger's Report of Travels with General Oglethorpe, 1739–42" (diary), in William D. Merenes, ed., *Travels in the American Colonies* (New York, 1916), 222–23; and William Stephens, *A Journal of the Proceedings in Georgia, Beginning October 24, 1737. . . ,* 2 vols. (London, 1742), 2: 128–30 (this journal was also reprinted in Candler and Northern, *Colonial Records*, vol. 4). This last document is closest in time, dated September 13, 1739, just four days after the revolt.

6. Some of these events are reported in Stephens, *Journal*, 2: 77, 78. In retrospect, Stephens was glad that earlier they had stopped a priest on the Georgia coast; 130.

7. The earlier incidents are detailed in Wood, *Black Majority*, 309–12; on runaways in Spanish Florida, see Jane Landers, "Gracia Real de Santa Teresa de Mose: A Free Black Town in Spanish Colonial Florida," *AHR*, 95 (February 1990): 9–30.

8. Candler and Northern, "Account of Negroe Insurrection," 233.

9. Candler and Northern, "Account of Negroe Insurrection," 234–35; Stephens, *Journal*, 128.

10. Stephens, *Journal*, 129, 235.

11. Andrew Leslie to Philip Bearcroft, January 7, 1740, quoted in Stephens, *Journal*, 318–19; see also Frank Klingberg, *An Appraisal of the Negro in Colonial South Carolina* (Washington, D.C., 1941), 80.

12. Wood, *Black Majority*, 271–320.

13. For a full discussion of the legal strictures as well as the substantial smuggling, see Joseph C. Miller, *Way of Death: Merchant Capitalism and the Angolan Slave Trade, 1730–1830* (Madison, Wis., 1988), 245–83.

14. A general survey of the English trade of this coast is presented in Phyllis Martin, *The External Trade of the Loango Coast, 1576–1870* (Oxford, 1972), 75–130.

15. David Galenson, *Traders, Planters, and Slaves: Market Behavior in Early English America* (Cambridge, 1986), 164–65.

16. James Barbot, "Abstract of a Voyage to the Kongo River and Kabinda in 1700," in Thomas Astley, ed., *A New General Collection of Voyages and Travels . . . ,* 5 vols. (London, 1746), 3: 202–09.

17. Cherubino da Savona, "Breve ragguaglio del 'Regno di Congo, e sue Missione' scritto dal Padre Cerubino da Savona, Missionario Apostolico Capuccino" (MS of

1775), fols. 42, 44; mod. edn. in Carlo Toso, ed., "Relazioni inedite di P. Cherubino Cassinis da Savona sul 'Congo e sue Missioni,'" *L'Italia francescana*, 45 (1975): 136–214. A French translation is available, Louis Jadin, "Aperçu de la situation du Congo en 1760 et rite d'élection des rois en 1775, d'après le P. Cherubino da Savona, missionaire au Congo de 1759 à 1774," *Bulletin, Institute historique belge de Rome*, 35 (1963): 343–419.

18. For a detailed discussion on trading networks in Angola and its eastern regions, see Miller, *Way of Death*, 207–83.

19. See Martin, *External Trade*, 130; Miller, *Way of Death*, 200–03.

20. On the Nzombo traders, see da Savona, "Breve ragguaglio," 136–214.

21. For an assessment of the Lunda expansion, see John Thorton, "The Chronology and Causes of Lunda Expansion to the West, ca. 1700–1852," *Zambia Journal of History*, I (1981): 1–13. Kongo (presumably Nzombo) participation in the trade of Lunda slaves was noted in 1756 by the Portuguese traveler Manuel Correia Leitão, "Relação brêve summário da viagem que eo, o sargento-mor dos moradores do Dande fiz as remotras partes de Cassange e Olos . . . 15 de agosto de 1756," in Gastão Sousa Dias, "Uma viagem a Cassange nos meados do século XVIII," *Boletim da sociedade de Geográfia de Lisboa*, 56 (1938): 19–20, 25. Note that Cherubino da Savona had Lunda (Mollua) as one of Kongo's neighbors by 1760; da Savona, "Breve ragguaglio," fol. 41v.

22. A description of the Maleba Pool markets in the late seventeenth and early eighteenth centuries can be found in Luca da Caltanisetta, "Relatione del Viaggo e Missione fatta per me Fra Luca da Caltanisetta . . . nel 1691 al . . . " (MS of 1701), fols. 55–60v; published in Romain Rainero, ed., *Il Congo agli inizi del settecento nella relazione di P. Luca da Caltanisetta* (Florence, 1974); French translation, François Bontinck, *Diaire congolaise, 1690–1701* (Brussels, 1970). See also Marcellino d'Atri, "Giornate Apostoliche fatte da me Fra Marcellino d'Atri, Predicator Cappuccino nelle messioni de Regni d'Angola e Congo . . . 1690" (MS of 1708), fols. 306–34; mod. edn., Carlo Toso, *L'anarchia Congolese nel Sec. XVII: La relazione inedita di Marcellino d'Atri* (Genoa, 1984). For the history of the commercial group upriver, see Robert Harms, *River of Wealth, River of Sorrow: The Central Zaire Basin in the Era of the Slave and Ivory Trade* (New Haven, Conn., 1981).

23. Miller, *Way of Death*, 277–78, 582–85.

24. See, for example, Anselmo da Castelvetrano, "Relatione dello stato in cui presentmente si trovano le Missioni Cappuccini in Regno di Congo," October 14, 1742, Scritture riferite nel Congregazioni Generali, vol. 712, fols. 296–305, Archivio "De Propaganda Fide" (Rome). Also, *ibid.*, Acta, vol. 112 (1742), fol. 422. On the general state of the Capuchin mission, and other ecclesiastical bodies in Kongo and Angola, see Graziano Saccardo [da Leguzzano], *Congo e Angola, con la storia del missione dei Cappuccini*, 3 vols. (Venice, 1982–84), vol. 2, *passim.*

25. An extreme example comes from Kasanje in the 1660s; see Giovanni Antonio Cavazzi, "Missione Evangelica al Regno di Congo" (MS of 1665), Book 3, MSS Araldi Family (Modena).

26. Beatrix Heintze, "Luso-African Feudalism in Angola? The Vassal Treaties of the Sixteenth to Eighteenth Centuries," *Revista Portuguesa de História*, 18 (1980): 111–31.

27. da Savona, "Breve ragguaglio," fol. 42.

28. Documents cited and quoted in Jorge Palacios Preciado, *La Trata de negros por Cartagena de Indias* (Tunja, 1973), 349.

29. John K. Thornton, "Demography and History in the Kingdom of Kongo, 1550–1750," *Journal of African History*, 18 (1977): 507–30. See the revealing comments of Luca da Caltanisetta, "Relatione del Viaggio," fols. 15, 25v. See the French translation by Bontinck, *Diaire congolaise*, for supporting references to Christianity, especially the rigorous following of the sacraments (particularly marriage) as distinctively Kongolese attributes.

30. For the origin and development of Christianity in Kongo, see John Thornton, "The Development of an African Catholic Church in the Kingdom of Kongo, 1491–1750," *Journal of African History*, 25 (1984): 147–49.

31. Hilton, *Kingdom of Kongo*, 179–98; Wyatt MacGaffey, *Religion and Society in Central Africa: The Bakongo of Lower Zaire* (Chicago, 1986), 198–211; Andrea da Pavia, "Viaggio Apostolico alla Missione" (MS *ca.* 1690), MS 3165, Biblioteca Nacional de Madrid; da Savona, "Breve ragguaglio," *passim*; Rafael Castello de Vide, "Viagem do Congo do Missionário Fr. Raphael de Castello de vide, hoje Bispo do São Tomé" (MS of 1788), MS Vermelho, 296 fol. 77 and *passim*, Academia das Ciências (Lisbon).

32. For example, see the account of da Savona, "Breve ragguaglio," fols. 42v, 43, 45, 45v. Also see Castello de Vide, "Viagem do Congo," fols. 53, 64, and *passim*.

33. François Bontinck, "Les Croix du bois dans l'ancien royaume de Kongo," *Miscellanea historiae pontificiae*, 50 (1983): 199–213.

34. In addition to the correspondence of Antonio de Salas cited above, see John Thornton, "On the Trail of Voodoo: African Christianity in Africa and the Americas," *The Americas*, 44 (1988): 268–69.

35. Landers, "Gracia Real de Santa Teresa de Mose," 27, citing a baptismal register entry of January 26, 1748. The catechism text was reprinted with French translation and annotation by François Bontinck and D. Ndembe Nsasi, *Le Catéchisme kikongo de 1624: Reédition critique* (Brussels, 1978). Italian clergy introduced a new edition in 1650, and copies were extant in the nineteenth century.

36. See Rui da Pina's untitled account (in an early sixteenth-century Italian translation), fol. 99rb–100vb, photographically reproduced in Francisco Leite da Faria, "Uma relação de Rui de Pina sobre o Congo escrita em 1492," *Studia*, 19 (1966), which quotes a letter of the king of Kongo written about September or October 1491. The author of the letter is likely to have been a Kongolese who had visited Portugal between 1488 and 1491, "a black Christian who knew how to read and write, who began to teach the young men (*moços*) of the Court and children of the nobility, which is a great number"; Rui da Pina, *Cronica de Rey D. Joham I* (*ca.* 1515), cap. 63, excerpted in António Brásio, ed., *Monumenta Missionaria Africana*, 1st ser., 14 vols. (Lisbon, 1952–81), 1: 136.

37. For a summary of Capuchin educational work, see Saccardo [da Leguzzano], *Congo e Angola*, 1: 402–15.

38. On literacy, see John Thornton, *The Kingdom of Kongo: Civil War and Transition, 1641–1718* (Madison, Wis., 1983), 67–68; Anne Hilton, *The Kingdom of Kongo* (Oxford, 1985), 79–83, 205, 217; Susan H. Broadhead, "Beyond Decline: The Kingdom of the Kongo in the Eighteenth and Nineteenth Centuries," *International Journal of African Historical Studies*, 12 (1979): 633–35.

39. Jean-Luc Vellut, "Relations internationales au moyen-Kwango et d'Angola dans la deuxième moitié du XVIIIe siècle," *Etudes d'histoire africaine*, 1 (1970): 82–89.

40. This was a constant complaint of mid-eighteenth-century governors; see, for example, Memorial of Francisco Innocencio de Sousa Coutinho, 1765, Fundo Geral, Códice 8554, fol. 28, Biblioteca Nacional de Lisboa. This and other complaints ought to be taken as indications of the failure of the Portuguese government to replace Kimbundu as the language of the colony, rather than that Kimbundu and not Portuguese were known, for Sousa Coutinho took Brazil, a completely Lusophonic country (in his opinion), as a model.

41. This use had religious implications; see Thornton, "On the Trail of Voodoo," 271–73.

42. Wood, *Black Majority*, 127.

43. Wood, *Black Majority*, 126–27, proposed that African soldiers may have been brought to the Americas and cited the use of firearms in Africa, although the evidence relates to the Gold Coast rather than Angola.

44. da Caltanisetta, "Relatione del Viaggo," fol. 99v.

45. da Caltanisetta, "Relatione del Viaggo," fol. 20v.

46. Thornton, *Kingdom of Kongo*, xiv–xv. Slaves in the New World known as "Congos" were typically transshipped through the country from farther east and exported either through Kongo ports or by Angola-based merchants who crossed Kongo to buy slaves.

47. For a detailed account, see Thornton, *Kingdom of Kongo*, 69–96.

48. See Thorton, *Kingdom of Kongo*, 97–113; for a general discussion of the late eighteenth century and the pattern of wars, see Broadhead, "Beyond Decline," 635–36.

49. Angelo Maria da Polinago to Dorotea Sofia di Neoburgo, August 16, 1733, Raccolta manuscritti, busta 49, Viaggi, fol. 3, Archivio di Stato, Parma.

50. Candler and Northern, "Account of Negroe Insurrection," 233.

51. For a general survey of the situation, see John Thornton, "The Art of War in Angola, 1595–1680," *Comparative Studies in Society and History*, 30 (1988): 373–75.

52. Thornton, *Kingdom of Kongo*, 75.

53. Dionigio Carli da Piacenza, *Viaggio del P. Michelangelo de' Guattini da Reggio et del P. Dionigi de' Carli da Piacenza al regno del Congo* (Reggio, 1671).

54. Theodore Ropp, *War in the Modern World* (New York, 1962), 37–60.

55. Ray Kea, *Settlements, Trade and Polities on the Seventeenth-Century Gold Coast* (Baltimore, Md., 1982), 154–68.

56. Alexandre Elias da Silva Corrêa, *História de Angola* (MS *ca.* 1789), 2 vols. (Lisbon, 1937), 1: 48–62, a general account of techniques of war in the 1770s illustrating an event (of 1774) based on contemporary records as preserved in a recension of the "Catálogo do Governadores de Angola." For further textual history, see Joseph C. Miller and John Thornton, "The Chronicle as Source, History and Hagiography: The *Catálogo dos Governadores de Angola*," *Paideuma*, 33 (1987): 359–90.

57. Filippo Bernardi da Firenze, "Ragguaglio del Congo, cioè viaggi fatti da' missionarij apostolici cappuccini della provincia di Toscana a' regni del Congo, Angola, Matamba, ecc . . . " (1711), Archivio Provinciale de' Cappuccini da Provincia di Toscana, Montughi Convent, Florence, p. 619.

58. Prince António Baretto da Silva to Pope Clement XI, October 4, 1701, Scritture refirite nelli Congressi, Africa-Congo, vol. 3, fols. 288–88v. Archivio "De Propaganda Fide."

59. Anton Felice Tomassi da Cortona to his brother, Anibal Tomassi, November 20, 1734, Papers of the Tomassi Family, Cortona, fol. 2. Luca da Caltanisetta also noted that arrows were still used along with muskets in the last years of the seventeenth century; "Relatione del Viaggo," fol. 17 (Incident of 1694).

60. Castello de Vide, "Viagem do Congo," fol. 118.

61. Castello de Vide, "Viagem do Congo," fol. 93.

62. Thornton, *Kingdom of Kongo*, 42.

63. Tomassi da Cortona to Anibal Tomassi, November 20, 1734, Tomassi Papers, fol. 2; Angelo Maria da Polinago to Dorotea Sofia Neoburgo, August 16, 1733, Raccolta manoscritti, busta 49, Viaggi, fol. 2, Archivio di Stato, Parma.

64. Miller has argued that firearms were less important in central Africa than proposed here. His main basis for this is the conclusion that firearms imports were insufficient to arm more than about 20,000 soldiers in the whole of central Africa (*Way of Death*, 86–94), even though he estimated that as many as 60,000 guns were imported per year. This low number derives from a pessimistic judgment of the capacity of Africans to repair defective imports or maintain existing weapons. I believe Miller is wrong in part because of the eyewitness evidence of large armies armed with muskets cited in previous notes and also on the grounds that his estimates of imports, number of serviceable weapons at any time, repair capacities of African smiths, and average life span of weapons are all considerably too low.

65. Candler and Northern, "Account of Negroe Insurrection," 234. Wood proposed a religious interpretation for the banners, *Black Majority*, 316, n. 30, even though no eighteenth-century source mentions the sort of cultic devotion to flags that he suggested. Unit flags were commonplace, however, in seventeenth-century armies; see Thornton, "Art of War," 366–67; and Castello de Vide mentioned them as always being a part of any force in the later eighteenth century; de Vide, "Viagem do Congo," fols. 93, 96.

66. Candler and Northern, "Account of Negroe Insurrection," 234.

67. It is so used, for the seventeenth century, even in sources by Europeans; see Mateus Cardoso, "Relação do alevamento de Dom Afonso, irmão del Rey Dom Alvaro

III de Congo" (January 1622), Assistencia Portugal, vol. 55, fol. 115v, Archivum Romanum Societatis Iesu (Rome).

68. Paulo Martins Pinheiro de Lacerda, "Noticia da campanha e paiz do Mosul, que conquistou o Sargento Mor Paulo Martins Pinheiro de Lacerda" (1790–91), *Annaes Maritímos e Colonais*, 6 (1846): 129–30. Miller, *Way of Death*, 91, n. 57, cited this account as evidence that the Kongo possessed few guns and still fought with their traditional weapons. In fact, he pointedly praised their skill with firearms in a way that suggests it was their principal weapon, noting the use of the "arma blanca" as a secondary weapon. The use of musket fire is also clear in other accounts by Pinheiro de Lacerda, which describe the actual battles of the same campaign in greater detail; see Angola, Caixa 76, doc. 28 (May 20, 1791), Arquivo Histórico Ultramarino (Lisbon); and doc. 34, service record of Felix Xavier Pinheiro de Lacerda (his son), enclosure by Paulo Martins Pinheiro de Lacerda.

69. da Caltanisetta, "Relatione de Viaggo," fols. 9, 25v; Castello de Vide, "Viagem do Congo," MS Vermelho 296, fols. 98, 119, Academia das Ciências. He also witnessed a *sangamento* in a village, which he compared to these military dances, and was told that the people were in fact dancing to make war on the Devil; fol. 137.

70. Documents summarized in Wood, *Black Majority*, 318–20.

71. Candler and Northern, "Account of Negroe Insurrection," 235.

72. William H. McNeill, *The Pursuit of Power: Technology, Armed Force and Society since 1000* (Chicago, 1982), 125–39. When fighting with Native Americans, and even during the colonial wars, colonial militias sometimes abandoned these principles, however, much to the chagrin of their professional leaders or opponents.

73. Thornton, "Art of War," 363, 374.

74. The best description involves a southern Kongo army fighting Portuguese-led forces in the mid-eighteenth century; Silva Corrêa, *História de Angola*, 2: 48–62. See the interesting description of tactics in Pinheiro de Lacerda, "Noticia da campanha," 131–32.

FOUR

Slave Runaways in Colonial
North Carolina, 1748–1775

MARVIN L. MICHAEL KAY AND LORIN LEE CARY

When slaves fled, "stole themselves," they dramatically denied the power-lessness defined by their status and challenged the carefully crafted controls their masters molded to regulate the lives, labor, and destinies of human property.[1] Slaves probably frequently understood the political implications of their actions, no matter how psychologically battered or physically threatened, maltreated, or constrained they might be and no matter how different their individual reasons for flight.[2] Obsessive reference to runaways in colonial laws demonstrates slave owners' profound anxiety about the problem.[3]

The political manifestations of running away had universal significance among New World slaves, but variations in geography, demography, and the social and psychological makeup of individual slave populations affected specific runaway patterns.[4] A number of scholars have analyzed such factors in other mainland British colonies, but none has done so for North Carolina.[5] This essay attempts to fill part of this gap by examining the province's runaways for the years 1748–1775. It compares North Carolina runaways with those from neighboring Virginia and South Carolina to clarify the North Carolina story, to identify broader implications, and to buttress statistics obtained from a too limited sample. Unlike North Carolina, more substantial samples are available for bordering colonies.[6]

Slaves who ran off to or formed maroon settlements best illustrate the importance of setting as well as the political dimensions of running away. At times these slaves settled among Indians or sought the security offered by other European powers such as the Spanish in Florida. Because they were closer to both the Spanish and the Indians in Florida than were the slaves of

North Carolina or Virginia, many South Carolina slaves successfully fled southward. As a result, confrontations between runaways and whites frequently occurred. Such tensions, in turn, tended to make South Carolina slaves particularly receptive to open revolt, as was the case in the Stono Rebellion of 1739.[7] The more limited and dangerously unpredictable chances of escape to the westward and the Cherokee, on the other hand, normally constrained North Carolina's slaves.[8]

Other distinctive opportunities for maroons in South Carolina led to further differences between slave experiences there and in colonies to the north. The economic immaturity and the relative absence of a political and legal infrastructure in the South Carolina backcountry in the 1750s and 1760s created a milieu in which whites and some blacks, a portion of them runaway slaves, lived as hunters and marginal farmers and joined together to practice social banditry. Through direct action and the establishment of legal and political institutions, the Regulators—more substantial farmers importantly tied to the norms and values of commercial agriculture and the potentialities of slavery—sought to subdue the counterculture that threatened them.[9] Although divided by other problems during this period, North Carolina's backcountry ordinarily was made secure against such social banditry, as was Virginia's, by a well-organized system of county courts, militias, and constabularies.[10]

Yet, neither Virginia nor North Carolina was impervious to problems caused by maroons. The Great Dismal Swamp, stretching southward from Norfolk, Virginia, to Edenton in the Albemarle Sound region of North Carolina, was an ideal hideout.[11] Runaways deep in the watery isolation of the swamp were "perfectly safe, and with the greatest facility elude the most diligent search of their pursuers," J.F.D. Smyth noted in 1784, and blacks had lived there "for twelve, twenty, or thirty years and upwards, subsisting . . . upon corn, hogs, and fowls . . ."[12] If by chance they were discovered, Elkanah Watson observed in 1777, "they could not be approached with safety" because of their belligerence.[13]

Regions other than those within the Great Dismal Swamp were also threatened by groups of runaways. In September, 1767, the New Hanover County court in North Carolina learned "that upwards of Twenty runaway Slaves in a body Arm'd . . . are now in this County . . ." The court promptly ordered "that the Sheriff do immediately raise the power of the County not to be less than Thirty Men well Arm'd to go in pursuit of the said runaway slaves and that the said Sheriff be impowered to Shoot to kill and destroy all such of the said runaway Slaves as shall not Surrender themselves."[14] Since the records are silent beyond this report, it is unlikely that a confrontation took place between the runaways and the posse comitatus. Perhaps the slaves escaped or returned to South Carolina.

Still, North Carolina slaves apparently had fewer opportunities than South Carolina slaves to form maroon communities, and this situation helped to restrict the growth of conditions necessary to spark a revolt.[15] But this did not deny political dimensions to running off, or prevent close interrelationships between running away and other forms of slave resistance in North Carolina, or elsewhere.

The matter may be understood even more holistically. Slaves lived organic lives in both a psychological and sociological sense, as do all human beings in touch with reality. To whatever degree they compartmentalized elements of their existence, they integrated their experiences and comprehended the intricate interrelationships that exist among institutions, roles, values, and behavior. Slaves thus interwove in complex, profound, if often hidden ways, patterns of resistance and adjustment that historians commonly view as disparate slave responses to bondage: murder, arson, sabotage, flight, truancy, as well as a sustaining religiosity and powerful marital, familial, and communal ties. Confronted by apparently identical or similar situations, some slaves resisted and others did not; some ran off and others murdered or committed suicide; and the actions of individuals could also vary dramatically over time.[16]

Running away, therefore, offers important insights into the psychological and social situations that impelled many slaves to resist bondage. Why, how, when, and to what destinations did slaves try to escape? Quantifying the runaways' behavior is difficult. There are few extant records for North Carolina that shed light on these fundamental questions. Yet as this analysis will demonstrate, there are several possible explanations for such behavior.

Newspapers are the richest sources of information on runaways in every colony. Unfortunately, the surviving issues of colonial North Carolina newspapers are scattered unevenly across the years, are not properly representative of the several regions in the province, and account for under 7 percent of the issues published between 1748 and 1775.[17] The practices followed by masters to recapture their runaways compound the problem. First, owners living closest to where the existing newspapers were published were most likely to advertise.[18] Second, owners wherever they lived tended to advertise as a last resort, except when they lived near a newspaper and thought their runaways were lurking about the neighborhood. Generally, owners first relied upon their own devices and the services of the county courts to retrieve runaways.[19] Jacob Wilkinson of Wilmington typified this approach. In November, 1766, he wrote Colonel Alexander McAllister that his "Negro Fellow Jack" had run off and was probably headed for Cumberland County. Wilkinson, who had purchased Jack there, urged McAllister to "Scheame so as to have him apprehended" and promised to pay the costs involved.[20] For these reasons it is impossible to extrapolate from the 134 cited runaways to determine approximately how many slaves actually ran off during this period.

Data deficiencies also prevent a quantitative determination of the effects of the growing Revolutionary crisis upon runaway patterns in the colony. Since 30 percent of the runaways between 1748 and 1775 escaped during the last three years of the survey, for instance, it might be concluded that the

TABLE 1

Frequency Distribution of Ages and Median Age
of Seventy-One Runaways in North Carolina, 1748–1775

Age-Year	Number	
7.0[a]	2	
10.0[b]	1	
10.5	1	
18.0[c]	6	
20.0	5	
21.0	1	
22.0	3	
23.0	3	
24.0	2	
24.5	1	
25.0	5	
26.0	2	
27.0	1	
27.5	2	
28.0	4	Median Age=28
30.0	8	
31.0	1	
32.5	1	
35.0	5	
37.0	1	
37.5[d]	3	
38.0	2	
39.0	1	
40.0	4	
45.0	3	
50.0	1	
51+[e]	2	

[a]Two runaways were listed only as "child."
[b]This slave simply was listed as a "girl."
[c]Includes four runaways designated only as "young."
[d]These slaves were listed only as "Younger than 40."
[e]These runaways were designated as "Elderly" and "Old."

crisis prompted slaves to run off in greater numbers. A more plausible explanation is that 37 percent of the extant North Carolina newspapers date from these same three years, 1773–1775.[21]

Whatever diachronic trends actually occurred, the paucity of available data also hinders a social and psychological description of the runaways. The most detailed information appears in formal outlaw notices for 10 runaways and in advertisements placed by masters of 61 runaways. Newspaper notices for 39 captured fugitives and 1 advertisement placed by a sheriff about an escape contain much less information but are more detailed than the brief references to 23 other runaways that appear in county court minutes, records of the colony's Committee of Public Claims, private correspondence, an inventory, and a newspaper story.

Information most often included in these diverse sources concerns readily observable characteristics—sex, ability to speak English, and age, in that order. Masters and captors alike also noted traits such as family ties, scars, height, color, and demeanor and often commented in varying detail upon motives for flight and possible destinations. Occupations were listed when they distinguished particular runaways from others and hence served as important clues to identification.[22] Occasionally, bits of detail about the runaways' perspectives appear in these sources.

At times African origins are cited in the notices, but most often one must infer African nativity from a combination of characteristics such as scarification and the degree of facility in English. Masters noted origins other than African only when that information might lead to capture. For instance, a Virginia-raised slave might be thought to be headed for his home plantation. The origins of less than half of the runaways could be learned.[23]

Despite the limitations of the data, it is likely that the resultant samples fairly accurately reflect for the years 1748 to 1775 the runaways' actual ages, sex distribution, occupational characteristics, and geographical origins. The ages of North Carolina runaways correspond with the pattern in other colonies: They were disproportionately young adults, 20 to 35 years of age (see table 1). Forty-four (62 percent) of North Carolina's runaways were in this age category, although this population group comprised only about 30 percent of the colony's slave population. Slaves 36 years of age and older ran away slightly more frequently than their percentage of the population would indicate: 24 percent of the runaways and 20 percent of the colony's slave population. At the other extreme, slaves under 20 comprised about 50 percent of the slave population but only 14 percent of North Carolina's runaways (see table 1).[24]

The vast majority of slave runaways in North Carolina, 89 percent, were males. This is identical with Lathan A. Windley's and Gerald W. Mullin's estimates for Virginia, but Windley, Philip D. Morgan, and Daniel C. Littlefield compute percentages for males in South Carolina that range from 7 to 11 percentage points less than was the case in the two more northern provinces (see table 2). Whatever the cause of these differences, since male preponderance among runaways is far greater than sex ratios would suggest in all the surveyed colonies, other factors must substantially explain this disparity. Indeed, South Carolina with the highest sex ratios also had the lowest discrepancy between male and female runaways.[25]

Familial considerations influenced many runaway slaves, inducing some to flee in order to join spouses, families, or prospective mates. The death of an owner or a direct sale of slaves, both of which often led to the separation of spouses or, more likely, children from parents, was significantly related to slave runaway patterns. The effects of such uprootings are suggested by the

TABLE 2

Distribution of North Carolina, South Carolina, and Virginia Runaways by Cohort and Gender

Province and Period	Number and Percentage of Males	Number and Percentage of Females
North Carolina[a]		
1748–1775	114 (89.1%)	14 (10.9%)
South Carolina[b]		
1732–1739	422 (81.9%)	93 (18.1%)
1740–1749	492 (79.3%)	128 (20.7%)
1750–1759	675 (77.7%)	194 (22.3%)
1760–1769	1,208 (85.6%)	203 (14.4%)
1770–1779	1,605 (83.8%)	310 (16.2%)
Total	4,402 (82.6%)	928 (18.4%)
South Carolina[c]		
1732–1775	3,147 (82.4%)	671 (17.6%)
South Carolina[d]		
1732–1774	1,360 (78.1%)	381 (21.9%)
Virginia[e]		
1730–1774	659 (88.8%)	83 (11.2%)
Virginia[f]		
1736–1801	1,138 (89.0%)	141 (11.0%)

[a]The gender of 6 of North Carolina's 134 runaways could not be determined.
[b]Extrapolated from table 12 in Philip D. Morgan, "Black Society in the Low Country, 1760–1810," in Ira Berlin and Ronald Hoffman (eds.), *Slavery and Freedom in the Age of the American Revolution* (Charlottesville: University Press of Virginia, 1983), 100, hereinafter cited as Morgan, "Black Society in the Lowcountry."
[c]Daniel C. Littlefield, *Rice and Slaves: Ethnicity and the Slave Trade in Colonial South Carolina* (Baton Rouge: Louisiana State University Press, 1981), 144, hereinafter cited as Littlefield, *Rice and Slaves*. The gender of 52 slaves in his sample could not be determined.
[d]Lathan A. Windley, "Profile of Runaway Slaves in Virginia and South Carolina from 1730 through 1787" (unpublished doctoral dissertation, University of Iowa, 1974), 65, hereinafter cited as Windley, "Profile of Runaway Slaves." The gender of 1 slave could not be determined.
[e]Windley, "Profile of Runaway Slaves," 65. The gender of 14 slaves could not be determined.
[f]Gerald W. Mullin, *Flight and Rebellion: Slave Resistance in Eighteenth-Century Virginia* (New York: Oxford University Press, 1972), 89, 103, hereinafter cited as Mullin, *Flight and Rebellion.*

fact that over a third of the skilled slaves and 17 percent of the field-hand runaways had been owned by more than one master.[26]

Many owners acknowledged that slaves ran off to be with mates or families.[27] George Moore advised readers of the *Virginia Gazette*, for example, that Bristol, a field hand, "is supposed to have made his way for *Richmond* county, in VIRGINIA, where he has three brothers, whom the subscriber sold to Col. Tayloe, one of his Majesty's Council." Jacob Wilkinson of New Hanover wrote a friend in Cumberland County that his field hand, Jack, whom he had recently purchased, was "undoubtedly" headed in that direction as "I was told When I bought him that he was about getting a molatto wench of Jeff Williams for a Wife . . ." Five other North Carolina field hands fled, their masters indicated, chiefly for family reasons. Another 17 North Carolina field hands ran off as familial groups: 3 couples, a father and a son, and 2 families consisting of 4 and 5 members respectively. Presumably family reasons also played important roles in prompting their escapes.[28] Among field hands, therefore, at least one fifth of the slaves who ran away probably did so to maintain family relationships. Yet, this already high figure is clearly an underestimate. Given the masters' desire to pinpoint where the runaways might be, it was logical for them simply to designate where the slaves' previous owners lived without including information about the slaves' families. This practice apparently explains why, in the small available sample for nonfield slaves, advertisements for 6 of these runaways (35 percent of the sample) list information about the slaves' previous owners, while in only one instance involving a domestic, did the master imply that familial ties might have motivated flight.[29]

The great importance of marriage and the family to slaves and the consequent large number of slaves who ran away to rejoin spouses and kin also help to explain the predominance of males among runaways. Since husbands and fathers usually were the ones separated from their families, it was they who most often ran off to be reunited with wives and kin. The converse was also true. Marital and familial obligations limited the number of female slaves who ran away. Since females most frequently remained behind with those members of slave families not sold or sent off, that which drove males to run away prevented females from doing so.

Males also ran away in greater numbers because their experiences tended to enhance their knowledge of the countryside and their social sophistication to a greater extent than was the case among females. Males probably were hired out more frequently, and only males worked on the roads and were boatmen, ferrymen, guides, porters, and teamsters. Particular job skills, especially artisanal, often made it easier for males to be hired as "free laborers" than for females who, on the average, had fewer marketable skills. Male field hands even could pass more readily as free blacks because employers were more inclined to hire them than female hands. The possibilities, therefore, either prompted or favored male runaways in what was at best an extremely risky enterprise.

TABLE 3

Slave Runaways in North Carolina, 1748–1775, by Occupation and Sex[a]

Gender	Occupation	Number	Percentage
Both	Field hands	117	87.3
	Artisans	13	9.7
	Watermen	3	2.2
	Domestics	1	0.8
	Total	134	100.0
Males	Field hands	102	85.7
	Artisans	13	10.9
	Watermen	3	2.5
	Domestics	1	0.8
	Total	119	99.9
Females	Field hands	15	100.0
	Artisans	0	0
	Watermen	0	0
	Domestics	0	0
	Total	15	100.0

[a]The sex of six field hands could not be determined. They were prorated between male and female field-hand slaves in accordance with their respective percentages of the total numbers of field hands.

While North Carolina's small runaway sample makes suspect an analysis of the frequency distribution of various occupations among the colony's runaways, most of the findings in this article appear plausible when comparatively analyzed with those for colonies for which larger samples have been compiled. Field hands in North Carolina ran away in numbers slightly less than their proportion of the colony's slave population would suggest, comprising about 87 percent of the runaways and perhaps 90 percent of the slave population (see tables 3 and 4). Although some of the sex-specific details between the two colonies differ, these figures closely parallel what occurred in South Carolina where field slaves ran away in numbers about 1.5 percent less than one would predict from their proportion of the slave population (see tables 5 and 6).

Domestics ran off in North Carolina in relatively few numbers, comprising 0.8 percent of the colony's runaways and 3.7 percent of the slave population. This ratio of about 1 to 5, however, is suspect because of the especially small sample involved. South Carolina's statistics, obtained from a much more substantial sample, reveal that domestics ran away roughly in

TABLE 4

Occupational Breakdown of North Carolina's Male and Female Slaves on the Pollock Plantations, 1770–1809[a]

Gender	Occupation	Number	Percentage
Both	Field hands	145	90.1
	Artisans	9	5.6
	Watermen (Ferryman)	1	0.6
	Domestics	6	3.7
	Total	161	100.0
Males	Field hands	70	87.5
	Artisans	8	10.0
	Watermen (Ferryman)	1	1.3
	Domestics	1	1.3
	Total	80	100.1
Females	Field hands	75	92.6
	Artisans (Weaver)	1	1.2
	Watermen	0	0
	Domestics	5	6.2
	Total	81	100.0

[a]Table 4 is based on lists of slaves owned by the Pollock family between 1770 and 1809. These slaves worked on at least three plantations: Mount Rose, Connecanara, and Looking Glass. The Pollocks were one of the oldest and wealthiest families in eastern North Carolina. A total of 161 slaves of working age were included in this sample. The sample is admittedly biased for a province-wide analysis. It overestimates nonfield slaves and represents large plantations in later years. Yet, it provides the most complete available data. See List of Negroes at Mount Rose, March 27, 1809, List of Negroes at Connecanara and Looking Glass, March 27, 1809, and Inventory of "Sundry Negroe Slaves" by Thomas Pollock, March 27, 1770, recorded at New Bern, May 25, 1770, Private Collections, Thomas Pollock Papers, PC 31.1, Archives, Division in Archives and History, Raleigh.

proportion to their percentage of the colony's slave population. Perhaps, then, too much should not be made of the discrepancy revealed by North Carolina's statistics.

It is essential that a sex-specific analysis be used for artisans because almost all were males, and it was preponderantly male slaves who ran off. In North Carolina male artisans fled in slightly greater numbers (just under 11 per-cent of the male runaways) than their proportion of the male slave popula-tion (10 percent). A substantially smaller percentage ran off in South Carolina: there they totaled about 8 percent of the male runaways but 12.3 percent of the colony's male slave population.

These findings do not substantiate Gerald W. Mullin's arguments that acculturated slaves, especially those with skills, chose to flee slavery in

TABLE 5

Occupational Breakdown of South Carolina's Male and Female Runaway Slaves, 1732–1779[a]

Gender	Occupation	Number	Percentage
Both	Field hands	4,612	87.1
	Artisans	352	6.6
	Watermen	187	3.5
	Domestics	100	1.9
	Town	27	0.5
	Agriculture	8	0.2
	Miscellaneous	12	0.2
	Total	5,298	100.0
Males	Field hands	3,746	85.5
	Artisans	352	8.0
	Watermen	187	4.3
	Domestics	54	1.2
	Town	21	0.5
	Agriculture	8	0.2
	Miscellaneous	12	0.3
	Total	4,380	100.0
Females	Field hands	866	94.3
	Artisans	0	0
	Watermen	0	0
	Domestics	46	5.0
	Town	6	0.7
	Agriculture	0	0
	Miscellaneous	0	0
	Total	918	100.0

[a]Table 5 is an extrapolation of tables 12 and 13b in Morgan, "Black Society in the Lowcountry," 100, 102. Morgan included a category "hired slaves" (22 males and 10 females) within his "tradesmen" (artisan) grouping. These slaves have been omitted since it is equally possible that they were field hands.

disproportionately large numbers because of greater chances of escaping successfully. Moreover, it is questionable if his figures for Virginia's artisans and domestics, equaling respectively 14.8 and 7.8 percent of the slaves who ran away during the period 1736–1801 (see table 7), actually support his contentions, for he does not estimate the two groups' numbers in the colony's slave population. Indeed, given Virginia's comparative economic maturity and the fact that Mullin calculates occupational patterns for runaway male slaves only, it is quite possible that his reckonings—at least for the runaway

TABLE 6

Occupational Breakdown of South Carolina's Male and Female Inventoried Slaves, 1730–1779[a]

Gender	Occupation	Number	Percentage
Both	Field hands	9,969	88.7
	Artisans	809	7.2
	Watermen	110	1.0
	Domestics	249	2.2
	Town	10	0.1
	Agriculture	88	0.8
	Miscellaneous	5	0.0
	Total	11,240	100.0
Males	Field hands	5,502	83.7
	Artisans	809	12.3
	Watermen	110	1.7
	Domestics	53	0.8
	Town	10	0.2
	Agriculture	88	1.3
	Miscellaneous	5	0.1
	Total	6,577	100.1
Females	Field hands	4,467	95.8
	Artisans	0	0
	Watermen	0	0
	Domestics	196	4.2
	Town	0	0
	Agriculture	0	0
	Miscellaneous	0	0
	Total	4,663	100.0

[a]Table 6 is an extrapolation of tables 11 and 13a in Morgan, "Black Society in the Lowcountry," 99, 101.

artisans—are commensurate with their proportion of the slave population. Such a conclusion is less likely for domestics who ran off; it is doubtful that they comprised as much as 8 percent of the male slave population.

An investigation of watermen who fled slavery adds to the element of doubt. North Carolina's statistics are again suspect because of the small sample. Since watermen were males, a sex-specific analysis is once more required, with only 1.3 percent of the colony's slaves reckoned as watermen in contrast with 2.5 percent of its runaways. These findings, however, are similar to those for South Carolina, where watermen comprised 1.7 percent of the male slave population but 4.3 percent of the colony's runaways (see

TABLE 7

Slave Runaways in Virginia by Cohort, Work, and Origin

	1730–1787[a]		1736–1801[b]	
	Number	*Percentage*	*Number*	*Percentage*
Work				
Artisans	163	14.6	168	14.8
Watermen	58	5.2	85	7.5
Domestics	89	8.0	89	7.8
Industrial	0	0	17	1.5
Miscellaneous	9	0.8	0	0
Field	795	71.4	779	68.4
Total	1,114	100.0	1,138	100.0

	1730–1774[a]		1775–1787[a]		1736–1801[b]	
	Number	*Percentage*	*Number*	*Percentage*	*Number*	*Percentage*
Origin						
Mainland colonies	165	59.1	70	68.0	1,113	87.0
Africa	88	31.5	26	25.2	141	11.0
West Indies	26	9.3	7	6.8	25	2.0
Total	279	99.9	103	100.0	1,279	100.0

[a]Data adapted from Windley, "Profile of Runaway Slaves," 68, 70, 71, 138. Windley gives occupational breakdowns for males only. He could not determine the national origins of 279 and 103 slaves respectively for the years 1730–1774 and 1775–1787. Moreover, for the two time periods Windley respectively gives figures of 114 and 33 "non-country" born slaves, i.e., slaves not born in the thirteen colonies. For purposes of this analysis the "non-country" slaves have been distributed according to the relative proportions of Africans and West Indians among those runaways whose origins were specified. Windley's discussion of facility with English is not comparable with this analysis.
[b]Mullin, *Flight and Rebellion,* 94–96, 103–105, 108–109. Mullin's occupational breakdown for runaways is only done for male slaves. He does not attempt to determine occupational distribution for the total slave population. His discussion of the slaves' facility with English is not comparable with this analysis.

tables 5 and 6). Despite the lack of comparative figures concerning the percentage of slaves who were watermen in Virginia, Windley's and Mullin's percentages for these runaways, 5.2 and 7.5 respectively, are sufficiently high to suggest that watermen there also ran off in disproportionately large numbers (see table 7).

Special characteristics prompted watermen to run away in large numbers and to do so with relative success. As with artisans and domestics, they had

TABLE 8

Slave Runaways in North Carolina, 1748–1775, by Origin and Facility with English

	Number	Percentage
Origin[a]		
Mainland colonies	26	42.6
Africa	33	54.1
West Indies	2	3.3
Total	61	100.0
Facility with English[b]		
Good	54	53.5
Some	33	32.7
None	14	13.9
Total	101	100.1

[a]The national origins for 73 slaves in the sample of 134 could not be determined.
[b]The facility with English for 33 slaves in the sample of 134 could not be determined.

the advantage of being relatively acculturated, and like artisans they were able to sell their skills on the free labor market more readily than most other slaves. Even so, because of their preferred jobs and status, all three groups— watermen, artisans, and domestics—had more to lose than did field slaves if they ran off. Although the skilled slaves' very knowledge of whites added to their capacity to escape successfully, it could paradoxically raise their level of apprehension. Skilled slaves understood precisely the power of whites and whites' willingness to use it, if pressed, without stint of violence. The special talents of watermen, their boating skills, and especially their geographical sophistication, nevertheless mitigated those inhibitions and enabled them to run off with uncommon frequency. Lastly, there is some evidence to suggest a high incidence of Africans among watermen.[30] Because Africans tended to run off with disproportionate frequency, the probability of watermen absconding was compounded.

Field slaves in the Carolinas, despite slender chances of success, fled in numbers only slightly less than their proportion of the slave population. Perhaps they chose to flee in such large numbers because they were less cognizant of the full scope of white power, had fewer material advantages to lose than skilled slaves and had only limited legal alternatives to relieve harsh circumstances. But perhaps of even greater significance, a larger number of field hands were Africans.

African-born slaves in the Chesapeake declined from about one third of

TABLE 9

Slave Runaways in South Carolina by Cohort, Origin, and Facility with English

	1732–1774[a]		1775–1787[b]		1732–1775[c]		1760–1775[d]	
	Number	Percentage	Number	Percentage	Number	Percentage	Number	Percentage
Origin								
Mainland colonies	209	33.0	104	55.3	364	27.4	–	–
Africa	386	61.0	76	40.4	907	68.3	–	68.5[e]
West Indies	38	6.0	8	4.3	58	4.4	–	–
Total	633	100.0	188	100.0	1,329	100.1		68.5
Facility with English								
Good	–	–	–	–	348	44.6	–	–
Some	–	–	–	–	200	25.6	–	–
None	–	–	–	–	232	29.7	–	–
Total					780	99.9		

[a]Windley, "Profile of Runaway Slaves," 68, 70, 71. Windley could not determine national origins for 1,109 and 1,601 slaves respectively for the years 1732–1774 and 1775–1787. He does not deal with the slaves' facility with English.
[b]See note a above.
[c]Littlefield, *Rice and Slaves*, 129–131, 151–158. Littlefield could not determine the national origins or facility with English respectively for 2,536 and 3,090 slaves.
[d]Morgan, "Black Society in the Lowcountry," 92. Morgan only gives the percentages of the runaways who were Africans and does not deal with the runaways' facility with English.
[e]Mean of means for years 1760, 1770, 1775. Morgan, "Black Society in the Lowcountry," 92.

the adult slave population in the 1750s to one tenth in the 1770s. In North Carolina during these years the proportion dropped from two thirds to one third. In South Carolina Africans constituted 45 percent of the adult slave population in the 1760s and 49.1 percent in 1775. During the years 1730–1774, Windley estimates that about 31.5 percent of Virginia's runaways were Africans, suggesting a comparatively high propensity for flight. Mullin presents a considerably lower estimate, 11 percent, which perhaps can only partially be explained by the different time span he reviews, 1736–1801 (see table 7). North Carolina's percentage of African runaways between 1748 and 1775, 54.1 percent, accords with the province's larger African slave population and the relative frequency with which Africans escaped (see table 8).[31] Although estimates for South Carolina vary somewhat with the investigator and the time span studied—40.4 percent to 68.5 percent for the period 1732–1787—the high percentages also tend to reflect the comparatively large number of Africans in the colony's slave population and their greater propensity than creole slaves to abscond (see table 9).[32]

Africans, then, despite their greater difficulties of traveling in a strange land, communicating, and passing as free, still ran off in relatively large numbers. They did so because of the especially wrenching separations and traumas they had experienced. Torn from their families, parents, and spouses, shipped to a foreign continent, treated as objects, sold to masters who could not understand them, often isolated within the slave community, they reacted predictably. If opportunities existed, they fled. When they did, they fell back on their African sense of communality and family and tended to run away in groups.

One third of the North Carolina runaways, all of them field hands, escaped in groups, and 88 percent of the group runaways whose origins are known were African.[33] The presence of so many Africans among the group runaways accounts for the fact that few of these slaves had facility in English. Among the group runaways whose linguistic abilities could be determined, half spoke some English, and fully 36 percent spoke none, while only 14 percent spoke good English (see table 10).

The experience of five Africans, possibly shipmates, who fled from Edward Batchelor of Craven County illustrates both the limits confronting such Africans and their tenacity in the face of adversity. Kakchee, Beebum, Ji, and Sambo Pool, all males, and Peg Manny, an aged female, ran off early one Sunday morning in February, 1775; none spoke English. Batchelor advertised for them the following day, an unusual step but one that produced immediate results. The five managed to travel only ten miles before being captured by William Gatling of Break Creek. But matters did not end there. Two months later two of the men, now described as Kauchee and Boohum, fled again. In the interval, William Gatling had purchased Peg Manny, perhaps with the reward money, and Batchelor thought that Kauchee and Boohum would be "lurking about" Gatling's farm.[34] The runaways' fate is not known.

The bulk of North Carolina runaways, 67.2 percent, including 11 identified as African-born field hands, fled alone (see table 10). Caesar, an Angolan, and Jack, an African of unidentified tribal origins, were more experienced with whites than the other Africans who escaped in this fashion: both had had prior owners, Caesar in South Carolina and Jack in Pennsylvania. The other Africans had been in the colony long enough to learn some English, but they undoubtedly shared with those imported more recently the distinct disadvantage of unfamiliarity with whites and their ways. Still, the Africans used their knowledge of the natural world to good advantage, if only temporarily. A Coromantee slave owned by John Dunn of Rowan County, for example, made his way to Wilmington, more than 200 miles to the southeast, before he was captured in August, 1759. Jikowife displayed similar capabilities, escaping after being captured with a *"French* musket" in Chowan County near Mattacomack Creek in June, 1774. Late that August he was recaptured in Hyde County, across Albemarle Sound. Quamino, the only individual runaway who clearly spoke no English, may have had more success. Only 4 feet, 10 inches tall, this dynamic thirty-year-old African with filed teeth and country marks fled in August, 1774, with "a Collar about his Neck with Two Prongs, marked P.G. [Public Gaol], and an iron on each leg." Ten months later Henry Young of Wilmington gave up hope that Quamino would falter in his bid for freedom and placed an advertisement in the *North Carolina Gazette.*[35]

TABLE 10

Origin and Facility with Language among 134 North Carolina Runaways, 1748–1775, Related to Occupation and Mode of Escape

Origin	How Escaped[a]				Number and % Who Were Individual Runaways[b]		Number and % Who Were Group Runaways	
	Alone		Group		Including	Excluding	Including	Excluding
	Nonfield	Field	(All Field)	Total	Unknown	Unknown	Unknown	Unknown
Mainland	5	19	2	26	24	24	2	2
colonies	19.2%	73.1%	7.7%	100%	26.7%	66.7%	4.5%	8.0%
Africa	0	11	22	33	11	11	22	22
		33.3%	66.7%	100%	12.2%	30.6%	50.0%	88.0%
Elsewhere	0	1	1	2	1	1	1	1
		50.0%	50.0%	100.0%	1.1%	2.8%	2.3%	4.0%
Unknown	12	42	19	73	54	-	19	-
	16.4%	57.5%	26.0%	99.9%	60%		43.2%	
Total	17	73	44	134	90	36	44	25
	12.7%	54.5%	32.8%	100%	100%	100.1%	100%	100%
Facility with English								
Good	16	33	5	54	49	49	5	5
	29.7%	61.1%	9.2%	100%	54.4%	75.4%	11.4%	13.9%
Some	0	15	18	33	15	15	18	18
		45.5%	54.5%	100%	16.7%	23.1%	40.9%	50.0%
None	0	1	13	14	1	1	13	13
		7.1%	92.9%	100%	1.1%	1.5%	29.5%	36.1%
Unknown	1	24	8	33	25	-	8	-
	30%	72.7%	24.2%	99.9%	27.7%		18.2%	
Total	17	73	44	134	90	65	44	36
	12.7%	54.5%	32.8%	100%	99.9%	100%	100%	100%

[a]This portion of the table correlates the number and percentage of slaves who escaped individually or in groups with their national origins and facility with English. The "total" for each category equals the full number of slaves, nonfield slaves and field hands, who escaped individually and in groups. For example, among the 26 slaves identified as being born in the mainland colonies, 5 (19.2 percent) nonfield slaves fled alone, 19 (73.1 percent) field hands escaped individually, and 2 (7.7 percent) field hands ran off together. The totals for all categories equal the percentage of field hands or nonfield slaves, regardless of their origins or facility with English, who fled as individuals or in groups. Thus, among the 134 runaways, all 17 of the nonfield slaves who ran off (12.7 percent) fled alone, 73 of the field hands fled alone (54.5 percent), but 44 field hands fled in groups (32.8 percent).

[b]This portion of the table correlates for each category the number and percentage of slaves who ran off as individuals or in groups with their national origins and facility with English. It does so by both including and excluding in the calculations those slaves who cannot be identified with respect to their national origins or facility with English. Totals here equal the number who escaped either individually or in groups for all categories. For example, among the 90 slaves who ran off individually, 49 (54.5 percent) could speak good English, 15 (16.7 percent) spoke some English, 1 (1.1 percent) spoke no English and the linguistic capabilities for 25 (27.7 percent) could not be determined. Or, calculating only for those whose linguistic ability could be discerned, 75.4 percent of the individual runaways could speak good English, 23.1 percent spoke some English, and 1.5 percent spoke no English.

Quamino, Jikowife, and the other Africans were atypical of the 90 North Carolina slaves who fled as individuals. Most were either American-born and spoke English well or had distinctive qualities or needs. In all, 16 nonfield slaves and 33 field hands handled English easily among the 101 slaves whose facility with English could be determined. Another 15 slaves, all of them field hands, spoke some English. Thus, over 70 percent of the slaves who ran off individually either spoke English well or could make themselves understood. Similarly, 64.5 percent of the individual runaways whose origins can be determined were born in the Americas.

The national origins and linguistic patterns that prevailed among runaway artisans, in turn, necessarily reflect how slave artisans were selected to pursue their trades and their subsequent special characteristics as slaves. Chosen from those who apparently were best equipped to learn and benefit from their experiences, slave craftsmen tended to be young creoles who handled English with relative skill and quite possibly often had fathers or other relatives who already were artisans.[36] Thus, the records reveal that even the youngest of the skilled runaways spoke English well. Eighteen-year-old George, for instance, was so proficient with the language that William Person described him as "a very artful Fellow" who would "impose upon any Person that will credit what he says," a lesson his master must have learned firsthand. Over time the varied work experiences of such slaves, who were often hired out, and their relative freedom to move from place to place further enhanced their command of English, their knowledge of geography, and their ability to deal with whites. Along the way they sometimes picked up other skills that would facilitate escape. Thomas Boman, for instance, could "read, write, and cypher."[37]

Understanding whites, language skills, and the consequent capacity to deceive whites obviously enlarged the chances of nonfield slaves for successful escape. Yet, many field hands shared such qualities. Since about 75 to 85 percent of the slaves outside the Cape Fear region lived on units of less than 20 slaves during the years 1748–1775, interracial contact must have been common.[38] Field hands also were hired out, worked on road gangs, or acquired experience with whites as a result of a change of owners. These diverse experiences help to account for the differences in the patterns among individual and group runaways. Only 2 of the 21 field hands identifiable as American-born fled in groups, both of them children who ran off with their parents.[39] The other 19, all of whom spoke good English, ran off by themselves.

Why some field hands fled alone related not only to origin or facility with English but also to how they perceived their situations. As already seen, at least 7 fled to be with mates or families. Two others, both of whom spoke good English, fled after their masters died. One headed back to his home plantation and the other, a middle-aged male who had been hired out, was thought to be "lurking about." Two young men, also believed to be "lurking about," fled at times of peak work. Two other males went "visiting" friends or relatives.[40] Seven of the field-hand runaways, however, set out to pass for free, a goal that must have seemed easier to achieve as an individual.

This last clustering of field-hand runaways, all but one clearly American-born, was unique in several respects. Included were one Negro born in Virginia, a mustee woman, a mustee male, a full-blooded Indian male, and a woman born in New England.[41] Because of their distinct backgrounds and experiences, they undoubtedly confronted the prospect of passing for free in a white-dominated world with a greater self-confidence than most field hands. Each of them had social and verbal skills similar to those of all non-field-hand runaways. Like artisans, they had a better chance of succeeding in passing for free than did the bulk of field-hand runaways. Not all eluded capture, of course, but their decision to run off and the methods they used to escape reflected a rational assessment of the risks involved balanced against their talents and needs.

Artisans normally were acculturated, but along with mariners, riverboatmen and other skilled slaves who were not field hands, they also possessed highly salable expertise. Since their success in passing as free workers hinged upon not calling undue attention to themselves, all 16 artisan runaways as well as all the riverboatmen and sailors ran off as individuals (see table 5). Although information is not available for most runaways, many artisans and sailors made use of their special abilities by seeking sanctuary in the relative anonymity of towns and at considerable distances from their homes in order to ply their trades.[42]

In puzzling over the question of why some slaves chose to flee enslavement, it is not surprising that some white North Carolinians, despite overwhelming evidence to the contrary, doubted that slaves could plot their own escapes. Edward Batchelor, a merchant in New Bern, Craven County, for instance, announced with opaque if familiar certainty that the five "newly imported" slaves who escaped from him in February, 1775, had not done so on their own. "As they are incapable of muttering a word of English, have [been] extremely well fed, and very little worked," he observed, "it is surmised they have been invegelied away by some infamously principled Persons, of a fairer Complexion, but darker Disposition than theirs." Robert Snow of Cape Fear lacked Batchelor's gift with words but shared his unwillingness to attribute self-motivation to slaves. When London and Bess ran off in the fall of 1755, Snow concluded that they had been "decoyed away" by a former overseer.[43]

However soothing such fantasies may have been to whites, slaves almost invariably determined when they would run off, under which circumstances, and what goals they would pursue. If often goaded by anger and despair, they nonetheless attempted to evaluate rationally their options and then plot the particularities of their escapes. This is not to suggest that slaves were not open to examples set by others. They were, and fleeing indentured servants and apprentices may have animated some slaves, just as the converse may be true. Several slaves fled from owners who also had runaway indentured servants. For instance, the Rowan County court in August, 1769, ordered Paul Crosby to serve former sheriff Francis Locke for four extra years after his indenture expired "for absenting himself 2 years. . . ." Two months after Crosby's sentencing three of Locke's slaves also fled.[44] Perhaps the only relationship between these two escapes was the shared resentments against a disliked owner. But it would be strange if the behavior of one group did not affect that of the other. Even where such clear juxtapositions are not evident, slaves undoubtedly were well aware that servants regularly fled from their masters, that in some cases they were never captured, that others—like Crosby—managed to stay out for long periods of time, and that some who were caught fled again.[45] Servants were similarly aware of slave escapes.

Servants and slaves, therefore, acted as role models for one another, and each group affected its peers. Slave runaways by their actions compounded the burden of bondage felt by other slaves while heightening a sense of the possibility of escape. Still, slaves fled for specific reasons. Some sought freedom for its own sake. But they also fled as males or females and within the context of their occupational backgrounds and situational possibilities. Calculating their particular situations, some slaves ran off with designs to obtain more negotiable economic rewards for their labor. Newly imported Africans fled the terrible traumas of slavery, while many slaves escaped to reestablish marital and familial ties. This last, in turn, was related to slave discontent with changes of ownership. What prompted particular slaves varied, but they constantly assessed their situation and the opportunities available to them before deciding on a course of action. For the decision to flee was not an easy one. It involved considerable risk, and perhaps as often as it was spawned by a desire to rejoin families or friends, it heartrendingly demanded departure from a familiar community peopled by friends and family.

The brutality of enslavement at times could offset all other considerations. Evidence of how individual masters treated their slaves appears in a number of newspaper advertisements. Referring with equanimity to marks left by punishments, owners revealed the cruelty to which they subjected their human chattel. Samuel Johnston, noted Revolutionary leader, advertised that his field hand Frank was "branded on the left Buttock with a P," while another master wrote that Bess was "branded in the breast." In such cases the assumption that this information would be useful in identifying the runaways is a revealing commentary on a system designed to strip blacks of personal dignity.[46] Nor did highly prized skilled slaves, for whom larger rewards were tendered, escape such cruelties. Riverboatman Frank's back had "frequently undergone the Discipline of the Whip," as his wealthy master Richard Quince observed.[47]

It is nonetheless not clear in each case that punishment prompted flight. Any number of additional reasons could spark running away, which no amount of punishment could deter. Field hand Frank was an "old Offender and a great thief," who presumably had fled before. Charles's master specified that the brands on his cheeks "were fresh given him by the Person of whom I bought him, and not cured when he left me," raising the possibility that Charles was not only "incorrigible" but that he also fled because of a desire to return "home" to relatives and friends—however brutal his past master.[48]

Bondage also produced psychological scars. Behind the decision to flee, indeed, there sometimes lay a festering frustration born of an acute sense of self-worth and knowledge of the inherent limits of slavery. Some of the riverboatmen displayed behavioral traits such as stuttering that could be interpreted as outward signs of such turmoil, but Thomas Boman, a blacksmith, was "slow of Speech" and Rob, a cooper, had a "flaw of speech, as if he had an impediment. . . ."[49] It is possible, of course, that these "flaws" stemmed from physiological rather than psychological reasons. Other run-

TABLE 11

Dates of Flight and Capture of North Carolina Runaways

Date of Flight[a]	Number	Percentage	Date of Capture[b]	Number	Percentage
February–April	17	29.3	February–April	14	24.6
May–August	15	25.9	May–August	17	29.8
September–November	23	39.6	September–November	20	35.1
December–January	2	5.2	December–January	6	10.5
Total	58	100.0	Total	57	100.0

[a]Dates of flight as given by masters.
[b]Dates of capture were determined from advertisements for captured slaves and from county court and Committee of Claims proceedings involving killed runaways. Where runaways appeared in more than one source, the earliest date was used.

aways, in any case, both field hands and artisans, bore expressions such as "an ill look," which could indicate buried hostility.[50] Ned, a "good sawyer and hewer, and part of a carpenter" with a "very good sense," retained a "bold look" even after repeated brandings before he fled from James Barnes of Halifax County in April, 1768.[51]

Whatever inner conflicts existed, slaves often tried to conceal their animosities. Outward appearance and behavior could be deceptive. As numerous masters learned all too well, slaves could hide their innermost thoughts behind deferential, dissembling, even stuttering masks. The "Negro Wench" Joan, for instance, had "a smiling Countenance," "outlandish" Jack "a pleasant countenance," and a slave who called himself Tom Buck "an uncommon flippant Tongue, full of Complement."[52] All were runaways.

The timing of departure is further evidence of how slaves rationally assessed their opportunities as runaways and often carefully planned their escapes. Masters did not always specify when their slaves had absconded. Indeed, slave owners generally took their time placing notices. But some observations can be drawn from the pattern evident for 58 slaves for whom escape dates were given (see table 11). The most popular periods for running away were the harvesting season of September to November, when 23 slaves (or 40 percent of the 58) fled, followed by February–April, the months during which the slack season ended and spring planting began. Seventeen slaves, or 29 percent, ran off at this time. Another 15 fled during the four months of May to August, and only 3 ran during the winter months of December and January. No significant variation in the timing of escape set nonfield runaways apart from field hands who fled. Most North Carolina runaways thus timed their departures to avoid both work and bad weather. This pattern, however, differs somewhat from the timing of flight among both Virginia and South Carolina runaways (see tables 11 and 12).[53]

TABLE 12

Months of Flight: North Carolina Runaways Compared with Those in South Carolina and Virginia

| | Virginia, 1730–1787[a] | | North Carolina, 1748–1775 | | South Carolina, 1734–1787[a] | |
	Number	Percentage	Number	Percentage	Number	Percentage
February–April	218	24.2	17	29.3	217	20.3
May–August	399	44.2	15	25.9	468	43.7
September–November	178	19.8	23	39.6	215	20.1
December–January	106	11.8	3	5.2	170	15.9
Total	901	100.0	58	100.0	1,070	100.0

[a]Windley, "Profile of Runaway Slaves," 175.

What runaways wore and took with them not only hinted at prior planning, but it also reflected the varying conditions of slaves. Typically, skilled runaways were better clothed and equipped than other runaways. Blacksmith Thomas Boman, however, was unusual even among skilled slaves. He carried away with him "about fifty or sixty Pounds in Cash, and a grey Roan horse, Bridle and Saddle, a Pair of Money-Scales and Weights, and one Pair of Sheets, three Coats, one a Broad-Cloth or Sarge, one a Bear-Skin Cape Coat, of a grey Colour, one a Home-spun Coat, a Blue Jacket, and a great many other Cloaths. . . ."[54] Some field hands, including Africans, wore more than the stock issue, dressed in finery, or carried extra clothing with them to guard against inclement weather and to disguise themselves.[55] Usually, however, field hands fled wearing only the seasonal issue of clothing. Thus, Will wore "Negro Cottens" when he ran off in the spring, whereas Peter and Abraham, who fled in November, wore woolen jackets and trousers and osnaburg shirts. Most recent immigrants had the least clothing of all. This lack of clothing could mean that they discarded what they regarded as cumbersome garments, that they had not had time to accumulate clothes, or that their owners provided a minimal amount of clothing to them, perhaps in the belief that it would hinder their escape. Two Africans captured in Craven County in July, 1767, wore "nothing . . . but an old Negro cloth jacket, and a blue sailors jacket without sleeves," and four other Africans each had nothing on but a "striped Dutch blanket" when captured in October, 1769.[56]

Whether they took little or considerable clothing, North Carolina runaways usually traveled sparely. Quantities of goods would have attracted too much attention. Jemmy, an Ibo, and Jikowife, an African whose tribal origin is not indicated, were atypical: both fled with guns.[57] Wishing not to appear too unusual and lacking access to other forms of transportation, the overwhelming majority of runaways fled on foot. Only two slaves rode off on stolen horses, and apparently two Africans were the only ones who escaped by canoe.[58] Many runaways, whatever their occupation or origin, used the waterways as escape routes and as means of sustenance. Sambo, who fled from a Moravian owner in Wachovia and "had wandered for several weeks in the wilderness along the Catawba River," for instance, "had suffered much from hunger" and was "willingly taken and brought back here." At least twelve other runaways were captured or sought to escape captors near rivers, lakes, or other bodies of water. Sam displayed considerably less willingness than Sambo when he was captured in Craven County; while being taken back to his Johnston County master he "broke out of Custody . . . near the *South-West* Bridge."[59]

The determination of slaves is also apparent when one considers their destinations. Thirty-six of the 100 runaways who were captured or for whom a destination was given tried to or did escape from the province. Included were 29 field hands and 7 nonfield slaves.[60] Whatever their exact purposes may have been collectively these 36 runaways shared many characteristics. Fifteen can be identified as American-born, and they as well as 8 other slaves spoke fluent English. The one identifiable African in this group had had two previous masters in South Carolina, and a West Indian–born slave had been owned in New York. Eleven of the 36 runaways who fled the colony left in groups, and all of them were captured—a family of 4 in South Carolina, a family of 5 in Williamsburg, and 2 males in Middlesex, Virginia.[61] In all, 16 of these runaways, or 44 percent of the 36, were actually captured outside of North Carolina.

The 64 runaways known to have remained in North Carolina stayed for various reasons and displayed no less resolution than those who actually crossed into neighboring colonies. Twelve were thought to be headed for or were actually captured in locations outside, and sometimes at quite a distance from, their home counties. Another 22 slaves were apprehended in North Carolina, their home counties unknown. Finally, 10 of the 64 were thought to be "lurking about" their home plantations or seeking to get to other places within the same county. Whether they lived as outliers or were harbored by relatives and friends, those who stayed close by risked more than recapture. They might also be declared outlaws, which subjected them to possible summary execution. Eleven of the 18 runaways caught in their home counties were killed or committed suicide.[62]

While place of capture is not proof of where runaways intended to go, the 64 slaves who remained in North Carolina differed sharply from the 36 runaways who escaped from the province. All but 2 were field hands, and 17, all Africans, fled in groups. The others—including 7 Africans and 4 American-born slaves, 2 of them artisans—fled alone. Only 4 others, besides the American-born, spoke English well. Twelve spoke some English, and 14 could not speak it at all. Neither the origin nor the facility with English of the remaining slaves could be determined.

In all, 61 field hands and 3 artisans were captured or killed, 48 percent of the 134 North Carolina runaways. Twenty-four of the 33 African-born runaways, or 73 percent, were among those who failed in their bid for freedom. Among the 40 percent captured or killed field hands whose ability to speak English could be determined, only 5, or 9 percent, spoke it well. That Africans and those who spoke little or no English stood a poor chance of escaping is hardly surprising. Those slaves who could manipulate the language and their environment and most readily market their skills stood the best chance of eluding captors.[63]

Slaves in the Americas who ran off, as masters and slaves alike knew, seriously threatened the authority of slave owners and the order necessary for a smooth-functioning and productive labor system. Flight from bondage thus necessarily had significant political implications, which were most evident when slaves joined or formed maroon settlements.

The ability of slaves to flee to maroon communities, however, varied with each region's particular geographic, political, economic, and demographic circumstances. Slaves in North Carolina and Virginia had fewer opportunities than did South Carolina's slaves to establish maroon settlements because they were a minority of each colony's population, were less concentrated on large plantations than slaves in South Carolina, lacked an outlet for escape commensurate with that of Florida, and had county governments organized in their provinces' western regions. Thus, despite frequent escapes to the fastness of the Great Dismal Swamp, North Carolina's and Virginia's slaves, unlike those in South Carolina, did not foment significant eighteenth-century colonial rebellions or seriously become involved in social banditry.

Ecology also helped shape other slave runaway patterns. Males, for instance, heavily predominated among slaves who ran away in all three colonies and probably for similar reasons. Their training prepared them better than female slaves to run off successfully. And since males most frequently were separated from mates or families, it was they who normally escaped to rejoin wives and relatives. Conversely, familial ties and obligations frequently prevented females from absconding. Sex ratios perhaps played some role in explaining this phenomenon; although in South Carolina where sex ratios were highest, males made up a smaller percentage of the runaways, between 78 and 82, than in either North Carolina or Virginia, where 89 percent of the slave runaways were males.

Occupational patterns among runaways in the three colonies, if perhaps less predictable than those concerning gender, do not sustain the argument that acculturated slaves, especially those with marketable skills, ran off in disproportionately large numbers because their chances of escape were greater than those for other slaves. Except in the case of watermen in each of the colonies and domestics in Virginia, skilled slaves in the Carolinas and Virginia did not escape in disproportionately large numbers. Despite their acculturation, marketable skills, and greater capacity to deal with whites, such slaves were inhibited from running off by their relative well-being and their detailed comprehension of the white power apparatus. Nevertheless, the special characteristics of watermen—their boating and geographical skills and the comparatively large proportion of Africans in this occupation—enable them, more than either artisans or domestics, to transcend the fears and inhibitions all three groups shared.

The large number of field slaves who absconded casts further doubt upon an analysis of occupational patterns among runaway slaves that simply stresses the greater proclivity of acculturated and skilled slaves to flee because they more readily could make good their escape. Field hands, at least in North and South Carolina, fled in numbers that were only slightly less than their respective proportions of each colony's total slave population. Despite overwhelming odds against successful escape, field hands were often emboldened to run off because of oppressive conditions aggravated by a comparative lack of lawful means to rectify problems and consequent desperation or heightened frustrations. Moreover, the large number of field hands who were Africans exacerbated the situation, for Africans tended to run off more frequently than did American-born slaves.

Africans, despite the most limited chances of success, fled in disproportionately large numbers in the Carolinas and probably in Virginia because of the special problems that beset them as an uprooted folk. The shock of being enslaved, instead of immobilizing them, spurred many to escape or to resist in other ways. And given their keen sense of communality and desperate need for family and friends to sustain them in the trials of escape, they frequently ran off in groups.

Another major theme in this story is that slaves, in spite of fears, frustrations, or desperation, rationally sensed their situational possibilities and planned their escapes accordingly. Skilled slaves in North Carolina, for instance, fled with the most ample stock of clothes and Africans with the least. Within these two extremes, which were obvious manifestations of the varying conditions of slaves, field hands usually escaped with only the seasonal issue of clothing. The province's slaves, to avoid attracting too much attention, ordinarily took little beside clothing and fled on foot, although waterways often served as effective escape routes.

Records do not reveal the statistical relationship between ill treatment and runaway patterns. Undoubtedly, if some slaves were deterred from running off by maltreatment or the threat of harsh reprisals, others were impelled to leave by the same conditions. Slaves shrewdly chose the most opportune times for flight. They ran off during the seasons when work was hardest and the weather most propitious. In so doing, the skilled and acculturated, more frequently than other runaways in North Carolina, covered long distances, many attempting to leave the colony.

Though their chances of success remained dubious, all slaves ran off seeking to protect what was sacred or inviolable. The fact that they often ended up captured, whipped, tortured, or dead only sadly testifies to the strength of their dreams and the indomitableness of their wills.

NOTES

1. The phrase is from Peter H. Wood, *Black Majority: Negroes in Colonial South Carolina from 1670 through the Stono Rebellion* (New York: Alfred A. Knopf, 1974), 239, hereinafter cited as Wood, *Black Majority*. This work remains, after more than a decade, the premier analysis of colonial slavery. The author's ability to understand and conceptualize the essential characteristics of slavery has been enhanced by Orlando Patterson's recent impressive study: *Slavery and Social Death: A Comparative Study* (Cambridge, Mass.: Harvard University Press, 1982).

2. For an overview of the legal condition of blacks in the thirteen mainland British colonies, see William M. Wiecek, "The Statutory Law of Slavery and Race in the Thirteen Mainland Colonies of British America," *William and Mary Quarterly*, XXXIV (April, 1977), 258–280. See also Elsa V. Goveia, "The West Indian Slave Laws of the Eighteenth Century," *Revista de Ciencias Sociales*, 4 (Marzo, 1960), 75–105; Elsa V. Goveia, *Slave Society in the British Leeward Islands at the End of the Eighteenth Century* (New Haven: Yale University Press, 1965), 152–202; Orlando Patterson, *The Sociology of Slavery: An Analysis of the Origins, Development, and Structure of Negro Slave Society in Jamaica* (London: MacGibbon and Kee, 1967), 70–93, hereinafter cited as Patterson, *The Sociology of Slavery*.

3. Two basic slave and servant codes were passed in North Carolina in 1715 and 1741. Five of the 21 articles in the 1715 law pertained directly to or mentioned runaways, and 22 of the 58 detailed articles of the act of 1741 were devoted to the problem. Walter Clark (ed.), *The State Records of North Carolina* (Winston and Goldsboro: State of North Carolina, 16 volumes, numbered XI–XXVI, 1895–1906), XXIII, 62–66, 191–204, hereinafter cited as Clark, *State Records*. For subsidiary laws passed in 1753, 1758, and 1764, see Clark, *State Records*, XXIII, 388–390, 488–489, 656.

4. For a detailed analysis of slave demography in North Carolina during the colonial period, see Marvin L. Michael Kay and Lorin Lee Cary, "A Demographic Analysis of Colonial North Carolina with Special Emphasis upon the Slave and Black Populations," in Jeffrey J. Crow and Flora J. Hatley (eds.), *Black Americans in North Carolina and the South* (Chapel Hill: University of North Carolina Press, 1984), 71–121, hereinafter cited as Kay and Cary, "A Demographic Analysis of Colonial North Carolina."

5. See, for example, Wood, *Black Majority*, 239–268; Gerald W. Mullin, *Flight and Rebellion: Slave Resistance in Eighteenth-Century Virginia* (New York: Oxford University Press, 1972), 34–123 and notes, hereinafter cited as Mullin, *Flight and Rebellion*.

6. Analyzing this time span makes the research demands manageable. It also stops short of the American Revolution, the severe disruptions of which had momentous effects upon slaves. Fortunately, much of this last question has already been examined by Jeffrey J. Crow in two admirable studies: *The Black Experience in Revolutionary North Carolina* (Raleigh Division of Archives and History, Department of Cultural Resources, 1977), hereinafter cited as Crow, *The Black Experience in Revolutionary North Carolina*; and "Slave Rebelliousness and Social Conflict in North Carolina, 1775 to 1802," *William and Mary Quarterly*, XXXVII (January, 1980), 79–102. See also Peter H. Wood, "'Impatient of Oppression': Black Freedom Struggles on the Eve of White Independence," *Southern Exposure*, 12 (November/December, 1984), 10–16; Sylvia R. Frey, "Between Slavery and Freedom: Virginia Blacks in the American Revolution," *Journal of Southern History*, XLIX (August, 1983), 375–398.

Using statistics from other colonies to bolster the findings of this study has obvious pitfalls. It may be used, for instance, to substantiate intercolonial similarities among runaway patterns while masking differences. But whatever its potential for misapplication, it remains a necessary tool.

7. See Wood, *Black Majority*, 304–326. To argue in the above manner is not to deny that other conditions, especially demographic factors, helped induce slave uprisings in South Carolina. In no other British colony in North America, for instance, were slaves in the majority. Slaves in South Carolina also were most heavily concentrated on large

plantations. See Wood, *Black Majority*, 131–166; Kay and Cary, "A Demographic Analysis of Colonial North Carolina," 71–87; U.S. Bureau of the Census, *Historical Statistics of the United States: Colonial Times to 1957* (Washington, D.C.: Government Printing Office, 1960), series Z 1–19, p. 756.

8. See Theda Perdue's "Red and Black in the Southern Appalachians," *Southern Exposure*, 12 (November/December, 1984), 17–24; *Slavery and the Evolution of Cherokee Society, 1540–1866* (Knoxville: University of Tennessee Press, 1979), especially 36–49.

9. For works on the South Carolina Regulators see Richard J. Hooker (ed.), *The Carolina Backcountry on the Eve of the Revolution: The Journal and Other Writings of Charles Woodmason, Anglican Itinerant* (Chapel Hill: University of North Carolina Press, 1953); Richard Maxwell Brown, *The South Carolina Regulators: The Story of the First Vigilante Movement* (Cambridge, Mass.: Harvard University Press, 1963); Rachel N. Klein, "Ordering the Backcountry: The South Carolina Regulation," *William and Mary Quarterly*, XXXVIII (October, 1981), 661–680. The summary in the text most closely follows the Woodmason narration and Klein analysis. For other South Carolina examples of maroons, see Philip D. Morgan, "Black Society in the Lowcountry, 1760–1810," in Ira Berlin and Ronald Hoffman (eds.), *Slavery and Freedom in the Age of the American Revolution* (Charlottesville: University Press of Virginia, 1983), 138–139, hereinafter cited as Morgan, "Black Society in the Lowcountry."

The term "social bandit" may not appropriately describe the bandits of the South Carolina backcountry, since they do not conform to Eric Hobsbawm's definition of social banditry. In his classic analyses of this form of resistance to authority, he differentiates social bandits from other bandits by noting that the former were "peasant outlaws whom the lord and state regard as criminals but who remain within peasant society" and are viewed by that society "as champions, avengers, fighters for justice, perhaps even leaders of liberation, and in any case as men to be admired, helped and supported." Eric Hobsbawm, *Bandits* (New York: Delacorte Press, 1969), 13–23; Eric Hobsbawm, *Primitive Rebels: Studies in the Archaic Forms of Social Movement in the Nineteenth and Twentieth Centuries* (New York: Frederick A. Praeger, 1959), especially 13–29, hereinafter cited as Hobsbawm, *Primitive Rebels*. Although the term "peasant" can be ascribed with some validity to the farmers of the South Carolina backcountry who lived within a significantly precapitalistic and hierarchical world, it is nonetheless true that the "bandits" of the region, rather than being representative and supportive of the main body of peasants (farmers, Regulators), preyed upon them and, in turn, were bitterly opposed by them. The term, still, appears to be peculiarly applicable to the backcountry bandits in that they emanated from frontier social types—hunters and marginal farmers—who were in the process of being superseded by farmers with more economically mature characteristics. The successful appeal to blacks, free or enslaved, who had access to the bandit communities is not difficult to comprehend since the bandits did not draw the color line. The relatively open race relationships at times practiced in frontier South Carolina helped to ensure the integration of the bandit groups, as did the recruitment needs of the bandits themselves. See Wood, *Black Majority*, 95–130.

See the following works, which collectively suggest feudal manifestations in the colonies; the precapitalistic economy and *mentalité* that tended to prevail, certainly in the rural colonial South; and the complementary idea of a peasantry in the colonies: Rowland Berthoff and John M. Murrin, "Feudalism, Communalism, and the Yeoman Freeholder: The American Revolution Considered as a Social Accident," in Stephen G. Kurtz and James H. Hutson (eds.), *Essays on the American Revolution* (Chapel Hill: University of North Carolina Press, 1973), 256–288; Robert S. Duplessis, "From Demesne to World-System: A Critical Review of the Literature on the Transition from Feudalism to Capitalism," *Radical History Review*, 3 (Fall, 1976), 3–41; Michael Merrill, "Cash Is Good to Eat: Self-Sufficiency and Exchange in the Rural Economy of the United States," *Radical History Review*, 3 (Fall, 1976), 42–71; Kenneth A. Lockridge, *A New England Town: The First Hundred Years* (New York: W. W. Norton, 1970); James A. Henretta, "Families and Farms: *Mentalité* in Pre-Industrial America," *William and*

Mary Quarterly, XXXV (January, 1978), 3–32; Edward Countryman, "'Out of the Bounds of the Law': Northern Land Rioters in the Eighteenth Century," in Alfred F. Young (ed.), *The American Revolution: Explorations in the History of American Radicalism* (DeKalb: Northern Illinois University Press, 1976), 37–69, hereinafter cited as Young, *The American Revolution*; Eric Wolf, *Peasants* (Englewood Cliffs, N.J.: Prentice-Hall, 1966); Marvin L. Michael Kay, "An Analysis of a British Colony in Late Eighteenth-Century America in the Light of Current American Historiographical Controversy," *Australian Journal of Politics and History*, XI (August, 1965), 170–184; Marvin L. Michael Kay, "The North Carolina Regulation, 1766–1776: A Class Conflict," in *The American Revolution*, 71–123, hereinafter cited as Kay, "North Carolina Regulation"; Marvin L. Michael Kay and Lorin Lee Cary, "Class, Mobility, and Conflict in North Carolina on the Eve of Revolution," in Jeffrey J. Crow and Larry E. Tise (eds.), *The Southern Experience in the American Revolution* (Chapel Hill: University of North Carolina Press, 1978), 109–151.

10. The North Carolina Regulators used other means to protest or seek relief. See Kay, "North Carolina Regulation"; Charles S. Sydnor, *American Revolutionaries in the Making: Political Practices in Washington's Virginia* (Chapel Hill: University of North Carolina Press, 1952; New York: Free Press, 1965), 86–106.

11. Crow describes maroon settlements in the Great Dismal Swamp in eighteenth-century North Carolina in *The Black Experience in Revolutionary North Carolina*, 41–42.

12. J. F. D. Smyth, *A Tour in the United States of America* (Dublin: Price, Moncrieffe, 2 volumes, 1784), I, 101–102.

13. Elkanah Watson, *Men and Times of the Revolution* . . . (New York: Dana and Co., 1856), 51–52, hereinafter cited as Watson, *Men and Times of the Revolution*.

14. Minutes of the New Hanover Country Court of Pleas and Quarter Sessions, 1738–1769, 1771–1772, Archives, Division of Archives and History, Raleigh, hereinafter cited as Court Minutes, with appropriate county and dates.

15. For an account of maroons and the more expansive possibilities they exploited in the Caribbean and Brazil, see Eugene D. Genovese, *From Rebellion to Revolution: Afro-American Slave Revolts in the Making of the Modern World* (Baton Rouge: Louisiana State University Press, 1979), 51–81. For details concerning the story in the British West Indies, see especially Michael Craton, *Testing the Chains: Resistance to Slavery in the British West Indies* (Ithaca, N.Y.: Cornell University Press, 1982). See also Patterson, *The Sociology of Slavery*, 269–283. For elaborations of the discussion in the text concerning maroons on the mainland, see Wood, *Black Majority*, 238–326 passim; Gary B. Nash, *Red, White, and Black: The People of Early America* (Englewood Cliffs, N.J.: Prentice-Hall, 1974), 290–297; John W. Blassingame, *The Slave Community: Plantation Life in the Antebellum South* (New York: Oxford University Press, 1972), 206–215, hereinafter cited as Blassingame, *The Slave Community*; Herbert Aptheker, *American Negro Slave Revolts* (New York: Columbia University Press, 1943), 162–292 passim; Kenneth Wiggins Porter, *The Negro on the Frontier* (New York: Arno Press, 1971); Herbert Aptheker, "Maroons within the Present Limits of the United States," *Journal of Negro History*, XXIV (April, 1939), 167–184; Herbert Aptheker, "Additional Data on American Maroons," *Journal of Negro History*, XXXIII (October, 1947), 452–460; J. Leitch Wright, "A Note on the First Seminole Wars as Seen by the Indians, Negroes, and Their British Adviser," *Journal of Southern History*, XXXIV (November, 1968), 565–575. Maroons are not cited in the North Carolina records used to develop the statistical relationship presented in the current study. Yet, the same records reveal that many slaves ran off in groups. Some of the latter obviously were maroons as were many others not listed in the few extant records.

16. The work of various scholars of British and French history has contributed to this analysis. Especially useful are E. P. Thompson, "Patrician Society, Plebeian Culture," *Journal of Social History*, VII (Summer, 1974), 382–405; E. P. Thompson, "The Moral Economy of the English Crowd in the Eighteenth Century," *Past and Present*, 50

(February, 1971), 76–136; Douglas Hay and others, *Albion's Fatal Tree: Crime and Society in Eighteenth Century England* (New York: Pantheon, 1975); Hobsbawm, *Primitive Rebels*, especially 1–56; Jeffry Kaplow, *The Names of Kings: The Parisian Laboring Poor in the Eighteenth Century* (New York: Basic Books, 1972); and Olwen H. Hufton, *The Poor of Eighteenth-Century France, 1750–1789* (Oxford, Eng.: Clarendon Press, 1974).

17. The *North Carolina Magazine and Universal Intelligencer*, published in New Bern between 1764 and 1768, had 260 possible issues of which 27, or 10 percent, remain. Twenty-four of the surviving issues date from 1764, 3 from 1765. The record of the *Cape Fear Mercury* is worse. Published in Wilmington between 1769 and 1775, it too had 260 issues. Only 17 unevenly dispersed issues (7 percent) have survived: 2 for 1769, 5 for 1770, 3 for 1773, 2 for 1774, and 5 for 1775. The other Wilmington paper, the *North Carolina Gazette*, appeared between 1764 and 1766. Its last extant issue is numbered 72, and only 4 issues (6 percent) remain: 2 for 1765, 2 for 1766. The colony's major journal, the *North Carolina Gazette*, published by James Davis in New Bern between 1751 and 1759 and again between 1768 and 1778, has a similar problem. Davis published some 200 issues during the first period and over 450 in the second. Only 26 (4 percent) have survived: 1 for 1751, 2 for 1752, 2 for 1753, 1 for 1757, 1 for 1759, 2 for 1768, 1 for 1769, 1 for 1773, 5 for 1774, and 10 for 1775. In other words, 62 percent of the surviving issues of Davis's paper are for the period 1773–1775. Collectively, there are 70 extant issues of North Carolina newspapers for the years under study, and 37 percent of them date from the years 1773–1775.

18. The surviving issues of the *North Carolina Magazine* and *Universal Intelligencer* (New Bern), hereinafter cited as *North Carolina Magazine*, contain only 2 notices, both placed by masters in Craven County. Only 1 of the 6 extant advertisements and 1 proclamation of outlawry in the *Cape Fear Mercury* (Wilmington), hereinafter cited as *Cape Fear Mercury*, were placed by masters who did not live in the Cape Fear counties of New Hanover, Brunswick, and Bladen. No advertisements for runaways appeared in the short-lived *North Carolina Gazette* (Wilmington), but the drawing power of James Davis's *North Carolina Gazette* (New Bern), hereinafter cited as *North Carolina Gazette*, is illustrated by the wider geographical distribution of the 25 masters who placed in the paper notices for runaways (19) or proclamations of outlawry (6). Of these, 10 came from Craven County and 3 from other Neuse-Pamlico counties. The remaining 12 notices were placed by masters living in a cross section of the colony's regions. North Carolina owners who placed notices in South Carolina and Virginia papers exemplified the same geographical patterns as those who advertised in North Carolina papers other than the *Gazette* published by Davis. Thus, masters from the Cape Fear counties closest to Charleston accounted for all 6 notices placed in the *South Carolina Gazette* (Charleston), hereinafter cited as *South Carolina Gazette*, while 13 of the 15 notices placed by North Carolina owners in the *Virginia Gazette* (Williamsburg), hereinafter cited as *Virginia Gazette* with appropriate publishers, came from counties abutting or near the Virginia border.

19. For nonfield runaways the time lag between escape and placement of an advertisement averaged just under 4 months, the amount of elapsed time ranging from 10 days to 7 months. With field hands the lag averaged just over 4 months, and the range of elapsed time was 7 days to 2 years. See also Rosser H. Taylor, "Humanizing the Slave Code of North Carolina," *North Carolina Historical Review*, II (July, 1925), 328; Mullin, *Flight and Rebellion*, 56, 192 n. 84; Wood, *Black Majority*, 240; Daniel E. Meaders, "South Carolina Fugitives as Viewed through Local Colonial Newspapers with Emphasis on Runaway Notices, 1732–1801," *Journal of Negro History*, LX (April, 1975), 290.

20. Jacob Wilkinson to Col. Alexander MacAllister, November, 1766, McAllister Papers, Southern Historical Collection, University of North Carolina Library at Chapel Hill, hereinafter cited as McAllister Papers. See also *Virginia Gazette* (Rind), September 6, 1770.

21. Forty of the 134 runaways for whom records exist fled during the years 1773–1775.

22. Since only slaves other than field hands had their occupations listed, all slaves without listed occupations were counted as field hands. For a supportive discussion relating to the listing and nonlisting of slave occupations in inventories, see Herbert G. Gutman and Richard Sutch, "Sambo Makes Good; or, Were Slaves Imbued with the Protestant Work Ethic?" in Paul A. David and others, *Reckoning with Slavery: A Critical Study in the Quantitative History of American Negro Slavery* (New York: Oxford University Press, 1976), 78 n. 30. Only 1 percent of Virginia and 0.7 percent of South Carolina male runaways between 1730 and 1787 were explicitly described by their masters as field hands. Lathan A. Windley, "Profile of Runaway Slaves in Virginia and South Carolina from 1730 through 1787" (unpublished doctoral dissertation, University of Iowa, 1974), 138, hereinafter cited as Windley, "Profile of Runaway Slaves."

23. See table 8 in the text.

24. Kay and Cary, "A Demographic Analysis of Colonial North Carolina," 71–121. Herbert G. Gutman, in *The Black Family in Slavery and Freedom, 1750–1925* (New York: Random House, 1976), 265, suggest that the absence of older slaves among runaways related to the binding ties of marriage; this study will be cited hereinafter as Gutman, *The Black Family in Slavery and Freedom*. Allan Kulikoff interprets the predominance of young males as part of a search for spouses. See his essay "The Beginnings of the Afro-American Family in Maryland" in Aubrey C. Land, Lois Green Carr, and Edward C. Papenfuse (eds.), *Law, Society, and Politics in Early Maryland* (Baltimore: Johns Hopkins University Press, 1977), 187. Numerous other studies at least agree on the youthfulness of runaways, including Eugene D. Genovese, *Roll, Jordan, Roll: The World the Slaves Made* (New York: Pantheon, 1974), 798 n. 2, hereinafter cited as Genovese, *Roll, Jordan, Roll*; Blassingame, *The Slave Community*, 202; Edgar J. McManus, *Black Bondage in the North* (Syracuse, N.Y.: Syracuse University Press, 1973), 111–113; Windley, "Profile of Runaway Slaves," 79–86.

25. Sex ratios in the Chesapeake, North Carolina, and the South Carolina low country probably averaged respectively during the years 1750–1775 about 117, 125, and 130. Without putting too fine a point on it, perhaps the higher sex ratios in South Carolina indirectly and paradoxically caused a higher percentage of female slave runaways in that province. Higher sex ratios reflected higher proportions of Africans in the slave population. Since African women were more prone to run away with their husbands or friends, the greater percentage of female slave runaways in South Carolina than was the case for its neighbors to the north is perhaps attributable to the colony's larger proportion of Africans. However, the almost identical percentages of female runaways in North Carolina and the Chesapeake despite the former's greater percentage of African-born slaves remains a puzzle. Clouding the issue further are the more substantial differences in sex ratios and proportions of Africans in the population between South Carolina and the Chesapeake than was the case between South Carolina and north Carolina. See the following for sex ratios and proportions of African-born slaves in the three regions: Kay and Cary, "A Demographic Analysis of Colonial North Carolina," 76–78, 93–103; Allan Kulikoff, "A 'Prolifick' People: Black Population Growth in the Chesapeake Colonies, 1700–1790," *Southern Studies*, 16 (Winter, 1977), 393–396, 403–406; Morgan, "Black Society in the Lowcountry," 90–92. See note 32 below for a contrasting view concerning the propensity of African women to run off.

26. Windley found that 22 percent of Virginia and 30 percent of South Carolina runaways had had at least one previous owner. Windley, "Profile of Runaway Slaves," 132–136. Mullin points to a "correlation between multiple owners, mobility, and running away" and notes that by 1770 half of all artisan runaways in Virginia were described by their masters as having had previous owners. Mullin, *Flight and Rebellion*, 89–91. Wood singles out change of ownership as a crucial immediate reason for fleeing among all runaways, not just non-field slaves. Wood, *Black Majority*, 248, 253–254. See also George M. Frederickson and Christopher Lasch, "Resistance to Slavery," *Civil War History*, 13 (December, 1967), 315–329; Gutman, *The Black Family in Slavery and Freedom*, 264–265, 318–319, 553–554 n 33. For examples in North Carolina see Committee of Claims Reports, Governors Papers, Arthur Dobbs, 1760–1764, State

Archives, hereinafter cited as Committee of Claims Reports; Clark, *State Records*, XXII, 836–840; *North Carolina Gazette*, March 24, July 14, 1775; *Cape Fear Mercury*, August 7, 1775; *North Carolina Magazine*, late June, 1764.

27. For other colonies see Gutman, *The Black Family in Slavery and Freedom*, passim, but especially chapter 8; Allan Kulikoff, "Tobacco and Slaves: Population, Economy, and Society in Eighteenth-Century Prince George's County, Maryland" (unpublished doctoral dissertation, Brandeis University, 1976), 226–228, 302–307, hereinafter cited as Kulikoff, "Tobacco and Slaves"; Mullin, *Flight and Rebellion*, 43, 103, 106, 109–110; Wood, *Black Majority*, 139–141, 248–249, 266. In "Profile of Runaway Slaves" Windley scarcely mentions the family.

28. *Virginia Gazette* (Purdie and Dixon), July 9, 1767, July 4, 1771, April 2, 1772; *North Carolina Gazette*, May 5, December 22, 1775; *Virginia Gazette* (Dixon and Hunter), June 24, 1775; Jacob Wilkinson to Col. Alexander MacAllister, November, 1766, McAllister Papers; *South Carolina Gazette*, May 16–25, 1748; *Virginia Gazette* (Hunter), February 21, 1751; *South Carolina Gazette*, November 27–December 4, 1775; *Virginia Gazette* (Purdie and Dixon), November 5, 1767; *North Carolina Gazette*, November 10, 1769.

29. It is also likely that owners at times carelessly neglected to mention past owners in their advertisements. The skilled slave referred to in the text was an eighteen-year-old Virginia-born waiter, George. *Virginia Gazette* (Purdie and Dixon), December 5, 1771. For the others see *North Carolina Magazine*, early June, late June, 1764; *Virginia Gazette* (Purdie and Dixon), November 3, 1769, August 7, 1775.

30. For contemporary comments that suggest the frequent use of Africans as watermen, see William Attmore, *Journal of a Tour to North Carolina by William Attmore, 1787*, edited by Lida T. Rodman (Chapel Hill: University of North Carolina Press, 1922), 44–45; Watson, *Men and Times of the Revolution*, 43.

31. The techniques used to identify African-born slaves in table 8 may have been too conservative. In addition to the 33 slaves identifiable as Africans, for example, 12 other field hands had African or African-derived names: 2 Mingos, 2 Jacks, 2 Cudgoes, Jemmy, Jamey, Jem, and 3 probable variations of Quash. Jem is specifically identified as "country born," but in all of the other cases the evidence is insufficient to determine origin. Some must have been African. The same is probably true of several of the 8 field-hand runaways whose names are not cited in contemporary records. For the 12 with African names see *South Carolina Gazette*, January 15–22, October 14–21, 1756, June 1, 1769; Committee of Claims Reports, 1760–1764; Clark, *State Records*, XXII, 823–827, 855–863; *Virginia Gazette* (Hunter), February 21, 1751; New Hanover County Court Minutes, October 4, 1768; *Cape Fear Mercury*, December 8, 1769, January 13, 1773; *North Carolina Gazette*, May 5, 1775. For the 8 unnamed runaways see Rowan County Court Minutes, July, 1755; Carteret County Court Minutes, December 6, 1757; Bertie County Court Minutes, July 24, 1759; *Cape Fear Mercury*, December 8, 1769; *Virginia Gazette* (Purdie and Dixon), July 9, 1767, December 14, 1769; *Virginia Gazette* (Rind), September 6, 1770, October 21, 1773; Inventory of John DuBois Estate, New Hanover County, July, 1768, North Carolina Wills, 1663–1789, Secretary of State's Papers, State Archives, hereinafter cited as John DuBois Estate.

32. See Wood, *Black Majority*, 289–292, 301–302, 314, for a discussion of African contributions to resistance in colonial South Carolina. For the prevalence of African runaways in Jamaica see Patterson, *The Sociology of Slavery*, 262–263. Daniel C. Littlefield adds a conflicting note to the issue, for he had found that African women in South Carolina were less prone to run off than "country-born" women. He also discusses which Africans were most prone to flight; the fragmentary nature of the evidence precludes such an analysis for North Carolina. See Daniel C. Littlefield, *Rice and Slaves: Ethnicity and the Slave Trade in Colonial South Carolina* (Baton Rouge: Louisiana State University Press, 1981), 12–33, 145, hereinafter cited as Littlefield, *Rice and Slaves*.

33. See, for example, *Virginia Gazette* (Hunter), October 17, 1755; *North Carolina Gazette*, November 10, 1769. A Similar proportion of South Carolina runaways fled in

160

groups—39 percent in the 1760s and 32 percent in the 1770s. See Morgan, "Black Society in the Lowcountry," 130.

34. *North Carolina Gazette,* February 24, May 5, 1775. Such determination was not uncommon among newly arrived Africans. See *North Carolina Gazette,* May 5, 1775, for the case of a "short well set Negro man" about thirty years of age with "Country marks in his Temples, and his Teeth filed sharp" who fled from an unknown master, was captured and jailed in Carteret County, escaped, and was then recaptured in adjoining Craven County.

35. *Cape Fear Mercury,* September 22, 1773; *North Carolina Gazette,* November 10, 1769, January 7, 1774, February 24, May 5, 1775; *South Carolina Gazette,* March 18–April 1, 1751; *Virginia Gazette* (Purdie and Dixon), September 28, 1769.

36. See, for example, *South Carolina Gazette,* October 2–6, 1758, July 12–19, 1760; *Virginia Gazette* (Purdie and Dixon), December 5, 1771. On the selection of nonfield hands, a process only partially documented, see Kulikoff, "Tobacco and Slaves," especially chapter 7; Mullin, *Flight and Rebellion,* 83–94; Herbert G. Gutman, *Slavery and the Numbers Game: A Critique of* Time on the Cross (Urbana: University of Illinois Press, 1975), 77–81, hereinafter cited as Gutman, *Slavery and the Numbers Game.*

37. See *Cape Fear Mercury,* November 24, 1769, December 8, 1769, August 7, 1775; *North Carolina Gazette,* March 13, 1752, May 5, 1775; *North Carolina Magazine,* early and late June, 1764; *South Carolina Gazette,* February 26–March 5, 1754. October 2–6, 1758, July 12–19, 1760; *Virginia Gazette* (Purdie and Dixon), November 3, 1768, December 5, 1771, June 24, 1773.

38. See Kay and Cary, "A Demographic Analysis of Colonial North Carolina," 91.

39. *South Carolina Gazette,* May 16–25, 1748. The origins of the parents could not be determined. The father is listed as Jemy, an African name, but he could have been American-born. The mother's name is not given.

40. *South Carolina Gazette,* May 16–25, 1748, November 22–29, 1760, July 18–25, 1761; *North Carolina Magazine,* January 4–11, 1765; *Virginia Gazette* (Purdie and Dixon), July 9, 1767, July 4, 1771, April 2, 1772; *North Carolina Gazette,* March 24, May 5, 12, October 6, 1775; *Virginia Gazette* (Dixon and Hunter), June 24, 1775. See Windley, "Profile of Runaway Slaves," 205–218. In South Carolina the percentage of runaways thought to be "visiting" either friends, acquaintances, or relatives was quite high—70 percent for 1760–1769, 72 percent for 1770–1779, and about the same proportion down through 1806. See Morgan, "Black Society in the Lowcountry," 129–130. Morgan does not distinguish among occupational groups in this instance.

41. *Virginia Gazette* (Purdie and Dixon), August 15, 1766, June 7, 1770; *Cape Fear Mercury,* December 29, 1773; *North Carolina Gazette,* April 7, December 22, 1775; *Virginia Gazette* (Dixon and Hunter), April 29, December 2, 1775; *Virginia Gazette* (Pinckney), June 15, 1775.

42. *Cape Fear Mercury,* November 24, 1769; *North Carolina Gazette,* March 13, 1752; *South Carolina Gazette,* February 26–March 5, 1754, July 12–19, 1760; *Virginia Gazette* (Purdie and Dixon), November 3, 1768, June 24, 1773; William L. Saunders (ed.), *The Colonial Records of North Carolina* (Raleigh: State of North Carolina, 10 volumes, 1886–1890), I, 975–976. For a discussion of the willingness of whites to use the labor of runaway skilled slaves, see Littlefield, *Rice and Slaves,* 165–166.

43. *North Carolina Gazette,* February 24, 1775; *South Carolina Gazette,* November 17–December 4, 1755. London and Bess fled with a slave owned by a nearby planter.

While Snow and Batchelor's assumption that whites had stolen or "decoyed away" their slaves flowed from a common bias that denied slaves the capacity of decision making, it nonetheless was not made totally without cause. The theft of slaves did occur in some instances, although with the exception of the two notices cited above, no other references to this practice appear in North Carolina records before the Revolution. It is highly unlikely that more than a few slaves were "invegelied" away by unscrupulous whites under the pretense of helping blacks escape to freedom. Slaves usually were far too aware of the ways of whites to believe in the fantasies projected by their masters.

For evidence from South Carolina concerning the theft of slaves, see Wood, *Black Majority*, 242; Windley, "Profile of Runaway Slaves," 43. North Carolina law provided heavy penalties for such thefts. See Clark, *State Records*, XXIII, 196–197. A 1778 act dealt specifically with the "promiscuous practice" of stealing slaves, as well as free blacks and mulattoes, and provided the death penalty in case of conviction. Clark, *State Records*, XXIV, 220–221. County court cases after 1741 suggest, however, that the earlier act was aimed chiefly at preventing the theft of black or mulatto servants and apprentices. In each instance free black or mulatto servants and apprentices were the targets of whites who sought to exploit their vulnerable status and illegally enslave them. See Kay and Cary, "A Demographic Analysis of Colonial North Carolina," 112–117, 121 n. 37.

44. Rowan County Court Minutes, August, 1769; *North Carolina Gazette*, November 10, 1769, advertisement dated October 13. See also Rowan County Court Minutes, February, 1769, in which it was recorded: "Mr. Frances Lock came into Open Court & approved his property to a certain negro Wench now in the possession of the Sheriff . . ." For other examples, see *North Carolina Gazette*, April 15, 1757, and June 24, 1768, for an Irish servant woman and a Negro slave owned by James Davis, the colony's printer; *South Carolina Gazette*, May 28–June 4, 1750, and June 1, 1769, for a "Dutch" (German) servant and a Negro slave; and *North Carolina Gazette*, May 5, 1775, for two white servants and a Negro slave owned by Henry Young.

45. Thirty-four servant and apprentice runaways are recorded in newspaper advertisements and a sample of county court minutes, the sources in which such individuals appear most frequently, for the period in question. As in the case of slaves, this total understates the number who actually ran off. Of the 34, 6 were designated as American-born (3 blacks, 1 Indian, and 2 whites), 2 as "Dutch" (German), 2 as English, 7 as Irish, and 1 as Scottish. Included among these were 2 free black and 4 Irish women. The origins of the remaining 16, all but 1 of them males, are not known. As might be expected, most of the 34 were young; the average for the 17 whose ages are given was 24 years. Thirteen of the 34 had been recently brought to North Carolina. No capture notices for servants and apprentices appeared in the colony's newspapers, but county court minutes make it evident that white servants stood a better chance of escaping than did black or mulatto servants and apprentices. Fourteen cases of captured servants appear in these records, 3 involving blacks. The latter were gone relatively short periods: 11 days, 1 month, and 2 months. White servants tended to be out longer before being captured; the average was 6 months for the 7 for whom such information is indicated. The Indian servant who fled, Joseph Leftear, was out 8 months. In addition to the sources cited in the last two notes, see Cateret County Court Minutes, September 16, 1769; Chowan County Court Minutes, July 23, 1748; Craven County Court Minutes, May, 1758; April, 1762, April, 1765; Rowan County Court Minutes, October, 1753, March and July, 1754, July and October, 1755, April 20, 1756, October 1768; *Cape Fear Mercury*, September 22, December 29, 1773; *North Carolina Gazette*, April 15, 1757; *North Carolina Magazine*, July 13–20, 1764; *South Carolina Gazette*, May 28–June 4, 1750; *Virginia Gazette* (Purdie and Dixon), September 23, 1773, February 17, 1774; *Virginia Gazette* (Rind), April 14, 1768.

46. In all, 8 of the 117 field hands bore signs of past punishments. Not included are 7 others with scars, which may or may not have been caused by punishments, and 2 slaves with neck collars. See *North Carolina Gazette*, November 15, 1751, June 24, 1768, April 7, 1775; *Virginia Gazette* (Hunter), October 17, 1755; *South Carolina Gazette*, November 27–December 4, 1755; *Virginia Gazette* (Purdie and Dixon), June 7, 1770, January 10, July 4, 1771. For a similar discussion about Virginia and South Carolina runaways, see Windley, "Profile of Runaway Slaves," 90–97. For the frequency of brands as identification among South Carolina runaways, see Littlefield, *Rice and Slaves*, 123.

47. *Virginia Gazette* (Purdie and Dixon), November 3, 1768. See also *Cape Fear Mercury*, December 8, 1769; *Virginia Gazette* (Purdie and Dixon), June 24, 1773. Three of the 17 nonfield runaways had scars from past punishments.

48. *Cape Fear Mercury*, November 24, December 8, 1769; *North Carolina Gazette*,

November 15, 1751, April 7, December 22, 1775; *Virginia Gazette* (Purdie and Dixon), November 3, 1768, June 7, 1770; *Virginia Gazette* (Dixon and Hunter), April 29, 1775.

49. Mullin, *Flight and Rebellion*, 98–103; *North Carolina Gazette*, March 13, 1752; *South Carolina Gazette*, October 2–6, 1758. Mullin's list of stutterers includes no blacksmiths, shoemakers, or carpenters, craftsmen who "characteristically worked by themselves, at their own pace and with a minimum of direct and persistent supervision." Mullin, *Flight and Rebellion*, 100–101. Windley, "Profile of Runaway Slaves," 157–161, found occupations listed for 12 of the 47 stutterers in Virginia (1736–1787) and 10 of the 40 stutterers in South Carolina (1732–1787). Mullin's generalization that waiting men and sailors were uniquely afflicted with stuttering because of their constant and stressful contact with whites is not supported by the range of occupations in either colony.

50. *Virginia Gazette* (Hunter), October 17, 1755; *North Carolina Magazine*, early June, 1764; *Virginia Gazette* (Purdie and Dixon), December 5, 1771; Kenneth Stampp, "Rebels and Sambos: The Search for the Negro's Personality in Slavery," *Journal of Southern History*, XXXVII (August, 1971), 391–392. See also Genovese, *Roll, Jordan, Roll*, 646–647; Robert W. Fogel and Stanley L. Engerman, *Time on the Cross: The Economics of American Negro Slavery* (Boston: Little, Brown, 2 volumes, 1974), I, 152–153; II, 118. Fogel and Engerman argue that slavery weighed most heavily on skilled slaves. For a contrasting view, see Gutman, *Slavery and the Numbers Game*, 74–75.

51. *Virginia Gazette* (Purdie and Dixon), November 3, 1768. See also *Virginia Gazette* (Purdie and Dixon), June 24, 1773; *Cape Fear Mercury*, December 8, 1769.

52. *Virginia Gazette* (Purdie and Dixon), November 26, 1772; *North Carolina Gazette*, November 10, 1769, September 2, 1774.

53. The times of flight are based on specific data for 51 field hands and 6 nonfield runaways, and 1 whose occupation is unknown. The 57 slaves listed as "captured" include those who were killed; the dates refer to the date of the capture notices or proceedings of the county court of Committee of Claims, whichever was earlier. Only 3 nonfield hands were among those captured or killed. Although capture dates are not an accurate guide to the time of flight, since at least 17 of those captured were Africans, most of them recent imports, and since over half of the remaining captured or killed slaves spoke little English, it seems plausible to suggest that most of those who were captured or killed had been out relatively short periods of time. See Windley, "Profile of Runaway Slaves," 171–176. Cheryl Ann Cody calculates that 30.8 percent of South Carolina runaways advertised in the *South Carolina Gazette*, 1725–1799, fled during May, June or July, the period of hardest labor in the rice fields. Morgan's findings, however, are the basis of her remarks. See Cheryl Ann Cody, "Slave Demography and Family Formation: A Community Study of the Ball Family Plantations, 1720–1896" (unpublished doctoral dissertation, University of Minnesota, 1982), 109.

54. *North Carolina Gazette*, March 13, 1752. See also *Cape Fear Mercury*, November 24, 1769.

55. *Virginia Gazette* (Hunter), October 17, 1755; *Virginia Gazette* (Dixon and Hunter), April 29, December 2, 1775; *North Carolina Gazette*, November, 1751; *Virginia Gazette* (Purdie and Dixon), November 26, 1772. See also *North Carolina Gazette*, November 10, 1769, September 2, 1774; *Cape Fear Mercury*, December 29, 1773; *Virginia Gazette* (Dixon and Hunter), June 24, 1775; *Virginia Gazette* (Pinckney), June 15, 1775.

56. *North Carolina Gazette*, June 24, 1768, November 10, 1769, January 7, 1774, February 24, 1775; *North Carolina Magazine*, January 4–11, 1765. See also *North Carolina Gazette*, November 15, 1751, September 2, 1774, February 24, May 5, 1775; *South Carolina Gazette*, October 14–21, 1756; *Virginia Gazette* (Purdie and Dixon), August 15, 1766, November 5, 1767, September 28, 1769; *Cape Fear Mercury*, January 13, September 22, 1773; *Virginia Gazette* (Dixon and Hunter), February 25, 1775.

57. *Virginia Gazette* (Hunter), October 17, 1755; *North Carolina Gazette*, September 2, 1774.

58. *Virginia Gazette* (Dixon and Hunter), December 2, 1775; *North Carolina*

Gazette, March 13, 1752, January 7, 1774. Three masters did fear that their runaways might flee the colony by boat or head for port towns in Virginia. *North Carolina Gazette,* June 24, 1768; *Virginia Gazette* (Rind), October 21, 1773; *Virginia Gazette* (Dixon and Hunter), April 29, 1775. See also *North Carolina Gazette,* February 24, 1775. In Virginia 39 fled on horseback and 7 in boats, 3 percent and 0.6 percent respectively of the 1,276 runaways. In South Carolina 21 rode off and 19 used boats, 1 percent and 0.8 percent respectively of the 2,424 runaways.

59. Adelaide L. Fries, Douglas LeTell Rights, Minnie J. Smith, and Kenneth G. Hamilton (eds.), *Records of the Moravians in North Carolina* (Raleigh: North Carolina Historical Commission, 11 volumes, 1922–1969), II, 858; *North Carolina Gazette,* July 17, 1753; New Hanover County Court Minutes, October 4, 1768.

60. The destination of nonfield hands specifically was discussed above.

61. *North Carolina Gazette,* June 24, 1768; *Cape Fear Mercury,* November 24, 1769; *South Carolina Gazette,* May 16–25, May 25–June 1, 1748, March 18–April 1, 1751, February 26–March 5, 1754, October 14–21, 1756, July 12–19, August 23–30, November 22–29, 1760, July 18–25, 1761; *Virginia Gazette* (Purdie and Dixon), July 9, 1767, November 3, 1768, June 7, 1770, July 4, 1773; *Virginia Gazette* (Dixon and Hunter), April 29, June 24, December 2, 1775; *Virginia Gazette* (Hunter), February 21, 1751; *Virginia Gazette* (Pinckney), April 13, June 15, 1775. Windley's data on destinations are not exactly comparable to this analysis. He deals only with the destinations presumed by masters and considers neither where slaves were captured or whether patterns varied by skill. Nonetheless, in Virginia prior to the Revolution, the patterns were almost identical to those in North Carolina. Of 406 runaways, for whom destinations were listed, 57 percent were thought to be staying in the colony, 37 percent to be heading out of it, and 6 percent either one or the other. In South Carolina, however, fully 86 percent of the 677 runaways for whom destinations were given were thought to be staying in the colony, only 10 percent to be leaving, and 4 percent either one or the other. Windley, "Profile of Runaway Slaves," 205–224.

62. For slaves whose destinations were not stated, see *North Carolina Gazette,* November 15, 1751, November 10, 1769, September 2, 1774, May 5, 1775; *Virginia Gazette* (Hunter), October 17, 1755; *South Carolina Gazette,* November 17–December 4, 1755, June 1, 1769; *Virginia Gazette* (Purdie and Dixon), July 9, 1767; *Cape Fear Mercury,* December 8, 1769, January 13, 1773; *Virginia Gazette* (Rind), September 6, 1770; *Virginia Gazette* (Dixon and Hunter), February 25, 1775; James Auld, "The Journal of James Auld," *Publications of the Southern History Association,* 7 (July, 1904), 262; John DuBois Estate, July, 1768.

For those thought to be lurking about, see *South Carolina Gazette,* January 15–22, 1750; Edgecombe County Court Minutes, June 27, 1758; *North Carolina Magazine,* January 4–11, 1765; *North Carolina Gazette,* September 2, 1774, February 24, March 24, May 5, 12, July 14, October 6, 1775.

For those thought to be headed for other parts of North Carolina, see *North Carolina Magazine,* January 4–11, 1765; *Virginia Gazette* (Purdie and Dixon), August 15, 1766; *North Carolina Gazette,* December 22, 1775; Jacob Wilkinson to Col. Alexander MacAllister, November, 1766, McAllister Papers.

For those slaves caught within North Carolina but in counties other than the counties from which they fled, see *North Carolina Gazette,* July, 1753, September 2, 1774, May 5, 1775; *South Carolina Gazette,* December 6–16, 1760; Lists of Taxables, Militia, and Magistrates, 1754–1770, undated, Governors Papers, State Archives; Clark, *State Records,* XXII, 836–849; *Virginia Gazette* (Purdie and Dixon), September 28, 1769; *Cape Fear Mercury,* December 8, 1769, December 29, 1773.

For those captured within North Carolina and whose home counties could not be determined, see Rowan County Court Minutes, July, 1755, February, 1772; Carteret County Court Minutes, December 6, 1757; Bertie County Court Minutes, July 24, 1759; *Virginia Gazette* (Purdie and Dixon), November 5, 1767, December 14, 1769, January 10, 1771; *North Carolina Gazette,* November 10, 1769, January 7, 1774,

February 24, 1775; *Cape Fear Mercury*, September 22, 1773; Stephen Blackman to Sheriff, Dobbs County, September 19, 1767, Private Collections, Colin Shaw Papers, PC 20, State Archives.

63. Littlefield notes that capture rates among slaves varied considerably. Ninety percent of the Mandingos, for example, were advertised as jailed rather than as fugitives, while under 20 percent of American-born slaves appeared in capture notices. Littlefield, *Rice and Slaves*, 128–133. Morgan, "Black Society in the Lowcountry," 131, makes no such distinctions, yet his figures are suggestive. Between 1760 and 1769, 36.9 percent of all advertised runaways appeared in capture notices. During the following decades, down to 1800, the percentages were 37.3, 34.9, and 22.4.

FIVE

Bearers of Arms: Patriot and Tory

SIDNEY KAPLAN AND EMMA NOGRADY KAPLAN

On the eve of the revolution, there were two and one half million Americans in the rebellious colonies. Of these, half a million were black—a few free, the rest slaves. It has been estimated that during the years of war some five thousand blacks served on the patriot side. The black soldier or sailor was, in fact, eager to fight on two fronts—for his own freedom and for the freedom of his country. Therefore, when white governors or generals running short of manpower in the army and navy, or white masters chary of risking their necks on the battlefield, promised a slave his freedom if he joined the ranks, he was more than willing to shoulder a musket.

The struggle for liberty by black people was not an innovation of 1776. Their attempts to shatter their chains had begun on the slave ships during the earliest years of the African diaspora, when some of the kidnapped and tortured were able to rise in revolt on the voyages across the Atlantic. Painful memories—some old, some fresh—of the middle passage, experienced at first or second hand, were still vivid in the minds of blacks, slave and free, who joined the patriot and Tory forces. A slip of a girl from Senegal whose African name is lost to history, destined to be the poet Wheatley, traveling as cargo in 1761 on a Boston schooner named *Phillis*, may have witnessed the tensions leading to insurrection. In his letter of instruction to the slaver's captain, the ship's owner cautioned him to be careful: "be Constantly Upon your Gard Night & Day & Keep good Watch that you may Not be Cutt of[f] by Your Own Slaves Neavour So Fiew on Board Or that you Are Not Taken by Sirprise. . . ."

The insurrections on the ocean did not cease during the time of the revolution, as a few entries in the logs of slavers of a single state make clear. Calculating their profits, two ship owners of Newport, Rhode Island, wrote to their brokers during the summer of 1774: "Pray get Insurance on the Brigt. *Othello*, George Sweet Mast'r, at and from hence to the Coast of Africa. . . . We have never made enquirty, if an Insurrection of the Slaves shou'd happen, and a Loss arise thereon, more or less, if your Underwriters pay in the Case. . . ." The Newport slave traders knew the risks of their business. During the fall of 1776 a worried report from the Rhode Island slaver *Thames*, anchored off the African coast near Accra, described in detail an event of Friday, November 8: "we had the misfortune to lose 36 of the best slaves we had by an Insurrection. . . . We had 160 Slaves on board [who] were that day lett out of the Deck Chaines in order to wash, about 2 Oclock. They began by siesing upon the Boatswain. . . . They continued to threw Staves, billets of wood etc. and in endeavoring to get down the Barricado, or over it for upwards of 40 Minutes, when finding they could not effect it, all the Fantee and most of the Accra Men Slaves jumped over board, in my opinion to get up abaft. . . ." There were other revolts aboard Rhode Island slavers in 1785 and 1796 as well as on two Massachusetts slavers, the *Felicity* in 1789 and the *Nancy* in 1793, another on a New London, Connecticut, ship in 1791.

Once landed on the soil of the colonies, the slaves from New York to Georgia continued their resistance in various modes of masquerade, sabotage, flight, conspiracy, and revolt. The documentation by historians of their freedom-seeking restlessness has grown year after year.

It was not easy for slave owners to arm their chattels, and two southern states resisted the idea to the end. Nor was the anxiety confined to the south. In Bucks County, Pennsylvania, during the summer of 1776, Henry Wynkoop wrote to the patriot Committee of Safety: "The people in my Neighborhood have been somewhat alarmed with fears about Negroes & disaffected people injuring their families when they are out in the Service. . . ." To quiet fears, he suggested that additional powder be sent to his neighbors.

As Lorenzo J. Greene once pointed out, the black population might have been assessed by both patriots and Tories as crucial in the balance of military power. But in July 1775, when Washington arrived in New England to take command, one of his earliest orders barred "Negroes" and "Vagabonds" from the army. Many months passed before the general and the Congress saw the light. Thereafter recruitment of black soldiers went on apace. During the winter of 1777 a German officer traveling through western Massachusetts was struck by the fact that a slave could "take the field in his master's place; hence you never see a regiment in which there are not negroes, and there are well-built, strong, husky fellows among them." In early spring of 1778 a Moravian farmer in Bethlehem, Pennsylvania, wrote in his diary: "From New England there arrived a company of soldiers, composed of whites, blacks and a few Stockbridge Indians, who were lodged over night." After the Battle of Monmouth, Adjutant General Alexander Scammell could report the names of over 750 black soldiers in fourteen brigades of the Continental Army. On the roll of Captain David Humphreys's black Connecticut company in 1781–83, among the forty-eight surnames, ten are Freedom, Freeman, or Liberty. On July 4, 1781, Baron Ludwig von Closen, an aide-de-camp to General Rochambeau, viewing the army at White Plains, noted in his journal: "A quarter of them were negroes, merry, confident, and sturdy."[1] Soon after the Siege of Yorktown, a young French sublieutenant sketched in watercolors in his notebook four foot-soldiers of the patriot army—one of whom is a black light infantryman of the First Rhode Island Regiment.

There were, of course, many blacks who fought with the Tories. The British, always short of men in spite of the large contingent of German mercenaries, saw clearly from the start the role that black power might play in the struggle ahead. When slaves abandoned their patriot masters in response to the blandishments of Lord Dunmore and Sir Henry Clinton, the decision to join the British was for them, as for their brothers on the opposite side, a blow struck against American slavery and for their own independence. It is possible that tens of thousands of slaves in South Carolina and Georgia went over to the British. Some blacks fled into swamps and the forests or conspired to fight their own battle for freedom. By the war's end, fourteen thousand black men, women, and children, some still bound to fleeing Tory masters, some now free and ready to begin new lives in new places, had been evacuated by the British from Savannah, Charleston, and New York, and transported to Florida, Nova Scotia, Jamaica, and later, Africa.

The black soldier and sailor of the revolution, whether he fought for Congress or king, served in a variety of ways—as infantryman, artilleryman, scout, guide, spy, pilot, guard, courier, wagoner, orderly, cook, waiter, able seaman, privateersman, and military laborer of all sorts. In a few cases, blacks formed their own units.

How many were killed or wounded, we can only guess. Some were heroes. Not long after they had fallen, most of them were forgotten. The white memory of things recorded in print and paint usually left them out.

A TRIO WITH THE GENERALS:
WILLIAM LEE, JAMES ARMISTEAD LAFAYETTE, AGRIPPA HULL

In 1768 George Washington bought a slave named William from Mary Lee. Seven years later, when Washington took command of the Continental Army, William Lee journeyed with him to Massachusetts and continued at the general's side as servant and orderly through thick and thin to the close of the war. In John Trumbull's portrait of Washington at West Point, painted in London in 1780, the artist shows young William, in a turban, holding the bridle of the general's horse. The fighting over, William returned to Virginia with Washington to serve the Mount Vernon household for the next twenty years. It is as a factotum of the Washington family—George and Martha with their grandchildren—that Edward Savage portrayed the black veteran in 1796. The genre of both these paintings, white master and black servant— a traditional one for the white artist—perhaps conceals the deep feeling that Washington had for his revolutionary comrade. When William in 1784 asked the general if he could bring to Mount Vernon his wife, Margaret Thomas, a free woman of Philadelphia, Washington reluctantly agreed: "I cannot refuse his request . . . as he has lived with me so long and followed my fortunes through the War with fidility."

Washington's soul-searching about the rightness of slavery is well known. There was "not a man living," he wrote to two friends in 1786, who wished more sincerely than he "to see some plan adopted by which slavery may be abolished by law." When he died in 1799, his will provided that upon Martha's death all his slaves should be liberated, but "to my Mulatto man William (calling himself William Lee) I give immediate freedom. . . . I allow him an annuity of thirty dollars during his natural life . . . and this I give him as a testimony of my sense of his attachment to me, and for his faithful services during the Revolutionary War."

In June 1804 on a visit to Mount Vernon, the artist Charles Willson Peale, who would later paint a vivid portrait of the black Muslim Yarrow Mamout, sought out the aged William Lee, whom he found in an outbuilding, crippled, cobbling shoes. The two sat down together and talked about old times and how to live a long, healthy life.

In March 1781 Washington rushed General Lafayette to Virginia in an effort to stop Cornwallis. Shortly thereafter, a slave by the name of James, in New Kent County, asked his master, William Armistead, for permission to enlist under the French major general. That spring and summer, Lafayette felt a crucial necessity to recruit black troops. He called for four hundred laborers and wagoners, and wrote frantically to Washington: "Nothing but a treaty of alliance with the Negroes can find us dragoon Horses . . . it is by this means the enemy have so formidable a Cavalry." As a master spy, James gave yeoman service. After the surrender at Yorktown, when Cornwallis visited Lafayette's headquarters, he was amazed to see there the black man he had believed to be *his* spy.

The war over, in November 1784 James met Lafayette in Richmond. In his own hand the Frenchman wrote a testimonial which he handed to James, certifying that the ex-spy had rendered "services to me while I had the honour to command in this state. His intelligence from the enemy's camp were industriously collected and more faithfully delivered. He perfectly acquitted himself with some important commissions I gave him and appears to me entitled to every reward his situation can admit of." It is barely possible that James, whose "situation" was still that of a slave, by his very presence played a certain part in clarifying the thinking of the marquis about race and slavery. It was about this time that Lafayette began to develop the outlook that would move him in 1783 to propose to Washington a plan "which might greatly benefit the black part of mankind. Let us unite in purchasing a small estate where we may try the experiment to free the Negroes and use them only as tenants." Five years later in Paris, Lafayette would be a fervent sponsor of the Society of Friends of the Blacks.

During the autumn of 1786 the General Assembly of Virginia, echoing Lafayette's words — "at the peril of his life found means to frequent the British camp, and thereby faithfully executed important commissions entrusted to him by the marquis" — emancipated James, ordering that his master be compensated at the going auction-block figure. When thirty-odd years later the freeman, "now poor and unable to help himself," petitioned for relief, the state gave him sixty dollars and finally placed him on the regular pension list.

In 1824 Lafayette, on a triumphal return visit to America, came to Richmond. The black veteran, who for a long time had called himself James Lafayette, and the French nobleman who had survived *his* revolution, greeted each other. The scene can be imagined the more vividly because it was probably during this year that the artist John B. Martin, whose portrait of Chief Justice John Marshall hangs in the Supreme Court, painted the aging James Lafayette in a military coat.

During the summer of 1844 Francis Parkman spent a few days in Stockbridge, a town in western Massachusetts. On July 7 he recorded in his journal: "The old Negro . . . had been a soldier in W's army. He had four children in the churchyard, he said with a solemn countenance, but 'these are my children' he added, stretching his cane over a host of little boys. 'Ah, how much we are consarned to fetch them up well and virtuous' etc. He was very philosophical and every remark carried the old patriarch into lengthy orations on virtue and temperance. He looked on himself as father to all Stockbridge." The old patriarch was Agrippa Hull, a black veteran who, sixty years before his conversation with the noted historian, had served as orderly to the noble Pole, General Tadeusz Kósciuszko, who, the story goes, wanted to take him to Poland after the revolution. To this day, Hull is a legendary figure in the Berkshire town where his portrait, complete with cane, in the historical room of the library broods over memorabilia of the past.

Agrippa Hull was born free in Northampton in 1759. At age six — so the story goes — a black man by the name of Joab, former servant to Jonathan Edwards, brought him to Stockbridge. On May 1, 1777, the eighteen-year-old youth — "5 ft. 7 in.; complexion, black; hair wool" — enlisted for the duration as a private in the brigade of General John Paterson of the Massachusetts Line. For two years he served as an orderly for Paterson, and then for another four years and two months for Paterson's friend, the Polish patriot, in spheres of action ranging from Saratoga to Eutaw Springs. In South Carolina, assigned to assist the surgeons, Hull always remembered with horror the bloody amputations. In July 1783 at West Point he received his discharge, signed by George Washington.

Back home in Stockbridge he farmed a small plot, did odd jobs, acted as butler for the local gentry and as major domo at weddings, and adopted as his daughter the child of a runaway slave from New York, one Mary Gunn, whose posterity still lives in Stockbridge. The town historian, who knew him well, recorded in his marriages: "Not long after the case of Mum Bett [Elizabeth Freeman] had been decided, Jane Darby, the slave of Mr. Ingersoll of Lenox . . . left her master and took refuge in Stockbridge. She and Agrippa soon agreed to tread life's path in company; but her master endeavored to seize her. Agrippa applied to Judge [Theodore] Sedgwick for aid, and obtained her discharge. She was a woman of excellent character, and made a profession of her faith in Christ. Some years after her death, Agrippa married Margaret Timbroke, who still lives respected among us." He became the village seer. In 1797, when Kósciuszko visited the United States, Hull traveled to New York. There was an affectionate reunion; no doubt both smiled as they recalled the time the general surprised the orderly dressed in his commander's uniform in the midst of a party Agrippa had thrown for his black friends. It was on this visit in 1797 that Kósciuszko, a lover of liberty, was awarded a gift of land in Ohio, which he directed to be sold to found a school for blacks.

In 1828, when Hull was seeking to have his soldier's pension mailed directly to his home, his friend Charles Sedgwick wrote to the official in charge: "I enclose his discharge & take the liberty to request that it may be returned—and also to mention as an interesting fact in regard to this man that I have obtained his permission to send it with great difficulty, he declaring that he had rather forego the pension than lose the discharge." Ten years later, after a long illness, he died.

Agrippa Hull "had a fund of humor and mother-wit," recalled the novelist Catharine Maria Sedgwick, "and was a sort of Sancho Panza in the village, always trimming other men's follies with a keen perception, and the biting wit of wisdom." After his death he was remembered as having "no cringing servility" in his makeup, always feeling "himself every whit a man." He would argue: "It is not the *cover* of the book, but what the book *contains.* . . . Many a good book has dark covers," or, "Which is the worst, the white black man, or the black white man? to be black outside, or to be black inside?" He was once overheard "in his public prayers" giving "thanks for the kind notice of his 'white neighbors to a poor black nigger.'" (The eavesdropper was unaware of the ploy of irony.) Another anecdote gives the measure of his character: "Once, when servant to a man who was haughty and overbearing, both Agrippa and his master attended the same church, to listen to a discourse from a distinguished mulatto preacher [Lemuel Haynes?] . . . the gentleman said to Agrippa, 'Well, how do you like nigger preaching?' 'Sir,' he promptly retorted, 'he was half black and half white; I like *my* half, how did you like *yours?*'"

A MUSTER OF BRAVE SOLDIERS AND SAILORS

After the fireworks were over on July 4, 1847, John Greenleaf Whittier, poet laureate of antislavery, was moved to right a historic wrong. The result was a lead editorial in the *National Era* entitled "The Black Men of the Revolution of 1776 and the War of 1812." "The return of the Festival of our National Independence," Whittier began, "has called our attention to a matter which had been very carefully kept out of sight by orators and toast-drinkers. We allude to the participation of colored men in the great struggle for Freedom." As a pacifist Quaker, he had no desire "to eulogize the shedders of blood, even in a cause of acknowledged justice," but

> when we see a whole nation doing honor to the memories of one class of its defenders, to the total neglect of another class, who had the misfortune to be of darker complexion, we cannot forego the satisfaction of inviting notice to certain historical facts, which for the last half century have been quietly elbowed aside. . . . Of the services and sufferings of the colored soldiers of the Revolution, no attempt has, to our knowledge been made to preserve a record. They have no historian. With here and there an exception, they all passed away, and only some faint tradition of their campaigns under Washington, and Greene, and Lafayette, and of their cruisings under Decatur and Barry, lingers among their descendants. Yet enough is known to show that the free colored men of the United States bore their full proportion of the sacrifices and trials of the Revolutionary war.

The faces of William Lee, Agrippa Hull, and James Lafayette have come down to us in paint because they were closely and valuably linked with famous generals. Such portraits are rare. The thousands of black rank and file who fought on the patriot side—who marched, sailed, spied, piloted, scouted—remain almost invisible, often nameless, except as we can feebly try to reconstruct their reality from a few, sometimes grudging, words scattered here and there in the meager (where black is concerned) records of the time. As Benjamin Quarles puts it, "The typical Negro soldier was a private, consigned as if by caste, to the rank and file. Even more than other privates, he tended to lack identity. Often he bore no specific name. . . ."

On board the Connecticut warship *General Putnam* were at least five black crewmen: Joseph Colly, Cato Jones, Cesar Landon, Cesar Sabens, and Cuff, the cook. When, in March 1781, Maryland needed ships, a tidewater patriot replied to the plea of the Council that he would send "his schooner Cheerfully," but with "a Negro Skipper, as no white man would go." We would like to know more about this fearless black skipper even as we understand more clearly why General Washington, two years earlier, had written to Major Henry Lee: "I have granted a Warrant for the 1000 Dolls. promised the Negro pilots. . . ." The vigorous portraits of two nameless seaman have survived to attest to the reality of the black presence in the revolutionary navy.

In John Marshall's *Life of George Washington* there is a description of an episode in which General Daniel Morgan, outnumbered, routed the British dragoons under Tarleton. Lieutenant Colonel William Washington, leader of the patriot cavalry and a relative of General Washington, was about to be cut down by a British sword "when a waiter, too small to wield a sword, saved him by wounding the officer with a ball from a pistol." In 1845 William Ranney painted the scene, perhaps out of Marshall, perhaps from tradition, with the youth as a bugler. The Continental Congress awarded General Morgan a gold plaque for his triumph at Cowpens, but we do not even know the name of the brave black lad rendered so vigorously by the imagination of the artist.

Sometimes the record has the laconic eloquence of an epitaph: "Zechery Prince now ded, Recd his freedom"—so reads a brief line on a payroll of Simsbury, Connecticut, troops in the spring of 1779. In the log of the ship-of-war *Ranger*, at anchor in Charleston harbor on February 25, 1780, there is this entry: "at 10 this Night a Negro Called Cesar Hodgsdon died." But who *was* Zechery Prince? And who *was* Cesar Hodgsdon? We grope for the man and have to be content with a phrase. Here is a cluster of vignettes, short and long, randomly assembled, which, read together as a collective profile, furnish a sketchy portrait of a sizable group of black soldiers and seaman of the revolution.

Garshom Prince

The biblical name Garshom refers to the son of Moses and his wife Zipporah, daughter of Jethro, who tradition records was black. The revolutionary soldier Garshom Prince was born around 1733 in Rhode Island or Connecticut, slave or servant of Captain Robert Durkee, with whom he fought in the French and Indian War and in the revolution. At Quebec he made himself a powder horn. Later, in the Battle of Wyoming, Pennsylvania, in 1778, he lost his life. The horn was taken from his lifeless body on the field. Carved with sketches of houses and ships, it bore the inscriptions: "GARSHOM PRINCE his horn made at Crown Point Septm. ye 3rd day 1761" and "PRINCE NEGRO HIS HORNM."

Harry, Cupid, Aberdeen

The armed schooner *Liberty* in the navy of Virginia, commanded by Captain James Barron (later to be Commodore Barron, senior officer of the United States Navy), fought twenty sharp actions during the war. When in his old age the commodore put down his memories of the *Liberty*, he wrote of the "courageous patriots who had served on board her during the war. Amongst these, I take pleasure in stating there were several coloured men, who, I think, in justice to their merits should not be forgotten. Harry (a slave, belonging to Captain John Cooper) was distinguished for his zeal and daring; Cupid (a slave of Mr. William Ballard) stood forth on all occasions as the champion of liberty, and discharged all his duties with a fidelity that made him a favorite of all the officers. It is well known, indeed, in Virginia, that many of the African race were zealous and faithful soldiers in the cause of freedom, and one of them, in particular, named Aberdeen, distinguished himself so much as to attract the notice of many of our first officers and citizens, and among them, of Patrick Henry, who befriended him as long as he lived." In 1783, in its "Act directing the Emancipation of certain Slaves who have served as Soldiers," the Virginia General Assembly freed Aberdeen, who had "labored a number of years in the public service at the lead mines. . . ."

Jupiter

On a fading scrap of paper, miraculously preserved, a Virginia colonel by the name of George Muter certifies on March 29, 1781, that "Jupiter (negro) saved four guns during the time the enemy were in Richmond, which he afterwards delivered to me & for which he has received no reward."

Antigua

In March 1783 a slave by this name was lauded by the General Assembly of South Carolina for his skill in "procuring information of the enemy's movements and designs." He "always executed the commissions with which he was entrusted with diligence and fidelity, and obtained very considerable and important information, from within the enemy's lines, frequently at the risk of his life." To reward him, the assembly liberated his "wife named Hagar, and her child." Presumably Antigua remained a slave.

Prince Whipple

There are two well-known paintings that depict the crossing of the Delaware on that wintry Christmas Eve in 1776. The earlier of the two, a huge canvas, was painted by Thomas Sully in 1819 for the state of South Carolina. It shows Washington astride a mettlesome white horse on a snowy riverbank attended by four mounted men, three of them white officers, the fourth a young black solider. The other, more familiar, picture, painted by Emanuel Gottlieb in 1851, shows the general standing in a rowboat moving through the ice. One of the oarsmen is black. According to a tradition there seems no reason to question (and first put into print by Nell in 1851) the black trooper who crossed the river with Washington and who is thus depicted by Sully and Leutze is Prince Whipple, "body-guard to Gen. Whipple, of New Hampshire, who was Aid to General Washington."

Nell recounts something of Whipple's life: "Prince Whipple was born at Amabou, Africa, of comparatively wealthy parents. When about ten years of age, he was sent by them, in company with a cousin, to America, to be

Latchom, still a slave, played a heroic role. The colonel's biographer has preserved the details:

> During the fight the militia retreated, leaving Cropper and a negro named George Latchom, who were in advance of the rest, engaged actively with the invaders. These two kept up the firing, until the foe were within a few rods of them, when they were compelled to fall back. Cropper had to retreat through a sunken, boggy marsh, in which he struck fast up to the waist in soft mud, the enemy at the time being so close as to prepare to bayonet him.
>
> At this critical juncture the faithful colored man fired and killed the foremost man, and seized hold of Cropper and dragged him by main strength out of the mud, and taking him on his back, carried him safely to dry land. This required great strength upon his part, Cropper weighing in the neighborhood of two hundred pounds.

Cropper thereupon bought Latchom from his owner, set him free, and "befriended him in every way he could, as an evidence of his gratitude, till Latchom's death."

Black Samson

In the folklore of Delaware there is preserved the figure of a black patriot, unlisted on any muster roll, who fought well at the Battle of Brandywine in September 1777. As the story is told, he had witnessed near Chadds Ford the brutal murder by British troops of a white man who had befriended him, and in "the fight at Brandywine next day, Black Sampson, a giant Negro, armed with a scythe, swept his way through the red ranks like a sable figure of Time." His schoolmaster friend "had taught him; his daughter had given him food. It is to avenge them that he is fighting." Over a century later, the black poet Paul Laurence Dunbar would be moved by the legend to put it into verse:

> Straight through the human harvest,
>   Cutting a bloody swath,
> Woe to you, soldier of Briton!
>   Death abroad is his path.
> Flee from the scythe of the reaper,
>   Flee while the moment is thine,
> None may with safety withstand him,
>   Black Sampson of Brandywine.

Edward Hector

Another black hero of the Battle of Brandywine was an artilleryman, Edward Hector, thirty-three years old, a private in Captain Hercules Courtney's company, Third Pennsylvania Artillery of the Continental Line. He died in 1834, a nonagenarian. The *Free Press* of Norristown carried his obituary:

Edward Hector, a colored man and a veteran of the Revolution. Obscurity in life and oblivion in death, is too often the lot of the worthy—they pass away, and no "storied stone" perpetuates the remembrance of their noble actions. . . . During the war of the revolution, his conduct, on one memorable occasion, exhibited an example of patriotism and bravery which deserves to be recorded. At the battle of Brandywine he had charge of an ammunition wagon, attached to Col. Proctor's regiment, and when the American army was obliged to retreat, an order was given . . . to abandon them to the enemy. . . . The heroic reply of the deceased was uttered in the true spirit of the revolution: "The enemy shall not have my team; I will save my horses, or perish myself!" He instantly started on his way, and as he proceeded, amid the confusion of the surrounding scene, he calmly gathered up . . . a few stands of arms which had been left on the field by retreating soldiers, and safely retired with wagon, team and all, in the face of the victorious foe. Some years ago a few benevolent individuals endeavored to procure him a pension, but without success. The Legislature of Pennsylvania, however, at the last session, granted him a donation of $40.00, which was all the gratuity he ever received for his Revolutionary services. . . .

Enough to bury Edward Hector.

Lambert Latham and Jordan Freeman

On Groton Heights, across the Thames from New London, the state of Connecticut in 1830 erected a granite shaft "in memory of the brave patriots who fell in the massacre at Fort Griswold near this spot on the 6th of September, A.D. 1781, when the British under the command of the traitor Benedict Arnold, burnt the towns of New London & Groton." On that shaft, inscribed on a marble tablet, are the names of the eighty-four patriots slain that day; at the top is the name of Lieutenant Colonel William Ledyard, their commander; at the bottom, segregated by the label "Colored men," are the names of Sambo Latham and Jordan Freeman. On the day the shaft was dedicated a black man in the crowd, William Anderson of New London, recollecting what "two veterans who were present at the battle" had told him of the event, reflected somewhat bitterly on the inscription: "One of these men was the brother of my grandmother, by the name of Lambert, but called Lambo,—since chiseled on the marble monument by the American classic appellation of 'Sambo.'"[2]

Lambert worked for a farmer named Latham and when the alarm came the two men were out in the field taking care of the cattle. The assault by the British was a deadly one: "Finally, the little garrison was overcome, and, on the entrance of the enemy, the British officer inquired, 'Who commands this fort?' The gallant Ledyard replied, 'I once did; you do now,'—at the same time handing his sword, which was immediately run through his body to the hilt. . . . Lambert, being near Col. Ledyard when he was slain, retaliated upon the officer by thrusting his bayonet through his body. Lambert, in return, received from the enemy *thirty-three bayonet* wounds, and thus fell, nobly avenging the death of his commander." According to a tradition in the

Latham family, "Lambo fought manfully by his master's side up to the time he was slain. In the hottest of the conflict he stood near his master, loading and discharging his musket with great rapidity, even after he had been severely wounded in one of his hands."

On that same day, an eyewitness recalled, the British commander of the assault, Major Montgomery, as he scaled a wall of the fort, "was killed by spears in the hands of Captain Shapley and a black man named Jordan Freeman," who was Colonel Ledyard's orderly.

Jack Sisson

Reports of the derring-do capture of British Major General Richard Prescott at his headquarters near Newport, Rhode Island, in July 1777 by a patriot team of commandos soon got into song and ballad. In the annals of the time, the black volunteer who played an important part in this caper goes by several names—Jack or Tack Sisson, and Prince. (He would later enlist for the duration as a private in Colonel Christopher Greene's First Rhode Island battalion.) Lieutenant Colonel Barton, states one of the earliest newspaper reports of the event, "selected and engaged about forty men to go with him on a secret expedition, by water in five batteaus . . . he told them his design, acknowledged it was hazardous. . . . If any of them were unwilling to engage in the enterprize, they were then at full liberty to decline it. . . . On putting the matter to their choice, they unanimously resolved to go with him, and told him to lead them on to honor. They then set off with muffled oars on a dark night. . . ." With Sisson as one of the boat steerers, they "passed the enemy's forts," slipped through his "ships of war," and landed near Prescott's headquarters. "The col. went foremost, with a stout active Negro, close behind him, and another at a small distance. . . ." Barton and Sisson made short work of the single sentinel at the door. With "the rest of the men surrounding the house, the Negro, with his head, at the second stroke, forced a passage into it, and then into the general's chamber . . . the colonel calling the general by name, told him he was a prisoner, he replied he knew it, and rising from his bed desired time to put on his clothes. The colonel told him to put on his breeches. . . ."

Legend has it that not long after Prescott's exchange for the American general Charles Lee, he was dining aboard the British admiral's ship off Newport and called for a song by a Yankee lad, a prisoner, thirteen years old. The ballad he sang was allegedly composed by a Newport sailor.

> A tawney son of Afric's race
> Them through the ravine led,
> And entering then the Overing house,
> They found him in his bed.
>
> But to get in they had no means
> Except poor Cuffee's head,

Who beat the door down, then rushed in,
And seized him in his bed.

Stop, let me put my breeches on,
The general then did pray.
Your breeches, massa, I will take,
For dress we cannot stay.

Catherine Williams, the biographer of Colonel Barton, wrote down a dozen years after Sisson's death her memory of him in his last years. Through her genteel racism one can glimpse the old veteran: "A black servant of the Colonel . . . a faithful attendant and shrewd fellow, and one who, in his own opinion at least, formed a very important personage in the expedition . . . he continued to regret to the day of his death, that his name had never appeared in any account of the transaction. After the capture of Prescott, [Jack] was made a drummer. . . . He was remarkably small. . . . On all public days he usually made his appearance on the parade ground, dressed in complete uniform, and his appearance was a perfect holiday to all the little urchins about street, who would immediately crowd around, to listen to his stories, and hear him in his cracked voice sing the old Ballad, beginning 'Brave Barton.'"

The *Providence Gazette* of November 3, 1821, published his obituary: "In Plymouth (Mass.) . . . a negro man, aged about 78 years. He was one of the forty brave volunteers. . . ."

Quaco

During the British occupation of Newport, Quaco's Tory master sold him to a colonel in the king's army. Quaco fled to the patriot line with valuable information. In January 1782 the General Assembly of Rhode Island, in recognition that "the information he then gave, render[ed] great and essential service to this state and the public in general," declared him "a freeman."

Pompey Lamb

The brilliance of "Mad" Anthony Wayne in his assault at Stony Point on the Hudson in 1779 is well known. The legend of Pompey, slave of Captain Lamb, who guided Wayne's troops and made the assault possible has faded away—even though Washington Irving in his *Life of George Washington* singled out Pompey Lamb for praise:

> About eight in the evening, they arrived within a mile and a half of the forts, without being discovered. Not a dog barked to give the alarm—all the dogs in the neighborhood had been privately destroyed beforehand. About half-past eleven, the whole moved forward, guided by a negro of the neighborhood who had frequently carried fruit to the garrison, and served the Americans as a spy. He led the way, accompanied by two stout men disguised as farmers. The

countersign was given to the first sentinel. . . . While the negro talked with him, the men seized and gagged him. . . .

Saul Matthews

As spy and guide, this slave proved himself of inestimable value. In 1781 Josiah Parker, colonel of the Virginia militia, said that he "deserved the applause of his country." Luther P. Jackson, historian of the black soldier in revolutionary Virginia, has sketched Saul's career at the front:

> This slave of Thomas Matthews "shouldered his musket" and went over to the American side in the early months of the war . . . in 1781 during the campaign of the British in the vicinity of Portsmouth, Saul, at the risk of his life, was sent into the British garrison. . . . He brought back military secrets of such value to Colonel Parker that on the same night, serving as a guide, he led a party of Americans to the British garrison. . . . On another occasion in 1781, when Saul's master and many other Virginians had fled into the adjoining state of North Carolina, he was sent by them to Norfolk to secure similar intelligence concerning the movement and plans of the British troops. For his services as a spy and a soldier such distinguished army officers as Baron von Steuben, Lafayette, Peter Muhlenburg, and General Nathaniel Greene praised him to the highest.

After the war Saul's master changed, but he continued to labor as a slave. In 1792 he petitioned the Virginia legislature for his freedom and in November of that year, "in consideration of many very essential services rendered to this Commonwealth during the late war," he was granted his "full liberty and freedom . . . as if he had been born free."

Austin Dabney

Patriots in Georgia were wary of arming their slaves. Only a few instances have turned up of the emancipation of black veterans for their service in the war. David Monday was one emancipated soldier; Georgia paid his owner 100 guineas and freed him.

Another was Austin Dabney. In the Battle of Kettle Creek early in 1779, "the hardest ever fought in Georgia," Dabney, an artilleryman who had been given his freedom in order to serve in his master's place, fought in Colonel Elijah Clark's corps. "No soldier under Clark," wrote a former governor of Georgia in 1855, "was braver, or did better service during the revolutionary struggle." Shot in the thigh, Dabney was rescued and nursed back to health by a white soldier named Harris. In gratitude, Dabney worked for the Harris family; out of his own pocket he sent his rescuer's eldest son through college and then arranged for his legal training.

Although Dabney was a pensioner, because he was black he was denied a chance in the lottery for land open to revolutionary veterans in 1819. When the legislature finally granted him 112 acres for his "bravery and fortitude" in "several engagements and actions," a group of whites in Madison County protested the award, claiming "it was an indignity to white men, for a mulatto to be put upon an equality with them in the distribution of the public land."

Austin Dabney existed gingerly, a friend of a few upper-class white veterans of the revolution. "He owned fine horses, attended the racecourse, entered the list for the stake. . . ." In his old age, in "the evening after the adjournment of the court in Danielsville, he usually went into the room occupied by the judges and the lawyers, where, taking a low seat, he listened to what was said, or himself told of the struggles between the Whigs and the Tories in upper Georgia and South Carolina. His memory was retentive, his understanding good, and he described what he knew well."

Caesar Tarrant

For four years, Caesar, a slave in the Tarrant family of Hampton, Virginia, served in the state's navy as a pilot on the armed *Patriot*, steering the vessel in its most important engagement south of the Virginia capes. Throughout the action, he "behaved gallantly." Other black seamen on the *Patriot* were David Baker, Jack Knight, Mark Starlins, Pluto, and Cuffee. The last, a pilot, died from injuries received in service. Tarrant was abroad the *Patriot* when she captured the *Fanny* on its way to Boston with supplies for the British.

In 1789 the Virginia legislature set Caesar Tarrant free, because he had "entered very early into the service of his country, and continued to pilot the armed vessels of this state during the late war." During the next half dozen years, the ex-slave and veteran bought several pieces of property in Hampton, and in 1796, when he died, willed houses and lots to his "loving wife." Thirty-five years later, the government granted to his daughter Nancy, 2,666 acres of land in Ohio in recognition of her father's crucial part in the operations of the Virginia navy.

Jude Hall

Nell tells the story of a black who enlisted for the war as a private in the Second Battalion of New Hampshire troops, commanded by Colonel Nathan Hale: "Jude Hall was born at Exeter. . . . He served faithfully eight years, and fought in most all the battles, beginning at Bunker Hill. He was called a great soldier, and was known in New Hampshire to the day of his death by the name of 'Old Rock.'" Nell goes on to relate the history of Jude Hall's family: "Singular to relate, three of his sons have been kidnapped at different times, and reduced to slavery. James was put on board a New Orleans vessel; Aaron was stolen from Providence, in 1807; William went to sea in the bark *Hannibal*, from Newburyport, and was sold in the West Indies, from whence he escaped after ten years of slavery, and sailed as captain of a collier from Newcastle to London."

Titus

Not exactly a brave soldier, but an interesting person. Hundreds of black seamen served on patriot privateers. Titus, of Salem, Massachusetts, served as a business agent for the privateers and he did well in his job according to the entry of August 13, 1781, in the diary of William Pynchon: "Fair and cool. News that Mrs. Fairfield's son died in the prison ship at New York. Three more privateers are taken. . . . Mrs. Cabot makes her will; in it gives Titus, her negro, £40 and his freedom in case he shall continue in her service henceforth till her death. Titus cares not, as he get money apace, being one of the agents for some of the privateersmen, and wears cloth shoes, ruffled shirts, silk breeches and stockings, and dances minuets at Commencement; it is said he has made more profits as agent than Mr. Ansil Alcock. . . ."

Minny

The short and simple annals of the brave—and black. Scene: Convention of Delegates of Virginia, Saturday, June 15, 1776. Business: "A petition of Lucretia Pritchett . . . setting forth that in late attack on a piratical [British] tender in Rappahannock river, Minny, a negro man . . . voluntarily entered himself on board a vessel commanded by Mr. Hugh Walker, and being used to the water, and a good pilot, bravely and successfully exerted himself against the enemy, until he was unfortunately killed, whereby the estate of the said Joseph Pritchett was deprived of a valuable slave . . . since the said slave was lost by means of a meritorious act, in defence of the country, she [asks to be reimbursed] the value thereof." Two weeks later, the Virginia delegates awarded Lucretia Pritchett one hundred dollars for the death of her slave Minny.

"Captain" Mark Starlins

Another reminiscence of Commodore James Barron in his old age is all there is to furnish a glimpse into the life of the black Virginia pilot, Mark Starlins, who called himself "Captain." The commodore remembered "a very singular and meritorious character in the person of an African, who had been brought over to this country when he was young, and soon evinced a remarkable attachment to it; he was brought up as a pilot, and proved a skilful one, and a devoted patriot," who sometimes "allowed his patriotism to get the better of his judgment." The "noble African," wrote Barron, "lived and died a slave soon after the peace, and just before a law was passed that gave freedom to all those devoted men of colour who had so zealously volunteered their services in the patriotic cause." Starlins was held in high estimation "by all worthy citizens, and, more particularly, by all the navy officers of the State."

John Peterson

As he begins his tale of the capture of the British spy Major André, Nell relates that Peterson (like James Forten) was a prisoner in the "notorious Prison Ship" at New York, until one dark night he tied a bundle of clothes on his head, crept down the anchor chains, and slipped into the water. But Nell's main concern is the way in which the black private has been omitted in the usual accounts of the André affair, and he reprints from the Westchester *Herald* the long obituary, which, he suggests, is "worthy of republication a hundred times. . . ." Here is the obituary, somewhat reduced:

> John Peterson, a colored man (mulatto) departed this life October 2d, at his late residence in the village of Peekskill, aged 103 years. Peterson was brought up in the family of . . . Isaac Sherwood [who] had entered the Continental army, as a first lieutenant, and Peterson . . . begged the privilege of accompanying him into the service. . . .
>
> This regiment was in the memorable battle of Stillwater, in Saratoga county, at the time Gen. Burgoyne surrendered his whole army. . . . Lieut. Sherwood, who always sought the post of danger, received in the action a mortal wound. Peterson watched over this brave officer with untiring perseverance, night and day, until he expired, and after his death, followed his remains to the public burying-ground in the city of Albany. . . . The devoted attachment of Peterson to the gallant and much-lamented lieutenant was observed by Col. Van Cortlandt, who, without solicitation, gave him his discharge from the service, to enable him to return home with the effects which belonged to the lieutenant. . . .
>
> On the morning of the 21st of September, 1780, Moses Sherwood and Peterson were engaged in making cider, at Barrett's farm, in Cortlandt. . . . they had taken their arms with them. . . . It was on that day that the Vulture sloop-of-war came to anchor . . . having brought up André for the purpose of holding an interview with the traitor Arnold. . . . [Moses Sherwood] saw a barge filled with armed men from the Vulture, in company with a gun-boat, approaching the shore . . . whereupon they seized their guns and . . . concealed themselves behind some rocks, and as the barge came sweeping along towards the place where they were lying, Peterson fired. His aim had been well directed, for an oar was seen to drop from the hands of one of the men on board, and much confusion was observed among them. A second shot from Sherwood compelled them to return to the Vulture, which they did under cover of canister and grapeshot from the gun-boat. . . . Many [armed townsmen] now hastened to the end of Teller's Point with a field piece. . . . They erected a small redoubt, and opened a well-directed fire on the Vulture, and she fired in return several broadsides directed towards the redoubt.
>
> André . . . saw from his window the Vulture slip her cable and make sail for New York. This circumstance prevented him from returning to the city by water . . . which led to his capture at Tarrytown. But for the firing of Peterson and Sherwood upon the barge, it is more than probable he would have returned to the Vulture in safety.

Peterson received a pension from the United States for his military services, and General Philip Van Cortlandt gave him a house and lot in

Cortlandt town, where he lived until he moved to Peekskill. "He retained through a long life" his obituary concludes, "the character of an honest man and a faithful soldier, and was much esteemed by all who knew him."

Jehu Grant

In 1832, when he was almost eighty, a black veteran living in Connecticut wrote to the War Department claiming a federal pension. His name was Jehu Grant. His initial letter of application and a second letter buttressing his claim reveal not only his life in the army as a wagoner and waiter but also his frustration when he was refused a pension—for an incredible reason:

> he was a slave to Elihu Champlen who resided at Narragansett, Rhode Island. At the time he left him, his master was called a Tory and in a secret manner furnished the enemy when shipping lay nearby with sheep, cattle, cheese, etc., and received goods from them. And this applicant being afraid his master would send him to the British ships, ran away sometime in August 1777 . . . he went right to Danbury and enlisted . . . was put to teaming with a team of horses and wagon, drawing provisions and various other loading for the army for three or four months until winter set in, then was taken as a servant to John Skidmore, wagon master general, and served with him until spring, when the troops went to the Highlands . . . on the Hudson River, a little above the British lines . . . sometime in June, when his master either sent or came, this applicant was given up to his master again, and he returned. . . .

In 1834, two years later, proslavery bureaucrats in the Pension Office in Washington rejected Jehu Grant's claim. Their reason? During his time of service in the patriot army he had in fact been a fugitive slave! It took old Grant another two years to recover from the rebuff. In 1836, in an angry, ironic reply signed with his mark, he wrote to the Commissioner of Pensions:

> In April 1834 I received a writing from Your Honor, informing me that my "services while a fugitive from my master's service was not embraced in the Pension Act of June 1832," and that my "papers were placed on file" . . . I now pray that I may be permitted to express my feelings more fully. . . .
>
> I was then grown to manhood, in the full vigor and strength of life. . . . when I saw liberty poles and the people all engaged for the support of freedom, I could not but like and be pleased with such thing (God forgive me if I sinned in so feeling). And living on the borders of Rhode Island, where whole companies of colored people enlisted, it added to my fears and dread of being sold to the British. These considerations induced me to enlist into the American army, where I served faithful about ten months, when my master found and took me home. Had I been taught to read or understand the precepts of Gospel, "Servants, obey your masters," I might have done otherwise, notwithstanding the songs of liberty that saluted my ear, thrilled through my heart. But feelings of conscious that I have since compensated my master for the injury he sustained by my enlisting, and that God has forgiven me for so doing, and that I served my country faithfully, and that they having enjoyed the benefits of my service . . . I cannot but feel it becoming me to pray Your Honor to review my declaration. . . .

> . . . I must be upward of eighty years of age and have been blind for many years, and, notwithstanding the aid I received from the honest industry of my children, we are still very needy and in part are supported from the benevolence of our friends. . . . I humbly set my claim upon the well-known liberality of government.

Perhaps Jehu Grant died soon after he sent off this letter. Whether he ever got his pension is not known.

THREE BLACK UNITS

There were two all-black units in the Continental Army; a third unit voyaged from Haiti with the French. Colonel Christopher Greene's First Rhode Island Regiment distinguished itself for efficiency and gallantry throughout the war—perhaps the war would have ended sooner if its example had been heeded. Little is known about the Bucks of America, a Massachusetts company, except that John Hancock chose it for special honor. The Black Brigade of Saint Domingue, Haiti, in this day of Pan-African aspiration, needs to be better known.[3]

The Black Regiment of Rhode Island came into being because that state was not able to supply its quota of white troops to the Continental Line—and because blacks wanted to fight for their own freedom. The rationale of the decision to create this unit is of some interest. Since history had supplied "frequent precedents of the wisest, the freest, and bravest nations having liberated their slaves, and enlisted them as soldiers to fight in defence of their country," and since the British had "taken possession of the capital, and of a greater part" of the state, it was simply "impossible . . . to furnish recruits. . . ." Therefore Rhode Island's legislature in February 1778 voted that any slave volunteering for the new battalions would be declared "absolutely free" and entitled to the wages and bounties of a regular soldier.

Colonel Christopher Greene, with Washington's blessing, hurried north from Valley Forge and before the spring was over he had begun to train the black soldiers who made up this extraordinary unit. The test of fire for the Black Regiment came all too soon in the Battle of Rhode Island, which General Lafayette called "the best fought action of the war." General John Sullivan, with six brigades, confronted a powerful force of British and Hessian troops. The Black Regiment—with its core of ninety-five ex-slaves and thirty freedmen, most of them raw recruits—assigned to what turned out to be one of the hottest sectors of the American right wing, was the special target of repeated Hessian charges. But here the Germans "experienced a more obstinate resistance than they had expected," noted an on-the-spot observer. "They found large bodies of troops behind the work and at its sides, chiefly wild looking men in their shirt sleeves, and among them many negroes." "It was in repelling these furious onsets," wrote a Rhode Island historian in 1860, "that the newly raised black regiment, under Col. Greene,

distinguished itself by deeds of desperate valor. Posted behind a thicket in
the valley, they three times drove back the Hessians who charged repeatedly
down the hill to dislodge them." The day after the battle, the Hessian colonel
"applied to exchange his command and go to New York, because he dared
not lead his regiment again to battle, lest his men shoot him for having
caused so much loss." On the day after the battle, General Sullivan announced that "by the best Information the Commander-in-Chief thinks that
the Regiment will be intituled to a proper share of the Honours of the day."

This was the Black Regiment's first action—but not its last. One of the
few American units that enlisted for the entire war, it proved itself again at
Red Bank, Points Bridge, and Yorktown. "In the attack made upon the American lines, near Croton river, on the 13th of May, 1781," wrote Nell, "Colonel Greene, the commander of the regiment, was cut down and mortally
wounded: but the sabres of the enemy only reached him through the bodies
of his faithful guard of blacks, who hovered over him to protect him, *and
every one of whom was killed.*"

Traveling in Connecticut in 1781, the Marquis de Chastellux noted in
his journal on January 5: "At the ferry-crossing I met with a detachment of
the Rhode Island regiment. . . . The majority of the enlisted men are Negroes or mulattoes; but they are strong, robust men, and those I saw made
a very good appearance." When the victorious American army passed in
review at Yorktown during the following July, Baron von Closen observed
that "three-quarters of the Rhode Island regiment consists of Negroes, and
that regiment is the most neatly dressed, the best under arms, and the most
precise in its maneuvres."

About all that is now known of Boston's all-black unit was recorded by Nell
in 1855:

> At the close of the Revolutionary War, John Hancock presented the colored
> company, called the "Bucks of America," with an appropriate banner, bearing
> his initials, as a tribute to their courage and devotion throughout the struggle.
> The "Bucks," under the command of Colonel Middleton, were invited to a
> collation in a neighboring town, and, *en route* were requested to halt in front
> of the Hancock Mansion, in Beacon street, where the Governor and his son
> united in the above presentation.

Three years after Nell gave his account, there took place in Boston an
exhibition of "interesting relics and mementoes of the olden time," including the banner of the black company as well as "a flag presented to an
association of colored men, called the 'Protectors,' who guarded the property
of Boston merchants" during the revolution. Sitting in the audience was
"Mrs. Kay, daughter of the Ensign who received the banner" from Hancock.
During the Civil War, Nell, who had purchased the banner from Mrs. Kay,
presented it to the Massachusetts Historical Society, whose proceedings for
1862 describe it as "a silk flag, bearing the device of a Pine-tree and a Buck,

with the initials 'J. H.' and 'G. W.' over a scroll, on which appear the words, 'The Bucks of America.'" And there was also a silver badge with the initials of the soldier, to be pinned on his coat, with the same pine tree, buck, and thirteen stars stamped on one side of it—on the other, a shield with the French fleur-de-lis, perhaps a salute to Lafayette.[4]

The role of the Bucks of America and of its black colonel during the revolution is somewhat elusive; military records have not so far revealed documentary evidence for such a unit. Perhaps the Bucks were simply another name for the Protectors, to which Wendell Phillips alluded as an "association of colored men . . . who guarded the property of Boston merchants." Nor does Colonel Middleton (or any other black officer) appear in the army or militia records, although it has been said that Middleton witnessed the Battle of Groton Heights in Connecticut in 1781. It may have been that the rank of colonel was bestowed on Middleton by Governor Hancock himself to identify him as the commander of a volunteer black posse comitatus to patrol Boston during the war and protect the city from Tory sabotage.

But whatever the military obscurity of *Colonel* Middleton during the war years, the *man* George Middleton did exist, and after the fighting was over he lived a long, full life as a solid citizen engaged in the struggle for civil rights in the Boston community.

George Middleton's name, apart from a record of his marriage in 1778, first appears in 1779 as a leading member of Prince Hall's African Lodge of Freemasons, and from then on, as a close coworker of Hall's in the activities of the African Lodge. The census of 1790 lists Middleton as head of a family of three. When black Masons in Philadelphia organized themselves into a lodge with Absalom Jones as Master, the vote to approve their warrant was taken at a gathering in George Middleton's house on Pinckney Street. In 1796, with Hall and forty-two other black men, Middleton organized a Boston African Benevolent Society and was licensed by the city as a teacher for the Society. In 1800, when sixty-seven blacks signed a plea for the establishment of an African school for their children, it was Middleton who submitted the petition to the Boston town meeting. After the death of Prince Hall and his successor Nero Prince, George Middleton would be elected to the office of third Grand Master of the African Lodge of Freemasons in Boston.

Lydia Maria Child has left us a sketch of George Middleton, whom she knew well in his hale old age when he played the violin and still retained his skill as a "horse-breaker." She tells a story in which he displays his youthful revolutionary fire in "subduing" some "mettlesome colts." The occasion was the celebration of an anniversary of the abolition of the slave trade, held annually by the blacks of Boston:

> It became a frolic with the white boys to deride them on this day, and finally . . . to drive them . . . from the Common. The colored people became greatly

incensed by this mockery of their festival, and rumor reached us . . . that they were determined to resist the whites, and were going armed with this intention. . . . Soon, terrified children and women ran down Belknap street, pursued by white boys, who enjoyed their fright. The sounds of battle approached; clubs and brickbats were flying in [all] directions. At this crisis, Col. Middleton opened his door, armed with a loaded musket, and, in a loud voice, shrieked death to the first white who should approach. Hundreds of human beings, white and black, were pouring down the street. . . . Col. Middleton's voice could be heard above every other, urging his party to turn and resist to the last. His appearance was terrific, his musket was levelled, ready to sacrifice the first white man that came within its range. The colored party, shamed by his reproaches, and fired by his example, rallied. . . .

The names of the Bucks of America (with one exception), their visages, their exploits of "courage and devotion" are so far lost to history. What remains is the bright banner and badge.

The Volunteer Chasseurs, another black outfit, from far-off Haiti—a brigade of the seaborne French expedition that supported General Lincoln in Georgia during the autumn of 1779—fought first in the American Revolution and then went on to join the struggle for nationhood in their own country, the second to achieve independence from Europe in the New World.

The aim of the Franco-American army was to evict the British from Savannah. In early September, a French fleet of thirty-three sail, under the command of the comte d'Estaing, anchored off the Georgia coast and debarked its troops. As reported in the *Paris Gazette*, there were 2,979 "Europeans" and 545 "Colored: Volunteer Chasseurs, Mulattoes, and Negroes, newly raised at St. Domingo," the latter called the Fontages Legion after its French commander.

Among the colored volunteers in the patriot cause were young men destined to become famous in the Haitian revolution—among them were Andre Rigaud and Louis Jacques Beauvais, noncoms at Savannah; Martial Besse, a general under the Versailles Convention; Jean-Baptiste Mars Belley, deputy to the convention; and Henri Christophe, future king. Many tales are told of twelve-year-old Christophe at Savannah—that he volunteered as a freeborn infantryman, that he was orderly to a French naval officer, and that he had been a slave and earned his freedom by his service in the Black Brigade.

To dislodge the well-entrenched enemy, Lincoln and d'Estaing decided to attack. But the British fought well, aided, it must be said, by hundreds of "armed blacks"—gathered from the countryside to build redoubts, mount cannon, and serve as guides and spies. "Having fallen in with a Negro named Quamino Dolly," wrote a participant in the siege, "Colonel Campbell induced him, by a small Reward, to conduct the Troops, by a private Path through the Swamp, upon the Right of the Americans."[5] Georgian patriots, however, fearful of slave revolt, always refused to give their bondsmen guns in exchange for liberty. As the French and Americans, raked by heavy fire, pulled back in retreat, the British, determined to wipe them out, charged. It was now that the Black Brigade, stationed as a reserve in the rear guard, showed its mettle by preventing the annihilation of the allied force. Count Casimir Pulaski, at the head of the cavalry, fell in this action. Martial Besse and Henri Christophe returned to Saint Domingue with slight wounds.

There is an ironic sequel. Eighteen years later when General Besse visited the United States on official business, he disembarked at Charleston, "dressed in the uniform of his grade," and was forced by the authorities to put up a bond as required by the law of South Carolina for all incoming blacks. It was only after the French consul in Charleston protested that General Besse was a representative of his government, and that, moreover, he had been wounded at the siege of Savannah, that the bond was remitted.

IN THE SERVICE OF THE KING

During the time of the revolution, white patriots, north and south, had to confront the hard fact that black people were doing some deep thinking about which side, if any, they should join. In one of his "Landscapes" of New York life near his homestead in Orange County, St. John Crévecour, the "American farmer," has the chairwoman of the local patriot committee lecture the slaves of a Loyalist: "Well, Nero. . . . They say you are a good fellow, only a little Torified like most of your colour." And there is the well-known anecdote of the slave of General Sullivan of New Hampshire, related by Nell in 1855: "When his master told him that they were on the point of starting for the army, to fight for liberty, he shrewdly suggested, that it would be a great satisfaction to know that he was indeed going to fight for *his* liberty. Struck with the reasonableness and justice of this suggestion, Gen. S. at once gave him his freedom." The general was an unusual person, but the anecdote suggests why some two hundred slaves volunteered to join Greene's First Rhode Island Regiment in the cause of American independence, while four times that number in Virginia fled their patriot masters to join Dunmore's Ethiopian Regiment in the king's cause.

For slaves, the idea of freedom of body and soul was more important than tea and taxes. In a war between white patriot and white Tory, both upholders of the abominable institution, the question for Africans, enslaved in America for a century and a half, was clear enough: In which camp was there a better future for black freedom? The question was a simple one; the answer, always framed in terms of freedom, was often complex and perilous, dependent on place, time, and opportunity; one had to size up promises made by whites, Whig and Tory, desperately in need of black manpower for their own purposes. All blacks, slave or free, did not make the same choice, and there were some who sought their own path in flight or revolt.

Among the black Whitecuffs, a free family in New York, there was (as

Herman Melville would say later in a Civil War poem) a "conflict of convictions." The story emerges from the evidence in hearings held in 1784 by a parliamentary commission to look into the claims of Loyalists—among them one "Benjamin Whitecuff (a Black)," a twenty-year-old New Yorker: "He says he was born at Hempstead in King's County . . . his Father was a Freeman and he was born a Freeman.—At the beginning of the Troubles he was a Farmer,—and worked with his Father on his Farm—His Father took the American side and was a Sargeant in their Service. He would have persuaded him to go too but he refused. His older Brother went with him [the father] . . . he was employed for 2 years as a Spy by Sir Henry Clinton and Sir William Ayscough. . . . He says he was hung up by the Rebels at Cranbury in the Jerseys . . . for three minutes but was saved by Detachment of the 5th light Company. . . . He has heard his Father was killed at Chestnut Hill. His Brother was killed at German Town. . . . He can't read—his Memorial was drawn out by a Lawyer."

Of course, black resistance to oppression was not a new phenomenon in the south. At Christmastide 1769, a few months before the Boston Massacre, in Hanover County, Virginia, an outraged slave, whipped by an overseer, slashed at him with an ax. Gerald W. Mullin, citing the news story in the *Virginia Gazette*, has sketched the outcome: "He missed, but a group of slaves jumped on the white and administered such a severe beating that the 'ringleader' [the whipped slave] intervened and saved his life. The overseer ran off in search of reinforcements; and instead of fleeing or arming themselves, the slaves tied up two other whites and 'whipped [them] till they were raw from neck to waistband.' Twelve armed whites arrived, and the slaves retreated into a barn where they were soon joined by a large body of slaves, 'some say forty, some fifty.' The whites 'tried to prevail by persuasion,' but the slaves 'deaf to all, rushed upon them with desperate fury, armed wholely with clubs and staves.' Two slaves were shot and killed, five others were wounded, and the remainder fled." Such possibilities were perceived fearfully by slave owners on the eve of the revolution, as a letter written by the chairman of the Safety Committee in Chatham, North Carolina, on July 15, 1775, makes clear. From Beaufort County word had arrived of "an intended insurrection of the negroes against the whole people. . . . We immediately sent off an Express to Tarborough to alarm the inhabitants there . . . and appointed upwards of one hundred men as patrolers. . . . By night we had in custody and in gaol near forty under proper guard." The Safety Committee found the affair "a deep laid Horrid Tragick Plan for destroying the inhabitants of this province without respect of persons, age or sex . . . five negroes were whipt this day by order." The next day the Committee "ordered several to be severely whipt and sentenced several to receive 80 lashes each, to have both Ears crapd which was executed in the presence of the Committee and a great number of spectators." Reports came in of "negroes being in arms on the line of Craven and Pitt [county] and prayed assistance of men and ammunition which we readily granted. We posted guards upon the roads, for several miles that night."

The anxious writers see a plot of the Tories to seduce the slaves of patriots, to line them up on the British side in the looming struggle. "We keep taking up, examining and scourging more or less every day; from whichever part of the County they come they all confess nearly the same thing, Vizt that they were one and all on the night of the 8th inst to fall on and destroy the family where they lived, then to proceed from House to House (Burning as they went) until they arrived in the Back Country where they were to be received with open arms by a number of Persons there appointed and armed by Government for their Protection, and as a further award they were to be settled in a free Government of their own." There is a P.S. at the end: "In disarming the negroes we found considerable ammunition."

Three years before the ex-bondsmen of the Ethiopian Regiment donned their British uniforms, Dunmore had explored the critical question of slave loyalty as a matter of military-political strategy. What jogged his thinking was probably Lord Mansfield's opinion in the Somerset case which, in effect, freed all slaves entering England, reports of which had reached the colonies by the summer of 1772. The news was in the *Virginia Gazette*. In 1773 an advertisement for a runaway couple claimed they were on their way to Britain, "where they imagine they will be free (a Notion now too prevalent among the Negroes, greatly to the vexation and Prejudice of their Masters)." A year later, a similar notice complains that a fugitive Bacchus has fled his master in frontier Georgia and would attempt "to board a vessel for Great Britain . . . from the knowledge he has of the late Determination of Somerset's Case." Responding in 1772 to the colonial secretary, Dunmore remarked that some American slave owners, "with great reason, trembled at the facility that our enemy would find in Such a body of men, attached by no tye to their Master nor to the Country. . . . It was natural to Suppose that their Condition must inspire them with an aversion to both, and therefore are ready to join the first that would encourage them to revenge themselves, by which means a Conquest of this Country would inevitably be effected in a very short time. . . ."

In late April 1775, as Salem Poor was making his way to Bunker Hill, a group of Virginia blacks, presented with a new possibility of winning freedom without fleeing across the Atlantic, sought out the royal governor and offered to fight for the crown. In June General Thomas Gage sounded the alarm to Lord Barrington, the colonial secretary in London: "Things are now come to that crisis, that we must avail ourselves of every resource, even to raise the Negros, in our cause." Lord Dunmore was not yet ready, although for six months he had pondered the idea, feeling that "all the Slaves" were "on the side of the Government."[6] In mid-November a detachment of Dunmore's troops with black privates among them whipped the colonial militia at Kemp's Landing and slaves captured one of the patriot colonels.

The time and place were right—on November 7 at the scene of the victory, Dunmore proclaimed "all indented Servants, Negroes, or others, (appertaining to Rebels) free, that are able and willing to bear Arms" in the king's cause. That the proclamation accelerated the flight of slaves to the British is reflected a week later in an advertisement in the *Virginia Gazette* for the return of "Charles, who is a very shrewd, sensible fellow, and can both read and write," who ran away from his master because of a "determined resolution to get liberty, as he conceived by flying to lord Dunmore."

The phrase "appertaining to rebels" is crucial—only the slaves of patriots are offered their freedom. The fugitive slaves of Tories will remain on their plantations or be sent back to their owners. As John Adams noted in his diary after a conversation with two southerners, the British had a problem: "These gentlemen gave a melancholy account of the State of Georgia and South Carolina. They say that if one thousand regular troops should land in Georgia, and their commander is provided with arms and clothes enough, and proclaim to all the negroes, who would join his camp, twenty thousand negroes would join it from the two Provinces in a fortnight. The negroes have a wonderful art of communicating intelligence among themselves; it will run several hundred miles in a week or fortnight. They say, their only security is this; that all the king's friends, and tools of government, have large plantations, and property in negroes; so that the slaves of the Tories would be lost, as well as those of the Whigs."[7]

As the *Virginia Gazette* appealed to the slaves with frantic arguments to cling to their kind masters—"Be not then, ye negroes tempted by his proclamation to ruin your selves"—Patrick Henry assailed the proclamation as "fatal to the publick Safety" and counseled "early and unremitting Attention to the Government of the Slaves." A broadside to the plantations strongly advised that "Constant, and well directed Patrols" were "indispensably necessary" to prevent the runaways from flocking to the royal standard. Meanwhile, blacks piloted Dunmore's amphibian guerrilla forays, helped man his crews, and foraged widely to keep him in food. Within a week, five hundred bondsmen had answered his call. He gave them guns "as fast as they came in." By the first of December nearly three hundred blacks in uniform, with the words "Liberty to Slaves" inscribed across their breasts, were members of "Lord Dunmore's Ethiopian Regiment."

For the patriotic slave masters of Virginia and points south, the Ethiopian Regiment was a terrifying version of the old nightmare of black revolt. In mid-December the Virginia Convention published its answering proclamation: pardon to runaways who returned to their masters; a warning to the "seduced" that the penalty for slave insurrection was death without benefit of clergy. It should be noted that four months earlier the royal governor of South Carolina had reported to Lord Dartmouth the execution of Thomas Jeremiah, a black pilot and fisherman of Charleston: "under colour of Law, they hanged and burned, an unfortunate wretch, a Free Negroe of considerable property, one of the most valuable & useful men in his way in the

Province, on suspicion of instigating an Insurrection. . . ." Henry Laurens, patriot president of the Provincial Congress, was of the opinion that Jerry *had* conspired to foment an insurrection, as was testifed by one Sambo, another harbor worker: "there is a great war coming soon," said Jeremiah; "what shall we poor Negroes do in a schooner?" asked Sambo—to which Jeremiah replied: "set the Schooner on fire, jump on shore and join the soldiers . . . the war was come to help the poor Negroes." Even more damaging had been the testimony of Jemmy, a slave Jeremiah first denied knowing but who was shown to be his wife's brother, for Jemmy had sworn that Jeremiah was to have "the Chief Command of the said Negroes, that . . . he had Powder enough already, but that he wanted more arms. . . ." The Virginia Convention also decreed that slaves taken in arms would be sold in the West Indies— this from patriots who indicted his majesty for supporting the slave trade. But the fugitives, perhaps a thousand strong, all too willing to strike a blow for their freedom, were not to be bribed or frightened.

Yet the Tory operation "Liberty to Slaves" was only a partial success. Blacks could understand the hollowness of Dunmore's libertarian pretenses—he offered freedom only to the "able and willing" slaves of rebels and helped Tory masters retrieve their runaways—and knew that he had blocked the colony's effort to halt the slave trade. On December 9 at the Battle of Great Bridge—the Lexington of the south—the British force of six hundred, nearly half of which was black, was thrown back by Woodford's Second Virginia Regiment. Dunmore then retreated to his ships with his troops and there continued to train black soldiers in the use of small arms. But in March Dunmore had to advise the secretary of state that although recruitment of blacks was going on "very well, a fever crept in amongst them which carried off a great many Very fine fellows." In July it was reported to the Maryland Council of Safety that some black deserters from the British had smallpox. "The shores are full of dead bodies, chiefly negroes." By spring's end only "150 effective Negro men" were left. Had not the fever killed off "an incredible number of our people, especially blacks," Dunmore reported in June, the Ethiopian Regiment might have grown to two thousand. In August the harassed British fleet was forced to abandon the Virginia coast. Seven ships sailing northward had aboard some three hundred black soldiers who would fight on other fields.

But Dunmore's defeat did not alter basic British policy. In fact, southern slaves were everywhere joining the British. At Savannah a patriot colonel wrote to Washington: "The men-of-war at Tybee . . . [are] encouraging our slaves to desert to them, pilfering our sea island for provisions." Almost two hundred slaves from various plantations had answered the call to desert. When the news, via "a negro hired to ride post in the Continental Service," reached Henry Laurens in Charleston, it ruffled his humanitarian soul. Although it was "an awful business . . . to put even fugitive & Rebellious Slaves to death," he advised the Council of Safety in Georgia "to seize & if nothing else will do to destroy all those Rebellious Negroes upon Tybee

Island or wherever they may be found." Two years later, in June 1778, Pennsylvania Tory Joseph Galloway, formulating grand strategy for the earl of Dartmouth in a report on the "Strength of America in Respect to Her Number of fighting Men," reiterated the Virginia governor's early appraisal:

> The Negroes are truly intestine Enemies, and must in proportion to their Numbers subtract from the Strength of the Colony where they are, because they are Slaves, and desirous of recovering their freedom, and are ever ready to embrace an opportunity of doing it, and therefore it is but just, in determining on the strength of America, to deduct their Number of fighting Men, which is 150,000. . . . And let it be further added, that in the Class of fighting Men among the Negroes, there are no men of property, none whose Attachments would render them averse to the bearing of Arms against the Rebellion—and that more fighting Men might be raised among them, upon proper Encouragement, than among the whites, though they amount to three times their Number.

Mrs. Galloway, like Abigail Adams, also worried. In her diary for December 9, 1778, she wrote: "She talked to me about keeping slaves, but I oppos'd her. I am not convinced it is right . . . dream'd of our Negroes & cou'd not get them out of My Mind . . . am Uneasy about them . . . ye slaves runs in my mind . . . took an Anodine but had no good rest."

The judgment of Dunmore and Galloway was reaffirmed a year later when Sir Henry Clinton, commander-in-chief of the king's forces, proclaimed from his Westchester, New York, headquarters that he would guarantee to any slave coming over to the British his full freedom and choice of military assignment. "Their property [slaves] we need not seek," echoed John André, the ill-fated English spy, "it flies to us and famine follows." One of these items of property, "Duncan a Negro belonging to Mr. Dill a Carpenter in Charlestown," André told Sir Henry, "run away from thence last night by going up Cooper River . . . whence he got a Canoe" and brought crucial intelligence of the situation inside the besieged city.

Anguished patriots agreed with André: a pseudonymous Antibiastes in a broadside of 1777 urged the Americans to liberate their black servicemen: "Our non-emancipated soldiers are almost irresistibly tempted to desert to our foes, who never fail to employ them against us." In his journal for September 20, 1777, Henry Melchior Muhlenberg, a Lutheran pastor, set down a conversation with two blacks, servants of an English family leaving Philadelphia: "They secretly wished that the British army might win, for then all Negro slaves will gain their freedom. It is said that this sentiment is almost universal among the Negroes in America." Certainly this sentiment was pervasive among blacks south of the Potomac. In May 1776, in North Carolina, a committee to prevent the desertion of blacks recommended to the provincial congress that all masters "on the south side of *Cape-Fear River* . . . remove such male slaves as are capable of bearing arms, or otherwise assisting the enemy, into the country, remote from the sea. . . ." A few months later, in Georgia, slave owners publicly worried about "the vast number of

Negroes we have, perhaps of themselves sufficient to subdue us." Writing to the president of Congress in February 1777, General Robert Howe recommended that seven to eight thousand regulars be retained in South Carolina at all times to control the "numerous black domestics who would undoubtedly flock in multitudes to the Banners of the enemy whenever an opportunity arrived." (In 1770 Lieutenant Governor William Bull of South Carolina had stated that in time of "great danger the militia is to be reenforced with a number of Trusty Negroes, and we have many such, not exceeding one-third of the corps they are to join." Apparently seven years later, these "Trusty Negroes" had diminished in number.) In 1778 the Georgia Assembly, afraid that "grave danger might rise from insurrections," ordered one-third of each county's troops to serve as a permanent local patrol.

In spite of the desperate ingenuity of the colonial governments—even New York had its "Commission for Detecting and Defeating Conspiracies" —the runaways bolted. An American prisoner on board the British ship *Roebuck* in Delaware Bay on May 26, 1776, wrote out an eyewitness report of the operation:

> On that night there came three negro men from the shore in a canoe, who were shaked hands with, and kindly received and entertained. . . . [an officer] afterwards asked them if there would come more of their people on board; that if they did they would be well used. The negroes said there would. He then asked them if there were any shirtmen or forces lying near; they told him there were none nearer than six miles. He then asked them if there were any cattle near the shore on the main; they said there was plenty. He then asked them if they thought there was any danger in landing to get them; they said there was no danger. He then asked them if they could get some fowls that night for the officers . . . they said they could get fowls and sheep. He then told them they should be well paid; and, besides, should be free when this disturbance was over, which he expected would be very soon, and then each of them should have a plantation of Rebels' land. After which one of the negroes went and brought some fowls and geese, which this deponent heard making a noise coming up the side of the ship; and also brought his wife and two children, and another negro man. . . .

Sometimes the black fugitives were caught, as a South Carolina trial record makes clear. In early spring of 1776, two whites asleep in the forecastle of their schooner tied to a wharf on the Potomac were surprised about midnight by four slaves from four nearby plantations. The slaves demanded that the boat be sailed to the Coon River and that "they should have the Guns to go on shore with . . . promising no hurt should be done. . . ." But "the negroes, not being able to Manage the Vessel," their white prisoners "stered to Maryland," where three of the slaves were captured. Charles and Kitt were sentenced to hang and Harry to receive thirty lashes on his bare back. Five springs later, in 1781, John Tayloe's slave Billy, accused of waging war against Virginia "in an armed vessel," was found guilty of high treason by a patriot court. He was sentenced "to be hanged by the neck until dead and his head to be severed from his body and stuck up at some public cross road on a pole." Two of the six judges dissented: "a slave in our opinion Cannot Commit treason against the State, not being Admitted to the Privileges of a Citizen [a slave] owes the State No Allegiance. . . ." Governor Thomas Jefferson apparently concurred, reprieving Billy until the legislature decreed that a slave could not be found guilty of treason.

More often, probably, the fugitives got through. In December 1777, a Baltimore newspaper described a spectacular escape from a Potomac plantation. Twenty-one blacks—fifteen men, two women, and four children— broke into a barn in which the master kept his boat and used the vessel to sail to the British. Three news items in patriot papers of 1780 related the exploits of a black guerrilla leader, a veteran of Virginia's Ethiopian Regiment, operating in Monmouth County, New Jersey. During the first week of June, "Ty with his party of about 20 blacks and whites, last Friday afternoon took and carried prisoners Capt. Barns Smock and Gilbert Vanmater," spiked the four pounder, and ran off with the artillery horses. A fortnight later, "Ty with 30 blacks, 36 Queen's Rangers, and 30 refugee tories, landed at Conascung . . . got in between our scouts" undiscovered, and "carried off" several whites and blacks as well as "a great deal of stock." There were casualties on both sides. In September, "72 men, composed of New-Levies, Refugees and Negroes . . . about an hour before day, attacked the house of Captain Joshua Huddy." The *brave Negro Tye* [one of Lord Dunmore's crew]" was among the wounded, and news of his guerrilla strikes no longer appears in the press, yet even after the surrender of Cornwallis, black Loyalists continue their forays: "We hear from Monmouth," reported the *New Jersey Gazette* on June 5, 1782, that "a refugee landed with about 40 whites and 40 blacks, at Forked-River, and burnt Samuel Brown's salt-works, and plundered him; they then proceeded Southward towards Barnegat, for the purpose of burning the salt-works along shore between those places."

Thus, tens of thousands of slaves chose *their* way of striking for freedom. Most of them served the British—always short of men—as an indispensable labor force, in some cases armed with shovels and muskets. Many served as orderlies, mechanics, and artisans—and as cooks, carpenters, sawyers, teamsters, wagoners, turnwheelers, and blacksmiths. Some served as spies, guides, man-of-war men, and pilots. So rare are their names in the annals of the time, that two at random must suffice to hint at the host. In July 1776 Christopher Gadsden, in reporting a victory in southern waters over an enemy squadron, appended a postscript: "As soon as the action began, the *Commodore* [a British ship] ordered to be put into a place of safety, negro Sampson, a black pilot." Six months later, north of New York, a patriot colonel complained to his general that "a scouting party . . . brought in a stout negro fellow, the property of a Tory (one Peck), who is now with the enemy; and the negro has been employed as a spy to bring them accounts of our motions." Sampson and Peck were not at all unique.

Many, drilled in the manual of arms, saw action in the field. In April 1782 General Nathaniel Greene informed Washington that the British had armed and put in uniform at least seven hundred blacks. The Ethiopian Regiment was not the only black unit. That same spring two members of a black cavalry troop, about a hundred strong, were killed in a skirmish at Dorchester, South Carolina. Evacuating Boston, the royal army sailed to Halifax with a "Company of Negroes." Philadelphia had a "Company of Black Pioneers." A Brunswick contingent under Baron von Riedesel, supporting Burgoyne, took back to Germany its corps of Afro-American drummers. And just as blacks had fought with the British in the first skirmishes of the war, so they also fought in the last—and for the same reasons. In 1781 the General Assembly of British East Florida had offered to liberate any slave who showed courage in battle and to outfit him with a red coat and silver badge. Nine days after the signing of the Treaty of Peace in April 1783, a Tory colonel, Andrew Deveux of South Carolina, with a task force of 220 men sailed out of St. Augustine in five privateers to recapture the Bahamas from Spain. The troops that debarked near Nassau and demanded the surrender of the Spanish fortress were both black and white.

It seems probable that most of the blacks serving with the British left the country of their own will. (When Isaac and Kitt, in New York, were urged by their Virginia master to return to the plantation—he promised to forget that they had run away—they both spurned the idea; Isaac said he had heard that slaves who went back were "treated with great severity.") When the king's armies departed from the United States at the war's end, there went with them at least fourteen thousand blacks—six thousand from Charleston and four thousand each from Savannah and New York. Some were still the slaves of Tories; most were ex-slaves whose possible path to freedom, in their eyes, had led to the losing camp of Dunmore, Clinton, and Cornwallis. They sailed to Halifax, Jamaica, St. Lucia, Nassau, and England, grimly hopeful of the chance to begin a new life. "If anything," Quarles adds, "these figures are a bit low, and they do not, of course, include those who went off with the French, nor the thousands—perhaps around five thousand—whom the British carried away prior to the surrender of Yorktown." There were also some forty-five hundred black refugees who had fled South Carolina and Georgia and made their way to East Florida.

Some of the royal army's black soldiers and laborers—victims of callous treatment by redcoat officers—did not leave in the British ships. A sequence of events jotted down in his journal by the Hessian captain Johann Ewald, campaigning in Virginia in 1781, might be seen as a pattern of betrayal, sad enough to touch even a mercenary's heart:

> [April 17] Because I lacked some cavalry . . . twelve Negroes were mounted and armed. I trained them as well as possible and they gave me thoroughly good service, for I sought to win them by good treatment, to which they were not accustomed.
>
> [June 21] . . . Lord Cornwallis had permitted each subaltern to keep two horses and one Negro, each captain, four horses and two Negroes, and so on, according to rank. . . . this order was not strictly carried out. . . . Every officer

had four to six horses and three or four Negroes, as well as one or two Negresses for cook and maid . . . I can testify that every soldier had his Negro, who carried his provisions and bundles. This multitude always hunted [foraged] at a gallop, and behind the baggage followed well over four thousand Negroes of both sexes and all ages. . . . They had plundered the wardrobes of their masters and mistresses, divided the loot. . . . a completely naked Negro wore a pair of silk breeches, another a finely colored coat, a third a silk vest without sleeves, a fourth an elegant shirt, a fifth a fine churchman's hat, and a sixth a wig.— . . . one Negress wore a silk skirt, another a lounging robe with a long train. . . . If one imagines all these variegated creatures on thousands of horses, then one has the complete picture. . . .

[October 14] I would just as soon forget to record a cruel happening. On the same day of the enemy assault, we drove back to the enemy all of our black friends, whom we had taken along to despoil the countryside. We had used them to good advantage and set them free, and now, with fear and trembling, they had to face the reward of their cruel masters. Last night, I came across a great number of these unfortunates. In their hunger, these unhappy people would have soon devoured what I had . . . we should have thought more about their deliverance at this time.

There were other black soldiers and laborers who, after the war was over, were either abandoned by the British or chose to continue their fight for freedom at home. A Georgia historian recorded in 1859 the known facts about a "corps" of some three hundred "runaway negroes, the leaders of which, having been trained to arms by the British during the siege of Savannah, still called themselves the 'King of England's Soldiers,' and ravaged both sides of the Savannah River, plundering and murdering, to the great alarm of the people; who also feared that the presence of this body of free-booters would lead to a general and bloody insurrection of the slaves in that vicinity." On May 6, 1786, a detachment of Georgia and South Carolina militia, guided by a few Catawba Indians, stormed the maroons in their improvised fortress, which consisted of a rectangular breastwork of logs and cane about a hundred yards wide and half a mile long. Many of the King of England's Soldiers were killed or captured; some escaped into the tangled brakes.

This was not the end of the resistance. In November, the *Massachusetts Gazette* printed a report from Georgia:

October 19. A number of runaway negroes (supposed to be upwards of 100) having sheltered themselves on Bellisle Island, about 17 or 18 miles up Savannah river, and for some time past committed robberies on the neighbouring Planters, it was found necessary to attempt to dislodge them . . . a small party of militia landed and attacked them, and killed three or four; but were at last obliged to retreat for want of ammunition, having four of their number wounded. Same evening, about sunset, 15 of the Savannah Light Infantry, and three or four others, drove in one of their out-guards; but the Negroes came down in such numbers, that it was judged advisable to retire to their boats from which the Negroes attempted to cut them off. Lieut. Elfe . . . had a field piece on board, which he discharged three times with grapeshot, and it is thought either killed or wounded some of them, as a good deal of blood was afterwards seen. . . . On Friday morning Gen. Jackson, with a party, proceeded to their camp, which they had quitted precipitately on his approach. He remained till Saturday afternoon, when he left the island having destroyed as much rough rice as would have made 25 barrels or more if beat out, and brought off about 69 bushels of corn, and 14 or 15 boats or canoes from the landing. He also burnt a number of the houses and huts, and destroyed about four acres of green rice. The loss of their provisions, it is expected, will occasion them to disperse about the country, and it is hoped will be the means of most of them being soon taken up.

The saga of the black men, women, and children who sailed to Nova Scotia with the British deserves to be better known as part of the history of the African diaspora and the American revolution. Here is a brief account of a figure of some stature in that history.

Thomas Peters fought for his freedom in the service of the king, but that is only part of the saga of this black Moses—a cluster of fact and legend that relates him to the times of Martin Delany and Marcus Garvey. Peters was an Ebga of the Yoruba tribe, of royal birth and "strong, far beyond the ordinary man," claim his descendants now living in Freetown, Sierra Leone. In the 1760s, he was kidnapped by the slave ship *Henri Quatre* and ended up on an American plantation, perhaps in Louisiana. He was then in his twenties. Legend has it that his master kept him shackled. After his first attempt to escape, he was forced to wear a broad iron belt from which hung two massive linked chains which connected the ankle bands. He was whipped after each dash for liberty; the third time he was branded.

On the eve of the revolution, Peters was the slave of one William Campbell in Wilmington, North Carolina. When Lord Dunmore dangled the bait of freedom, he ran away into the British lines. Three years later, Sally, his wife-to-be, fled her master in Charleston, South Carolina. Peters fought with the British for the entire war and was twice wounded. No doubt his commitment to freedom, his courage, and his ability to lead brought him to the fore. His name appears as "Petters" with the rank of sergeant in "a Return of the Companies of Black Pioneers" for September 13, 1783. He later described himself as "a free Negro and late Serjt. in the Regiment of Guides and Pioneers serving in North America under the Command of Genl. Sir Henry Clinton."

The war over, Peters and his veteran comrades asked the British to keep their promises. In May 1784 the king's ships landed them in Nova Scotia. True, they were free, but where were the pledged farms? Peters hoped to work as a millwright. The reality was weasel words instead of farms, un-clearable land for a few, slavelike apprenticeships to white Tories. In August, Peters and Murphy Steel, another ex-sergeant in the Black Pioneers, peti-tioned the royal government for an immediate grant of the promised acre-age—to no avail. After six years of struggle, in which he was supported by his people, he determined to go to London. As he later wrote, the trip was one of "much Trouble and Risk"; he was fifty years old, carrying a complaint against the hostile governor, an ex-slave voyaging alone.

In London, after initial hardship, it is possible that he received his first help from a brother African, ex-slave Ottobah Cugoano, a Fanti who had been sold in the West Indies and brought to London as a servant. Four years earlier Cugoano had written a celebrated book, *Thoughts and Sentiments on the Evil and Wicked Traffic of Slavery and Commerce of the Human Species.* It was Cugoano who probably introduced Peters to the great English abolitionists Granville Sharp, William Wilberforce, and Thomas Clarkson. Peters found his old commander-in-chief, Sir Henry Clinton, sympathetic to his cause. The upshot was that the abolitionists agreed to support the petition that Peters had brought with him over the ocean, in which, "on Behalf of himself and others [of] the Black Pioneers and loyal Black Refugees" of Annapolis and New Brunswick, he demanded a "competent Settlement." He was "Attorney" for two groups: those "Black People . . . earnestly desirous of obtaining their due Allotment of Land and remaining in America," and those who were "ready and willing to go wherever the Wisdom of Government may think proper to provide for them as free Subjects of the British Empire." The British secretary of state endorsed the petition and ordered the governor of Nova Scotia to comply.

Meanwhile another path had opened up for Peters—a path back to Africa. A few years earlier, English abolitionists, appalled by the hard lot of the black poor in England, had helped some four hundred blacks begin a new life on the coast of Sierra Leone. A company had been formed to promote the idea. Why not offer the plan to the stranded, outraged black Nova Scotians— transportation to Sierra Leone and twenty acres for each settler? Peters said yes, returned to Canada, and rounded up his own group of eighty-four emigrants, including his wife and six children. In January 1792 some twelve hundred settlers in fifteen ships sailed from Halifax for Freetown.

The rest belongs to the early history of the modern state of Sierra Leone. Although Thomas Peters died of fever only four months after returning to his native land, his name is imperishably linked to its history: kidnapped slave, branded fugitive, Tory soldier seeking his own freedom, early organizer of his own people for their return to the homeland, and finally, as his biographer noted, a founding father of Sierra Leone.[8]

NOTES

1. Von Closen has other first-hand observations of blacks in his journal. In 1782 he records a meeting with "a slave ship, under an Austrian flag, coming from the Guinea coast and bound for the Cape. . . . The commerce . . . in negroes is an abominable and cruel thing, in my opinion. On board these ships they are treated worse than beasts; men are on one side, and women on the other, in the forepart of the ship. There is an iron

chain which crosses from one side to the other, to which they all are attached, 2 by two, except for the few who are necessary for assistance in the maneuvers. All these unfortunate beings are naked, and at the least movement that does not suit the Captain, they are beaten to a pulp. . . . the loss of a fifth of them, from sickness or despair during a voyage of 2 or 3 months, is expected."

2. Parker Pillsbury, the New Hampshire abolitionist, wrote to Nell in 1855 about "the two brave men of color" who fell with Ledyard: "All the names of the slain, at that time, are inscribed on a marble tablet, wrought into the monument—*the names of the colored soldiers last,*—and not only last, but a blank space is left between them and the whites; in genuine keeping with the 'Negro Pew' distinction—setting them not only below others, but by themselves, even after that. And it is difficult to say why. They were not the last in the fight. . . . And the name of Jordan Freeman stands away down, last on the lists of heroes—perhaps the greatest hero of them all."

3. In Louisiana, a colony of Spain during the revolution, two black companies of militiamen fought against the British. "Assigned the mission of driving the British from the Gulf Coast and the banks of the Mississippi, Bernardo Gálvez [governor of Louisiana] mobilized a task force of 670 men of all nations and colors of whom eighty were free blacks. . . . These troops, a company of Pardos (or mulattos) and Morenos (or Negroes) [helped] to capture Baton Rouge in 1779, Mobile in 1780, and Pensacola in 1781. . . . Gálvez specifically cited the blacks. 'No less deserving of eulogy are the companies of Negro and Free Mulattoes' who 'conducted themselves with as much valor and generosity as the white.'" (Roland C. McConnell, "Louisiana's Black Military History, 1729–1865," in *Louisiana's Black Heritage*, ed. Robert R. Macdonald, John R. Kemp, Edward F. Haas [New Orleans, 1979], 34–35)

4. In 1781 Isaiah Thomas's *Massachusetts Spy* (Worcester) adopted a new device for its masthead which embodied in part a chain of thirteen links, a star in each link, and the fleur-de-lis of the French alliance. (Joseph T. Buckingham, *Specimens of Newspaper Literature* . . . [Boston, 1852], 1:240)

5. These black allies of the British suffered terribly in the aftermath. A French officer in Savannah, after its later evacuation by the British, recorded in his journal: "The large number of negroes they had requisitioned as laborers spread the plague in town. These miserable creatures could be found in every corner, either dead or dying. No one took the trouble to bury them, so you can imagine the infection this must have engendered. Still, a large number of them survived. Most were reclaimed by the inhabitants. Negroes without masters found new ones among the French, and we garnered a veritable harvest of domestics. Those among us who had no servant were happy to find one so cheap."

6. Dunmore's strategy had a tradition in British military history. Captain Woodes Rogers, preparing for a battle in the summer of 1709, wrote in his journal for August 16: "This Day I muster'd our Negroes [slaves] aboard the *Duke*, being about 35 lusty Fellows; I told them, That if we met the *Spaniards* or *French*, and they would fight, those that behav'd themselves well should be free Men; 32 of 'em immediately promis'd to stand to it, as long as the best *Englishman*, and desired they might be improv'd in the Use of Arms, which some of them already understood; and that if I would allow 'em Arms and Powder, these would teach the rest. Upon this I made *Michael Kendall*, the *Jamaica* free Negro, who deserted from the *Spaniards* to us at *Gorgona*, their Leader . . . and to confirm our Contract made them drink a Dram all round to our good Success; at the same time I gave 'em Bays for Clothes, and told them they must now look upon themselves as *Englishmen*, and no more as Negro Slaves to the *Spaniards*, at which they express'd themselves highly pleas'd. . . ."

7. As Silas Deane wrote to John Jay on December 3, 1776, the Americans could use the same ploy: "*Omnia tentanda* is my motto, therefore I hint the playing of their own game on them, by spiriting up the *Caribs* in St. *Vincent's*, and the negroes in Jamaica, to revolt."

8. In the latest treatment of Thomas Peters, Gary B. Nash refers to him "as a leader of as great a stature as many a famous 'historical' figure of the Revolutionary era. Only

because the keepers of the past are drawn from the racially dominant group in American society has Peters failed to find his way into history textbooks. . . ." The history of another colonial slave, Boston King of South Carolina, who fled to the British, is self-told. After the war, King struggled for a living on the land in Nova Scotia and as a crewman on an American whaler. He ended up as a cleric and schoolmaster in Sierra Leone. The story is told in "Memoirs of the Life of Boston King, a Black Preacher, Written by Himself . . ." (1798), published in his lifetime.

PART TWO

NEGOTIATING
OUR
LABOR:
SLAVE
AND
FREE

SIX

Disciplining Slave Ironworkers in the Antebellum South: Coercion, Conciliation, and Accommodation

CHARLES B. DEW

When John C. Calhoun learned in 1845 that his son-in-law, Thomas Clemson, was planning to break up his plantation and rent out his slave force, Calhoun promptly reminded him of the probable human consequences of such a move. The hirer of the slaves would have no incentive to "take good care of them," Calhoun warned. "The object of him who hires, is generally to make the most he can out of them, without regard to their comfort or health," he continued, and Calhoun was so convinced of the evils of slave hiring that he offered to buy the slaves himself if Clemson could not find other decent masters who would purchase them.[1]

Several historians of American slavery who have commented recently on slave hiring, and particularly on the hiring of slaves for industrial purposes, share Calhoun's bleak assessment of this phase of the South's peculiar institution. "The overwork of hired slaves by employers with only a temporary interest in their welfare was as notorious as the harsh practices of overseers," notes Kenneth M. Stampp. "Slaves hired to mine owners or railroad contractors were fortunate if they were not driven to the point of where their health was impaired."[2] In the view of Stampp and a number of other scholars, slave hiring and industrial slavery were among the most brutal and exploitive aspects of the American slave system; these historians tend to see hiring out and industrial employment, like slave trading, as areas where the business aspects of the institution were most highly developed and where the humanity of the slaves was most likely to be ignored.[3]

Other recent students of slavery, particularly Clement Eaton and Richard

B. Morris, have suggested a somewhat different picture. "Court records . . . contain rather frequent references to cruel treatment, overwork, and neglect of hired slaves," writes Professor Eaton. "Yet considerable evidence . . . indicates that many of the plantation slaves of the Upper South desired to be hired in the cities and in industries to secure the privileges, social opportunities, rewards, and freedoms which they could not enjoy on the plantation."[4] Both Eaton and Morris see slave hiring and industrial work contributing to the development of improved living conditions for slave laborers and argue, in Morris's words, that these improvements represented a "trend toward upgrading slaves into a shadowland of quasi-freedom" in the late antebellum era.[5] Although there is considerable doubt about some of the implications of the Eaton-Morris analysis, particularly their suggestion that this trend toward greater freedom posed a threat to the continued existence of slavery itself, they would seem to be on the right track. A close examination of one phase of Southern industrial slavery that used large numbers of hired bondsmen—the manufacture of iron—reveals a complex relationship between master and slave that rested more on a subtle process of mutual compromise and accommodation than on excessive use of physical force and coercion. This is not by any means intended to suggest that force was not used, for it clearly was, or to suggest that the slave ironworker lived and labored as a free person; he or she was still a slave, and in Southern industrial slavery, as in all slave systems, the master ultimately possessed far superior weapons if a test of wills threatened to go beyond what the master considered reasonable bounds. But unless an outright threat to the master's authority or a direct challenge to the slave system itself occurred, the Southern iron men examined for this article proved, for a number of reasons, to be willing to meet their slave hands in a rather vague and nebulous middle ground where black and white could live with and work alongside each other and where the slave had considerable influence over his working conditions, his family arrangements, and the course of his everyday life.

In order to present this thesis in as clear and brief a fashion as possible, this article concentrates on the operations of William Weaver and several other ironmasters whose furnaces and forges lay in the Valley of Virginia. More detailed evidence is available on the antebellum Virginia iron industry than for any other Southern state, but research in the surviving records of iron establishments that were located in other areas of the South indicates that Virginia's labor practices were characteristic of the industry throughout the slave states.[6] The emphasis on a specific group of men in a specific area also reflects a conviction that only through close and detailed case studies of the ways in which slavery functioned on a day-to-day basis can we begin to understand what it meant to be a slave in any phase of the American slave system, industrial or agricultural, urban or rural. One of my purposes is to suggest that the material for studies in microcosm of this sort is available and that records generated in the daily functioning of the system can give us some insight into the slave's own reaction to his or her bondage. Perhaps an imaginative use of primary sources of this kind can free historians from an almost exclusive dependence on published fugitive accounts or the Slave Narrative Collection of the Library of Congress in our renewed efforts to get inside the most peculiar of American institutions.[7]

William Weaver was something of a legend in his own lifetime. Although born in Pennsylvania, he spent most of his adult life in the valley region of Virginia where he amassed, for his day, a sizable fortune from his iron, farming, and milling operations. In 1860 Weaver, then seventy-nine years old, estimated to the federal census taker that his real and personal property was worth over $130,000, a figure that was probably reasonably accurate since Weaver owned thousands of acres of land and held sixty-six slaves in 1860 —thirty-one adult men, fifteen adult women, and twenty children.[8] Weaver's scientific farming experiments on the steep slopes of the North River and Buffalo Creek in his home county of Rockbridge gained wide notoriety and earned him a reputation as an innovating and successful farmer.[9] But it was in the iron trade that Weaver concentrated his energies, his financial resources, and the bulk of his slave labor force.

During the 1850s Weaver operated two iron manufacturing installations, both of which employed slave labor extensively and both of which were typical of the slave-manned furnaces and forges that dotted upland areas in Virginia, Tennessee, Kentucky, North and South Carolina, Georgia, Alabama, and Missouri prior to the Civil War. Weaver centered his operations at Buffalo Forge, near Lexington, Virginia, where a picked group of slave operatives worked four fires and two water-powered hammers that annually produced about one hundred tons of bar iron for the Lynchburg and Richmond markets. The pig iron to sustain the operations at Buffalo Forge came from Weaver's Etna Furnace, a charcoal blast furnace located in an adjoining county, which produced some seven hundred tons of pig iron per year. The Etna pig iron not consumed at Weaver's forge was sent by boat down the James River and Kanawah Canal and offered for sale by commission merchants in Lynchburg and Richmond.[10]

Iron manufacturing in the antebellum South was a labor-intensive industry. Since Weaver's Etna Furnace, like practically all Southern blast furnaces, used charcoal for fuel, dozens of workers were needed to chop wood, man charcoal pits, and haul the charcoal frequently long distances to the furnace site. At the ore banks, which might also be several miles from the furnace, miners dug iron ore, while other miners were needed to extract limestone to use as flux in the manufacturing process. When an adequate supply of what furnace men referred to as "stock"—ore, charcoal, and limestone—had been assembled, a process that often required two or three months, the furnace was "blown in" and the production of pig iron begun. Once in operation, workers fed measured amounts of iron ore, charcoal, and limestone into the blast furnace day and night until the blast was completed. Since blasts frequently lasted four to five months, and sometimes longer, and since farming operations were also conducted at most Southern iron works, including Weaver's installations, a constant interchange of slave labor between industrial and agricultural tasks took place at furnaces and forges throughout the South and allowed ironmasters to employ their extensive labor force year round.

At most Southern blast furnaces slave labor played a large role in almost all phases of pig iron production. As founders, colliers, miners, teamsters, wood choppers, and general furnace hands, slaves constituted the bulk of the laboring force. An average charcoal blast furnace required some sixty or seventy slave workers, in addition to a white manager and a handful of skilled laborers, usually but not always white, who were responsible for supervising various stages of production. Since Weaver owned only thirty-one adult male slaves in 1860 and many of these worked at his forge he, like most Southern iron men, was forced to hire a considerable number of slaves each year—as many as ninety or a hundred hands—in order to sustain both of his iron-making enterprises and his farming operations.[11]

The labor demands at Buffalo Forge were less than those at Weaver's blast furnace. At the forge a force of slave heaters and hammermen turned Weaver's pig iron into "merchant bars," the term used in the nineteenth century to describe refined iron that had been hammered or rolled into standard-size bars. A number of slave hands at Buffalo Forge were highly skilled artisans owned by Weaver: Henry Mathews, who was proficient as a blacksmith, rough carpenter, forge hand, and farmworker; Jim Garland and a slave named Tooler who operated Weaver's chafery and refinery forges and there worked the iron prior to its being wrought into bars; two heaters, Henry Towles and Henry Hunt, Jr., the son of one of Weaver's older slaves of the same name who had evidently been brought up in the iron trade at Buffalo Forge; Sam Williams, an exceptionally skilled ironworker who apparently hammered out finished bars; and Mark, Charles, Garland, and Warder who each had responsibility for a six-mule team and wagon. Weaver's select group of forge hands and teamsters was supplemented by an additional force of slave workers hired by the year to work in less skilled forge operations, in Weaver's flour mill at Buffalo Forge, and as agricultural laborers on Weaver's extensive and scattered farm properties.[12]

The necessity for an accommodation between William Weaver and his slaves, both those he owned and those he hired, lay ultimately in Weaver's dependence on these men for the success of his operations. First of all, to carry on his various manufacturing and farming activities he needed large numbers of slave hands, not all of whom could he afford to purchase. As mentioned previously, he annually sought as many as ninety to a hundred slaves, and the process of hiring so many hands was by no means routine or automatic. A number of difficulties were involved, and these difficulties were compounded in the late antebellum period by the fact that slave labor was becoming increasingly scarce and expensive in Virginia. In the 1820s Weaver normally paid $45 to $50 per year to hire slave hands, with the $50 hire representing Weaver's upper limit for superior workers.[13] By the mid-1850s, however, the price had risen well above those levels, as Weaver's hiring agents reported to him in December 1855:

> They [the owners] are asking $135 to $150 for good hands, no one can tell what the price will be, untill new years day. . . . you have no idea of the trouble there is in hiring hands here, at this day, there is all sorts of trickery and management, I don't expect to be able to hire more than thirty or forty hands, we may get fifty; but I can assure you, the prospect is very glomy.[14]

One of Weaver's nephews, James C. Davis of nearby Gibraltar Forge, seeking hands in the same neighborhood, a few days later reported similar difficulties and explained the reason for the troublesome situation. "Hands are hiring a little higher this year than last; the cause of it is the high price of the produce of farms & the consequent demand for their labor in that direction."[15] "There are not so many Iron & no more railroad men in the field," he wrote two days later, "but the farmers make a formidable phalanx of opposition. Some of them are giving $140 to $150 for men, & $70 to $90 for women," he added. "Women are higher than ever known before."[16]

As these letters indicate, the competition among various industrial and agricultural groups for slave labor was stiff in Virginia in the mid-1850s, but this was by no means a novel situation. In the 1820s and 1830s canal-building and gold-mining interests had offered strong hiring competition, and bursts of railroad construction in Virginia in the 1840s and 1850s brought another major employer into the field. Throughout the late antebellum decades agents for the urban tobacco factories and the Richmond area coal mines, cotton mills, and iron works also sought large numbers of slave hands each year.[17]

Given the increased problems involved in hiring an adequate labor force, it was imperative that Weaver and the other ironmasters avoid the reputation that they abused slaves in their employ. If slaves returned home to their owners with stories of hard driving and excessive punishment, an iron man like Weaver could be seriously handicapped in his efforts to hire in subsequent years. That ironmasters were sensitive to any suggestion that they abused slaves and that they sought to avoid excessive physical punishment if at all possible is indicated by an exchange of correspondence in 1849 between the manager of an iron furnace in Rockbridge County and the owner of a hired slave who claimed the manager had mistreated him. First, the letter from the slaveholder to the ironmaster, Francis T. Anderson of Glenwood Furnace:

> My boy Edmond that I hired to . . . you got here the eight of this month [November 1849], he says that your overseer is so cruel that he could not stand him. I have hired him out for the three years and the Gentleman was very much pleased with him. I know he will do his work as well as any negroe unless the person that overlooks him is barbourse I write this to let you know that I have given him a pass and started him back to you, this morning, if you thrash

him do not be two rough and I know he will do his work as well as any other negroe at your furnice.[18]

After receiving this letter, the furnace owner had his manager draft a statement concerning the conduct of this worker and the circumstances surrounding his punishment and subsequent departure from the furnace:

> Your letter under date of 9th Nov. is before me and contents noticed, in answer I must inform you that your man Edmund has behaved very badly & told you lies.
>
> I have never struck him one lick on account of his work, the place he lived at last year Mr. Stevens is in the neighborhood of our Furnace, where he had some 2 or 3 wives and would be there nearly every night in the week and Mr. Stevens complained to me that Edmund kept a continual uproar and fighting with other negroes, and that he could not stand it. I then told Edmund not to go there, and I also told Mr. Stevens if it happened again to take Edmund and bring him to me which he did and I gave him a good dressing and have not seen him since, which was the early part of the summer. Since that time he has been plundering the neighborhood & steeling & lying in peoples barns and robing their spring houses&c.
>
> You will please inquire of the negroes which came from the same neighbourhood namely—Ben Swan, Randle Swan, Fister, Burbage, and Beverly Beasly all of them will prove the correctness of my statement.[19]

There are a number of significant points in this exchange, but two elements deserve special mention: first, that Edmond, the slave, knew he could get the ear of his master by pleading, in effect, "ironmaster brutality," and although his owner sent him back to the furnace, he did so with the admonition that Edmond not be severely punished; and second, that the owner of the furnace kept a copy of his manager's explanation in his files to protect himself and his enterprise from the charge that slaves were abused at his iron works.

A runaway incident that occurred at Weaver's Etna Furnace in the 1850s led to a similar revealing exchange of correspondence. A hiring agent who had secured several slave wood choppers to work at the furnace had just learned some disturbing information, as he noted in a letter to Weaver dated November 11, 1857:

> I received a letter from some one with no name to it saying that Robert had left you and the reason assigned was that your [furnace] manager wished him to work in the Ore Bank and it was so dangerous that all your white hands had quit on that account. if so I am surprised for I had always thought you a different man and had always represented you as being one of the safest men to hire to as regards the treatment in the Vallie and besides I have always hired Robt William & Prince as wood choppers and I have no doubt it was done without your knowledge. if Robt has left please let me hear from you immediately as I dont want the Boy to give either of us any trouble.[20]

Weaver immediately asked his furnace manager for an explanation and received a full account of the difficulty concerning Robert:

> On inquiry I find there is something in relation to Bob from which a tale could

be manufactured, to wit. On Tuesday a week William [W. Rex] requested Bob to go to the Bank (he picking him out on a/c of being near his wife's) William thinking all [was] right left, but afterwards finding that he did not go up, saw him again on Tuesday last at which time Bob said very imputantly that you had a letter at the forge to the effect that a particular understanding was made that he (Bob) was not to work in the Bank. If that is the case (says William) I dont expect you to work there. He William at the same time requesting him (Bob) to come [to the] Furnace stating to Bob that he would write to you & if it was not in your hands he bob might expect a punishment. That was all that was said & the last & Bob is now away. Of course there is not one word of truth in regard to white hands in [the] Bank & *no danger there either.*[21]

Once again, the ironmaster's inquiry and the manager's detailed explanation of the incident that employers were well aware that they could not afford to ignore charges that they neglected owners' instructions about working conditions or that they dealt too severely with slave laborers.

Although ironmasters apparently tried to avoid excessive reliance on harsh physical punishment, there is ample evidence that the whip was employed at antebellum iron works in Virginia. The point seems to have been not to overuse the lash, to employ it to the extent that the slaves became recalcitrant or demoralized and owners became apprehensive over the health and safety of their hired bondsmen. One letter in particular touches on the entire question of discipline and coercion in such a revealing way that it deserves to be quoted at some length. The letter describes the trials of James C. Davis who was attempting to rehire a specific group of slave workers in eastern Virginia for another year's labor at his Gibraltar Forge near Lexington. His problem was not only to convince the master that they should go back to the forge but also to persuade the slaves, and one slave in particular, to return. He described his difficulties with this group of hands in a detailed letter addressed to his father, William Weaver Davis, at the forge, dated January 5, 1856:

There is some difficulty about Dickinson's hands & I hardly know how to act. When they came from over the mountain they wished to go back: & under the impression that they still wished so I hired them of Dickinson at the Ct House tuesday. Shortly after I hired them he came & told me that Elick did not wish to go, that a railroad man had offered him five dollars cash in his hands to go with him & that tickled his fancy.

But the owner thought that Elick would "get over that & be willing to go with you." If the slave's reluctance to return continued, however, Dickinson said that he would not force him to go but he promised at the same time to send the other hands. "But yesterday I received a letter from him saying that his boys had come to him & avowed they would not go, & if they did go they would run off after they got there," Davis continued. "Now I believe that this is nothing but an empty threat for the purpose of scaring their master & that it only required decisive measures to bring them straight." If the slaves actually carried out their runaway attempt, "they would be apt to run before they got there [Gibraltar Forge] & not after they crossed the blue Ridge [Mountains], for they know that they dont understand the country well enough to start when so far from home." And if they ran away before they reached the mountains, "they will come down in Dickinson's neighborhood & he will be perfectly willing to take them back & so no harm will result in that case." Davis was reasonably certain the hands would not try to flee after they reached the forge, because in addition to their "not being used to the country," they were not "skilled in the wiles of running away," and thus would be recaptured before they could get very far. "All this is on the hypothesis that Elick goes with them," Davis noted. "If he is cooled down & kept in Jail until I choose to let him off & the others sent on I dont apprehend any difficulty whatever: because he is the ringleader and has persuaded the other's . . . who were willing to go back up to last Monday when I saw them at the Ct House." Davis could not surrender his claim to these men because "the hands through the country are hired," and, in addition, he had gotten the slaves "cheaper than I could get hands again even if I could find any for hire." He then outlined his scheme for dealing with this difficult situation:

> I wrote to Mr Dickinson by this morning's mail that I could not let them off, but for him to take them to the Ct House monday morning, put Elick in Jail before the eyes of the others without saying a word as to the meaning of it, then take the others and send them on the [railroad] cars for Staunton with a pass to Gibraltar [Forge]: and after they are gone to take Elick out of Jail & hire him out there at the Ct House by the day, letting on to him that he (Dickinson) will hire him where he wishes to go when he finds a place, which he might do if I found I could make it suit to let him off; if not, I would take him over when I went. I think this plan will work.

In closing this letter the much-troubled ironmaster vented his anger and frustration with a verbal blast at Elick, the "ringleader":

> This negro's perversity is but another instance of the assimilation of the negro to the dog. Inorder to make a dog like and follow you, you must whip him occasionally & be sparing of favors, or he will turn at last & bite the hand that feeds him. So with this boy. Of all those five negroes he was the only one that escaped the lash: & frequently received favors that I would have denied the others. Now he not only turns from me but tries to lead them away likewise.[22]

Several things in this letter deserve comment. First, although five of the six slaves involved had been whipped by their employer, they initially expressed a willingness to return to the same man for another year's work. Since hands were scarce at this time, their master could have hired them out elsewhere with no difficulty and clearly would have done so if the men had objected earlier about going back to the forge. Even more significant, it would seem, is the psychological game the hiring agent was forced to play with Elick and the other slaves who looked to him for leadership. The ironmaster wanted and needed these hands, but he could not simply assemble them into a coffle and drive them over the mountains. Because the master did not want to force his slaves to work where they were unwilling to reside, the hirer planned a rather elaborate charade to isolate Elick, get the other men ("who are not skilled in the wiles of running away") on a train, and place them in unfamiliar country where they would probably be unable to find their way back home if Elick failed to follow them or if, after rejoining the group at the forge, he continued to create dissatisfaction among the other hands. The entire incident suggests a rather complex give-and-take between master, slave, and employer that rested not on brute force but on a series of adjustments and accommodations in which the slaves did anything but sit passively by while their fate was decided. Four days later Davis reported that the owner had indeed hired the men to another party, and young Davis urged his father to insist that the hands be delivered up to them as originally promised or that a damage suit be brought against the slaves' master; "there being no hands for hire I cannot hire others in [their] place," Davis told his father, and "consequently we cannot prosecute our business."[23]

This incident illustrates another key point: a vital factor in any industrialist's ability to hire slave labor was the willingness of the slave to reside at his work site for the year. Owners of slaves were reluctant to send their bondsmen to locations where slaves did not want to go, as one master told Weaver in 1828:

> Our agreement was, if Brandus was not willing to go to you, I should not force him and on seeing Mr. Brawly, who says the boy is anxious to remain with him therefore I cannot think of compelling him to go any where it is not his wish, as that has always been my rule.[24]

This master expressed his position in exceptionally strong language, but the position itself was by no means exceptional, as a hiring agent in eastern Virginia informed Weaver in 1854 when Weaver asked the agent to secure slaves for his iron works. "I am willing to hire hands for you," the man replied, and added that he would also be hiring for another Rockbridge County ironmaster, "but that will make no in[ter]ferance as persons let their [hands] go pretty much were they please," he assured Weaver.[25]

In addition to any humanitarian considerations, owners worried that a dissatisfied slave might run away, and there was no guarantee that a valuable slave hand would run back to the protection of his master when he left a furnace or forge. As a result owners, like Elick's master in the long letter cited above, frequently respected the wishes of their slaves and refused to hire them to places where they feared the slaves might be dissatisfied, as one slaveowner wrote Weaver in 1830:

> I am sorry to inform you that one of the men I hired you (Isaac) has expressed such an unwillingness to return to you, that I feared should I send him over he would run away, and perhaps be of little or no service to you during the year — I therefore thought it best to hire him in Amherst [County] where he is willing to stay, for the same you were to give — I return your bond for him in this letter. I am very sorry this has happened as perhaps it may put you to some in-

convenience, but I hope not much. When I hired him I was under the impression he would be willing to serve you,—but I find he is not.

Another slave belonging to this same owner was also reluctant to return to Weaver's employ but agreed to do so under certain circumstances:

Sam has requested me to ask the favor of you, to permit him to stay at the establishment at which you live; he says he greatly prefers it. He also was unwilling to return; but says he would have no objection, provided, he could live at your own establishment. I hope, if it will not put you to much inconvenience, you will grant his request.[26]

The slaves' wishes obviously counted for something, and the industrial employer who was unwilling to meet the basic requests of his laboring men was risking present difficulties with his work force and future problems with his hiring.

Even after an ironmaster secured an adequate slave force, he faced other serious problems. Key factors in the success of any manufacturing concern were the efficiency, skill, and productivity of the workers; industrialists employing slave labor on a large scale faced a formidable task in attempting to discipline and, even more important, motivate unfree labor. Weaver, of course, had the power to inflict physical punishment on any recalcitrant or troublesome slave worker, but excessive dependence on force could easily backfire and lead to even greater evils: further demoralization among his slaves, a rash of runaways, an unsavory reputation among slaveowners, slave abuse of draft animals, theft, arson, or acts of industrial sabotage carried out by skilled artisans, any of which could seriously disrupt normal furnace and forge operations. The slaves, in short, were in a position to do considerable physical and financial damage to Weaver's interests, even if they limited their activities to passive forms of resistance like work slowdowns or slipshod performance of their duties. In an effort to deal with the closely related problems of discipline and motivation, Weaver very early in his career as an iron manufacturer (at least as early as the 1820s when surviving records begin) instituted an incentive system to encourage slaves to meet and exceed their tasks. Men who did more than their required amount were rewarded with payment, in either cash or goods, for their extra labor, or "overwork" as it was called. In adopting this incentive system Weaver was instituting a technique that had been used in Southern iron works as early as the 1790s and that continued to be used until the end of the Civil War.[27] The object of the overwork system was to make the industrial slave a disciplined and productive worker without having to rely heavily on physical coercion.

Payment of wood choppers for overwork illustrates the way the system operated for almost all slaves at Weaver's installations. The normal task for a wood chopper in the Virginia iron region was 1½ cords per day, working a six-day week—Sunday was a traditional day of rest. Both employer and slave seem to have recognized the 1½ cord requirement as the standard task, and any ironmaker who attempted to increase the customary amount of work would be engaging in a risky enterprise that might well result in extra trouble instead of extra wood. For any wood that a slave chopped over and above his 1½ cord task, he was given credit on the company's books at the rate of 40 cents per cord, the same rate at which white wood choppers were paid. The same general system operated for every job at Weaver's furnace and forge: skilled slave ironworkers could earn overwork payments for producing more than their required quota of iron, ore-bank hands could mine and wash extra ore, colliers could tend the charcoal pits in their time off, shoemakers could make additional shoes, and even unskilled hands could earn credit, at the rate of 50 cents per day, for working at night, on Sundays, and over the traditional Christmas holidays. Other means of earning credit included weaving coal baskets; raising hogs, chickens, and eggs; packing pork; and growing corn on individual plots. Emergency situations also provided the slaves with the opportunity to earn money: if a mine had to be emptied of water, a road needed to be repaired after a storm, or a dam had to be rebuilt after a freshet.[28] Finally, some slaves were credited with a small "allowance," in effect a regular wage for, evidently, assuming responsibility for various phases of the furnace or forge operation. The highest allowance paid by Weaver, $5 a month for twelve months, went to a hired slave named Joshua Crews who worked at Etna Furnace. The exact nature of Crews's duties is unclear, but since another slave was credited for "5 Sundays at Furnace under Joshua" and since Crews's compensation was exceptionally high, $60 for the year, it seems certain that he held an important supervisory post at the furnace, perhaps a job similar to that performed by a black driver on a large plantation.[29] Other slave hands who were paid allowances of lesser amounts whose duties can be determined include Washington Coleman, a collier, who probably received his $8 "coaling allowance" in 1857 for supervising one or more charcoal pits, and Bill Jones, who was paid $1 a month for "ore carts" and was evidently in charge of the mule-drawn ore train at Etna Furnace that brought ore to the furnace site from a bank some ten miles distant.[30]

Entries in the Buffalo Forge and Etna Furnace "Negro Books," as these ledgers were called, indicate that most of the slave hands, both skilled and unskilled, used the overwork system to earn their own money. The most significant thing about these entries is the way in which they suggest how a sizable number of blacks took advantage of the system to carve out something of a private and individual life for themselves. Admittedly, in the process of earning overwork compensation the slaves were in one sense doing the ironmaster's bidding; they finished their required tasks before they began working for themselves and thus responded positively to the employer's attempt to motivate them. But on another level the slaves were, it seems fair to say, being their own men. They could do extra work if they wished, or they could take their time off as leisure. Even in the simple act of accepting or rejecting the overwork system, they were achieving, in at least one small phase of their existence, some measure of self-choice. If they did choose to do additional labor, the sums they earned were theirs to control, and they gained an even greater measure of personal initiative. An examination of several individual accounts will perhaps indicate what is being suggested here.

In 1858 one of Weaver's hiring agents secured four hands—Jack, Jim, Bill, and Dabney Willoughby—from a family in eastern Virginia to work for the year. The four men were assigned to Etna Furnace where they labored as wood choppers and miners. During the year the four built up overwork credits on Weaver's books for sums ranging form $10.50 to $13.50. They drew against their credit at the company store for small "luxury" items like coffee and sugar, but in June three of the men decided to use part of their money to buy themselves vacation time at home. Their request for leave was granted, and they left the furnace. While they were away they were debited at the standard overwork rate of 50 cents per day for their time off—ten days for two of the men and two weeks for the third. They returned to Etna at the end of their stay at home and served out the balance of the year. The fourth member of this group, Jim Willoughby, evidently decided not to spend his money in this fashion in order to draw as much cash as possible at the end of the year. In December, just before the four men returned home for Christmas, he drew his remaining credit in cash, which amounted to $10.[31]

Husbanding of cash was characteristic of a number of slave hands; men like Mat Robinson, a miner, earned $5.00 in overwork in one year, spent a carefully allotted 50 cents of it for tobacco, and then drew $4.50 in cash in December; Elec the Collier, as he was listed in the books, earned $13.75 for extra coaling and by raising a hog in 1857 and collected $10.00 in cash at the Christmas break. At the other end of the spectrum was a slave like John Sims, a furnace laborer, who spent his overwork faster than he could earn it on tobacco, coffee, and clothing. Sims ended the year 1858 owing the company store $6.84 but was able to work off his debt the following year by Sunday labor and ore washing, and he made enough additional compensation to continue his purchases of coffee and tobacco on a fairly regular basis.[32]

Sims's case illustrates a second major intent of the overwork system. In addition to motivating the slaves to become efficient and productive workers, it could be used by the employer as a disciplinary tool. Sims had a taste for consumer goods that outran his ability to pay for them, and the furnace manager allowed him to indulge himself to the point where Sims was forced to do extra work in order to pay off his debt. The ledgers also show that slaves who failed to meet their normal task could have the value of their unfinished work deducted from whatever credit they had built up. Two hired slaves, Reubin and Dudley Camack, were, respectively, five and seven cords of wood short when a check of wood choppers was made in August 1858. As a result, they were debited for their shortages at the rate of 40 cents per cord, the same amount paid for cutting extra wood. Several other slaves suffered similar deductions for unfinished tasks as miners and wood choppers. In all of these cases, however, the slaves were able to work off their debt and build up additional credits in their favor, usually by turning to some alternative form of labor for which they received payment. The two Camack slaves, for example, removed their debt for unfinished wood chopping by Sunday labor. In fact it may be that these two men purposely came in short on their wood cutting, intending to make up their deficiency by working together on Sundays. This is suggested by the fact that most of the slave choppers met the 1½ cords per day task with relative ease, and, in this particular case, both of the men worked the same number of Sundays, twenty. They drew on their accounts for flour, coffee, sugar, and tobacco during the year and ended their term of service in December with cash coming to them.[33] Wood choppers were not highly skilled workers in the charcoal iron industry, but they still could amass considerable amounts of overwork credit if they chose to do so. To cite one example, over a two year period a black chopper named Daniel Henry working at Glenwood Furnace in Rockbridge County cut 248½ cords over his required task, worked 36 Sundays, and made 36 standard-size charcoal measuring baskets in his spare time. His overwork earnings for the two years totaled $127.66, which he drew mainly in coffee and other store purchases during the year, but he had enough credit remaining at the end of each year to make fairly substantial Christmas purchases—$22.58 in 1847 and $13.50 in 1848.[34]

The slaves who were generally in the best position to take advantage of the overwork system, however, were the more skilled artisans. Weaver's own forge hands regularly earned relatively large sums by heating, working, and finishing extra tonnages of iron at Buffalo Forge. Sam Williams, Henry Towles, Jim Garland, Henry Mathews, Tooler, and Henry Hunt, Jr., all slave ironworkers owned by Weaver, were paid from $3 to $5 per ton for their overwork, and all of these men used their exceptional position to good advantage. Henry Towles, for example, who was a heater at the forge, was credited with $31.80 in overwork in 1852, $36.16 in 1853, $55.28 in 1855, and $93.53 in 1856. In 1858, when his account was transferred to a new ledger, he carried a balance of $102.53 in his favor to the new book. Towles drew most of his overwork in cash, but another of Weaver's forge hands, Henry Hunt, Jr., used the credit he earned primarily to buy quality clothing, like three $6 coats and a $4 pair of pants in 1850 and "1 fine suit (coat & pants)" valued at $18 in 1854.[35] The individualism of each slave shows through clearly in these and other accounts: John White, who chopped 43¼ extra cords of wood in 1856, Allen Jackson, who devoted his off hours in 1856 to raising chickens and a hog, and Landis Cartmill, a skilled basket weaver who earned $17.32 in 1857 by making fifty-two charcoal baskets for Etna Furnace.[36]

The case of Sam Williams demonstrates the degree to which a skilled industrial slave could use his training and ability to live a life that probably deserves to be called quasi-free, or something like it. Williams worked molten iron into finished merchant bars at Buffalo Forge and received the highest overwork rate paid to any of Weaver's forge hands, $5 per ton. He, like a number of Weaver's skilled slaves, also had individual plots of land at the forge that were laid off and planted in the spring by the regular force of agricultural workers. These farm hands, including the white overseer, a white agricultural laborer, and several slaves, planted the plots along with Weaver's own fields as part of the spring corn planting.[37] Williams and the other forge hands then worked their own lots during the summer, and when they brought in their crops they could either sell them to Weaver or consume them themselves. By working extra tonnages of iron, growing corn, and raising hogs, Williams earned enough cash during the 1850s to supplement his own and his wife's diet with regular purchases of sugar and coffee, buy "3 yds. cotton cloth for Nancy," his wife, to cite one 1855 entry, and, most surprisingly, open a savings account at a Lexington bank.[38] Williams, who was forty years of age in 1860, played an important part in establishing the high reputation that Weaver's "W" brand bar iron enjoyed among Virginia blacksmiths and commission merchants, and Williams obviously used his skills to improve materially the quality of life he and his wife were able to lead under slavery.[39]

One of the most significant ways in which the overwork system allowed male slaves to achieve some measure of personal dignity and pride was the opportunity it gave men like Sam Williams to provide cash or small luxuries for their wives. Tooler, a skilled slave artisan who had been raised at Buffalo Forge, drew $5 in cash to send to his wife in 1850, and other entries in his account show that he used part of his overwork credit in 1852 to make three trips to Lynchburg, perhaps to see his wife. Other examples of men using their overwork credit to acquire items for their wives include Bill Jones, the ore cart supervisor at Etna Furnace, "1 pair Brogans for his wife," $2, and for a slave identified as "Daniel Dumb Boy," several entries for "cash to Louisa."[40]

Additional evidence of slave marriages appears elsewhere in the records of Weaver's enterprises. A number of slaves, both hired and owned by Weaver, who had wives in the vicinity regularly left Buffalo Forge after the work day ended on Saturday to visit their wives and returned in time for work on Monday morning.[41] Slave men whose wives lived longer distances away sometimes tried to deal with this separation in their own way. Booker, a slave chopper at Etna in 1854, was noted in the furnace timebook as having "lost two weeks going to see his wife." Perhaps he had permission to make this trip, however, since his overwork account shows that he was docked only 50 cents, one day's pay, on April 28, 1854, as a "day lost going to see his wife."[42] Even more revealing is a letter from Weaver's manager at Etna Furnace describing his difficulties with two hands in 1862:

> You asked about Griffen. I consider him a triffling hand. — He laid up here very often & for long periods — but it was only when we worked him about the Furnace[;] he laid up so often that we had finaly to take him away. Par objected

to changing so often. tell him that you will put him in the wood chopping when he gets well. & I will guarantee he will soon be out—that is his object now in laying up. I found that he laid up very seldom when he could get a chance to run to his wife.[43]

The incidence of slave resistance at Weaver's installations is difficult to judge, but if this letter is indicative, the problems of slave motivation and efficiency were not by any means completely solved by the overwork system. In order for the system to work, Weaver's slave hands had to exceed their required tasks voluntarily, and if the slave were a skilled artisan, Weaver and his managers were apparently willing to tolerate a certain amount of neglect of duty in order to avoid difficulty with key black personnel. This point can be illustrated by the work records of several of the Buffalo Forge slaves contained in a daily journal kept by Weaver's nephew-in-law and second in command, Daniel C. E. Brady, from October 1860 to June 1865. Tooler, one of Weaver's heaters, is frequently described by Brady as "loafing," but there is no indication that Tooler was disciplined, physically or otherwise, for his performance; when he was running out iron or drawing bars he regularly earned substantial overtime credit that was not docked for his slipshod work on other occasions. Edgar, a miller who worked at Weaver's flour mill, is another slave who is listed as "loafing" on numerous occasions, again with no record of punishment. Most of the Buffalo Forge slave hands, however, are regularly listed at their jobs with no indication that Weaver or Brady were dissatisfied with their performance. Sam Williams is typical of this larger group; "Sam at work" is the most consistent entry in Brady's journal, perhaps because Williams was putting something away for himself at that bank in Lexington.[44]

Unskilled slave workers had much less leverage with Weaver and his managers, of course, but they did have the power to accept or reject the master's incentives and they had rights set by tradition if not by law—like a reasonable daily task, Christmas holidays, and Sundays off—that they would go considerable lengths to defend. The slaves' insistence on their annual Christmas vacation is demonstrated in a report Weaver's furnace managers made in November 1830 explaining why they would not be able to keep the furnace in blast during the entire month of December:

> We had thought [of] blowing through the Christmas holy days and going on as long as possible, but as our white hands are few and the most part of the blacks will be going home and the few remaining not willing to be closely confined we have concluded to stop up for a short time during Christmas.[45]

Similarly, a potentially explosive altercation at Etna Furnace in 1854 showed the risks one of Weaver's own slaves was willing to take in order to maintain Sunday as a day he alone controlled.

> Anthony was told saterday evening to start to [Buffalo] forge this morning [Sunday]—I waited till about 10 oclock and finding that he had not started I asked him the reason[.] he said it was Sunday and that he was not going till

> tomorrow—with some other impudence to me I collared him and he resisted
> & struck me—I struck him on the head with a rock, you please will see about
> the matter.

The irate manager closed his letter with a significant postscript: "He said that this was Sunday and his day and that he was not going [to] take it up in going to your place."[46] Unfortunately there is no other information in surviving records that reveals whether Weaver inflicted further punishment on his bondsman, but the incident shows clearly the determination of one slave to preserve his day of rest and probably speaks for a view that was universally held among Southern slaves, industrial or otherwise.

The most serious labor difficulties at Weaver's installations were caused by slaves running away, but this evidently did not become a major problem until late in the Civil War. Between 1829 and 1861 at least thirteen slaves ran off from Weaver's employ, with the bulk of these flights (ten of the thirteen) occurring during several years in the late 1820s and early 1830s when a manager at one of Weaver's iron works evidently caused a considerable amount of dissatisfaction among the slave force. All but one of these run-aways were hired slaves who returned to the counties in eastern Virginia from which they had been secured and there either hid out in the vicinity of their homes until recaptured or, in several instances, came in to their owners with accounts of mistreatment by overseers, sickness, or bad food.[47] But the runaway problem did not seriously endanger Weaver's furnace and forge operations at any time during the antebellum period, and this was true of the first three years of the war as well.[48] In June 1864, however, a large scale cavalry raid by Union forces commanded by General David Hunter swept through the valley iron district and provided several of the Buffalo Forge slaves with an opportunity to gain their freedom. "I regret to inform you that your boy Beverly went off with the enemy upon that raid through this country on 12 June," Daniel Brady informed the owner of a hired slave. "I lost three of my own men at the same time," he continued, and "I was fortunate in escaping myself & sustaining no loss of other property."[49] In all, five Buffalo Forge slaves made it to freedom with Hunter's troopers; and included in the three escaped slaves who had belonged to Weaver was Warder, a skilled teamster who had hauled pig iron and supplies between Etna Furnace and the forge for a number of years. More of the Buffalo Forge hands undoubtedly would have fled had they not been moved to an isolated farm on the day the federals occupied Lexington.[50] The forge property itself escaped destruction, and Union troops did not reappear in the vicinity for the remainder of the war.

When a reasonably good chance for successful escape presented itself, black ironworkers, like the vast majority of slaves throughout the South, wasted little time in striking for freedom. In the absence of such an opportunity, however, Weaver's black artisans and laborers appear to have learned how to live with, and cope with, industrial slave conditions. Perhaps the most impressive evidence underscoring this point came in the transition. from slavery to freedom at the close of the Civil War. Three brief entries in journals kept at Buffalo Forge by Daniel Brady describe events of monumental significance for the black men, women and children working and living there:

> Friday May 26, 1865 Declared free by order of the military authorities.
> Saturday May 27, 1865 All hands quit work as they considered themselves free. I made a speech to them, & read the order No 2 of Genl Gregg. J G Updike, Alex Hamilton, Jno D Ewing, W W Rex & Thos Edwards present.
> Monday May 29, 1865 Commenced work on free labor.[51]

Brady, who assumed ownership and primary direction of all of Weaver's properties when Weaver died in March 1863, did not write down what he said in his address, but subsequent events make clear that he told the newly freed blacks that he intended to keep Buffalo Forge in operation and continue farming on the Weaver lands. Those workers who wished to keep their jobs could do so, and they would be paid on a piecework or wage basis depending on the specific position they held. The general orders that Brady read to the assembled workers had been issued by General J. Irvin Gregg, the federal commander of the military subdistrict of Lynchburg, on May 18, 1865, and they were published in the Lynchburg press five days later. Gregg's orders contained both a declaration of the former slaves' rights and a statement of their responsibilities:

> The operation of existing laws is to make them *free*, but not to give them any claim whatever upon, or rights in connection with the property of former owners. They are at liberty to make any contract or agreement concerning themselves that a white man may, and equally bound to abide by it.

The former masters had "the right to refuse them anything that he might deny to a perfect stranger," the orders continued, "and is no more bound to feed, clothe, or protect them than if he had never been their master." The freedmen might "remain with him if he and they both desire it, and agree on the terms, in which case each party is equally bound by the contract." The orders concluded by admonishing blacks "that they must work for their support now, the same as before they were free; in some instances, perhaps, even harder" and informed them that "destitute" rations would not be issued to able-bodied laborers unless they could show they had tried but were unable to obtain work. A final paragraph read:

> All colored persons living in the country, are informed that it is much better for them to remain there than to come to the already over-stocked city, and that they will not be permitted to come here for work or subsistence, unless they cannot obtain them where they are.[52]

With Brady offering continued employment and with the military authorities in Lynchburg telling the freedmen in rather blunt language to keep their present jobs, some forty-three men and women, almost the entire black work force at Buffalo Forge when emancipation occurred, accepted labor contracts. Work resumed "on free labor," as Brady described it in his journal on May 29, 1865, three days after the slaves learned officially that they were free.[53]

The length of time the freedmen remained at Buffalo Forge offers the only real evidence as to their motives for staying on. For some, the military's position seems to have been a deciding factor. Two men who had been hired at the beginning of 1865 left within a matter of days after signing their contracts and two of Weaver's former slaves quit in mid-July. Six men who had been hired from the same household—George, Bob, John, William, Alfred, and Stephen Glasgow—all signed three-month contracts to chop wood, served out the terms of their agreement, and then departed. Perhaps Gregg's General Orders No. 2 had some influence on them and on the remainder of those who did not work beyond 1865; eleven of the forty-three who signed initial contracts had left by August 30 and seven more departed by the end of the year. For the twenty-one who can be identified as working into 1866 and beyond, however, the decision to remain seems to have been a choice they themselves made. Included in this number were almost all of the skilled artisans who had drawn and hammered Weaver's iron during the antebellum and Civil War years.[54]

For those freedmen who began working at Buffalo Forge on the morning of May 29, 1865, conversion to a wage basis presented few problems since all the laboring force was familiar with the overwork system. Now the men would be paid for all the work they did, and they would assume the responsibility of providing for themselves and their families. Sam Williams, Henry Towles, Henry Mathews, Henry Hunt, Jr., and Tooler all signed contracts to work for three months at $4 per ton for all the iron they produced, while they furnished their food and other supplies out of their wages. Sam Williams's wife, Nancy, went to work as a dairymaid at $4 a month. Williams and his wife were still working at Buffalo Forge in 1872, as were Towles, Mathews, and Hunt, when their accounts were transferred to a new ledger, and they can no longer be traced in surviving records; Tooler's accounts were closed in December 1868. Most of the remaining freedmen at Buffalo Forge who had once belonged to Weaver also accepted initial contracts of three months' duration for work as forge hands, wood choppers, shoemakers, carpenters, teamsters, and farmworkers. As mentioned above, employment was also offered to those men who had been hired at the beginning of 1865 for a year's labor. A number of these men had been employed by Weaver and Brady on a regular basis for a considerable length of time, some since the 1850s, and they formed the bulk of the freedmen who signed on as wood cutters, at the rate of 66²/₃ cents per cord. Generally those men who had been hired as slaves stayed for shorter periods of time than the more skilled workers who had previously been owned by Weaver. But a sizable number of the former hired slave hands served out their three-month contracts, others remained until the end of the year, and several worked for two or three years.[55]

Looking back over the entire black labor existence at Weaver's iron works, the smooth and rapid conversion to a free labor situation in 1865 seems particularly significant. Both skilled and unskilled workers in appreciable numbers made the transition to a wage basis at the jobs they had held as slaves, a pattern that was repeated by slave artisans and laborers at other iron works not only in Virginia but elsewhere in the South.[56] Even though local military officers might not like it, those workers who did not wish to remain at Buffalo Forge could leave; some did so at once, some left after several weeks or at the expiration of their initial contracts, and some stayed for years. Those who remained for more extended periods did so not because of military compulsion or because slavery had infantilized them or rendered them incapable of making a decision without white guidance; they stayed, it seems clear, simply because they saw an opportunity to use the skills they had acquired under slavery to earn a living for themselves and, for those with wives and children, for their families. Equally important, it seems fair to say that they had not been so mistreated as industrial slaves that they could not continue to work in the same job at the same place after emancipation. This is not meant to suggest that slavery under Weaver, Brady, and their various managers was an institution that lay lightly on the shoulders of the black laborers who worked Weaver's furnace, forge, and fields. Weaver's slaves were sometimes whipped,[57] black (and white) ironworkers occasionally suffered from the poor quality or inadequate food and clothing available at the blast furnace site,[58] and Weaver was not above selling several slaves into Louisiana in the late 1850s when he thought their conduct warranted it.[59] Perhaps most important of all, the black men and women who manned Weaver's operations had to cope psychologically with the prospect that the rest of their lives would in all likelihood be spend in bondage. But at the same time, day in and day out, the central tendency at Weaver's installations was for slavery to function more through mutual accommodation than outright repression. Because Weaver had to go into a tight hiring market year after year and because the success of his various enterprises was, in many ways, controlled by the slaves he employed, measures like compensation for overwork grew into features of primary importance in the functioning of his slave system. And because of things like the overwork system, black and white managed to find a way to live together at Weaver's iron works without maltreatment and excessive use of physical force permanently poisoning relations between the two groups. In this instance, industrial slavery did not totally degrade and brutalize the black workers; in fact it seems in some ways to have done something quite different, to have provided these men with an environment in which they could develop some sense of personal dignity and individual initiative in spite of the psychological and physical confines of their bondage. Or at least so it appears. If this analysis is correct, then we clearly need to take a closer look at the industrial phase of the South's peculiar institution. Such an examination may tell us a good deal about the nature of slavery in the American South.

NOTES

1. J. C. Calhoun to T. G. Clemson, Oct. 27, 1845, John C. Calhoun Papers, Clemson University Library, Clemson, S.C.

2. Kenneth M. Stampp, *The Peculiar Institution: Slavery in the Ante-Bellum South* (New York, 1956), 84.

3. Robert S. Starobin, *Industrial Slavery in the Old South* (New York, 1970), especially chs. 3 and 4, and his article "Disciplining Industrial Slaves in the Old South," *Journal of Negro History*, 53 (1968): 111–28; Samuel Sydney Bradford, "The Ante-Bellum Charcoal Iron Industry of Virginia" (Ph.D. dissertation, Columbia University, 1958), especially chs. 4 and 5, and his article "The Negro Ironworker in Ante Bellum Virginia," *Journal of Southern History*, 25 (1959): 194–206.

4. Clement Eaton, "Slave-Hiring in the Upper South: A Step toward Freedom," *Mississippi Valley Historical Review*, 46 (1960): 668–69; Richard B. Morris, "The Measure of Bondage in the Slave States," *ibid.*, 41 (1954): 231–39.

5. Morris, "Measure of Bondage," 239.

6. The employment of slave labor at iron works outside Virginia is discussed in detail in the Louisa Furnace Account Books, which deal with operations of a Tennessee blast furnace, in the Southern Historical Collection, University of North Carolina, Chapel Hill, N.C.; the Shelby Iron Works Collection, which describes the operations of a major Alabama iron complex, in the University of Alabama Library, University, Ala.; and the Lucy Wortham James Collection, which contains most of the extensive records of the Maramec Iron Works of Missouri, in the Western Historical Manuscripts Collection, University of Missouri, Columbia, Mo. On the use of slave ironworkers in Georgia, see the Augusta *Daily Constitutionalist*, Oct. 29, 1859, and the material relating to the Etowah Iron Works in "Confederate Papers Relating to Citizens or Business Firms," War Department Collection of Confederate Records, Record Group 109. National Archives. Washington, D.C. See also Starobin, *Industrial Slavery*, 100–01; Lester J. Cappon, "Iron-Making—A Forgotten Industry of North Carolina," *North Carolina Historical Review*, 9 (1932): 340–41; and Ernest M. Lander, Jr., "The Iron Industry in Ante-Bellum South Carolina," *Journal of Southern History*, 20 (1954): 350–51. I wish to thank Dr. Robert H. McKenzie of the University of Alabama for kindly providing information on the slave labor practices of the Shelby Iron Works.

7. Two suggestive studies that rely heavily on the Slave Narrative Collection and fugitive accounts have recently appeared. See George P. Rawick, *From Sundown to Sunup: The Making of the Black Community* (Westport, Conn., 1972); and John W. Blassingame, *The Slave Community: Plantation Life in the Ante-Bellum South* (New York, 1972).

8. Manuscript Population and Slave Schedules, Rockbridge County, Virginia, Eighth Census of the United States, 1860, National Archives Microfilm Publications, M653.

9. "Farming of Mr. William Weaver, of Rockbridge County, Virginia," *Farmers' Register*, 10 (1842): 411–13.

10. For a description of Weaver's iron properties, see J. P. Lesley, *The Iron Manufacturer's Guide to the Furnaces, Forges and Rolling Mills of the United States* (New York, 1859), 73, 181.

11. William Weaver to James D. Davidson, Jan. 10, 1855, James D. Davidson Papers, McCormick Collection, State Historical Society of Wisconsin, Madison, Wis.

12. See entries in Buffalo Forge Negro Books, 1850–58 and 1865–72, Weaver-Brady Records, University of Virginia Library, Charlottesville, Va.

13. James C. Dickinson to Weaver, Jan. 2, 1828, William Weaver Papers, *ibid.* (hereafter these papers will be cited as Weaver Papers, Virginia).

14. Henry A. McCormick to Weaver, Dec. 29, 1855, *ibid.*

15. James C. Davis to William W. Davis, Jan. 5, 1856, William W. Davis Papers, University of Virginia Library, Charlottesville, Va.

16. J. C. Davis to William W. Davis, Jan. 7, 1856, Jordan & Davis Papers, McCormick Collection, State Historical Society of Wisconsin, Madison, Wis.

17. See John Chew to Weaver, Dec. 5, 1830; and James Coleman to Weaver, Feb. 5, 19, 1856, both in William Weaver Papers, Duke University Library, Durham, N.C. (hereafter these papers will be cited as Weaver Papers, Duke); Tuyman Wayt to Jordan & Irvine, Jan. 6, 1830; and Pallison Boxley to Jordan & Irvine, Jan. 13, 1831, both in Jordan & Irvine Papers, McCormick Collection, State Historical Society of Wisconsin, Madison, Wis.; see also advertisements of companies seeking to hire slave hands in Richmond *Daily Dispatch*, Jan. 5, Dec. 18, 31, 1853; Dec. 22, 1856; Jan. 1, 1857; Jan. 7, Dec. 10, 31, 1858; and Apr. 6, 1859.

18. John T. Day to Shanks, Anderson & Anderson, Nov. 9, 1849, Anderson Family Papers, University of Virginia Library, Charlottesville, Va.

19. T. H. Burns, agent for Shanks & Anderson, to John T. Day, Dec. 18, 1849, *ibid.*

20. Thomas R. Towles to Weaver, Nov. 11, 1857, Weaver Papers, Duke.

21. Charles K. Gorgas to Weaver, Nov. 17, 1857, *ibid.* William W. Rex, a nephew of Weaver's, was one of the managers at Etna Furnace.

22. James C. Davis to William W. Davis, Jan. 5, 1856, Davis Papers.

23. James C. Davis to William W. Davis, Jan. 9, 1856, Cyrus H. McCormick Papers, McCormick Collection, State Historical Society of Wisconsin, Madison, Wis.

24. C. Wiglesworth to Weaver, Dec. 31, 1828, Weaver Papers, Duke.

25. T. R. Towles to Weaver, Nov. 27, 1854, *ibid.*

26. William Stapes to Weaver, Jan. 4, 1830, Weaver Papers, Virginia.

27. Starobin, *Industrial Slavery*, 101; see also Charles B. Dew, "David Ross and the Oxford Iron Works: A Study of Industrial Slavery in the Early Nineteenth-Century South," scheduled for publication in the *William and Mary Quarterly*, April 1974.

28. See entries in Etna Furnace Negro Books, 1854–61 and 1857–60, and Buffalo Forge Negro Book, 1850–58, both in Weaver-Brady Records, Virginia.

29. See entries for Joshua Crews and Tom Duecen, Etna Furnace Negro Books, 1854–61 and 1857–60.

30. Etna Furnace Negro Book, 1857–60.

31. *Ibid.*

32. *Ibid.*

33. *Ibid.*

34. Glenwood Furnace Negro Book, 1847–49, Anderson Ledgers, University of Virginia Library, Charlottesville, Va.

35. Buffalo Forge Negro Book, 1850–58.

36. Etna Furnace Negro Book, 1857–60.

37. Entries for Apr. 23, 27, 1861, Daniel C. E. Brady, Home Journal, 1860–65, McCormick Collection, State Historical Society of Wisconsin, Madison, Wis.

38. Buffalo Forge Negro Book, 1850–58; John A. Rex to J. D. Davidson, Feb. 25, 1855, Davidson Papers. The text of the letter from Rex, another one of Weaver's nephews, to Davidson, a Lexington lawyer, reads as follows: "I wish to ask you one question whether Sam Williams can draw his money from the Savings Bank or if he cannot. As Sam and Henry Nash has got a bet for his watch against the said Nash['s] watch. It is my opinion that he can draw his money if he gives the Directors of the Bank 10 days notice. After he receives the money he wishes to show it to Henry Nash, and then he will return the said money back to the Bank again. As I was witness to the said bargain." Davidson noted on the rear of this letter that he had directed Rex "to confer with Wm Weaver" about the matter. Henry Nash was a free black cooper who lived in the vicinity of Buffalo Forge. Manuscript Population Schedules, Rockbridge County, Virginia, Eighth Census of the United States, 1860.

39. William's age is given in a "Descriptive List of Negroes at Buffalo Forge, Rockbridge, Co., Va.," 1865, Weaver Papers, Duke; he is described as five feet ten inches

tall and his color is listed as "yellow." On the quality of Weaver's iron, see William D. Couch to Weaver, Feb. 9, 1859; McCorkle & Co. to Weaver, Feb. 22, 1859; and Thomas G. Godwin to Weaver, Mar. 2, 1859, all *ibid.*

40. Buffalo Forge Negro Book, 1850–58, and Etna Furnace Negro Book, 1857–60; Jordan Davis & Co. to Weaver, Oct. 11, 31, 1831, Weaver Papers, Duke.

41. See entries in Brady, Home Journal.

42. Etna Furnace Time Book, and Etna Furnace Negro Book, 1854–61, Weaver-Brady Records, Virginia.

43. W. W. Rex to Brady, Mar. 22, 1862, Weaver Papers, Virginia.

44. Entries in Brady, Home Journal.

45. Jordan Davis & Co. to Weaver, Nov. 24, 1830, Weaver Papers, Duke.

46. John K. Watkins to Weaver, July 30, 1854, *ibid.*

47. William Watson for Joel W. Brown, Jailor, to Post Master, Lexington, Va., Apr. 19, 1829; W. E. Dickinson to Abraham Davis, Apr. 19, 1829; James C. Dickinson to Weaver, May 10, 1829; James Rose to Weaver, Mar. 8, 1830; Elizabeth Mathews to Weaver, Mar. 29, 1830; Lewis Rawlings to Weaver, Aug. 22, 1832; Charles Perrow to Weaver, Sept. 17, Oct. 26, 1833; and John A. Turpim to Weaver, Aug. 28, 1854, all in Weaver Papers, Duke; Henry A. McCormick to Weaver, Dec. 29, 1855, Weaver Papers, Virginia; see also entries under "Lawson," Etna Furnace Negro Book, 1857–60.

48. Two slaves tried to escape in 1863 but were apprehended in Lynchburg. Brady to James D. Davidson, Dec. 9, 1863, Davidson Papers.

49. Brady to James Stewart, July 7, 1864, Weaver Papers, Virginia.

50. Entries for June 11, 12, 14, 1864, Brady, Home Journal.

51. Buffalo Forge Journal, 1859–66, Weaver-Brady Records, Virginia; Brady, Home Journal.

52. Lynchburg *Daily Virginian*, May 23, 1865.

53. Buffalo Forge Negro Book, 1865–72.

54. *Ibid.* In the case of four of the forty-three who signed contracts, it is impossible to determine from their accounts how long they remained.

55. *Ibid.*

56. Records documenting the transition of a large number of black workers from slave to free labor almost identical to that which occurred at Buffalo Forge can be found in the Graham Ledgers and Papers, dealing with the operations of David Graham's iron works in Wythe County in southwestern Virginia, in the University of Virginia Library, Charlottesville, Va.; see especially Ledgers "L" 1857–59, "M" 1859–64, "N" 1864–68, and "E" 1868–71. For the post-war use of a substantial force of former slave workers by the most important Richmond iron manufacturer, see Charles B. Dew, *Ironmaker to the Confederacy: Joseph R. Anderson and the Tredegar Iron Works* (New Haven, 1966), 313–14; for a similar transition of black labor from slavery to freedom at a major Alabama iron works in 1865, see Robert H. McKenzie, "The Shelby Iron Company: A Note on Slave Personality after the Civil War," *Journal of Negro History,* 58 (1973): 341–48.

57. At least two instances of hired slaves being whipped can be documented; see Jordan Davis & Co. to Weaver, May 26, 1830; and William W. Rex to Brady, Oct. 26, 1860, both in Weaver Papers, Duke.

58. See Jordan Davis & Co. to Weaver, Mar. 25, Aug. 11, 1830; Jordan Davis & Co. to Abraham W. Davis, Aug. 24, 1830; Charles K. Gorgas to Brady, Mar. 11, Apr. 2, 1860; William W. Rex to Brady, May 29, June 29, Sept. 6, 21, 26, Oct. 13, 1860; and Rex to Weaver, Aug. 7, 1860, all *ibid.*; Gorgas to Weaver, Mar. 29, Apr. 6, 1859; and Rex to Brady, Mar. 15, 1861, Weaver Papers, Virginia.

59. J. E. Carson to Weaver, Mar. 12, May 30, June 27, 1859; William W. Rex to Weaver, Aug. 15, 1860; and G. W. Johnson to Weaver, Oct. 29, 1860, all in Weaver Papers, Duke.

SEVEN

Skilled Blacks in Antebellum
St. Mary's County, Maryland

BAYLY E. MARKS

It is well known that the overwhelming majority of the inhabitants of the slave states were engaged in agriculture. Yet throughout rural areas in the antebellum South men and women, slave and free, also held a wide variety of other occupations. The following article focuses on rural blacks in St. Mary's County, Maryland, from 1790 to 1864 and poses and answers a variety of questions about their skills and occupations. How many blacks worked outside farming? How do their numbers compare with the black population as a whole? What was the nature of their work? Why did blacks dominate certain occupations and not others? Did the number of blacks working outside agriculture change over time? How did free blacks who were not farmers compare materially with their white counterparts?

Using a wide variety of sources it is possible to construct a comprehensive skills profile for this rural southern Maryland county. This profile indicates that while the majority of adults of both races were engaged in farming, there were many opportunities to earn a living outside farming between 1790 and 1864. In all nearly eighty different occupations were pursued by county residents during the seventy-four years covered by this study. But only twenty-eight of those occupations were followed by blacks.

Occupations of free blacks and slaves have been the subject of several major works. Ira Berlin's *Slaves Without Masters* mentions skilled free blacks in rural areas but focuses on urban areas, where much of the free black population was concentrated. Robert E. Perdue's *Black Laborers and Black Professionals in Early America, 1750–1830* also discusses skilled free blacks

TABLE 1

St. Mary's County Population, 1790–1870

Date	Slaves	Free Blacks	Whites	Total
1790	6,985	343	8,216	15,544
1800	6,399	622	6,678	13,699
1810	6,000	636	6,158	12,794
1820	6,047	894	6,033	12,974
1830	6,183	1,179	6,097	13,459
1840	5,761	1,393	6,070	13,224
1850	5,842	1,633	6,223	13,698
1860	6,549	1,866	6,798	15,213
1870	——	7,726	7,218	14,944

Source: J. Thomas Scharf, History of Maryland From the Earliest Period to the Present Day (3 vols.; Philadelphia, 1879, rpt. ed., Hatboro, Penn., 1967), 780–81.

as well as slaves. Berlin and Perdue's sources, which are by necessity drawn largely from urban areas, suggest that from 20 to 25 percent of free blacks worked outside of agriculture. Perdue also found that the proportion of skilled slaves on the plantations he studied ranged from 5 to 14 percent. In their controversial work Time on the Cross Robert W. Fogel and Stanley L. Engerman use computer-generated statistics to answer many questions about slavery, including the proportions of skilled and semiskilled slaves to field hands. They conclude that approximately 26 percent of the male slaves in "the agriculture sector" followed occupations other than field labor. Herbert G. Gutman takes strong exception to their conclusions. In Slavery and the Numbers Game he argues that the sources used by Fogel and Engerman biased the data on skilled slaves upwards, and more important, he argues that they ignored questions of change in occupational structure over time. All these works raise as yet unanswered questions about the proportions of skilled slaves and free blacks in the rural black population, and none of them directly compares rural skilled blacks with their white contemporaries. There is a paucity of rural sources, and the sources they did use — plantation accounts, city directories, newspapers, records of sales and manumissions — may have overemphasized the proportion of skilled blacks and masked changes in the occupational structure over time.[1]

No substantial claim can be made that St. Mary's County was typical of its region, much less of the entire antebellum South (see table 1). For example, the county's agricultural base, originally dominated by tobacco, had diversified to include wheat, with mixed success. This diversification encouraged the development of related occupations, such as milling, and brought an increase in prosperity in the early years of the nineteenth century that stimulated building. With salt water on three sides, the county always had a varied maritime economy. In the early years most maritime occupations related to coastal trade and transport. By the 1830s, though, Baltimore, some 135 miles up the Chesapeake Bay by steamboat, had come to dominate county trade and transport. This helped shift the county's maritime economy to fishing and oystering. In addition, resorts at Piney Point and Point Lookout were attracting urbanites by the mid-1850s to the county's stimulating salt air.[2]

Residents of St. Mary's County also made some attempts at industrialization. Along the St. Mary's River in the county's second electoral district there were several mills and an industrial enclave called Clifton Factory. Clifton existed from 1810 to 1959, although its heyday was in the decades prior to a forced sale and reorganization in 1834. During its growth period the factory employed a large number of men and women in its sawmill, tannery, gristmill, and cotton yarn operations, and rented space to shoemakers, blacksmiths, and storekeepers. Thus of all the districts in St. Mary's County, the second was the most occupationally diverse. By 1860 there were also two small "factories" in the vicinity of Leonardtown (the county seat) that manufactured cigars and coaches respectively.[3]

Constructing a skills profile for a rural area like St. Mary's County and determining the race and status of those men and women who earned a living outside farming is difficult. Although before 1850 there is no handy list of rural occupations followed by a free population, and although census takers completely ignored the skills of slaves, enough information survives in county records, supplemented by censuses and private accounts, to make construction of a skills profile possible.

County records consulted includes volumes of indentures, estate inventories, and administration accounts. Because skilled slaves were assessed at higher rates than other slaves, county tax records are invaluable. They also make it possible to compare populations of skilled slaves to those slaves who worked in agriculture and to trace slaves from master to master. While exact occupations were not recorded in the federal censuses before 1850, the censuses of 1820 and 1840 show the numbers of individuals in the categories of agriculture, commerce (in 1840 maritime commerce formed a separate category), and manufacturing. Some private accounts survive, the most valuable of which are the records of the Jesuit plantations of St. Inigoes and Newtown and those of Clifton Factory. Although the county newspaper, the *St. Mary's Beacon*, does not survive before 1852, it too provides occupational information. The appendix contains a complete explanation of the strengths and weaknesses of each of these sources.

In all some 1,628 individuals, master and apprentice, free black and slave, can be positively identified as having been engaged in a skill or occupation other than farming. Another 152 individuals were counted in the census but could not be otherwise identified by name, trade, or craft. This list includes 537 blacks, slave and free. Non-farming occupations in which blacks appear can be divided into four groups: skilled crafts, maritime occupations, semi-

TABLE 2

Proportions of Individuals in Selected Occupations, St. Mary's County, 1790–1860

	Slaves		Free Blacks		Whites		Totals
	Number	Percent	Number	Percent	Number	Percent	
Skilled Crafts							
Blacksmith	70	43	5	3	88	54	163
Bricklayer	1	3	7	18	32	80	40
Carpenter	144	43	36	11	156	46	336
Cooper			1		2		3
Miller	6	14	1	2	37	84	44
Shoemaker	5	5	7	7	89	88	101
Tailor	2	3			67	97	69
Unspecified	36	24	13	9	102	68	151
Total	264	29	70	7	573	63	907
Maritime							
Waterman	2	11	2	11	14	77	18
Sailor	36	13	40	14	210	73	286
Fisherman/Oysterman			7	9	71	91	78
Total	38	10	49	13	295	77	382
Semiskilled							
Brickmaker	1	11	3	33	5	55	9
Ditcher			4	21	15	79	19
Groom	1	17	4	66	1	17	6
Painter			2	29	5	71	7
Woodcutter			15	47	17	53	32
Total	2	3	28	38	43	59	73
Women							
Cook	7	15	33	73	5	11	45
Laundress			17	71	7	29	24
Midwife			13	30	30	70	43
Seamstress	1		3	1	252	98	257
Spinner/Weaver	12	8	4	3	135	89	151
Total	20	4	70	13	429	83	520

skilled jobs, and occupations of women. Table 2 gives total numbers of individuals in each occupation.

Of the 537 blacks known to pursue these occupations, 220 were free blacks and 317 were slaves. Of these, 334 (264 slave and 70 free) were in manufacturing, working as blacksmiths, bricklayers, carpenters, coopers, millers, shoemakers, and tailors. The maritime occupations of waterman (bay craftsman), sailor, fisherman, and oysterman counted 87 blacks (49 free and 38 slave). Jobs that might be considered semiskilled at the time—barber, brickmaker, ditcher, musician, groom, sawer, tanyard worker, woodcutter, carter, and painter—were held by 30 blacks (28 free and 2 slave). Some of these jobs may have occupied most of a person's working day; others were probably tasks engaged in as additions to agricultural labor. This supposition is supported by comparing occupations given by free blacks in the 1850 and 1860 censuses. In 1860 eleven of the men who had given their occupations as "laborer" in 1850 were more specific as to what this "labor" involved— carpentry, ditching, woodcutting, oystering, and fishing.[4]

Black women were also found in occupations other than agriculture. They cooked, sold cakes, spun thread, wove cloth; they were laundresses, seamstresses, midwives, and nurses. In general it is difficult to uncover women's occupations. Many planters owned girls and women who must have helped in the kitchen, yet inventories only record seven slave cooks. When a master was an innkeeper like John T. Yates of Leonardtown, he must have employed at least one of his three slave women in the kitchen. Yet between 1790 and 1864 only eighty-four black women could be found with known occupations outside farming, seventy of whom were free and only fourteen slave.[5]

Among those occupations followed by both blacks and whites, blacks formed the majority of carpenters (53 percent) and 46 percent of the blacksmiths. Cooks and laundresses were nearly always black women, and many woodcutters were free blacks. Black occupations seem to reflect either occupations that were convenient or profitable for their masters or those that were low paying, probably low status, and therefore avoided by whites. Thus poor white women spun, wove, and sewed to earn money, but they did not hire themselves out as cooks or take in laundry.

Entry into some crafts was limited for blacks because the occupation required a period of apprenticeship. A master craftsman might train his slave as a helper, or a slaveowner might arrange for someone to teach his slave a necessary or profitable skill, but free blacks had only a minuscule number of black craftsmen to teach them. Most apprentices came from the Alms House or were bereft of fathers and were bound out by the St. Mary's County Orphans Court. This was the result of a practice, dating from colonial times, of teaching orphaned children a trade. No free black, however, appeared among the master craftsmen, and only eleven young free blacks were apprenticed in a trade. Race was clearly the determining factor. Of 371 total apprenticeships recorded between 1801 and 1840, 143 (38 percent) were in farming, but more than half (58 percent) of the farmers' apprentices were black. Children of both sexes were, like Ann Monk, apprenticed to learn "all the necessary branches of common labour suitable for a child of her colour."[6] The differences in numbers between whites, free blacks, and slaves in skilled occupations thus likely reflect the difficulty young free blacks had in finding apprenticeships, the generational passage of skills within the slave community, and the master's needs.

Maritime occupations required both familiarity with the sea and capital

TABLE 3

Proportions of Skilled Slaves to Adult Male Slaves, St. Mary's County, 1804–1860

	1804	1813	1820	1821	1830	1831	1840	1850	1860
Slave Males 14–15	1,276	1,177		1,194		942			
Skilled Males under 45	46	60		51		74			
Percentage	3.6%	5%		4.3%		7.9%			
Slave Males over 16			1,673		1,616		1,419	1,671	1,809
Skilled Males			106		95		53	28	26
Percentage			6.3%		5.9%		3.7%	1.6%	1.4%

for equipment. Records are unclear whether "bay craftsman" and "water-man" mean "sailor" or "fisherman," although they were among occupations needing apprenticeships. Oystering and fishing required capital as well as skill. Inventories do not show slave fishermen, but there is a great deal of evidence that slaves worked seine nets, particularly during spawning runs, and tonged for oysters. But for a free black to work as an oysterman he needed capital for a boat and "oyster paws." Otherwise he had to sign on with a captain willing to hire blacks. That only two of the sixty oystermen counted in the 1860 census were black suggests that most captains would not hire them. Black sailors may have faced the same prejudice. Most slave sailors were owned by mariners; these captains might have hired free blacks to fill out their crews. Avenues for escape, however, opened up to sailors, which may have made captains reluctant to hire free blacks for fear they were really aiding in the escape of a slave.[7]

Outside of blacksmithing and carpentry, then, blacks, who formed more than half the adult male population of St. Mary's County, were disproportionately underrepresented in nonfarming occupations. They did, however, constitute more than a third (37 percent) of the skilled craftsmen and 23 percent of those persons engaged in maritime occupations. Blacks appear to have dominated semiskilled jobs, but these figures may be suspect; many semiskilled tasks could be and probably were performed by some of the men who listed "laborer" as their occupation. Black women seem to have been employed largely in agriculture, for they represented only 18 percent of the women who used their housewives' skills to earn extra money for their families.

Focusing on slaves, what proportion were employed in occupations other than farming? Since information on slave women is so sparse, only men can be used as a basis for comparison. Assessors placed a higher value on slaves who were blacksmiths, carpenters, millers, masons, and sailors. Taking the assessments of 1804, 1813, 1821, and 1831, comparisons can be made between all slave males fourteen to forty-five and those engaged in skilled occupations (see table 3). The returns for 1813 and 1831 appear to be more complete, thus yielding higher proportions. Nevertheless, if the tax records of St. Mary's County are at all accurate, only a very small proportion of the adult male slaves were engaged in nonfarming occupations.

Census data gives only a slightly different picture (see table 3). Except for 1820 and 1840 there is no way to be positive that skilled slaves present in probate and tax records were active in census years, so numbers are possibly too low. With these cautions in mind, census figures indicate only a slightly higher number of skilled male slaves than do the assessments. They also indicate that the decade of the 1830s was a watershed; after that date the number and proportion of skilled slaves declined to the point that by 1860 only 1 percent of the adult male slaves appear to have worked outside farming.

If skilled slaves made up only a small portion of the total adult male slave population, might they not represent a higher proportion of the adult slaves on their own plantations? When Charles Carroll of Carrollton, the largest slaveowner in Maryland, died in 1832, he possessed 338 slaves, of whom 206 were men and women over age sixteen. Twenty of his male slaves were listed in nonfarming occupations; that is, 9.7 percent of his adult slaves, or 16.5 percent of his adult males, were not engaged directly in agriculture. Given these statistics, how then do the plantations of St. Mary's County compare to Carroll's plantations?[8]

The eighty-eight inventories of county slaveowners between 1795 and 1864 that recorded skilled and semiskilled adult slaves listed a total of 2,238 individuals. Of these, 1,213 were over the age of sixteen, and 153 were recorded with occupations. Most of their masters were wealthy planters with large numbers of slaves, at least in terms of county slaveholdings. While the size of holdings ranged from 2 to 216, the average number of slaves on these plantations was 27, the median 16. Among the total adult population, 12.6 percent (or 20 percent of the men over sixteen) were working outside farming. These inventories suggest that a far higher proportion of adult slaves were working outside farming than was actually the case. Since fifty-five (67 percent) of the inventories showed only a single skilled slave, one can only conclude from these inventories that slaves on large plantations were more likely to be engaged in crafts than were those who lived on small plantations.[9]

Table 4 shows the estimated number of skilled and semiskilled slaves, arranged by occupation, present in each census year. Carpenters were consistently the largest group and the most desirable investment for slaveholders. Sixty percent of the inventories with skilled slaves listed carpenters. The assessments show a similar pattern, with 55 percent of the owners of skilled slaves possessing carpenters. The preponderance of slave carpenters

TABLE 4

Occupations of Skilled and Semiskilled Slaves in St. Mary's County in Census Years 1790–1860

	1790	1800	1810	1820	1830	1840	1850	1860
Blacksmith	11	18	24	26	21	14	6	6
Bricklayer			1					
Carpenter	16	30	35	59	69	31	20	19
Miller	1	2	3	2				
Shoemaker		1	2	2				
Tailor		1						
Sailor	2	2	3	13	2	5		
Waterman				1	2	2	2	1
Barber			1	1				
Carter	1	1	2	1				
Groom		1	1					
Tanyard worker				1	1	1		
Cook		2	2			2	1	
Seamstress						1		
Weaver		3	4	3	2			
Totals	31	61	78	109	97	56	29	26

reflects the needs of a rural agricultural society. For example, most farmers possessed carpentry tools when they died. While free carpenters were widely available in the county, owning a slave carpenter could be one way to save money as well as be convenient. Administration accounts refer to constant repairs to farm buildings and tenements. In fact, if the condition of buildings described in probate valuations is indicative of those in the county, carpenters should have found constant employment.[10]

Carpenters were also the most valuable of slaves, skilled or otherwise. In 1808 a prime twenty-three to twenty-six-year-old field hand was worth $300. John Reeder's carpenter, Charles, age twenty-eight, had a value of $400. Differences remained over time. Francis Piles's carpenter, Harry, age forty-eight, was valued at $800 in 1837 when a prime field hand was worth only $600. John T. Hawkins's thirty-eight-year-old carpenter, Edward, had a value of $1,000. These values reflected earning power. In the second decade of the nineteenth century the hire of field hands averaged $45 a year. From 1812 to 1814 carpenter Stephen, who belonged to Henry Abell, was hired out for $100 a year. Carpenter Isaac earned $290 for his master's estate in 1824. Peter Gough charged $100 plus board for the services of Clem, who was both a carpenter and a miller. For most of the years between 1812 and 1829 a slave carpenter was hired out for $100 plus room and board. Thus investing in a slave carpenter was potentially more profitable than buying a field hand. This raises the question of how much work was available off the plantations, since slave carpenters were competing with free men, black and white. Ad-

TABLE 5

Comparison of Blacks and Whites in Skilled Trades by Decade, St. Mary's County, 1790–1860

	1790		1800		1810		1820		1830		1840		1850		1860	
	No.	Percent	No.	Percent	No.	Percent	No.	Percent	No.	Percent	No.	Percent	No.	Percent	No.	Percent
Blacksmiths																
Slaves	11	73	18	64	24	60	26	44	21	64	14	52	6	33	6	18
Free Blacks			3	8							1	4			2	6
Whites	4	27	10	36	13	33	33	56	12	36	12	44	12	67	25	76
Bricklayers																
Slaves			1	17												
Free Blacks									1	20	3	38	4	50	3	30
Whites	4	100	6	100	5	83	6	100	4	80	5	63	4	50	7	70
Carpenters																
Slaves	16	55	30	49	35	42	59	49	69	59	31	40	20	22	19	18
Free Blacks	1	3			7	8	12	10	6	5	6	8	16	18	15	14
Whites	12	41	31	51	42	50	49	41	42	36	40	52	54	60	71	68
Millers																
Slaves	1	50	2	67	3	75	2	67								
Free Blacks							1	33							1	9
Whites	1	50	1	33	1	25					1	100	3	100	10	90
Shoemakers																
Slaves			1	8	2	11	2	8								
Free Blacks	1	10	1	8	1	5	1	4	1	6	3	13	5	23	1	8
Whites	9	90	10	83	16	84	21	88	17	94	21	88	17	77	13	93
Tailors																
Slaves			1	7									1	25	1	20
Free Blacks					1	10	1	8	1	13	1	5				
Whites	2	100	13	93	9	90	12	92	7	88	21	95	3	75	4	80
Unspecified																
Slaves							9		4		22		2			
Free Blacks					3		8		3		7					
Whites					6		49		13		59					

ministration accounts and private letters indicate owners actively sought work off their plantations for their skilled slaves. Edmund T. Maddox wrote James Thomas in 1831 requesting two of Thomas's carpenters to work on his corn house when they completed other work in the neighborhood. He offered to pay the "customary monthly wage."[11] The windmill at St. Inigoes was built by "Charles a blackman from St. Thomas Manor . . . he had no instructions from anyone—the windmill is well built and appears to answer well."[12] Apparently slave carpenter were competitive with free men both in wages and in skills.

The second most numerous and most valuable group of skilled slaves was blacksmiths. Slaves clearly dominated the craft of blacksmithing before 1850 (see table 5). Blacksmiths appeared in 35 percent of the inventories that contained skilled slaves and in 22 percent of the assessments with skilled slaves. Like carpenters, blacksmiths were more highly valued than field hands and retained their value into their forties. Joseph Millard's blacksmith, Nace, age forty-four, was worth $300 in 1810. Nicholas Sewall's Joshua, fifty-three years old in 1814, was valued at $180, while Luke W. Barber's forty-nine-year-old blacksmith, Jake, had a valuation of $275 in 1831. George, who belonged to William Bean, was forty-three in 1838 and had a value of $600, the same value as that recorded in 1825, when he was twenty-nine.[13]

Most planters who owned blacksmiths had their own plantation smithies and did work for themselves as well as for neighbors. The Jesuit plantation of St. Inigoes had a succession of slave blacksmiths from 1806 to 1838. Accounts show that the majority of work done was for the plantation, but neighbors and tenants brought iron items to be mended when the blacksmith was not otherwise employed. Only a very few owners of slave blacksmiths appear to have used them primarily for commercial work. Merchants Bennet Walker of Clements, Henry G. Garner of Chaptico, and Richard H. Miles of Milestown all had smithies operated by slave blacksmiths near their stores. Several mill owners also owned blacksmiths and may have had them operating a shop near the mill. Planter George Slye actually rented Philip Key of Tudor Hall's blacksmith shop at Chaptico but then apparently decided it was more profitable to hire out his blacksmith. While only one white blacksmith appears to have owned a slave blacksmith, others clearly rented them, sometimes with unfortunate results, like the man who leased George Reeder's Bill along with $37 worth of tools in 1818: "the man failed & I lost the Hire."[14]

Slave sailors made up the largest of the maritime occupational groups. Many of these men were owned by pilots or by mariners, although sailors were also possessed by masters who had distinctly land-bound occupations. If their masters did not follow the sea, slave sailors were probably rented out, like George Reeder's Miley Dixon, listed in 1813 as "a good sailor." Sailors, like carpenters and blacksmiths, made well above the prevailing agricultural wage: Jack Bell was hired by George Guyther for $101 in 1839, although for the next six years his annual hire fell to $60. One might ask why, in a county with a maritime economy, there were not more slave sailors. The answer may lie in the opportunities offered thereby for escape, although none of the known runaways from St. Mary's County were sailors.[15]

No other occupational group was as prominent as carpenters, blacksmiths, or sailors. Some groups like fishermen/watermen and cooks were probably undercounted, for while sailors were assessed at the same rate as other skilled slaves, fishermen and cooks were not. Slaves clearly fished and oystered. Joseph Mobberly of St. Inigoes remarked, "They also, in defiance of authority, gathered oysters on Sundays and holidays, which they sold to ships etc."[16] Catching alewives for fertilizer and herring to be salted for food were seasonal occupations that also employed slaves. Seine nets were an expensive item and appear in the inventories only of the wealthiest men, who were also slaveowners. Slave fishermen might also have been hired out. Those men who advertised alewives for sale in the 1860 St. Mary's Beacon either owned slaves themselves or lived in close proximity to large slaveowners who may have rented slaves to them.[17]

The numbers of skilled and semiskilled slaves in most occupational categories rose until 1820, then declined sharply. Some of this decline might be

TABLE 6

Age Categories of Carpenters and Blacksmiths in the Taxes
and Censuses, St. Mary's County, 1804–1860

	1804	1813	1821	1831	1840	1850	1860
Under 20	1		1				1
20–30	5	10	7	7	4	7	2
31–40	15	15	15	18	14	6	4
41–50	6	13	17	9	19	9	5
Over 50	6	6	5	11	7	9	6

attributed to the available data. Yet comparable data available for 1820 and 1840 shows that the number of slaves working outside farming was halved. Declines in some occupational categories can be attributed to technology. By the 1830s regular steamboat service from Baltimore to St. Mary's County lessened the demand for homemade shoes and cloth and therefore for local shoemakers, tanners, and weavers. In fact, as table 5 shows, these occupations declined in general between 1820 and 1840.[18]

Declines in the numbers of skilled slaves after 1820 can also be attributed to a decline in the general agricultural economy. High prices for the country's two staples, tobacco and wheat, encouraged the residents of St. Mary's County to build and to invest in consumer goods in the years following the War of 1812. Then came the long depressions following the panics of 1819 and 1837. Prices of staples fell. Tobacco never really recovered, being worth $3.04 per hundred-weight in 1822 and only $2.70 in 1860. Wheat suffered even more. In the early nineteenth century St. Mary's County farmers, encouraged by prices of over $1.00 per bushel, expanded the county's wheat acreage. Wheat prices were generally below $1.00 per bushel in the 1820s to the mid-1830s and again in the 1840s. Competition from the new western wheat farms had depressed the market. In addition, county wheat was hard hit by "rust" in the 1850s. There may not have been enough work off the plantations to justify training skilled slaves, particularly if wages for free craftsmen were low. By 1850 even carpenters and blacksmiths do not appear to have been good investments for slaveowners.[19]

By combining assessment, inventory, and census data on ages, a clear pattern of the "greying" of the population of carpenters and blacksmiths appears (see table 6). The highest proportion of younger men (under 25) occurs in the decade of the teens—a period, at least after the war, in which the county was prosperous and highly skilled slaves ought to have been a good investment. Nearly all studies of slave craftsmen have found a disproportionate number of older men. The suggestion is that most plantations could only support one man in a craft, and owners did not move to train a successor until age made it difficult for him to continue his trade. Older craftsmen were clearly in the majority in St. Mary's County, most falling into the thirty-to-forty-year-old range, with the forty-to-fifty-year-old range close behind. Yet the near absence of young craftsmen in the 1840s as well as the decline in the number of slave craftsmen suggest that owners were not even replacing older men as they declined or died.

There is general agreement that slave craftsmen tended to be older men. The area of disagreement is why. Fogel and Engerman believe that the late age of entry into crafts is explained by such an occupation being viewed as a "reward" for earlier good behavior or good service. Yet the small number of skilled slaves in St. Mary's County, where nearly half the population was enslaved, argues against such a "safety valve" system of reward. Moreover, it would seem that if occupation in a craft was a reward independent of the master's needs, the proportion of skilled slaves would not have declined over time. Herbert Gutman's hypothesis that the late entry of slaves into crafts was related to a limited need for craftsmen seems to be supported by the situation in St. Mary's County. Masters did not replace artisans until older men died. Gutman also suggests that young craftsmen were often the sons of craftsmen who had learned their skills from their now deceased fathers.[20]

Gutman's suggestion raises the question of how the slaves in St. Mary's County learned their skills. Slave names are completely absent from re- corded apprenticeship agreements. Only three young slaves are referred to as apprentices in any extant records. Carpenter Bernard Medley had a slave apprentice, Clement, in 1793. Blacksmith Joe, twenty-one, who belonged to John Thompson, was probably apprenticed to Thompson's other black- smith, thirty-two-year-old Henry. It is not known to whom Michael Fenwick's twenty-two-year-old blacksmith, "Little Bill," was apprenticed.[21]

Africans could have brought such traditional skills as carpentry, metal working, and weaving to America. How many Africans were present in late- eighteenth or early-nineteenth-century St. Mary's County is not known. About 1823 Joseph Mobberly of St. Inigoes remarked that "about 35 years ago, it was very common to hear of murders committed by Negroes. At that time the Negroes in Maryland were chiefly Africans . . . ,"[22] and Charles Ball's paternal grandfather was an African. None of the craftsmen in this study had African names, but this does not preclude their having been in- troduced to traditional crafts by African forebears.[23]

On Charles Carroll's plantation sons learned craft skills from their fathers or from other kin. Unfortunately, kinship links among St. Mary's County slave craftsmen cannot at present be proven. Only thirteen inventories between 1795 and 1864 show more than one slave in the same craft. Six blacksmiths and eleven carpenters worked with one or more companions. Five of the blacksmiths and six of the carpenters worked with men young enough to have been their sons. Assessments show that on twenty-one plantations two or more men worked at the same trade. Four blacksmiths worked with another, two possibly with their sons. Twenty carpenters had co-workers, but in only eight cases do the ages suggest a father-son team. Sons, of course, could have been trained by fathers who were dead by the time these records were made. But as the number of craftsmen declined over time, fewer and fewer men were left to pass their skills on to the next generation.[24]

Some slaves may have learned their trades from their masters. Five carpenters owned slave carpenters whom they probably trained. Thomas Cadden clearly taught his slave Frank the tailor's trade. Blacksmith William Harrison owned a slave blacksmith who may have apprenticed under him. Men who followed the sea—three pilots, nine ship captains, and a sailor— owned slave sailors and might have taught them seamanship. White craftsmen also rented slaves. It is possible that the blacksmith and the nine carpenters who rented slaves in 1820 and 1840 were actually training them. In 1850 carpenter James W. Burch had seven adult male slaves in his household, while carpenter Gustavius Greenwell had four. Were these slaves carpenters or apprentice carpenters? We will never know.[25]

Because the focus of this essay is skilled blacks and not their masters, this is not the place to discuss masters' occupations and wealth. Suffice it to say that most owners of skilled slaves were wealthy planters, usually in the top 10 percent of the county's assessables. They invested in skilled slaves as a convenience or to maximize profits. Without a detailed study of sales and inheritance patterns for all county slaves it is difficult to say if craftsmen were treated differently from other slaves. It is their higher value that allows one to trace skilled slaves over time and from master to master.

Of the total of 317 known skilled and semiskilled slaves, 155 can be traced from master to master. By far the largest number, ninety-one (58 percent), were willed to kin who remained in St. Mary's County. Only six went to kin who resided out of the county or who subsequently moved. Ten slaves were freed by their masters, while three others went to kin who later freed them. Jesse Floyd's blacksmith named Peter remained in the Floyd family until 1856, when at the age of sixty-six he was sold to free black John F. Taney, perhaps one of the rare cases of a free black buying a relative out of slavery. Five skilled slaves ran away, but it is impossible to draw conclusions that craft skills made escape easier or more likely to be successful.[26]

Forty-three (27 percent) of the skilled slaves were sold—eighteen in the county, twelve out of the county, and thirteen out of the state. At this point it cannot be determined if the possession of craft skills influenced a master's decision to sell or retain a particular slave. With rare exceptions, slaves were sold individually or in small lots. Some sales were clearly the results of settling an estate, for slaves were sold by their late master's executor or by heirs not long after the estate was settled. Four of the thirteen skilled slaves sold out of state left St. Mary's County when the Society of Jesus sold all its chattels to Henry Johnson of Louisiana in 1839. Most sales were in the period between 1820 and 1840; nearly all out-of-county and out-of-state sales occurred in the late 1830s. It is difficult to assess individual motives, but hard times were certainly a factor influencing sales. These decades were also the period during which slave traders as well as individual southern planters

TABLE 7

Percentage of the Male Population Engaged in Manufacturing or Maritime Occupations in St. Mary's County, 1790–1860

	1790		1800		1810		1820		1830		1840		1850		1860	
	No.	Percent	No.	Percent	No.	Percent	No.	Percent	No.	Percent	No.	Percent	No.	Percent	No.	Percent
Total Males Over 16							3,529		3,648		3,382		3,839		4,453	
Slave Males							1,673		1,616		1,419		1,671		1,809	
Free Black Males							231		244		247		412		547	
White Males	2,100		1,703		1,536		1,625		1,788		1,716		1,756		2,097	
Total Males in Manufacturing	69		137		193		319	9.0	210	5.8	195	5.7	152	4.0	233	5.2
Slave Males	29		54		69		92	5.5	91	5.6	46	3.2	26	1.6	25	1.4
Free Black Males	2		2		15		32	13.9	12	4.9	22	8.9	32	7.8	42	7.7
White Males	38	1.8	81	4.8	109	7.0	195	11.7	107	5.9	127	7.4	94	5.4	166	7.9
Total Males in Maritime	37		92		120		151	4.3	71	1.3	102	3.0	119	3.0	171	3.8
Slave Males	2		2		3		14	.8	4	.2	7	.5	2	.1	1	
Free Black Males					3		11	4.8	6	2.4	16	6.5	33	8.0	17	3.1
White Males	35	1.7	90	5.3	114	7.4	126	7.8	61	3.4	79	4.6	84	4.8	153	7.3
Total Males in Manufacturing & Maritime*	106		229		313		470	13.3	271	6.2	297	8.8	271	7.0	404	9.0
Slave Males	31		56		72		106	6.3	95	5.9	53	3.7	28	1.7	26	1.4
Free Black Males	2		2		18		43	18.6	18	7.4	38	15.4	65	15.8	59	10.8
White Males	73	3.4	171	10	223	14.5	321	19.8	158	8.8	206	12.0	178	10.0	319	15.2

*For sources of information see Appendix on Sources.

were most successful in persuading Maryland slaveowners to sell their chattels. Yet sales out of state were only a very small proportion of all county slave sales, even in these two most active decades.[27]

When skilled slaves were manumitted they became part of a small but growing community of free blacks, many of whom had been slaves. Free black craftsmen found limited opportunity in St. Mary's County. Only 9 percent of the craft apprentices were free blacks. These included two blacksmiths, a carpenter, a shoemaker, and a bricklayer. Only one free black was apprenticed in a seagoing occupation. Most of the free black children were apprenticed as farm workers, although a handful trained as seamstresses, house servants, or waiters. Some children learned their skills from their fathers. Others learned from white employers without formal apprenticeship agreements. Carpenter James W. Railey of Great Mills advertised in the 1854 St. Mary's Beacon that he "wanted two or three boys to learn the Carpenter's trade from 16 to 18 years of age, Colored boys preferred."[28] A large portion of the free blacks of St. Mary's County had been slaves and carried their crafts into freedom.[29]

While the number of free black males who worked at skilled and semi-skilled tasks was small, their proportion compared to the free black male population over the age of fifteen was higher—peaking in 1850 at 15.7

TABLE 8

Opportunity to Acquire Land and Taxable Property in Selected Occupations in St. Mary's County, 1790–1860

	Total Numbers	Acquired Land Percent	Acquired Taxable Property Percent	Acquired Both Percent
Black Carpenters	37	8	19	27
White Carpenters	192	31	41	73
Black Bricklayers	6	33	16	50
White Bricklayers	23	39	34	74
Black Shoemakers	7	14	14	28
White Shoemakers	57	19	47	49
Black Tailors	1	0	0	0
White Tailors	31	29	42	71
Black Woodcutters	14	28	35	64
White Woodcutters	3	66	33	100
Black Fishermen	7	14	0	14
White Fishermen	76	14	21	35
Black Sailors	30	3	3	6
White Sailors	117	9	21	30
Skilled Manufacturing				
Blacks	51	17	10	27
Whites	303	29	42	71
Maritime				
Blacks	37	8	2	11
Whites	193	11	21	32

percent—than the proportion of either slaves or white males who had similar occupations (table 7). Statistically, at least, free blacks had more opportunities to work outside farming than did slaves or whites. On the other hand, when the careers of free blacks are traced over time, that "advantage" is purely statistical.

Taking three areas of success—the ability to acquire taxable property, the ability to acquire land, and a decision to remain in the county—how did free blacks compare with whites? Table 8 compares the proportion of skilled blacks and whites with taxable property and land. Only 10 percent of the free blacks had taxable property compared to 42 percent of the whites. While 29 percent of the white craftsmen managed to acquire land, only fourteen blacks—a mere 17 percent—were able to become landowners.

Free black craftsmen do not appear to have been able to take full advantage of the opportunities their skills might have afforded. Some managed to succeed. The most successful was carpenter Abraham Barnes (later McClain), who was twenty-nine years old and had a wife and three children when he was freed in 1808 by the will of Colonel Richard Barnes. His skills were in immediate demand, as he is mentioned in several administration accounts for making repairs and for constructing outbuildings. By 1819 he had saved enough money to purchase 268 acres, which he retained to his death. His land and taxable wealth of $440 placed him just barely in the top half of assessables. Compared to his white contemporaries he was moderately prosperous, although when he died in 1841 his estate of $328 in personal property was quite small.[30]

No other black craftsman did as well as Abraham Barnes McClain. The other landowners all had fewer than 200 acres. Direct comparisons of the value of taxable property between blacks and whites in the same occupations show that blacks were consistently poorer. There is no real correlation between trade and ability to acquire land. The largest occupational group of black landowners was the woodcutters listed in the 1860 census. All lived in an area of the county known for its heavily timbered but thin-soiled uplands. It is likely they found their farms more suited to timber than to tobacco.

Traced from census to census, the career paths of many black craftsmen led downhill. Frank Cadden (later Thompson) learned the tailor's trade from his master, who freed him in 1804 and gave him thirty square feet across the end of his lot in Leonardtown upon which to build a house. Frank Thompson appears as a householder in the 1830 and 1840 censuses engaged in agriculture, not manufacturing. It is unlikely he built his house, for he never acquired taxable property. Another example is William Brian (Bryon) who had been apprenticed as a shoemaker in 1811 at the age of twelve. He was apparently still working at that trade in 1840. But in 1836 he and his wife were forced to bind out three of their children to farmers because they were "in indigent circumstances." Four carpenters, a shoemaker, and three sailors did not continue their trades from census to census. The sailors may have left the sea because of age, but why the carpenters discontinued their trade is an open question.[31]

If skilled and semiskilled free blacks failed to acquire property, did they then opt to leave St. Mary's County? Among the county's white population there was a direct relationship between ability to acquire property and the decision to remain in the county. Among farmers and craftsmen alike propertyless tenants were most likely to migrate. Examination of the careers of white craftsmen and their apprentices reveals that 47.8 percent remained in the county for at least a decade, and 43.3 percent resided there until death. Nearly all (72 percent) of those men who remained until they died owned land or some form of taxable property.[32]

It is quite difficult to trace the careers of free blacks or determine if they remained in St. Mary's County until they died. Propertyless men leave few records in life or in death. Yet 53.4 percent of the free black craftsmen could be found living in the county for a decade or more, although only 24 percent appear to have remained there until they died. Nearly all of these men were without any form of assessable property; only four of the fourteen who probably remained in the county until death appear on tax rolls. That a slightly higher proportion of black craftsmen remained in St. Mary's County for more than a decade, and that these men were nearly all propertyless, likely reflects lack of opportunities for them outside the county. Whites could and did migrate westward or to cities. Blacks, however, may have perceived that the atmosphere outside their home county was a hostile one. In a slave state free blacks who left their community where they were known were objects of suspicion and might become victims of kidnapping. So free blacks remained longer in St. Mary's County in a futile search for financial security, while propertyless whites left.

What conclusions can be drawn from a study of rural skilled blacks in a border state like Maryland? While their numbers were small relative to the black male population, a higher proportion of blacks than whites possessed craft skills. Indeed, blacks dominated certain crafts like blacksmithing and carpentry. The position of black craftsmen, however, seems to have eroded as the antebellum period progressed. Was this situation unique to St. Mary's County? Were there fewer skilled blacks because of the stagnation in tobacco and wheat prices, because of the importation of urban manufactured goods, or because whites "conspired" to limit black opportunities? One is tempted to attribute the decline to economic causes, but why then did the numbers of white craftsmen rise between 1850 and 1860?

As far as the free black population is concerned, why were more engaged in nonfarming activities? The answer probably lies in low wages for free agricultural workers in an economy that, after all, was dominated by slave labor. A free black likely had to possess a variety of skills and be willing to attempt any available job simply to survive. He could not look forward to acquiring land and to "retiring" from his craft to become a farmer. That numbers of skilled free blacks listed their occupations in 1850 as "laborer" is indicative of the lack of opportunity, at least in St. Mary's County.

Is St. Mary's County representative? Possibly not. But there needs to be far more research into the black craft population of rural areas before 1850. Only then can definitive statements concerning the role played by skilled blacks in the rural antebellum economy be made.

APPENDIX ON SOURCES

As social historians turn to statistics in their attempts to understand and interpret the past, we become more and more aware of what can and cannot be done with numbers. It may be a truism, but people in the past did not keep records with future historians in mind. The case of skilled blacks in rural areas of the antebellum South exemplifies the difficulty of constructing a comprehensive rural crafts profile before the 1870 census. There is no simple way to proceed, and no single source can be viewed as reliable. Moreover, if the records of St. Mary's County are representative, statistical sampling techniques can be misleading.

Knowing that there is no comprehensive picture of rural free black skills before the 1850 census and that slave skills were ignored by the census takers in 1850 and 1860, how can a historian proceed? This essay argues for in-depth studies of representative counties. Maryland is particularly fortunate in possessing a wealth of surviving county probate, land, and tax records. Some are contained in courthouses, but many of the originals, as well as microfilm copies, are housed at the Maryland Hall of Records in Annapolis. Unless otherwise stated, all references in this article are to collections at the Hall of Records. It must also be noted that the staff of the Hall of Records has provided invaluable assistance to this author over the years.

St. Mary's County may not be completely representative of southern Maryland, but its nineteenth-century records are remarkably complete despite a courthouse fire in 1831. It is the completeness of those records that makes the construction of a skills profile possible. Also, as Maryland's mother county, St. Mary's has been the subject of a good deal of recent research, and many source materials have been published.

The major source for the names and occupations of the county's white craftsmen is the series of Valuations and Indentures, 1809–29, 1826–1908. These are by no means comprehensive. No black master craftsman appears among those taking apprentices, nor in fact is every white craftsman present. The indentures, however, are an important beginning.

Inventories are also an excellent source of information. While most farmers owned simple carpentry tools, and those who lived on the water had fishing and oystering equipment, men who made their living from these occupations had a considerably larger investment in tools than an ordinary farmer. Often a craftsman's tools made up the largest component of his inventoried wealth. Surviving inventories begin in 1795; there are seventeen volumes to 1864. To give some examples of investment in tools, proportions ranged from 2 percent to more than half of the value of craftsmen's estates, depending less on the value of the tools themselves and more on the absence or presence of slaves. In the 1810s a farmer might have $2 to $5 worth of carpentry tools, while a carpenter would have between $20 and $50 invested in tools (Inventories, 1810–14, 1814–18, 1817–24).

One might assume that most craftsmen who remained in the county until they died would have had inventories, particularly since inventories in Maryland were taken to protect creditors as well as to ensure an equitable distribution of the deceased's estate. Yet of some 158 skilled individuals whose date of death is known, only 112 (70 percent) had inventories. Since not all men went through probate, other sources must be consulted to confirm their deaths. Fortunately Margaret K. Fresco has compiled marriage and death records to 1900 in *Marriages and Deaths: St. Mary's County, Maryland, 1634–1900* (Ridge, Md., 1982), thus making it possible to determine that a man indeed died without probate. Sometimes the tax collector also noted "heirs" in the margin of assessment records.

Not all county craftsmen, however, left inventoried estates that contained the tools of their trade. The single free black craftsman whose estate was inventoried did not contain the tools of his trade (see Abraham Barnes McClain, Inventories, GC 2, p. 29).

A third source of information on free craftsmen is the U. S. census, specifically the Manuscript Census Returns, Fourth and Sixth Censuses of the United States, 1820 and 1840, St. Mary's County, Maryland, Population Schedules. In these years census takers recorded the number of individuals in occupational categories. By careful comparison of adult men and women in each household with the total number of individuals in each occupational category in that household, more skilled workers were discovered. In many cases the one individual who listed an occupational category other than agriculture was clearly the head of the household. In 1820 free black Charles Davis reported five people in the household, one of whom was engaged in manufacturing. He must have been that one, for he was the only adult male, two other males being under the age of ten (Fourth Census, 1820, St. Mary's County, Population Schedule, 264). Thus the names of 439 individuals, including 30 free blacks, who were engaged in occupations other than agriculture were uncovered. In many cases there were other records of that person and his or her occupation as well as records of apprentices or other household members known to have been craftsmen. Thus even before 1850 the census can be used to discover as well as to confirm the presence of rural craftsmen. In the cases of those craftsmen, like Charles Davis, who left no record of their presence other than the 1820 or 1840 censuses, no specific occupation could be determined. There were sixty-two individuals listed under "manufacturing" in 1820 and eighty-three in 1840. These numbers may include some men whose names and occupations were known but who could not be located in the census.

The most commonly used source of information about rural craftsmen in the South is surviving plantation records. There are very few plantation account books surviving in St. Mary's County, but fortunately the records of two Jesuit plantations, St. Inigoes near the Potomac River in the southeastern part of the county and Newtown off Bretton Bay in the center, are nearly complete for the late eighteenth and early nineteenth centuries. Part of the Maryland Province Archives, now housed at Georgetown University Library, St. Inigoes's accounts include six volumes, 1784–1850 (170 C-H), and Newtown's accounts consist of seven volumes, 1768–1851 (171 B-H) and five volumes, 1818–42 (100 + F, vols. I–V). The skilled and semiskilled workers they employed came from a wide area of the county.

Most of the plantation accounts consulted were in the form of Administration Accounts, eleven volumes, 1798–1843, and Guardian Accounts, eight volumes, 1787–1839, recorded by the county register of wills. Only the most conscientious administrators or guardians took the time to have individual transactions with craftsmen recorded. Those who did recorded transactions with individuals who were not necessarily St. Mary's County residents. Everyone listed in these accounts had to be traced in census or tax records to determine where they lived. In most cases the accounts confirmed occupations of individuals already known to be engaged in manufacturing or commerce. But sixty-four men whose last names suggest they were from St. Mary's County appeared only in these accounts.

The task of discovering the occupations of free persons becomes easier after 1850. Both the 1850 and 1860 censuses for St. Mary's County have been transcribed, indexed, and published: The Genealogy Committee of the St. Mary's County Historical Society, comp., *The 1850 Census of St. Mary's County, Maryland* (Leonardtown, Md., 1979); and Shirley Evans Colleary, Harvey L. Lineback, and David Roberts, comps., *The 1860 Census of St. Mary's County, Maryland* (Valley Lee, Md., 1982). In addition, craftsmen and professionals advertised in the *St. Mary's Beacon*. Microfilm of the paper from 1852 is now available at the Maryland Hall of Records.

All sources—probate records, indentures, censuses, private accounts and correspondence—enabled the creation of a master list of free people who worked outside agriculture. In most cases one source merely confirmed another—i.e., accounts or inventories confirmed the occupation of a householder listed in the census as engaged in "manufacturing" or "commerce." All these men and women were then traced through county records until they died or left the county. Great care was taken to be certain that two or more individuals with the same name were not confused.

Discovering slave craftsmen poses even greater problems than discovering free craftsmen. The most commonly used source for skilled slaves is probate inventories. Between 1790 and 1864 a total of eighty-eight inventories noted the presence of skilled slaves. Yet inventories, at least in St. Mary's County, give a very incomplete picture of slave occupations. Not all slaveowners were inventoried when they died. The estate of Richard Barnes, the county's largest landowner and slaveholder, was not inventoried when he died in 1804 (see St. Mary's County Wills, JJ 3, p. 46; Orphans Court Proceedings, 1809–26, pp. 1–22). This was because an individual's heirs could post bond equal to the deceased's indebtedness and thus avoid an inventory. The case of Governor James F. Thomas of Deep Falls, who died in 1845, is similar (Wills, GC 2, p. 180). Both men were known to have owned skilled slaves. Moreover, some slaves, like Luke W. Barber's carpenter Sam, were known from other sources to have had craft skills, yet no mention of these skills appeared in the inventory. Sam is recorded as a carpenter in Certificates of Slaves returned to the county assessor in 1813, 1821, and 1831 and is probably one of four in Barber's household engaged in "manufacturing" in 1820, yet he is not in Barber's 1830 inventory (Inventories, EJM 2, p. 255, EJM 3, p. 22).

Skilled slaves are also mentioned in other county probate records. Administration and Guardian Accounts regularly report the renting of slaves from others as well as the hiring out of slaves. Skilled slaves always commanded greater hire rates than those who were agricultural workers, and a careful reading of accounts is useful in discovering their names, occupations, and owners.

The most useful source on the total population of skilled slaves is related to the county assessments. These exist in a nearly complete series of forty-four volumes (St. Mary's County Assessments, 1793–1845). All taxable property, including land and slaves, is described and valued. After 1845 only changes in assessable property and total tax liability were recorded on an annual basis. Because skilled slaves were assessed at a higher rate (for example, between 1813 and 1841 a skilled male between fourteen and forty-five years of age was assessed at $250, an unskilled male at $125), they were subject to special attention on the part of the assessors. In 1804, 1813, 1821, and 1831 reassessments were made, requiring certificates from all slaveowners stating the name, age, and occupation (if relevant) of each slave in their possession. The occupations, although not the names, of skilled slaves were recorded in the actual assessment books in 1804, 1813, 1821, and 1831. Comparing the assessment books with the certificates of slaves shows gaps in the surviving certificates, but enough certificates exist to make it possible to construct an age and occupational profile of skilled slaves and to compare them to other adult slaves and to free craftsmen.

Assessment records are also a good source for tracing skilled slaves over time. When any form of assessable property changed hands the transaction and the circumstances were recorded in Minute Books, five volumes, 1807–30, or in Alienations and Transfers, six volumes, 1786–1829, 1832–64. Thus with a list of the names of slaves and their owners drawn from probate records and the slave certificates, many of those slaves can be traced from owner to owner until they died or were sold out of the county. It must be emphasized that the collection of certificates is not complete, and at times the tax records are frustratingly vague—recording the transfer of an adult male slave valued at twice what field hands were assessed for without any additional information, or noting the name and age of the slave but giving the occupation simply as "mechanick." At times transfers that seemingly should have been recorded are not there. Yet enough transfers are fully recorded to make tax records, in conjunction with probate records, a rich source of information about skilled slaves.

The most disappointing records were the lists of slaves taken in 1867 (St. Mary's Commissioner of Slave Statistics, Slave Statistics, 1867–69). By joint resolution of Congress compensation was proposed for loyal slaveowners. The state recorded lists of slaves and their ages and occupations at the time of emancipation in 1864 (Lewis Mayer, *Supplement to the Maryland Code* . . . [Baltimore, 1868], 111–15). So few craftsmen were recorded—ten, all carpenters—among the adult slaves that one's suspicion is aroused. Could the number of slave craftsmen have fallen so sharply from the 1840s? The answer, as it turned out, is yes.

A final source for skilled slaves is, surprisingly, the U.S. census. It bears repeating that no slave occupations were recorded in 1850 and 1860. The 1820 and 1840 censuses did record occupational categories. As names of household heads were checked against the free population's known individuals in "manufacturing" and "commerce," it became clear that some of those listed in the above categories were slaves. This assumption was confirmed by tax and probate records, for fifty-seven known skilled slaves were recorded in their masters' households. There were also cases where the head of household listed skilled individuals who by age could only have been slaves. When the assessments were consulted it became clear that some of these householders did not own adult male slaves, evidence, then, that skilled slaves were hired out. It is indeed unfortunate that there are no occupational clues for slaves in the 1850 and 1860 censuses, for there are tantalizing suggestions that skilled slaves were still being leased by craftsmen.

From these various sources a master list of men and women, slave and free, who worked outside agriculture was compiled and those individuals traced through time. Once data had been assembled, a clearer picture of black skills and opportunities could be drawn.

NOTES

1. Berlin, *Slaves Without Masters: The Free Negro in the Antebellum South* (New York, 1974), Chap. 7; Perdue, *Black Laborers and Black Professionals in Early America, 1750–1830* (New York and other cities, 1975), 42–43; Fogel and Engerman, *Time on the Cross: The Economics of American Negro Slavery* (Boston, 1974), 38–43 (quotation on p. 39); Gutman, *Slavery and the Numbers Game: A Critique of* Time on the Cross (Urbana, Chicago, and London, 1975), 47–84.

2. For agricultural diversification prior to 1840 see Bayly Ellen Marks, "Economics and Society in a Staple Plantation System, St. Mary's County, Maryland, 1790–1840" (Ph.D. dissertation, University of Maryland, 1979). Aggregate statistics for St. Mary's County in the censuses of 1840, 1850, and 1860 show that county wheat production rose dramatically—more than doubling between 1840 (68,372 bu.) and 1850 (156,369 bu.) and almost doubling again by 1860 (296,703 bu.). County tobacco production actually fell between 1840 (2,872,052 lbs.) and 1850 (1,763,882 lbs.) but recovered significantly by 1860 (5,774,975 lbs.). For 1840 see Manuscript Census Returns, Sixth Census of the United States, 1840, St. Mary's County, Agricultural Schedules. State agricultural statistics for 1850 and 1860 are taken from manuscript volumes entitled Seventh Census, Agriculture, 1850, Maryland; and Products of Agriculture, Maryland, 1860, located at the Maryland State Law Library, Annapolis. Both volumes give farm by farm agricultural statistics. For Baltimore's domination of southern Maryland trade see Bayly Ellen Marks, "Rural response to urban penetration: Baltimore and St. Mary's County, Maryland, 1790–1840," *Journal of Historical Geography*, VIII (April 1982), 113–27. The approximate mileage between Baltimore and Leonardtown by water is 135. To Cedar Point on the Patuxent River the distance is only eighty-one miles. According to the 1860 census hotels at Piney Point and Point Lookout were open. Advertisements in the *St. Mary's Beacon* in 1854 suggest that the hotel at Piney Point was newly built while that at Point Lookout was advertised as new in 1860.

3. For Clifton Factory see Bayly Ellen Marks, "Clifton Factory, 1810–1860—An Experiment in Rural Industrialization," *Maryland Historical Magazine*, LXXX (Spring

1985), 48–65. Julius Rubin, "Urban Growth and Regional Development," in David T. Gilchrist, ed., *The Growth of the Seaport Cities, 1790–1825* (Charlottesville, Va., 1967), 3–21, believes that the industrial cities of the Northeast rather than slavery undermined the position of skilled craftsmen in the South. He suggests that the farther from established transport routes, the longer the craftsmen or small manufacturer was able to retain a share of the market. This was certainly the case with St. Mary's County.

4. There is a valid argument to exclude these semiskilled workers on the grounds that their tasks could be performed by any farmhand. I have included them because these individuals identified themselves, or were regularly identified by others, as following particular occupations. Moreover, these semiskilled tasks paid above the prevailing agricultural wages.

5. For a full title and description of the manuscript sources used in this article see the Appendix on Sources. Yates's inventory is found in Inventories, 1815–26, p. 90. It might be noted that few women, black or white, gave occupations in 1850, while in 1860 nearly every woman gave her occupation. The difference probably stems from the way the census takers asked for occupational data.

6. Indenture of Ann Monk to Richard Wainwright, 1816, Indentures, 1809–29.

7. Seine nets were quite expensive. For example, inventories in the 1820s show values of nets ranging from $15 to $60. Canoes, particularly old ones, could be found for under $10; oysterman Ephraim Chesser owned oyster rakes, $2.50, a canoe and sail, $10, a canoe with two sails, $6, and the vessel *Telegraph* worth $275 (Inventories, GC 4, p. 228). Joseph Mobberly, a lay brother who managed the Jesuit plantation of St. Inigoes in the 1820s, commented on slaves tonging for and selling oysters, using plantation equipment but keeping all profits. See Joseph Mobberly, Journal I, p. 133 (Archives of Georgetown University, Georgetown University Library, Washington, D.C.; repository hereinafter cited as GUL). The most renowned escape of a Maryland slave, that of Frederick Douglass, was made with the aid of a sailor's pass. Yet on examination of all St. Mary's County records in which the escape of a slave was attempted or succeeded, none reveals the escape of a sailor.

8. A list of Carroll's slaves that names them and gives age, occupation, and family relationship can be found in Carolyn Vehrendt, "Charles Carroll of Carrollton, Inventory of Property, Slave List," *Maryland Geographical Society Bulletin*, XXIII (Winter 1982), 328–39.

9. The most skilled slaves were found in inventories of the decade between 1800 and 1809. A total of 281 estates were inventoried, possessing 464 male slaves between the ages of fourteen and forty-five. There were 41 skilled male slaves (another 8 were over forty-five), making those skilled slaves 5 percent of the prime males inventoried, close to the 1804 assessment figure of 3.5 percent for skilled prime males.

10. The estate of James Forrest may be taken as representative. A valuation of the property taken in 1827 showed fifty-five structures on eighteen pieces of rental property. Fully half were in need of some sort of repair. Valuations, 1826–41, St. Mary's County Courthouse, Leonardtown, Md. Within one year his administrator had employed at least eight men and spent $287 on repairs. Administration Accounts, 1829–31.

11. Edmund T. Maddox to James Thomas, [1831], No. 296, G 176, Thomas Papers, Gift Collection (Maryland Hall of Records, Annapolis). See the inventories of John Reeder, Francis Piles, and John T. Hawkins in Inventories, JFR, p. 187, GC 1, p. 216, EJM 3, p. 467. For carpenter Stephen see estate of Henry Abell, Guardian Accounts, 1806–17. In the period from 1811 to 1816, John Reeder's carpenter, Charles, earned $60 a year. Estate of George Reeder, Administration Accounts, 1834–36. Carpenter Isaac was in the estate of William Bennett of Joseph, Administration Accounts, 1823–26. Clem can be found in Clifton Factory Day Book, 1817–28.

12. St. Inigoes Accounts, 1804–32, 170 E-G, Maryland Province Archives (GUL).

13. See inventories of Joseph Millard, Nicholas Sewall, Luke W. Barber, William Bean (I), and William Bean (II) in Inventories, JFR, p. 446, JF S, p. 628, EJM 2, p. 255, 1824–26, p. 199, and GC 1, p. 289.

14. Estate of George Reeder, Administration Accounts, 1834–36 (quotation). Bill's

hire was $60 in 1811, $100 in 1812, $120 in 1813, $60 in 1814 (in Frederick, Md.), $80 in 1815, and $120 in 1816. For Walker, Garner, and Miles see Inventories, JF R, p. 24, JTMR 1, p. 216; Certificates of Slaves, 1831; and Minute Book, 1827–30. For Slye see the administration account of Philip Key, Administrations, 1823–31; and Inventories, GC 2, p. 266.

15. Certificates of Slaves, 1813 (quoted phrase). Dixon was freed in 1819 (Registry of Certificates of Freedom, 1806–51), and appears in the 1850 census as Miley "Decisan," age 65. For Bell see estate of Benjamin Hewett, Administration Accounts, 1838–43, 1843–47.

16. Joseph Mobberly, Journal I, p. 131.

17. Charles Ball wrote of his youth on the Patuxent River, about 1793: "as we fortunately lived near both the Patuxent river and the Chesapeake Bay, we had abundance of fish in the spring, and as long as the fishing season continued." [Charles Ball], *Slavery in the United States* . . . (New York, 1837), 26. Joseph A. Magill, William E. Hooper, Benjamin Tucker, Bennet R. Abell, and George C. Tarlton all advertised alewives. With the exception of Tucker, who was an oysterman, all the others listed their occupation in 1860 as "Farmer." Eighth Census, 1860, St. Mary's County, Slave Schedule, shows Tarlton with fifteen slaves, Hooper with five, and Magill with one. Tucker did not own slaves. Several neighbors in the sixth electoral district along the Patuxent River owned between ten and sixteen slaves.

18. For details of Baltimore's domination of St. Mary's County's trade see Marks, "Rural response to urban penetration."

19. For details of the county's agricultural economy see Marks, "Economics and Society in a Staple Plantation System," Chap. 2. Prices for tobacco appear in *Baltimore Prices Current*, 1803–30; *Baltimore American and Commercial Daily Advertiser*, 1831–44; and *Lyford's Baltimore Prices Current*, 1844–50. The prices quotes are an average of the year's prices for common tobacco, and were checked against values of tobacco crops in county inventories. Wheat prices were compiled directly from county inventories. Wheat prices recovered in the decade of the 1850s, rising at times to $1.50. Yet a reading of the *St. Mary's Beacon* for that decade shows hopes for fine harvests frequently dashed by the "rust," actually a virus. Thus the steady increase in wheat production shown in the censuses may not equate to a steady increase in prosperity.

20. Gutman, *Slavery and the Numbers Game*, 79–81.

21. Bernard Medley's apprentice is mentioned in Accounts, 1793–96, 110 S 10, George Fenwick Papers, Maryland Province Archives. The other apprentices appear in the inventories of John Thompson and Michael Fenwick, Inventories, JF R, p. 212, JF Q, p. 165.

22. Joseph Mobberly, Journal I, p. 77.

23. [Ball], *Slavery in the United States*, 15, 19, 21–24. Peter H. Wood's article, "Whetting, Setting and Laying Timbers: Black Builders in the Early South," *Southern Exposure*, VIII (Spring 1980), 3–8, discusses the survival of African building skills.

24. For kinship among Carroll's craftsmen see Allan Kulikoff, "The Beginnings of the Afro-American Family in Maryland," in Aubrey C. Land, Lois Green Carr, and Edward C. Papenfuse, eds., *Law, Society, and Politics in Early Maryland* (Baltimore and London, 1977), 171–96. Kulikoff finds that on Caroll's plantations 33 percent of artisans learned skills from their fathers, and another 22 percent from other kin (p. 186).

25. For Cadden see Wills, JJ 3, p. 32. William Harrison's Jesse first appears in Certificates of Slaves in 1804 when he was ten years of age. Harrison (who listed himself and eleven slaves in the 1820 census, two in "manufacturing") sold Jesse to John T. Hawkins in 1825 (Minute Books), and he appears as a blacksmith in Certificates of Slaves, 1831. For James W. Burch and Gustavius Greenwell see the Seventh Census, 1850, St. Mary's County, Slave Schedule (note Burch's name is spelled "Birch"). In the 1850 census Burch has a free black apprentice, William H. Warren (age sixteen). Greenwell was not even a householder in 1850, although in 1843 he was credited in the Assessment with land and a single male slave. Burch apparently lacked taxable property.

26. Jesse Floyd's servant Peter first appears in Certificates of Slaves, 1804, aged twelve.

Jesse died in 1813 (Inventories, JF S, p. 581), and Peter went to his wife, Elizabeth, then to his son William, then to James R. Floyd, in whose estate he appears in 1854, Certificates of Slaves, 1821, Alienations and Transfers, 1835; Inventories, GC 4, p. 510. In the Seventh Census, 1850, St. Mary's County, Population Schedule, there were two John F. Taneys (spelled Tauney), one free black farmer aged thirty, the other a free black laborer aged twenty-three, In the Eighth Census, 1860, St. Mary's County, Population Schedule, only one John F. Taney is shown, occupation farmer, aged thirty, with $200 worth of land. Peter cannot be located.

27. The sale of the Jesuits' slaves is recorded in a document, "slaves sold on all estates," 112, W O, Maryland Province Archives. Between 1820 and 1840 Alienations and Transfers and Deeds record the sales of 2,062 slaves. Out-of-state sales accounted for 245 (12 percent)—this includes 127 owned by the Jesuits. Out-of-county sales were 463 (22 percent). These figures are similar to those uncovered by William Calderhead, "How Extensive Was the Border State Slave Trade? A New Look," *Civil War History*, XVIII (March 1972), 42–55. It is interesting that a higher proportion of skilled slaves were sold out of the county or out of the state. It may mean that demand for slave craftsmen was so low in the county in the late 1830s that ready buyers were not available. If there was no local market for men who already possessed skills, there was clearly no incentive to train younger slaves in crafts.

28. *St. Mary's Beacon*, May 4, 1854.

29. For the origins of St. Mary's County's free black community see Marks, "Economics and Society in a Staple Plantation System," 437–39.

30. For Barnes see Orphans Court Proceedings, 1809–26, pp. 1–22; Assessments, 1813–43; and Inventories, GC 2, p. 29. In 1850 his widow, Elizabeth, 75, was still alive, and their daughter Lydia was credited with the land.

31. Thomas Caden, Wills, JJ 3, p. 32. For Brian see Indentures, 1809–29. He appeared in the Sixth Census, 1840, St. Mary's County, Population Schedule in the second electoral district engaged in "manufacturing," and in the Clifton Factory Day Book, 1831–32, as a shoemaker. For the indentures of his children see Indentures, 1826–1908 (quoted phrase).

32. For the economic aspects of the decision to migrate see Marks, "Economics and Society in a Staple Plantation System," 563–75. Craftsmen who appeared after 1840 were traced via the 1850 and 1860 censuses, county probate records to 1864, and Margaret K. Fresco, *Marriages and Deaths: St. Mary's County, Maryland, 1634–1900* (Ridge, Md., 1982).

EIGHT

Peter Hill, the First
African American Clockmaker

SILVIO A. BEDINI

I

The annals of clockmaking appear to identify but a single instance of an African American clockmaker, although there may be others who escaped the attention of historians. The number of African Americans, either as slaves or freemen, who were enabled to work in the skilled crafts was limited, and of this small number even fewer succeeded in achieving a degree of independence that enabled them to establish their own shops and clienteles.

African American artisans and mechanics, as distinguished from skilled craftsmen, were relatively prevalent in the American colonies and the new republic. The majority were working as slaves or free artisans assisting white men in their trades, however. Black bricklayers, bakers, blacksmiths, carpenters, cobblers, cooks, coopers, tailors, and weavers were at work in some of the colonies as early as the 17th Century. They were most frequently to be found in the Middle Colonies, and they also played an important role in Southern plantations.

Occasionally a relatively wide range of skills might be combined in the same individual. A house carpenter might also be capable of working as either a turner, a cooper, or a cabinetmaker, as the need arose. Less frequently an African American freeman or slave was given the opportunity to demonstrate a particular ability in one of the skilled crafts, such as goldsmithing, silversmithing, or clockmaking. Although several colonial silversmiths are known to have employed African American slaves of considerable ability, only a few of them have been identified, and then usually only by a first name. As an example, the Philadelphia silversmith and jeweler William Ball was forced to seek new shop help in 1778 when three of his black assistants, including "Tom, by trade a silversmith," left his employ to join the British army.[1]

Clockmaking was one of the more skilled professions in which African Americans were not to be found. Well known to the annals of African American history is the achievement of Benjamin Banneker (1731–1806), a free black man of Baltimore County, Maryland, who successfully constructed a wooden striking clock. He was not a clockmaker in the true sense, however, despite claims to the contrary, for he produced but a single clock. Instead, his major contribution was as an amateur astronomer who calculated ephemerides for almanacs that were published over a period of six years.[2]

It is remarkable, therefore, to be able to identify the single known instance of an African American clockmaker, whose name has been almost obliterated by the passage of time. This unusual craftsman was Peter Hill (1767–1820) of Burlington, New Jersey. As with most of the figures in early African American history, few details of Hill's life and work are known. His biography consequently consists of a mosaic assembled from bits and pieces gleaned from the most exhaustive examination of civic records in community, county, and state repositories.

II

For a full understanding of the significance of Hill's achievement, it is necessary to review briefly the state of free and slave African Americans in New Jersey in the 18th and early 19th Centuries.

By the 18th Century, slavery in the American colonies had become a serious economic problem. It was particularly apparent in the province of New Jersey, which had the largest slave population of any of the Northern colonies except New York. The condition of the black slave and freeman was far more favorable in western New Jersey than in the eastern section of the province, which had been settled by New Englanders and the Dutch, who gravitated around New York City as their center of commerce and social activity. In contrast, western New Jersey developed in a manner quite similar to the plantation life of Maryland and Virginia, with Philadelphia as its center of activity. There was considerable emphasis to be found on the betterment of the African American's lot.[3]

Contemporary accounts reported that the conditions of the slaves in New Jersey were not as poor as those in other colonies. In 1790 New Jersey contained 11,423 African American slaves, and in general they were said to receive relatively good treatment. According to the Presbyterian clergyman John Witherspoon (1723–94) and other commentators of the period, they were fed and clothed as well as free persons who lived by daily labor, and lived in a state of relatively mild servitude. Male black slaves were engaged in farming and maritime pursuits as well as in mining and lumbering, and related types of employment. Female slaves were employed in domestic activities in the home. Despite the reportedly favorable conditions, however, existing laws were not always adequate to protect the slaves from injustice and inhumane treatment.[4]

By 1800 the situation of African American slaves was substantially better in Burlington County than elsewhere in New Jersey, but in that year there were only 188 slaves in that county, out of a total of 12,422 slaves in the entire state.[5]

The Society of Friends in Burlington County made organized efforts to educate and train them, but inevitably it encountered many problems, which had to be solved one at a time. Among the first obstacles was confusion concerning the purpose of baptism. Although there was no basis for such an assumption, it was widely believed that baptism of American Indian and African American slaves removed them from their slave status. So persistent and widespread was the claim that the Friends were seriously hampered in their efforts to provide them with an education. So prevalent was the assumption that in 1704 the New Jersey legislature found it necessary to affirm that baptism of Indians and African Americans did not set them free.[6]

The Society of Friends, meanwhile, continued to encourage its membership to dispense with slaves they owned. Progress was slow, but little by little Quaker slave owners reduced their holdings and at the same time cooperated with the Burlington Monthly Meeting in providing their slaves with the rudiments of an education and religious instruction. This movement had its beginnings in 1688 in Germantown, Pennsylvania, and spread somewhat like a crusade under the name of the Germantown Protest. Among its leading supporters was John Woolman, a Quaker resident of Mount Holly, New Jersey. He subsequently dedicated himself entirely to the cause of African American freedom, and was instrumental in developing the position taken by the Burlington Yearly Meeting in 1755 with respect to slaves. The Meeting voted not to engage any longer in the importation and purchase of slaves, and also agreed to free the slaves already owned by its members. In Philadelphia, meanwhile, Anthony Benezet had determined that African American slaves were being denied even the most basic education, and undertook a program for the establishment of schools for their children.[7]

These several actions exercised a great influence upon the Society of Friends in Burlington County, and in 1759 the Burlington Quarterly Meeting reported that slaves were no longer being imported or purchased in its community, and that in fact some of the Friends had taught slaves to read and brought them to meetings on occasion. Nevertheless, progress remained slow. Although a large number of the Society of Friends in Burlington had agreed to manumit their slaves at once or when they came of age, the promise was not promptly fulfilled.[8]

By 1780, however, subscription funds and permanent school funds had been established by Friends in a number of New Jersey communities to provide education for African American adults by means of the newly established Society for the Instruction of Orderly Blacks and People of Colour. Burlington followed this example, and in the following year the Burlington Meeting had enrolled twenty-six adult students in a program of its own. A First-Day School was provided during the summer and continued through the winter months. It was so successful that it remained in existence until almost the close of the century.

It was not until the year 1788, however, that the Society of Friends successfully prevailed upon the New Jersey legislature to enact a bill requiring that slaves and servants under the age of twenty-one be taught to read.[9]

The concerted efforts made by Friends in Burlington County to improve the condition of the African Americans was directed primarily to providing an education, and in 1798 the Society in Burlington reported some progress with its aims and achievements. New Jersey was distinguished in this period by its indifference to the maintenance of schools and for its lack of provision by legislation for education in general, except as was supported by private and denominational groups. By 1801 the township of Burlington succeeded in establishing a school for the children of the poor, which was attended by both black and white. The school was supported by funds from an estate that had been willed for that purpose.[10]

With all the emphasis on manumission of slaves in New Jersey during this period, it is useful to review the state of the free African American. According to the 1790 census, 2,762 free persons of color were registered in the state, of which number 598 were residents of Burlington County.[11]

In general, the free African American had a well-established role in the community, and there is adequate evidence that he was considered to be better than a member of the poorer class of white men. They were hired and paid in the same manner as white laborers, at a rate of fifty cents per day plus board. Many free African Americans chose to work on a monthly arrangement at a rate of three pounds during the summer, or at a daily rate of three shillings per day.[12]

The situation of the free African American man in New Jersey during the late 18th Century had its hazards as well as its advantages, however. He occupied an intermediate position in society, a position that is clearly reflected by his treatment in the courts and in relation to education. His social position was on a level somewhere between that of slaves and that of free white inhabitants. A free African American had physical freedom, but with defined limitations, and he had the right to earn wages. Social and intellectual advancement were nevertheless severely hampered by prejudice. Manumitted slaves, if convicted of felony or of petit larceny twice within the same month, were forced to leave the state and live elsewhere permanently after they were released from imprisonment. No African American manumitted in another state was permitted to reside in or to travel in New Jersey. If an African American manumitted in New Jersey wished to leave the county in which he had received his freedom, a certificate of permission was required from two justices of the peace. Although persons of color of full age and owning property valued at fifty pounds or more were permitted to vote for a few years after the Constitution of 1776, the law was revised after 1807 to limit the voting privileges to only free white adult male citizens.

In 1788 the French journalist and revolutionary leader Jean Pierre Brissot (1754–93) visited the United States with a plan for the development of the antislavery clause on behalf of Les Amis des Noirs, the society that he had founded in Paris for this purpose. He undertook a special study of the progress that had been made in effecting laws for the emancipation of African Americans. He reported in particular on their social position, and noted that they generally undertook one of a limited number of occupations:

> The free Blacks in the Eastern States are either hired servants, or they keep little shops, or they cultivate the land. You will see some of them on board of coasting vessels. They dare not venture themselves on long voyages, for fear of being transported and sold in the islands. As to their physical character, the Blacks are vigorous, of a strong constitution, capable of the most painful labor, and generally active. As servants they are sober and faithful. Those who keep shop live moderately, and never augment their affairs beyond a certain point.[13]

Although Brissot commented on the fact that free African Americans were enabled to maintain small shops, extremely few if any such shops were known, because in Brissot's own words there was too great

> an interval between them and the Whites, especially in the public opinion. The reason is obvious; the Whites though they treat them with humanity, like not to give them credit to enable them to undertake any extensive commerce, nor even to give them means of a common education, by receiving them into their counting-houses. If, then, the Blacks are confined to the retail of trade, let us not accuse their sagacity, but prejudices of the Whites, which lay obstacles in their way.[14]

III

Peter Hill proved to be the exception to the general rule. This was due in large part to the fact that he lived and worked in Burlington Township in Burlington County. In that community the influence of the Society of Friends was combined with the efforts of the New Jersey Society for the Abolition of Slavery to bring about a substantial change in the status of the African American within its borders.

The Burlington Township of the 18th Century was a modest little farming community in western New Jersey. Situated along the Delaware River a short distance from Philadelphia, it had been founded in the 17th Century by members of the Society of Friends emigrating from England. The Township was incorporated in 1784, and by 1797 it consisted of 214 houses and 1,714 inhabitants. By 1814 these numbers had been swelled to about 500 houses and a population of 3,200. The major occupations in the town were farming, shoe manufacturing, and iron founding. It remained a predominantly Quaker settlement, and the residents were distinguished for their piety, intelligence, and abstinence.

The state of the African American within the county at the end of the century was briefly but impressively described in a *Report of the Acting Committee of the New Jersey Abolition Society, in the County of Burlington, relative to such parts, as were refer'd to them of the requisitions contained in the Address of the Convention of Delegates holden at Philadelphia the 1ˢᵗ Day of the 12ᵗʰ mo. 1769.*

The *Report* noted that there were then approximately 128 "Africans and People of Colour in Slavery" or under indenture for a term of years, and that approximately 100 of that number were within the townships of Burlington and Nottingham. Although some of them were in comfortable circumstances, there were some painful exceptions. In addition to the foregoing, the *Report* noted,

> There are about 430 Free Africans and Mulattoes. In too many instances they are given to Idleness, Frolicking, Drunkenness, and in some few cases to Dishonesty. The liberal mind, which can make the necessary allowance for the various disadvantages under which they have in time past and still do labour will not admire at this; and yet it is matter of doubt whether a larger share of the above enumerated vices, ought to be ascribed to this People than strictly appertains to their more enlightened White Neighbours. On the other hand, perhaps the greater part may be stiled Industrious, faithful to the trust reposed in them,—a considerable number of them sober, economical, and in various other respects good examples for imitation.

Then followed a list of twenty-four married couples and ten single men who had demonstrated outstanding qualities of industry, frugality, and sobriety and who had established themselves as useful members of the community. It was reported, "In all, we reckon 93 Householders, and 16 Freeholders."[15]

The earliest record relating to Peter Hill is a certificate of manumission that was recorded in 1795 and filed among the Burlington Township property records. From this document is derived the fact that Hill was an African American slave owned by the Quaker clockmaker, Joseph Hollinshead, Jr., of Burlington Township. Hill was born on July 19, 1767, presumably on Hollinshead's property and the son of slaves he owned.

As a boy and youth in the Hollinshead household, young Peter was trained by his master in the intricate craft of clockmaking so that he could assist in the latter's shop. In 1794, at the age of twenty-seven, Peter was manumitted by Hollinshead and became a free African American. His freedom was certified in the following spring when he was presented before a committee consisting of two Overseers of the Poor of the Township and two Justices of the Peace of the County. This impressive document entered among the County Property Records, reads as follows:

State of New Jersey. To all whom it may concern I do hereby for myself & my Heirs Manumit and set free my Negro or Mulatto Man Peter Hill aged twenty seven years the 19th of July 1794.—In Testimony whereof I have hereunto set my Hand & Seal at Burlington the place of my dwelling the 16th day of April 1795.

Jos. Hollinshead (Seal).
Sealed and delivered in the presence of John Thompson.

County of Burlington—We do hereby certify that on this first day of May A D 1795 Joseph Hollinshead of the Township of Burlington in the County of Burlington brought before us two of the Overseers of the Poor of said Township and two of the Justices of the Peace of said County his slave named Peter Hill who on view and examination appears to us to be sound in mind and not under any bodily incapacity of obtaining a support and also is not under twenty one years of age nor above thirty five. In Witness whereof we have hereunto put our hands the first day of May 1795.

Nath.¹ Fitz (Seal)}   Overseers of the Poor of
Sam.¹ Stockton (Seal)}   the Township of Burlington

W.ᵐ Love Jun.ʳ (Seal)}   Justices of the Peace for
Tho.ˢ Adams (Seal)}   the County of Burlington.[16]

Joseph Hollinshead, Jr. was a clockmaker by profession and a prominent citizen of 18th-Century Burlington. He was a member of the fourth generation of Hollinsheads, a dynasty founded by John Hollinshead (I) who had brought his family to Burlington from London in about 1680. Soon after his arrival he acquired a considerable amount of land and established himself as a merchant and ships chandler. One of his sons, John (II), the father of Joseph Hollinshead, Sr., was the first of several clockmakers in the family. Joseph served an apprenticeship with Isaac Pearson (1685–1749), also of Burlington, who was one of the first clockmakers in the American colonies and a silversmith as well. Upon completing his apprenticeship, Joseph Hollinshead, Sr. married his master's daughter, Sarah Pearson, on May 17, 1740 at the Burlington County Meeting.

In the same year that he married, young Hollinshead inherited from his father's estate the plantation in Wisham on which his father had lived, and which he in turn had inherited from the first John Hollinshead. His father's entire "personal estate and negroes and mulattoes" were devised to his widow as long as she remained unmarried. A curious aspect of the will of John Hollinshead, Jr. was Item 7, which specified

It is my mind that the while Indian Peter remain with thy family, and that there be what is necessary allowed him from me estate.[17]

Although that item has no relationship to the story of Peter Hill, it is included here as a curious note in the history of the Hollinshead family. The will made a definite differentiation between "negroes" and "mulattoes" and Indian Peter was apparently an American Indian and a ward of the family.

Joseph Hollinshead, Sr. subsequently became Pearson's partner in the clockmaking business as well as his son-in-law. His wife, Sarah, had died at some time within the first decade of their marriage, and there were no children. Pearson died in 1749 and in the same year Hollinshead was married for a second time, to Martha Howe. He was immediately disowned by the Burlington County Meeting for having married against the Quaker discipline. Seven children subsequently resulted from the marriage, five sons and two daughters. Hollinshead, Sr. served the community for several years as sheriff of Burlington County and in 1762 was elected a member of the Council of the West Jersey Proprietors.

Two of his sons, Joseph, Jr., and John (III), followed his own profession of clockmaker, and both served an apprenticeship with the father. Joseph, Jr., who was Peter Hill's master, was born in Burlington in 1751 and worked part of the time as an independent clockmaker and part of the time in association with his brother John, who had established himself as a clockmaker in the same community.[18]

Peter Hill's manumission document specified that this act was made in accordance with the prevalent law concerning the liberation of slaves who had achieved the legal age of twenty-one years, but had not reached the age limit for manumission of thirty-five. As a slave in the Hollinshead household, Hill had served a form of apprenticeship in clockmaking from about the age of fourteen until he was twenty-one, after which he probably worked on salary as a skilled assistant in the shop, or perhaps as a journeyman clockmaker, for the next six years until he achieved his freedom.

One of Hill's first acts as a free man was to marry. On September 9, 1795, four months after his manumission was formalized, Hill married Tina Lewis in Burlington Township. As noted in the town records:

> County of Burlington SS. These are to certify that on the 9th day of Sept. 1795 I the subscriber one of the Justices of the Peace in and for the County of Burlington joined Peter Hill of the City of Burlington Clock & Watch Maker and Tina Lewis of the same place Spinster (being free People of Colour) in the holy bonds of Matrimony and them pronounced Man and wife. Given under my hand this 6th day of October 1795.
>
> Tho.ˢ Adams J. P.[19]

All marriages were entered in chronological order of occurrence in the County *Marriage Book* regardless of color, the marriages of African Americans being identified in the manner indicated.[20]

Three years prior to her marriage, the name of Peter Hill's bride appeared in the records of the Burlington Society of Friends, which was then making a concerted effort "to instruct and improve" the African Americans in their community by providing free schooling. In 1790 the enrollment consisted of twenty-six pupils. The school was maintained through the winter months and in 1792 an average attendance of about fourteen students was reported. Many of them had made substantial improvement in writing and arithmetic.

In a communication to Philadelphia's Society for Free Instruction of the Friends, the Burlington Society forwarded a sample of the writing of one of its pupils, Tenah [sic] Lewis, to demonstrate the remarkable progress she had made over a period of four months.[21]

An impressive description of Hill and Tina was included among descriptions of married couples in the report of the Acting Committee of the New Jersey Abolition Society already noted:

> Peter Hill (Clock & Watch maker) & Wife. A reputable exemplary Couple. Peter was a Slave untill several Years above twenty, and his Master being a Clock and Watch Maker, Peter learn'd the Trade of him. By a stipulation with the Master, wherein he engaged to Pay what was demanded for him in a limited time, Peter was enabled to set up his business and successively to accomplish his own purchase and that of his Wife whom he married whilst a Slave. He appears now to be doing very well, gets considerable to do at Clock Making and Cleaning, & carries on a clever Trade in the Sale of Watches. His stock in Trade is supposed to be worth at least . . . 300 [£300.00].[22]

It is readily apparent from this report that Hill was virtually unique as an example of a freed slave engaged in trade. Not only was he distinguished for having been trained in a technical profession in which he later worked independently, but he had been provided with an opportunity while still a slave to enable him to purchase not only his own freedom but that of his wife and to establish himself in business.

The date that Hill first opened his own clock repair shop cannot be determined from surviving tax and other community records, but from the Abolition Society's report it appears that Joseph Hollinshead assisted him in developing his own business and opening a shop before his manumission, prior to 1795. Several locations of Hill's shop are given in the local histories of Burlington and neighboring Mount Holly, leading to considerable confusion as to when or whether he lived and worked in one or the other community. The fact of the matter is that he lived and worked in both, first in Burlington Township and then in Mount Holly.

Hill's home and shop in Burlington were on the east side of High Street, below Broad Street. His building was situated directly opposite the residence of Rowland Jones and nearly opposite the Friends' Meeting House. It was several doors north of the shop of the cabinet maker George Deacon, who constructed the cases for Hill's clocks. The building that housed his home and shop no longer remains, but the Meeting-House survives.[23]

All evidence in the local histories, meager though it is, indicates that Hill maintained his own clockmaking business in Burlington Township throughout the entire period of twenty-three years and more that he lived there. The possibility must be considered, of course, that during at least a part of this time he may have continued to be employed as a clockmaker in the shop of his former master, Joseph Hollinshead, Jr., or in that of the latter's brother, John Hollinshead. Although John Hollinshead was included in the tax listing for 1796, his name did not appear thereafter, and he may have died in that year. Some confirmation is to be found in the fact that in the next year, 1797, a property listing appeared for a "Mrs. Hollinshead," who owned only a house and a lot, and was taxed five shillings. Her name did not appear on the tax records thereafter. If Hill did indeed begin his career as a free man in the employment of John Hollinshead, he may have continued to work for the widow for a short period after his employer's death, and then purchased the good will in trade and/or the shop for himself.

Hill's name is to be found in the Burlington Township tax lists for the first time in 1796, as a householder with a tax levy of six shillings. It is interesting to compare this tax with that listed at the same time for Joseph Hollinshead, Jr., in which the latter is identified as a householder and owner of a house and lot taxed at £2.1.4.

In the following year Hill was listed again as a householder and as the owner of one head of cattle, with a tax levy of 6s. 6d. Joseph Hollinshead, Jr. was again included in the tax lists for that year as a person of considerable substance. For some reason not determined, Hill's name was not found in the tax records from 1798 through 1801.[24]

In an indenture dated March 3, 1801, Hill bought land in Burlington Township from Charles Ellis for the price of $500. In the property transfer, he was described as a "clock and watchmaker." The tract consisted of a piece of land

> ... bounded ... on the East by the ditch that divides the said lot from Manuel Eyres low meadow on the South & Southwest by the canal that surrounds the Island of Burlington on the West by a ditch that divides said lot from the low meadow of the late Samuel B. Eyres now belonging to the said Charles Ellis, & on the North by the Upland of the said Charles Ellis as the fence now stands which piece or lot of land is the same piece of Creek or low meadow called lide meadow ... & is supposed to contain two acres & an half be the same more or less together with the free use & privilege of a one rod road leading from Washington street to said meadow. . . .[25]

This acquisition was reflected in the tax assessments for 1802 listing Hill as a householder owning one horse and one head of cattle, presumably a cow.[26]

The records for 1803 and 1804 did not include Hill's name, but in 1805 he was shown to own two acres of land, valued at $100 per 100 acres and a house and lot valued at $20. He was taxed for one horse and two head of cattle, and was identified as a householder once more, although not as a shopkeeper. In 1806 Hill's status remained the same, and the same items were noted except that the number of heads of cattle was reduced to one.[27]

Hill's situation appears to have improved somewhat in 1807. His two acres of land and house and lot remained the same, but he had acquired a second horse. With constantly increasing properties, in 1808 Hill reported four acres of land valued at $80, and his house and lot were valued at $20, in addition to a horse and two head of cattle.[28]

The additional property listed for Hill in this year is identified as a tract of two acres one rood and nine perches of land that was formerly part of a larger tract called Tanner's Run, purchased on April 1, 1808 from the heirs of Anna Rodman, deceased, for the amount of $89.94. Hill's property remained the same in 1809, with the exception that the evaluation of his four acres increased to $100.[29]

There is no tax listing for Hill in 1810. In 1811 he owned four acres, but not "a House & Lots of 10 Acres & under" as before. He continued to own one horse and one head of cattle. The lack of an entry for a house and lot may have been due to the manner of listing, however. In 1813 he is clearly shown to own not only two acres, but also one house and lot, a horse and one head of cattle.[30]

Hill "and Tina his wife" sold the property at Tanner's Run, which they had acquired from the Rodman heirs, to Joseph McIlvaine of Burlington on April 9, 1813, for the amount of $90, realizing a total profit of six cents on the transaction. The lack of profit from the sale, made five years after their purchase of the land, suggests that Hill may not have been prospering during this period and had need to sell. In the listing of his property in 1814, his holdings were once more reduced to two acres of land in addition to his house and lot, one horse, and one head of cattle "three years or older."[31]

There is no mention of Peter Hill in the tax listings or other community records of Burlington Township during the next five years. His name is next encountered five years later, in 1819, pursuing his profession of clockmaker in nearby Mount Holly. He maintained ownership of his property in Burlington Township during this period, however, and the absence of his name from the Burlington tax listings and other records may have been due to an oversight. On February 12, 1819, Hill sold to Charles Ellis the same two and one-half acres of land with buildings and improvements that he had purchased from Ellis in 1801, eighteen years earlier, for the same amount he paid for it, namely, $500. The indenture identified "Peter Hill of Mount Holly in the County of Burlington and the State of New Jersey Clockmaker & Tenah his wife," thus providing the first documentation of Hill's removal from Burlington Township to Mount Holly.[32]

Mount Holly is a village in Northampton Township situated seven miles from Burlington. It was settled in 1676, also by members of the Society of Friends emigrating from England. It derives its name from a high hill almost two hundred feet above sea level that dominates the community and was formerly distinguished for the abundance of holly trees that grew naturally on its slopes. Despite its remoteness and small size, Mount Holly has had an interesting history. It was the home of such notables as Stephen Girard, John Woolman, and printer William Bradford, among others, and, like Burlington, it played a momentarily important role in the American Revolution because of its strategic location. In 1795 it became the county seat of Burlington County. The village experienced a very slow growth until late in the 18th Century, when many refugees flocked to the town to escape the yellow-fever epidemic in Philadelphia. At approximately the same time an uprising among slaves in San Domingo developed into a massacre and brought to Mount Holly an influx of French and other refugees.

There was little noteworthy about the industrial life of the community in the 18th Century. In addition to farming, the village had its customary grist mills and sawmills as well as a fulling mill built during various periods of its early development. An ironworks was established in 1730 by Isaac Pearson, Joseph Hollinshead's father-in-law, which after his death was continued by others. A paper mill still flourished there in the early 19th Century, and in about the same period a short-lived steamboat company was formed for transporting freight and passengers between Mount Holly and Philadelphia.

An unpublished manuscript history of Mount Holly compiled by Dr. Zacharias Read in the 19th Century identified the location of Hill's home and shop in Mount Holly for the first time. In a description of residences then surviving on Main Street, Read noted,

> Next is the premises of Daniel Love, and now is in the possession of some of his descendants. Rev. Gamaliel Bailey lived here about the year 1815 or 1816, he was a silversmith. After him Peter Hill a colored man lived here, and carried on the Clock and Watch business. . . . [33]

This account formed the basis for the several other published references to Peter Hill. In a history of Burlington County that appeared in 1883, Woodward and Hageman wrote:

> Above the old Zachariah Rossell tavern, west side of Main Street, was the Daniel Love property, subsequently occupied by Gamaliel Bailey, a silversmith, and Peter Hill (colored) a watch-maker.[34]

Hill's house and shop, as had been reported, were in a building formerly owned and used as a residence and shop by Gamaliel Bailey. It was situated on the west side of High Street (now Main Street) not far from Hill Street and just above the large wooden frame building of the Black Horse Tavern maintained by Zacharias Rossell. Next door to Hill's shop was the home of Hannah Stakes (or Stokes) and just beyond it was the building constructed for the use of the State Legislature and in which it met in 1779. This structure was subsequently converted into shops. On the other side of that building was a lot owned by the Crossed Keys Tavern, a public house established in 1731 by Thomas Clark on the western side of Main Street.

Gamaliel Bailey, the former owner of Hill's shop, was a prominent member of the community. An early follower in America of John Wesley, he was a traveling Methodist preacher in addition to plying the trade of silversmith. Immediately after settling in Mount Holly in 1807, he organized a class that became the basis for the Methodist Episcopal Church in that community. After purchasing the house and property formerly owned by David Love, he established his residence and shop therein and remained there as long as he lived in Mount Holly. Eventually he sold the property and moved elsewhere, presumably to Philadelphia, where he is known to have worked between 1828 and 1833.

Following the period during which the property was owned by Bailey and later by Hill, it continued to be used for shops. A hat shop later maintained there by John Love was succeeded by an ice cream parlor kept by his daughter, Ann. Later it accommodated the restaurant of Harry Justin. The building was razed in 1854.

Although such an assumption is without documentation, it is possible that Peter Hill may have moved to Mount Holly to take over the clockmaking business of Hugh Hollinshead III, another member of the family of his former master. Hollinshead maintained his shop on the west side of Main Street near Washington Street from about 1805 until about 1810, when he moved to Chester Township (now Moorestown) and continued in the same trade.[35]

Hill's shop was near the location of Hollinshead's place of business. It is not known with certainty when Hill first established his residence and shop in Mount Holly, but it was probably in 1814 or shortly thereafter. His name appeared as a property owner in Northampton Township, of which Mount Holly formed a part, for the first time in the tax lists of 1820. Hill's color became a consideration for the first time in his business career, inasmuch as he was listed in a separate section of the tax ratables under the title "Blacks." The entry indicated that he did not own any improved or unimproved land, but that he was the head of a household, and that he owned a sulky. He was one of twenty-six African Americans owning property in Mount Holly in that year, although seven of that number did not have specific property listed after their names.[36]

On February 29, 1820, after the tax listing had been returned, Hill invested the proceeds from his sale of property made two weeks earlier in a new house he purchased from Eunice Ridgway. It was an important step for Hill to make. The house was a brick dwelling, with one or more outbuildings and a fenced garden and lawn, situated on the south side of New Street. It was a substantial purchase, and although a copy of the indenture has not been found, the price for the property was probably $300 and it may have been more.

Unfortunately, Hill did not live long enough to enjoy his new home. He died suddenly in late December of the same year, cause not reported. He was fifty-three years of age. He left no will and testament and, curiously enough, his wife is not mentioned in any of the documents relating to his estate. It is not known whether she was a cosigner in the purchase of the Ridgway dwelling earlier in the year. It is possible that she had died a short time prior to Hill's death or at the same time.

An inventory of Hill's property was made during the first week of the following January by two members of the community assigned by the court, Job Bishop and Jeremiah J. Haines, as follows:

A true and perfect Inventory of all and singular the goods and chattles, rights and credits of Peter Hill late of Mount Holly in the County of Burlington and State of New Jersey deceased, made this 5th day of the First Month of January, 1821,

Wearing apparel	5..00
Desk, Tables, Chairs, Bed and sundry House hold goods and kitchen furniture in the first story of House	34..05
Beds, Beding Draws & in Chamber	10..50
Meal & Tubs in Garrett	6..50
A Ten Plate Stove & Barrells & c. in the Cellar	8..50
A Mare, saddle, bridle, sulky and harness	22..50
3 vices & other tools in the shop	19..12-½
A Time Peace	16..00
	$122..17-½

Appraised by us}   Job Bishop
             }   Jeremiah J. Haines.[37]

The inventory appears to have been handwritten by Job Bishop, one of the appraisers, and it is clearly dated as having been made on January 5, 1821. The two counter-signatures by the same justices of the peace, however, both bear the date of January 6, 1820. Most probably this official, accustomed to signing both documents in the course of his work, continued to sign the year "1820" from habit.

Something of Hill's status and life-style at the time of his death can be derived from this inventory. Mention is made of the furniture and furnishings on the first floor, indicating that his house had at least two stories in addition to an attic and basement. The references to the garret and cellar suggest that his was a residence of substantial size. The presence of a desk among the first-floor furnishings implies that it was probably where he kept his business accounts and that Hill could read and write. Beds were listed in the plural on the second floor in addition to a quantity of bedding, plus another bed on the first floor, suggesting that his family may have included one or more members other than his wife. The tax records always listed Hill as a "householder," but never specified the number of people in the household. Did he have children? The presence of a ten-plate stove not in the kitchen but in the cellar indicates that cooking may not have taken place in the kitchen, or that the cellar was used as a summer kitchen. Strangely enough, although the inventory listed a mare, sulky, and harness, the mare was not included in Hill's final tax assessment in Northampton Township in 1820. The inventory makes no mention of the contents of a separate shop building, implying that a shop was part of his residence, or in an attachment to the building separated from his living quarters. It is reasonable to assume that he did not maintain a separate shop in this period. The final item, a timepiece of substantial value, was probably his shop regulator used to adjust his clients' clocks and watches.

Inasmuch as Hill left no will, an administrator of his estate, Daniel Wills, was appointed by the Surrogate Court, so designated by the Surrogate, Abraham Brown:

> I, Abraham Brown Surrogate of the County of Burlington, do certify that on the sixth day of January in the year of our Lord one thousand and eight hundred and twenty-one, administration of the goods and chattels rights and credits which were of Peter Hill late of the County of Burlington, who died intestate was granted by me to Daniel Wills of the County of Burlington, who is duly authorized to administer the same according to law witness my hand and seal of office the sixth day of January in the year of our Lord one thousand eight hundred and twenty one.[38]

When an accounting of Hill's business affairs had been completed, it was discovered that he was deeply in debt. Wills accordingly filed a formal "Rule to shew cause on application for sale of real estate":

> The said administrator having exhibited to this court on solemn affirmation a just and true account of the personal estate of the said deceased, and also of his debt so far as we have discovered the same, by which account it appears, that the personal estate of the said deceased is insufficient to pay said debts; Whereupon on application of the said administrator, setting forth, that the said Peter Hill died seized in fee simple of lands, tenements, hereditaments and real estate in the county of Burlington and praying the aid of the Court in the premises—it is ordered, that all persons interested in the lands, tenements, hereditaments and real estate of the said deceased, do appear before the Judges of this Court on the first day of August next at three o'clock in the afternoon to show cause if any they have, why so much of the real estate of the said deceased should not be sold as will be sufficient to pay off his debts which remain unpaid.[39]

After the necessary period of time had elapsed, the Court handed down its decree on the rule, as stated in the following:

> It appearing to the Court that the said administrator hath caused the rule entered in this cause at the last term to be set up and published as the law directs. And now at this Term no one appearing to show any cause against the prayer of the said administrator. And it also appearing to the Court on full examination that the personal estate of the said deceased is insufficient to pay his debts—Therefore it is ordered and decreed by this Court that the said administrator do sell and dispose of according to law, all the following described real estate whereof the said deceased died seized in fee simple in the County of Burlington, or so much thereof as may be necessary for the purpose of paying off the debts of the said deceased which remain unpaid viz: All that Brick dwelling house and lot of ground situate on the South side of New Street in Mount Holly in the County of Burlington aforesaid containing forty four hundred and sixty six square links be the same more or less which Eunice Ridgway by deed dated 29 February 1820 conveyed to the said Peter Hill intes[tate].[40]

No record has been found of the cause of Hill's death, nor of the further disposition of his estate. Having left no family or heirs to arrange for his burial, and presumably since no funds for it were available, the Society of Friends made the final arrangements. Hill was buried in the Friends' Burial-Ground adjacent to the Friends Meeting-House in Burlington Township, in a plot situated almost directly across the street from Hill's former residence and shop. In a survey made of the cemetery and published in 1900, it was noted

> PETER HILL—Was a "Colored Clockmaker." He was in the employ of the "Hollingsheads" [*sic*], who were prominent clockmakers in Burlington, and they taught him the trade. After their retirement from business, he succeeded them. A number of his clocks are still in the neighborhood. His shop was on High Street, nearly opposite Friends' Meeting-house. Section XXVIII. No. 1.[41]

Adjacent to Hill's grave was the burial site of Caroline Loango, a young African American girl who had been kidnapped by slave traders in Loango, a former African kingdom in the interior, and brought to New Jersey. Hill's burial in the Friends' Burial-Ground was not particularly unusual in this period. It was not until 1826 that an African American church was established at Mount Holly and prior to that time the Society of Friends occasionally furnished ground for burial of indigent members of the Negro race. Hill's former association with members of the Hollinshead family, who were prominent Quakers, also may have provided some basis for the arrangement, although no members of the Hollinshead family were buried in that graveyard.

The burial ground of the Burlington Society of Friends has had an interesting history. It is believed to have been used for burials from the earliest period of settlement in the late 17th Century, and it may in fact be on the site of an ancient Indian burial ground. The oldest headstones surviving to the present are of the early 18th Century, and a number of personages of local prominence are buried in that yard. Among them are the American scholar John Gummere (1784–1845), author of *A Treatise on Surveying* (1814) and *An Elementary Treatise on Astronomy* (1822) and other works on mathematics. Another buried there is Stephen Pike, author of *Pike's Arithmetic.*

In the *Discipline* of the Society published in 1834, it was specified that "no monuments either of wood or stone be affixed to graves in any of our burial-grounds; and if any remain therein that these shall be forthwith removed, so that no cause of uneasiness on this account may exist or partiality be justly charged to us." This ruling apparently led to the removal of many existing headstones or to their concealment by burial beneath the ground. During the late 19th Century churchyard sextons discovered a number of such stones covered over in this manner, which were subsequently replaced into their proper position. Later in the century the *Discipline* of the Society was modified by a clause permitting the marking of graves with simple unornamented stones at the head and foot of the plot, rising not more than six inches above ground level, and containing only the name and age or dates of birth and death of the individual interred. The burial ground was originally enclosed with a fence of palings on the east and a close-board fence along the south-side driveway. No careful record of interments had been maintained prior to 1828, when the first map of the graveyard was prepared. Consequently, when in about 1860 the fences were removed, some of the landmarks for identifying grave sites were eliminated. Since the removal of the fencing created difficulties in identifying grave sites, another plan of the burial ground was made in 1870 by William F. Newbold. He surveyed the area and divided it into twenty-eight sections, the corners of which are marked with marble posts inscribed with section numbers. It is on this map that Hill's grave is clearly marked as No. 1 in Section XVIII.[42]

A recent search made of the burial ground has failed to reveal a gravestone or other marker on Hill's grave, and it has been determined conclusively that no headstone for his grave has existed since at least 1879.[43]

IV

Five clocks made by Peter Hill are presently known. The clocks are equipped with eight-day striking movements made of brass in the common English style of the period. The brass movements of four of the clocks are virtually identical, of standard construction, with time and strike trains operated by separate weights. The movement of the clock having the serial number "30" is quite different in workmanship than the others. It may have been an attempt by Hill to experiment with another form, or it may be a movement made by another that he acquired and adapted. Several of the front plates of the movements bear evidence that the brass available to Hill was of less than premium quality and possibly were made from reused brass, a common practice at the time. Hill employed two styles of clock hands, which were English imports and which he apparently purchased in quantity. The wheels are engine-cut, indicating that he owned a wheel-cutting engine, which was an expensive item of shop equipment in that period.

The dials, which are 12½ inches in diameter, consist of cast-iron sheets painted in white enamel and decorated with floral motifs in the spandrels. All of these are imports of English manufacture, made by various firms including Osborn and Wilson. From about 1780 American clockmakers began to replace the customary engraved brass dials commonly in use until then with painted iron dials that were cheaper, for brass remained at a premium in the new republic until it could be produced locally, after about 1837.

In four of the dials used by Hill, a box opening above the chapter ring accommodates the phases of the moon separated by English country scenes revolving behind maps of the two hemispheres. This feature is lacking in one example, which features a painted rose instead of an opening for the moon phases. A seconds dial appears within the chapter ring and a semicircular opening for a calendar dial is featured below the winding holes. To the hand-painted dials Hill generally had his name and place of work added— *Peter Hill / Burlington*—as well as a serial number. Following the custom of most clockmakers, Hill probably did not begin numbering the clocks he made from the digit "1," but may have begun with "10" or even a higher number. Several of the surviving clocks are not numbered, one of them known to have been made a decade later than most of the others.

Each clock is housed in a tall case made of fine wood evidencing excellent craftsmanship. Hill arranged with George Deacon, a cabinetmaker with a shop several doors away from his own, to make the cases for him or he referred clients purchasing his clocks to Deacon to provide the case. During this period of handcrafting, the case was generally considered to be an item quite separate from the clock itself and had to be ordered by the purchaser from the local cabinetmaker or the clockmaker and made to order according to the clients' specifications. The cases were generally ninety-nine inches in height, made of matched veneers of walnut and mahogany with boxwood or yew inlay.

The earliest of the known clocks associated with Hill was noted in 1933 by the local historian George DeCou as the property at the time of a Miss Mary Deacon of Mount Holly. She is believed to have been a descendant of George Deacon, the cabinetmaker who constructed the clock cases for Hill, and the clock may in fact have been originally made for him. The clock was inherited by David Deacon, a relative, who married a daughter of a Southern minister and moved to Atlanta. It was acquired more than twenty years ago from David Deacon by Mr. W. Thomas Camp of Sharpsburg, Georgia. The clock is housed in a walnut case with boxwood inlay. No name, place, or serial number appears on the dial, but scratched on the reverse side of the dial plate are the words "Constructed by Peter Hill in November 1803." Also scratched on the back of the dial plate are names of several repairers with dates from 1820. The dial plate is stamped with the name of the British maker, "Wilson Birmingham." The case is elaborately decorated with inlay of the hood and the door. The hood of the walnut case has small oval windows on each side from which the movement can be viewed.[44]

The clock having the lowest serial number, "29," presently owned by Paul and Susan Kleinwald of Great Barrington, Massachusetts, features a gilt brass finial and rosettes on the hood. The reverse of the dial plate bears the names of some half-dozen clockmakers who cleaned or repaired the movement with dates ranging from 1805 to 1881. It was cleaned or repaired twice in 1805 and again in 1817 and 1820.

Another tall case clock made by Peter Hill, marked with the serial number "30" on the dial, is in the collections of the National Museum of American History of the Smithsonian Institution. The movement and dial are similar in all features to the others, except that the movement is substantially different in details of construction, suggesting that, although it was made by Hill, he experimented with another form, or perhaps that it had been made by another and adapted by Hill. Six-pointed stars are inlaid in the terminals of the pediment.

The only other known Hill clock bearing a serial number is owned by Mr. Don Moser of Woodbury, New Jersey. It also is decorated with inlays of six-pointed stars in the pediment. A puzzling feature is the serial number "99," so much greater than the other known examples, and suggesting that Hill produced almost a hundred clocks in the course of a little more than two decades.

A Hill clock owned by Westtown School in Westtown, Pennsylvania, can trace its provenance to its original owner. Although a signature does not appear on the dial, a marking is visible at the lower right corner of the front plate that includes the letter "H" between two bars and possibly several other letters. It was formerly the property of Rowland (Jones) Dutton of Burlington. A statement handwritten by Dutton dated March 11, 1890, recorded the

History of this Clock

It was made for Rowland Jones about the year 1812.

The works were made by Peter Hill—a colored man, who learned the trade of J. Hollingshead [sic], and whose shop was on High St. below Broad St. East Side Burlington, N. J. directly opposite my residence.

The Case was made by George Deacon whose Cabinet Shop was opposite Friends Meeting House and a few doors South of Peter Hill's shop.

The Clock stood at the head of the Stairs of this house which was occupied by R. Jones until he built the house now occupied by Richard F. Mott on Wood St. at the rear of this lot.—It was moved there in 1836.—One year after the death of R. Jones, i.e., in 1868 it was removed to its original position in this house, where it has remained to the present time.

Rowland Jones is my authority in regard to the makers.

Burlington, N. J. 3 mo. 11 1890. /s/Rowland J. Dutton.[45]

Peter Hill has been mentioned as a clockmaker in various accounts of New Jersey silversmiths and clockmakers as well as in local histories, all references apparently derived from the brief mention in Read's *Annals* already cited.[46]

Distinguished primarily as the only African American clockmaker presently known to have been at work in the late 18th and early 19th Centuries, Hill made no major contributions in invention or art to the craft of clockmaking, but his work demonstrates professional quality reflecting excellent training. Hill's membership in a skilled profession and position as an independent businessman were in large part due to the happy accident of his residence in communities in which the Burlington Society of Friends had dedicated themselves to the improvement of the state of African Americans. Undoubtedly he was included in that small group reported in the Minutes of the New Jersey Society for Promoting the Abolition of Slavery, a number of free African Americans who were examples of uprightness, sobriety, industry, and economy, who regulated their families well and were respected by white inhabitants: ". . . some of them hold real estate, free and disencumbered, and a considerable number [who] support themselves comfortably."[47]

NOTES

1. *Pennsylvania Gazette*, September 1, 1778; Leonard F. Stavisky, "Negro Craftsmanship in Early America," *Journal of Negro History* 54, no. 2 (January 1949): 315–25.

2. "Account of a Negro Astronomer: A Letter from Mr. James McHenry to the Editors of the Pennsylvania, Delaware, Maryland and Virginia Almanack, containing particulars respecting Benjamin Banneker, a free Negro," *New York Magazine, or Literary Repository* 2 (1791): 557–58; Martha E. Tyson, *Banneker, the Afric-American Astronomer: From the Posthumous Papers of Martha E. Tyson, Edited by her Daughter* (Philadelphia: Friends' Book Association, 1884); and Silvio A. Bedini, *The Life of Benjamin Banneker* (New York: Scribner's, 1972; rept. Rancho Cordova, Calif.: Landmark Enterprises, 1985).

3. Marion M. Thompson Wright, *The Education of Negroes in New Jersey* (New York: Columbia University Teachers College, 1941), pp. 1–6, 198–201.

4. William W. Woodward, ed., *Works of the Rev. John Witherspoon* (Philadelphia: William W. Woodward, 1803), p. 306.

5. Thompson Wright, *Education of Negroes*, pp. 98–203.

6. *Laws of New Jersey* (1709), p. 8.

7. George S. Brookes, *Friend Anthony Benezet* (Philadelphia: University of Pennsylvania Press, 1937), pp. 46–47.

8. Society of Friends, Burlington County Meeting, *Minutes*, 27/VIII/1759.

9. *Laws of New Jersey* (1788), p. 488.

10. Haverford College Library, Manuscripts Division, The New Jersey Society for Promoting the Abolition of Slavery, Burlington Branch, 1793–1809, *Minutes of the Meeting of April 24, 1798.*

11. *United States Census, 1790, 1800* (Washington, D.C.: U.S. Government Printing Office, 1802), pp. 38–40.

12. François Alexander Frédéric de La Rochefoucauld-Liancourt, *Travels Through the United States of North America, the Country of the Iriquois and Upper Canada in the Years 1795, 1796 and 1797* (London: R. Phillips, 1799), vol. 2, pp. 418, 543–44.

13. Jacques Pierre Brissot de Warville, *New Travels in the United States of America Performed in 1788* (London: Printed for J.S. Jordan, 1794), pp. 238–39.

14. Brissot, *New Travels*.

15. Philadelphia, Historical Society of Pennsylvania, Manuscripts Division, *Pennsylvania Abolition Society Papers*, vol. 5, folder 13, pp. 127–29, Burlington County, New Jersey, 1796. Report prepared and signed by Robert Smith, junior clerk of the Acting Committee, dated April 23, 1798.

16. Mount Holly, N.J., County Court House, Records of the County of Burlington, *Property Records* (1795), Book C, p. 33. The writer is indebted to Mrs. Betty Walker of *The Burlington County Record* for locating this item.

17. Trenton, N.J., Office of the Secretary of State, *Probate Records*, Book 4, p. 221, last will and testament of John Hollinshead, Jr., probated March 12, 1740.

18. A. M. Stackhouse, *Some Genealogical Notes of the Hollinshead Family* (n.p., privately printed, 1911), pp. 21–22.

19. Mount Holly, N.J., Burlington County Court House, *County Clerk's Records 1795–1840, Marriage Book A*, p. 5. Also listed in H. Stanley Craig, comp., *Burlington County New Jersey Marriages* (Merchantsville, N.J.: By the author, n.d.), p. 113.

20. Among these were marriages of Jeremiah Hill to Lydia Davis on October 23, 1803, and of John Hill to Sally Riley on June 9, 1833. Whether either of these were related to Peter Hill could not be established.

21. Philadelphia, Penn., Society of Friends, Department of Records, *Papers Relating to a School for Adult Colored Persons deposited for Joseph W. Lippincott in the Department of Records, Society of Friends*, correspondence addressed to the Society, nos. 2 and 4, letter dated March 3, 1792.

22. Philadelphia, Historical Society of Pennsylvania, *Pennsylvania Abolition Society Manuscripts*, vol. 5, pp. 127–29.

23. Trenton, New Jersey State Library, *Burlington Township, Burlington County Tax Records June–August 1796*, no. 177, pp. 11–12. These and copies of subsequent tax records for Peter Hill were made available by Mrs. Rebecca B. Colesar, Reference Librarian.

24. *Burlington County Tax Records June–August 1797*, no. 178, pp. 15–16.

25. Mount Holly, N.J., Burlington County Courthouse, *Record of Deeds for Burlington Township, Book I*, p. 545. Courtesy of Mrs. Betty Walker.

26. Mount Holly, N.J., Burlington County Courthouse, *Burlington Township Tax Records*, no. 179, September 1802, p. 15.

27. *Burlington Township Tax Records*, no. 180, September 1805, p. 17; and no. 181, 1806, p. 12.

28. *Burlington Township Tax Records*, no. 182, 1807, p. 25; and 1808, no. 183, *Tax Ratables*, p. 15.

29. Mount Holly, N.J., Burlington County Courthouse, *Burlington County Land Records, Book S*, pp. 393–95, indenture dated April 1, 1808, for the sale of land by heirs of Anna Rodman, deceased, to Peter Hill; and *Burlington Township Land Records*, no. 184, 1809, *Tax Ratables*, p. 21. This and other land records were made available by Miss Anna Hawthorne, office of the County Clerk.

30. *Burlington Township Land Records* no. 185, 1811, p. 20; and no. 187, 1813, pp. 22.

31. *Burlington County Land Records Book A-2*, p. 2; and *Burlington Township Tax Records*, no. 188, 1814, p. 21.

32. *Burlington County Land Records, Book I-2*, February 12, 1819, p. 253.

33. Mount Holly, N.J., Burlington County Historical Society, Manuscripts Division, Zacharias Read, M.D., *Annals of Mount Holly* (1859). Typewritten copy of unpaginated and unpublished manuscript.

34. Major E. M. Woodward and John E. Hageman, *History of Burlington and Mercer Counties, New Jersey, With Biographical Sketches of Many of Their Pioneers and Prominent Men* (Philadelphia: Everts and Peck, 1883), p. 182.

35. George DeCou, "Colonial Clockmakers of Burlington County," *The Mount Holly Herald*, June 16, 1933, sec. 2, p. 4.

36. Mount Holly, N.J., Burlington County Courthouse, *Burlington Township Tax Records*, no. 286, 1820, n.p.

37. Mount Holly, N.J., Burlington County Courthouse, Office of the Surrogate, *Records of Wills and Inventories, Northampton Township*, Inventory of the property of Peter Hill, January 6, 1821. Courtesy of the Clerk of the Surrogate Office.

38. *Records of Wills and Inventories*, Records of the property of Peter Hill, 1821, p. 197.

39. *Records of Wills and Inventories*, "Rule to shew cause on application for sale of real estate (Peter Hill, deceased)," p. 206.

40. *Records of Wills and Inventories*, p. 206.

41. Rowland J. Dutton, "Friends' Burial-Ground, Burlington, New Jersey," *Pennsylvania Magazine of History and Biography* 24, no 2 (July 1900): 155.

42. Henry J. Cadbury, "Negro Membership in the Society of Friends," *Journal of Negro History* 21 (1936): 161–62. Communications concerning the Burlington burial ground from Mr. Corson Poley and Mr. Charles A. Doehlert, clerks of the Burlington County Meeting, Burlington Society of Friends, are gratefully acknowledged.

43. The writer is greatly indebted to Mr. Warren J. Danzenbaker of Annandale, Virginia, who not only made a grave-by-grave search of the Friends' Burial-Ground for Hill's burial plot, but also explored and photographed sites associated with Hill's career in Burlington and Mount Holly.

44. George DeCou, *The Historic Rancocas: Sketches of the Towns and Pioneer Settlers in Rancocas Valley* (Moorestown, N.J.: *News Chronicle*, 1949), pp. 130–31; and Read, *Annals*, unpaginated.

45. Document pasted inside the clock case. Through the efforts of Miss Sarah E. Mickle, the clock was donated to the School on September 25, 1919, by Miss Edith H. Dutton of Burlington, daughter of Rowland Dutton. The assistance of Mr. Donald H. Byerly and of Miss Mary O. Hogenauer of Westtown School is gratefully acknowledged.

46. George DeCou, *The Historic Rancocas: Sketches of the Towns and Pioneer Settlers in Rancocas Valley* (Moorestown, N.J.: *News Chronicle*, 1949), pp. 130–31; DeCou, "Colonial Clockmakers," sec. 2, p. 4; Carl E. Drepperd, *American Clocks and Clockmakers* (New York: Doubleday, 1947), p. 235; Carl M. Williams, *Silversmiths of New Jersey 1700–1825* (Philadelphia: MacManus, 1949), p. 72; *Early Furniture Made in New Jersey 1690–1870, an Exhibition* (Newark, N.J.: Newark Museum Association, 1958), p. 60; Henry C. Shinn, *The History of Mount Holly, N.J.* (Mount Holly, N.J.: *Mount Holly Herald*, 1957), pp. 15, 117; and William E. Drost, *Clocks and Watches of New Jersey* (Elizabeth, N.J.: Engineering Publishers, 1966), p. 123.

47. *Minutes of the Proceedings of the Seventh Convention of Delegates from the Abolition Societies* (Philadelphia, 1801), p. 12.

NINE

"Sweep O! Sweep O!":
African-American Chimney Sweeps
and Citizenship in the New Nation

PAUL A. GILJE AND HOWARD B. ROCK

"Sweep O! Sweep O!" New Yorkers of the early nineteenth century woke to this call breaking the quiet of dawn. The characteristic street cry of the chimney sweeps seeking work, it was sung out in a lyrical voice by a flamboyantly dressed master and his apprentices and often interspersed with popular tunes. Romanticizing the sweeps, popular writers and artists recorded their calls and their picturesque appearance in songs, rhymes, and drawings.

Behind these images lay a hard reality. African-American chimney sweeps clung to the edge of society and earned their living as best they could by work that was laborious, dangerous, and dirty. Masters and apprentices alike were black; both groups lived under conditions of exploitation that the masters applied in turn to their young apprentices.

New York City offers a window into this shadowy world. At the turn of the century many of the city's African Americans moved from slavery to freedom and began to claim an independent identity. Simultaneously, officials and reformers grappled with problems that emerged with the establishment of a republic. They worried about how to deal with the new "free persons of color." They also confronted the question of how to regulate the increasingly free market and capitalist urban environment. These concerns led to several attempts to reorganize the sweeping of chimneys in New York City from 1800 to 1820. In turn, these efforts at reform eventually elicited a striking response from African-American master sweeps that included the assertion of their rights as citizens. "Sweep O!" masks an important tale marked by strife and controversy. Examination of the debates swirling around the sweeps provides a measure of the pervasiveness and success of the ideas of liberty and freedom during the era of the early republic.[1]

Chimney sweeping became an important occupation when sixteenth-century Englishmen began to abandon the wide hearth fireplace for smaller, more efficient models with narrower chimneys as the major source of heat and illumination.[2] To maintain an adequate supply of oxygen, to prevent soot from building up and causing fires, and to draw smoke out of the room, flues had to be cleaned regularly. By the eighteenth century, English builders further revolutionized housing design by including fireplaces in almost every room. These fireplaces had vents extending to the chimneys that dotted Georgian roofs. The dimensions of vents decreased to an average of nine by fourteen inches, with some as tiny as six or eight inches square, and the vents often bent and turned as they made their way to the roof.[3]

American construction largely followed the English example, and Georgian homes, although ordinarily not as complex or as large as their English counterparts, were common in early nineteenth-century New York. Their chimneys had to be swept to operate efficiently and cleanly and to prevent fires. This second point became crucial in a compact city like New York because fire could quickly spread with devastating effects.[4]

Cleaning these chimneys was hazardous and dirty work. While older chimneys with adequate width could be swept by an adult standing on the roof and passing brushes through the flue, the smaller, zig-zag chimneys common in 1800 were not amenable to such methods. Rather, a young sweep had to climb through the chimney with a scraper prying soot from the flue and brushing it down. After reaching the top and letting out a yell of triumph and relief, he would reverse the climb back to the entrance of the flue, scraping and brushing along the way. The soot at the bottom was collected in the apprentice's blankets and sold as fertilizer. In order to pass through the smallest openings, a sweep wore no clothing but his underwear and a stocking cap with eye slits to cover his face, however inadequately. Soot collected over the sweeps from head to toe. Eventually their bodies became calloused with scar tissue from lacerations, and their skin developed an armorlike leathery texture.[5] Sweeps also had a tendency to develop "cancer of the scrotum" from infections caused by imbedded soot. This "sooty wart," as the "cancer" was called, led to sterility, and occasionally, death. Soot lodged under the eyelids, causing infections and leaving the telltale "red-rimmed eye." Finally, there was enormous danger of consumption, or tuberculosis, from soot in the boys' lungs.[6]

The sentimentalized portrait of the chimney sweep reflected some of this harsh reality. The popular children's book *Cries of New York*, first published in 1808, featured illustrations of street callers captioned with poems. Prominent among the engravings is a depiction of the chimney sweep. The 1812 edition describes the sweeps' cry:

> Sweep, O—O—O—O. / From the Bottom to the Top,
> Without a ladder or a rope, / Sweep, O—O—O—O.

The book notes that this "uncouth sound" early in the morning came from "figures . . . unpleasant to the sight," who were "a necessary and suffering class of human beings . . . much to be pitied."[7] Others picked up on the subject. The dress of the masters is suggested by Alexander Anderson's woodcut engraving used in early editions of *Cries* and by a painting of a Philadelphia sweep from the 1830s. The master is wearing the black hat and tailcoat that were the characteristic dress of European master sweeps as early as the sixteenth century.[8] Both illustrations indicate the poor condition of the apprentice, a theme also apparent in Niccolino Calyo's watercolor depicting a sweep at rest and in Thomas Eaton's *Review of New York*:

> Next we meet a chimney sweep, / Who in the street had
>   been asleep,
> Enrob'd in rags, with sooty cap, / And issues from his
>   mouth a clap
> Of shrill alarm, which, understood, / Bespeaks a
>   disposition good
> To sweep the chimneys at a nod / To gain a crum, or
>   shun a rod.
> All cold and hungry I have seen / These helpless negroes
>   screen
> Themselves from chastisement, by oath / Denying cold
>   and hunger both.[9]

In Eaton's lines we detect the pathos elicited by the apprentice sweep, barely earning a survival wage while striving to avoid punishment from his master's rod.[10]

These images reinforce one of the fundamental and sad truths about the trade: whoever contracted to sweep chimneys needed child labor. In England, horror stories abounded of kidnapped and abused youths held in virtual bondage by master sweeps.[11] In New York, where slavery was well entrenched in the eighteenth century, the bondage was real. Sometime before 1800, slaveowners began to hire out their slaves, including children, for this work. Given the high demand for labor in New York, there was little competition from free white workers, who had no taste for difficult tasks in a notorious and degrading trade. Although whites originally worked as sweeps, by the beginning of the nineteenth century not only the labor but also the contracting was performed by African Americans.[12]

During and after the American Revolution, New York's African Americans experienced the transition from slavery to freedom. There were many paths out of bondage. The British, who occupied the city from 1776 to 1783, offered freedom to slaves who abandoned their patriot masters. Some slaves owned by tories obtained freedom when the British evacuated the city. In the postwar years, others living in the surrounding countryside ran away to the city. Also important were the egalitarian aspirations that swept the country. Both blacks and whites could see the contradiction between the ideal of liberty and the shackles of slavery. For some years, New York leaders hesitated to act upon this ideal because they were unwilling to deprive slave owners of costly property and feared that newly emancipated slaves would become unruly, even dangerous. In 1799, the state legislature enacted a gradual emancipation law that, with revisions in 1817, brought freedom to all the state's slaves by 1827. Long before that date, blacks freed under the provisions of the 1799 law, runaways, and those emancipated by private manumissions that began in the 1780s and accelerated in the 1790s and early 1800s, greatly increased the number of free blacks in the city. By 1810, nearly 7,500 free African Americans lived in New York—about 8 percent of the population and 84 percent of the black community.[13]

Cast into the free labor market, these blacks scrambled to earn a living. A few took up artisanal trades they had learned as slaves; many more remained domestic servants or ran oyster cellars, barber shops, and other small-scale enterprises. Others became day laborers or used their newfound mobility to go to sea. One occupation offering an income and a modicum of respect was that of master chimney sweep.[14]

The master's involvement in the drudgery of sweeping chimneys varied from individual to individual. By the late 1810s there were about sixty masters, including at least three women and one ninety-six-year-old man, as well as 150 apprentices. Some masters scaled the rooftops and joined in the physical labor when chimneys could be cleaned without requiring a climbing boy. Others limited their activity to providing tools—ladder and cleaning equipment—and contracting the work. A few masters maintained an office and were listed in the city directories with the apparent intention of having a permanent location for the convenience of their customers. Several of these masters, and many others without offices, also traversed the streets with their apprentices soliciting business by crying "Sweep O! Sweep O!" Through their colorful attire and high public profile these masters displayed their status as independent entrepreneurs. Indeed, the distinctive dress, with its ties to an era when the profession of master sweep had had some prestige, in contrast to the notoriety it had acquired in England by 1800, was, for an aspiring black person, a statement that the occupation constituted a promising career.[15]

The master sweep did not have full control of his occupation. This trade was one of several that were closely regulated by the municipality. The Common Council was concerned because sweeping directly affected the public welfare. Magistrates were responsible for protecting citizens from the monopolization of vital goods such as bread and firewood, from fraudulent practices such as inaccurate weighing or the selling of spoiled meat, and from hazards to the public health and safety, especially fire.[16] Accordingly, from the seventeenth century, the city corporation set requirements for cleaning chimneys.

New York City experienced tremendous growth during the early national period: the population increased from just over 33,000 in 1790 to more than 200,000 in 1830.[17] To house this multitude, buildings were constructed and the city expanded up Manhattan Island. Much of the new housing was made of wood and slapped up as cheaply as possible. Fire periodically swept through entire sections of the city.[18]

Confronted with this danger, the Common Council repeatedly tinkered with its fire prevention regulations, including the cleaning of chimneys. During the 1790s, officials reissued regulations that all citizens maintain swept chimneys. If a fire broke out because of a faulty vent, the householder was subject to a $5.00 fine.[19] The council also established special officers in 1791 to help enforce fire codes. These fire wardens, two to each ward, were entrusted with regular announced inspections of homes to determine whether fire buckets were in place and chimneys and stoves in sound condition. They were also responsible for directing firemen at the site of any fire in their ward and met as committees to discuss the state of fire safety.[20] In 1801, the council ordered the fire wardens to notify a magistrate of any dirty chimneys. The magistrate would then compel the offender to clean the chimney or pay a $1.25 fine.[21]

A council action of 1804, intended to rationalize fire protection further, also threatened to do away with the African-American occupation of master sweep. The council voted to create a new position, superintendent of sweeps, with a monopoly of the trade. No other person was permitted to solicit sweep work under penalty of a steep fine of $55 plus court costs. (When the offender was an "infant apprentice servant" or a slave, the master sweep or owner of the slave would be liable for the fine.) City residents were required to register at offices established by the superintendent and have their chimneys swept by his boys at set intervals. Any inhabitant not complying was subject to a fine. The superintendent had to pay the penalty if a chimney fire broke out in the dwelling of a resident who was in compliance with the ordinance. The ordinance also charged the superintendent with responsibility for the welfare of the boys (all of whom were blacks) he employed.[22]

The Common Council appointed Adolph Degrove, a hatter by trade, as superintendent. Degrove was the first of several white entrepreneurs in the early 1800s who tried to gain control of the trade and probably owed his appointment to political connections. He invested over $800 in the business, but less than three months after enactment, the council repealed the law.[23] No reasons were given, but it is possible that the fire ordinance proved too comprehensive to be workable in a society that expected government to be minimal.

Although the city once again heard "Sweep O!" as the master sweeps regained their standing under the provisions of the previous ordinance, problems remained.[24] In 1808, the Common Council increased the fines for dirty chimneys to $25 on discovery and $5 a day until the situation was corrected.[25] But the difficulties, the magistrates came to believe, went beyond the householders. Soon they began to examine charges that the sweeps were too lackadaisical in their work. In late 1810, the Committee of Fire Wardens noted in its annual report that "because the practice of those who undertake the sweeping of chimneys [is] attended with very many, and great impositions on the public," a chimney would often catch fire within days after it had been swept. To ensure that master sweeps were doing a proper job, the wardens proposed a licensing system to hold the sweeps responsible for fires.[26]

While the Common Council pondered this suggestion, a white man again intruded upon the world of the sweeps. In 1811, John Boyreau, a 1792 French immigrant and now a citizen and merchant, offered a detailed plan under which he would take over sweeping chimneys. Boyreau capitalized on the city's dissatisfaction with the master sweeps and reinforced his position by attacking their treatment of their apprentices. He argued that the sweeping was "for the most part very carelessly and imperfectly done" and declared that consideration of "the miserable state of the poor objects who have to earn bread for their employers and seldom receive any of the comforts, and for the most part are scantily supplied with even the necessities of life" demanded action. Boyreau planned to employ seventy sweeps, aged nine to eighteen, selected from those currently at work and "from among boys of colour, such as now are employed as such or may be paupers in the Alms House." He would act as general supervisor; the sweeps would report to an inspector in each ward.[27]

The Boyreau plan appealed to the Common Council, but difficulties arose. Wondering whether it had the power to institute such a comprehensive system of inspection, the council sought authorization from the state government. Albany quickly gave permission, but the committee charged with drafting a new law had trouble negotiating the terms of the contract with Boyreau. There was also opposition within the council to registering every chimney and thereby extending governmental power into the homes and hearths of all New Yorkers. When an ordinance along the lines suggested by Boyreau came up for a vote on May 31, 1811, it was defeated, 7–5.[28]

In 1804, the Common Council barely had mentioned the treatment of apprentice sweeps during its discussion of the trade. In the deliberations in 1810 and 1811, the welfare of the boys became a compelling issue. Reformers believed that education and training of black youths was crucial to the success of gradual emancipation. More important from the viewpoint of the council, if these apprentices were not adequately provided for, they would burden society as adults and thus represent a failure of freedom.

The situation of these boys was grim. Masters often overcame the boys' understandable reluctance to climb hot and sooty chimneys by brutal discipline. The boys were usually covered with sores and bruises and, seldom having the means to wash other than occasional plunges in the river, were liable to disease and infection. Their only garments were tattered rags, and their only protection against the cold was the blanket that they used to collect soot. Although apprentices were children or young adolescents, we cannot be sure where they lived. Some did not reside in their master's household. Reports indicate that many slept in the same cellars that housed the soot or in doorways and on the streets, where a number of artists captured their plight.[29]

By 1811, rising interest in the well-being of the young blacks brought with it strong condemnation of the perceived behavior of the master sweeps. Members of the Common Council declared that the conduct of the "miserable corps who at present manage" the sweep business violated "order and decency"; the master sweeps were "cruel taskmasters," who treated their boys with ruthless brutality. The condition of the apprentices was a central theme in the council's petition to the state legislature seeking authority for greater regulation. The magistrates described the boys' plight as "destitute, miserable, and depraved." After their daily labor, these youths "are left to themselves; they enjoy none of the advantages arising from the care of persons willing to afford them opportunities for improvement, or desirous to preserve them from the contagion of evil example, and idleness."[30]

This concern represented both an extension of English efforts to aid chimney sweeps in that country and white American interest in the future of newly freed African Americans in New York City. American reformers often modeled themselves after their English counterparts. In Great Britain, sweeps became the focus of a reform movement around 1800 that brought the issue onto the pages of William Blake and Charles Dickens and into the halls of Parliament. Englishmen first began to discuss publicly the treatment of young chimney sweeps in the 1770s, and in 1788 Parliament considered a bill to protect the "climbing boys." That measure failed in the House of Lords. In 1803, an English society "to supersede the necessity of employing climbing boys" was organized, and in 1817, the House of Commons issued a massive report on the subject. By that time, however, English reformers were hoping that new machinery would supplant child labor.[31]

Americans knew of these efforts, but, a writer observed in the New York Morning Chronicle, "in this country, where that calling is chiefly confined to blacks, the evil excites less sympathy."[32] In England and America, chimney sweeps represented a despised trade. In both nations the apprentices came from the lowest classes. The main difference was the segregation of the trade by race in America. In the same way that cartmen staunchly opposed the entry of any blacks into their ranks, even the poorest of whites may have stayed away from chimney sweeping because of the stigma of race.[33]

During the closing months of 1811, the New York City Manumission Society began to investigate the treatment of the city's sweeps. This society was organized in 1785 to protect free blacks from kidnapping and reenslavement and to lobby for the end of slavery. It worked to secure adoption of the state's gradual emancipation law of 1799. Founded by Quakers, the organization was led by people such as Alexander Hamilton, John Jay, and others from the highest echelon of New York society. These Federalist merchants, lawyers, and businessmen approached their task with caution, hesitating to push too hard because they feared that too rapid emancipation would create social havoc and disorder. Some members wanted to take free black youths from their parents and apprentice them as domestic servants in white families that were "better qualified" to provide care, guidance, and good morals. Although its paternalism was laced with racism and could be overbearing, the society took an active interest in the future of New York's black community. Society members registered manumissions, helped establish schools, and sought to prevent the exportation of slaves in violation of state law. It was in this role as guardian of the city's African Americans that the organization turned its attention to the chimney sweeps.[34]

After completing its inquiry, the Manumission Society delivered a strongly worded memorial to the Common Council. Ignoring the master sweeps, the report focused on the apprentices, "a class of sufferers, whose condition is peculiarly unhappy." The boys were "compelled to begin their work at a very early hour in the morning; whereby this abridgement of their natural rest, together with the want of necessary clothing and other accommodations, renders them not only liable to be weakly and diseased, but subjects of commiseration and care." Surely, "the compassion and sympathy of a benevolent mind" must be excited by the misery of the apprentice sweeps, a misery resulting from the "cruel effects of inhumanity and avarice . . . in combination with the natural evils of the Trade."[35]

The voice of these influential men was heard. The Charity Committee of the Common Council drew up a response in the same spirit as the Manumission Society's memorial, reporting that "the situation of the poor sweeps" and the conduct of the trade "require the interference of this Board as much perhaps as any subject whatever." While the committee did not propose detailed regulations, it recommended licensing.[36]

The Common Council acted quickly. On May 11, 1812, it passed a licensing law that addressed all the major complaints that had emerged since the previous year. The new ordinance required master chimney sweeps, with "satisfactory evidence of their good character," to obtain permits. They were not to employ boys younger than twelve or allow them to labor in the morning earlier than six o'clock in the winter or five the rest of the year. Five-dollar fines were prescribed for employing underage apprentices, for failing properly to clothe or feed the boys, or for working without a license. Master sweeps would be held responsible for any fire in a chimney swept within the previous month. All masters and apprentices were to wear numbered badges for identification.[37]

The Manumission Society and the Common Council blamed the masters for their apprentices' misery. Did these men have a voice in measures that affected their lives? We cannot be sure. The struggle to reform the trade in 1804, 1810, and 1812 produced little evidence of their views. The Common Council minutes for these years reveal that some master sweeps exercised their rights as citizens by petitioning for special favors or for remissions of fines.[38] But if masters responded to the charges for careless work and abuse of apprentices, the record is silent until 1816.

The early national era was a critical period for northern blacks. Not only did they gain freedom from slavery, but they asserted an independent identity. Confronted by growing racism, African Americans molded their own institutions and created their own community. In New York City, black Methodists broke away from their white co-religionists by 1796 and chartered the African Methodist Episcopal Zion Church in 1801. Seven years later, black Baptists established their own church on Anthony Street, and the New York African Society for Mutual Relief began collecting money and assisting members in need. Other black self-help societies did the same. By 1813, African Americans had organized their own schools, independent of the control of the Manumission Society.[39]

African Americans also exhibited an outspoken public presence. They convened meetings to rouse the black community in support of emancipation throughout the United States.[40] In 1808 they gathered to celebrate the end of the slave trade. In August 1814, "free people of color" fulfilled their obligations as citizens by meeting to volunteer their services in constructing fortifications for the defense of the city.[41] Despite efforts by Democrats to disfranchise them, propertied blacks participated in politics, usually supporting Federalist candidates associated with the Manumission Society.[42]

As part of this movement, master sweeps demonstrated their own sense of civic potency. From 1816 through 1818, in a flurry of petitions and counterpetitions, they asked for the privileges due American citizens. Once again the issue was municipal regulation. Some master sweeps hoped to raise their social and financial status through expanded supervision. Others perceived this as a threat to their livelihood. In the middle was the Common Council, concerned as always with the need to prevent fires and maintain order. The result was series of exchanges that expressed African-American values based on the ideals of the Revolution.[43]

Early in 1816, nine master sweeps took the initiative in a petition to the Common Council. These men—only two of whom could sign their names—admitted that their "hold in society is very humble," but, seizing on the egalitarian rhetoric of the day, they declared that they were persuaded that the councilmen wanted to show themselves "as the friends and guardians of every class in the community without regards to poverty and riches." Consequently, they wished to be treated "in the same manner as you have thought proper to do in respect to Cartmen, porters, measurers, &c." Black tradesmen, they were saying, had the same right to paternal municipal regulation and protection as their white counterparts.

These masters asked the council to revise the sweep statues, set rates, limit the number of licenses to eighteen at most, and appoint an "Inspector of Chimney Sweepers." They complained that the current regulations were followed only "by the honest part of the licensed sweepers" and "altogether unattended to by the others." Interlopers, "who go about sweeping chimneys, without any license," ignored the laws. Along with these requests for more stringent regulation, the masters sought the easing of one requirement. Noting that "there are many vents in this city, which are so extremely narrow, that they never can be cleaned by a boy of twelve years, unless he should be an absolute dwarf," they wanted the minimum age for apprentices lowered from twelve to eleven. The reasoning of the petition, and perhaps the influence of a few white friends, impressed the magistrates. On April 22, 1816, the Common Council enacted all of the proposed measures except the limitation on licenses.[44]

The triumph of these masters appeared complete. Indeed, the Common Council also accepted their suggestion that Adam Marshall, a master who had not signed the petition, be appointed inspector. Inspired by this success, the masters organized the United Society of Chimney Sweeps (USCS) to provide a fund for the "mutual relief" of "sick & superannuated members; for the burial of deceased members and for the assistance of their widows & orphans." New York City, like other urban areas at the time, had many similar associations. Some organizations were based on race or ethnicity, others on a trade. The mutual relief associations set up by white mechanics often expanded their role by policing their members' economic activities to ensure that they were in line with the overall goals of the trade. Following this model, the USCS masters claimed that their society maintained "mutual controul over the members."[45]

Establishing a trade association and keeping control of the trade turned out to be two different operations. By the summer of 1816, USCS members had set up twenty-nine officers across the city. The USCS, however, did not include all the city's sweeps, nor were all its members in complete agreement.[46] Divisions appeared after August 1816, when Marshall made a further bid for the respectability of his trade and the material circumstances of the USCS masters who had gotten him his position. Arguing that anyone who wanted a chimney swept could go to one of the USCS offices, Marshall asked the Common Council to do away with the wailing of itinerant chimney sweeps. Early morning street calling, he maintained, was "distressing" to the sick and "very unpleasant" to those who "wish to enjoy repose." Invoking the council's concern for the apprentices, Marshall also pointed out that the young sweeps were "subject to abuses in consequence of their bawling." With no purpose any longer served by "these disagreeable screamings," he asked the council "for the sake of the public quiet" to punish any sweep "who shall disturb the citizens, by making a noise in the manner now so common."[47] On August 26 the council passed an ordinance declaring that any master who was guilty of "crying aloud or singing in the public streets," either personally or through his apprentice, would "forfeit his license."[48]

Flexing their newfound civic muscle, Marshall and the USCS had hoped to stifle competition. But the attempt to suppress itinerancy created disagreement within the masters' ranks. In December 1816, fourteen USCS members, joined by twelve other masters, presented the Common Council with their own petition, asking for the repeal of the anticrying law. Among those who put their marks to the document were three women. "From Delicacy and the defference due," the law's opponents chose to "forbear using any argument" against the "evils attending their crying out." Still, they asked the council to take into consideration "that the means of gaining a living for the sweeps and their families is very much lessened" without the right to solicit in the streets. "Fully trusting in the kindness and wisdom" of the council, they sought repeal. Marshall's effort on behalf of the USCS to eliminate street cries in order to monopolize the trade and to move the sweep masters closer to social and financial equity with white tradesmen had made it more difficult for some masters to compete.[49]

Late in 1816, the Common Council repealed the regulation against street crying, except in the relatively affluent second and third wards. It is likely— debate within the council is not recorded—that the aldermen were concerned that the new ordinance might turn some of New York's working class into dangerous vagrants.[50] Six weeks later, a new memorial against crying from Inspector Marshall was tabled, even though "a number of our most respectable citizens" sent a petition supporting Marshall and stating that the cries continued to create a nuisance throughout the city. The audible trademark of the occupation remained.[51]

The repeal of the anticrying law represented the first of a series of problems for the USCS. The Common Council in 1817 considered an ordinance similar to the one that had been in force for three months in 1804 that put all sweeps under a single employer, and thereby again threatened to end the livelihood of the master sweeps. The primary concern of the magistrates once more centered on the boys. The licensing law had evidently failed to end the abuse of apprentices. Consequently, a special investigative committee of the council proposed the creation of an office of Superintendent of Sweeps. The superintendent, salaried by the city, would become the sole employer of the apprentice sweeps, aged ten to twenty-one. He would establish citywide offices that would be open daily to register all chimneys and to note the number of fireplaces, the nature of the fuel used, and when they were last swept. Sweeps would service chimneys on a regular basis, and fines would be levied if the sweep was not let in. Rates charged for sweeping remained the same as in previous ordinances.[52]

The committee issued a scathing description of the plight of the boys, whose sustenance, it declared, depended not on the benevolence of their masters but on "the charity of those whose chimneys are swept." This was only a small part of their miseries:

the soot and dirt which collect on their bodies from year to year defend them
from inclement weather nearly as well as their tattered cloathing; which barely
preserves them from freezing until they can attain the heights of their enjoyment by being warmed in a chimney. Cleanliness being so very necessary for
the preservation of health being wholly unattended to and from the corrosive
property of the soot and ashes with which they are covered it follows that
disease finds in them apt subjects . . . , a disease of the most virulent nature is
peculiar to them called Chimney Sweepers Cancer.

The committee urged the council to take responsibility for the "little
sufferers." It recommended that the superintendent not employ apprentice
sweeps before 4 A.M. or after noon. He should provide good accommodation,
bedding, and garments. Clothing would be changed immediately after work,
and the boys would be required to wash. A competent schoolmaster would
teach them daily from two to five in the afternoon. Half the proceeds from
fees would go to the superintendent, and the other half would be set aside as
a fund for the boys after they completed their indentures. It was vital, the
committee resolved, that the "poor wretches" be trained for an occupation
that would provide an "honest and useful life," rather than allowing them to
return to the street as "thieves and vagabonds."[53]

The Common Council's special committee had no faith in the ability or
desire of master sweeps to treat their charges with decency. The city fathers
dismissed all masters as a class occupying a "condition in life" that was "but
one remove from the lowest of all—the oppressed sweep." The council
believed that the master sweeps could not provide the paternal care expected
of other master craftsmen.[54]

Faced with the loss of their income, the master sweeps of the USCS responded vigorously. They had learned much in their political struggles the
previous year. Now many dissident masters who had opposed the anticrying
law joined forces with the USCS. Together they worked to save their profession when the new plan reached the Common Council.

The masters attacked on several fronts. They argued that such an ordinance would "deprive them of their employment" and would make them
and their families a "burthen to the public." The master reminded the
Common Council that the 1816 law had led to the formation of the USCS.
The organization not only policed its own ranks but also eased the potential
welfare costs by offering relief to sick members and aid to orphans and widows. In other words, the current system, which allowed these free African-
American citizens to regulate and support themselves, was working well.
Therefore, "in the opinion of the chimney sweeps, as well as the citizens at
large," the 1816 ordinance was answering "every useful purpose," and "any
innovation would be prejudicial rather than beneficial to the community."[55]

The USCS admitted that there were problems. Competition among
masters was intense, and some masters cut costs by treating apprentices
poorly. Accordingly, the USCS wanted city authorities to distinguish be-

tween honest and disreputable masters. They urged the Common Council to enact an ordinance requiring masters who desired a license to "give reasonable security" for the "faithful performance of their duty," especially in regard to apprentices. This included treating them "with humanity," providing "good & wholesome food," clothing them "in a comfortable manner," sending them to Sunday school, and giving them a quarter's tuition at a school each summer.[56] If it did this, the "respectable part" of the sweep masters would be "kept together" while the "worthless part," unable to afford the security, would be forced out of the trade and "no longer be a stigma on the body." Consequently, "an effectual reformation" would be achieved.[57]

It was one of the many ironic twists of this controversy that, by 1817, the apprentices were members of the so-called free labor market. The masters informed the magistrates that most of these youths "were free" and received a "certain sum" each week. Because of this arrangement, masters did not have "that controul over them which could be wished," and "if on the Lord's day, they are found lying about the streets, it is impossible for them to prevent it." Members of the USCS claimed that they did their best under difficult circumstances and did not neglect education, "as it is a rule in their society, that every one of their boys shall be sent to school for one quarter during each summer."[58] Agreeing that more attention ought to be given to the "moral and religious habits" of the boys, the masters promised "to do everything in their power" to keep them off the streets on the Sabbath and "if possible, prevail on them to go to school."[59] The plan of the special committee, in contrast, would render the behavior of the boys "much worse," because "one hundred & fifty boys, without education & of depraved morals [would be] convened together and boarded in one place."[60]

Along with the arguments predicting an increase in the public dole and the worsening of the condition of apprentices, the master sweeps attacked the committee's proposal on the ground that it violated their rights as citizens. The USCS asserted that its members were on the same level as other regulated tradesmen—all of whom were white—such as cartmen, bakers, and butchers. The relationship between the masters and the city was reciprocal; each side had its responsibilities and its privileges. Thus, the masters reasoned, the 1816 law not only provided for the "publick good" but also protected "the rights and interests of the Chimney Sweeps."[61] This compact ought not to be broken.

Laying claim to the heritage of the American Revolution, the master sweeps reminded the Common Council that "several of their numbers have served in the revolutionary war & some of them received wounds in consequence of which they are rendered incapable of any kind of hard labour." Did the magistrates, through ill-advised reforms, have the right to take away the employment of these veterans and "reduce them to indigence & want" when at an "advanced age"?[62] Recognizing the revolutionary changes that had led to a more egalitarian sense of citizenship, the master sweeps declared that "your Petitioners, to be sure, are men of colour, a class of people, who

have heretofore been greatly despised; but they now live in a more enlightened period, and are fully persuaded, that Your Honorable Body will treat
every man, whether white or black, according to his deserts."[63] The sweeps,
as free blacks, citizens, and licensees of the City of New York, claimed their
rights. The city should not break a reciprocal trust by removing the livelihood of tradesmen who were fulfilling their duty as workers and members of
civil society.

The effect of these arguments on the Common Council is difficult to
gauge. In the early months of 1818, the reform proposals became mired in
the bureaucratic maze of council procedure. Perhaps some aldermen,
repeating arguments that had surfaced when the council considered earlier
measures, believed that this reform would entail too much regulation of the
lives of the city's residents. A few influential whites lobbied in support of the
master sweeps. After failed amendments and three postponements, the
measure was returned to committee, where it died.[64]

The master sweeps' victory was brief. Two months after the defeat of the reform measure, the special committee on sweeps issued a new report urging
the aldermen to support the efforts of Benjamin Bruff to devise a machine to
clean chimneys without requiring a boy to climb the flue. The documents
do not describe Bruff's device, but it was probably similar to English patent
machines that cleaned chimneys with collapsible rods attached to brushes
and scrapers. With some enthusiasm the Common Council paid Bruff
seventy-five dollars to develop his invention. In the following months other
tinkerers applied for assistance. By the early 1820s, several men had secured
permission from the council to use their machines to clean chimneys in New
York. These men were white entrepreneurs who planned to hire African-
American masters to do the actual chimney sweeping. The master still used
apprentices, but they worked together from the rooftop, and the boy did not
need to enter the flue.[65] Chimney sweeping was far from the only nineteenth-century craft to be radically transformed by the introduction of
machinery. It differed from others, however, in that the Common Council,
concerned for the welfare of the apprentice sweeps, actively supported
efforts at mechanization.[66]

These developments threatened the livelihood and independence of the
USCS masters. The USCS now began to recede but not without one final
effort. In June 1821, sixteen masters, led by a new inspector, Benjamin
Haskell, petitioned the Common Council concerning competition from
sweeps using machines. They argued that they had complied with the
regulations of the council, "to promote the convenience of the citizens in
general." Yet, they lamented, "those men, who call themselves *Patent
Sweeps*," were not subject to such restrictions. Moreover, the patent sweepers
treated the traditional masters with "every kind of indignity, deeming themselves, as it were, a privileged order and us an inferiour and degraded race of
beings." The exact intent of these words remains vague since it is not clear if

the patent sweepers referred to in the petition were the white entrepreneurs or the blacks hired by them. Regardless, the spread of machinery threatened the independent status of the USCS members. They therefore asked that "in justice" the patent sweeps ought to be under the same regulations. Denying that they were "actuated by any malignant or improper motives," the masters declared that they were "persuaded that the old mode of sweeping chimneys is much preferable to this new scheme." They believed that, because they were citizen tradesmen who did "their duty," the city was obliged to protect them in their employment.[67]

The Common Council responded by requiring all sweeps to abide by the city's ordinances. This did not halt the advance of machinery, and more sweeps soon adopted it. Many masters, however, continued to employ the old method. Both systems operated in the city throughout the first half of the nineteenth century. The 1825 edition of *Cries of New York* suggests that sweeps continued to evoke a sentimental pathos. The illustration still depicts a master and apprentice, this time burdened with machinery. The call of the sweep remains, but with an explanation that the machinery is to "relieve the boys of the hard and sometimes fatal business of sweeping chimneys." The features of both individuals in the picture appear to be African American.[68]

What do we learn from the travail of New York's chimney sweeps in the opening decades of the nineteenth century? Scholars have delineated two key trends in African-American history during these years. First and foremost is the impact of the age of revolution on the institution of slavery. The wartime experience, which offered slaves a variety of opportunities for freedom, combined with egalitarian ideals to challenge the very notion of slavery. One by one, northern states moved to abolish the institution within their borders. Even many southerners came to see slavery as dying. The second development served as a counter to the first. By the beginning of the nineteenth century, the expansion of the cotton kingdom strengthened the economic base of slavery in the South, entrenching the institution further in the region's culture. Meanwhile, in the North, whites put political, economic, and social impositions on free blacks.[69]

Historians have traced the effects of these grand trends on the lives of blacks in northern cities. After a period of quasi-servitude under the paternalism of white benefactors, African Americans began to assert their identity and express faith in the ideals of the Revolution, only to run up against the stone wall of racism by the 1820s. Historians' understanding of the assertion of African-American identity in this period and in the difficult years thereafter relies heavily upon the articulate expressions of such leaders as Richard Allen and Absalom Jones in Philadelphia and William Hamilton, John Teasman, and Peter Williams, Jr., in New York.[70]

Study of New York's chimney sweeps enables us to see deeper into the African-American world. On the one hand, the political activity of the master sweeps reveals the penetration of the egalitarian ideals of the American Revolution into one of the lowliest trades and exhibits the desire of a group of aspiring African Americans to claim the rights of citizenship. On the other hand, their aspirations were not fulfilled. The entry of the patent machine sweeps ended the regular sweeps' monopoly of the trade and reduced their leverage. Consequently, the masters lost the civic voice so well expressed in their petitions from 1816 to 1818. After 1821, they forwarded few memorials to the municipality. Nothing more is heard of the United Society of Chimney Sweeps. The ideals of the Revolution may yet have held sway among these African-American workers, but the conditions of their employment and the racism of the age militated against public expression and effective organization.

We also gain some understanding of the interaction between African Americans and whites during this period. Three groups of white New Yorkers played an important role in this drama: city officials, philanthropists, and entrepreneurs who hoped to control the sweep trade. Protection of the city from fires remained uppermost for the Common Council. The difficulty lay in guaranteeing efficient and inexpensive sweeping of chimneys without excessive regulation. Although the city had a long history of monitoring key trades, there was some reluctance to intrude too actively on the daily lives of New Yorkers. The guardians of the public welfare also became concerned with the treatment of the sweep apprentices. Repeatedly, then, the council felt compelled to tinker with sweep ordinances in an attempt to limit fires and, after 1810, aid free black youths. The push and pull of these factors, as well as the lobbying of African-American chimney sweep masters, led to changes in ordinances but only modest improvement for master and apprentice sweeps.

The philanthropists of the Manumission Society appear briefly in the record concerning chimney sweeps. Their petition to the Common Council represented just a small component of their reform activities but fits into a larger pattern of interaction with New York's African-American community. The Manumission Society in these years worked to stifle the self-assertion of adult blacks and strove to gain control over youths in order to train them to be compliant and deferential. Although there is no direct evidence indicating that this motivation lay behind their concern with sweep apprentices, it may well have had some influence over the Manumission Society's interest in the apprentice's plight.[71]

The entrepreneurs—men such as Adolph Degrove, John Boyreau, and the inventor Benjamin Bruff—pursued economic goals: monopoly of the trade offered the possibilities of profit. The entrepreneurs had no intention of cleaning chimneys themselves but planned to hire African Americans who had always done the real dirty work. In some instances they described their efforts—perhaps not altogether insincerely—as a reform to alleviate the condition of the apprentices. The exact nature of their relationship with the

African-American masters remains obscure, but it could not have been cordial. Although the early white entrepreneurs failed to get a monopoly, others managed to gain entry into the field through the use of machinery.

Sweep apprentices remain virtually anonymous. Critics of the masters had a point when they focused on the treatment of the boys. Competing for business, some masters badly abused their apprentices, who lived at the very edge of subsistence. But like white youths who refused paternal guardianship of their employers in this period, many young sweeps apparently relished their independence and rejected the USCS efforts at guidance and education. The free labor market thus made it difficult to control the apprentices off the job. White masters in other trades had similar problems but escaped the opprobrium heaped on the black master sweeps.[72] The advent of patent machinery meant that the proportion of masters requiring climbing boys diminished. This development suggests that fewer black youths had to cripple themselves climbing sooty flues, though some would lose employment.

African Americans, whether using the old-fashioned method or patent machinery, continued sweeping chimneys and occupied a special labor niche that other New York workers avoided at any cost. Only the introduction of central heating liberated master and apprentice sweeps from a dangerous, difficult, and degraded trade. For much of the remainder of the nineteenth century the streets of New York echoed with the cry "Sweep O! Sweep O!"

APPENDIX: IDENTIFYING THE MASTER CHIMNEY SWEEPS, 1815–1820

While researching this essay we found that there were many questions that the sources either did not address or answered only incompletely. In particular, we wish we had more information on the identity of the New York chimney sweeps. Unfortunately, the apprentices remain anonymous, and the masters almost so. Perhaps some day more biographical data about these African Americans will come to light. We drew up a list of master sweeps based on the names appended to the documents and a list of licensed sweeps compiled in the file papers in 1816. When we checked the directories and the New York City Census and Jury List for 1819 we found a few additional names of masters and their addresses. The results, summarized here, demonstrate how difficult it is to trace individuals like these masters. Of the fifty-nine individuals listed, we have little more than the names of twenty-two. We have found more information on thirty-seven of the sweeps. We know the ages of fifteen master sweeps in 1819. They ranged from age twenty-six to ninety-six, with a median age of forty-eight. At least three women served as masters, and only three of the male sweeps could sign their own name.

In some instances, the information we have is tantalizingly suggestive. Some sweeps lived near each other or even in the same building. In 1816, both Betsy Henry and Peter Marsh were licensed sweeps living at 87 Bancker Street, across the way from James Green at 84 Bancker Street. In 1819, none of them was listed as a head of household. In that year, however, Roger Orange and John Giles, of 95 Bancker Street, are given as masters on the Jury and Census List. We can only conjecture as to the relationship among these people. Did they work as partners or competitors? How did they view each other on a daily basis? We have just enough information to imagine some interactions but not enough to come to any certain conclusions.

We can also ask about occupational loyalty and mobility. Did some sweeps work at two occupations or move from one occupation to another? A James Simmons appears in the 1814 directory as a shoemaker residing at 9 Bancker Street. A James Simmons held a license as a sweep in 1816 and is listed as living on Bancker Street. This name does not appear in subsequent directories. Was Simmons the shoemaker in 1814 the sweep master in 1816? Or were they two different people? What happened to James Simmons after that year? We cannot answer these questions with great precision. Regardless of the problem in resolving the issue of James Simmons, the difficulty in tracing individuals from year to year suggests that some sweep masters did not stay long in the profession.

We have also been careful about delineating any patterns concerning the residence of the masters. Although a few masters, like Richard Garrison whose office was at 33 Henry Street, retained the same address for several years, most changed addresses frequently. Residential mobility, however, was not unusual for New Yorkers. Whites and blacks both were famous for shifting addresses, especially on the annual moving day of May 1.

If the residential mobility of the master sweeps was unexceptional, so was their overall geographic distribution. There were no segregated African-American neighborhoods in early-nineteenth-century New York. Blacks could be found throughout the city, but there were certain neighborhoods, streets, and even houses in which African Americans clustered. Thus sweep masters, like other African Americans, sometimes lived among whites and sometimes with others of their race. Hercules Schurman, for instance, resided at 47 Lispenard Street in 1819. The neighborhood and street were largely white with many artisans living there. Schurman's address was just a few blocks from Chapel Street, where many more blacks lived. Indeed, John Patterson, another master sweep, lived at 74 Chapel Street. This building was in a series of houses (numbers 72, 74, 78, 80, 82, but not 76) that were all occupied by African Americans, comprising a total of eleven families with forty people. A few areas, like the neighborhood around Chapel Street in the Fifth Ward, had several sweeps and concentrated numbers of African Americans. Besides the Chapel Street area, African Americans and sweeps congregated in the Five Points district (at the intersection of Cross, Orange, and Anthony Streets) of the Sixth Ward and the Bancker Street area of the Seventh Ward. All three neighborhoods were crime ridden and contained marginal housing.

Finally, we offer a word of caution. The whole process of identifying individuals such as master sweeps is tenuous and complex. In several instances, for example, city directories list more than one person with the same name. If none of these had a sweep occupation, we left the person unidentified, even though the directory sometimes gives no occupation for people we knew were sweeps. We also strove to simplify the following list by not indicating which petition the name appeared on. However, we did indicate whether we knew individuals belonged to the USCS or held office in that organization and if they opposed the antisweep ordinance. Multiple and single sources of an address are indicated on the list. We include this material because we want to illuminate some of the difficulties in finding information on the sweeps and, in some measure, to bring to life these otherwise anonymous individuals who struggled in the early nineteenth century to assert their identity as tradesmen and citizens.

ALLEN, ROBERT: He was a member of the standing committee of the USCS, 1817. Before 1817 the directories list only a mariner under this name. In 1817–1818 he is listed as having a sweep office, 51 Oak St. The 1819 Jury and Census List indicated that a Richard Allen (probably the same person), age 48 and a sweep, resided at 328 Water St.

ARDEN, JACOB S.: No positive identification made. There was a physician listed under this name, 1814–1819, at 42 Walker St.

BAILEY, EDWARD: He opposed the anticrying law. He was a licensed sweep in 1816, at 27 Duane St., 5th Ward.

BRIGGS, ELIJAH: He was a member of the USCS. But no positive identification made. The only person the directories list by this name was a grocer.

BRYAN, NATHANIEL: He was a USCS member but opposed the anticrying law. He was a licensed sweep in 1816, at 38 Chapel St., 5th Ward. The 1816 directory lists him at the same address with no occupation.

BUNN, WILLIAM: The 1815 directory lists him as having a sweep office at Pump St.

BUTLER, EDWARD: He was a USCS member. We have no other information on him.

COLE, JAMES: He was a USCS member. We have no other information on him.

COOPER, JOSHUA: We have no information on him.

COURTWRIGHT, JACOB: He opposed the anticrying law. He was a licensed sweep in 1816, at 93 Duane St., 6th Ward. The 1814–1818 directories list him, at the same address, as having no occupation. In the 1819 directory he has a sweep office on Catherine Lane. In 1819 the Jury and Census List indicated that he was age 96 and operating a sweep office at 30 Catherine Lane.

COX, CHARLES: He was a USCS member and listed with the title "Attendant on the Sick" as part of that organization. He opposed the anticrying law. He was a licensed sweep in 1816, on Spring St., 8th Ward. The 1814–1818 directories list him as having a sweep office on Spring St., and the 1817–1819 directories list his sweep office at Christopher and Herring Sts.

COX, HUNT: We have no information on him.

CUMMINGS, ABRAHAM: No positive identification made. The 1814–1815 directories list a person by this name and no occupation at 21 Oak St. (Greenwich).

DODGE, CHARLES: He was a member of the standing committee of the USCS but opposed the anticrying law. He was a licensed sweep in 1816, at 177 Division St., 6th Ward. The 1814–1819 directories list him with no occupation. In 1814 he resided at 3 Jefferson St. In 1815 he resided at 182 Grand St. In 1816–1819 he resided at 167 Division St. In 1819 the Jury and Census List indicated that he was 40 years old.

EDSALL, PETER: He was a USCS member. No other positive identification made. The 1814–1819 directories list a person by this name whose occupation was shoemaker and who moved three times during those six years.

EVERETT, JOSEPH: We have no information on him.

FREEMAN, JOHN: He was a USCS member but opposed the anticrying law. He was a licensed sweep in 1816, with no address listed. The 1814 directory lists him as a master and residing at 33 Jay St. Other John Freemans are listed 1816–1819 with different occupations at different addresses.

GARRISON, JOHN: He was a USCS member. The directories list several person with this name, but none of them are sweeps.

GARRISON, RICHARD: He was a USCS member but opposed the anticrying law. He was a licensed sweep in 1816, at Henry St., 7th Ward. The 1814–1819 directories list him as a sweep at 33 Henry St.

GERALD, JAMES: He was a USCS member. We have no other information.

GILES, JOHN: In 1819 the Jury and Census List indicates that he was age 46, a master, and residing at 95 Bancker St.

GREEN, JAMES: He was a licensed sweep in 1816, at 84 Bancker St., 7th Ward.

GREEN, TOBIAS: He was a USCS member but opposed the anticrying law. The 1818 directory lists him as having a sweep office at 12 Frankfort St. The 1819 Jury and Census List does not include his age but indicates that he was a master residing at 49 Mulberry St.

HASKELL, BENJAMIN: He was a USCS member and was inspector of sweeps in 1821. The 1818–1819 directories list him as having a sweep office at 47 Mulberry St. The 1819 Jury and Census List indicated that he was age 50 and living at 49 Mulberry St.

HENRY, BETSY: She opposed the anticrying law. She was listed as a licensed sweep in 1816, at 87 Bancker St., 7th Ward. An Elizabeth Henry is listed in the 1816, 1818, and 1819 directories. In 1816 she is listed as a widow with a sweep office at 113 Bancker St. In 1818 she is listed as a widow with no occupation at 7 Hudson St., and in 1819 she is listed as a widow with no occupation, living on Hudson St., corner of Charlotte St.

HENRY, JOHN: The 1819 Jury and Census List indicates he was age 44, a master, and residing at 118 Bancker St.

HUNT, JOHN: He was a USCS member but opposed the anticrying law. He was listed as a licensed sweep in 1816, at 12 Frankfort St., 4th Ward. He was listed as a master in the 1816–1819 directories, at 12 Frankfort St. in 1816, to 44 Augustus St. in 1818, and at 173 Spring St. in 1819.

JACKSON, [DAVID]: He opposed the anticrying law. He was a licensed sweep in 1816, on Thomas St., 5th Ward.

JAMISON, JAMES: We have no information on him.

JERREL, JAMES: He was a USCS member but opposed the anticrying law. He was a licensed sweep in 1816, on Nassau St., 2d Ward.

JOHNSON, HAZARD: The 1819 Jury and Census List indicates he was age 35, working as a "sweeper," and residing at 11 Orange St.

JOHNSON, PETER: We have no information on him.

JOHNSON, SUSAN: She opposed the anticrying law. She was a licensed sweep in 1816, at 16 Sixth St., 10th Ward. In 1815 there were two "widows" listed with this name. In 1816 there was only one widow, no occupation listed, who resided at 16 Sixth St. By 1817 she had moved to 98 Christie St., and by 1819 she lived at 8 Harmon St.

JOHNSON, WILLIAM: He was a USCS member and could sign his name. We have no other information on him.

LAWSON, ABRAHAM: He opposed the anticrying law and could sign his own name. We have no other information on him.

LAWSON, HENRY: He was a USCS member but opposed the anticrying law. He was inspector of sweeps in 1817 and a licensed sweep in 1816, at 98 Cross St., 6th Ward. The 1816–1819 directories list him as a master, at the Cross St. address. The 1819 Jury and Census List indicates that he was age 36 and residing at 45 Cross St.

LEIGE, TIMOTHY: The 1819 Jury and Census List gives no age but indicates he operated a sweep office on Bedford St.

MARSH, PETER: He was a USCS member but opposed the anticrying law. He was a licensed sweep in 1816, at 87 Bancker St., 7th Ward. The directories list several people with this name involved in maritime activities. None is listed as a sweep or at the Bancker St. address.

MARSHALL, ADAM: He was a USCS member. He was inspector of sweeps and was a licensed sweep in 1816, at 177 Duane St., 5th Ward. The directories list his sweep office at that address, 1815–1816, and at 38 Chapel St., 1817–1819. The 1819 Jury and Census List indicates that he was age 40.

MELLIARNS, JORDAN: He was a licensed sweep in 1816, at 71 Pump St., 10th Ward.

MINIS, QUACCO, JR.: We have no information on him.

MOORE, HANNAH: She opposed the anticrying law. She was a licensed sweep in 1816, at 60 Henry St., 7th Ward.

MOORE, HENRY: He was a licensed sweep in 1816, on Bancker St., 7th Ward. The directories list several individuals with this name but no sweeps and none at a Bancker St. address.

MOORIS, JAMES: He opposed the anticrying law. He was a licensed sweep in 1816, at Sixth St., 10th Ward. The 1815 directory lists him as a master, 184 Grand St. The 1819 Jury and Census List indicates that he was age 66.

MYER, ENOS: He was a USCS member. We have no other information on him.

ORANGE, ROGER: He was a USCS member but opposed the anticrying law. He was a licensed sweep in 1816, on Orange St., 6th Ward. The 1814 directory lists a person with this name with no occupation at 18 Mott St. The 1819 Jury and Census List indicates that he was age 68, a master, and residing at 95 Bancker St.

ORR, JOHN: We have no information on him.

PATTERSON, JOHN: He was a USCS member but opposed the anti-crying law. He could sign his own name. He was a licensed sweep in 1816, at 74 Chapel St., 5th Ward. The 1815–1816 directories list him with a sweep office at the same address. The 1817 directory lists him with a sweep office at 71 Chapel St. Thereafter there is no sweep listing under this name. There are several John Pattersons listed at different addresses with different occupations. The 1819 Jury and Census List does not give his age but indicates that he was a master residing at 74 Chapel St.

SCARLETT, JOHN E.: He was a USCS member. He was a licensed sweep in 1816, at 9 Orange St., 7th Ward. The 1816 directory lists him at this address with no occupation. The 1819 Jury and Census List includes a John Scarlet at 9 Orange St., age 26. He is African American; his occupation is listed as "speculator."

SCHURMAN, HERCULES (sometimes used the name Cornelius): He was vice president of the USCS but opposed the anticrying law. In 1816 he was a licensed sweep, at Lispenard St. near Church St., 5th Ward. The 1816 directory lists him with a sweep office on Lispenard St. The 1819 Jury and Census List indicates he was age 60, a master, and residing at 47 Lispenard St.

SHEPARD, THOMAS: He was a member of the USCS standing committee but opposed the anticrying law. In 1816 he was a licensed sweep, at 7 Republican Alley, 6th Ward. The 1817 directory lists him as a master at 38 Hester St. The 1814–1816 and 1818–1819 directories list a person with this name as either a laborer or with no occupation. The person listed has a different address almost every year. No address matches those listed above.

SIMMONS, JAMES: He opposed the anticrying law. He was listed as a licensed sweep in 1816, on Bancker St., 7th Ward. The 1814 directory lists a shoemaker with this name at 9 Bancker St. We cannot be sure that this individual is the same as the chimney sweep. In 1815 there are two persons listed with this name.

SMITH, HENRY: He opposed the anticrying law. The 1814–1817 directories list him as having a "chimney office" at 8 Ferry St. In 1818–1819 the office was listed at 54 Augustus St. The 1819 Jury and Census List indicates that he was age 35.

SMITH, TIMOTHY: He opposed the anticrying law. He was listed as a licensed sweep in 1816, at 88 Elizabeth St., 6th Ward. The 1814–1819 directories list him as having a sweep office at Elizabeth and Grand Sts. The 1819 Jury and Census List indicates he was age 60 and operating a "chimney office" at 88 Elizabeth St.

STEWART, CHARLES: He was a licensed sweep in 1816, at Gold St. near Eden's Alley, 2d Ward. The 1814 directory lists him as master at 83 Warren St.

WARNER, LEONARD: He was a USCS member. We have no other information on him.

WESTERVELT, HENRY: He was a USCS member. We have no other information on him.

WILLIAMS, MOSES: He opposed the anticrying law. We have no other information on him.

WILLIAMS, HENRY: He was a member of the USCS standing committee. We have no other information on him.

Sources: List of Chimney Sweeps, [1816], File Papers, NYCMA; Petition of Chimney Sweeps, Dec. 2, 1816, ibid.; Petition of Cornelius Schurman et al., Dec 11, 1816, ibid., Petition of Chimney Sweepers to the Common Council, n.d. (in 1818 box but clearly from 1815–1816), ibid; Petition of Henry Lawson et al., Jan. 5, 1818, ibid.; Petition of Henry Lawson et al., Feb. 23, 1818, ibid.; Petition of Sweep Masters, Apr. 23, 1821, ibid.; *Longworth's Directory* (New York, 1814–1819); New York City Jury and Census List, 1819, NYCMA.

NOTES

The authors thank Kenneth R. Cobb, director of the Municipal Archives of the City of New York, and his staff for their assistance. The authors also thank Ira Berlin, Daniel Cohen, Graham Hodges, and Jon Sensbach for critical comments and help on this essay.

1. This essay focuses on New York City because of the unique documentation offered in the Municipal Archives and Records Center of the City of New York outlined below. For a fuller descriptive discussion of chimney sweeps throughout the nation see George Lewis Phillips, *American Chimney Sweeps: An Historical Account of a Once Important Trade* (Trenton, N. J., 1957). See also Jonathan A. Glickstein, *Concepts of Free Labor in Antebellum America* (New Haven, Conn., 1991), 179–180.

2. Phillips, *England's Climbing-Boys: A History of the Long Struggle to Abolish Child Labor in Chimney-Sweeping* (Cambridge, Mass., 1949), 1–2; John Crowley, "Artificial Illumination in Early America and the Definition of Domestic Space and Time," in Barbara Karsky and Élise Marienstras, eds., *Travail et Loisir dans Les Sociétés Pré-Industrielles* (Nancy, Fr., 1991), 59–69.

3. Phillips, *England's Climbing-Boys*, 1.

4. See Paul A. Gilje and Howard B. Rock, eds., *Keepers of the Revolution: New Yorkers at Work in the Early Republic* (Ithaca, N. Y., 1992), 13, and Augustine E. Costello, *Our Firemen: A History of the New York Fire Departments, Volunteer and Paid* (New York, 1887).

5. Phillips, *England's Climbing-Boys*, 24. The best single description of sweep working conditions is in the testimony of Dr. Stephen Lushington before the House of Lords in 1818. See Lushington, "The Reply of Dr. Lushington, in Support of the Bill of the Better Regulation of Chimney-Sweepers and their Apprentices. . . ," in *Improving the Lot of the Chimney Sweeps: One Book and Nine Pamphlets, 1785–1840* (New York, 1972). New York sources cited throughout the article support this description.

6. Phillips, *American Chimney Sweeps*, 12–27. Sources concerning English sweeps are the most explicit on the dangers to sweeps. See Phillips, *England's Climbing-Boys*; *Report from the Committee of the Honorable House of Commons on the Employment of Boys in Sweeping Chimneys . . .* (London, 1817), 5, 63; and *Improving the Lot of the Chimney Sweeps*.

7. *Cries of New-York* (New York, 1812), 38–39.

8. Ibid.; *Metropolitan Museum of Art Bulletin* (Nov. 1942). James Cross Giblin, *Chimney Sweeps: Yesterday and Today* (New York, 1982), 9–13.

9. Eaton, *Review of New York, or Rambles Through the City. Original Poems. Moral, Religious, Sarcastic, and Descriptive* (New York, 1813), 124.

10. Phillips, *American Chimney Sweeps*, 32–48.

11. Glickstein, *Concepts of Free Labor*, 107–112.

12. The authors have not found any documentation on the exact timing of these developments. The Minutes of the Common Council for the colonial and early national eras list some disbursements for cleaning chimneys at jails and public buildings. The individuals paid, however, were minor city officials who probably contracted out the sweeping. All that can be conclusively asserted is that before 1800 Euro-Americans identified the trade as fit only for African Americans. According to Phillips's research, this was true not only in New York but throughout the northern seaports. He dates the changeover to the mid- to late eighteenth century, though he notes that in a few cities, such as Boston and Baltimore, there were white apprentices. New York had none. Phillips argues that the cause of the switch to black sweeps was the use of slave labor to do such work in the South along with the notoriety of the trade. See Phillips, *American Chimney Sweeps*, 12–27, 49–51, and *Minutes of the Common Council of the City of New York, 1784–1831*, 21 vols. (New York, 1917–1930) (hereafter cited as MCC).

13. Ira Berlin, "The Revolution in Black Life," in Alfred F. Young, ed., *The American Revolution: Explorations in the History of American Radicalism* (De Kalb, Ill., 1976), 349–382; Leonard D. Curry, *The Free Black in Urban America, 1800–1850: The Shadow of the Dream* (Chicago, 1981); David Brion Davis, *The Problem of Slavery in the Age of Revolution, 1776–1823* (Ithaca, N. Y., 1975); Rhoda Golden Freeman, "The Free Negro in New York City in the Era Before the Civil War" (Ph.D. diss., Columbia University, 1966); Sylvia R. Frey, *Water from the Rock: Black Resistance in a Revolutionary Age* (Princeton, N. J., 1991); Leo H. Hirsch, Jr., "The Negro and New York, 1783 to 1865," *Journal of Negro History*, XVI, No. 4 (1931), 382–473; Graham Russell Hodges, "The Black Revolt in New York City and the Neutral Zone: 1775–1783," in Gilje and William Pencak, eds., *New York in the Age of the Constitution, 1775–1800* (Rutherford, N. J., 1992), 20–47; Sidney Kaplan and Emma Nogrady Kaplan, *The Black Presence in the Era of the American Revolution*, rev. ed. (Amherst, Mass., 1989); Vivienne L. Kruger, "Born to Run: The Slave Family in Early New York, 1626 to 1827" (Ph.D. diss., Columbia University, 1985); Leon F. Litwack, *North of Slavery: The Negro in the Free States, 1790–1860* (Chicago, 1961); Edgar J. McManus, *A History of Negro Slavery in New York* (Syracuse, N. Y., 1966); Gary B. Nash, "Forging Freedom: The Emancipation Experience in the Northern Seaport Cities, 1775–1820," in Berlin and Ronald Hoffman, eds., *Slavery and Freedom in the Age of the American Revolution* (Charlottesville, Va., 1983), 3–48; Roi Ottley and William J. Weatherby, eds., *The Negro in New York: An Informal*

Social History (New York, 1967), 31–91; Aaron Hamlet Payne, "The Negro in New York Prior to 1860," *Howard Review*, I (1923), 1–64; Benjamin Quarles, *The Negro in the American Revolution* (Chapel Hill, N. C., 1961); Quarles, "The Revolutionary War as a Black Declaration of Independence," in Berlin and Hoffman, eds., *Slavery and Freedom*, 283–301; Shane White, *Somewhat More Independent: The End of Slavery in New York City, 1770–1810* (Athens, Ga., 1991), 173–177; Arthur Zilversmit, *The First Emancipation: The Abolition of Slavery in the North* (Chicago, 1967).

14. American Convention for Promoting the Abolition of Slavery and Improving the Condition of the African Race, *Minutes of the Proceedings of the Fourth Convention . . .* (Philadelphia, 1797.); Curry, *Free Black in Urban America*, 15–36; Arnett G. Lindsay, "The Economic Condition of the Negroes of New York Prior to 1861," *J. Negro Hist.*, VI, No. 2 (1921), 190–199; White, *Somewhat More Independent*, 150–184, and "'We Dwell in Safety and Pursue Our Honest Callings': Free Blacks in New York City, 1783–1810," *Journal of American History*, LXXV (1988), 445–470.

15. This description of the work of the masters is a composite drawn from documents in City Clerk, File Papers, Municipal Archives and Records Center of the City of New York (hereafter cited as File Papers, NYCMA), Phillips, *American Chimney Sweeps*, and various illustrations. Of special help was Petition of Henry Lawson et al., Feb. 23, 1818, File Papers, NYCMA.

16. Jon C. Teaford, *The Municipal Revolution in America: Origins of Modern Urban Government, 1650–1825* (Chicago, 1975); Hendrik Hartog, *Public Property and Private Power: The Corporation of the City of New York in American Law, 1730–1870* (Chapel Hill, N. C., 1983); Arthur Everett Peterson and George William Edwards, *New York as an Eighteenth-Century Municipality* (Port Washington, N. Y., 1967; orig. pub. 1917); Rock, "A Delicate Balance: The Mechanics and the City in the Age of Jefferson," *New-York Historical Society Quarterly*, LXIII (1979), 101–111.

17. Ira Rosenwaike, *Population History of New York City* (Syracuse, N.Y., 1972), 14–32.

18. Elizabeth Blackmar, *Manhattan For Rent, 1785–1850* (Ithaca, N.Y., 1989), 184–199.

19. In 1793 and 1797 the fine was set at 40 s.; in 1799 this was converted to 5 dollars. [New York City], *Laws and Ordinances . . .* (New York, 1793), 23–24; [New York City], *Laws and Ordinances . . .* (New York, 1797), 32; [New York City], *Laws and Ordinances . . .* (New York, 1799), 24–25.

20. Sidney I. Pomerantz, *New York: An American City, 1783–1803: A Study of Urban Life* (New York, 1938), 237–246.

21. [New York City], *Laws and Ordinances . . .* (New York, 1801), 39–40.

22. MCC, III, 473, 493, 505, 589, 603, 609. See also Petition of A. L. Degrove, Feb. 4, 1805, File Papers, NYCMA.

23. Repeal left conditions much as they had been before the law's passage. Degrove, facing financial ruin, persuaded his friends on the council to allow him to keep a monopoly of sweeping in one district for 3 years. Petition of Degrove, Feb. 4, 1805, File Papers, NYCMA; Report of [the] Committee on [the] Petition of Adolph Degrove, Mar. 13, 1805, ibid.

24. [New York City], *Laws and Ordinances . . .* (New York, 1805), 70–71. The one new provision allowed the fire wardens to issue fines without the magistrates' mediation.

25. [New York City], *Laws and Ordinances . . .* (New York, 1808), 52–53.

26. Report of the Committee of Fire Wardens, Nov. 19, 1810, File Papers, NYCMA.

27. Boyreau had his plan privately printed; Boyreau, *Plan for Establishing a General Chimney Office in the City of New-York* (New York, 1811), Mar. 4, 1811, File Papers, NYCMA.

28. Report of Committee on Sweeping of Chimneys, Apr. 21, 1811, File Papers, NYCMA; MCC, VI, 606.

29. The 1820 U. S. census included 14 sweep households: 6 had no male youths under age 14; one had one male youth; 6 had two male youths; and one had 6. The census does not indicate whether any were apprentices. It appears that there was no clear pattern of

residence for apprentice sweeps. See also Phillips, *American Chimney Sweeps*, 59, and Giblin, *Chimney Sweeps*, 17–18.

30. Report [of the] Committee on [the] Plan of J[ohn] Boyreau, Mar. 18, 1811, File Papers, NYCMA; Memorial to Legislature on the Subject of Sweeping Chimneys, May 18, 1811, ibid. Passage of the act is noted in *MCC*, VI, 357–358.

31. Phillips, *England's Climbing-Boys*, 1–56; Report from the Committee . . . on the Employment of Boys in Sweeping Chimneys . . . ; James Montgomery, ed., *The Chimney-Sweeper's Friend, and Climbing-Boy's Album* (New York, 1978; orig. pub. 1824). A good sampling of the English reform literature is found in *Improving the Lot of the Chimney Sweeps*. Final passage of a comprehensive reform act did not occur until 1840.

32. [New York] *Morning Chronicle*, Sept. 8, 1803.

33. Rock, *Artisans of the New Republic: The Tradesmen of New York City in the Age of Jefferson* (New York, 1979), 224.

34. Edwin Olson, "Social Aspects of the Slave in New York," *J. Negro Hist.*, XXVI, No. I (1941), 66–77; John L. Rury, "Philanthropy, Self Help, and Social Control: The New York Manumission Society and Free Blacks, 1785–1810," *Phylon*, XLVI (1985), 231–241; Robert J. Swan, "John Teasman: African-American Educator and the Emergence of Community in Early Black New York City, 1787–1815," *Journal of the Early Republic*, XII (1992), 331–356; Harry B. Yoshpe, "Record of Slave Manumissions in New York During the Colonial and Early National Periods," *J. Negro Hist.*, XXVI, No. I (1941), 78–107; White, *Somewhat More Independent*, 81–88. See also "Records of the New York City Manumission Society," microfilm, New-York Historical Society.

35. Memorial of Society for Manumission of Slaves on Subject of boys employed as Sweeps, Dec. 23, 1811, File Papers, NYCMA. See also Minutes of the New York Manumission Society, Nov. 13, 1811, "Records of the New York City Manumission Society," microfilm reel II, 278, 296–298.

36. Report of Charity Committee, Jan. 17, 1812, File Papers, NYCMA. Clerk John Morton noted that the council would report an ordinance agreeable to the report of the committee. Report of John Morton, Apr. 27, 1812, ibid.

37. *MCC*, VII, 138. For the ordinance see [New York City], *Laws and Ordinances* . . . (New York, 1817), 121–123.

38. *MCC*, V, 673, 681.

39. Gilje, *The Road to Mobocracy: Popular Disorder in New York City, 1763–1834* (Chapel Hill, N. C., 1987), 153–158; Gilje and Rock, eds., *Keepers of the Revolution*, 208–243; Ottley and Weatherby, eds., *Negro in New York*, 53–56; Nash, "Forging Freedom"; Daniel Perlman, "Organizations of the Free Negro in New York City, 1800–1860," *J. Negro Hist.*, LVI, No. 3 (1971), 181–197; Swan, "John Teasman"; George E. Walker, *The Afro-American in New York City, 1827–1860* (New York, 1993); John J. Zuille, *Historical Sketch of the New York African Society for Mutual Relief* (New York, 1892). See also Christopher Rush, *A Short Account of the Rise and Progress of the African Methodist Episcopal Church in America* (New York, 1843), 9–29.

40. See, for example, the report of the celebration of congressional prohibition of the international slave trade in *New York Evening Post*, Dec. 16, 1807.

41. White, *Somewhat More Independent*, 150–151.

42. Dixon Ryan Fox, "The Negro Vote in Old New York," *Political Science Quarterly*, XXII (1917), 252–275; Herman D. Bloch, "The New York Negro's Battle for Political Rights, 1777–1865," *International Review of Social History*, IX (1964), 65–80.

43. The petitions and documents discussed below were transcribed for the master sweeps and reflect the language of officialdom. James Hardie identified himself as the amanuensis on one petition, and his handwriting appears on most of the others. Hardie, born and educated in Scotland, had an eclectic career in New York City as an educator, author, and literary jack-of-all-trades. His publications indicate that he was familiar with all levels of society in the city. Despite the fact that Hardie gave a certain cast to the language, we believe that the ideas, emotions, and even many of the words reflect the intentions of the sweeps. "James Hardie," in Francis S. Drake, *Dictionary of American*

Biography, Including Men of the Time . . . (Boston, 1872), 406–407. Hardie's publications on New York included *An Account of the Malignant Fever, lately Prevalent in the City of New-York [1798]* . . . (New York, 1799); *An Account of the Malignant Fever which Prevailed in the City of New-York during the Autumn of 1805* . . . (New York, 1805); *An Account of the Yellow Fever, which Occurred in the City of New-York, in the Year 1822* . . . (New York, 1822); *A Census of the New Buildings Erected in this City, in the year 1824* . . . (New York, 1825); and *The Description of the City of New-York* . . . (New York, 1827).

44. Petition of Chimney Sweepers to the Common Council, n.d., (in 1818 box but clearly from 1815–1816), File Papers, NYCMA.

45. The master sweeps described the functions of this mutual relief society in several petitions to the Common Council, Petition of Henry Lawson and Cornelius Schurman, Feb. 19, 1818 (misdated 1817), File Papers, NYCMA; Petition of Cornelius Schurman et al., Dec. 11, 1817, ibid.; Remonstrance of Chimney Sweeps, Dec. 15, 1817, ibid.; Petition of Henry Lawson, et al., Jan. 5, 1818, ibid.; and Petition of Henry Lawson, et al., Feb. 23, 1818, ibid. On black associations see Perlman, "Organizations of the Free Negro," 181–197. On artisan associations see Rock, *Artisans of the New Republic*, 128–143, 273–275.

46. For the identity of those who opposed the anticrying law and a discussion of efforts to identify master sweeps see the appendix [p. 290].

47. Memorial of Adam Marshall, Aug. 26, 1816, File Papers, NYCMA.

48. *MCC*, VIII, 613, 620; Resolution of the Common Council, Aug. 26, 1816, File Papers, NYCMA.

49. Petition of the Chimney Sweeps, Dec. 2, 1816, File Papers, NYCMA; Memorial of Citizens in Support of Sweep Masters, Sept. 6, 1818, ibid.

50. In the same year, 1817, citizens petitioned the Common Council to keep swine from running freely in the street, where they posed a serious hazard to pedestrians. Once the council passed such an ordinance, the poor and their advocates countered that they would have no food in the winter nor would the garbage be removed from their streets. Again the council reversed itself and allowed the pigs to roam, which they continued to do in many wards until the 1850s; Rock, ed., *The New York City Artisan, 1789–1825: A Documentary History* (Albany, N. Y., 1989), 35–36, 41–44, 101–111.

51. Petition on Sweeps, Feb. 7, 1817, File Papers, NYCMA; *MCC*, VII, 625, 700, 718, 724, IX, 12.

52. The rate structure elaborated in earlier laws detailed charges depending on the number of floors in a building and the kind of stove in the fireplace. For each chimney swept, the master was paid 15½ cents for the uppermost floor, 18½ cents for the next floor, 25 cents for the next floor, 30¼ cents for the next floor, 37½ cents for the next floor, and 40 cents for the next floor. If there was a Franklin stove, coal grate, or jack—a machine inserted in the chimney that took advantage of drafts to turn a roasting spit— a further 12½ cents was due. [New York City], *Laws and Ordinances* . . . (New York, 1817), 121–123.

53. On Dec. 22, 1817, the committee on chimney sweeps filed its report. Report of the Special Committee of the Common Council, Dec. 22, 1817 (appended to proposed ordinance), File Papers, NYCMA. On Feb. 16, 1818, a printed ordinance similar to the Dec. 22 proposal was put before the Common Council. An Ordinance Relative to the Sweeping of Chimneys for the Prevention of Fire in the City of New York and for the Appointment of a Superintendent of Sweeps, ibid.

54. An Ordinance Relative. . . , Feb. 16, 1818.

55. Remonstrance of Chimney Sweeps, Dec. 15, 1817, Petition of Lawson and Schurman, Feb. 19, 1818 (misdated 1817), File Papers, NYCMA.

56. Petition of Lawson and Schurman, Feb. 19, 1818 (misdated 1817). The documentation does not indicate which school they were to attend. They could have attended the Manumission Society's African Free School. But in 1812 African-American leaders in New York City, disgruntled over the paternalism of the Manumission Society, began organizing their own schools. The reference to tuition suggests that the sweeps were to attend the latter. Swan, "John Teasman"; Charles C. Andrews, *History of the New-York*

African Free Schools . . . (New York, 1969; orig. pub. 1830); Enid Vivian Barnett, "Educational Activities By and in Behalf of the Negroes in New York, 1800–1830," *Negro History Bulletin,* XIV (1951), 99–102, 113–114.

57. Petition of Lawson et al., Jan. 3, 1818, File Papers, NYCMA.

58. Remonstrance of the Chimney Sweeps, Dec 15, 1817, ibid.; Petition of Lawson et al., Jan. 3, 1818.

59. Remonstrance of the Chimney Sweeps, Dec. 15, 1817.

60. Petition of Lawson, Feb. 23, 1818.

61. Memorial of the Chimney Sweeps, Dec. 11, 1817, File Papers, NYCMA, Petition of Lawson and Schurman, Feb. 19, 1818 (misdated); Petition of Lawson, Jan. 3, 1818. On the place of licensed trades in New York see Rock, *Artisans of the New Republic,* chap. 8; Rock, *The New York City Artisan,* 161–178; and Hodges, *New York City Cartmen, 1667–1850* (New York, 1986).

62. On the political rights of blacks see Gilje and Rock, eds., *Keepers of the Revolution,* 208–212, 237–243; White, *Somewhat More Independent,* 150–151; and Petition of Lawson and Schurman, Feb. 8, 1818 (misdated 1817).

63. Petition of Lawson, Jan. 3, 1818.

64. Report of the Special Committee, Dec. 22, 1817, File Papers, NYCMA; *MCC,* IX, 390, 393, 425, 431, 438, 450, 474, 478, 483, 491, 500, 512, 536, 548.

65. The race and method of operation of the men who introduced machinery into the trade had to be pieced together from a variety of sources. Three of the 6 men were identified in the city directories and jury lists; they were clearly white. Another came from Boston explicitly to peddle his machinery. One of the "inventors" was a merchant, another a doctor. A third set up several offices in the city during the 1820s. *MCC,* IX, 601, 620, 690, X, 67, 75, 645, 659, 678, XI, 323. *Longworth's Directory* (New York, 1817–1819); New York City Jury and Census List, 1819, NYCMA. See also *N. Y. Evening Post,* May 29, 1818, and Phillips, *American Chimney Sweeps,* 68–73.

66. On the transformation of artisan crafts after 1820 see Sean Wilentz, *Chants Democratic: New York City and the Rise of the American Working Class, 1788–1850* (New York, 1984), chap. 3.

67. Petition of the Sweep Masters, Apr. 23, 1821, File Papers, NYCMA. The petition was referred to the Committee on Public Offices, which on June 11 recommended registering patent sweeps. *MCC,* XI, 685, 726. For a similar controversy see ibid., XVI, 592.

68. One reason that the traditional method was still in use was that patent machines could not clean all flues with right angle turns unless adjusted at each angle. Phillips, *American Chimney Sweeps,* 40, 69.

69. Among many works on this subject are Davis, *Problem of Slavery;* Frey, *Water from the Rock;* Berlin and Hoffman, ed., *Slavery and Freedom;* Nash, *Forging Freedom: The Formation of Philadelphia's Black Community, 1720–1840* (Cambridge, Mass., 1988); Nash, *Race and Revolution* (Madison, Wis., 1990); and White, *Somewhat More Independent.*

70. Nash, *Forging Freedom;* White, *Somewhat More Independent.* See also Julie Winch, *Philadelphia's Black Elite: Activism, Accommodation, and the Struggle for Autonomy, 1787–1848* (Philadelphia, 1988).

71. Snow, "John Teasman," 339–343.

72. Rock, *New York City Artisan,* 195–198.

PART THREE

NINETEENTH-CENTURY
BLACK
MALE
CULTURE

TEN

Black Musicians from Slavery to Freedom: An Exploration of an African-American Folk Elite and Cultural Continuity in the Nineteenth-Century Rural South

PAUL A. CIMBALA

During the nineteenth century, black instrumentalists enjoyed a special position in the rural black community of the American South. In the antebellum slave quarters, they earned the status of a folk elite because of their contribution to community life.[1] Like their sacred counterpart, the preachers, "musicianers," as their neighbors called them, provided opportunities for slaves to come together to recreate a sense of community in one of the few social outlets available to them—the frolic, the secular counterpart of the Sunday prayer meeting. Emancipation, however, brought new challenges to that community and the transition from a pre-political slave community to a freedmen's community that was acutely aware of the importance of political activity placed new demands on its leaders.[2]

Musicianers did not respond to the political challenge of Reconstruction in ways that broke clearly with their old roles in African-American society. Consequently, they did not participate in any substantial way in the new political dimension of rural black life in which ex-slaves would attempt to define the parameters of freedom. Nevertheless, war, emancipation, and Reconstruction had not completely altered black community life in the rural South. Musicians, the community's secular ministers, continued to play a central role in African-American social and cultural life, a role that may have had a greater impact than politics on the continued strength of the African-American community prior to the era of the civil rights movement. The frolic became the fish fry, house party, or picnic. Reels, jigs, and ballads eventually made way for the more individualistic blues. Guitars replaced fiddles as the most popular instrument. But musicians remained at the center of their folk culture and rural black society by providing the southern black community with the opportunity to come together to revive its collective spirit on a regular basis. In this respect, well into the twentieth century, Virginia Piedmont, Mississippi Delta, Texas, and other blues musicians continued a tradition that had its roots in the slave quarters of the antebellum South.[3]

Before the Civil War, slave musicianers, like other skilled slaves, were uniquely qualified to set themselves apart from most of their neighbors. Because of their talent, they could lay claim to privileges associated with freedom that ordinary field hands could not. Since the job of musician was a menial one by the standards of the upper orders of white southern society and since white Southerners needed musicians to entertain at their social functions, slave musicianers used their talents to their advantage much as any slave craftsman might have done. Consequently, musicians enjoyed more freedom of movement than the average slave, because they received passes to travel to and perform at various white social functions. While performing their art, they escaped constant white supervision, earned a steady if small source of income, gained confidence and self-respect, and generally loosened their personal bonds of slavery.[4]

The rewards earned by serving the needs of their white masters clearly impressed fellow bondsmen, but they were only partially and secondarily responsible for the status of slave musicianers. More important than any privilege won from white society were the services that they performed for their own people.[5] In the antebellum slave quarters, musicianers claimed the status of a folk elite primarily because of their contributions to community life. As performers, slave musicians assumed an indispensable role in the frolic, one of the two most important widespread and regularly held social events in the slave South, the other being the prayer service.

Interestingly, while there is some evidence of tension between the sacred and secular in the slave community, frolics coexisted peacefully with religious services. There are examples of slaves attending dances on Saturday night and prayer meetings on Sunday mornings. In fact, the two could easily find themselves on different points of the same social continuum. Ex-slave Eli Coleman, for example, recalled that the slaves would dance until their master came to tell them to get ready for Sunday services.[6] And there are examples of slaves, like Ol' Tom, a resident of a Fayette County, Texas plantation, who served their communities as both preacher and musician.[7]

The frolic, like its sacred counterpart, provided opportunities for African Americans to come together to recreate themselves as a community.[8] Importantly, it was a community whose boundaries spread beyond the confines of one plantation, as masters often allowed slaves to visit other plantations for these festivities.[9] Texas ex-slave Andy McAdams noted the wide draw the frolic would have when he remembered that slaves came "from all around to have a good time" at a function "that was the only time that the slaves ever had to get together."[10]

As McAdams suggested, the frolic provided slaves with one of the few social occasions where they could enjoy themselves and "do as we pleased."[11] Often the frolic provided slaves with the opportunity to escape white supervision or observation, thereby functioning as one means for subverting white authority. At the frolic there was "no one to bother or interfere with us," John McAdams, another ex-slave, noted. "The white people they never bothered with us on these times at all unless we raised too much hell."[12] Mary Gaffney, an ex-slave who reviewed the events of her life about ninety years after her birth in Mississippi, fondly remembered the frolic for these very reasons:

> "That was the happiest time of the slaves because the rest of the time it was like being a convict, we had to do just like Maser told us. We would get together and dance, talk and have our fun, Maser he would not be there to holler instructions at us. I will never forget them old dances out there in the woods . . . These dances lasted all night long as they was no one to bother us and the next day was a holiday."[13]

Anna Lee, a former slave from Tennessee, confirmed Mary Gaffney's assessment.

> "That was about the only time we ever were allowed to be together and have some fun," she recalled. "You know we had to have some way to see the other sex and be together, and that was the only time that our Maser allowed us to be together just among ourselves, and we sure made the best of it cause we generally danced, hollered and had our fun all night long."[14]

The musicianers' role as the facilitator of the frolic placed them at the center of this communal gathering. And like the location of the preachers at the front of their congregations, the actual position of the musicians at frolics—usually a make-shift stage that allowed them to be heard and seen above the crowd—is suggestive of their central role in the social life of the slave community.[15] Aware of their role as performers, they further attracted attention to themselves by wearing costumes, some cutting impressive figures in bright-hued, long-tailed coats accented with gilt buttons and fancy shirts.[16] But most important for attracting attention to the players, of course, was the musicianers' ability to perform. Once center stage and in front of energetic dancers, slave instrumentalists did not simply make music—they entertained, understanding very well that they were the critical element for a successful frolic.[17]

When the music began, the players exercised a potent force over the crowd, and the audience's appreciative response to their tunes only encouraged their confidence. Kate Betters, who was born in Mississippi in 1848, told of her experiences with one musician:

"An dey'd fotch ole Jim Long from 'cross de ribber to play. He'd come wid he fiddle, grinnin' an scrapin' cause he shore wuz a notable fiddler. When dat old 'him 'ud shake dat bow, you couldn't help you foot a-pattin a leetle, excusin ef you wuz a member of de church. In er minute, dey all 'ud be flyin roun de room an' old Jim, he 'us be a-rockin like a boat on de ribber . . . he big foot set way out, er-pattin to keep de time." No wonder Jim's face lit up, "he teef a-grinnin like de full moon."[18]

He was playing his audience as much as he was playing his instrument.

Caught up in the sweeping excitement of a frolic and always eager to impress their audiences, musicians seemed to drive the crowd on to greater heights of activity by their own acrobatics. The Sea Island slaves of Pierce Butler, for example, were treated to "the feats of a certain enthusiastic banjo player, who seemed to thump his instrument with every part of his body at once."[19] And a dexterous Alabama slave "could scrape the fiddle and dance on, all at the same time."[20] Uncle Whit, an eighty-year-old ex-slave who danced and sang while playing, duly impressed a young W. C. Handy. Handy later explained that "A less expert fiddler . . . would have stomped both heels simultaneously, but a fancy performer like Uncle Whit could stomp right heel and left foot, making four beats to the bar."[21]

At times the excitement provided by the musicians at slave frolics was heightened by what some modern jazz musicians refer to as "cutting contests." Sam Forge, an ex-slave from Texas, was about fifteen years old "w'en freedom cum." He recalled a fiddlers' contest that could have taken place before or after the Civil War but undoubtedly had its roots in the antebellum slave quarters:

"W'en de leader say 'Go', to de fiddlers, dey all start to fiddlin' at once, dey play dey own tunes, an' each one of dem pat his foot to keep time to dey music. Den dey all stop an' let one of de fiddlers play by himself, he would flip his fiddle over his head, den behin his back an' away on hit, den he raise hit over his head, den under his right, den his left leg, an' keep right on a playin' till de leader calls on him to 'Halt'. Den dey all line up for dey contest."

After this warm-up, Forge noted that "each man plays his best" usually with someone accompanying the featured musician with straw beating or guitar playing or in ensemble playing, each musicianer striving to "show what dey kin do." "Dey play each by turn on an' on for two, three hours." Finally, "dey has de judges to call off who won de first place, an' dey most always has hit to be somebody dat pleases dem all."[22]

When not vigorously entertaining their friends and neighbors in this manner, musicianers also served their communities in the role of folklorists and teachers. While these roles were not exclusively the domain of the musicianers, their place in the community suggests that they probably were important communicators of tradition. Mack Chaney's father, for example, played his fiddle for dances, but the son remembered him singing emotionally about the father's mother, who had been left behind in "Africa—Dat Good Ole Land."[23] And a Tennessee slave fiddler named George passed along black folk culture in the singing and dancing lessons he gave to the children in his slave community. In this case, the white observer who recorded George's activities gave the impression that the musicianer, at least on this particular plantation, dominated this type of activity. The other adult slaves may have deferred to George's talent at least in the more formal instructions that he gave to the youngsters.[24]

Of course, slave musicians contributed most obviously to the continuity of African-American folk life by passing on their skills and songs to a new generation of players. In this role, they guaranteed that the community would continue to come together to recreate itself at the frolic. While many players were self-taught, many of those were probably inspired by the example of older players while many others learned how to handle an instrument under the direction of a more experienced slave musicianer. Ex-slave William Grant "learned to fiddle after the fiddler on the place" and Margaret Hughes remembered an uncle who taught other slaves how to play the fiddle.[25] Another slave musician impressed a Northern governess with a beautiful violin solo he had learned from his father.[26]

Because of these activities, musicians identified themselves by their skill and took pride in their ability, which they considered a special talent.[27] But a feeling of self-importance is not enough if one is to be considered a member of an elite. The community itself must acknowledge the specialist's contributions.[28] Complicating matters for slave musicians in the area of recognition was the fact that active community participation in musical pastimes, like the active participation of worshippers at a Sunday service, could easily blur the boundaries between performer and audience. Good dancers, juba patters, and singers were numerous and enjoyed recognition in their own right. Musicianers, however, commanded a degree of prestige enhanced by the fact that most slaves did not perform on an instrument. As Uncle Warrie, an old fiddler who had been a slave on a plantation near Lancaster, North Carolina, understood, that particular talent was not equally distributed. "Co'se, if a man ain't got music in him, 't ain't no use fo' him ter fiddle," he explained. "Music is bawn in er man. . . . If he's musical, he *is* [*sic*], an' de good Lawd's responsible. If he ain't den he better set an' lessen to de others playin'."[29]

The slaves themselves agreed, critically appraising the music they heard. Even a homely row of quills became a recognized medium for virtuoso performers who sometimes organized themselves into ensembles dignified with the leadership of a most accomplished "captain."[30] While these cane pan's pipes were simple enough for children to construct and use, skillful musicians played them effectively and won high praise for their grand dance music.[31]

Ex-slave Sam Forge no doubt expected much of a musician after his experiences with Texas fiddlers who "put de life dey lives into de music of de fiddle, you kin hear de wild coyotes call an' de panthers shrill scream, de lowin' of de cattle in de fiddle's music."[32] Unsurprisingly, for some former slaves who recalled the music of their past, the modern sounds they heard emanating from radios or phonographs could not hold a candle to the tunes played by their musicians. Willie Black, a former South Carolina slave who claimed to be 103 years old in 1937, after recalling the words to "Run, Nigger, Run," the widespread antebellum song about slave patrols, emphatically pronounced his judgment:

> "Ise tell you right now, de music dem words am set to make dese Cab Calloways of today git to de woods an' hide. Long's a man warnst so drunk he's plum out, he jus' have to git up an' jig or dance w'en dat music starts. Yes suh! I aint foolin' a-tall."[33]

In the antebellum South, slaves further recognized the musicianers as important members of their community by acknowledging the fact that their skills demanded some kind of reward. Rarely was cash available to pay for performances, but slaves proffered other tokens of their esteem and special privileges as concrete signs that they appreciated what their musicianers were doing for them.[34] Young women paid special attention to them.[35] Importantly, some community members acknowledged talent by remembering individuals specifically as "musicianers" even if those players, like South Carolina ex-slave Ben Horry's father and uncles, had other plantation jobs or by adding the sobriquet "fiddler" to their names.[36] These naming practices contributed an attractive distinction among slaves who were part of an institution that had as one of its implicit goals the destruction of black pride, confidence, and identity, all qualities joyfully personified in the "musicianer."

Finally, slaves paid special tribute to their musicianers by making their favorite trickster, Br'er Rabbit, a fiddler and by recounting stories concerning their musicians in the same style as the animal trickster tales. Interestingly, Lawrence W. Levine, in his thorough study of slave culture, clearly describes the importance of the trickster but fails to make any connection with slave musicians.[37] Also, Bennet Siems in a recent article makes a strong connection between the twentieth-century bluesman and the slave trickster but completely misses the fact that slaves were recounting stories about their musicianers in this manner long before bluesman Robert Johnson went down to the crossroads.[38]

In one animal tale from Texas, for example, Br'er Fox schemed to hurry Br'er Rabbit to his demise by having his wife request that Br'er Rabbit "git he fiddle and play de las chune [tune] ober Bre'r Fox' head" while Br'er Fox played 'possum. Br'er Rabbit, fiddle in hand, divined the plot, tricked Br'er Fox into revealing himself, and escaped Br'er Fox's clutches.[39] Importantly, Br'er Rabbit's musical talent was central to Br'er Fox's plot, and not incidental to the story.

Alabama ex-slave Jake Green recalled an event that placed the musician in a role with which the trickster rabbit would have been quite comfortable. Slave Dick, "what claim sick all de time," earned a reprieve from all labor from his master. "He was a fiddler," Green explained, "so dey jes' tuck his vittuls to him for seven years," revealing in the telling the worth that slaves ascribed to musical talent. But even a clever slave, like Br'er Rabbit himself, could fall victim to hubris. This cautionary story ended unhappily for the fiddler: "Den one day, Old Massa say to de overseer man, 'Let's slip up dere an' see what Dick doin'.' So dey di an' dere sot Dick, fat as he could be a playin' de fiddle an a singin'[:]

> 'Fool my Massa seben years.
> Gwiner fool him seben mo'.
> Hey diddle, de diddle, de diddle, de do'.'"

The master quickly put Dick back to work.[40]

Thus during slavery, musicianers triumphed, relaxing the physical and psychological restraints of their own personal bondage while gaining the respect of their communities for contributing to the social, cultural, and psychological well-being of the group. The musicianer's role in the slave community, however, could be viewed in two contradictory, although not necessarily mutually exclusive, ways. There is no evidence that musicianers used their status to attack—in the modern sense of political or violent resistance—the institution that suppressed them. In fact, by presenting the slave community with an emotional outlet and by making the community aware of itself and what it had to lose if its members actively challenged the system, musicianers could be viewed as a conservative force.

On the other hand, one must understand that the slave community was a pre-political community deprived of the conventional avenues through which leadership is usually expressed. By acting as entertainers and teachers, musicianers helped maintain a black culture and, most importantly, a sense of community that helped the slaves of the American South endure. In the role of the facilitator of culture and of community identity, in fact, musicianers could be considered subversive in that they actively nurtured resistance to the white domination of the black soul. It is this interpretation that is more considerate of slave life and of the role played by musicians in the preservation of the African-American community.

With emancipation, leadership in the freedmen's community found expression in roles that had never before been open to the old slave elite. The pre-political slave community adapted to the new circumstances and became very much aware of the new political opportunities—indeed, requirements—of freedom. On the Georgia coast, which came under Union control before the end of the Civil War, black residents established local plantation-based governments, and in the Ogeechee district in Chatham County near Savannah, Georgia, freedmen elected representatives from their neighborhoods to form a board of advisors to the area's federal agent.[41] Immediately after the conclusion of the war, ex-slaves expressed their expectations in a convention movement that swept across the South; the slave elite joined northern black missionaries and teachers in what historian Leon Litwack called "the political debut of southern blacks."[42] In Georgia, for example, such a convention established the Georgia Equal Rights and Education Association, which formed local chapters across the state and thus gave politically inexperienced freedmen the opportunity to explore more formal leadership roles.[43] Finally, the South-wide commencement of Congressional Reconstruction in 1867 provided the political climate in which freedmen were able to elect some of their numbers to constitutional conventions as well as local, state, and national office.[44] In other words, these conventional positions of leadership and status provided opportunities for the black elite to assume modern political leadership roles that had been unavailable during slavery time.

During this period of political change, the social context in which musicians had acted as cultural leaders during slavery did not remain untouched by the transition to freedom. The ex-slaves' quest for autonomy, for example, led them to withdraw from white-dominated churches and establish congregations of their own. That quest for autonomy also prompted the freedmen to place much of their energy and resources into formal education. Significantly, it motivated the freedmen to bargain for new labor arrangements that ultimately encouraged them to break up the old slave quarters and scatter their homes among the plots of land they came to sharecrop, tenant farm, or rent.[45] Consequently, while emancipation provided opportunities, it also challenged the black status quo of the slave quarters.

Some things, however, did not change. Within this transformation of the black rural community from one of slaves to one of free individuals, musicianers continued to function in their traditional roles of repository of folk culture and lightning rod of community identity. Ex-slave musicians, for example, continued to pass on their skills to a new generation of performers just as they had done before emancipation. Simpson Campbell, who had been born a slave in Harrison County, Texas, in 1860, recalled, "One of the oldest fiddlers of slavery time teached my brother Flint to play the fiddle."[46]

Sometimes, just the presence of musicians in a neighborhood inspired youngsters like the Louisiana native and famous jazzman Kid Ory to learn the craft by watching and listening to the adult musicians play, a practice that should not discount the importance of the adult musicians' role as the transmitter of musical skill.[47] Texas guitarist Mance Lipscomb claimed to be a self-taught musician. "I started out by myself, just heard it and learned it," he bragged. "Ear music. And nobody didn't learn me nothin'." Yet his father, an ex-slave, was a popular fiddler with whom Lipscomb performed. Lipscomb's "ear music" was more likely than not his father's music.[48]

Sam Chatmon, who along with his brothers, became well-known in the South as the Mississippi Sheiks, "started out from [his] parents." He explained that "it's a gift we had in the family. Our mother and our father they could both play. And see, he was an old musicianer in slavery time."[49] Henderson Chatmon, the patriarch of this musical clan, was also the father of Charley Patton, the purported founder of Mississippi Delta–style blues. Not surprisingly, Patton picked up the basis for his vocal and instrumental techniques from his father's generation of Chatmons.[50]

The practice of an older generation of musicians passing on their skills and songs to a younger one certainly outlived the last slave musicianer. Rural black musicians continued to teach their children, grandchildren, and friends, serving as a repository for the community's musical tradition well into the twentieth century. John Cephas, a Virginia Piedmont bluesman and a recent winner of a W. C. Handy award, recalled that his inspiration was his grandfather John Dudley, "a guitar player, a gambler, [and] a ladies' man," who showed him the "true essence" of music.[51] And Jo Jo Williams, another twentieth-century bluesman, believed that his family roots had determined his destiny, although family example probably had more to do with his interest in music: "A lot of my foreparents was musicians, as far as I understand, so for that particular reason I guess it's just something that fell on me."[52]

Clearly, the link with the past remained strong even as tastes and styles changed. As a new generation of bluesmen emerged in the rural black community during the 1920's, 1930's and 1940's, their members continued to learn from the older black fiddle, guitar, and banjo pickers,[53] who in turn had been influenced by their slave and freedmen friends and relatives. As Archie Edwards, another contemporary Virginia Piedmont bluesman, explained, "But I still play a lot of the songs I learned when I was a kid. I picked up on all the old-timers."[54]

After emancipation, the "foreparents" of Jo Jo Williams, Sam Chatmon, and John Cephas carried on their business within the freedmen's community much as they had done during slavery. The social context for performing changed little and consequently the musicianers' source of status remained available. Musicians like Mance Lipscomb's father continued to travel to social functions—black and white—earning their musical reputations as they earned money above and beyond the wages of their "day jobs." But while whites provided musicians with the prestige that could come with extra income, black audiences continued to provide plenty of opportunities for their musicianers to assume the mantle of community celebrity. Historian Vernon Wharton, for example, notes in his study of Blacks in Mississippi during the latter part of the nineteenth century that the African-American community enjoyed picnics that were day-long affairs. Ex-slaves and their children gathered to gossip, feast, play ball, listen to and make speeches, and, of course, dance to the tunes of their musicianers.[55] In Louisiana, Kid Ory and his fellow musicians went one step further; they held their own fish fries to draw an audience together.[56] Incidentally, as Dave Evans has documented in his observations of black fife and drum bands, the tradition of marathon get-togethers continued in Mississippi at least into the 1970's with the African-American community participating in weekend-long gatherings that featured music and dancing in the evenings.[57]

Functions such as these Mississippi picnics—fish fries, house parties or whatever name the gathering assumed—drew the freed black community together to recreate itself much as the ante-bellum frolics had done. In 1867 in Clarke County, Alabama, freedpeople gathered to listen and dance to the music of a fiddler who wore his musicianer's uniform of top hat and tails.[58] Even after new labor arrangements drew some of a community's members away from their antebellum residences, traditional gatherings brought them back home again. F. J. Jackson recalled returning to his old plantation on the Georgia coast for the "big times" at Saturday night dances after work had drawn him away from the home place.[59] And Harry Johnson, an ex-Arkansas slave who moved to Texas after the war, remembered dancing all night and then riding thirty miles the next day to return home, suggesting that the postbellum frolic helped to define a community that stretched beyond the boundaries of local towns or plantations.[60]

Like the Sunday church meeting, its sacred counterpart, the frolic gave the ex-slaves an opportunity to identify themselves as a community. And just as before the war, the frolic had its symbolic and real focal point in the musicians who performed for the community, musicians who could shine as the most important element of the evening's entertainment, musicians who could assume their position of importance at center stage. The cocky attitude of the musicians and their art of performance survived as well. At a Georgia corn shucking probably held in the late 1870's or early 1880's the fiddler assumed an air common to antebellum musicians. As a white observer noted, "The fiddler is the man of most importance on the ground. He always comes late, must have an extra share of whiskey, is the best-dressed man in the crowd, and unless every honor is shown him he will not play."[61]

Unsurprisingly, the cultural and social role of the musician in the rural black community remained fairly consistent into the middle of the twentieth century. One only has to read interviews with John Cephas, Archie Edwards, and other blues musicians to come across descriptions of performance venues, performance practices, and audience reaction that are remarkably similar to descriptions gathered from ex-slaves.[62] For example, David "Honeyboy" Edwards, who began playing blues in 1930, recalled that people still had respect for musicians at that time. "If they knew you played music they were nice to you," he explained, "bought you drinks, talk to you, and have a nice time."[63] John Cephas also noted that he was the "center of attraction" at many house parties, which often led to fights over women.[64] His experiences with women, except perhaps for the fights with jealous boy friends and husbands, were not all that different from those of some slave musicians. "All I got to do is get up there and sing good one night and kind of look at this woman and that's my woman," he explained.[65] At times it seems as if the bluesmen are paraphrasing the words of their slave ancestors.

While the cultural and social importance of the musicianer remained as it had been in slavery, there appears to have been no guarantee that this traditional and pre-political status and the confidence that went along with it were sufficient to encourage or allow musicianers to assume a more politically sophisticated leadership position in the freedmen's community. Undoubtedly, some musicians found their way into the local and state freedmen's meetings and conventions during 1865 and 1866; all sorts of freedmen did so, although specific examples of musicianers attending the gatherings are elusive. The political campaigns that drew large numbers of freedmen into electoral politics during 1867 and 1868 certainly found musicians participating in these events. Nevertheless, their role for the most part remained very traditional. Peter Hines, for example, led a band of black musicians who played for political rallies in Dougherty and Lee counties in the southwestern part of Georgia, one of the most dangerous areas in the state for black and white Republicans. Their fife and drum music attracted crowds of freedmen who would then listen to white and black politicians make their speeches. This kind of participation was not insignificant; in fact, it was essential for illiterate freedmen in rural areas where communication relied more on what was heard that on what was read. This role was also fraught with danger, since whites generally directed violence at individuals who conspicuously challenged their control. When a riot erupted at Camilla, Georgia, in September 1868, whites directed their first volley of gunfire at the bandwagon. No musician in Peter Hine's group escaped injury; one was killed.[66]

Still, while Hines and men like him played an important role in black political life, they were not the individuals making the speeches. When a Congressional committee conducted an investigation of Ku Klux Klan violence in the South, it heard testimony from many black leaders who had suffered because of their prominent political positions. Only James Alston, a freedman from Tuskegee, Alabama, identified himself as having been a slave musician.[67]

Of course, the dearth of musicians giving testimony to congressmen in Washington and at other cities in the South does not mean that the black community automatically excluded this traditional elite from the post-emancipation role of politician. Texas ex-slave Peter Robinson made the transition. However, his career suggests that the freedpeople's community quickly developed a degree of sophistication in assessing its political needs based on the new requirements and aspirations that developed during Reconstruction. Robinson, according to his wife Mariah, "played de fiddle all over de country" before and after the Civil War. Clearly, this activity allowed the musician to become better known among the slaves and the freedmen in his neighborhood than blacks who did not have this kind of mobility and visibility. But Robinson had other qualities that allowed him to become involved in the institution building of the freedmen's community. His wife remembered him as being " 'telligent and 'liable and de good man," one who worked hard and succeeded—probably with some assistance from the money he made playing at dances—in becoming what most blacks hoped to become in freedom: a landholder. Significantly, Peter Robinson "could write de plain hand." A hard worker known to the community, Robinson had a skill and a sense to use it. He became a teacher and a founder of the first black church in Meridian, Texas, the Cumberland Presbyterian Church. These two activities—education and institution building—placed Robinson at the center of the most important concern of ex-slaves: how to become autonomous of the white man. And while the recognition he received as a musician certainly helped, literacy and its uses in school and church matters probably moved Robinson into politics. According to his wife, he became a county trustee and eventually a state elective official.[68]

The role of politician, then, attracted individuals who held the respect of their people and at the same time were able to assume the more sophisticated styles of leadership demanded by a political culture defined by the majority society. It is not surprising to find that ministers, school teachers, free blacks, and northern blacks, who were more likely to be literate and involved in institution building than the musicians, assumed prominent positions in the political life of the southern black community. But remember: the period in which the freedmen actually participated in politics in significant numbers was short. By the end of the 1870's, southern states had shed themselves of Republican governments that had for the most part themselves allotted only a small portion of their power to black politicians.[69] And while into the next century a number of Blacks continued to participate in politics, voting and winning office in some localities, disfranchisement effectively excluded most freedmen and their children from extensive political participation until the second Reconstruction of the 1960's. The African-American community of the South once again was a community deprived of political expression. The black community would never forget the meaning of the word freedom, but, without politics, it returned to a social and cultural life that was closer to what it had known in slavery.

In the end, musicianers in slavery and freedom were much more than the stereotypical song-and-dance men of the minstrel stage. They were talented individuals who stretched the limits that a racist society attempted to impose on them. Furthermore, they were essential performers in the southern black community's efforts to persevere, acting as facilitators of communal recreation, comfort, and identity. Musicianers eased the troubled minds of their people and reminded them on regular occasions that they could smile. Most importantly, they were central figures at and the facilitators of the occasions that helped keep southern Blacks in touch with their sense of being a people. Even if not one of their number had stood for public office, they all had contributed to their community's resistance to white society's efforts to deprive the black South of its soul.

Chalmers Archer, Jr., a black educator, recalled growing up in Mississippi before the Civil Rights movement once again brought African Americans into the full political life of the nation and in the process testified to the long-lasting central role of the musician. The first house party that he attended — incidentally, he was from a church-going family — left a vivid impression on his memory. To celebrate graduation and a successful performance of a high school play, he and his friends made their way to the home of Mr. Joe, the "Blues Man," to participate in a "'downhome' country breakdown." Truly impressed by the experience, he became a life-long fan and frequenter of the blues house party. Importantly, he also grew to understand that there was more to the house party than fun: "I realized, later, that those gatherings communicated our values, our good times and bad times, and gave us a real sense of community."[70] Clearly, within the context of a community deprived of what white Americans would have considered to be acceptable avenues for leadership expression and community advancement, the more traditional role of musicianer remained an important force.

NOTES

1. Vocalists and even preachers may be considered musicians. However, in the context of this article, with its emphasis on individuals who brought their communities together in the frolic, instrumentalist, musician and "musicianer" are used interchangeably to refer to an individual skilled in performing on an instrument.

2. For information on the social arrangements of the slave community see John W. Blassingame, *The Slave Community: Plantation Life in the Ante-Bellum South* (New York, 1972); Eugene D. Genovese, *Roll, Jordan, Roll: The World the Slaves Made* (New York, 1974); and Leslie Howard Owens, *The Species of Property: Slave Life and Culture in the Old South* (New York, 1976). Historians of slavery and African-American music have generally ignored the role of the slave musician but Blassingame in *The Slave Community* (p. 56) notes that musical talent could earn a slave prestige within his community, praise from his white overlords, and some important self-esteem. Owens in *This Species of Property* (pp. 165–9) also briefly deals with the role of the musician. Gifted bondsmen, he explains, not only used their musical skill to gain the respect of both slaves and masters, but used their talent to stretch the limits of their own personal bondage. Both treatments are limited. Two of the most comprehensive treatments of African-American music, Eileen Southern's *The Music of Black Americans: A History*, 2nd ed. (New York: W. W. Norton & Co., 1983) and Dona J. Epstein, *Sinful Tunes and Spirituals: Black Folk Music to the Civil War* (Urbana, Illinois, 1977), acknowledge the importance of black musicians but their primary purpose is not to explore the slave musician's role in relation to the social structure of the black community. For the fullest discussion of slave musicians before the Civil War, see Paul A. Cimbala, "Fortunate Bondsmen: Black 'Musicians' in the Antebellum Southern United States" (M. A. thesis, Emory University, 1977) and Paul A. Cimbala, "Fortunate Bondsmen: Black 'Musicianers' and their Role as an Antebellum Southern Plantation Elite," *Southern Studies* (Fall 1979): 291–303.

3. The purpose of this article is not to provide an analysis of the changes in the music performed by the musicianers, although as discussed below there was a greater degree of continuity than suggested by the emphasis placed on Mississippi Delta blues during its rediscovery during the blues revival of the 1960's and 1970's. For a sample of the variety of music sung and played in the American South prior to this revival, one may consult the recordings presented in Alan Lomax's 1993 four compact disc set of field recordings originally issued on record in 1960 entitled *Sounds of the South: A Musical Journey from the Georgia Sea Islands to the Mississippi Delta* (Atlantic 7 82496-2) as well as numerous compact disc reissues from Yazoo Records of recordings made during the 1920's and

1930's including *Memphis Jug Band* (Yazoo 1067); Mississippi Sheiks, *Stop and Listen* (Yazoo 2006); *Don't Leave Me Here: The Blues of Texas, Arkansas, and Louisiana, 1927–1932* (Yazoo 1004); *East Coast Blues* (Yazoo 1013); *The Georgia Blues, 1927–1933,* (Yazoo 1012); and *The Roots of Robert Johnson* (Yazoo 1073). For a good example of recently recorded Virginia Piedmont blues, see Archie Edwards with Richard "Mr. Bones" Thomas featuring Mark Wenner's harmonica, *Blues 'N Bones* (Jazz Heritage 51295Y). From the written record, from the fact that slave musicians played for white dances, from the types of instruments used, and from the emphasis that many musicians placed on continuity with the past, it would be reasonable to assume that black dance music sounded close to how the Mississippi Sheiks and the Memphis jug bands sound on the above-noted recordings.

4. For an exploration of how slaves determined status, see John W. Blassingame, "Status and Social Structure in the Slave Community: Evidence from New Sources," in *Perspectives and Irony in American Slavery,* ed. Harry P. Owens (Jackson, 1976), 137–51. For a good example of how a slave used his talent to secure perquisites from his master, see Solomon Northup, *Twelve Years a Slave,* edited by Sue Eakin and Joseph Logsdon (Auburn, 1853; reprint, ed., Baton Rouge, 1986), 28–32, 181, 183, 196, 216. For a full treatment of the slave musicians' relationship with their masters, see Cimbala, "Fortunate Bondsmen: Black 'Musicians' in the Antebellum United States," 27–41. Also see Joseph Boskin, *Sambo: The Rise and Demise of an American Jester* (New York, 1986), 42–64, for details about the roles all slaves played as entertainers for white society in the antebellum plantation South. Boskin overemphasizes the desires of whites in shaping the role of entertainer and does not focus in detail on the social and cultural roles of the slave musicians within the black community, but he makes some interesting observations about black humor.

5. This is a point stressed by Blassingame, "Status and Social Structure," 137–51.

6. George P. Rawick, ed., *The American Slave: A Composite Autobiography* (supplement series 2, 10 vols., Westport, Conn., 1979), vol. 3: *Texas Narratives,* pt. 2, 843.

7. Rawick, ed., *American Slave,* supplement series 2, vol. 6: *Texas Narratives,* pt. 5, 2111.

8. The best account to date of the significance of a particular social event in the formation and preservation of African-American culture and the use of such occasions as a means for resisting white domination is Roger D. Abrahams's study of the corn shucking in *Singing the Master: The Emergence of African American Culture in the Plantation South* (New York, 1992). Abrahams makes an important contribution to the understanding of how the slave community functioned but concentrates on a social event that was seasonal by nature and not part of the normal routine throughout the year. He acknowledges that it was not "universally practiced throughout the plantation South" (*Singing the Master,* xxv). On the other hand, the frolic was held on a regular basis, was common throughout the South, and drew together individuals from beyond distinct plantation boundaries. Consequently, by the antebellum era the less frequently held social functions such as corn shuckings and weddings reinforced a culture and a community identity that was more frequently nurtured at the Saturday night frolic. For a treatment of black dance forms that were part of the frolic, see Katrina Hazzard-Gordon, *Jookin': The Rise of Social Dance Formations in African-American Culture* (Philadelphia, 1990).

9. For example, see, Rawick, ed., *American Slave,* supplement series 2, vol. 3: *Texas Narratives,* pt. 2, 498; vol. 2: *Texas Narratives,* pt. 1, 200–1; vol. 4, *Texas Narratives,* pt. 3, 1083, 1281; vol. 5: *Texas Narratives,* pt.4, 1561; and vol. 10; *Texas Narratives,* pt. 9, 4164.

10. Ibid., vol. 7: *Texas Narratives,* pt. 6, 2451.

11. Ibid., vol. 9: *Texas Narratives,* pt. 8, 3520.

12. Ibid., vol. 7: *Texas Narratives,* pt. 6, 2467.

13. Ibid., vol. 5: *Texas Narratives,* pt. 4, 1448.

14. Ibid., vol. 6: *Texas Narratives,* pt. 5, 2281.

15. William B. Smith, "The Persimmon Tree and the Beer Dance," *Farmers' Register*

6 (April 1838): 9, reprinted in Bruce Jackson, ed., *The Negro and His Folklore in Nineteenth-Century Periodicals* (Austin, Texas, 1967); J. H. Ingraham, ed., *The Sunny South; or, the Southerner at Home, Embracing Five Years' Experience of a Northern Governess in the Land of Sugar and Cotton* (Philadelphia, Pa.: G. G. Evans, 1860), 144; [Isaac D. Williams], *Sunshine and Shadow of Slave Life: Reminiscences as Told by Isaac D. Williams to "Tege"* (East Saginaw, Mich., 1885; reprint ed., New York, AMS Press, 1975), 61–62; Hanna Hardeman Meade, *When I Was a Little Girl: The Year's Round on the Old Plantation* (Los Angeles, 1916), 70, and George P. Rawick, ed., *The American Slave: A Composite Autobiography,* (19 vols., Westport, 1972), vol. 17; *Florida Narratives,* 244; and vol. 16; *Maryland Narratives,* 8.

16. Rawick, ed., *American Slave,* vol. 16: *Kentucky,* 95; and vol. 18: *Fisk University,* 251.

17. Ibid., vol. 16: *Ohio,* 3; and vol. 8: *Arkansas,* pt. 2, 109; and Orlando Kay Armstrong, *Old Massa's People: The Old Slaves Tell Their Story* (Indianapolis: Bobbs-Merrill Co., 1931), 141.

18. Rawick, ed., *American Slave,* supplement series 2, vol. 2: *Texas Narratives,* pt. 1, 262–3.

19. Frances Anne Kemble, *Journal of a Residence on a Georgian Plantation in 1838–1839,* ed. with an Introduction by John A. Scott (New York, 1962), 131.

20. Rawick, ed., *American Slave,* vol. 10: *Arkansas Narratives,* pt. 6, 327.

21. W. C. Handy, *Father of the Blues: An Autobiography,* ed. Arna Bontemps, with a Forward by Abbe Niles (New York, 1942), 6.

22. Rawick, ed., *American Slave,* supplement series 2, vol. 4: *Texas Narratives,* pt. 3, 1373–4.

23. George P. Rawick, ed., *The American Slave: A Composite Autobiography,* (supplemental series 1, 12 vols.; Westport: Greenwood Press, 1977), vol. 9: *Mississippi Narratives,* pt. 4, 1416–1418, 1428.

24. J. H. Ingraham, ed., *The Sunny South; or, the Southerner at Home, Embracing Five Years' Experience of a Northern Governess in the Land of Sugar and Cotton* (Philadelphia, 1860), 104.

25. Rawick, ed., *American Slave,* vol. 9: *Arkansas Narratives,* pt. 3, 12; and vol. 2: *South Carolina Narratives,* pt. 2, 327.

26. Ingraham, ed., *Sunny South,* 106.

27. Rawick, ed., *American Slave,* vol. 8: *Arkansas Narratives,* pt. 2, 109; vol. 16: *Ohio Narratives,* 3; and supplement series 2, vol. 6: *Texas Narratives,* pt. 5, 2408.

28. Alan P. Merriam, *The Anthropology of Music* ([Evanston], Illinois, 1964), 125.

29. Orlando Kay Armstrong, *Old Massa's People: The Old Slaves Tell Their Story* (Indianapolis, 1931), 141.

30. Rawick, ed., *American Slave,* vol. 13: *Georgia Narratives,* pt. 3, 206.

31. George Washington Cable, "The Dance in Place Congo," *Century Magazine,* 31 (February 1886), reprinted in Bruce Jackson, ed., *The Negro and His Folklore in Nineteenth-Century Periodicals* (Austin and London, 1967), 193; Rawick, ed., *American Slave,* vol. 2: *South Carolina Narratives,* pt. 2, 175; vol. 10: *Arkansas Narratives,* pt. 5, 161; vol. 12: *Georgia Narratives,* pt. 1, 99 and pt. 2, 197; and vol. 13: *Georgia Narratives,* pt. 3, 206.

32. Rawick, ed., *American Slave,* supplement series 2, vol. 4: *Texas Narratives,* pt. 3, 1374.

33. Ibid., vol. 2: *Texas Narratives,* pt. 1, 312.

34. Rawick, ed., *American Slave,* vol. 4: *Texas Narratives,* pt. 1, 79; James Hungerford, *The Old Plantation and What I Gathered There in an Autumn Month* (New York: Harper & Bros., 1859), 199; and Northup, *Twelve Years a Slave,* 217.

35. Rawick, ed., *American Slave,* supplement series 1, vol. 8: *Mississippi Narratives,* pt. 3, 1236–7; and A. J. H. Christensen, [comp.], *Afro-American Folk Lore Told Round Cabin Fires on the Sea Islands of South Carolina* (Boston: J. G. Cupples, Co., 1892), 3.

36. Rawick, ed., *American Slave,* vol. 2: *South Carolina Narratives,* pt. 2, 308; Charles Perdue, Jr., Thomas E. Barden, and Robert K. Phillips, eds., *Weevils in the Wheat:*

Interviews with Virginia Ex-Slaves (Charlottesville, Virginia, 1976), 225; Hungerford, *The Old Plantation*, 125; and Garnett Andrews, *Reminiscences of an Old Georgia Lawyer* (Atlanta, 1870), 21.

37. Lawrence W. Levine, *Black Culture and Black Consciousness: Afro-American Folk Thought from Slavery to Freedom* (New York, 1977), 81–135.

38. Bennet Siems, "Brer Robert: The Bluesman and the African American Trickster Tale Tradition," *Southern Folklore* 48 (1991): 141–58.

39. Rawick, ed., *American Slave,* supplement series 2, vol. 5: *Texas Narratives*, pt. 4, 1621.

40. Rawick, ed., *American Slave*, vol. 6: *Alabama Narratives*, 168.

41. Paul A. Cimbala, "The Freedmen's Bureau, the Freedmen, and Sherman's Grant in Reconstruction Georgia, 1865–1867," *Journal of Southern History*, 55 (November 1989): 602–3.

42. Leon Litwack, *Been in the Storm So Long: The Aftermath of Slavery* (New York, 1979), 503–24; quotation on 507.

43. Edmund L. Drago, *Black Politicians and Reconstruction in Georgia: A Splendid Failure* (Baton Rouge, 1982), 28.

44. Kenneth M. Stampp, *The Era of Reconstruction, 1865–1877* (New York, 1965), 155–85.

45. See Eric Foner, *Reconstruction: America's Unfinished Revolution, 1863–1877*, (New York, 1988) for a complete examination of the impact of freedom.

46. Rawick, ed., *American Slave*, supplement series 2, vol. 3: *Texas Narratives*, pt. 2, 612, 614.

47. Kathy J. Ogren, *The Jazz Revolution: Twenties America and the Meaning of Jazz* (New York, 1989), 27–8.

48. Paul Oliver, *Conversation with the Blues* (London, 1965), 27 (quotation), 38; Paul Oliver, *Savannah Syncopators: African Retentions in the Blues* (New York: Stein and Day, 1970), 85–6.

49. Oliver, *Conversation*, 45.

50. John Fahey, *Charley Patton* (London, 1970), 18.

51. Barry Lee Pearson, *Virginia Piedmont Blues: The Lives and Art of Two Virginia Bluesmen* (Philadelphia, 1990), 148.

52. Jeff Todd Titon, *Early Downhome Blues: A Musical and Cultural Analysis* (Urbana, 1977), 37.

53. This is a point B. B. King makes. See William Ferris, *Blues from the Delta* (New York, 1978; reprint ed., New York: Da Capo, 1984), 46.

54. Titon, *Early Downhome Blues*, 37.

55. Vernon L. Wharton, *The Negro in Mississippi, 1865–1890* (Chapel Hill, 1947), 268.

56. Ogren, *Jazz Revolution*, 27–8.

57. David Evans, "Black Fife and Drum Music in Mississippi," *Mississippi Folklore Register*, 6 (Fall 1972): 94–107.

58. See the unattributed etching in Giles Oakley, *The Devil's Music: A History of the Blues* (London, 1976), 18–19.

59. Georgia Writers' Project, *Drums and Shadows: Survival Studies among the Georgia Coastal Negroes* (Athens, Georgia, 1940; reprint ed. Athens, Georgia, 1986), 100.

60. Rawick, ed., *American Slave*, supplement series 2, vol. 6: *Texas Narratives*, pt. 5, 1194.

61. David C. Barrow, Jr., "A Georgia Corn-Shucking," *The Century Magazine*, 24 (October 1882): 878.

62. For example see Pearson, *Virginia Piedmont Blues*, passim; Barry Lee Pearson, *Sounds So Good to Me: The Bluesman's Story* (Philadelphia: University of Pennsylvania Press, 1984), passim; William Barlow, *"Looking Up at Down": The Emergence of Blues Culture* (Philadelphia, 1989), 4–5; but especially Zora Neale Hurston, *Mules and Men* (1935; reprint edition, New York, 1990), 60–5 for comments on musicians and frolics.

63. Pearson, *Sounds So Good to Me*, 12, 14 (quotation).

64. Pearson, *Virginia Piedmont Blues*, 164.

65. Ibid., 158.

66. Affidavit of Peter Hines, Sept. 23, 1868; affidavit of William Outlaw, Sept. 24, 1868; and affidavit of Howard Bunts, Sept. 24, 1868, roll 22, Records of the Assistant Commissioner for the State of Georgia, Bureau of Refugees, Freedmen, and Abandoned Lands, National Archives Microfilm M798.

67. *Report of the Joint Select Committee to Inquire into the Condition of Affairs in the Late Insurrectionary States* (Ku Klux Klan Hearings) (13 vols., serials 1484–96, Washington: Government Printing Office, 1872). James Alton's testimony is in vol. 9: *Alabama*, pt. 2, pp. 1016–22.

68. Rawick, ed., *American Slave*, vol. 5: *Texas Narratives*, pt. 3, 254–5.

69. Foner, *Reconstruction*, 590–2; and J. Morgan Kousser, *The Shaping of Southern Politics: Suffrage Restriction and the Establishment of the One-Party South, 1880–1910* (New Haven: Yale University Press, 1974).

70. Chalmers Archer, Jr., *Growing Up Black in Rural Mississippi: Memoirs of a Family, Heritage of a Place* (New York: Walker and Company, 1992), 121.

ELEVEN

The Black Church:
Manhood and Mission

WILLIAM H. BECKER

Students of the black Christian church today tend to emphasize its long and honorable association with the cause of black liberation, its tradition of protest, whether overt or covert, against white racism. "The Black Revolution was born in the 'invisible' Black Church of the slave era." "The independent Black Church emerged as a protest—a protest against the racist theology and the racist ecclesiology of the church in America."[1]

This emphasis, as Vincent Harding has pointed out, serves as a necessary counterbalance to "classic" interpretations of the black church, by such scholars as Benjamin Mays and E. Franklin Frazier, as passive, other-worldly, not inclined to struggle for racial justice. Any definite judgment on the black church will undoubtedly have to give some weight to both these interpretations, thereby recognizing what Harding terms "the ambiguity, the doubleness, of black religious experience, indeed of all religious experience."[2]

Yet even recognition of this "doubleness"—this polarity between religion as an opiate and religion as a stimulus to protest—does not constitute a full appreciation of the contribution the black church has made to the earthly liberation of its people. That contribution goes beyond the simple either/or of passive submission and active resistance to encompass the realm of communal nurture in which a people develops and symbolizes its answer(s) to the question, What does it mean to be a man? Every human community defines and authenticates those models of manhood that serve to guide its members in their growth toward mature humanity, and within the black community the church has played a key role in this process.

Manhood is an important term in the tradition of the independent black church (Bishop B. W. Arnett described the organizing conference of the African Methodist Episcopal Church in 1816 as "the Convention of the friends of Manhood Christianity"),[3] and there can be no doubt that the models of black manhood provided by the black church constitute one of its most important contributions, over the years, to the cause of black liberation. These models are delineated in the biographies, sermons, histories, and conference minutes of the black churches, and are manifested in the lives and work of significant black churchmen such as Daniel A. Payne and Henry M. Turner.

It is proper to speak here of models and not a single model. The changing situation of the black church in different periods of its history, the varying temperaments of its leaders, the ebb and flow of white racism—these and other factors have led to the development in their church of different styles of black manhood. While we cannot, therefore, speak of some single model of manhood, we can begin to identify various aspects of manhood which have been (and are) emphasized by the black church, and embodied in its heroic figures. This essay represents a preliminary effort in that direction.

There are four distinguishable but interrelated aspects of manhood, as manifested in the black church tradition, to be discussed here: (1) leadership, self-assertion, (2) independence, (3) black identity, and (4) vocation. With the reminder that these are understood as interdependent and not as mutually exclusive, it may be suggested that the first aspect is especially prominent in the slave preacher, the first three are prominent in the founders of the black church, and all four are evident in the developed black church, especially as it defines its role as a missionary church following Emancipation.

The two interrelated theses of this essay are that (1) the definition and assertion of black manhood has been a conscious motive and dominant theme throughout the history of the black church, and that (2) the assertion of black manhood was in turn a conscious motive and dominant theme in the black appropriation of the common nineteenth century dogma that it was the black American's special providential calling to win his African brother to Christianity. Black manhood and black mission in Africa came to be tied together in the black Christian mind, and they remain tied together (though with some different emphases) to this day.

THE SLAVE PREACHER

The policy of white slaveholders concerning the religious instruction of their slaves varied greatly, not only from region to region, but even from one plantation to the next. Some forbade any religious instruction or practice; some required attendance at prayer services and Sunday worship.

It was not long after slaves began to appropriate the Christian faith as their own that there stepped forth from among them effective, although often illiterate, preachers of the Gospel. We do not know very much about these "prophets" and "judges" of the black church, but we know enough to realize that they were among the first slaves who had opportunity to assert themselves in a public, dramatic role of leadership. Where slaves' meetings were prohibited and, therefore, held secretly in the woods or slave quarters, the charisma of the slave preacher was known only to those whom he led. Where slave worship was permitted, an able preacher might become widely known among both blacks and whites. Several known preachers attracted considerable white audiences, and sometimes, as in the cases of George Lisle, Andrew Bryan, Josiah Bishop, and "Uncle Jack," white persons either manumitted slave preachers of recognized ability or raised money to purchase their freedom.[4]

Leadership by charismatic preachers is, according to W. E. B. DuBois, one of three dominant characteristics of slave religion (the other two being music and "frenzy" or shouting).

> The Preacher is the most unique personality developed by the Negro on American soil. A leader, a politician, an orator, a "boss," an intriguer, an idealist—all this he is, and ever, too, the center of a group of men, now twenty, now a thousand in number.[5]

It is the preacher's place at "the center of a group of men" that especially concerns us here. As one who knew something of the Bible's sacred mysteries, who had the power to transform biblical imagery into the affections of the heart, who had the confidence to stand before others with shouting voice and pounding fist, the preacher was manifestly a man and a leader of men. In addition to whatever other symbolic functions he had, he symbolized self-assertive masculinity and integrity for the slaves who watched and heard him.

Unconsciously at least, he may also have symbolized the slave's previous independence in Africa, in that he was an Afro-American reincarnation, DuBois suggests, of the "Priest or Medicine-Man" who played such a central role in African social organization.

THE INDEPENDENT BLACK CHURCH

Separate black congregations led by black preachers were formed in the eighteenth century, the first one between 1773–75 by Baptists in Silver Bluff, South Carolina. But it was not until the formation of the African Methodist Episcopal Church in 1816 that any black church achieved complete independence—i.e., control of its own property and freedom from the jurisdiction of white denominational officials. Because it was the first fully independent black denomination, and also because there is more published historical material available on it than on any other denomination, the A. M. E. Church will be the focus of study in this essay.[6]

What we know of the causes and motives which led to the founding of the

A. M. E. Church suggests that two interrelated factors, one negative and one positive, were primarily responsible. Undoubtedly these two factors, accompanied sometimes by others, were present in the formation of virtually all separate black churches. The negative factor is of course discrimination by whites against black fellow-worshippers. The positive factor is the assertion by black men of their essential dignity as men, as children of God, as citizens of the nation.

Richard Allen reports that soon after he arrived in Philadelphia in February, 1786, he saw the necessity of establishing a separate meeting house for "our colored brethren [who] were destitute of a place of worship [and] were considered as a nuisance" in the St. George's Methodist Church where some did worship. White discrimination and black pride collided in that dramatic incident in 1787, in which the trustees of St. George's sought physically to remove Absalom Jones, Richard Allen, and other blacks from a "white" section of the gallery in which they were on their knees at prayer. What someone has called the first "freedom march" occurred when the "prayer was over, and we all went out of the church in a body, and they were no more plagued with us in the church."[7]

Daniel Coker, with Richard Allen a founder of the A. M. E. denomination, in 1816 compared the newly independent churchmen with "the Jews in Babylon [who] were held against their will" but then gained their freedom. Like many A. M. E. spokesmen who were to come after him, he hoped and assumed that the A. M. E. Church would serve to build the unity, and therefore enhance the security, of the black people. "May the time speedily come, when we shall see our brethren come flocking to us like doves to their windows. And we as a band of brethren, shall sit down under our own vine to worship, and none to make us afraid."[8]

Given these dramatic beginnings, it is not surprising that the A. M. E. Church has viewed itself, its very existence as an independent, black-controlled denomination, as a manifestation of black self-assertion. Bishop Daniel A. Payne (1811–1893), the first official historian of the A. M. E. Church, says that the separation of that black denomination from the predominantly white Methodist Episcopal Church was "beneficial to the man of color" in two ways. "First: it has thrown us upon our own resources and made us tax our own mental powers both for government and support." So long as he was simply a small minority within the A. M. E. Church, Payne argues, the colored man "always was, still is, and ever must be a mere cipher." His dependent status tended to "confirm the oft-repeated assertions of his enemies, that he really is incapable of self-government and self-support." In Payne's view, "the existence of the African Methodist Episcopal Church" constitutes a "flat contradiction of this slander."

The second benefit of separation is closely related to the first: It gave the black man "an independence of character which he could neither hope for nor attain unto, if he had remained as the ecclesiastical vassal of his white brethren." It has produced "independent thought," "independent action," and an "independent hierarchy," and the latter "has made us feel and recognize our individuality and our heaven-created manhood."[9]

Bishop Payne did more than simply write about the "heaven-created manhood" nurtured within the A. M. E. Church. Like the black preacher of slavery times, he *embodied* that manhood—in a career as teacher, pastor, and A. M. E. Bishop. He had numerous occasions during that career to display his personal courage and commitment. As an educator he overcame his own bitter discouragement at the enforced closing of his flourishing school in Charleston, South Carolina, a closing forced upon him in 1835 by the "white backlash" which followed Nat Turner's uprising (1831). As pastor and bishop, he fought—against determined opposition within his own church—on behalf of some important causes: an educated ministry, racial inclusiveness in the church, sound planning in foreign missions.[10] When he was in his seventies he once chose to get off a train and walk, carrying his luggage, rather than be seated in Jim Crow conditions. "Before I'll dishonor my manhood by going into that car, stop your train and put me off," he said.[11]

Charles Spencer Smith (1852–1922) who like Payne was both a bishop and the official historian of the A. M. E. Church, produced Volume Two of the History of the A. M. E. Church in 1922. It covers the period from the end of Payne's history (1856) through World War I. A dominant theme of Smith's history is precisely the one we are discussing: the self-assertive manhood manifest in the leaders and spirit of the A. M. E. Church. The book begins with this dedication, "To the Trailblazers, whose self-sacrificing and heroic labors made possible the expansion and development of the African Methodist Church in the West and South." It ends with a chapter entitled "After-war Problems" which quotes the well-known, militant poem of Claude McKay:

> If we must die, let it not be like hogs
>   Hunted and penned in an inglorious
> spot,
>
> Like men we'll face the murderous, cowardly pack
>   Pressed to the wall, dying—but
> fighting back![12]

In at least three different ways Smith associates black manliness and integrity with the A. M. E. Church. First, in the words he characteristically uses to describe the leaders (pastors, missionaries, and bishops) of the Church during the period treated. Elder William P. Quinn, missionary to states west of Ohio (1840), "had the faith and daring of Paul, the intrepidity of Francis Asbury, and the blood and iron of Bismarck. He was matchless in heroism, superb in courage, and relentless in his attacks on the foes of his people. He was a militant soldier of the Cross. He was a giant in his day." James Lynch and J. O. S. Hall, the first A. M. E. missionaries to South Carolina (1863), are characterized as men of "courage, daring and self-sacrificing spirit." The Rev. A. W. Wayman, preaching in Norfolk, is "another Daniel [who by going South did] dare to enter the lion's den of American slavery." Wayman, J. M. Brown, and D. A. Payne are a "trio of red-blooded pioneers."[13]

> May 15, 1865, when Bishop Daniel Alexander Payne proceeded to organize the South Carolina Annual Conference, a new Chapter was opened in the history of the African Methodist Church, . . . one filled with deeds of heroism, daring, self-sacrifice, and indomitable will, which matches the story of the Crusaders.[14]

In highlighting the Church's continuing protest against slavery and (after Emancipation) against white racism and lynching, Smith finds a second way to associate the A. M. E. Church with what is now termed black liberation. Bishop William P. Quinn (1851): "Nine times out of ten when we look into the face of a white man, we see our enemy. . . . Our hope is in God's blessing on our own wise, strong, and well-directed efforts."[15] Resolutions on Civil Rights adopted unanimously by the General Confederate of 1872:

> Resolved, that we, the representatives of the largest body of Christians of the African race in this country, hereby enter our solemn protest against this relic of barbarism and American slavery [i.e., Southern Jim Crow railroad laws]. . . .
>
> Resolved, that we hereby pray the Congress of the United States, now in session, to pass the "Civil Rights Bill," now pending, . . . to the end that equal rights may be awarded to every American citizen traveling on the highways of the nation.[16]

A memorial to the Congress of the United States from the "Commission on After-War problems of the African Methodist Episcopal Church" (1919): Many black American citizens have "sworn by the blood of their kinsmen who fell on the battlefields of France . . . to help make the world safe for democracy, that they will no longer tamely submit to a denial of the rights guaranteed them by the National Constitution."[17]

MANHOOD AND MISSION IN AFRICA

There is yet a third way in which C. S. Smith suggests an association of the A. M. E. Church with black manhood—an association more subtle than the two already discussed, but nevertheless highly significant. This association has to do with those closely related aspects of manhood we have called identity and vocation. As the nineteenth century unfolded, the identity of the A. M. E. Church came to be more closely associated in the minds of its leaders with the idea of a special vocation to evangelize Africa.

The General Conference of 1872, for example, adopted the following statements in a report on Church Union:

> We are now more than ever convinced that the African Methodist Episcopal Church has yet a mission to perform, not only in the elevation and religious

training of our long-neglected people in the United States, but in the perfect
evangelization of Africa and the islands of the seas. . . .

When prejudice on account of color shall be swept from the Church and shall
disappear . . . then, and not until then, will the grand mission of the African
Methodist Episcopal Church, as a separate organization, be at [an] end."[18]

Affirmation of blackness over against white prejudice necessitates the existence and constitutes the identity of the A. M. E. Church; the mission of the
Church, correlative with this identity, is to evangelize the black man, including those in Africa.

There is no surprise, of course, in the fact that the A. M. E. Church was
concerned with missionary work. Such work was seen as the responsibility of
all Christians, deriving from Christ's Commandment in Matt. 28:19–20.
The Methodist Episcopal Church, parent body of the A. M. E., had a strong
missionary tradition, and Richard Allen was himself a M. E. home missionary preacher during the 1790's, before he organized his own church. Moreover, the nineteenth century was the "great century" for Christian missionary expansion, and the black church, in its missionary fervor, reflected the
fervor of the white Christian bodies surrounding it. Nor is it surprising that
the black church should focus its missionary efforts on black men. There the
need was greatest, the opportunities most obvious—especially after Emancipation in 1863—and the prospects of success highest.

What is surprising, at least at first blush, is the emphasis on *African
mission*. Why should the independent black church—dependent upon a
constituency of the poorest classes for its support, faced with great financial
difficulties and a shortage of educated leaders, confronted in 1863 with the
task of serving literally millions of newly freed slaves—undertake foreign
missions across the seas in Africa? Why look so far, when the need is so great
at one's back door—indeed, in one's own house?[19]

There were those within the A. M. E. Church who raised these very
questions, as is illustrated by these words from the Episcopal Address to the
General Conference of 1856:

The cause of missions demands our serious and careful consideration. But
whether we are able to cultivate the foreign as well as the home field is a grave
and important question. Some think we ought to cultivate both. One thing
however is certain, for it is a fact of history that we have made two attempts to
occupy foreign fields [i.e., "in Africa and Hayti"] but have never maintained
ourselves in them.[20]

Bishop Daniel Payne argued in 1884 that, rather than attempt to re-establish
its foreign ministry efforts in Africa, the A. M. E. Church should concentrate
its efforts on its already existing mission in Haiti. "The A. M. E. Church is too
poor to attempt to establish more than one college at a time," Payne insisted,
and the same principle must be applied to foreign missions. "The A. M. E.
Church ought not to establish a mission in Africa until she has made her
mission in the island of Haiti a grand success." Moreover, Payne warned

against what he saw as a tendency toward "Ecclesiastical Imperialism" in missions at a time when "thousands of our own churches are suffering for lack of moneys to support them. All of our schools are suffering for lack of endowment."[21]

But Payne's words of caution were not heard in the black church during the 1880s and 90s, at least not on the subject of missions in Africa. During 1891, Bishop Henry M. Turner (1834–1915) travelled to West Africa, organizing the Sierra Leone Annual Conference of the A. M. E. Church on November 10 and the Liberian Annual Conference on November 23. In the eleventh of his series of fourteen "African Letters" (dated December 4) Turner said of Africa, "There is no reason under heaven why this continent should not or cannot be brought to God in twenty-five years—say thirty at most."[22]

In part, of course, Turner's enthusiasm for African mission simply echoed that of white churchmen. Whites were already missionizing blacks in Africa—why should the black church exclude itself from this task? As Bishop Nazrey said in 1856: "We have as much right to look after perishing Africa and the West India Islands as any other Christian Church upon the face of the earth."[23] The Episcopal Address to the General Conference of 1896 puts it more strongly: "Our church is better adapted to the redemption of Africa than any other organization."[24]

Moreover, black churchmen were being told over and over again during the 1880s and 90s, by both blacks and whites, that they were "better adapted" and in fact divinely commissioned to play the key role in missionizing Africa. As part of the "African fever" which gripped Europe and the U.S. during the period 1880–1900, it was widely assumed by statesmen, educators, journalists—as well as churchmen—that Africa would be Christianized "in this generation," and that the Afro-American would bear a major responsibility in this task.

This latter idea was not new; it had been broached before by the New England divine Samuel Hopkins, and by the American Colonization Society, organized in 1817. But following emancipation the idea was put forward with new force, and by a great variety of spokesmen. These appeals for black mission in Africa, as Josephus Coan has pointed out, generally emphasized one or more of the following points: (a) the American black man has been prepared for mission work by divine providence, through Christianization and education in the U.S.; (b) being thus blessed by God, Afro-Americans are obligated to bring these blessings to their African brothers; (c) Afro-Americans possess a "superior fitness" for African mission because of their racial kinship with Africans and because they can adapt to the African climate more successfully than white missionaries.[25]

But, acknowledging the pervasiveness and appeal of these arguments, why should the black church have accepted them—given its pressing tasks at home? Why didn't the A. M. E. Church respond to them with a resounding

"No," as it had to earlier arguments, put forward by the American Colonization Society, that the proper destination of the American black man was
Africa?[26]

The basic answer, I think, has to do with the issue of black manhood:
African mission provided a dramatic symbol of the Afro-American as man, as
leader, as authoritative carrier of God's word to those racial brothers who do
not possess it. The power of this symbol can be seen in an engraving used as
the frontispiece in the Arnett book, which shows a group of dark-skinned
peoples — Orientals, Africans, American Indians — approaching a preacher
with the question, "Which way to God?" The preacher holds in his right
hand an open Bible, and with his extended left arm points to a cross on a
distant mountain peak, a cross from which radiate the words, "Lo I am the
Way." The preacher is a young, vigorous, American black man. He is tall and
well built; he stands a full head taller than any of the other figures. He is
manifestly a man, and he is showing the way to the other men. The caption
reads: "The Special Mission of the A. M. E. Church to the Darker Races is
to 'Teach the Mind to Think, the Heart to Love, the Hand to Work.'"

This symbol of the black man as missionary to other men of color had
appeal for both black and white Americans. It was a symbol which portrayed
the Afro-American as exercising leadership and independence, as having a
definite identity (educated, Christian, chosen of God) and a definite vocation (to evangelize the "darker races," especially in Africa). It was a symbol
which sought to make some sense of the suffering of a slave past (that past was
a preparation for this vocation), and which held out high hopes for the future
(God will reward his faithful missionaries, and no man will be able to doubt
their courage or effectiveness). Moreover, and this is a vital point, here is a
symbol which, by dramatizing the manhood of the Afro-American *in another
land*, made it clear, at one and the same time, that he was a man, but that he
had to leave America to be recognized as a man.

All these aspects of the symbol, which are implicit in the engraving,
become fully explicit in numerous statements by A. M. E. churchmen
during this period. The Reverend S. F. Flegler, who as pastor led a group of
thirty A. M. E. settlers to Liberia in 1878, addressed the South Carolina
Conference of the Church in 1890 as follows:

> Africa is the home of the Negro, the land where he is free, and where he has
> the best opportunity for the best development. It is much in need of the
> Gospel. What the Church expends in the interests of missionary operations in
> Liberia will return to you in glory and grandeur. The work is before us, and we
> will do it if we are possessed of race pride. I would not be here today, if I could
> have induced my family to have joined me when I was in Africa. I have too
> much soul in me to be satisfied with the condition that presents itself here. I
> recognize no man to be my superior, nor any race to be naturally in advance
> of ours. . . . God Almighty never made a soul with more elements of manhood
> than mine; and I thank God there is sufficient African blood in me to thrill me
> with aspirations of manhood.[27]

In addition to the motifs already mentioned, one detects in this quotation a certain ambivalence concerning Africa, a double-mindedness which follows from what DuBois calls the "twoness" of the American Negro. On the one hand, Africa is viewed positively: it is "home," the place of freedom and "opportunity," the source of "manhood." In these respects, the American black can identify with and affirm Africa. On the other hand, Africa is not source and giver, but in need of what the Afro-American has to give. It is "much in need of the Gospel. . . . The work is before us, and we will do it, if we are possessed of race pride." If this "race pride" includes the effort to Christianize Africa, as well as a proper affirmation of what Africa is, it is clearly a complex concept, involving ambivalence.

To recognize this complexity and ambivalence is to understand the basis for significant differences which emerged between blacks of this period as to exactly what constitutes the mission (and consequently, the manhood) of the black missionary to Africa. Most A. M. E. leaders reflected the dominant biases of western culture, assuming that the role of the missionary was to replace African darkness with Western Christian light. "Pursuing our onward march for the Dark Continent," says the Episcopal Address at the A. M. E. General Conference of 1896,

> we will speak to more than two hundred million of men and women, bone of our bone, and flesh of our flesh, and say to them, "Arise, and shine, for the light of civilization is waiting for thee."[28]

L. J. Coppin, A. M. E. Bishop of South Africa, writing on the topic "The Negro's Part in the Redemption of Africa," said in 1902 that "In their isolated condition, the people [of Africa] have for long centuries become the victims of customs and habits not in keeping with the better life which is the result only of Christian civilization."[29]

But there were a few A. M. E. leaders, the most noteworthy being Bishop Henry M. Turner, who were convinced that Africa had as much to give the American black as he had to give Africa — perhaps more. As a bishop, Turner was concerned with Christianizing Africa, and he devoted great effort to raising funds for African mission work, especially through publications such as the *Voice of Missions*, which he founded in 1893 and edited until 1900. But he went beyond missions, seeing emigration to Africa as the only satisfactory solution to the race problem in America, and he promoted and even sponsored various African colonization programs.

Turner saw the American black, surrounded as he was by a racist white majority, as schooled in contempt for himself, and as inevitably passing on this feeling of inferiority to his own children.

> Any people oppressed, proscribed, belied, slandered, burned, flayed and lynched will not only become cowardly and servile, but will transmit that same servility to their posterity, and continue to do so *ad infinitum*, and as such will never make a bold and courageous people.[30]

Therefore Turner concluded (in italics), *"There is no manhood future in the United States for the Negro.* He may eke out an existence for generations to come, but he can never be a *man*—full, symetrical and undwarfed."[31] In contrast, the African black impressed Turner as embodying manliness in his very posture. "One thing the black man has here," he wrote from Africa, "and that is manhood, freedom and the fullest liberty. He feels like a lord and walks the same way."[32]

In Turner's view, Afro-American manhood could not be fulfilled simply by mission *to* Africa; it required mission *in* Africa, i.e., a large scale back-to-Africa movement by American blacks. "I believe that two or three millions of us should return to the land of our ancestors, and establish our own nation, civilization, laws, customs . . . and cease to be grumblers [in] the white man's country, or the country he claims and is bound to dominate."[33]

Like Turner, Professor Edward W. Blyden, who was among other things a clergyman, scholar, and Liberian government official, put forward in its most uncompromising form the argument that the manhood and mission of the black man was not here but in Africa. In his view, God had allowed African slaves to be brought to America so that they could be educated in Christianity, and then return home to Christianize Africa. In this way, Africans would receive Christianity through the tutelage of other Africans, instead of via the white man. "God sent us here to be trained that we might return to the land of our fathers and take charge of it, develop it and defend it."[34]

As these words suggest, Blyden went further in his analysis of divine providence than most black churchmen of the time: American blacks will not only teach Africa, they will emigrate to Africa and govern that land.

> You see then the field that lies before you. You see the reason that God is giving you this schooling. It is to train you for the important duties, not here, but where there is a welcome field for your talent.[35]

Since the American black has this divine commission, he violates God's will when he seeks to deny his blackness.

> I have taken so much care, says the Lord, to preserve these black skins, and they are trying to extinguish themselves. You ought to see the importance of trying to preserve your race as purely as you can.[36]

African mission requires a pure black race, and black manhood will be fulfilled when it carries out its providential African mission.

MANHOOD AND MISSION TODAY

In the past the black church has, as we have seen, defined and embodied models of black manhood, and has associated that manhood with mission to Africa. This past tradition, so obviously relevant to many concerns of the contemporary black community, poses many questions for today's black church. Four such questions will be stated in this concluding section; the first two pertain to models of manhood, the second two have to do with the concept of mission to Africa.

1. Does the black church possess within itself, potentially if not actually, models of manhood adequate for the present, or must it look outside itself— to other black movements or ideologies—for models fully adequate for today?

This may seem at first like a strange question, one which must obviously be answered in the affirmative. But the answer is not so obvious. Criticism of the black church by black militants has forced some churchmen to be very sensitive, even defensive, about the church's "establishment" character. "To some Black people, especially many of the young Blacks, the very life, thought and style of the Black Church is seen as a gigantic sell-out of Black people."[37] Some black pastors have felt a pressure to identify with programs initiated by militants outside the church, or to turn over church facilities for use in these programs, without much time to ask whether the church has (or should have) its own program, and whether the church's program, if articulated, would harmonize with the militant one.

Some contemporary black theologians, while stressing the church's past contributions to the realization of black manhood, seem ready now to argue that, in the future, the church's contributions must be judged according to criteria from outside the church per se.

> It is this common experience among black people in America that Black Theology elevates as the supreme test of truth. To put it simply, Black Theology knows no authority more binding than the experience of oppression itself. . . . Concretely, this means that Black Theology is not prepared to accept any doctrine of God, man, Christ or Scripture which contradicts the black demand for freedom now.[38]

Other black theologians show more awareness of the genuine tension that will and must continue to exist between the church, which has traditional manhood models of its own, and non-church black groups with which the church must now work.

> Coalition formation is not always easy or smooth. It involves give and take. . . . The Black Church will be pushed perhaps more than it will pull. . . . As coalitions are formed, Black churchmen will need to clarify the distinct contribution they have to offer out of their religious or theological perspective. . . . How does the Black Church distinguish itself from other organizations, even in coalitions, so that it can be itself and make its unique contributions?[39]

It seems clear that deciding between these two perspectives, or working out some viable compromise between them, constitutes a major task for the black church in the immediate future.

2. To what extent, and in what ways, can/does Jesus the Christ function in the black church as a model of manhood adequate for the present, and what interpretative terms and symbols are required for a contemporary black christology?

Again, a strange-sounding question. If Jesus the Christ is not an adequate model of manhood for the black church, who would be? In earlier decades, such an answer—which dismisses the question—would have been quite appropriate. Daniel Payne, for example, was quite clear that "the glorious manhood of Jesus Christ is the only true type of real manhood. . . . Study him, study him as your model; study the perfect model of manhood until he shall be conformed in you."[40]

Today Payne's words are not sufficient because they take no account of what Vincent Harding has called "the deep ambivalence of American Negroes to the Christ we have encountered here."[41] This ambivalence has been there from the beginning (see David Walker's *Appeal* of 1829), but only now is it fully and freely articulated by blacks, many of whom are influenced by Malcolm X's forceful attacks on Christianity in his *Autobiography*. Addison Gayle, for example, addresses this charge to the Christ: "You are the greatest slave master of them all. You taught us to be good to our enemies, to love them, to forgive them. Holding out promises of heaven, you tied our hands and made us weak."[42]

Now that blacks, including black theological students, are speaking out against a Christ who has been co-opted as divine guardian of a white racist society (who has himself been "painted white and pink, blond and blue-eyed—and not only in white churches but in black churches as well"), the question is, Can Jesus the Christ function in the black church as a model of manhood adequate for the present, and if so, what interpretive terms and symbols will be most helpful in disclosing the "Black Messiah"?[43]

3. How should the black Christian church in America today understand its relation with black Africa: is the church a giver, or is it the recipient of Africa's gift?

I pose the question in this either/or form advisedly. Of course the black church may be *both* giver and receiver, just as it was in time past when, as we noted above, it recognized Africa as both the source of the black American's manhood and as in need of what the black American church had to give. But I am not sure the black church has ever, either in the past or the present, clearly recognized and analyzed its complex and perhaps ambivalent relation to Africa.

Most often the church of the past has spoken confidently of itself as the giver, as in the Episcopal Address of 1896 quoted above which invited Africa to "Arise, and shine, for the light of civilization is waiting for thee." Today black theologians reject such language as unconsciously reflecting the white-supremacist, Western-supremacist ideology so pervasive in white American Christianity. My question seeks to get at the issue: after this language is rejected, what language *should* be used? If Africa does not receive her light from the (Western) church, does she receive anything? If so, what? Does the black church in America receive from Africa? If so, from Christian Africa, or "traditional" Africa? And what does she receive?

These are anything but merely abstract questions. When John S. Mbiti, an African Christian theologian from Uganda, addressed black students at the Interdenominational Theological Center (October, 1970) on the topic "African Traditional Religions," the first question asked—and one that recurred again and again in a series of discussion sessions with Mbiti—was, Did Christian missionary work in Africa serve only to destroy African traditional religion and values, or did it also have some positive effects? Were this question posed by a black who has rejected the church, e.g., a Muslim, it would not be an expression of ambivalence. But when it is asked by a young black man preparing to enter the ministry of the Christian church, it is an expression of profound ambivalence toward the church and its mission. It suggests the need for some radical reflection on the relation between the black church and black Africa.

4. Does the black church (and more broadly, the black community) in America today possess a special mission beyond America, and if so is that mission best understood as having primarily a literal or a rhetorical-symbolic character?

This is a complex question, and one which receives quite divergent answers from different voices within the black community today. Some of these voices insist that the American black should abandon all thought of any mission to others, and concentrate his efforts on healing himself.

> We still have too much missionary zeal. We want to *light the lamp* for other nonwhites and whites as well. . . . It may be viewed as a come-down, as a withdrawal to halt our rhetoric (we still use it!) about showing the way for the balance of humanity but until we fully realize our responsibility to self, we'll be the laughing stock of the oppressed portion of the world.[44]

More common is the view that the American black should see his struggle as part of and essentially identical with the struggle of "oppressed," "colonized," "non-white," or "Third World" peoples the world over. "We black Americans are . . . part of that fellowship of the disinherited which will surely inherit the earth in this century."[45]

It is easy to move from thinking of oneself as part of the oppressed to thinking of oneself as that vanguard which leads the oppressed (and perhaps the oppressor also) to freedom. "We are the ones who will save the world and bring a new day, a brilliantly alive society that swings and sings and rings out the world over for decency and honesty and sincerity and understanding and beauty and love. . . ."[46]

This view has had great impact on the thought of black churchmen and theologians. It led Martin Luther King, Jr., for example, to associate the black freedom movement with the worldwide struggle of the oppressed, and to suggest the possibility that the American black might constitute, through his non-violent protest, the "new spiritual dynamic" required to save the world from self-destruction.

It makes a considerable difference, though, whether the black American's unity with the Third World and his special mission in that world is under-stood as having primarily a literal or a rhetorical-symbolic character.[47] If the unity/mission concept is understood literally, we would not expect to find *fundamental* dissimilarities in the experiences, motives, concerns and ide-ologies of black Americans and other non-whites. If on the other hand the concept is rhetorical and symbolic, it may have great ideological value and significance, while still allowing for many and real differences to exist between the peoples involved.

To give a specific example, "Black Theology" is often discussed as if it were literally universal, a theology applicable to oppressed and/or non-white peoples the world over. Yet as David G. Gelzer has pointed out, "black the-ology and African theology are by no means the same." African theology was not born of slavery, does not aim at liberation from white racism, is "not a theology of blackness as forged by blacks for blacks," and does not in general pursue its task in a "hostile society."[48]

The concept of the unity of the darker races and of a special black mission in Africa has in the past had a tremendous rhetorical and symbolic signifi-cance within the black church and community. The power of the concept Black Mission in Africa during the period 1890–1900 went, as we have seen, far beyond the black church's actual, very limited commitment of funds and personnel to foreign mission work. It may be that this concept will continue to be of significance in the black church primarily for its symbolic rather than its literal truth, primarily for its expressive rather than its descriptive value.

NOTES

1. *Christianity and Crisis*, 30/18 (Nov. 2 and 16, 1970), 225, 229.

2. Vincent Harding, "Religion and Resistance Among Antebellum Negroes, 1800–1860," in August Meier and Elliott Rudwich (eds.), *The Making of Black America*, I (New York: Atheneum, 1969), p. 181.

3. B. W. Arnett (ed.), *Proceedings of the Quarto-Centennial Conference of the A. M. E. Church of South Carolina, May 15–17, 1889* (Charleston, S.C., 1890), p. 384.

4. Cf. Chapter 3, "Pioneer Negro Preachers," in Carter G. Woodson, *The History of the Negro Church* (Washington, D.C.: Associated Publishers, 1921).

5. W. E. B. DuBois, *The Souls of Black Folk* (New York: Fawcett Publications, 1961), p. 141.

6. While it is true that the concept of black manhood and the explicit association between that manhood and mission to Africa are more pervasive and emphatic in the A. M. E. tradition than in that of other black churches, this is a difference of degree and not of kind. Study of historical works on other black denominations, both Baptist and Methodist, indicates that the generalizations which follow apply, in greater or lesser degree, to these as well as to the A. M. E. Church. This view will be documented in appropriate places by footnotes which refer to the National Baptist Convention, U. S. A., Inc., which is the largest of the black Baptist Churches—even as the A. M. E. Church is the largest black Methodist body.

7. Richard Allen, *The Life Experience and Gospel Labors of the Rt. Rev. Richard Allen*, n.d. (reprinted New York–Nashville: Abingdon Press, 1960), p. 25.

8. David Coker, "Sermon Delivered . . . January, 1816 . . . ," in Herbert Aptheker (ed.), *A Documentary History of the Negro People in the United States,* I (New York: Citadel Press, 1951), p. 68.

9. Daniel A. Payne, *A History of the A. M. E. Church, I, 1816–1856* (Nashville: A. M. E. Sunday School Union, 1891; reprinted New York: Arno Press, 1968), pp. 9–10, 12.

10. Cf. Josephus R. Coan, *Daniel Alexander Payne: Christian Educator* (Philadelphia: A. M. E. Book Concern, 1935).

11. Daniel A. Payne, *Recollections of Seventy Years* (Nashville: A. M. E. Sunday School Union, 1888; reprinted New York: Arno Press, 1968), p. 287.

12. Charles S. Smith, *A History of the A. M. E. Church, II, 1856–1922* (Philadelphia: A. M. E. Book Concern, 1922; reprinted New York: Johnson Reprint Corp., 1968), p. 395.

13. *Ibid.,* pp. 17, 52, 54.

14. *Ibid.,* p. 67. Similar language is found in the histories of the National Baptist Convention, U. S. A., Inc. Edward A. Freeman, in his *The Epoch of Negro Baptists and the Foreign Mission Board* (Kansas City, KA: The Central Seminary Press, 1953), describes John Jasper, one of the pioneer Baptist preachers, as a "personality who towers like a mighty oak above the horizon of the past and his contemporaries." He was "full of dangerous energies, almost gigantic in his muscles, . . . with a self-assertion that made him a leader within the circles of his freedom. . . . He was too decided, too aggressive . . . to be popular" (pp. 39–40). Freeman quotes a contemporary of the Baptist preacher Walter H. Brooks, who wrote: "Dr. Brooks . . . believed in Negro manhood; he opposed anything or anybody who antagonizes the manly development of the Negro" (p. 54). *The Story of the National Baptists,* by Owen D. Pelt and Ralph L. Smith (New York: Vantage Press, 1960), treats the early black Baptist preachers in a chapter entitled "The Heroic Age," arguing that, given the conditions under which they had to work, "the early pioneers of the Negro Baptist Church can certainly be called heroes—heroes both in mind and of spirit" (p. 34).

15. Smith, *History of the A. M. E. Church,* p. 22.

16. *Ibid.,* pp. 101–02.

17. *Ibid.,* p. 395.

18. *Ibid.,* p. 102–03.

19. It must be stressed that the question being posed here has to do, not with the *quantity* of effort and treasure expended by the black church in Africa (which was relatively small), but rather with the issue, why did the church attempt *any* effort in Africa, and why did the church make that effort so central in its missionary rhetoric, given its shortage of money and trained leaders, and the tremendous mission task it faced at home. The black church was terribly poor, and in spite of eloquent pleas and programs, never mustered either a large number of missionaries, nor sufficient funds to support them. The *Voice of Missions* published many poignant letters sent home by A. M. E. missionaries in Liberia and Sierra Leone during the 1890s, letters which plead for financial support from the church, and which sometimes betray the disappointment of troops who feel abandoned in the field.

The average annual receipts of the Department of Missions (*both* home and foreign) of the A. M. E. Church during the period 1881–84 were $8,702.95, less than 3% of the $381,878 appropriated for missions by the Methodist Episcopal Church in 1884. (Cf. Coan, *Expansion of Missions,* p. 39.)

The Foreign Missionary Board of the National Baptist Convention, Inc., raised a little more than four thousand dollars in 1897, about eighty-five hundred dollars in 1901. (Cf. Freeman, pp. 118, 122.)

20. Smith, *History of the A. M. E. Church,* p. 332.

21. Daniel A. Payne, "The Past, Present, and Future of the A. M. E. Church," *A. M. E. Church Review,* I/4 (April, 1885), 314–15, 318–19.

22. Smith, *History of the A. M. E. Church,* p. 178.

23. *Ibid.,* p. 26.

24. Josephus Coan, *The Expansion of Missions of the African Methodist Episcopal Church in South Africa, 1896–1908.* Unpublished doctoral dissertation (Hartford Seminary Foundation, 1961), p. 50.

25. Cf. *Ibid.*, p. 61.

26. Cf. Smith, *History of the A. M. E. Church,* p. 21. Black Baptists were speaking and hearing similar calls to African mission during this same period. W. W. Colley, who had served as an African Missionary (commissioned by the Southern Baptists) from 1875–79, returned to the South in 1879 to organize the Foreign Mission Convention of black Baptists. "He urged upon his brethren the moral responsibility that, since God had blessed them with the light of his Word, it was their sacred responsibility to send it to their brethren in that benighted land." (Freeman, *Epoch of Negro Baptists,* p. 70.) The Preamble of the Convention's Constitution, adopted in 1880, contains the statement that "African Missions claim our most profound attention, and [we feel] that we are most sacredly called to do work in this field and elsewhere abroad" (p. 73). Since the organization of this missionary convention preceded, and to some extent precipitated, the organization of the National Baptist Convention, Inc., in 1895, Pelt and Smith conclude that "it is hardly an exaggeration to say that the wish to do missionary work in Africa created the National Baptist Convention" (*Story of National Baptists,* p. 149). This wish sometimes led Baptists, as it did the A. M. E.'s, to put aside home mission tasks for the sake of African mission. "In view of the low state of our funds, and the importance of the prosecution of the African Missions, therefore we recommend that our strength and means be mostly directed to that field until the mission there is established." (C. C. Adams and Marshall A. Talley, *Negro Baptists and Foreign Missions* [Philadelphia: National Baptist Convention, U.S.A., 1944], p. 31.)

27. Arnett, *Proceedings,* p. 139.

28. Coan, *Expansion of Missions,* p. 51.

29. L. J. Coppin, "The Negro's Part in the Redemption of Africa," *A. M. E. Church Review,* 19/2 (Oct., 1902), p. 507.

30. Henry M. Turner, "The American Negro and the Fatherland," in J. W. E. Bowen (ed.), *Africa and the American Negro: Addresses and Proceedings of the Congress on Africa, December 13–15, 1895* (Atlanta: Franklin Press, 1896), p. 197.

31. *Ibid.*, p. 195.

32. Turner as quoted in Edwin S. Redkey, *Black Exodus: Black Nationalist and Back-to-Africa Movements, 1890–1910* (New Haven: Yale Univ. Press, 1969), p. 44.

33. Turner, *American Negro and Fatherland,* p. 196.

34. Arnett, *Proceedings,* p. 133.

35. *Ibid.*, p. 136.

36. *Ibid.*, p. 135–36.

37. *Christiantiy and Crisis,* 30/18, p. 232.

38. James H. Cone, *Black Theology and Black Power* (New York: Seabury Press, 1969), p. 120.

39. *Christianity and Crisis,* 30/18, p. 234.

40. Charles S. Smith (ed.), *Sermons Delivered by Bishop Daniel A. Payne Before the General Conference of the A. M. E. Church* (Nashville, 1888), pp. 58, 64.

41. Vincent Harding, "Black Power and the American Christ," *Risk,* 4/1 (1968), p. 26.

42. Addison Gayle, *The Black Situation* (New York: Horizon Press, 1970), p. 132.

43. For some preliminary efforts to deal with this question see Albert B. Cleage, Jr., *The Black Messiah* (New York: Sheed and Ward, 1968); James H. Cone, *A Black Theology of Liberation* (New York: J. B. Lippincott Co., 1970), especially chap. 6; and W. H. Becker, "Black Power in Christological Perspective," *Religion in Life* 38/3 (Autumn, 1969).

44. Robert Bowen in a letter published in *The Black Scholar,* 2/4 (December, 1970), p. 55.

45. John Oliver Killens, as quoted in Vincent Harding, "The Religion of Black Power," *The Religious Situation: 1968,* ed. by Donald Cutler (Boston: Beacon Press, 1968), p. 14.

46. Ronald Fair, as quoted in Vincent Harding, "The Religion of Black Power," *The Religious Situation: 1968*, ed. by Donald Cutler (Boston: Beacon Press, 1968), p. 14.

47. In our literalistic (yet somehow also fantastic) age, I should stress that I use the terms rhetorical and symbolic as terms of high value, and in no sense pejorative. Rhetoric, according to Webster, is "the art of expressive speech or of discourse, originally of oratory"; the symbol, according to Tillich, points beyond itself to some other reality, "participates in that to which it points," and thereby "opens up levels of reality which otherwise are closed for us."

48. David G. Gelzer, "Random Notes on Black Theology and African Theology," *The Christian Century*, 87/37 (September 16, 1970), 1091–92.

TWELVE

The Free-Slave Phenomenon:
James P. Thomas and the Black
Community in Ante-Bellum Nashville

LOREN SCHWENINGER

Considering the recent proliferation of scholarship concerning blacks in the ante-bellum South, perhaps, as one historian suggests, there should be a ten-year moratorium on any future study of slavery. Though characterized by interpretational differences, the writing offers a new perspective on several important aspects of American Negro slavery: blacks in bondage attained a relatively high degree of flexibility within the system; they resisted as well as accommodated themselves to their condition in a myriad of subtle and ingenious ways; and they maintained a distinct Afro-American cultural heritage, despite the institutional barriers of the "peculiar institution."[1] That such generalizations can now be made rests largely on a closer scrutiny than ever before of various groups of bondsmen and women: investigations, for example, of field hands, house servants and mammies, of drivers and overseers, artisans and mechanics, rebels and runaways, as well as children and old folks, wives and mothers, husbands and fathers.[2] In all, the recent literature has greatly expanded our understanding of the Afro-American past.

Yet, one significant group of bondsmen and women has received scant attention: free-slaves. This is not surprising, as even the term seems incongruous: how could slaves also be free? In many respects, of course, they could not, and even legally emancipated blacks are considered by many historians as only "quasi-free." In addition, as their livelihoods depended upon secrecy, or deception, or at the very least, a tacit illegal agreement with a prominent white benefactor, it is extremely difficult even to identify, much less uncover information about, such slaves. Owners were reluctant to acknowledge that bondsmen in their charge roamed about unsupervised, undermining the foundations of the system; the unsuspecting foreign traveller, or northern visitor, or southern defender of slavery believed these blacks to be either slaves or free Negroes; and free-slaves themselves refused to admit, much less advertise, their situation. Consequently, the journals of the slave-holding class, descriptions by outside visitors, writings of white southerners, and to a large extent, even the autobiographies of nineteenth century blacks, contain only fleeting references to these quasi-free bondsmen.[3]

But there were slaves in the ante-bellum South who achieved an amazing degree of self-sufficiency.[4] Numbering perhaps many thousands, living in nearly every region of the South (though especially in urban centers) and attaining a remarkable degree of upward mobility within the caste system, they came and went as they pleased, earned their own living, hired out and ran their own businesses, and lived outside the purview, and sometimes the control, of their master.[5] Though always cognizant of their precarious and anomalous condition, these virtually free slaves achieved a large measure of spiritual, intellectual, and material independence, so much that even some whites envied their self-confidence, self-reliance, and economic mobility.[6] Though a close examination of one such free-slave, James P. Thomas, as seen in a collection of slave letters, notes and autobiographical reminiscences, is only the study of a *single bondsman*, it perhaps reflects the activities and attitudes of other slaves who lived nearly as free men.

"My recollections of early life are many, but none are so vivid as the one instance when I was loaded in a vehicle of some sort, bound for Charlottesville," Thomas began his autobiography, "there to be turned over to one of the rightful heirs of one Thomas."[7] It seems that James and his mother, Sally, slaves belonging to the trust estate of Charles S. Thomas, a friend and neighbor of Thomas Jefferson in Albemarle County, Virginia, changed hands in 1835, becoming the property of one John Martin, an affable young man who was looking to sell off portions of his inheritance for a quick profit. As it happened the two slaves were returned to Nashville. "We went home, that is, to the house where I was born, and where mother lived years before I was born, . . . at 10 Deaderick street."[8] Despite the fact that James's father had been the famous Tennessee judge John Catron, a short time after their arrival in the capital, an advertisement appeared in a local newspaper: For Sale. Likely Mulatto Boy. Eight Years of age. Reasonable Terms.[9]

Sally had faced such a predicament on two different occasions, but in both instances she had been able to prevent the sale of her child. When it became clear that her first son, John, a mulatto who also belonged to the Thomas estate, was about to be sold in 1818, she advised him to hire-out to barge-captain Richard Rapier, who was plying the Cumberland, Tennessee, and Mississippi River trade between Nashville, Florence (Alabama), and New Orleans. After several years of devoted service, the young bondsman, who had taken the surname Rapier and established himself as a barber in Florence, was emancipated by the barge-master.[10] And when fifteen years later she saw that her second son, Henry, a mulatto who was property of the same estate, was about to be put up for sale, she urged him to flee from the South. Though captured near Louisville and put in chains, he escaped, crossed the Ohio River, and eventually opened a barber shop in Buffalo, New York.[11] Now she acted quickly to prevent the sale of her third son.

Seeking an audience with a prominent Tennessee lawyer, Ephraim Foster, she asked for assistance: "Will you talk with [Martin] and see what he will take for [James?]." "Very well, Aunt Sally," Foster replied, "I will see him and let you know what can be done." A few days later Foster told her that he wanted $400. "I have saved only $350," explained Sally, who had hired out as a cleaning woman to earn the money, "but if you, Col. Foster, will pay the fifty and make it four hundred, have the bill of sale made to yourself, you can hold [James] until I return the money. I want you to be his protector." Foster agreed and the bargain was sealed. Relinquishing the debt in 1836, she received a bill of sale, free papers, for her son.[12] But even then James was not free. According to the state law, emancipated slaves were required to secure manumission papers from the county court, and thereupon immediately leave Tennessee.[13] Thus, despite having freedom papers, young James, who had now taken the surname Thomas, was by law still a slave.[14]

As a young boy he performed a variety of chores for his slave mother, running errands, keeping salt in the hopper for making soap, cutting wood for the fire place, and delivering cleaned clothes to various parts of the city. He also attended school. Sitting on rickety benches, in a drafty, one-room school house, without paper, pencils, books, or even proper clothing, he listened to lessons given by free black instructors Daniel Watkins, Rufus Conrad, and Samuel Lowery. "But often," he recalled, "there was no school because there was no teacher." About 1837 a free Negro teacher, described as "a fine scholar," was taken out by white toughs and whipped nearly to death. Such occurrences were common. And even upper-class white aristocrats generally opposed educating blacks, who, they contended, might forge passes and escape from bondage. Yet, despite these vicissitudes, the school remained open several months each year, and young Thomas, who had an intense desire to learn, quickly mastered the rudiments of mathematics, reading and writing.[15]

Other blacks were also eager to learn. At the fall session in 1850, thirty Negro "scholars" crowded into the small classroom, and later that same year, enrollment jumped to nearly fifty.[16] Black youngsters, slave and free, walked miles through the dense woods of the Cumberland River Valley "to get some learnin'," and two brothers, John and James Rapier, children of Sally's first slave son John H. Rapier, Sr., travelled all the way from Florence, Alabama, to attend the school.[17] The progress of the Rapier boys during the 1844–45 session gave their father such satisfaction that he wrote: "James [age 8] reads well for a lettle Boy. John has wrote me two letters. He writes very plain for a boy of his age [10 years] and practice, and has as much taste for reading as any child I know off and very good in arithmetic."[18] The school was so popular among blacks that free Negro Harriett P. Young stipulated in her will that her niece, Mary Jane, should receive an education there.[19] In 1850, perhaps 25 percent of the slaves, and according to the compilations of census officials, 158 of 264 adult free blacks in the city (60 percent) could read and write, a literacy rate among the latter slightly lower than among southern whites.[20]

But the school was responsible not only for creating an educated free and quasi-free black populace; a number of black Reconstruction lawyers, doctors, government officials, politicians, ministers, and even Congressmen received their first training at the Nashville school. Treasury Department official and black banker James Carroll Napier, for instance, took his early training there,[21] as did Reconstruction lawyer Samuel Lowery, who was admitted to argue a case before the United States Supreme Court, and Nelson Walker, who served as President of the 1865 Tennessee Negro suffrage convention.[22] The free black educator Daniel Watkins, who later served as pastor of the First Colored Christian Church, not only taught at, but attended the school. "Watkins is one of the most eminently progressive and well educated colored men in the State," a Reconstruction newspaper proclaimed.[23] The Rapier brothers also gained distinction. John served as an army surgeon at the Freedmen's hospital in Washington, D.C. (1864–65), and James entered the United States Congress from Alabama (1873–75).[24] "You know Jim does not require much education," James Thomas said describing future Congressman Rapier's progress in the city. "Some polish would not hurt. He has improved very much. I am quite anxious for you [John Rapier, Jr.] to see a letter he wrote me. It is a model."[25] In all, a generation of black children secured a rudimentary education at the Nashville Negro school.

As suggested by Thomas's genuine delight at the educational progress of his namesake James (Thomas) Rapier, the Thomases and Rapiers were an intimate family. Though separated by hundreds of miles, though forbidden to travel in certain regions, and though denied postal privileges, they kept in constant touch. "Mother looks as young as she did 8 years ago and works as hard and hardly takes time to talk to you," John Rapier, Sr., who had taught himself to write by using a system of phonics, noted with some chagrin after a visit to the Tennessee capital in 1843.[26] Journeying northward two years later to see his brother, Henry, who had moved to Canada, he explained, "I am fearful that Brother will come to want in that country, as I am of the opinion [it] is poor farming country."[27] Meanwhile, he sent all four of his sons to attend the Nashville school and stay with their free-slave grandmother. "I entend to go up to Nashville in the course of ten or twelve days," Rapier wrote, "and See them all."[28]

If other family members could not travel quite so extensively, they continually communicated by letter. "Mama and Papa are well, as is the rest of the family," Sarah Thomas, Henry's eldest daughter, wrote from Canada, "and they send their compliments."[29] "All the family is well," her father generally concluded his correspondence, "and wishes to be remembered to you."[30] "A letter from your hands affords me a great deal of pleasure," admitted James Thomas, writing John Rapier, Jr., "to say nothing of the [family] news it imparts."[31] It seems that physical separation and legal restrictions, the very forces designed, in part, to destroy the black family— gave impetus, not to disintegration and disunity, but to an extraordinary feeling of family loyalty.

About 1841 Thomas hired out as an apprentice barber. Working for free-slave Frank Parrish, who had earlier established a barber shop on the public square, he quickly learned the trade. "James [is] still with Frank Parrish and has the character of a good barber, So a Gentleman toald me," John Rapier said of his brother in 1843. "[He] is well though[t] of by the Gentlemens. James has manners to please almost any one who do not let their prejudice go to fair on account of color." Two years later James was still with Parrish, earning $12 a month. At the same time he began lessons on the violin with a local Negro musician, Gordon McGowin. "James will make a man of musick, I think. He seems to be very fond of it."[32] And in 1846, having served a five-year apprenticeship, he opened his own barber shop. The 19-year-old slave established his new business in the house where he had grown up (and where his mother still operated her cleaning business) at 10 Deaderick Street.[33] The location was ideal.[34] Within a few steps of several banking houses, newspaper buildings, and law firms, as well as the county court house, Market Square, and the Capitol, "the place on Deaderick," he explained, "[is] convenient to bankers, merchants, editors, lawyers, politicians, and other professional men."[35] He listed among his customers several famous Tennesseans: ex-governor William Carroll, businessman E. S. (Squire) Hall, plantation owner William Harding, Whig political leader Ephraim Foster, William G. (Parson) Brownlow, later the Civil War governor, and Francis Fogg, a well-known Davidson County lawyer, who visited the Thomas shop daily.[36] "He returns to us in the evening," Mrs. Fogg noted approvingly, "with face smooth and curls nicely arranged."[37]

And his reputation soon spread beyond Davidson County. In 1848 he received an offer from Maury County plantation owner Andrew Jackson Polk to serve as his barber on a trip to New York. "I told the Col. that I had just bought a business and I didn't think I could go. 'Don't tell me about your business,' [he retorted.] 'I'll buy it and shut it up.'" So he made arrangements to leave, subsequently journeying with Polk by stage coach, river-packet, canal-barge, railroad, and steamboat, 1100 miles, from Nashville, to Louisville, Cincinnati, Buffalo, Albany, and New York City. At every stop, he was asked: "Are you a slave?" "Who is your master?" "Is [Polk] any relation to the President?" Admitting he was a bondsman, he explained that he ran his own affairs, which included managing a business and negotiating contracts, including the one with his companion A. J. Polk—the brother of Bishop Leonidas L. Polk, a distant cousin of the President, and a man who owned some 300 slaves and a large cotton plantation in Tennessee. "Several advised me to leave Mr. Polk," he said, "showing that they didn't believe what I had said as to being [virtually] free." But Thomas had roots and family in the South, and further, he quickly experienced the extreme hostility of some northerners toward Afro-Americans, being greeted nearly everywhere by jeers, hoots, and derisive comments such as "Black cloud risin'." In addition, he was denied accommodation on the omnibus, asked to leave museums, and refused admission to the theatre. "Such things never occurred in the south," he pointed out, bitterly assailing the hypocrisy of northerners who professed to be the black man's best friend, but who refused to accept him as a man. "In fact the southern people never laughed at the Negro because he was a negro, but would laugh at his pranks and foolishness." Yet, he was also realistic about the oppression of blacks in the South. As he passed through Washington, D.C., Alexandria and Richmond, on his way home, he lamented the selling of Negro children on the auction block, and recalled the ubiquitous slave trader. "About every five minutes on the train, some ugly fellow, loudly dressed, would say: 'Who do you belong to boy?'" Thomas would then point to the aristocratic Polk, knowing it was not true, but "thus ending the conversation." After the trip he received a handsome remuneration, had "a few pictures to hang up, some New York clothes, and had to answer many questions about the people of the north." It was not long afterwards (1851) that he accompanied Polk on a second northern sojourn, travelling to Saratoga, Boston, Newport, and again New York City.[38] Such travel was a remarkable experience for Thomas, who, by law, was still human chattel; he never forgot the antipathy northerners felt toward blacks.

Perhaps because of these experiences, he now began to listen more attentively to the conversations that took place among his customers. "They had time to talk in the barber shop. Nobody seemed in a great hurry. Everything was discussed—social, commercial, political and financial." He remembered conversations about the advancement of cotton on the Liverpool market, the magnetism of Andrew Jackson, plantation acreage along the Mississippi, and the abolitionist movement as well as fugitive blacks. Once, he was sharply questioned on the subject of runaway slaves. "'You have a brother [Henry Thomas] living in Buffalo, New York, I believe,'" William Harding, owner of the beautiful Belle Meade plantation, told him gruffly. "'Well, he treated me in a [brusque] manner. I went to ask him if he knew anything about a boy who ran off from me. I told him I only wanted to see him; I had come to Buffalo for that purpose. I received a very cold and indifferent reply.'" The free-slave barber could do little except apologize for his brother's "rudeness."[39] Though usually remaining silent when the conversation turned to such emotion-charged issues, on occasion he ventured a personal opinion, as was the case in 1846 when he boldly informed a young Virginia lawyer (who was taking a shampoo) that he heartily approved of the Wilmot Proviso, halting the expansion of slavery. "The set back I got caused me to be careful in the future. Among other things he told me that I had no right to listen to gentlemen's conversations."[40] Despite such "set backs," Thomas built up a flourishing business. Charging 20¢ for a haircut, 15¢ for a shave, and $1 for occasionally extracting a tooth, he operated one of the most prosperous "tonsorial establishments" in Nashville. And in the city's first business directory, published in 1853, he advertised in large boldface print: "JAS. THOMAS, BARBER SHOP, 10 Deaderick St."[41]

Offering an opportunity for economic independence, the barbering trade was an attractive one for Nashville blacks. In fact, of the eight barbers advertising in the 1853 directory, six were Negroes,[42] and among them, perhaps the best-known and most flamboyant was Thomas's friend and mentor Frank Parrish, a tall, handsome, well-dressed free-slave who had travelled (with his master Edwin H. Ewing) to England, Scotland, the Germanies, Persia and Egypt.[43] "Frank was an elegant dresser, by nature polite and gentlemanly, and [a] most conspicuous character," explained Thomas, who greatly admired the older Parrish. "Everywhere in Europe and the Orient [sic] he was taken for the principal man of the party. All rushed to take care of him. It kept Frank busy trying to explain that 'I am not the one,' but the people though[t] he was modest and heaped more attention on him."[44] As early as 1836 Parrish had established a bath house–barber shop in Nashville. Advertising that customers could be accommodated to tepid, cold, and shower baths, and could indulge in "the greatest luxuries," he claimed that on his staff were barbers who had no superior in the country.[45] Later, he married Sarah Jane, a virtually free slave belonging to David M. Harding, moved his barber shop to the basement of the St. Cloud Hotel (the most elegant in the city), and in 1853, at 48 years of age, he purchased his freedom, though he had been living as a quasi free Negro since childhood.[46]

Other nearly free slaves in ante-bellum Nashville also prospered as independent entrepreneurs. Bondsmen Jerry Stothard and Peter Lowery (Samuel's father), hack drivers in the city, owned their own coaches, horses, and had saved $2000 by the time they purchased freedom papers for themselves and their families.[47] A third hackman, James Wilson, who advertised low prices, prompt service, and coaches always ready to accommodate city residents needing conveyance, also started out as a slave and later bought his freedom.[48] Free-slave construction boss York Freeman earned a good living building houses in Davidson County,[49] while bondswoman Sarah Estell managed a popular ice-cream shop in a small log cabin near the McKendree church in Nashville.[50] Slaves also worked as stonemasons, brickmasons, mechanics, coopers, wagoners, hostlers, confectioners, and in numerous other capacities.[51] In all, one of four bondsmen in the city hired out, and despite the constraints of slavery, perhaps several hundred legally enslaved Afro-Americans became successful private entrepreneurs.

Nor was such black enterprise limited to central Tennessee. In every region of the South slaves hired their own time, chose their own employers, made their own housing arrangements, and lived as de facto free blacks. The constant demand for laborers (both skilled and unskilled) allowed bondsmen to profitably peddle their skills, making contracts by the month or the year. In some instances, they lived completely outside the regulation of the master.[52] Such was the case in Mobile, New Orleans, St. Louis, and Baltimore, where city officials constantly complained about "quasi f. n.," "virtually free negroes," and masterless slaves moving about the streets seemingly oblivious to any law or regulation.[53] Even in isolated rural areas observers noted the presence of such bondsmen. "Although they are slaves," a startled Tennessee planter explained, describing a small out-of-the-way community of blacks, "they have been living to themselves for about twenty years, . . . have supported themselves, . . . and are tolerable farmers."[54] Nothing seemed to dampen the enthusiasm, nor curtail the activities of these partially free black Americans, neither state laws, which, of course, prohibited such freedom, nor the periodic outcries of public officials. "There was a large number of slaves," Thomas recalled, "who managed to buy themselves, their families, and had money or property besides. . . . Some ran hacks, or drays, . . . some were [even] owners of Race horses."[55] Thus, with a tradition stretching back to the beginning of slavery in America, enterprising, resourceful, and self-sustaining slaves like James Thomas made a mockery of the timeworn concepts of racial inferiority.[56]

There were, of course, legal barriers to such activity. Blacks in bondage were not allowed to own personal property or purchase whiskey, much less earn money, buy real estate, and manage businesses. "No person shall hire any slave," one Nashville ordinance, typical of others in various southern cities, pronounced. At the same time, slaves were forbidden to gather "within the limits of the corporation" to dance, or for any other purpose, except white-supervised religious activity, and they were prohibited from travelling without a pass or socializing with free blacks. Nor were slaves allowed to rent property, and freed blacks, according to an 1831 statute, were to immediately leave the state. Failure to comply could mean a jail or prison sentence.[57]

But these legal restrictions failed to inhibit the activities of James Thomas, who accumulated personal property (furniture, mirrors, clothes, and about $1000 in cash), hired out, earned about $50 a month, and eventually managed one of the largest barbering businesses in the city, though still a bondsman.[58] He travelled to various parts of Nashville without a pass, entertained free blacks in his home, and attended black church gatherings. At one such meeting, he recalled the unsupervised congregation singing until 12 o'clock at night. "The owners," he wrote, "seemed to care very little how much religion their servants got. They seemed to encourage it." Later, he even journeyed outside Tennessee, returning without difficulty.[59]

Part of the reason Thomas could so easily circumvent the law was the acquiescence of whites. A number of Tennesseans, both slave holders and non–slave holders, entertained genuinely liberal sentiments toward blacks. The most conspicuous in Nashville was plantation owner Ephraim Foster, a lawyer, Whig politician, and United States Senator.[60] Praising Negroes as "remarkably steady and industrious workers," Foster assisted slaves in gaining their freedom for nearly a half century.[61] As early as 1818, he had appeared at the Davidson County Court seeking the manumission of the African-born slave Simon, who was "sober, industrious, hardworking, and a firm believer in the Christian religion."[62] Later he posted a $1000 security bond for Anna, a slave who was also honest, industrious, sober, and "strictly obedient to heredity."[63]

It was in the same courtroom, March 6, 1851, that Foster presented a petition for the emancipation of James Thomas, who, he said, had conducted himself in a manner to gain the respect of whites, had a reputation for honesty and integrity, and had always maintained "an exemplary character."[64] "Colonel Foster proved to be a staunch friend as long as he lived and his family were also good friends to me," Thomas wrote in praise. "He did all that he said he would do."[65] The testimony of such an eminent Tennessean apparently swayed the nine-judge panel hearing the case; they decreed, after a short deliberation, that "the slave James, otherwise called James Thomas, be emancipated and forever set free."[66]

Now able to address the court himself, Thomas quickly asked for immunity from the 1831 law requiring free blacks to leave the state. He had led a moral and productive life, had deported himself in a way "to require the good wishes of the community," and had always earned a good living. Having gained many faithful customers, he would "be greatly damaged having to Start anew in some Strange Country." Boasting that he could easily post the $500 good behavior bond, after some delay, he received immunity, thus becoming the first Negro in the county (and perhaps in the state), under the 1831 law, to legally gain both freedom and residency.[67]

In freedom Thomas expanded his barbering business and purchased some real estate in Nashville.[68] Later, he moved to St. Louis, bought a string of barber shops and bath-houses, began speculating in land and railroad stocks, and eventually acquired an apartment complex.[69] In 1868 he married Antoinette Rutgers, who had a good deal of property of her own.[70] At the height of his business career (1882), he controlled an estate valued at $400,000, including 42 apartment units, a large mansion over-looking the Mississippi River, a summer house in Alton, Illinois, and several hundred acres of valuable farm land near Memphis.[71]

Such success stemmed from his heritage in slavery. As a free-slave he had attended school, entered an apprenticeship, opened a barber shop, maintained close family ties, and acquired the values of hard work, frugality, and business enterprise. He had also ingeniously circumvented the web of legal restrictions, had rejected, sometimes overtly, white racist attitudes, and had cemented "friendships" with prominent whites to protect himself against the abuses inherent in the slave system. Through contrivance and deception, he had, in short, successfully compromised the caste system. But he also had taken with him from slavery the legacy of a vibrant black community where perhaps a majority of the Negroes had secured a rudimentary education, hired out or opened businesses, and maintained close family relationships. This vitality left a lasting impression.

In some respects, of course, Thomas was very fortunate, belonging to a permissive master, living in an urban environment (as did less than 10 percent of the southern black populace), and growing up with Sally, a determined and loving mother. Yet, like the vast majority of blacks in the ante-bellum South, he suffered the indignities and degradations inherent in human bondage, humiliations rooted in the pains of family separation, legal restrictions, fear of physical violence, and the necessity to employ subterfuge merely to survive. In this sense, then, his experiences shed light on the attitudes and activities of other Afro-Americans, who, like him, struggled from day to day, year to year, under the ominous burdens of "the peculiar institution." But for Thomas and other free-slaves in ante-bellum Nashville, such conditions resulted neither in infantilization, nor even demoralization, but gave impetus to an enormous inner strength and resiliency. It is thus perhaps ironic that the heritage of human bondage would, in this way, stand him in such good stead in the successful years ahead.

NOTES

1. John Blassingame, *The Slave Community: Plantation Life in the Ante-Bellum South* (New York, 1972); Stanley Engerman and Robert Fogel, *Time on the Cross: The Economics of American Negro Slavery* (Boston, 1974); Eugene Genovese, *Roll, Jordon, Roll: The World the Slaves Made* (New York, 1974); George Rawick, *The American Slave: A Composite Autobiography* (Westport, Conn., 1971); Robert Starobin, *Industrial Slavery in the Old South* (New York, 1970); Herbert Gutman, "The World Two Cliometricians Made," *Journal of Negro History*, LX (1975), 53–227; reprinted as *Slavery and the Numbers Game* (Urbana, 1975).

2. See especially Blassingame and Genovese above.

3. John Hope Franklin, *From Slavery to Freedom: A History of Negro Americans* (New York, 1974), Ch. XI; Ira Berlin, *Slaves Without Masters: The Free Negro in the Antebellum South* (New York, 1974), *passim*; and "The Structure of the Free Negro Caste in the Antebellum United States," *Journal of Social History*, IX (1976), 297–318.

4. See, for example, John Hope Franklin, "Slaves Virtually Free in Ante-Bellum North Carolina," *Journal of Negro History*, XXVIII (July, 1943), 284–310; John Hebron Moore, "Simon Gray, Riverman: A Slave Who Was Almost Free," *Mississippi Valley Historical Review*, XLIX (Dec. 1962), 472–484; E. Horace Fitchett, "The Origin and Growth of the Free Negro Population of Charleston, South Carolina," *Journal of Negro History*, XXVI (Oct. 1941), 435; Marina Wikramanayke, *A World in Shadow: The Free Black in Ante-Bellum South Carolina* (Columbia, S.C., 1973), p. 12; Berlin, *Slaves Without Masters*, pp. 32–33, 41–43, 49, 93, 143–149, 150–153, 328, 332, 350.

5. Kenneth Stampp, *The Peculiar Institution: Slavery in the Ante-Bellum South* (New York, 1956), pp. 72–73, 90, 147.

6. Richard C. Wade, *Slavery in the Cities: The South, 1820–1860* (New York, 1964), pp. 143–151.

7. "Autobiography of James P. Thomas: A Slave and Free Black in the Antebellum South," p. 1, Moorland-Spingarn Research Center, Howard University, Washington, D.C. (hereafter, "Thomas Autobiography").

8. *Ibid.*, 3–5, Records of Albemarle County Court, Deeds, Book XXXII (Jan. 2, 1835), p. 89.

9. "Thomas Autobiography," p. 51; the newspaper notice is only alluded to by Thomas, *ibid.*, 3–4.

10. *Ibid.*, Ch. 1; Records of the Lauderdale County Court, Wills, Vol. VI (June 3, 1824), 117; *Acts of the Eleventh Session of the General Assembly of the State of Alabama* (Tuscaloosa, 1830), p. 36; John H. Rapier, Sr., to Henry K. Thomas, Feb. 28, 1843, Rapier Papers, Moorland-Spingarn Research Center.

11. "Miscellaneous Notes of James P. Thomas," Moorland-Spingarn Research Center (hereafter, "Miscellaneous Notes"). Written on scraps of paper, backs of envelopes, and even shopping bags, the notes are not numbered by page. They were composed at various times between 1887 and 1902; A. M. Simmons to Henry K. Thomas, May 26, 1836, Rapier Papers, *Buffalo City Directory* (Buffalo, 1842), p. 213.

12. "Thomas Autobiography," 7, 9–11, 3–4.

13. Records of the Davidson County Court, Minutes, Book 1850–1853 (Mar. 6, 1851), 134–135. The earlier transactions were mentioned in Thomas's petition for legal manumission.

14. *Acts Passed at the First and Second Session of the Nineteenth General Assembly of the State of Tennessee* (Nashville, 1832), pp. 167–170.

15. "Thomas Autobiography," 1–6.

16. *The Seventh Census of the United States: 1850* (Washington, D.C., 1853), p. 582.

17. James P. Thomas, to John H. Rapier, Jr., Oct. 3, 1856, Rapier Papers; John H. Rapier, Sr., to Richard Rapier, Apr. 8, 1845, *ibid.*

18. John H. Rapier, Sr., to Richard Rapier, Apr. 8, 1845, Rapier Papers. For the activities of the Rapiers, see: Ira Berlin, pp. 280, 356, 387; Loren Schweninger, "John H. Rapier, Sr.: A Slave and Freedman in the Ante-Bellum South," *Civil War History*, XX (Mar. 1974), 23–34; and "A Slave Family in the Ante-Bellum South," *Journal of Negro History*, LX (Jan. 1975), 29–45.

19. Records of the Davidson County Court, Wills and Inventories, Vol. 11 (Feb. 1, 1838), 111, 112.

20. J. Merton England, "The Free Negro in Davidson County, Tennessee" (M.A. thesis, Vanderbilt University, 1937), p. 37; U.S. Office of the Census, "Free Inhabitants of the City of Nashville, 1850," *passim*, on microfilm at the Tennessee State Library and Archives, Nashville. Even compensating for the inaccuracies of the census takers, as well as the fact that some of these blacks could probably write only a few sentences, this is a high literacy rate. See: Bertram Wyatt-Brown, "Southern History Upside Down: Cliometrics and Slavery," *Reviews in American History*, II (Dec., 1974), 461. In other parts of the South, blacks also established schools. For the remarkable exploits of black educator John Chavis, see John Hope Franklin, *The Free Negro in North Carolina, 1790–1860* (Chapel Hill, 1943) pp. 73, 106–107, 170–171, 173–177.

21. "A Biographical Sketch of James Napier," Napier Papers, Special Collections, Fisk University, Nashville.

22. For biographical data on Lowery, see: Samuel Lowery, to Rutherford B. Hayes, Washington, D.C., Oct. 22, 1877, *General Records of the Department of Justice*, Records Relating to the Appointment of Federal Judges, 1877–1881, R. G. 60, Box #3, National Archives, Washington, D.C. In a letter to President Chester Arthur concerning an appointment as a United States Marshal for the Northern District of Alabama, Lowery boasted that he had recently been "admitted to practice before the Supreme Court of the United States." Samuel Lowery, to Chester Arthur, Sept. 29, 1881, *ibid.* For information on Nelson Walker, see: *The Colored Tennessean*, Aug. 17, 1865, Cincinnati *Daily Commercial*, Aug. 13, 1865; Nashville *Daily Press and Times*, Aug. 8, 1865.

23. *The Colored Tennessean*, Aug. 17, 1865; Nashville *Daily Press and Times*, Apr. 4, 1868; J. Merton England, "The Free Negro in Ante-Bellum Tennessee" (Ph.D. dissertation, Vanderbilt University, 1941), p. 32.

24. *Circular and Announcement of the Seventeenth Session of the Medical Department of Iowa State University* (Keokuk, Iowa, 1865), p. 48; John H. Rapier, Jr., Keokuk, Iowa, to U.S. Surgeon General, Washington, D.C., Apr. 21, 1864, *Records of the Adjutant*

Generals' Office, Medical Officer's File of John H. Rapier, Jr., R. G. 94, National Archives; John H. Rapier, Jr., to Andrew Johnson, Jan. 6, 1865, Andrew Johnson Papers, Manuscript Division, Library of Congress.

25. James P. Thomas, to John H. Rapier, Jr., Oct. 3, 1856, Rapier Papers. At the time, Rapier was on his way to Canada where he would spend the next eight years furthering his education. Loren Schweninger, "A Fugitive Negro in the Promised Land: James Rapier in Canada, 1856–1864," *Ontario History*, LXVII (June, 1975), 91–104.

26. John H. Rapier, Sr., to Henry K. Thomas, Feb. 28, 1843, Rapier Papers.

27. John H. Rapier, Sr., To Richard Rapier, Apr. 8, 1845, *ibid.*

28. John H. Rapier, Sr., to Henry K. Thomas, Feb. 28, 1843, *ibid.*

29. Sarah Thomas, to John H. Rapier, Jr., Mar. 10, 1857, *ibid.*

30. Henry K. Thomas, to John H. Rapier, Sr., Oct. 27, 1856, *ibid.*

31. James P. Thomas, to John H. Rapier, Jr., June 17, 1858, *ibid.*

32. John H. Rapier, Sr., to Henry K. Thomas, Feb. 28, 1843, *ibid.*; John H. Rapier, Sr., to Richard Rapier, Apr. 8, 1845, *ibid.*

33. "Thomas Autobiography," 7–11.

34. *Nashville General Business Directory* (Nashville, 1853), pp. 1–22; *ibid.* (1857), p. 3; "Diary of John Berrien Lindsley," Feb. 7, 1849, Lindsley Papers, State Library and Archives, Nashville.

35. "Thomas Autobiography," Ch. IV.

36. *Ibid.*; *Nashville General Business Directory* (1853), pp. 1–5; For the early business and financial activities of E. S. Hall in Nashville, see: John Claybrooke Papers, Manuscript Division, State Library and Archives, Nashville. And for the activities of the other whites mentioned, see: Phillip Hamer, *Tennessee: A History*, I (New York, 1935), 282, 370, 381, 435; "Leadership in Nashville: Biographical Sketches of 116 of the Most Prominent Citizens in Nashville," Catherine Pilcher Avery Papers, Manuscript Division, State Library and Archives, Nashville; J. G. M. Ramsey, *The Annals of Tennessee* (Charleston, S.C. 1853), pp. 293, 543; William B. Nicholson, "Biographical Glimpses of Early Nashville," in Nicholson Papers, Manuscript Division, State Library and Archives, Nashville.

37. Ellen S. Fogg, to E. H. Foster, Feb. 15, 1849, Ephraim Foster Papers, Manuscript Division, State Library and Archives, Nashville.

38. "Thomas Autobiography," Ch. VII. As there are no accurate page numbers in this chapter, the following references and quotes can be cited only with the chapter. For a more detailed examination of this second trip as well as an analysis of how southern travellers like Polk perceived the North, see John Hope Franklin, *A Southern Odyssey* (Baton Rouge, 1976), Ch. IV.

39. "Thomas Autobiography," 39–40, 44–45; 44, 45; Ridley Wills, II, "Letters from Nashville, 1862, I: A Portrait of Belle Meade," *Tennessee Historical Quarterly*, XXXIII (Spring, 1974), 70–84.

40. "Thomas Autobiography," Ch. IV.

41. *Nashville General Business Directory* (1853), p. 68.

42. *Ibid.*, p. 69.

43. "Thomas Autobiography," p. 64.

44. *Ibid.*, p. 65.

45. *Nashville Republican*, Apr. 21, 1836; Nashville *Daily Republican Banner*, Apr. 9, 1841.

46. "Thomas Autobiography," p. 64; Records of the Davidson County Court, Minutes, Book 3 (Oct. 4, 1853), 563, 564; *ibid.*, Wills and Inventories, Vol. 16 (Nov. 28, 1854), 428, 429; *ibid.*, Warranty Deeds, Book 22 (Oct. 9, 1855), p. 330; Book 19 (Dec. 23, 1854), 251–253; Book 33 (June 22, 1864), p. 366.

47. Legislative Papers, Petitions, Davidson County, "A Petition Asking to Emancipate Slave Peter Lowery," 1837, Tennessee State Library and Archives, Nashville; *ibid.*, "Petition of Peter Lowery Asking to Remain in the State," 1839, State Library and Archives, Nashville; Records of the Davidson County Court, Minute Book 1850–1853

352   LOREN SCHWENINGER

(Mar. 6, 1851), 135–137, 144, 175, 192. As Ira Berlin suggests, economic opportunity for
blacks was far greater in the South than in the North during the period. Ira Berlin, "The
Structure of the Free Negro Caste in the Ante-Bellum United States," *Journal of Social
History,* IX (1976), 297–318.

48. *Nashville General Business Directory* (1853), p. 22.

49. Records of the Davidson County Court, Wills and Inventories, Vol. 9 (July 7,
1832), p. 596; *ibid.,* Warranty Deeds, Book 2 (Mar. 12, 1840), 389, 390; Book 7 (Jan. 25,
1845), p. 247; *Private Acts Passed at the First Session of the Twentieth General Assembly
of the State of Tennessee* (Nashville, 1833), p. 96; *Nashville General Business Directory*
(1853), p. 13.

50. "Old Days in Nashville, Tennessee, Reminiscences by Jane Thomas," reprints
from the Nashville *Daily American,* 1895–1896, in Jane Thomas Papers, Tennessee
State Library and Archives, Nashville.

51. Nashville *Banner,* Jan. 26, 1858; *Nashville General Business Directory* (1853),
passim; "Thomas Autobiography," 15–35; U.S. Office of the Census, "Free Inhabitants
of the City of Nashville," 1840, 1850, 1860, *passim,* on microfilm at Tennessee State
Library and Archives, Nashville; Robert Fogel and Stanley Engerman, *Time on the
Cross,* p. 135; Eugene Genovese, *Roll, Jordan, Roll,* p. 391.

52. Clement Eaton, "Slave-Hiring in the Upper South: A Step Toward Freedom,"
Mississippi Valley Historical Review, XLVI (Mar. 1960), 663–678.

53. Richard C. Wade, *Slavery in the Cities,* pp. 40–43.

54. Quoted in Ira Berlin, *Slaves Without Masters,* p. 148.

55. "Thomas Autobiography," p. 54.

56. In Dutch New Netherlands (1624–1661) a system known as "half-freedom"
evolved whereby black slaves lived a portion of each year completely independent of
their master. Edgar J. McManus, *A History of Negro Slavery in New York* (Syracuse,
1966), pp. 13–15.

57. *Acts Passed at the First Session of the Fourteenth General Assembly of the State of
Tennessee* (Knoxville, 1821), p. 34; *Private Acts Passed at the Called Session of the
Nineteenth General Assembly of the State of Tennessee* (Nashville, 1832), pp. 5–6; *Public
Acts Passed at the First Session of the Twentieth General Assembly of the State of Tennes-
see* (Nashville, 1833), pp. 2–3, 75–76, 87, 94, 99–100, 215–216; William Imes, "The
Legal Status of Free Negroes and Slaves in Tennessee," *Journal of Negro History,* IV
(July, 1919), 260, 261; *Revised Laws of the City of Nashville* (1850), pp. 124–126; *ibid.*
(1854), pp. 147, 154–158.

58. "Thomas Autobiography," *passim.*

59. James P. Thomas, to John H. Rapier, Jr., Mar. 1, 1856, Rapier Papers; James P.
Thomas, to John H. Rapier, Jr., Oct. 3, 1856, *ibid.*

60. Philip May Hamer, *Tennessee: A History, 1673–1932,* I (New York, 1933), 264,
282, 298–299, 310, 370; "Leadership in Nashville: Biographical Sketches Listing 116 of
the Most Prominent Citizens in Nashville," Catherine Pilcher Avery Papers, State
Library and Archives, Nashville.

61. Ephraim H. Foster, Mrs. Jane Foster, July 30, 1847, Ephraim Foster Papers, State
Library and Archives, Nashville, Records of the Davidson County Court, Minute Book,
Apr. 1819 to October 1821 (Oct. 1821), p. 208; *ibid.,* Minutes Book, 1850–1853 (Mar.
6, 1851), 134, 135.

62. Records of the Davidson County Court, Minutes Book, Oct. 1816 to Jan. 1818
(Feb. 2–3, 1818), p. 457.

63. *Ibid.,* Minute Book, Apr. 1819 to Oct. 1821 (Oct. 1821), p. 208.

64. *Ibid.,* Minute Book, 1850–1853 (Mar. 6, 1851), p. 135.

65. "Thomas Autobiography," p. 7.

66. Records of the Davidson County Court, Minute Book, 1850–1853 (Mar. 6, 1851),
p. 135.

67. *Ibid.,* 135–136.

68. "Thomas Autobiography," p. 82; Records of the Davidson County Court, Warranty Deeds, Book 18 (June 1, 1854), 366, 367.

69. Cyprian Clamorgan, *The Colored Aristocracy of St. Louis* (St. Louis, 1858), p. 18.

70. Records of the St. Louis City Court, Marriage Records, Vol. 13 (Feb. 12, 1868), p. 222.

71. *Tax Book for the Year 1879, State of Missouri* (St. Louis, 1880), pp. 26–29, in Records of the St. Louis City Court, St. Louis, Missouri. Thomas died in St. Louis in 1913, rating a front-page story in the conservative St. Louis *Post-Dispatch*, Dec. 16, 1913.

THIRTEEN

"To Feel like a Man": Black Seamen in the Northern States, 1800–1860

W. JEFFREY BOLSTER

"Those beautiful vessels, robed in white, and so delightful to the eyes of freemen," remembered Frederick Douglass of the sailing ships he saw daily during this boyhood along the Chesapeake Bay, "were to me so many shrouded ghosts." Douglass contrasted the ships, "loosed from [their] moorings, and free," with his own condition—"fast in my chains, and . . . a slave!" And he swore, as he later recollected, "This very bay shall yet bear me into freedom."[1]

As it turned out, Douglass employed a seafaring subterfuge instead of a ship to escape his chains. Rigging himself out in "a red shirt and tarpaulin hat and black cravat, tied in sailor fashion, carelessly and loosely about my neck," he borrowed a seaman's protection certificate from a bona fide black sailor and brazenly struck out for Philadelphia by train. He succeeded that September day in 1838 largely because free black seamen were then so common as to cause few second looks.[2]

Frederick Douglass never went to sea. Yet as a skilled ship caulker he worked on the wharves in Baltimore (and later did odd jobs in New Bedford, Massachusetts) shoulder to shoulder with black and white sailors and, in his own words, "knew a ship from stem to stern, and from keelson to crosstrees, and could talk sailor like an 'old salt.'" No stranger to waterfront tales of hardship, brutality, and deprivation at sea, Douglass nonetheless persisted in his metaphorical view of ships as "freedom's swift-winged angels" because, unlike the white men who spoke movingly of the "slavery" aboard ship, Douglass knew real slavery firsthand.[3]

Whether ex-slave like Frederick Douglass or freeborn, all northern black men recognized seafaring as one of the few jobs readily available to them in the racially restricted employment market of the late eighteenth and early nineteenth centuries. Blacks then consistently signed aboard ship in disproportionately large numbers relative to their strength in the northern states' populations as a whole. Afro-American men filled between 17% and 22% of Philadelphia's seafaring jobs between 1800 and 1820, when blacks (both men *and* women) in the Pennsylvania–Delaware–New Jersey area were only 5% of the population. Black men occupied approximately 20% of the available berths in Providence, Rhode Island, during those years, when blacks constituted only 8.5% of that city's population and only 4% of the state's. Similar figures reflect a higher proportion of black seamen than black residents in New York, Connecticut, and Massachusetts. In a petition to the Massachusetts legislature in 1788, Afro-American sailors from Boston stressed the importance of the occupation for men of their race by arguing that shipping out provided one calling in which "thay might get a hanceum livehud for themselves and theres" (see table 1).[4]

Most black seamen's lives unfolded differently from those of other northern black workers precisely because of the specialized nature of seafaring, an occupation with significant psychological and social ramifications for its workers. This essay is attentive to those differences and to the unique appeal for black workers of the Atlantic maritime culture then prevalent aboard American ships. It shows how a partly separate subculture with its own mores and traditions, like that of Atlantic maritime workers, could offer minority men opportunities not available in the mainstream. It touches on the historical conditions that allowed a degree of freedom and opportunity for black men in the maritime industries of the late eighteenth and early nineteenth centuries, including a perpetual shortage of sailors and merchant shipowners' belief in a vertically ordered society in which the "mob," be it black or white, was expected to provide hands for ships. The essay concludes by examining the erosion of those conditions in antebellum America.

After 1840 in most northern states, individual blacks' positions aboard ship declined. Their numerical strength on specific ships in the early national period eroded; by the antebellum years, the black seafarer was often cook or steward alone amid an all-white crew. While seafaring had contributed economically to early-nineteenth-century black family stability and black community formation, blacks' declining position in the industry at mid-century made shipping out then a more casual occupation, less likely to return significant wages — or wage earners — to their home ports. That declension foreshadowed the constriction of blacks' opportunities at sea during Reconstruction and their virtual exclusion from the industry by Jim Crow unions in the late nineteenth century.[5]

Historians, like the train conductor who let Douglass slip by, have usually been blind to Afro-American sailors. Maritime historians have ignored the fact that foredeck gangs were substantially integrated, more so than most

TABLE 1

Allotment of Berths by Race

Year	% of Population African-American	% of Males African-American	% of Berths Held by African Americans	% of Berths Held by Whites	All Berths
			Providence		
1800	8.6	-	-	-	-
1803–1804	-	-	22.0	78.0	723
1807	-	-	23.0	77.0	381
1808	-	-	15.5	84.5	245
1810	8.6	-	21.5	78.5	683
1816	-	-	21.6	78.4	333
1818	-	-	18.7	81.3	609
1820	8.2	6.7	23.0	77.0	456
1822	-	-	19.0	81.0	788
1825	-	-	23.8	76.2	554
1829	-	-	23.3	76.7	459
1830	3.3	2.7	18.0	82.0	396
1832	-	-	22.5	77.5	517
1834	-	-	29.0	71.0	543
1836	-	-	30.5	69.5	246
1839	-	-	20.0	80.0	440
1840	5.6	4.8	16.0	84.0	361
1844	-	-	11.4	88.6	369
1846	-	-	15.0	85.0	342
1850	2.0	1.9	7.5	92.5	200
1853	-	-	11.0	89.0	277
1856	-	-	9.0	91.0	242
			New York		
1800	10.5	-	-	-	-
1803–1806	-	-	17.1	82.9	561
1810	10.2	-	-	-	-
1818–1819	-	-	17.4	82.6	688
1820	8.6	7.0	-	-	-
1825	-	-	18.2	81.8	734
1830	7.0	6.3	-	-	-
1835	-	-	13.8	86.2	523
1840	5.2	4.6	8.3	91.7	1407
1846	-	-	6.9	93.1	686
1850	2.7	2.4	-	-	-
1856	-	-	7.6	92.4	499
1860	1.5	1.3	-	-	-
			Philadelphia		
1800	10.3	-	-	-	-
1803	-	-	17.4	82.6	811
1810	11.8	-	22.4	77.6	1047
1820	11.8	10.3	18.4	81.6	1026
1825	-	-	19.5	80.5	1083
1830	8.3	7.5	17.0	83.0	862
1838	-	-	16.6	83.3	946
1840	7.7	6.2	15.4	84.6	643
1846	-	-	18.0	82.0	1039
1850	4.8	4.3	13.2	86.8	1127
1853	-	-	17.0	83.0	1029
1860	3.9	3.4	-	-	-

SOURCES: Providence Crew Lists, U.S. Customs House Papers, Providence, R.I., RG 28 (Manuscript Collection. Rhode Island Historical Society, Providence); New York and Philadelphia Crew Lists, Records of the U.S. Customs Service, RG 36 (National Archives); U.S. Census Office, *Return of the Whole Number of Persons within the Several Districts of the United States, According to an Act Providing for the Second Census or Enumeration of the Inhabitants of the United States* ([Washington], 1800), 26, 27, 35; U.S. Census Office, *Aggregate Amount of Each Description of Persons within the United States of America and the Territories Thereof, Agreeably to Actual Enumeration Made According to Law, in the Year 1810* [Washington, 1811], 23, 28, 51; U.S. Census Office, *Census for 1820, Published by Authority of an Act of Congress under the Direction of the Secretary of State* (Washington, 1821), 8, 13, 20; U.S. Census Office, *Fifth Census; or, Enumeration of the Inhabitants of the United States, Corrected at the Department of State, 1830* (Washington, 1832), 24–25, 54–55, 66–67; U.S. Census Office, *Sixth Census; or, Enumeration of the Inhabitants of the United States, As Corrected at the Department of State in 1840* (Washington, 1841), 54–55, 122–23, 156–57; J. D. B. DeBow, *Statistical View of the United States, Embracing Its Territory, Population–White, Free Colored, and Slave–Moral and Social Condition, Industry, Property, and Revenue; The Detailed Statistics of Cities, Towns, and Counties; Being a Compendium of the Seventh Census* (Washington, 1854), 278, 296; Joseph C. G. Kennedy, *Population of the United States in 1860, Compiled from the Original Returns of the Eighth Census* (Washington, 1864), 337, 432, 444.

early-nineteenth-century labor forces.[6] Even more surprising, given Herbert Aptheker's observation almost forty years ago that "maritime occupations were among the most important followed by Negroes," has been the neglect of black sailors by scholars of northern Afro-American communities. That oversight has implicitly reinforced the conventional notion that sailors were "beyond the pale," rather than the more accurate recognition that seafaring was inextricably entwined in the family life, community structure, and sense of self of northern blacks in the early republic.[7]

The few historians of black sailors have focused on the aggregate rather than the individual, on wholesale data—such as James Barker Farr's finding that in the 1850s "6,000 black men were serving in the American merchant marine"—rather than on the processes through which such men's sea experience changed, and the meaning that seafaring held for them.[8] Simply knowing that black men were part of ships' crews prompts questions about their commitment to seafaring, about their prestige in the black community, and about how their lives and careers may have differed from those of their white counterparts.

Observers along the wharves and aboard ship during the years of the early republic saw a variety of African-American mariners—green hands and old salts, casual laborers and committed professionals, adventuresome rakes and responsible providers. Contemporaries recognized the ambiguities and multiple realities of blacks' seafaring experience. Scholars should do the same and should resist the attempt to reconstruct that experience in entirely consistent terms. As seafarers, Afro-Americans experienced relative racial toleration and racial friction; they embraced the quintessential American appeal of economic mobility through seafaring wages, yet they expressed the opposition to shoreside norms common to many sailors; they felt the lure of the sea and the appeal of a manly life, along with the subjugation, tyranny, and iron discipline prevalent in life under sail.

One attraction in studying seamen is the possibility of transcending local particularity. Community studies indicate that members of similar ethnic and occupational groups rarely had identical experiences in different places. The arguments here rely on logbooks, literature, court records, and narratives from much of the American fleet, as well as on quantifiable shipping records from Providence, New York, and Philadelphia, and glimpses of such records from Boston, Newport, and New London.[9] The pattern that emerges has a local exception: blacks who shipped out of Philadelphia did not find shrinking opportunities in the 1840s as their counterparts east of the Hudson River did. Despite fierce competition from white labor, and despite a decided shift aboard ship from deck to galley duties, substantial numbers of black men continued to find employment aboard Philadelphia vessels.

However much this discussion draws on local Providence, New York, or Philadelphia data, the antebellum black seafaring experience cannot be understood without some reference to Atlantic maritime culture in its entirety.[10] Culture is understood here, in William Roseberry's words, "not sim-

ply as a product but also as a production"—a continuously evolving influence rooted in the changing conditions of daily life and work, and inextricably linked to power relationships. Since the age of the Roman Empire,
Atlantic and Mediterranean seamen (irrespective of nationality or race) had
been shaped by shipboard cultural forms that endowed them with distinctive
attitudes and perceptions. In common parlance, such forms evolved as the
traditions or usages of the sea. Samuel Taylor Coleridge acknowledged the
generation of a distinctive maritime culture by sailors

> Crowded in the rank and narrow ship,—
> Housed on the wild sea with wild usages.[11]

Following the work of Charles A. Valentine and Eric R. Wolf, it is quite
appropriate to regard men socialized in those shipboard usages as at least
bicultural, as having available simultaneously two or more distinct yet in-
tertwined cultural systems or resources, based on their origins and on their
international occupation.[12] Individuals belonging to bounded ethnic or
occupational groups often have multiple, and sometimes conflicting, allegiances and play multiple roles. Nineteenth-century black American seamen daily lived that multiplicity, maneuvering through white and black
societies ashore, and maritime society afloat. When under way in the company of other seamen, sailors' behavior was largely conditioned by their Atlantic maritime culture.

Seafarers' culture, as Marcus Rediker has vividly shown for the eighteenth
century, included strong "egalitarian impulses." That egalitarianism frequently confounded shoreside racial etiquette. Three white sailors from the
American brig *Neptune*, after being befriended in 1787 by a Georgian black
man named Charles, "thanked him, [and] shook him by the hand"—a
gesture unthinkable to the mass of white Georgians. During the war of 1812,
the crew of an American warship, invited to a theatrical performance in New
York City honoring their bravery in battle, "marched *together* into the pit,
and nearly one half of them were negroes." Forecastle culture evolved in
shipboard populations recruited by merchants with more of an eye to muscle
than complexion. While by no means either color-blind or without internal
frictions, Atlantic maritime culture created its own institutions and its own
stratifications, which could work to the relative advantage of black men. One
observer summed it up by writing, "The good will of 'old salts' to negroes is
proverbial."[13]

The written legal structures associated with the Atlantic maritime culture
stretched back to medieval codes, including Barcelona's thirteenth-century
Consolato del mare, and to the Rolls of Oléron, the basis of maritime
common law in the North Sea and the Atlantic Ocean. For centuries these
codes served foremost to protect the property of owners and shippers. The
legal emphasis was not on seamen's rights, but on their restriction and
punishment.[14] This is not to say that sailors succumbed without resistance to
a hegemony imposed by merchant capitalism. They did not. It is to say that

shipboard life and Atlantic maritime culture evolved around the concept of order—no matter how contested that order may have been. Today our language retains the word *shipshape* to connote compulsive orderliness. We acknowledge that a teacher, executive, or coach who runs "a taut ship" is not one with whom to trifle.

The seagoing workplace in which nineteenth-century black Americans found themselves placed its priority on shipboard order maintained through a precise "distinction of role and status." As Greg Dening points out, "In the total institution of a ship, persons were owed little. Role and rule were owed everything. . . . all was depersonalized."[15] The articles that each man signed indicated his position (mate, second mate, carpenter, cook, seaman, ordinary seaman, boy) almost immutably fixing his status on board. Boundary maintenance—between officers and men, between larboard and starboard watches, between idlers and watch standers, between skilled and greenhands—was the essence of life aboard ship, for boundaries delineated privileges, perquisites, and punishments. Though formal boundaries could flex to accommodate human relationships, they never entirely broke down, and they essentially defined the social combinations and conflicts at the heart of seafaring life. Racial boundaries certainly existed, but they were often secondary to those established by the institution of the ship.

For a black man, then, the ship provided a unique workplace where his color might be less a determinant of his daily life and duties than elsewhere. The power of the Atlantic maritime culture to offset racist norms was nowhere better dramatized than by a visitor's observation in New Orleans around 1800 that quadroon naval officers aboard ship might "give twenty lashes with the end of a rope to white sailors, but ashore they dare not even look them in the face." New Bedford whale ships—dirty, dangerous, isolated, and one of the few places black men might sail as officers—also upset established racial hierarchy. Young Frank T. Bullen found himself questioned by a black man moments after joining the *Cachelot* in 1875.

> I said "yes" very curtly, for I hardly liked his patronizing air; but he snapped me up short with "yes, *sir*, when yew speak to me, yew blank limejuicer. I'se de fourf mate ob dis yar ship, en my name's Mistah Jones, 'n yew jest freeze on to dat ar, ef yew want ter lib long 'n die happy. See, sonny." I *saw*, and answered promptly, "I beg your pardon, sir, I didn't know."[16]

Less compelling in their drama, but no less indicative of the fact that a seaman's billet meant more than his race when it came to pay and privileges, were the innumerable Yankee ships on which black men before the mast ranked higher and earned more than white co-workers. The best-paid sailor aboard the Rhode Island brig *Mary* sailing to Cuba in 1819 was Cato Burrill, a black veteran of twenty-five years at sea. Sixteen years later, when the *Panther* cleared for the East Indies, only one black man was aboard. Paid the same as the white sailors, he earned three times as much as the white "boys" and would not have deigned to stoop to their menial and unskilled tasks. The historical precedent arising from such black men's experiences and their shipmates' respect contributed to Herman Melville's introduction of a manly black as the archetypal Handsome Sailor in *Billy Budd*. "The center of a company of his shipmates," he was "on every suitable occasion always foremost."[17]

This is not to suggest that most white Americans' racial prejudice disappeared when they stepped over a ship's rail. Duncan McClellan, late supernumerary of the bark *Triton*, said of a shipmate in 1840: "Mr. Hansen was the most unpopular person on board, both with the officers and the men, more so than the nigger cook." Prejudice, the implication is clear, remained the norm among seamen as among other white Americans. When festering in a captain well beyond the law, it could be deadly.[18] But overtly racist actions by other sailors were often subordinated to the requirements of shipboard order, and the unprecedented toleration that existed at sea afforded black men a virtually unknown degree of equality with white co-workers.

Between the seventeenth and the late nineteenth centuries blacks worked aboard all sorts of vessels as sailors, stewards, and cooks. Slaves were forcibly packed off to sea by masters eager for their wages; runaways gravitated toward ships to make good their escape from bondage; freemen recognized an occupation in which they would receive equal wages with similarly skilled white men and in which they might escape the strictures or the taunts of white society ashore. The lucky few parlayed maritime work into a good subsistence. Born in Africa, Venture Smith was sold as a child to a slaveowner on Fishers Island, New York. He later earned his freedom and that of his family, made a profitable cruise on a whaler in the 1770s, and ended his days as a landowner in Haddam, Connecticut—in great part due to the success of his small-boat freighting ventures between Rhode Island, eastern Connecticut, and Long Island.[19]

Afro-Yankees more typical than Smith also sought a livelihood on the water. Providence-born Noah Brown was fortunate to survive a romantic career on coasters and transatlantic ships, including British impressment and prison, Spanish capture, and service under fire in the War of 1812. Elisha Carder, born in Warwick, Rhode Island, in 1779 was like Melville's heroic Bulkington: "the land seemed scorching to his feet." Carder shipped out of Providence as sailor or steward on international voyages seven times in the six years following 1803, with barely a respite ashore.[20]

These black Rhode Islanders sailed in part because they knew their prospects ashore were not very flattering. Noah Brown's son William recalled their plight. "To drive carriage, carry a market basket after the boss, or brush his boots, or saw wood and run errands, was as high as a colored man could rise." Limited to odd jobs and farm labor, Rhode Island's Afro-Americans naturally gravitated to the maritime labor force in the early nineteenth century as Narragansett Bay agriculture declined and shipping expanded. Blacks outside New England made similar moves. Those from the upper South flocked to Philadelphia to search for jobs on the ships that provided the single largest employment for black and mulatto men in the region.[21]

Seafaring wages were a strong drawing card for Afro-Americans. Though shipboard wages declined with the resumption of peace in 1815, they generally equalled or exceeded those paid shore-bound laborers through the 1850s.[22] Ships provided room and board too, an important consideration for poor laborers, and the irregularity of sailors' work was nothing new to black men. A job that promised to last several months was an almost unheard-of luxury in the black community.

Most significant, for both pride and pocketbook, black sailors generally received pay equal to that of whites in the same position. Aboard the brig *John* in 1806 each of the seamen—one black, one white, one mulatto—earned $18 per month, while the white cook and the ordinary seaman each earned only $14. Lays (that is, shares) on the whaleship *Bowditch*, whose complement in 1843 was about two-thirds black, were assigned by berth regardless of race: 1/185 for green hands and 1/150 for seamen. A man motivated to resist the temptation of substantial advances in foreign ports could be paid off handsomely at the end of a voyage. "My entire savings up to the period of my return from this voyage," remembered Moses Grandy of his trip to the East Indies aboard the ship *James Murray*, "amounted to $300. I sent it to Virginia and bought my wife." Men with less compelling reasons to save could also do so. The black cook and black steward of the ship *Lion* stepped ashore after twenty-two months round the world with $254 and $280 respectively, each having been paid as well as the best white sailors aboard.[23]

Though holding a job was a prime concern for every black worker, financial duress was not the sole incentive to go to sea. Like white men, blacks were "captivated with the tough stories of the elder seamen, and seduced as well by the natural desire of seeing foreign countries." John Malvin, a free-born Virginia black man who became cook and ultimately captain of Great Lakes coasting schooners, recalled his wanderlust. "In the year 1827 a spirit of adventure, natural to most young men, took possession of me and I concluded to leave Virginia." The prestige conferred on the traveler, the manliness associated with a robust calling, the sea's own ineluctable charm, and the sense of belonging to a small community all contributed to draw black men into the maritime labor market.[24]

Shipping, the most integrated and tolerant industry in the nation, still reflected the vindictive prejudice prevailing ashore in times of economic hardship. During the embargo, in Thomas Jefferson's second term, the proportion of integrated crews in Rhode Island dropped from three-quarters to one-half, and the number of available berths going to African Americans fell from 22 percent to 15.5 percent. Overt discrimination along the Providence waterfront began as soon as the embargo's restrictions took effect.[25]

Even in good years, well-defined limits established what a black man might do aboard American ships. With the extraordinary exception of Capt.

Paul Cuffe, the Afro-American quarter of the maritime labor pool had little chance of advancement outside of whaleships and small coasters. Black men's occupational mobility in merchant ships was all lateral at best, between cook and steward and seaman. Among a sample of thirty-five hundred crews outward bound from Providence, Philadelphia, and New York between 1803 and 1856, only three had nonwhite officers. George Henry, an ex-slave seaman who escaped Providence after years of commanding a coasting schooner in his native Virginia, curtly recalled in his autobiography, "I found prejudice so great in the North that I was forced to come down from my high position as captain, and take my whitewash brush and wheelbarrow and get my living in that way." The prestige and the honorific "Captain" associated with command were still too important in northern seaports to bestow on a black man.[26]

Despite the institutionalized obstacles to advancement, young blacks vainly aspired to officers' billets and sought the training necessary. Noah Brown attended a school in Providence whose Quaker teacher "was celebrated for teaching the Mariner's art." In the late 1820s the New York African Free School added navigation to its curriculum. A Scots traveler to the New World, who in 1833 published *Men and Manners in America*, did not miss the incongruity of a society that taught navigation to a class of men and then relegated them to the galley aboard ship.[27]

Stymied in their quest for promotion whether educated in "the Mariner's art" or not, black mariners nonetheless found another appeal in sea life — its roughhewn forecastle equality. Northern blacks had traditionally been barred from trades, and even road crews occasionally demanded segregated gangs for different tasks. Blacks ashore were regularly subject to insults and invective. "If you were well dressed they would insult you for that, and if you were ragged you would surely be insulted for being so; be as peaceable as you could there was no shield for you," recalled William J. Brown in his memoirs.[28]

The pervasive prejudice encountered in the workplace and on the street, and embodied by the government in its naval manning regulations, seems to have been ameliorated offshore. Despite the order of Secretary of the Navy Benjamin Stoddert in 1798 that blacks and mulattoes were not to be enlisted aboard ship, many were. Surgeon Usher Parsons wrote of his service on the *Java* in 1816 that "the white and Negro seamen messed together. About one in six or eight were Negroes." Parsons also noted that on the *Guerriere* three years later, "There seemed to have been an entire absence of prejudice against the blacks as shipmates among the crew." Others too noted a rare racial toleration off soundings. It could get under the skin of a pro-slavery Kentuckian like J. Ross Browne, who found himself before the mast in a Yankee whaler.

> It was . . . particularly galling to my feelings to be compelled to live in the forecastle with a brutal negro, who, conscious that he was upon an equality with the sailors, presumed upon his equality to a degree that was insufferable.

TABLE 2

African-American Seamen Working in Ships with All-African-American Crews

	Providence			New York	
Year	African-American Seamen Sampled	% of African-American Seamen Working in All-African-American Crews	Year	African-American Seamen Sampled	% of African-American Seamen Working in All-African-American Crews
1803–1804	160	27	1803–1806	96	9.3
1820	105	9	1818–1819	120	15.8
1830	71	18	1825	133	7.5
1836	75	41	1835	72	22.2
1839	89	20	1840	117	7.6
1840	58	7	1846	47	0
1853	30	0	1856	38	10.5
1856	22	0			

SOURCES: Providence Crew Lists, U.S. Customs House Papers, Providence, R.I., RG 28 (Manuscript Collection, Rhode Island Historical Society, Providence); New York Crew Lists, Records of the U.S. Customs Service, RG 36 (National Archives).

Personal grudges like the one this "Kentucky dandy" held against his black shipmate soured the peace in many shipboard societies. But the evidence indicates that blacks and white sailors fraternized easily early in the century. James Kelly, in his *Voyage to Jamaica*, recorded that in the 1820s and 1830s:

> Sailors and Negroes are ever on the most amicable terms. This is evidenced in their dealings, and in the mutual confidence and familiarity that never subsist between the slaves and the resident whites. There is a feeling of independence in their intercourse with the sailor. . . . In the presence of the sailor the Negro feels as a man.[29]

Black sailors must have appreciated the toleration extended them by white shipmates in their narrow wooden worlds, where food, danger, and duty were equally shared. They probably appreciated even more the chance to sail as part of all-black crews, whose forecastle life would reflect norms and behavior of their making. Eugene D. Genovese and Rhys Isaac have convincingly demonstrated that a desire for "community in labor" pervaded American slave society. A sense of community could exist for black men plowing furrows in the ocean as well as for those plowing furrows in the fields. In 1803 more than a quarter of the black men who sailed from Providence did so in ships where only the officers were white, and many other blacks made voyages from New York and Philadelphia to the Caribbean, to Europe, and to the coast of Africa with a black majority before the mast (see table 2).[30]

The fact that few black sailors kept journals precludes us from examining firsthand the social dynamics aboard predominately black ships. But crew lists such as the one left by the brig *John Josiah Arnold*, which sailed for Spain in 1803 with a white master and mate and five black men before the mast, speak eloquently enough. Those black sailors lived in the forecastle, a part of the ship reserved for them alone by custom and practice as ancient as the common law. No officer—on the *John Josiah Arnold*, no white man—concerned for his physical well-being or for the effectiveness of his authority would dare trespass in the men's domain without fair warning. The officers likewise kept their distance during the dogwatch, the leisurely two hours at the end of the day when the men gathered around the forebitts to smoke or sing, to yarn or just chat. Officers and men, in this case whites and blacks, each maintained their own sphere in their tightly ordered world afloat. Aboard the *Arnold* a black man controlled the cooking, an important post with immediate repercussions for sailors who wanted to dry their socks or light their pipes at his hearth, and unless the captain regularly stood a watch, a black man also had charge of the deck at times—officer de facto if not de jure.[31]

Black sailors on ships with a black majority before the mast, such as the *John Josiah Arnold*, had found a more congenial workplace than many of their brethren ashore. Sailors—black or white—had to create a pattern of existence as satisfying as possible under the constraints of their ship's demands for labor and its restraints on personal freedom. Black men who signed aboard ships with an entirely black crew were conscious of the opportunity (even within the inevitable hierarchy of the ship) to mold their own forecastle social life from the camaraderie of an isolated, masculine, and Afro-American world.

A black crew with white officers can be seen as a microscopic version of the societies that existed on such "sugar islands" as Jamaica in the seventeenth and eighteenth centuries. Though whites claimed proprietorship of "their" plantations or ships, though they extracted the profits, and though they remained in power through the threat or use of corporal punishment, it was the black culture that prevailed in those plantations and on those ships. At sea, the larger maritime culture tempered and adapted that black culture.

Culture is always inextricably entwined with work, but nowhere more intimately than aboard a ship, a "total institution" whose members work, sleep, and spend their leisure within its boundaries. The "total character" of shipboard life and its isolation wrenched men's terrestrial roots and bound those men through their Atlantic maritime culture to a society of their own making, a society which "was, for all its difficulties, quite select." It is probable that many black men chose seafaring precisely for this sociability in the workplace. When the number of all-black crews declined at midcentury, individual black sailors became increasingly isolated in the midst of otherwise white forecastle worlds. As late as 1839, however, a fifth of the black men sailing out of Providence did so in predominately black crews.[32]

Whether living and working at sea primarily among black shipmates or with whites, some black men cultivated an important occupational identity through repeated voyaging. Restricted from artisan trades ashore in the northern states, black sailors proudly picked up marlinespike and serving mallet instead. A decided hierarchy existed among Jack Tars, ranging from the "landsman" to the ordinary sailor who could "hand, reef, and steer," to the skilled able-bodied seaman (AB) who could turn in an eye splice, set up a deadeye, or send down a yard. Chief mates prized "old salts" who had mastered tools and skills essential to maintaining the tautness and integrity of their ships' rigging. Only racist exclusivity kept such men from advancing, a point acknowledged years later by the wife of schooner captain Fred Balano. Referring to a black man in their crew, she confided to her diary, "As Fred says, Dawson would be a captain if he were white."[33]

Acculturation to the world of the ship also conferred on professional black seamen—as it did on their white shipmates—a distinctive identity separate from that of common laborers. Seamen boasted to provincial acquaintances of their worldly travels and exotic encounters; they took a fierce pride in their technical competence; they cultivated a fatalistic stoicism in the face of frequent danger; and they valued pugilism and pluck, traits that stood them in good stead both in their rough-and-tumble waterfront world and in their routine defiance of ships' officers.[34]

Skilled able-bodied seamen versed in "the Mariner's art" were admittedly a minority among black seamen, but men like Daniel Watson, who was born and raised in Providence and who made five foreign voyages between 1803 and 1810, had a strong professional identity as seamen. Watson, and men of the next generation like African-born David O'Kee, an ex-slave who made at least eight voyages out of Providence in the 1830s, were fully socialized to the world of the ship, and possibly more at home there than ashore.[35]

The majority of black men who signed aboard early-nineteenth-century ships, however, were hardly regular seamen. William J. Brown's ten dollars per month as a deckhand on the sloop *Venus* was insufficient in his mind to compensate for nearly foundering, and Brown gladly went ashore. Seafaring for Brown was only one more job in a career path that had included every menial task. Drawn by the fleeting security of a few months' wages, black casual seamen like Brown flowed into the maritime labor market when it could absorb them and then drifted—or were bounced—back ashore to ditchdigging, boot blacking, wood chopping, and unemployment.[36]

Seafaring, both casual and committed, became a bulwark of employment for early-nineteenth-century Rhode Island blacks, including the black community's leaders. When the Providence African Union Society (the city's first black benevolent group) drafted its bylaws at the turn of the century, it acknowledged seafaring's importance to eminent black citizens by agreeing to a common sacrifice: members covenanted not to serve on slavers, despite those ships' prominence in the Newport and Bristol fleets. Even unmarried young men from the black community made a determined effort not to let

TABLE 3

Seamen's Ages

	1803		1820	1830		1850	
Ages	African-American	White	African-American	African-American	White	African-American	White
			Philadelphia				
To 19	10.8%	18.0%	3.8%	8.9%	20.1%	5.7%	-
20–29	62.5	62.8	46.7	47.9	45.4	37.5	-
30–39	20.0	16.2	29.1	30.2	24.2	30.7	-
40–49	5.0	2.3	16.5	7.5	8.3	20.4	-
50+	1.7	.7	3.9	5.5	2.0	5.7	-
	100.0%	100.0%	100.0%	100.0%	100.0%	100.0%	
N	120	513	182	146	566	88	-
			Providence				
To 19	15%	30.0%	-	11.0%	22.5%	-	22.0%
20–29	62	54.5	-	41.0	55.5	60.0%	53.0
30–39	17	12.0	-	35.0	16.0	33.0	19.5
40–49	6	3.0	-	11.0	5.0	7.0	5.0
50+	-	.5	-	2.0	1.0	-	.5
	100.0%	100.0%		100.0%	100.0%	100.0%	100.0%
N	48	167	-	46	157	15	153

SOURCES: Providence Crew Lists, U.S. Customs House Papers, Providence, R.I., RG 28 (Manuscript Collection, Rhode Island Historical Society, Providence); Philadelphia Crew Lists, Records of the U.S. Customs Service, RG 36 (National Archives).

seafaring's occupational hazards blemish their characters. When Jesse Almy applied for his Seaman's Protection Certificate in 1809 he simultaneously requested a letter from his Baptist congregation "to any sister church for transient membership."[37]

A substantial case, in fact, can be made in retrospect that seafaring was a pillar of support for the aspiring black "middle class," for blacks who owned property and were determined to improve their situation. Paul Cuffe, a Massachusetts merchant and shipmaster, and James Forten, a Philadelphia sailmaker with sea experience who patented a device for handling sails, best exemplified black Americans' maritime entrepreneurship. Elleanor Eldridge, a Rhode Island weaver whose prowess at the loom earned her modest wealth and property, was an example of the tiny black "middle class": she had been engaged to a man lost at sea. Yet an important question remains unanswered. To what extent did the "better sort" of black citizens look to the sea and ships as an avenue of advancement? It is fair to say that many an enterprising black man shipped out in the early nineteenth century; it is

TABLE 4

Persistence at Sea
(Men Making at Least Three Voyages from Providence in Seven Years)

N = Men Sailing in First Year/Men Still Sailing Seven Years Later

	African-American		White	
Years	N	%	N	%
1803–1810	48/10	21	167/43	26
1830–1837	45/11	24	156/27	17
1850–1856	15/1	7	153/19	12

SOURCE: Providence Crew Lists, U.S. Customs House Papers, Providence, R.I., RG 28 (Manuscript Collection, Rhode Island Historical Society, Providence).

probably fair to say as well that seafaring never attained the status of barbering, or other dignified professions, in the black community ashore. Henry Highland Garnet, a respected black preacher and abolitionist who had been to sea as a boy, castigated seafaring in 1852. Writing from Jamaica, Garnet asserted that "West Indian towns are generally notorious for immorality, and the reason is they are usually seaports."[38]

Many black men, however, chose maritime employment as a means to establish households and raise families. William J. Brown noted that his father was married in Cranston in 1805, "and commenced keeping house in that town, but being engaged in a seafaring life he removed to Providence and rented a house of Dr. Pardon Bowen." Noah Brown continued to ship out on deepwater voyages for another decade. The "Return of Coloured Persons Being Housekeepers" compiled in Providence in 1822 listed a number of black sailors, including Fortune Dyer, whose wife and child profited by a boarder's company in his absence. By the time the Providence city directory was published in 1832 one-quarter of the heads of African-American households were mariners. These Rhode Island sailors were by no means anomalies: city directories for seaports from Portland, Maine, to Baltimore consistently listed seafaring in the three most common occupations for black men.[39]

Seafaring, then, meant very different things to black men and white men in the early nineteenth century. White sailors—whether gentlemen's sons inspired to dare "an insight into the mysteries of a sailor's life" or ambitious boys eager to gain a command or "rebels who left the land in flight and fear"—were geographically mobile, unmarried, and unlikely to stick with the sea unless promoted. Black sailors were older than their white shipmates, more rooted in their home ports, more likely to be married, and more likely to persist in going to sea (see tables 3 and 4).[40]

All of these differences stemmed from black men's limited employment opportunities. With few other jobs at their disposal, they had to persist in seafaring. Blacks aged in the forecastle watching white youngsters parade through. In fact, a preponderance of "old salts" in the early republic's fleet were black men with no better place to go, seamen like Prince Brown, who in his midforties, during the era of neutral trade, made at least six voyages out of Providence.[41]

Black and mulatto sailors lived with the constant tension of separation from their families because seafaring provided rare support—bittersweet support—for a black family. Samuel Crawford's private entrepreneurial venture of four barrels of potatoes aboard the brig *John*, when added to his wages, put him far ahead of intermittent day labor ashore. So Crawford spent only a few days at home with his wife after a five-and-a-half-month trip to Europe aboard the *Columbia* before sailing to Havana aboard the *John* in 1806. Black men of the next generation were likewise forced financially to leave their wives alone on shore. John Gardner, who acknowledged in 1831 that he "follow[ed] the sea mostly," came to resent his calling. Until age thirty-two Gardner lived with his mother and sisters by the Canal Basin in Providence while ashore. Then, after a two-year courtship punctuated by voyaging, he married Mary Ann Elizabeth Stewart in a Presbyterian service at her father's house. She contributed to the household they established on Olney Lane by doing laundry for the steamboats and taking in sewing and washing from other black people in the Hardscrabble neighborhood. Always pressed financially, however, Gardner spent time in jail for debt and reluctantly shipped out again in 1835. During that absence three drunken white men gang-raped his wife.[42]

White sailors rarely had families to be threatened ashore in their absence, as Nathaniel Armes indicated in his *Nautical Reminiscenes*. "I do not know that I ever sailed in an American ship," he recalled, "with an individual before the mast that was a married man with the exception of one Negro cook of Boston." The fact that Rhode Island's black mariners had families ashore made them more likely than footloose white deckhands to ship out of a home port regularly, and to keep returning there (see table 4). It also meant that maritime tragedies struck directly at the black community struggling for stability and respectability on shore. Betsy Watson of Providence lost several husbands to the sea around the turn of the century; by 1822 she had married a fourth time—to seaman Henry Gray.[43]

The link between seafaring wages and black family formation so important in Rhode Island cannot be assumed elsewhere. Free blacks' rapid influx into Philadelphia and New York created black communities substantially different from the rather stable one in Providence. Preliminary investigation reveals that only an insignificant number of Philadelphia's black seamen had roots in the city itself and that among the twenty-two hundred black mariners enumerated in New York in 1846, less than 5 percent lived with their families.[44]

Until about 1840 the greatest impediment to free black men who opted for voyaging was the southern states' "Negro Seamen Acts." Passed in 1822, on

the heels of Denmark Vesey's plot, by the South Carolina legislature (varia-
tions were later enacted in North Carolina, Georgia, Florida, Alabama, and
Louisiana), the original "Act For The Better Regulation And Government of
Free Negroes And Persons Of Color" stemmed from fears that freemen—"a
dangerous class of persons"—would infect slaves with freedom's taint. The
South Carolina legislators were right on the mark. Black sailors as early as
1809 were smuggling abolitionist material into Charleston, and after David
Walker published his fiery *Appeal* in 1829, Afro-American seamen seem to
have carried it clandestinely to southern ports. The new law required that
free black sailors arriving in South Carolina be imprisoned until their vessels departed, with their captains paying the expenses of detention. Violators
could be sold on the auctioneer's block. Enforcement of this law was occasionally strict, and occasionally lax, but it led to hundreds of free black
soldiers being incarcerated in Charleston, some of whom became *causes
célèbres* in the abolitionist press.[45]

The negro seamen acts pressured black Americans working in what had
been one of their least pressured occupations. In effect, free black seamen
with an eye to self-preservation had to exclude themselves from the nation's
single most important antebellum domestic trade—freighting southern
cotton to northern ports. Limited prospects for employment ashore forced
some black seamen to risk a southern trip. Others found themselves in the
cotton ports when their ships were rerouted mid-voyage. By 1844 free black
sailors' situation in the Deep South had become so intolerable that Massachusetts appointed commissioners to both Charleston and New Orleans in
a futile attempt to look after the rights of its black mariners.[46]

Individual black sailors' fortunes took a decided turn for the worse in the
1840s. That development seems ironic considering changes in the nature of
seafaring itself. Once New England's economic mainstay, shipping declined
in relative importance as industrialization caught Yankee entrepreneurs'
imaginations and their investment capital. As one successful shipmaster
had put it earlier in the century, working at sea then appeared to be "the most
sure and direct means of arriving at independence." Consequently, in the
early national years it entailed a degree of social acceptability. Elmo P.
Hohman exaggerated when he wrote that early-nineteenth-century crews
were "drawn from the best stock of New England, and could look forward to
becoming officers and owners."[47] The Federalist *aristoi* who comprised "the
best stock of New England" would have resented the inference that their
ranks spawned common sailors, and most seamen actually came from the
laboring population. Yet in the early national period, seafaring did offer the
possibility of prestige and promotion to white men who could withstand its
rigors, and of regular, even tolerant, employment to blacks. Northern men
shipped out in large numbers, including the talented and ambitious from
each race.[48]

By midcentury, however, mariners experienced the "lowest degradation
of [free] labor" in American history. Herman Melville's Redburn, "the son

of a gentleman in the merchant service," portrayed seamen in 1849 with a hauntingly familiar ring.

> Consider, that, with the majority of them, the very fact of their being sailors, argues a certain recklessness and sensualism of character, ignorance, and depravity; . . . consider that by their very vocation they are shunned by the better classes of people . . . consider all this, and the reflecting mind must soon perceive that the case of sailors, as a class, is not a very promising one.[49]

Substitute "Negro" for "sailor" and "race" for "vocation," and few Americans at midcentury would have missed a beat. By then the sailor's status was increasingly conflated with that of the slave.

Describing themselves as "vassals," or "slaves of the lowest cast," seamen typically moaned: "And now I ask what slave at the south suffers more hardships or feels more keenly the bitterness of oppression than the poor care worne sailor." Uncontrollable captains like Frank Thompson, master of the brig *Pilgrim* on a voyage from Boston to California in 1834, drove the point home. Seizing up two men by their wrists to the main rigging, he laid on the stripes with a rope's end and screamed:

> You see your condition! . . . I'll make you toe the mark, every soul of you, or I'll flog you all, fore and aft, from the boy up! You've got a driver over you. Yes, a *slave-driver—a nigger-driver*! I'll see who'll tell me he isn't a *nigger* slave![50]

Shipboard institutions thus posed a dramatic conflict with the "equality" and "independence" white American men had come to expect from mid-nineteenth-century democratic rhetoric. Under such circumstances and in light of black Americans' traditional seafaring, it seems that America's most degraded caste of workers—black ones—might have shouldered more and more of the merchant fleet's burdens as those burdens became increasingly onerous to white Americans. Ironically, they did not. With Irishmen and other white foreigners "willing to submit to oppressive and despotic treatment," blacks' seagoing tradition seemed to count for little when it came to hiring time. Midcentury discrimination extended not only to new occupations in the expanding economy but also to carry-overs from the past, such as seafaring.[51]

Although black men would continue to work on American ships, the circumstances of their individual sea experience began to change after 1840. Fewer black men were found in many ships as time passed, and in Rhode Island at least, fewer all-black crews existed to provide the workplace sociability important to the previous generation (see table 5).

Black men throughout the North were increasingly relegated to jobs as cooks or stewards, jobs with potential problems for a man of any race. Cooks' power over the larder could lead to either favoritism or antipathy toward men in the forecastle, but stewards—the cabin servants—were easy scapegoats and were frequently perceived by sailors as captains' flunkies. The log kept by Amos Jenckes aboard the ship *Resource* on the ceremonial occasion of

TABLE 5

Crews with African-American Majorities

	Providence		New York	
Year	Crews Sampled	% of Crews with an African-American Majority	Crews Sampled	% of Crews with an African-American Majority
1803–1804	98	19.0	71[a]	8.5
1807	61	14.5	-	-
1808	29	6.4	-	-
1810	105	15.5	-	-
1816	52	15.5	-	-
1818	91	11.0	104[b]	5.8
1820	72	16.7	-	-
1822	121	7.5	-	-
1825	92	15.2	106	9.4
1829	82	13.4	-	-
1830	74	5.5	-	-
1832	87	15.0	-	-
1834	102	21.5	-	-
1835	-	-	60	5.0
1836	49	26.5	-	-
1839	84	13.1	-	-
1840	75	8.1	125	2.4
1844	58	8.6	-	-
1846	61	10.0	114	.9
1850	45	2.2	94	7.4
1853	68	8.9	-	-
1856	57	5.3	59	4.3

SOURCES: Providence Crew Lists, U.S. Customs House Papers, Providence, R.I., RG 28 (Manuscript Collection, Rhode Island Historical Society, Providence); New York Crew Lists, Record of the U.S. Customs Service, RG 36 (National Archives).
[a]1803–1806
[b]1818–1819

crossing the equator recorded a common sentiment: "and as the Ship Steward was by no means liked of, he was the last brought up and handled more rough than any of the rest."[52] Such billets' separation from the rest of the crew—both in bunking and in duties—reflected and reinforced black men's racial distinctiveness. Cooks and stewards were not always bona fide sailors with the skill to steer a ship and maintain its rigging, and in the antebellum years fewer blacks were initiated into the mysteries of the sailor's art. White workers' hegemony over shore-based crafts slowly extended to shipboard ones as well.

The cross-racial camaraderie and fraternization that had once characterized the forecastle seems to have been eroded as that part of the ship became increasingly the province of white men. "A negro in the forecastle of a British ship," commented an Englishman at sea in the 1870s, "is a lonely being. He has no chums."[53] The same might be said of blacks on American ships as the century wore on.

We must, of course, beware of inferring a state of mind from statistics. Individual black sailors in the midst of white forecastles may not have been completely isolated: interracial fellowship and tolerance formerly prevailed at sea. The single black man whose presence so disconcerted J. Ross Browne in the 1840s apparently did not offend the rest of the white sailors. It is safe to say, however, that after midcentury black sailors were generally dependent on white shipmates for companionship, a chancy situation hinging on such variables as individual personalities and racist proclivities. Perhaps some blacks continued to find congenial situations in predominately white crews, but after midcentury black men could no longer create their own shipboard communities to the degree they once had.

The degradation of the industry (including declining wages and increasing brutality) likewise worked against black family formation ashore. With conditions making it tougher to support a family through seafaring, black mariners became increasingly rootless and casual. No longer did a large number of black sailors aboard Providence-based ships have Rhode Island birthplaces, nor did many return to Providence as home port.

The most striking thing about the Rhode Island fleet in the 1850s was that black *sailors*—the real seamen who persisted in shipping out time and time again—had disappeared. Throughout the 1850s the black men aboard Rhode Island ships were all casual laborers, men who made one or two voyages at most.[54] The prominent group of black mariners who considered themselves professionals, the "old salts" in the two generations that had included Cato Burrill, Prince Brown, Daniel Watson, and David O'Kee, were gone. Though seafaring still provided casual employment to black men with limited options ashore, it was no longer a bastion of black professionalism, or a bulwark of the tiny black "middle class" (see table 5).

Historians have long recognized a similar trend among native-born white seamen and have attributed their lack of persistence in sailing as reflection of the industry's "degradation" and of their better options ashore. Black men had no better options ashore: it seems unlikely that they would voluntarily forsake the sea. As W. E. B. Du Bois wrote, "the question of economic survival [was] the most pressing of all questions" for nineteenth-century American blacks.[55] Yet the ranks of regular seafarers in New York, Massachusetts, Rhode Island, and Connecticut whitened noticeably at midcentury.

Charting historical phenomena is often more straightforward then explaining them. Trying to understand the midcentury squeeze on black seafarers prompts us to examine simultaneous changes in American society as a whole, in the northern seaport economies, and in the specifics of maritime hiring practices. Several sociological trends converged at midcentury to begin the transition from an American merchant marine manned prominently by blacks to one in which Jim Crow prevailed.

The replacement of regular black sailors with white ones, in Rhode Island at least, is partly attributable to the influx of "down east" ships in the port of Providence at midcentury. As Rhode Islanders diverted their capital into industry, they increasingly relied on out-of-state ships for their commerce, especially those from Maine. Not surprisingly, Maine men predominated among those ships' crews. And though crew turnover succeeded virtually every voyage, Maine skippers generally hired down easters, if they were available, before Rhode Islanders. That this put pressure on black employment prospects is undeniable, although Maine captains such as Edward Tilley of Eastport did occasionally hire black seamen; an all-black crew manned his brig *Nelson* to Pictou, Nova Scotia, for coal in 1834.[56]

The robust immigration and increasing class stratification that marked national society as a whole also eroded black mariners' prospects. White foreigners undoubtedly competed with black men for seafaring jobs. In 1845 the chairman of the Committee on Naval Affairs asserted (hyperbolically) that 90 percent of the men in the United States Navy and merchant marine were foreigners; the *Merchant's Magazine* that same year reduced the claim to only 66 percent. A few years before, Capt. Frederick Marryat concluded that exclusive of masters, mates, and other specialists who were native-born, about 70 percent of the men before the mast were foreigners. Although such "statistics" are not verifiable, the overwhelming impression of every observer was that as the century progressed fewer and fewer white Yankees sailed in American ships. "What [white] American," asked seaman Roland Freeman Gould, "would ever be content to rivet the chains of slavery upon himself?" But the mere presence of white immigrant and foreign labor does not satisfactorily explain why those whites were hired instead of the black Americans who had traditionally manned the fleet.[57]

Many historical studies of antebellum America contain an implicit "reason" for the decline of blacks' occupational opportunities: northern whites, ever more aware that a "race problem" jeopardized the Republic, increasingly discriminated against blacks. The real question is how and why that "climate of opinion" became embodied in discrete acts with real consequences for living people. In that light, it was probably quite significant for black seamen that the responsibility for hiring sailors increasingly shifted from shipowners and captains to "crimps," or shipping masters. Col. Thomas H. Perkins, a prominent Boston merchant, testified to a committee of the Massachusetts General Court in 1813 that for twenty years he had "always had the particular care of that part of our business which relates to the shipping of our seamen." Capt. Elijah Cobb recalled in his memoirs that in 1812 he had "visited the Sailors' boarding houses, where I shipped my crew." But by 1851, according to Richard Henry Dana, "Usually [the manner of shipping the crew] is left up to the shipping masters, who are paid so much a head for each of the crew, and are responsible for their appearance on board at the time of sailing." This specialized division of labor, long established in London and Bristol, became more common in the United States as seaport populations swelled.[58]

The frequent reliance on crimps to provide crews at midcentury signaled rising class stratification in northern seaports and probably made race more of an issue in sailors' employment than it had been formerly. As proprietors of taverns and inexpensive boardinghouses, crimps belonged to that shadowy lower-middle-class entrepreneurial group too long ignored by historians, a group increasingly significant in the expanding commercial economy. The growth of this urban petite bourgeoisie reflected the evolution, and increasing complexity, of antebellum social structure—a process that affected racial attitudes. Northern whites not only reacted consciously to what they perceived as a growing "race problem"; they also unconsciously evolved new assumptions about blacks as class stratification shaped the nation.

Whereas many captains and owners in the early republic had thought of themselves as the "better sort" and acted aloof and indifferent to labor in general—black or white—midcentury crimps displayed instead the aggressive egalitarianism and competitiveness of white democrats. The widespread conviction of equality among white men in antebellum America rested in part on a bellicose sense of superiority to blacks. Exemplifying this mentality, crimps seem to have become the agents by which the increased salience of race in antebellum America was translated into increasingly restricted employment options for Afro-Americans.[59]

The policy of "hiring white first" gained momentum in the maritime industry as a whole at midcentury. By 1869 the British consul in Baltimore was writing to the Foreign Office that "the Shipping Masters and the Boardinghouse Keepers have . . . determined not to ship a white man on board the same vessel with a colored man."[60] And indications are that as early as the 1840s and 1850s black men who might have preferred the little occupational stability and rewards that regular seafaring once offered men of their race were being consciously edged out of the industry.

Social historians—with their reluctance to treat society as an organic whole, and their preference for microscopic examination of its constituent parts— have chipped away at the assumption once implicit in much American historiography that our society had, or has, a single culture. Many scholars today regard it as more appropriate to consider the United States as pluralistic in culture. The intersection of Afro-American, white American, and Atlantic maritime cultures aboard ship, and the significance of the intersection for antebellum black seafarers, illuminate that multiculturality and some of its consequences.

The story of black seamen suggests how one culture that shaped daily life (the Atlantic maritime culture) exerted pressure on an extant social system (the racist American one). That occupational culture drove a wedge that provided several generations of black men a more tolerant work environment and better wages than they could find elsewhere. Forced by social constraint to accept jobs in what was for many an unenviable workplace — the ship — black Americans forged an occupational identity there and honed craft skills otherwise difficult to obtain. By tapping an international maritime culture that allowed them to "feel as men" in the presence of co-workers and to "presume upon their equality," they partially and temporarily circumvented the racist norms of American society. In Ralph Ellison's words, they "helped create themselves out of what they found around them."[61]

In the long run, however, the Atlantic maritime culture could boost black men's dignity and improve their material lives only to a limited degree. Distinctive subcultures exist in tension with the economic and social conditions in which they arise: once those conditions change substantially, cultural change is sure to follow. Black seamen's best years came to a close as the shipping industry underwent a transformation from its virtually medieval organization — in which merchant-shipowners despatched vessels to trade goods on their own account — to more rationalized and specialized business practices. That transformation, in conjunction with an apparently heightened race consciousness among the crimps who hired antebellum sailors and an influx of white immigrants to compete with black men for relatively fewer jobs aboard ship, spelled the end of blacks' best sea years.[62]

Seafaring remained economically important to northern blacks in 1860. But within the world of the ship the black man's position declined. Increasingly relegated to the galley or steward's department, and less likely each year after 1840 to serve aboard a ship manned predominantly by other blacks, the antebellum black seafarer became a lonely being. When maritime opportunity contracted at midcentury, blacks' maritime opportunity contracted even faster, dealing a serious blow to the antebellum Afro-American community and further restricting the avenues to self-esteem open to black men.

NOTES

1. Frederick Douglass, *Life and Times of Frederick Douglass, Written By Himself: His Early Life As a Slave, His Escape From Bondage, And His Complete History* (1892; reprint, New York, 1962), 125.
2. *Ibid.*, 199. Beginning in 1796 the federal government issued certificates to American sailors, black and white, as protection against impressment.
3. *Ibid.*, 199, 125.
4. "Protest against Kidnapping and the Slave Trade," in *A Documentary History of the Negro People in the United States*, ed. Herbert Aptheker (2 vols., Boston, 1951), I, 21. The numbers of black (including mulatto) mariners were derived from crew lists and from abstracts of applications for seamen's protection certificates. New York and Philadelphia crew lists, Records of U.S. Customs Service, RG 36 (National Archives); Providence crew lists, U.S. Customs House Papers, Providence, R.I., RG 28 (Manuscript Collection, Rhode Island Historical Society, Providence); Salem, Massachusetts, crew lists, Records of the U.S. Customs Service, RG 36 (National Archives, Boston Branch, Waltham, Mass.); abstracts of applications for seamen's protection certificates for New

London, Connecticut, *ibid.* For pioneering work using such records, see Ira Dye, "Seafarers of 1812—a Profile," *Prologue,* 5 (Spring 1973); and Ira Dye, "Early American Merchant Seafarers," *Proceedings of the American Philosophical Society,* 120 (Oct. 1976), 331–60; U.S. Department of Commerce, Bureau of the Census, *Historical Statistics of the United States: Colonial Times to 1970* (2 vols., Washington, 1975), I, 24–37; Edwin M. Snow, *Census of the City of Providence, Taken in July, 1855; With a Brief Account of the Manufacturers, Trade, Commerce, and Other Statistics of the City; and an Appendix, Giving an Account of Previous Enumerations of the Population of Providence* (Providence, 1856), 73.

5. William S. Swift, *The Negro in the Offshore Maritime Industry,* Part Three in *Negro Employment in the Maritime Industries: A Study of Racial Policies in the Ship-building, Longshore, and Offshore Maritime Industries,* ed. Lester Rubin, William S. Swift, and Herbert R. Northrup ([Philadelphia], 1974), 69–72.

6. For notable exceptions, see Dye, "Seafarers of 1812"; Dye, "Early American Merchant Seafarers"; Harold D. Langley, "The Negro in the Navy and Merchant Service, 1798–1860," *Journal of Negro History,* 52 (Oct. 1967), 273–86; Martha S. Putney, *Black Sailors: Afro-American Merchant Seamen and Whalemen prior to the Civil War* (Westport, 1987). For omission of black sailors, see Samuel Eliot Morison, *The Maritime History of Massachusetts, 1783–1860* (Cambridge, Mass., 1921); Robert G. Albion, *The Rise of New York Port, 1815–1860* (New York, 1939); Margaret Creighton, *Dog Watch and Liberty Days: Seafaring Life in the Nineteenth Century* (Salem, 1982); Robert G. Albion, William A. Baker, and Benjamin W. Labaree, *New England and the Sea* (Middletown, 1972); and Marcus Rediker, *Between the Devil and the Deep Blue Sea: Merchant Seamen, Pirates, and the Anglo-American Maritime World, 1700–1750* (Cambridge, Eng., 1987).

7. For the (exceptional) recognition of black sailors as part of the Afro-American community, see Gary B. Nash, *Forging Freedom: The Formulation of Philadelphia's Black Community, 1720–1840* (Cambridge, Mass., 1988); Shane White, "'We Dwell in Safety and Pursue Our Honest Callings': Free Blacks in New York City, 1783–1810," *Journal of American History,* 75 (Sept. 1988), 445–70. One author specifically excluded mariners from his study "because they were an unstable floating element in the city's population." See Robert Ernst, "The Economic Status of New York City Negroes, 1850–1863," in *The Making of Black America: Essays in Negro Life & History,* ed. August Meier and Elliott Rudwick (New York, 1969), 250–61, esp. 254. Black sailors' lives receive little more than mention in Leon F. Litwack, *North of Slavery: The Negro in the Free States, 1790–1860* (Chicago, 1961); Leonard P. Curry, *The Free Black in Urban America, 1800–1850: The Shadow of the Dream* (Chicago, 1981); Robert J. Cottrol, *The Afro-Yankees: Providence's Black Community in the Antebellum Era* (Westport, 1982); William D. Pierson, *Black Yankees: The Development of an Afro-American Subculture in Eighteenth-Century New England* (Amherst, 1988); Theodore Hershberg, "Free Blacks in Antebellum Philadelphia: A Study of Ex-Slaves, Freeborn, and Socioeconomic Decline," *Journal of Social History,* 5 (Winter 1971–1972), 183–209.

8. Swift, *Negro in the Offshore Maritime Industry;* James Barker Farr, "Black Odyssey: The Seafaring Traditions of Afro-Americans" (Ph.D. diss., University of California, Santa Barbara, 1982), 229.

9. On manuscript sources, see note 4. Noah H. Landau, "The Negro Seaman," *Negro Quarterly,* 1 (Winter/Spring 1943), 339, reports that 40% of Boston's free blacks were mariners in 1830, but only 15% in 1850. For Newport, see Martha S. Putney, "Black Merchant Seamen of Newport, 1803–1865: A Case Study of Foreign Commerce," *Journal of Negro History,* 57 (April 1972), 167. My analysis of the 3,879 seamen who applied for protection certificates from the port of New London, Connecticut, between 1803 and 1879 indicates a significant whitening of the work force after 1850. Abstracts of applications for seamen's protection certificates for New London, Records of the U.S. Customs Service, RG 36 (National Archives, Boston Branch).

10. Rhode Island figures largely in this account because for many years the American slave trade had been the Rhode Island slave trade, and blacks were common in the

Narragansett Bay area. See Jay Coughtry, *The Notorious Triangle: Rhode Island and the African Slave Trade, 1700–1807* (Philadelphia, 1981); and Jay Coughtry, "Creative Survival," in *Creative Survival: The Providence Black Community in the Nineteenth Century* (Providence, [1981]), 28–72.

11. William Roseberry, "Balinese Cockfights and the Seduction of Anthropology," *Social Research*, 49 (Winter 1982), 1013–29, esp. 1026; Gerald M. Sider, *Culture and Class in Anthropology and History: A Newfoundland Illustration* (Cambridge, Eng., 1986), esp. 10, 94; Samuel Taylor Coleridge, *The Piccolomini; or, The First Part of Wallenstein*, Act 1, sc. 6, epigraph in Richard Henry Dana, *Two Years Before the Mast: A Personal Narrative of Life at Sea* (1840; reprint, New York, 1981), 35.

12. Charles A. Valentine, "Deficit, Difference, and Bicultural Models of Afro-American Behavior," *Harvard Educational Review*, 41 (May 1971), 135–57; Eric R. Wolf, "Specific Aspects of Plantation Systems in the New World: Community Sub-Cultures and Social Classes" in *Plantation Systems of the New World: Papers and Discussion Summaries of the Seminar Held in San Juan, Puerto Rico* (Washington, 1959), 141–42. The analysis of culture and society in this essay also draws on Peter H. Fricke, "The Socialization of Crews aboard British Dry Cargo Merchant Ships" (Ph.D. diss., University of Wales, Cardiff, 1974), 87–95.

13. Rediker, *Between the Devil and the Deep Blue Sea*, 286; William Butterworth, *Three Years Adventure of a Minor in England, Africa, the West Indies, South Carolina and Georgia* (Leeds, [1831]), 205–11, esp. 211; William C. Nell, *The Colored Patriots of the American Revolution, with Sketches of Several Distinguished Colored Persons: To Which Is Added a Brief Survey of the Condition and Prospects of Colored Americans* (Boston, 1855), 314, emphasis added; S. G. Howe, *Report of the Freedmen's Inquiry Commission, 1864: The Refugees From Slavery in Canada West* (1864; reprint, New York, 1969), 75.

14. Elmo Paul Hohman, *History of American Merchant Seamen* (Hamden, 1956), 4; Frederic R. Sanborn, *Origins of the Early English Maritime and Commercial Law* (New York, 1930), 63, 64, 96.

15. Greg Dening, *Islands and Beaches: Discourse on a Silent Land, Marquesas, 1774–1880* (Honolulu, 1980), 158–59.

16. Ira Berlin, *Slaves without Masters: The Free Negro in the Antebellum South* (New York, 1974), 111; Cottrol, *Afro-Yankees*, 153–54, 161; Frank T. Bullen, *The Cruise of the Cachelot* (1898; reprint, New Haven, 1980), 4.

17. Providence crew lists, 1819–1821, 1831–1835, RG 28, U.S. Customs House Papers, Providence, R.I.; Edward Carrington & Co. "Seamen's Ledgers," 1819–1821, 1831–1835, Carrington Papers (Manuscript Collection, Rhode Island Historical Society); Herman Melville, *Billy Budd, Sailor (An Inside Narrative)* (Chicago, 1962), 43–44; Bullen, *Cruise of the Cachelot*, 198.

18. *Joseph M. Smith v. Barque Triton*, Aug. 1840, Final Record Book 8, U.S. District Court at Providence, Records of the U.S. District Court, RG 21 (National Archives, Boston Branch); Paul C. Nicholson, comp., *Abstracts from a Journal Kept aboard the Ship Sharon of Fairhaven on a Whaling Voyage in the South Pacific, 1841–1845* (Providence, 1953), 9–10.

19. Lorenzo J. Greene, *The Negro in Colonial New England* (New York, 1968), 100; Richard Peters, *Admiralty Decisions in the District Court of the United States for the Pennsylvania District* (2 vols., Philadelphia, 1807), II, 285–87; George P. Rawick, ed., *The American Slave: A Composite Autobiography* (13 vols., Westport, 1972), XVI, Maryland Narratives, Part 8, 63, Virginia Narratives, Part 17, 49; John W. Blassingame, ed., *Slave Testimony: Two Centuries of Letters, Speeches, Interviews, and Autobiographies* (Baton Rouge, 1977), 322, 340; Nash, *Forging Freedom*, 48–49, 54, 66, 85, 134, 138. "A Narrative of the Life and Adventures of Venture, a Native of Africa" (New London, 1798), in *Five Black Lives* (Middletown, 1971), 1–34.

20. William J. Brown, *The Life of William J. Brown of Providence, R. I., with Personal Recollections of Incidents in Rhode Island* (Providence 1883), 6–29; Providence crew lists, 1803–1807, U.S. Customs House Papers, Providence, R.I.; Herman Melville, *Moby Dick; or, The White Whale* (1851; reprint, New York, 1961), 115.

21. Brown, *Life of Brown*, 103; Coughtry, "Creative Survival," 40–42; Gary Nash, "Forging Freedom: The Emancipation Experience in the Northern Seaports, 1775–1820" in *Race, Class, and Politics: Essays on American Colonial and Revolutionary Society*, ed. Gary Nash (Urbana, 1986), 284–87. Delaware, Maryland, and Virginia provided at least one-third of Philadelphia's black seamen in the first half of the nineteenth century. Philadelphia crew lists, 1803, 1820, 1830, 1850, Records of the U.S. Customs Service, RG 36 (National Archives).

22. Stanley Lebergott, *Manpower in Economic Growth: The American Record since 1800* (New York, 1964), 74, 149–50, 241–47; Donald R. Adams, Jr., "Wage Rates in the Early National Period: Philadelphia, 1785–1830," *Journal of Economic History*, 28 (Sept. 1968), 409–22; Morison, *Maritime History of Massachusetts*, 110.

23. Relative pay for black and white sailors on many ships can be determined by comparing Providence crew lists, Customs House Papers, with Edward Carrington & Co. "Seamen's Ledgers," 1819–1835, Carrinton Papers. For ships' articles with wage data, see Ships' Articles, 1840s, 1850s, U.S. Customs House Papers, Providence R.I.; and New York crew lists, 1856, Records of the U.S. Customs Service, RG 36 (National Archives). *The John, Abner Mosher, Master (An Appeal from New Providence). Appendix. 1809* (pamphlet, Manuscript Collection, Rhode Island Historical Society). Moses Grandy, *Narrative of the Life of Moses Grandy, Late a Slave in the United States of America* (Boston, 1844) in William Loren Katz, ed., *Five Slave Narratives: A Compendium* (New York, 1968), 26.

24. Owen Chase, *Narrative of the Most Extraordinary and Distressing Shipwreck of the Whaleship Essex* (New York, 1821) reprinted in Thomas Farel Heffernan, ed., *Stove by a Whale* (Middletown, 1981), 18–19; John Malvin, *North into Freedom: The Autobiography of John Malvin, Free Negro, 1795–1880*, ed. Allan Peskin (Kent, 1988), 37.

25. Coughtry found that the Embargo had a similar impact on black seamen in Newport. See Coughtry, *Notorious Triangle*, 60.

26. Lamont D. Thomas, *Paul Cuffe: Black Entrepreneur and Pan-Africanist* (Urbana, 1986); Henry S. Sherwood, "Paul Cuffe," *Journal of Negro History*, 8 (April 1923), 153–229. For the lack of intergenerational success among colored seamen, see Cuffe's son's autobiography: Paul Cuffe, *Narrative of the Life and Adventures of Paul Cuffe, A Pequot Indian* (Vernon, Conn., 1839). George Henry, *Life of George Henry, Together with a Brief History of the Colored People in America* (1894; reprint, New York, 1971), 62.

27. Brown, *Life of Brown*, 49; Landau, "Negro Seaman," 334; Charles C. Andrews, *The History of the New-York African Free-Schools, from Their Establishment in 1787, to the Present Time; Embracing a Period of More than Forty Years; Also a Brief Account of the Successful Labors of the New-York Manumission Society* (1830; reprint, New York, 1969), 85–96; Thomas Hamilton, *Men and Manners in America* (1833; reprint, New York, 1968), 55–58.

28. Brown, *Life of Brown*, 126.

29. Seebert J. Goldowsky, *Yankee Surgeon: The Life and Times of Usher Parsons, 1788–1868* (Boston, 1988), 410; J. Ross Browne, *Etchings of a Whaling Cruise: With Notes of a Sojourn on the Island of Zanzibar* (New York, 1846), 108; James Kelly, *Voyage to Jamaica, and Seventeen Years' Residence in That Island: Chiefly Written With a View to Exhibit Negro Life and Habits* (Belfast, 1838), 29–30, quoted in Edward Brathwaite, *The Development of Creole Society in Jamaica, 1770–1820* (Oxford, 1971), 301.

30. Eugene D. Genovese, *Roll, Jordan, Roll: The World the Slaves Made* (New York, 1976), 324; Rhys Isaac, *The Transformation of Virginia, 1740–1790* (Chapel Hill, 1982), 305–8; Providence crew lists, 1803–1856, U.S. Customs House Papers, Providence, R.I.; cf. New York and Philadelphia crew lists, Records of the U.S. Customs Service, RG 36 (National Archives).

31. Brig *John Josiah Arnold* crew list, outbound, 1803, Providence crew lists, Customs House Papers; Elbridge S. Brooks, *The Story of the American Sailor* (Boston, 1888), 189.

32. Vilhelm Aubert, *The Hidden Society* (Totowa, 1965), 236–58; Fricke, "Socialization of Crews," 87–89; Creighton, *Dog Watch and Liberty Days*, 48.

33. Dorothea M. Balano, *The Log of the Skipper's Wife* (Camden, Maine, 1979), 69.

34. All of these traits, representative of Atlantic maritime culture, can be found in the journals, logs, and published memoirs of seamen. For the best accounts, see Dana, *Two Years Before the Mast*, 72–73, 78–79, 120–22, 250, 431; Rediker, *Between the Devil and the Deep Blue Sea*, 153–253; Creighton, *Dog Watch and Liberty Days*, 40–41, 48–50, 60–68.

35. Daniel Watson's voyaging can be traced in the Providence crew lists, 1803–1810; Providence crew lists, U.S. Customs House Papers, Providence, R.I. David O'Kee's voyaging can be traced in the Providence crew lists, 1830–1837, *ibid.*

36. Brown, *Life of Brown*, 97–98.

37. Coughtry, "Creative Survival," 52; Register of Seamen's Protections (Library, Rhode Island Historical Society); Register of Members, First Baptist Church, Providence, Manuscript Collection, *ibid.*

38. Thomas, *Paul Cuffe*; Philip S. Foner, *History of Black Americans from Africa to the Emergence of the Cotton Kingdom* (Westport, 1975), 339–40; Eleanor McDougall, ed., *Memoirs of Elleanor Eldridge* (Providence, 1838), 33–41; Henry Highland Garnet to Louis Alexis Chamerovzow, Oct. 2, 1854, in *The Black Abolitionist Papers*, ed. C. Peter Ripley (2 vols., Chapel Hill, 1985), II, 410; Sterling Stuckey, "A Last Stern Struggle: Henry Highland Garnet and Liberation Theory," in *Black Leaders of the Nineteenth Century*, ed. Leon F. Litwack and August Meier (Urbana, 1988), 129–49, esp. 130.

39. Brown, *Life of Brown*, 6; "Return of Coloured Persons Being Housekeepers," June 24, 1822, folio 118, vol. 112, Providence Town Papers (Manuscript Collection, Rhode Island Historical Society); *The Providence Directory, Containing Names of the Inhabitants, Their Occupations, Places of Business, and Dwelling-Houses; With Lists of the Streets, Lanes, Wharves, & c.* (Providence, 1832).

40. George Edward Clark, *Seven Years of a Sailor's Life* (Boston, 1867), 12; Jesse Lemisch, "Jack Tar in the Streets: Merchant Seamen in the Politics of Revolutionary America," *William and Mary Quarterly*, 25 (July 1968), 377. On black seamen's ages and relation to home ports, see Providence crew lists, 1803–1856, U.S. Customs House Papers, Providence, R.I.; and Philadelphia crew lists, Records of the U.S. Customs Service, RG 36 (National Archives).

41. On seamen's ages, see table 3. On Prince Brown, see Providence crew lists, 1803–1810, U.S. Customs House Papers, Providence, R.I.

42. Papers of the Brig *John* (Manuscript Collection, Rhode Island Historical Society); Deposition of John Gardner, Sept. 30, 1831, Richard Ward Greene Papers, *ibid.*; Depositions of John Gardner and Mary Gardner, "State vs. Fuller and Nobles," 1835, *ibid.*

43. Nathaniel Ames, *Nautical Reminiscences* (Providence, 1832), 38; Coughtry, "Creative Survival," 39. My discussion of black seafarers' families has profited greatly from a magisterial work: Herbert G. Gutman, *The Black Family in Slavery and Freedom, 1750–1925* (New York, 1976). Providence crew lists, 1803–1856, U.S. Customs House Papers, Providence, R.I.; Philadelphia crew lists, Records of the U.S. Customs Service, RG 36 (National Archives).

44. In 1803 only 3.3% of Philadelphia's black sailors had been born in the city; in 1820, 5%; in 1830, 3%. (The minimum sample size was 141.) See Philadelphia crew lists, Records of the U.S. Customs Service, RG 36 (National Archives). On New York, see *Sailor's Magazine and Naval Journal*, 18 (Aug. 1846), 382, cited in Langley, "Negro in Navy and Merchant Service," 285.

45. Philip M. Hamer, "Great Britain, the United States, and the Negro Seamen Acts, 1822–1848," *Journal of Southern History*, 1 (Feb. 1935), 3–28; Philip M. Hamer, "British Consuls and the Negro Seamen Acts, 1850–1860," *ibid.* (May 1935), 138–68; Alan F. January, "The First Nullification: The Negro Seamen Acts Controversy in South Carolina, 1822–1860" (Ph. D. diss., University of Iowa, 1976); John Oliver Killens, ed., *The Trial Record of Denmark Vesey* (Boston, 1970), 159–60; Herbert Aptheker, *"One Continual Cry": David Walker's Appeal to the Colored Citizens of the World (1829–1830), Its Setting and Its Meaning* (New York, 1965), 45; A. Mazyck, *The Law of Colored Seamen* (Charleston, 1851), 23.

46. For a black Rhode Island widow's fear that her son had been kidnapped into slavery while on a southern voyage in 1833, see George Turner to R. W. Greene, Aug. 8, 1834, Richard Ward Greene Papers (Manuscript Collection, Rhode Island Historical Society). On the danger of free black sailors being sold into slavery in New Orleans, see Blassingame, ed., *Slave Testimony*, 284, 690. Harold D. Langley, *Social Reform in the United States Navy, 1798–1862* (Urbana, 1967), 94; House no. 14, *Documents Printed by Order of the House of Representatives of the Commonwealth of Massachusetts during the Session of the General Court, A.D. 1845* (Boston, 1845).

47. Richard J. Cleveland, *Voyages and Commercial Enterprises of the Sons of New England* (New York, 1855), 26; Elmo P. Hohman, *Seamen Ashore: A Study of the United States' Seamen's Service and of Merchant Seamen in Port* (New Haven, 1952), 3.

48. My work on occupational mobility among Providence's white seamen, 1803–1856, indicated that virtually any white man making multiple voyages during the 1830s would be promoted. See David Montgomery, "The Working Classes of the Pre-Industrial American City, 1780–1830," *Labor History*, 9 (Winter 1968), 3–22, esp. 16.

49. Hohman, *History of American Merchant Seamen*, 7, 21–22; Elmo P. Hohman, *The American Whaleman: A Study of Life and Labor in the Whaling Industry* (New York, 1928), 48–49; Herman Melville, *Redburn; His First Voyage: Being the Sailor Boy Confessions and Reminiscences of the Son-of-a-Gentleman, in the Merchant Service* (1849; reprint, Garden City, 1957), 131–32.

50. Jacob A. Hazen, *Five Years Before the Mast; Or, Life in the Forecastle, Aboard of A Whaler and Man-of-War* (Philadelphia, 1854), 184; Browne, *Etchings of a Whaling Cruise*, 23; Gaddis Smith, "Black Seamen and the Federal Courts, 1789–1860," in *Ships, Seafaring, and Society: Essays in Maritime History*, ed. Timothy J. Runyan (Detroit, 1987), 321; Richard Henry Dana, *Two Years Before the Mast* (Boston, 1869), 116–17.

51. Browne, *Etchings of a Whaling Cruise*, 495; Cottrol, *Afro-Yankees*, 120–21, 151–52.

52. Log of the ship *Resource*, Dec. 29, 1803 (Manuscript Collection, Rhode Island Historical Society).

53. Joseph Conrad, *The Nigger of the "Narcissus"* (New York, 1908), ix. For the historical roots of Conrad's fiction, including experiences with black shipmates, see Jerry Allen, *The Sea Years of Joseph Conrad* (New York, 1965).

54. Providence crew lists, 1850–1856, U.S. Customs House Papers, Providence, R.I.

55. W. E. B. Du Bois, *The Philadelphia Negro* (Philadelphia, 1899), 97.

56. A midcentury increase in the number of vessels from Maine sailing out of Providence can be seen by comparing crew lists from the 1850s with those from the 1830s; Providence crew lists, U.S. Customs House Papers, Providence, R.I. Brig *Nelson*, outbound crew lists, Providence, 1834, *ibid.*

57. Lebergott, *Manpower in Economic Growth*, 26–27. Richard Henry Dana, J. Ross Browne, James Fenimore Cooper, and others made similar claims. Roland Freeman Gould, *The Life of Gould, An Ex-Man-of-War's-Man with Incidents on Sea and Shore, Including the Three-Year's Cruise of the Line of Battle Ship Ohio, on the Mediterranean Station, under the Veteran Commodore Hull* (Claremont, N.H., 1867), 191.

58. Carl Seaburg and Stanley Patterson, *Merchant Prince of Boston: Colonel T. H. Perkins, 1764–1854* (Cambridge, Mass., 1971), 146–47; Elijah Cobb, *Elijah Cobb, 1768–1848: A Cape Cod Skipper* (New Haven, 1925), 21–26, 66; Richard Henry Dana, Jr., *The Seaman's Friend: Containing a Treatise on Practical Seamanship* (Boston, 1851), 132; Stan Hugill, *Sailortown* (New York, 1967), 83; Testimony of Samuel Aldridge, 1807, Papers of the Brig *John* (Manuscript Collection, Rhode Island Historical Society).

59. My interpretation of the sociology of racial attitudes in antebellum America draws on Robert H. Wiebe, *The Opening of American Society: From the Adoption of the Constitution to the Eve of Disunion* (New York, 1984), 339–60.

60. Herbert G. Gutman, "Documents on Negro Seamen during the Reconstruction Period," *Labor History*, 7 (Fall 1966), 307–11, esp. 308. After about 1860 segregation aboard ship seems to have become more prevalent. Masters increasingly hired an all-

white or all-black crew or else split an integrated crew into watches by race. See Samuel Samuels, *From Forecastle to Cabin* (Boston, 1924), 292; Alfred John Green, *Jottings from a Cruise* (Seattle, 1944), v; Swift, *Negro in the Offshore Maritime Industry,* 65–66.

61. For Ralph Ellison's statement, see Gutman, *Black Family,* 326.

62. Sider, *Culture and Class,* 94; John G. B. Hutchins, *The American Maritime Industries and Public Policy, 1789–1914: An Economic History* (New York, 1941), 221–42.

FOURTEEN

Violence, Protest, and Identity: Black Manhood in Antebellum America

JAMES OLIVER HORTON AND LOIS E. HORTON

In his autobiography, Frederick Douglass recalled his confrontation with the slave breaker Covey as the first step on his escape to freedom. After regular beatings from Covey, to whom he had been hired, he had run away, and then returned to face certain and severe punishment. This time, though, the adolescent slave resisted, and the two became locked in a two-hour struggle that left both exhausted. Young Frederick was not subdued, and Covey never beat him again. This successful resistance changed the slave: "My dear reader this battle with Mr. Covey . . . was the turning point in my life as a slave . . . I was nothing before; I was a man now."[1] It was natural for Douglass to express his new-found power in terms of manhood, as power, independence, and freedom were often thought of as traits reserved for men in nineteenth-century America. To be a man was to be free and powerful.

Although the American man in the nineteenth century could choose from a variety of gender ideals, virtually all the combinations of characteristics, values, and actions constituting each ideal included self-assertion and aggression as key elements. Aggression, and sometimes sanctioned violence, was a common thread in American ideals of manhood. Charles Rosenberg believes that two masculine ideals exemplified the choices open to nineteenth-century men, the *Masculine Achiever* and *Christian Gentleman*. The Masculine Achiever ideal was closely associated with the rapid economic growth of the nineteenth century. As the rise of the market economy disrupted local relationships and tied formerly isolated communities to distant economic affiliations, this ideal provided American men with a dynamic model of behavior. The man of action was unencumbered by sentiment and totally focused on advancement, the quintessential individualist and the self-styled ruthless competitor. He was the rugged individual succeeding in the world of commercial capitalism.

The Christian Gentleman ideal arose in reaction to the Masculine Achiever and threats to the traditional values and relationships. Eschewing self-seeking behavior and heartless competition in the commercial world, this gentler ideal stressed communal values, religious principles, and more humanitarian action. It was a natural outgrowth of the religious revival that blossomed under the Second Great Awakening of the early nineteenth century and stressed self-restraint and Christian morality. Christian Gentlemen were not expected to be passive. Dynamic and aggressive action was assumed, but in the name of moral values and self-sacrifice, not personal greed.[2]

E. Anthony Rotundo argues that an additional ideal emerged among northern males in the nineteenth century—the *Masculine Primitive*. This ideal stressed dominance and conquest through harnessing the energy of primitive male instincts and savagery lurking beneath the thin veneer of civilization. This was a more physically aggressive ideal, based on the natural impulses of man's most primitive state, and violence was its confirming feature.[3] Although Rotundo sees this ideal as influential among northern men by the middle of the nineteenth century, southern historians have found a strikingly similar ideal in the South throughout the eighteenth and nineteenth centuries. Bertram Wyatt-Brown and Grady McWhiney describe the violence in defense of honor sanctioned by even the most genteel southerners. Elizabeth Fox-Genovese notes the simultaneous existence of gentility and savagery: "Southern conventions of masculinity never abandoned the element of force or even brutality. . . . This toleration of male violence responded to the perceived exigencies of governing a troublesome people. . . ." The behaviors believed necessary for managing the slave system were incorporated into the gender ideals for all southern white men.[4]

Black men growing up as slaves in southern society had an especially complex gender socialization. The gender ideals of white southern society overlaid the foundations of African cultural expectations and the intentional socialization imposed on slaves. The dual and contradictory genteel and savage images applied to southern white manhood paralleled characteristics whites imagined black men possessed. The happy, contented Sambo stereotype slaveholders wanted to believe existed was placed alongside the brute, savage Negro they feared. Slaveholders tried to cultivate a slave approximation of the Christian Gentleman ideal, typified by Harriet Beecher Stowe's Uncle Tom, all the while dreading the emergence of the barbaric Masculine Primitive. Thomas R. Dew argued in 1832 that Africans were by nature savage and that it was only the civilizing influence of slavery that restrained their brutish nature. According to William Drayton, another nineteenth-century apologist for slavery, only slavery checked the "wild frenzy of revenge, and the savage lust for blood" natural to the African and dramatically apparent in the Haitian Revolution. In 1858 Thomas R. R. Cobb alleged that once removed from the domesticating influence of slavery, Haitian blacks "relapsed into barbarism."[5]

Ever watchful for any outward signs of rebellion, white southerners went to great lengths to suppress black aggression and assertiveness. As one former slave recalled, "Every man [was] called boy till he [was] very old, then the more respectable slaveholder call[ed] him uncle." Actions expected of white men were condemned in black men. No black man could defend his family from a white attacker, "let him be ever so drunk or crazy," without fear of drastic reprisal. Yet a black man under the orders of white authority could legitimately use his strength against a white person. A slave directed by his overseer could strike a white man for "beating said overseer's pig."[6]

"A slave can't be a man," proclaimed former slave Lewis Clarke.[7] Slavery was designed to make it impossible for a man to freely express his opinions and make his own decisions. Yet many slave men asserted aspects of manhood even under the most difficult circumstances. William Davis refused to be whipped by his overseer. When the white man realized he could not administer the beating alone, he ordered three "athletic fellows" to assist him, but Davis served notice that he would not be taken easily. "Boys, I am only a poor boy and you are grown men, but if either of you touch me, I'll kill one of you . . . ," he warned. Davis was not whipped.[8]

Slave men found many ways to assert themselves. Even the threat of self-assertion could be effective. One man reported that he avoided being sold at auction by meeting the gaze of prospective buyers directly as they inspected him, an obvious sign of a hard-to-handle slave. Another stopped his master from beating slave children by standing beside them, glaring at the master as he began punishment. Among the slaves, men who refused to submit to the master's authority were accorded respect. Those who submitted too easily to the master's authority lost respect. "Them as won't fight," reported Lewis Clarke, "is called Poke-easy."[9] How could a man be both manly and a slave? A central theme in the abolitionists' attacks on slavery was that it robbed men of their manhood. The widely used antislavery emblem was a manacled slave kneeling in the supplication, "Am I not a man and brother?"[10]

David Walker, a free black North Carolinian who migrated to Boston, gained national attention and raised southern fears by urging slaves to prove their manhood, to rise up and take their freedom by force if necessary. His call to arms was issued in partial answer to Thomas Jefferson's suggestions that African Americans were an inferior species and could not be granted freedom. Walker asserted that the African American could not be domesticated like an animal and could never be held in slavery against his will. He goaded black men to action by rhetorically wondering how so many could be enslaved: "Are we Men!!! How we could be so submissive to a gang of men, whom we cannot tell whether they are as good as ourselves or not, I never could conceive." Blacks, he wrote, must not wait for either God or slaveholders to end slavery. "The man who would not fight . . . to be delivered from the most wretched, abject and servile slavery, that ever a people was afflicted with since the foundation of the world . . . ought to be kept with all his children or family, in slavery or in chains to be butchered by his cruel enemies."[11]

In his *Appeal* David Walker called upon the memory of the successful Haitian Revolution in 1804 as proof of the power of unity and manliness. "One thing which gives me joy," he wrote of the Haitians, "is, that they are men who would be cut off to a man before they would yield to the combined forces of the whole world." Black men demonstrated in Haiti, Walker contended, that "a groveling, servile and abject submission to the lash of tyrants" is not the African man's natural state. Walker believed that slaves could transform themselves into men through aggressive action. "If ever we become men," he said, "we must assert ourselves to the full."[12]

In his call to action, Walker claimed the physical superiority of black men. "I do declare," he wrote, "that one good black can put to death six white men." The assertion that slaves were stronger and better in combat than their masters was not new. It became part of the racial folklore of the period and was often cited in conjunction with rumors of slave uprisings. Yet this declaration posed problems for African Americans. The use of violence to assert manhood tended to reinforce white stereotypes of the "brutish African nature" only restrained by slavery.[13]

Despite David Walker's mysterious death in 1831, his advocacy of the use of violence as an acceptable tactic for the acquisition of freedom and equality, what were increasingly referred to as *manhood rights*, remained an important position among blacks throughout the antebellum period. At the time that Walker wrote his *Appeal*, the American imagination was captured by Greek revolutionaries seeking independence from Turkey, by rising Polish discontent with their Russian masters, and the revolutions in Latin America that, in 1826, brought the abolition of slavery to the former Spanish colonies. Thus he drew on more than the distant models of the American Revolution and the revolt in Haiti. He was undoubtedly aware that freedom was being sought through violence abroad and that revolutionary armies in Latin America included black soldiers bearing arms supplied by the Haitian government.[14]

Walker was not alone in using international illustrations to attack slavery or in considering the prospect of slave revolt. In 1825 in his commencement address at Bowdoin College, John Russwurm, one of the first African Americans to graduate from an American college, assailed the institution, taking as his paradigm the establishment of Haitian independence.[15] Later, as co-editor of *Freedom's Journal*, Russwurm speculated that if the federal government would stop providing protection for slaveholders, slaves might very well settle the question of slavery themselves. Ohio judge Benjamin Tappan shocked an acquaintance by inquiring rhetorically, "whether the slave has not a resort to the most violent measures, if necessary, in order to maintain his liberty? And if he has the least chance of success, are we not, as rational and consistent men, bound to justify him?" Historian Merton Dillon asserts that most antislavery proponents of the time accepted the right of slaves to strike for their liberty.[16]

The 1830s brought a new, more forceful critique of violent means in the fight against slavery as William Lloyd Garrison began publishing his newspaper, the *Liberator,* in Boston. His commitment to immediate emancipation for slaves and civil rights for free blacks was popular among African Americans who had worked toward these ends for decades with only marginal assistance from white reformers. Garrison was a nonresister—a pacifist opposed to cooperating with any government built on slavery and compromise with slaveholders. His pacifism led him to oppose government that forced citizens to participate directly or indirectly in violence, through, for example, war, imprisonment, or capital punishment. He opposed voting or participating in politics, and condemned the use of violence even to achieve freedom. The route to manhood, he believed, was through strength of character and principled action. In the pages of the *Liberator* he rejected Walker's call for slave revolt, and although he praised Walker personally, Garrison made clear that "we do not preach rebellion—no, but submission and peace." His stand on the use of violence by slaves was complex. He considered slaves "more than any people on the face of the earth" justified in the use of force and compared slave revolt to the American Revolution in the justice of its cause, but a just cause, Garrison believed, was no justification for violence.[17]

Garrison's strong commitment to nonviolence and his philosophy of nonresistance entered the continuing debate within black society over violent and nonviolent means for the abolition of slavery. African Americans had been influenced by arguments for nonviolence early in the colonial era. Quakers, some of their first allies, were pacifists. Blacks who became Friends often wrestled with the question of the practicality of nonviolence for a people violently deprived of their rights. Yet blacks were obliged to "become convinced of [Quaker] principles" in order to be accepted into the society. During the War of 1812, black Quaker David Mapps of Little Egg Harbor, New Jersey, demonstrated his pacifist principles and refused to transport cannon balls aboard his schooner, explaining, "I cannot carry thy devil's pills that were made to kill people."[18]

Although black Quakers were strongly committed to nonviolence, most African Americans expressed a great deal more ambivalence on this issue. At the opposite extreme from the Quakers, many continued to agree with David Walker that violence was the surest route to freedom and manhood. Some opposed the use of violence on practical grounds, others wrestled with moral issues and searched for alternative ways to assert themselves and to achieve dignity without the use of force. Garrison and his philosophy had become the center of this debate by the 1830s, but the debate was over means, not ends. All blacks agreed that freedom and equality were the goals, and most continued to equate these with manhood.

Speaking to a gathering of black Bostonians in 1831, black activist Maria W. Stewart echoed Walker's call to black men to assert their manhood: "O ye fearful ones, throw off your fearfulness. . . . If you are men, convince [whites] that you possess the spirit of men." Yet hers was not a call to violence. She called forth the "sons of Africa" to show their bravery, their intelligence, and their commitment to serving their community. "But give the man of color an equal opportunity . . . from the cradle to manhood, and from manhood to grave, and you would discover a dignified statesman, the man of science, and the philosopher."[19]

Maria Stewart urged a version of the Masculine Achiever ideal of manhood that incorporated achievement, autonomy, and "intensive competition for success in the marketplace."[20] Her ideal, however, was not completely individualistic. The object of success in the masculine competition was to prove black men the equals of other men. It was also important, according to Stewart, that successful men become assets to the black community and contribute to the struggle of black people. Even though Stewart was a friend and co-worker of Garrison, her appeal was not incontrovertibly nonviolent. The heroes she called upon to inspire black men to the competition included the black soldiers of the American Revolution and the War of 1812—and David Walker.

Garrison agreed that bondage and discrimination denied human dignity and pledged his efforts to combat these destructive forces. He was a pacifist, but his philosophy and style was neither passive nor apologetic. As he began the *Liberator*, Garrison promised to speak clearly and forcefully in words that could not be misunderstood. He was unequivocal in his opposition to slavery, but he also believed he had a responsibility to free blacks in the North. He dedicated himself and his paper to work for their "moral and intellectual elevation, the advancement of [their] rights, and the defense of [their] character." Less than two months after beginning publication, Garrison felt his venture had already met with success. He reported: "Upon the colored population in the free states, it has operated like a trumpet call. They have risen in their hopes and feelings to the perfect stature of men. . . ."[21]

Garrison's conception of manhood, characterized by intellectual achievement, personal dignity, and moral responsibility, was shared by many abolitionists, whose underlying antislavery motivation was religious. It had particular appeal for black abolitionists, who felt they carried the added burden of disproving the claims of black inferiority advanced by Jefferson and the proslavery interests. Yet even among black Garrisonians there was some ambivalence regarding total reliance on the pacific means of moral suasion. A widely circulated poem composed by the intellectual black abolitionist Charles L. Reason illustrates this ambivalence. Reason's poem, entitled "The Spirit Voice: or Liberty Calls to the Disfranchised," is filled with martial images but comes to a decidedly nonviolent conclusion. He wrote:

Come! rouse ye brothers, rouse! a peal now breaks,
From lowest island to our gallant lakes,
'Tis summoning you, who long in bonds have lain,
To stand up manful on the battle plain,
Each as a warrior, with his armor bright,
Prepared to battle in a bloodless fight.[22]

Respect for Garrison and his work kept many black abolitionists from openly questioning reliance on moral suasion, even when they harbored doubts
about its effectiveness. Some Garrisonians, of course, were committed to
nonviolence on principle; others saw it as a practical strategy. Throughout
the 1830s and early 1840s, the small band of antislavery crusaders was
continually under attack. Mobs broke up their meetings, attacked them in
the streets, and occasionally set fire to their lecture halls and homes. Slaveholders posted rewards for the most notorious abolitionists, dead or alive.
In the face of such opposition, taking the principled stance of moral suasion
had the additional practical benefit of attracting adherents while avoiding
inflaming even more violent reactions.

Yet some continued to proclaim the right of slaves to take their freedom
"like men." One of the most radical and elaborate schemes for the forcible
abolition of slavery came from a white sixty-year-old politician, Jabez Delano
Hammond, a jurist and former U.S. congressman from Cherry Valley, New
York. In 1839 Hammond proposed that abolitionists sponsor military acad-
emies in Canada and Mexico that would train blacks in military arts and
sabotage. The trainees would then be set loose in the South to commit
terrorist acts and to encourage and lead slave rebellions. Referring to these
infiltrators as potentially "the most successful Southern missionaries," Hammond explained that such steps were necessary because "the only way in
which slavery at the South can be abolished is by force."[23]

Many black reformers were also growing impatient with moral suasion as
the primary weapon against slavery and moral elevation as the surest route to
progress for free blacks. Peter Paul Simons spoke for a growing minority in
1839 when he challenged the efficacy of moral reform. Instead of lessening
the hold of slavery and prejudice on blacks, he believed, it had encouraged
timidity and self-doubt. African Americans do not suffer from lack of moral
elevation, he argued. "There is no nation of people under the canopy of
heaven, who are given more to good morals and piety than we are." He
contended that blacks suffered from a lack of direct "physical and political" action. They lacked confidence in one another, he said, and were thus
likely to depend on the leadership of whites, a not-so-subtle reference to the
willingness of many blacks to follow Garrison's lead. His argument continued, charging that black children learned passive acceptance not manly
action and leadership from parental examples. Action must be the watch-
word: "This we must physically practice, and we will be in truth an independent people."[24]

Although Simons stopped short of endorsing a David Walker–style call for violence in this pursuit of self-confident independence, his statements did signal the move toward a more aggressive posture. He was not alone. Many who worked most closely with fugitive slaves or on behalf of free blacks kidnapped into slavery were among those least able to accept the doctrine of nonviolence. Black abolitionist David Ruggles, an officer of the New York Committee of Vigilance, had never been totally committed to nonresistance. As early as 1836 he wrote that in dealing with slave hunters and kidnappers, "Self-defense is the first law of nature."[25] Gradually Ruggles grew more impatient with the slow pace of antislavery and civil rights progress. In the summer of 1841, he addressed a meeting of the American Reform Board of Disfranchised Commissioners, a New York protest group of which he was a founding member. In strident tones he rallied the group to action and explained that "in our cause" words alone would not suffice. "Rise brethren rise!" he urged the distant slaves. "Strike for freedom or die slaves!"[26]

Two years later at the Buffalo meeting of the National Negro Convention, twenty-seven-year-old black abolitionist minister Henry Highland Garnet echoed David Walker's exhortation, urging black men to act like men. Addressing himself to the slaves, he used provocative and incendiary language. "It is sinful in the extreme," he admonished, "for you to make voluntary submission." As Walker had accepted the necessity for a man to use violence in the assertion of manhood, so Garnet concluded that "there is not much hope of Redemption without the shedding of blood." Black men must not shrink from bloody confrontation—there was no escape. A mass exodus was not an option for African Americans, he argued. The solution must be found in America, and it might well be violent. "If you must bleed, let it come at once, rather, die freemen than live to be slaves." Garnet did not urge a revolution. "Your numbers are too small," he observed. But all slaves should immediately "cease to labor for tyrants who will not remunerate you." He assumed, however, that violence would be the inevitable result of this tactic. And when it came, he instructed, "Remember that you are THREE MILLIONS."[27]

As Maria Stewart had done a decade earlier, Garnet used black heroes as a standard for manhood, and he found contemporary black men wanting. Questioning the commitment of his fellows to the assertion of manhood, Garnet cut to the heart of masculine pride. "You act as though your daughters were born to pamper the lusts of your masters and overseers," he charged. Garnet continued forcefully: "And worst of all, you timidly submit while your lords tear your wifes from your embraces and defile them before your eyes. In the name of God, we ask, are you men? Where is the blood of your fathers? Has it all run out of your veins?"[28] Here Garnet drew upon one of the most powerful justifications for the link between physical prowess and masculinity in American gender ideals—the responsibility of men to protect their families. This responsibility was an important part of all male ideals in the society. Even those most committed to the Christian Gentleman ideal, even the most fervent black nonresisters had great difficulty arguing that nonviolence was the only recourse when one's family was in physical danger. Garnet's charge to the slaves forcefully affected the black and white abolitionists and observers in his audience as he evoked the universal images of manhood.

Garnet's speech split the convention; debate was heated. Ardent Garrisonians Frederick Douglass and Charles Lenox Remond spoke against endorsing his sentiments. They pointed to the bloody retribution slaves and free blacks, especially those in the border states, might suffer should the convention support such a radical call to violence. Although there was substantial support for Garnet's message, by a narrow margin the convention refused to endorse his words. For the time being the black Garrisonians remained convinced and had successfully blocked the open embrace of violent means.[29]

A commitment to nonviolence and a sense of the dangers the relatively powerless slaves faced continued to prevent most blacks from urging slaves to gain their freedom through physical force. Many black abolitionists had been slaves and were intimately familiar with the dangers involved. Even Frederick Douglass, who recounted the story of attaining his manhood through physical confrontation, was aware of the risks and continued to be reluctant to sanction calls for slave rebellion. A news story he printed in his paper in the late 1840s illustrated the horrors of slavery and made the point that resistance could be deadly:

> Wm. A. Andrews, an overseer of J. W. Perkins, Mississippi attempted to chastise one of the negro boys who seized a stick and prepared to do battle. The overseer told the boy to lay the stick down or he would shoot him; he refused, and the overseer then fired his pistol, and shot the boy in the face, killing him instantly. The jury of inquest found the verdict, "that the said Wm. A. Andrews committed the killing in self-defense."[30]

In the 1840s Garrisonian nonresistance came under fire from many quarters. There was a split in the abolition movement at the start of the decade, and many of those committed to political antislavery cast their lot with the newly formed Liberty party. Among white abolitionists there was also growing intolerance of what some saw as Garrison's unreasoned radicalism, not only attacking slavery but also condemning the Constitution, the entire federal government, and the national political system. Further, some criticized his support of women's rights as an unnecessary complication that made abolition even less palatable to the general public and threatened to blunt the central thrust of the movement. This fear was reinforced when feminist Abby Kelley was elected to be the first female member of the business committee of the Garrisonian-dominated American Anti-Slavery Society. Opposition groups sprang up to challenge this and other Garrisonian organizations.[31]

This debate between those who favored political participation and those who opposed it split the black abolitionist ranks. Despite their ambivalence, most black Bostonians remained personally loyal to Garrison. New York's *Colored American* attempted to remain neutral, but many black New Yorkers sided with the political abolitionists. Blacks in several northern states faced the curtailment or loss of their voting rights. The vote was an instrument of males' political power, and blacks viewed disenfranchisement as symbolic emasculation. Garrison himself conceded that where rights were in jeopardy, black voters should vote in self-defense.[32]

The debate was short lived among blacks, and even Boston blacks openly took part in electoral politics by the mid-1840s. There were Liberty party announcements inserted in the pages of the *Liberator,* and by 1848 the paper reported on meetings at which African Americans in Boston discussed the formation of an auxiliary to the Liberty party. William Cooper Nell, one of the most loyal of the black Garrisonians, allowed his name to be put into nomination as Free-Soil party candidate for the 1850 Massachusetts legislature.[33]

By the mid-nineteenth century, Garrisonians were also reassessing their stand on nonviolence. Among African Americans almost all reservations about the appropriateness of violence in the struggle against slavery were wiped away by the passage of the federal Fugitive Slave Law of 1850. This measure, which made it easier for fugitives to be captured and for free blacks to be kidnapped into slavery, was seen as a direct blow against all African Americans. It generated a strongly militant reaction even among those who had favored nonviolence. Charles Lenox Remond, who had opposed Garnet's call to arms in the early 1840s, a decade later demanded defiance of the law, protection of all fugitives, and the withholding of federal troops should the southern slaves rise against their masters.[34]

Douglass, who had joined Remond in voting against Garnet, published a novella in 1853 in which slaves killed the captain of a slave ship and a slave owner. In an editorial entitled "Is It Right and Wise to Kill a Kidnapper?" published in *Frederick Douglass' Paper* a year later, he was even more forthright. Violence, even deadly violence, was justifiable when used to protect oneself, one's family, or one's community.[35] At a community meeting in Boston, Nell cautioned African Americans to be watchful for kidnappers. If confronted, he urged them to defend themselves.

The defection from nonviolence was not limited to African Americans. Boston journalist Benjamin Drew suggested that when the government supported oppression, violence against the state might be reasonable.[36] Pacifist minister Samuel J. May and five fugitive slaves stood before an antislavery convention in Syracuse. In surprising tones for the longtime Garrisonian, May asked, "Will you defend [these fugitives] with your lives?" The audience threw back the answer: "Yes!"[37]

Most plans of action were far less offensive. New vigilance committees were formed to protect the safety of fugitives, and already established committees redoubled their efforts, publicly vowing that no slave would be taken. This was a manly pursuit it was said, for every "slavehunter who meets a bloody death in his infernal business, is an argument in favor of the manhood of our race."[38] Yet not all blacks viewed violent confrontation with slave catchers as the route to manliness. Former slave Philip Younger, who sought refuge in Canada in the 1850s, wrote that even more than in the free states, Canada offered a black man self-respect and dignity. "It was a hardship at first," he reported, "but I feel better here—more like a man—I know I am—than in the States."[39]

Some reformers, such as New York's Gerrit Smith, were critical of men who protected themselves and their families by escaping to Canada, viewing this as a cowardly act. Black abolitionist William Whipper took offense when Smith published such criticism, considering it a slur on the bravery of all black men. Whipper offered a combative reply, saying that he could not understand Smith's attack, considering that African Americans were leaving "a country whose crushing influence . . . aims at the extinction of [their] manhood."[40] Reactions to the Fugitive Slave Law of 1850 ranged from flight to confrontation—different, but each an assertion of personal dignity.

The rising anger at the attack by the "slave power" through its influence over the federal government went beyond militancy to an interest in military preparedness. The Negro Convention in Rochester in 1853 called for the removal of all restrictions on black enlistment in state militia. Sixty-five Massachusetts blacks petitioned their state legislature, demanding that a black military company be chartered. The right to bear arms for their state, they contended, was part of their "rights as men." Their petition was rejected, but a black military company called the Massasoit Guard was formed in Boston in 1854. The unit took its name, their second choice, from a powerful seventeenth-century Indian chief. Most would have preferred the name Attucks, in honor of the black revolutionary hero Crispus Attucks, but the name had already been taken by two other black military companies, the Attucks Guards of New York and the Attucks Blues of Cincinnati. Before the decade ended, there were several black military units in northern cities. Binghamton, New York, named its company after black abolitionist Jermain Loguen, an associate of John Brown, and Harrisburg, Pennsylvania, formed the Henry Highland Garnet Guards. Thus during the 1850s, black men armed themselves, poised to strike against slavery and to reaffirm their manhood through military action.[41]

The opinion in the Dred Scott decision in 1857, which declared that African Americans were not citizens of the United States, further inflamed antigovernment sentiment, as it placed African Americans in an even more perilous position. Increasing militancy and the continuing formation of black military companies led white abolitionist John Brown to believe that substantial numbers of northern free blacks might join a military attack on slavery. He was wrong; in 1859 only five blacks and sixteen whites (three of whom were Brown's sons) joined his attack on the federal arsenal at Harpers Ferry, Virginia. Despite the depth of the antislavery feeling, anger, and frustration, African Americans were not ready to join a private venture that seemed doomed to failure.

Within two years Brown's private war assumed national proportions. Although Lincoln firmly proclaimed preservation of the Union as his sole Civil War aim, northern blacks were convinced that abolition would be its outcome. Their immediate offer of service was refused, even though more than eighty-five hundred men had joined black militia units by the fall of 1861. Two years later, however, the U.S. casualties mounting and the nation bogged down in a protracted war, the government reversed itself and began active recruitment of African American troops. Black abolitionists became energetic recruiters. Jermain Loguen, William Wells Brown, Martin R. Delany, Garnet, and Douglass were among those who encouraged black men to provide their services to the forces of the United States. Victories in the abolition and civil rights struggles during the antebellum period had enhanced their self-image, and most viewed the war as another opportunity to prove themselves to a skeptical white populace. "The eyes of the whole world are upon you, civilized man everywhere waits to see if you will prove yourselves. . . . Will you vindicate your manhood?" challenged the *Weekly Anglo-African* in 1863. African Americans hoped that the war would do more than end slavery. Dignity awaited the black man who would "get an eagle on his button, a musket on his shoulder, and the star-spangled banner over his head."[42] Black men marched off to win freedom for slaves and respect and equality for those already free. War was the culmination of the aggressiveness emphasized in much of the resistance to slavery. It celebrated the instincts necessary for survival and reinforced the violence of the Masculine Primitive Ideal.

Given the realities of life for African Americans under slavery or in freedom during the antebellum period, the irony of using the term *manhood* to apply to the assertion of dignity or the acquisition of freedom is striking. All black people were aware that such action respected no lines of gender. Yet both black men and women used the term. Maria Stewart, David Walker, and Henry Highland Garnet used appeals to manhood to incite blacks to action, but it was not clear whether black women were included. Did calls for slave resistance include women? Were they expected to be "manly"?

Black women's resistance to slavery paralleled black men's, running the gamut from trickery to feigning illness to escape and physical confrontation.[43] Women's physical prowess was acknowledged and often admired within the slave community. Silvia Dubois was proud of the strength that enabled her to run a ferryboat better than any man on the Susquehanna River. As a child she endured her mistress' brutality, but when grown to five feet ten inches tall and weighing more than two hundred pounds, Silvia finally exacted her retribution by severely beating her mistress. After intimidating white spectators who might have subdued her, she picked up her child and made her escape from slavery.[44]

Women's rights advocate and abolitionist Sojourner Truth often spoke with pride of her ability while a slave to do the work of any man. She did not find her strength or her six-foot frame incompatible with being a woman. Nor did Frederick Douglass question the appropriateness of one slave woman's refusal to be beaten and her physical ability to stand her ground against any disbelieving master. When Douglass was resisting Covey, a slave woman named Caroline was ordered to help restrain him. Had she done so, Douglass believed her intervention would have been decisive, because, "she was a powerful woman and could have mastered me easily. . . ." Thus only because a women defied her master was Douglass able to assert his manhood.[45]

For black women no less than black men, freedom and dignity were tied to assertiveness, even to the point of violence. Slavery blurred distinctions between the gender expectations in black society and reinforced the broader economic and political roles provided to black women by their African heritage. Slavery attempted to dehumanize the slave without regard to gender. Both men and women resisted in concert with others and through the force of their individual personalities; dignity and respect could be achieved by remarkable individuals of both sexes. In freedom, black women protected themselves and their families from slave catchers and kidnappers. They were also aggressive wage earners, providing substantial portions of their household income. Scholars have described the independence and economic autonomy of women in precolonial West and Central Africa. As women's spheres and traits became increasingly differentiated from men's in nineteenth-century America, the experience and traditions of black women led them to depart from American gender expectations.[46]

There was no ideal in American society encompassing the experience or honoring the heritage of black women.[47] Perhaps the closest was the notion identified by Ronald W. Hogeland as *Radical Womanhood*, which allowed women a public role. But even this most extreme norm was not sufficient. It accepted the separation of feminine and masculine capabilities, granting moral superiority to women but reserving intellectual and physical power to men.

Accepting masculine traits as the opposite of feminine traits was one of many ways black men sought to establish and define themselves as men in the face of assaults by slavery and racial discrimination. Gender comparisons in Western society were carefully controlled to favor men, limiting women's sphere. Here black people participated in the ongoing effort in nineteenth-century America to construct gender roles in what Hogeland argued was a male-initiated attempt "not conceived of essentially to improve the lot of women, but [implemented] for the betterment of men." The argument set forth by black minister J. W. C. Pennington in opposition to the ordination of women into the African Methodist Episcopal Church illustrates this point. Pennington contended that women were unsuited for "all the learned professions, where mighty thought and laborious investigations are needed," because as "the weaker sex" they were "incapacitated for [them] both physically and mentally."[48]

The force of prevailing gender conventions outside the black community led some to promote gender expectations totally inappropriate for black women's lives. In the face of solid evidence to the contrary, several blacks, such as abolitionist Charles B. Ray, argued that the proper place for women was in the home, as "daughters are destined to be wives and mothers—they should, therefore, be taught to . . . manage a house, and govern and instruct children."[49] Even Douglass, who spoke at the Seneca Falls Convention in 1848 in favor of women's right to vote, asserted in that same year that "a knowledge of domestic affairs, in all their relations is desirable—nay, essential, to the complete education of every female. . . . A well regulated household, in every station of society, is one of woman's brightest ornaments—a source of happiness to her and to those who are dependent upon her labors of love for the attractions of home and its endearments."[50] Although this may have been an appropriate ideal for many white middle- and upper-class women of the time, it was unrealistic for white working women, and even more unrealistic for black women. Most black women did become wives and mothers, but for many their knowledge of domestic affairs was necessarily applied in someone else's home in exchange for wages to help support their families.

Of all the techniques for bolstering black manhood, this was the most internally destructive. It demanded that women affirm their own inferiority in order to uphold the superiority of their men. Not that every African American accepted these gender images, many did not, but they nevertheless became touchstones for gender conventions within black society. Moreover, women faced sanctions for disregarding them, for to do so was viewed as furthering the aims and continuing the effects of slavery, depriving black men of their manhood.[51]

There were women who recognized the dangerous consequences of counterposing male and female traits, but only the boldest voices were raised in opposition. One of those voices was Sojourner Truth's. In the aftermath of the Civil War, when Congress debated the Fifteenth Amendment and related legislation providing the franchise to black men but not to women, she warned of the dangers inherent in such a move: "I feel that I have a right to have just as much as a man. . . . if colored men get their rights and not colored women theirs, the colored men will be masters over the women, and it will be just as bad as before."[52]

NOTES

1. Frederick Douglass, *The Life and Times of Frederick Douglass* (London: Collier-MacMillian, 1962), 143. Also see David W. Blight, *Frederick Douglass' Civil War* (Baton Rouge: Louisiana State University Press, 1989). Ronald T. Takaki makes the argument

that because of Douglass's experience of cruelty at the hands of southern white men and relatively gentle treatment by white women he came to associate the brutality of slavery with white men in the South. It was this belief, Takaki argued, that led him later in life to suggest that perhaps violence alone would make white southern men understand that slavery must be ended. This is a suggestive and interesting thesis with which Blight disagrees and about which there is some question. See Ronald Takaki, *Violence in the Black Imagination: Essays and Documents* (New York: Putnam, 1972).

2. Charles Rosenberg, "Sexuality, Class and Role in Nineteenth Century America," in Elizabeth Pleck and Joseph E. Pleck, eds., *The American Man* (Englewood Cliffs, N.J.: Prentice-Hall, 1980), 219–57.

3. E. Anthony Rotundo, "Learning about Manhood: Gender Ideals and the Middle Class Family in Nineteenth-Century America" (Paper delivered at Smith-Smithsonian Conference on the Conventions of Gender, Smith College, South Hadley, Massachusetts, 16–17 February 1984).

4. Grady McWhiney, *Cracker Culture: Celtic Ways in the Old South* (University: University of Alabama Press, 1988); Bertram Wyatt-Brown, *Southern Honor: Ethics and Behavior in the Old South* (New York: Oxford University Press, 1982); Elizabeth Fox-Genovese, "Cavaliers and True Ladies, Bucks and Mammies: Gender Conventions in the Antebellum South" (Paper delivered at Smith-Smithsonian Conference on the Conventions of Gender, Smith College, South Hadley, Massachusetts, 16–17 February 1984).

5. Thomas Dew, *Review of the Debate of the Virginia Legislature of 1831 and 1832* (1832; reprint, Westport, Conn.: Negro Universities Press, 1970); William Drayton, *The South Vindicated From the Treason and Fanaticism of the Northern Abolitionists* (New York: Negro Universities Press, 1836), 246; Thomas R. R. Cobb, *An Inquiry into the Law of Negro Slavery in the United States of America* (1858; reprint, New York: Negro Universities Press, 1968), quoted in George M. Fredrickson, *The Black Image in the White Mind* (New York: Harper & Row, 1971), 54.

6. William Craft, *Running a Thousand Miles for Freedom: Or The Escape of William and Ellen Craft From Slavery* (London: William Tweedle, 1860), 14–15.

7. Published in two parts in the National Anti-Slavery Standard, 20, 27 October 1842, reprinted in Blassingame, *Slave Testimony*, 152.

8. *New York Times*, 14 January 1862, reprinted in Blassingame, *Slave Testimony*, 170.

9. William Still, *The Underground Railroad* (1872; reprint, New York: Arno Press, 1968); Benjamin Drew, *A North-Side of Slavery* (Boston: J. P. Jewett, 1856); Blassingame, *Slave Testimony*, 157.

10. For an analysis and discussion of this antislavery emblem, see Jean Fagan Yellin, *Women and Sisters* (New Haven: Yale University Press, 1989).

11. David Walker, *Walker's Appeal*, edited with an Introduction by Charles M. Wiltse, 3d ed. (New York: Hill & Wang, 1965), 16, 12.

12. Ibid., 21, 62.

13. Merton L. Dillon, *Slavery Attacked* (Baton Rouge: Louisiana State University Press, 1990), 146–47.

14. Walker had lived in Charleston, South Carolina, about the time that Denmark Vesey's slave rebellion plot was revealed. Historian Peter Hinks speculates that Walker was influenced by the arguments and general sentiment that gave rise to Vesey's actions. See Hinks, "'We Must and Shall Be Free.'"

Others also understood the link between the spirit of freedom overseas and the slaves' desire for liberty in America. In Baltimore white children anxious to aid Greek children turned their attention to the plight of the slaves upon learning that the Greeks no longer needed their help; Dillon, *Slavery Attacked*.

15. Benjamin Quarles, *Black Mosaic* (Amherst: University of Massachusetts Press, 1988).

16. Ibid., 165, 162.

17. Peter Brock, *Radical Pacifists in Antebellum America* (Princeton: Princeton University Press, 1968); *Liberator*, 8 January, 3 September 1831.

18. Henry J. Cadbury, "Negro Membership in the Society of Friends," *Journal of Negro History* 21–22 (April 1936): 151–213. There was considerable controversy among the Friends over the admission of blacks to the Society. Often African Americans were rejected on account of color, even though they were considered models of Quaker virtue. The implication is that those blacks who applied for membership were likely to be at least as acceptable on grounds of principle, including that of pacifism, as whites who did so. Many blacks were accepted into the Society.

19. Marilyn Richardson, ed., *Maria Stewart, America's First Black Woman Political Writer* (Bloomington: Indiana University Press, 1987), 57.

20. Rotundo, "Learning About Manhood," 6.

21. *Liberator*, 1 January 1831; William Lloyd Garrison to the Reverend Samuel J. May, 14 February 1831, in Donald M. Jacobs, "William Lloyd Garrison's *Liberator* and Boston's Blacks, 1830–1865," *New England Quarterly* (June 1971), 260.

22. Wesley, "The Negroes of New York," 96.

23. Dillon, *Slavery Attacked*, 205–6. Hammond also wrote a fictionalized autobiographical account of the life of Julius Melbourne in which black troops are recruited and funded by abolitionists for an attack on southern slavery. See Jabez Delano Hammond, *Life and Opinions of Julius Melbourne* (Syracuse, N.Y.: Hall & Dickerson, 1847).

24. Peter Paul Simons, "Speech Delivered before the African Clarkson Association," New York, 23 April 1839, reprinted in Ripley et al., *The Black Abolitionist Papers* 3: 288–93.

25. *Liberator*, 6 August 1836.

26. Ibid., 13 August 1841.

27. "Speech by Henry Highland Garnet delivered before the National Convention of Colored Citizens, Buffalo, New York, 16 August 1843," reprinted in Ripley et al., *The Black Abolitionist Papers* 3:403–412, quotes 408–10.

28. Ibid., 407, 410.

29. David Blight argued that Douglass was committed to nonviolence as a tactic rather than a moral position. In this way he was never a nonresistant in the Garrisonian sense of that term. See Blight, *Frederick Douglass' Civil War*.

30. *North Star*, 12 May 1848.

31. Foner, *History of Black Americans*, vol. 2.

32. For an excellent discussion of Garrison and his relationship with antebellum blacks in Boston, see Jacobs, "William Lloyd Garrison's *Liberator*" and Horton and Horton, *Black Bostonians*.

33. Horton and Horton, *Black Bostonians*; Smith, "William Cooper Nell," 182–99.

34. Horton and Horton, *Black Bostonians*.

35. William S. McFeely, *Frederick Douglass* (New York: W. W. Norton, 1991); *Frederick Douglass' Paper*, 2 June 1854.

36. Dillon, *Slavery Attacked*.

37. Jayme A. Sokolow, "The Jerry McHenry Rescue and the Growth of Northern Antislavery Sentiment During the 1850s," *Journal of American Studies* 16, no. 3 (December 1982): 427–45, 431.

38. *Liberator*, 7 July 1854.

39. Drew, *A North-Side of Slavery*, 248–51.

40. William Whipper to Gerrit Smith, Esq., Columbus, Pennsylvania, 22 April 1856, in Benjamin Quarles, ed., "Letters from Negro Leaders to Gerrit Smith," ed., Benjamin Quarles, *Journal of Negro History* 27, no. 4 (October 1942): 432–53, 450–51. Smith had issued his criticism in a speech entitled "Right of Suffrage" printed in *Frederick Douglass' Paper*. In his text he had used the term *black men* to refer to the objects of his remarks. Whipper obviously took offense at the use of the all inclusive term and in his answer he placed the words in quotation marks each time he used them. Whipper's reaction, perhaps overreaction, indicated his extreme sensitivity on the issue of black manhood.

41. Horton and Horton, *Black Bostonians*; Benjamin Quarles, *Allies For Freedom: Blacks and John Brown* (New York: Oxford University Press, 1974), 69.

42. *Weekly Anglo-African*, 31 January 1863; Douglass, *The Life and Times*, 338.

43. See Deborah Gray White, *Ar'n't I a Woman?* (New York: W. W. Norton, 1985). White argues that female slaves were more likely to feign illness to escape work than were men. Because childbearing was a primary expectation for slave women, this was a practical and effective tactic.

44. Silvia Dubois, "Silvia Dubois," in *Black Women in Nineteenth-Century American Life*, ed., Bert James Loewenberg and Ruth Bogin (University Park: Pennsylvania State University Press, 1976), 39–47. Many other examples might be cited. See Blassingame, *Slave Testimony*; Blockson, *The Underground Railroad*; Still, *The Underground Railroad*; Norrece T. Jones, Jr., *Born a Child of Freedom, Yet a Slave* (Hanover, N.H.: University Press of New England, 1990).

45. Jacqueline Bernard, *Journey Toward Freedom* (New York: The Feminist Press at The City University of New York, 1990); Douglass, *The Life and Times*, 142.

46. Bonnie Kettel, "The Commoditization of Women in Tugen (Kenya) Social Organization," in *Women and Class In Africa*, ed. C. Robertson and I. Berger (New York: Holmes & Meier, 1986), 50–51.

47. Barbara Welter's delineation of the "cult of true womanhood" identified a middle-class ideal that stressed piety, purity, and domesticity as the most natural and desirable nineteenth-century female characteristics. Ronald W. Hogeland expanded this view, calling the "true woman" *Romanticized Womanhood* and adding three additional ideals: The *Ornamental Woman*, typified by the ideal of genteel white womanhood in the Old South, was characterized by delicacy and decorum. *Evangelical Womanhood* was a practical response to the frontier, allowing women a more active role while engaged in social reform. And *Radical Womanhood*, an ideal that emerged before the Civil War, accepted the innate characteristics of true womanhood but encouraged the active assertion of feminine virtues in the public arena. Barbara Welter, "The Cult of Womanhood, 1820–1860," *American Quarterly* 18 (Summer 1966): 151–74; Ronald W. Hogeland, "'The Female Appendage': Feminine Life-Styles in America, 1820–1860," *Civil War History* 17, no. 2 (June 1971): 101–14.

48. Daniel R. Payne, *History of the African Methodist Episcopal Church* (Nashville: Publishing House of the AME Sunday School Union, 1891), 301.

49. Charles B. Ray, "Female Education," *Colored American*, 18 March 1837, Black Abolitionist Papers Microfilm, Reel 1, Frame 1008. For further discussion on this point and an analysis of black newspapers' contributions to gender education, see chapter 5, "Freedom's Yoke: Gender Conventions among Free Blacks."

50. *North Star*, 17 March 1848.

51. Hogeland, "'The Female Appendage,'" 113.

52. Truth quoted in Elizabeth Cady Stanton et al., *History of Woman Suffrage* (Rochester, N.Y.: Susan B. Anthony; Charles Mann, 1881–1922), 2, 152.

FIFTEEN

"Discipline to the Mind":
Philadelphia's Banneker Institute,
1854–1872

EMMA JONES LAPSANSKY

Nineteen-year-old Jacob C. White, Jr., was sure about what was needed, and on a spring day in 1856 he made it clear to his friends: "a library which, if properly kept up, would shed a halo of literary light throughout this city and reflect great credit on those who constitute this association."[1] In his capacity as recording secretary of the Banneker Institute, White outlined this objective in his annual report. The institute had been organized in 1853 by a group of some five dozen African-American men who had titled it "the Alexandrian Institute, a young men's instruction society."[2] In the ensuing years these men redefined their identity, replacing the classical title with one closer to the members' own heritage and aspirations. African-American mathematician Benjamin Banneker (1731–1806) had been born free in a slave society, had become educated through his own initiative and discipline, and had thereby been able to make a contribution to society, to "reflect great credit on those who constitute this [race]." Banneker had assisted Pierre L'Enfant in the surveying of Washington, D.C., and had published a series of almanacs well-respected in the United States and in Europe. Thomas Jefferson had brought Banneker's work to the attention of the French Academy of Sciences. In addition to these intellectual achievements, Banneker had been an outspoken champion of freedom and political rights for African Americans, having sponsored numerous petitions and pamphlets in their cause.[3] Banneker, then, symbolized the aspirations of the ambitious young men who took his name to describe their brotherhood: he had disciplined and developed his mind, he had taken a public stand for his principles, and he had contributed to international intellectual discourse.

The Banneker Institute had indeed set itself an ambitious mission. For nearly two decades the group kept detailed records as it pursued its mission, engaging the energies of scores of young black men in several countries, stimulating the minds of countless other men and women through public programs, and solidifying a network of family friendships that would transmit the institute's values to future generations.

The story of the Banneker Institute is an integral part of the story of the development of nineteenth-century urban discipline, of the development of African-American group consciousness, of industrialization, and of the relationship between these forces. Unremarkable in its time and place, the Banneker Institute is unique and valuable to the historian because of the survival of eighteen years of very meticulous records and because its membership included representatives of black families who were influential in the economic, religious, political, and intellectual sphere of their day and in succeeding generations.

As the urban areas of nineteenth-century England, France, and the United States made the transition to a standardized work day, punctuated by the scheduled hum of factories and routinized public transportation, so too did the nonwork activities of urbanites acquire a higher degree of regimentation and formality. In the increasing economic, ethnic, and racial diversity of such cities as London, Paris, New York, Philadelphia, Charleston, New Orleans, and Port-au-Prince, individuals became acutely conscious of the danger and isolation that could accompany a particular ethnic, class, racial, religious, political, or professional identity. In response, many individuals sought to join with others who shared their background or values. Traditional indicators by which an individual might have recognized identity and status—family membership, neighborhood or religious community, occupational camaraderie, etc.—were replaced by more "objective" measures of worth: economic power, professional or social connections, public visibility, and organizational affiliation.

A wide array of public agencies (hospitals, orphanages, banks, schools) were replacing functions that had previously been located in the informality of family, church, or community, thereby introducing artificial, professional protectors and comrades into situations where the "natural" allies had been friends and family. The resulting dislocations and disorientations were experienced as much by beneficiaries of the new order as by its casualties. Institutional loyalties replaced personal relationships, and institutional protocol produced group loyalty, discipline, and conformity in an otherwise fragmenting community. Thus, for many and diverse reasons, residents of western cities, besieged by a life of increased speed, greater regimentation, and heightened alienation, found relief by huddling in associations of persons like themselves.[4]

Impermeable—often incomprehensible—to "outsiders," such groups of self-limiting associates increasingly augmented or replaced the natural, informal medical, financial, educational, or emotional roles formerly filled by family or neighbors. An important distinction, however, between the old natural connections and the consciously created replacements was the introduction of regularized meeting times and agendas designed to coordinate with increasingly routinized schedules. Philadelphia's own American Philosophical Society, begun by Benjamin Franklin and some of his friends and modeled after the Royal Society of London, joined the proliferation of similar institutions that flourished after the mid-eighteenth century. These groups signaled the heightened value placed on the systematization of the pursuit and dissemination of knowledge.

An integral part of western industrial society, urban African Americans could not remain aloof from its collateral effects. The hunger for definition-by-association and for the systematization of knowledge was felt among them also. In the wake of the American Revolution, a half-dozen northern states had abolished slavery.[5] Now, for black residents of northern cities, there was the vague promise of inclusion in American life. Now, like Benjamin Banneker, northern African Americans would be born free into a slave society. The Banneker Institute, organized by and for black Philadelphians and their colleagues in British and Canadian cities, sought to maximize these larger modern trends. Publicizing its activities through broadsides and local newspapers, the group met weekly September through June. (Such seasonal scheduling was typical of group activities in Philadelphia. The summer humidity was oppressively unhealthy, and surviving broadsides suggest that Banneker Institute members and their peers fled the city in summer for the ocean air of Cape May and Atlantic City.)[6] Punctuated by rigid adherence to schedules, assignments, and behavioral codes, the story of the Banneker Institute offers insights into one African-American community's interpretation of the best way to maximize the new opportunities they perceived around them.

By the 1850s, when the Banneker Institute appeared, the tradition of voluntary intellectual organizations was well-established among Philadelphians—including black Philadelphians. An 1841 visitor to the city listed more than a dozen self-help and self-education groups sponsored by the African-American community. One such organization, the Gilbert Lyceum, established in the 1830s "for the encouragement of polite literature," numbered among its founders Jacob White's father.[7] In his involvement with the Banneker Institute, then, Jacob White, Jr., mirrored his father's aspirations.

If the existence of the Banneker Institute was not its claim to significance, its importance lies in the historical consciousness and scientific method of its record keeping that allows modern researchers to examine its goals and strategies. Statistics, correlations, and comparative analysis of trends are significant markers in the institute's records, and attempts to mold and shape the organization's future are clearly based on such predictors.[8] The organization's goals and its strategies for effecting those goals were sophisticated and tightly focused.

The catalyst and hub of the organization of the Banneker Institute was Jacob C. White, Jr., and it is White's energy, enthusiasm, imagination, and contacts that sustained the group for nearly two decades. White was only able to do this because he was at the center of an organized and dedicated group of young men who shared his dreams—if not always his convictions about methods. White and his cohorts sought to create what today would be called a "network," a structure through which a group of individuals could support each other in pursuit of their common goals. White and his colleagues hoped to use the adhesive of intellectual energy to create and cement a unified black consciousness that would, in turn, provide an informed social and political leadership for African Americans.

Seeking to display themselves in the best light, the institute leaders recruited those men who they believed were most likely to share their values and ambitions, values based on the belief that the first step in effective political action was self-education.[9] Hence, the Banneker Institute's entrance requirements included some demonstrated intellectual achievement. As with similar organizations, membership was by invitation only; one had to be nominated by people who were already members—a system designed to protect the exclusivity and close-knit structure of the group.

As literacy was a somewhat scarce commodity among nineteenth-century urbanites, the organizers of the Banneker Institute relied heavily for their early recruits upon the most prestigious black educational institution of the day, the Institute for Colored Youth (ICY) which had begun in the 1830s as a trade school. Over the ensuing two decades, the African-American families it served demanded a redefinition of its mission. By the 1850s ICY had a strong liberal arts curriculum and some black teachers on its staff.[10] These factors made ICY a natural recruiting ground for the Banneker Institute.

Jacob C. White, Jr., was himself a graduate of ICY, and he was joined in his mission by other ICY graduates. Octavius Catto, Jesse Glasgow, and Jacob White's own brother George had all been outstanding students at ICY before becoming leaders in the Banneker Institute. The Banneker Institute's membership also included Ebeneezer Bassett, John P. Burr, Stephen Gloucester, and Nathaniel Depee, all of whom had been associated with ICY, either through the governing board or faculty. This latter group was associated with the Banneker Institute for only one year, 1856, when they were all designated honorary members. These were all older, well-respected leaders, whose names no doubt offered an aura of respectability to the activities of the leaders-in-training.[11]

At mid-century Philadelphia had only a few hundred black families with sufficient disposable income to allow them the luxury of sustained discretionary expenditures of time and money. Membership in the Banneker Institute required a 50 cent entry fee and $2 in yearly dues. Attendance at lectures could cost an additional 5 cents, or perhaps as much as 25 cents. Thus, participation in the Banneker Institute involved a substantial financial commitment, and the 58 members listed on the Banneker Institute's 1856 rolls represented a significant number of those who might have been eligible to join.[12] Taking into account the literacy requirement and the narrow age grouping to which the Banneker Institute limited itself, this organization may be seen as an inclusive assemblage of one stratum of Philadelphia's black elite. From an initial membership of two dozen, the Banneker Institute showed strong growth for several years. After 1858, however, the membership declined and wavered between 32 and 45 members, finally dropping off sharply from 42 members in 1867 to 22 members in 1872, the last year for which records are available. Whether or not the organization dissolved after this time is unclear. It is clear that in this year, Jacob C. White, Jr., who had been the charismatic center of the organization, had many other issues on his mind. In 1872 White was in his sixth year of service as the first black principal of a city public school that faced a number of challenges. As if this were not enough, Octavius Catto, White's dear friend and close associate in organizing the Banneker Institute, had been murdered in a political race riot in the fall of 1871. Coincidentally, 1872 was also the year that Jacob C. White, Sr., died, leaving to his son a library, an "electrical machine," and the responsibility for administering a rather large and complex estate.[13]

    The small membership and the short life of the Banneker Institute should not mask its importance in cementing enduring relationships and values for nineteenth-century black Philadelphia. In total, some 105 different individuals held membership in the Banneker Institute. In addition, countless others benefitted and offered support by speaking or attending public lectures and by participating in performances, celebrations, or contribution drives. The leadership was provided by Jacob C. White, Jr., but White was assisted and supported by a nucleus of staunch supporters, each of whom brought an energy for reform and exemplary public service that had been nurtured in their own families. Robert Adger, eighteen years old in 1855, was the second child—the eldest son—of Robert Adger, Sr. The elder Adger, a china-store keeper, was a leader in not less than a dozen African-American self-help organizations over a long career that spanned the years from 1839 to 1890. His wife, Mary, a member of the Ladies Union Committee, was a model of public service in her own sphere. By the end of his life, Robert Adger, Jr., had amassed a large library of Afroamericana, 320 volumes of which were later donated to Wellesley College.[14] Adger served on the Banneker Institute's governing board and on many ad hoc committees over the years.

    Henry Black brought similar energy to the group. The son of Ebenezer Black, Henry was nineteen in 1855. Ebenezer, who owned significant real estate and personal property, was apparently quite literate; he served for some years as the corresponding secretary for the First African Presbyterian Church. He also joined the effort to recruit black soldiers for the Union Army. Ebenezer's son Henry served as the Banneker Institute's librarian, lectured on various natural science topics, and served repeatedly on the Banneker Institute's governing board.[15]

William Minton joined the Banneker Institute at the age of seventeen in 1857. He was the son of Henry and Emily Minton, natives of Virginia, who arrived in Philadelphia to establish themselves as successful restaurateurs. They willed several houses to their heirs. William Minton became treasurer of the Banneker Institute in 1859, the year before his father joined other black leaders in establishing the Civil, Social, Cultural, and Statistical Association of the Colored People of Philadelphia. Designed to "embrace the public interests of the colored citizens of Philadelphia" and to "diffuse a knowledge of the condition and wants of the colored people, and to remove prejudice in any directions where their civil rights are discriminated thereby," the association hoped to use logical and "scientific" arguments in pursuit of their political and social goals.[16] Clearly, Henry Minton and his son had similar intellectual notions. Not only did William Minton remain loyal to the Banneker Institute throughout its existence, but his younger brother, Theophilus, joined the group in 1865 when he was twenty years of age. Theophilus went on to have a distinguished career in providing leadership for the city's first black hospital.[17]

Jacob White, Jr., likewise inspired the loyalty of John W. Simpson, a shoemaker who was eighteen years old in 1855. Between 1855 and 1861 Simpson served the Banneker Institute in various capacities: president, vice-president, secretary, and member of the board of managers. He was an active participant in debates, and he was frequently a member of ad hoc committees to organize such special events as the West India Emancipation Day celebrations held annually on August 1.[18] Three other long-term members—Parker T. Smith, Joel Selsey, and George Burrell—gave loyal service to the institute as lecturers, officers, and members of the board of managers.

Perhaps the most intimate and cherished support to White came from Octavius V. Catto who was only fifteen years old when his father, William T. Catto, became a founding member of the Banneker Institute. Young Octavius, then an outstanding student at ICY, had his petition for membership denied because of his youth. The Catto family was connected to the White family through many close and overlapping ties. William T. Catto, long a champion of education and literacy and the author of a history of Philadelphia's black churches, was a close friend of the White family. Jacob C. White, Sr., was director of the Sunday School in the First African Presbyterian Church where the elder Catto served as pastor. The elder Catto was also on the board of managers of the Lebanon Cemetery, the White family business. Nevertheless, these close family connections did not secure young Octavius's membership until after his graduation from ICY. By 1859, however, Octavius was not only a member, but was listed as recording secretary. He remained a loyal supporter of the institute until his death in 1871.[19]

Octavius Catto's value to the Banneker Institute cannot be overrated. Echoing his father's passion for literacy, after graduation young Catto took a teaching position at ICY and threw his considerable energies into expanding and improving the curriculum and the physical plant at the school. At the same time, he became deeply involved in efforts to secure political power for the black community.[20]

Family tradition and cohesion were indeed important to the success of this group. Among the younger White's supporters were Jacob Glasgow and his younger brother, Jesse, Jr. Jesse Glasgow, Sr., was a whitewasher, who, like Jacob White, Sr., had been a founder of an intellectual organization a generation earlier. Like the younger White, the young Glasgows had been among ICY's best students. Also numbered among the founding members of the Banneker Institute was Joseph Brister whose father, in the 1830s, had been a founding member of the ephemeral Rush Library and Debating Society, an organization which, at its peak, boasted three dozen members and a 200-volume library.[21]

That their fathers had been unable to sustain such organizations as legacies to their sons did not seem to daunt these young enthusiasts. Indeed, there is no evidence to suggest that these organizations were even conceived as long-lived ventures. That such organizations sprang up, ran a course of years, and then disappeared suggests that they may have been instituted to serve a limited purpose—as a kind of "finishing school" or fraternity for a group of young men, assisting them until they had established a personal and political persona of their own. The typical Banneker Institute member in 1855 was young, unmarried, just beginning a career. By 1872 these same men were householders with time-consuming commitments to children and to multiple civic responsibilities.[22] Whatever their goals, these young men went about the task of reinventing their father's dreams with remarkable energy, dedication, and skill, and with a steady insistence upon high standards of behavior, loyalty, and involvement from which no member, no matter how well-connected, was exempt.

Mid-nineteenth-century Philadelphia saw a proliferation of young men's clubs catering to specific ethnic, religious, or other special interests. Calling their clubs "library companies," "fire companies," or similar labels, they rented rooms in which to hold "meetings," which were often characterized by gambling, swearing, harassing passersby, and, occasionally, unabashed street brawling.[23] The Banneker Institute, however, posted rules in the meeting room (rented after 1860 at a cost of $6.25 per month) that were intended to present a disciplined and purposeful air that would place the group a cut above the raucous activities of the more common clubs. The group hired a cleaning woman (at a cost of $6.00 per year) and installed bookcases and a bust of Abraham Lincoln to symbolize its values.[24]

In various years, a number of members were fined, suspended, or expelled. In 1856 twenty members—one-third of the membership—was expelled. Though no reason is recorded for these disciplinary measures, the institute had spent 87 cents to frame their list of rules, and the rules were prominently posted in the meeting room. The rules, which included prohibitions against "indecorous language," and against leaving one's seat without permission of the chairman, were an integral part of the group's concern with self-discipline. Presumably, then, the expulsions resulted from infractions of those rules.[25]

The Banneker Institute leaders worked hard, especially in the early years, to reach agreement on policies and procedures. Achieving and sustaining unity was no easy task, however, even among men whose educational background, goals, and ideals were compatible. Over the first several years, a good deal of meeting time was spent in setting protocol. It was necessary to set behavioral limits that would be stringent enough to define the group's specialness without being too rigid. For example, consistent with White's concern for discipline, members were exhorted to take seriously the commitment to prompt, regular attendance at meetings that were scheduled to convene promptly at 8:00 on Thursday evenings, and to adjourn just as promptly at 10:00.

Setting such goals was one thing; finding ways to discipline oneself and one's colleagues to adhere to such guidelines was yet another. Mechanisms for enforcing policies had to be delicately balanced between rules strict enough to define the group as selective, yet not so confining as to invite flagrant violation. Attempts to walk such a fine line sometimes produced stress. In the early years attendance was erratic. More than one member followed the lead of frustrated president Parker T. Smith who resigned from office in 1855 because "strict order and parliamentary etiquette has not been observed . . . [and] strife and contention predominated." In the same year, William H. Smith unseated himself from the same position because he could not meet the "demands of great punctuality."[26]

Hard pressed to maintain and support an intellectual community in a city that offered African Americans scant opportunity for intellectual exercise — a city which, in fact, constantly ridiculed such efforts[27]—Banneker Institute members persevered against the constraints of white aggression, uncertain finances, internal dissension, and competing demands on members' energies and resources. They were determined to provide a steady diet of intellectual stimulation and nourishment for black Philadelphia. To that end they employed both the carrot and the stick. Exhortations and fines, appreciation and suspension, accolade and expulsion peppered the career of many a Banneker Institute member. Through a combination of careful screening of potential members, and equally careful monitoring of current members, the group attempted to maintain high standards of programming, participation, behavior, and morale. This self-imposed discipline was the Banneker Institute's version of conformity to what one hopeful black Philadelphian termed "an age . . . fastidious in its taste."[28]

Apparently members accepted these disciplinary measures without rancor. Though Jacob Glasgow was expelled in 1856, his younger brother Jesse remained an active member. In the early 1860s, when Jesse emigrated to Scotland, he continued his membership as an equally active "corresponding" member until his untimely death from pneumonia in 1863. The elder Jesse Glasgow was, like the elder Catto, a member of the board of managers of the White family's Lebanon Cemetery, and he continued in that role while son Jacob was on furlough from the Banneker Institute. By 1866 Jacob was once again on the rolls, though the terms of reinstatement were never spelled out in the minutes.[29]

That the process of expulsion was an accepted and impartial part of discipline, engendering little hard feeling, is also suggested by the experience of Robert Adger. A loyal and committed member since the founding of the group, Adger promptly met his obligations to contribute books, time, and committee service, in addition to extra monetary gifts. Yet in 1855 he was expelled. Reinstated by 1858, he was given $15 from the group's treasury to underwrite his travel to the Equal Rights Convention in Harrisburg in 1865. Later that same year, he was again expelled. Two years later he donated $9 worth of bookcases.[30] The specifics of Adger's erratic relationship with the Banneker Institute are unknown, but the expulsion-reinstatement pattern was a part of many members' stories.

The vigor of the Banneker Institute was the result of the energy and dedication of people such as White, Adger, Simpson, Brister, and the Glasgows, men who seemed to place their commitment to improving the economic, social, and political well-being of the black community above their private tensions and disagreements, and who seemed, by and large, willing to abide by rules. The cohesion and intimacy of the Banneker Institute was aided also by geography; many of these men lived in the same neighborhood. Of the seven men who served with Jacob White as the stable nucleus of the institute, only one, Joel Selsey, lived more than a short walk from the rest of the group. The others lived within a three-block radius of the White family's Lebanon Cemetery at Tenth and Bainbridge streets. John W. Simpson, who served as president from 1854 to 1861, lived at 420 S. Seventh Street. William Minton lived in one of the two adjoining brick houses owned by his father in the 1100 block of Rodman Street. Henry Black lived at 612 Barclay; George Burrell, whose wife made her own independent monetary contribution to the institute, lived at 1309 Lombard. Robert Adger's address was listed as 835 South Street. George White, the older brother of Jacob White, Jr., lived at 1118 Rodman.[31]

Though young, these loyal friends and neighbors were serious about their responsibility to maintain the viability of the club. They served as its officers, staffed its subcommittees, organized its meetings, designed broadsides, and placed newspaper advertisements to publicize its lectures. They kept its records, railed at its shortcomings, donated time and books and bookshelves — and disciplined themselves and each other. Over the course of nearly two decades these eight men were always represented on the nine-member board of managers and always active on the library, debate, and program subcommittees of the organization.[32] In addition to their commitment to the institute, these men led full and active lives in many other arenas. Octavius Catto was active in the Pennsylvania Equal Rights League, and he joined White and Adger in organizing the Pythian Baseball League, Philadelphia's first

African-American ball club. While operating his china store, Adger worked with Minton, Catto, and White to recruit black troops for the Civil War.[33]

Similarly, the wives, sisters, and women friends of Banneker Institute members lent their support to the cause, even though many of these women were busy with their own enterprises. In the spring of 1867 Fanny Jackson, who was soon to become a principal at ICY, presented a lecture that yielded $8.10 for the institute's coffers. Sarah Mapps Douglass, also a teacher at ICY, lectured on anatomy one rainy evening in 1855, to an audience that was just "tolerable." The club netted a profit of only 45 cents. Douglass's daughter Grace and Caroline Harding, both teachers at ICY, are listed as "contributing members," and in 1855 a "Mrs. Stephens" (presumably the wife of member Alexander Stephens) contributed a volume on the life of Benjamin Franklin.[34]

As they set about the dual agenda of building internal unity and simultaneously seeking acceptance in the world outside their own community, these strategists knew they faced an uphill battle. In popular culture—in newspapers and on stage, in cartoons and in song—as well as in the system of exclusion of blacks from many educational institutions, white Americans mocked and thwarted their strivings.[35] In the spring of 1858 Jacob White petitioned to have the Banneker Institute included in the National Literary Congress, a city-wide consortium of similar organizations. When the Literary Congress lauded the program and format of the Banneker Institute but refused it membership, solely on the basis of race, White was deeply disappointed—but undaunted.[36]

Derision and exclusion were not the only challenges presented by the environment. Worried that their own social and economic vessels might run aground in the turbulent waters of industrialization, many urban white workers met the aspirations of upwardly mobile blacks with resentment and violence. The persons and property of aspiring blacks were repeatedly the targets of attack in the mid-century urban unrest. White, Catto, and Adger had all been children in Philadelphia during the repeated racial, ethnic, and religious riots of the 1830s and 1840s. Violent attacks on the families and property of their middle-class friends and neighbors were well-known to them. They knew that the meeting hall of the black masons had been destroyed in a steak of violence, and they knew that the city streets were populated with roving gangs that might, at any moment, unleash their frustration on the symbols of African Americans' dreams.[37]

In addition to these external threats, pressures within the group also challenged the institute's stability. Members were expected to make periodic contributions of intellectual fare to stimulate their peers, and there was a strict requirement on the payment of fees. In addition, each member was duty bound to educate himself on some subject and then lecture to the group. Often members were conscientious about living up to their commitments. In January 1859 a gathering of eleven members heard Davis Turner and George Burrell lead a debate on the subject of whether it is right "for lawyers to defend persons whom they know to be guilty of the crimes with which they may be charged?" In March of that same year, Henry Black lectured to eight people on the topic of mineralogy, botany, and Linneaus. A few weeks before, Jacob White, Jr., had used examples from Greek and Arab history to argue for competence in math for bookkeeping, navigation, surveying, and, most importantly, for providing "discipline to the mind." Isaiah Wears held forth on the subject of "Love, Courtship and Marriage" to a "tolerable" audience on a cloudy evening.[38]

The events in 1859, a year of typical institute activities, provided an intellectual menu that was stimulating and varied. Upon closer examination, however, it becomes possible to see how, even with the best of intentions, the consistent adherence to discipline was not easy. The minutes record only eleven regular business meetings at which the highest attendance was only fourteen of the members. Four meetings were canceled because of low attendance. In early May a meeting was called off because of the school examinations being held in the Institute for Colored Youth building, where the Banneker Institute sometimes met. Another meeting was canceled because it was scheduled for a night when Frederick Douglass was speaking in town. There is no entry or explanation for the other twenty-odd meetings that should have been scheduled.

Eleven public lectures were scheduled, of which only eight actually occurred. Octavius Catto twice refused to speak, once complaining that he had not been given enough notice, and once saying that he felt the audience was too small. William Johnson had to be rescheduled twice, once because he had forgotten it was his turn to lecture and a second time because he refused to speak before a small audience. When, however, his lecture praising Napoleon III opened the fall season, it was well received. Two members, Ralph Gilmore and the usually loyal George Burrell, failed to show up at all for their scheduled lectures. For one meeting all but one member arrived more than an hour late.

For the months of January–June, recording secretary Parker T. Smith meticulously kept track of attendance, topics, weather, and, sometimes, the gross income from the lecture events. But when William Minton took over as secretary after the summer hiatus, he adopted a terse style of record keeping that included neither attendance nor weather.[39]

If adherence to schedules and timing was a challenge, other rules presented equally difficult situations. By 1855 Robert Adger had made the first of two gifts of bookshelves, but the books to fill these shelves came slowly. Librarian Henry Black reported in January 1855 that only twelve volumes had been deposited in the previous twelve months. At that point a volume of French literature, given by member T.J. Harmon, set on the shelves alongside a biography of John Quincy Adams, contributed by George Burrell, a biography of George Washington, added by Alexander Stephens, and the biography of Franklin, donated by "Mrs. Stephens."[40]

It was a struggle, but the fact that things often went smoothly seemed to make it worth the effort. In the winter of 1855 Parker T. Smith lectured to a full house on "The History of Women," and William Wells Brown talked about "Mahomet and Confucius." Such titles, along with Parker T. Smith's discussion of Thomas Paine's *The Age of Reason*, make us wish that the speakers had complied with the secretary's request to deposit a transcript of their talks in the library.[41] The 1855 attempts to engage Massachusetts abolitionist senator Charles Sumner were unsuccessful, as was William Minton's 1869 telegram inviting Stephen Douglas to address the group (declined because "other engagements stood in the way"). On the other hand, the proceeds from an 1866 lecture by the Honorable J.M. Forney netted more than $170, and over the course of nearly twenty years White, Simpson, Selsey, Burrell, and their friends arranged more than 200 events that brought public attention and/or economic benefit to themselves and their audiences.[42]

Though the participation of individual members fluctuated somewhat, the institute's rhythm and programming remained firm throughout. Regular scheduling of events, September through June, remained the standard, even as the membership waned and the calendar could not always be filled. Likewise, the topics on the agenda showed a cerain consistency. A group such as this had a wide range of options for topics and the formats it might use for presentation. Poetry, drama, sports, social welfare, art, philosophy, politics, or natural science were all popular with the intellectuals of the day. The list of topics for lecture and debate suggests that much planning went into choosing topics. They should be stimulating but not offensive, controversial but not divisive, and within the scope of the constituency's experience and comprehension but not to the point of being pedestrian or repetitive.

Topics in both programming and in the library collections seemed to cluster around four areas: math/natural sciences, philosophy/history, business skills, and predictably, a variety of race-related issues. Jacob White recorded a "house crowded to overflowing" for Jeremiah Asher's discussion entitled "Does the Bible Sanction Slavery?" Pastor of Shiloh Baptist Church, Asher was actively involved in the underground railroad through William Still's "vigilance committee." He remained active in the black commuity throughout his lifetime, recruiting soldiers for the Civil War and preaching resistance rather than patience from his pulpit. An equally timely debate, led by Jacob White, Joel Selsey, George Burrell, and William Johnson, on the relative merits of slavery, brought a large crowd to partake of the spirited discussion. Johnson took the position that slavery was beneficial because it introduced "civilization" into Africa. White concurred, adding that slavery had brought Africans "under discipline." Turner took the other side, arguing that there could be no justification for the millions of people "sent to eternity" as a result of the slave system.[43]

The Banneker Institute's leaders clearly took seriously their self-imposed duty to find topics that would interest and edify the African-American population. However, owing to White's moderate, religious, and noncombative attitude toward racial injustice, perhaps controversial current events were approached infrequently, obliquely, and in a controlled, somewhat dispassionate format. The Banneker Institute's minutes show no response to the widely debated trial of escaped slave Anthony Burns, to the birth of the Republican party, to the Dred Scott case, or to the dramatic escape of Henry "Box" Brown who was uncrated, in Philadelphia, from the small box in which he had fled from Virginia slavery. In 1867 Octavius Catto and his fiancée, Caroline LeCount, were in the vanguard of the battle to end discrimination on Philadelphia streetcars. This battle went on *outside* the confines of the Banneker Institute meetings.[44]

Insulated from some of the political/racial activity of the time, the Banneker Institute was bold about promoting discussion of other issues. In November 1855 a crowded house greeted Mary Ann Shadd, the controversial African-American teacher who had recently begun her own newspaper. Member Isaiah Wears appeared on the platform with Miss Shadd, and together they had a discussion on the merits of emigrating to Canada, which Shadd had done several years before. And, within weeks of John Brown's 1859 attempt to muster a slave army at Harper's Ferry, the Banneker Institute had twice gathered to consider the implications of such a bold move. For each discussion strict discipline was kept, and the meetings adjourned promptly at 10:00.[45]

The library of the Banneker Institute reflected this same air of caution. There is a record of a subscription to *The Nation*, but there is no evidence that the group owned a copy of *Uncle Tom's Cabin*, nor is there any indication that the institute subscribed to the *Liberator*, the *Anti-Slavery Standard*, or to Frederick Douglass's paper. Even the black Philadelphia paper, *The Christian Recorder*, is not listed among the group's reading matter.

What might be inferred about the *unspoken* agenda of the Banneker Institute? Perhaps some clues may be found by examining the young men who *might* have been members but who were not. There were other groups of African-American intellectuals active in the city—most notable among these being the Philadelphia Library Company of Colored Persons. This rival group included wealthy coal-and-lumber dealers William Still and William Whipper and dentist James McCrummell. These men, though neighbors of White, Adger, and Catto, were generally somewhat wealthier and favored a political alignment with William Lloyd Garrison and his associates. This political alignment sought a strategy of "moral suasion" to accomplish a society in which there would be no "complexional institutions," that is, no segregated institutions. Jacob White and several of his associates in the Banneker Institute were quite outspoken about their more conservative approach, advocating alliances with white institutions but avoiding mergers. Presaging the later strategies of Booker T. Washington, White was more concerned with political rights than with immediate access to social rights.[46]

Consistent with this approach, the Banneker Institute maintained cordial diplomatic relations with the Library Company of Colored Persons but declined to merge with them. They cooperated in a number of joint projects —including the joint rental of a meeting room which they occupied on alternate evenings. On several occasions the two groups cosponsored public programs, sharing equally in production and publicity costs and in profits. A fall concert presented at the Franklin Institute and several celebrations of West Indian Independence day are typical of such collaborations.[47] Banneker Institute members, however, remained firmly opposed to moving from collaboration to merger.[48] Perhaps they were concerned that their agenda would be engulfed in the ideas of their more powerful and wealthier neighbors. Perhaps the political/strategical differences seemed insurmountable, even on the presumably neutral ground of intellectual inquiry. Whatever the impetus, the Banneker Institute members exercised their right to separateness.

With the coming of the Civil War, the energies of many Banneker Institute members were redirected into the war effort. They helped to recruit troops, fund and staff freedmen's education and relief efforts, and mapped out strategies to secure the vote. Also, even as public responsibilities tugged at the attention of this small cadre of activists, private lives brought increasing distractions. Demanding careers, teenagers to be educated, and the other tasks of adult life seemed to drain the vitality from the group.

Over the years, as membership waned, so too did the vigor with which high standards of participation were upheld. By the late 1860s expulsions dwindled, and so did attendance and record keeping. What became of the group after 1872 is unknown. Certainly, individuals from the group maintained their friendships and their business connections. Most of the members continued their active and visible leadership roles in the community: working to secure the vote, to establish an industrial school, to start newspapers, hospitals, and loan associations, and, in 1897, the Negro Historical Society, through which the records of the Banneker Institute survived. These men passed on their ideals to their sons and daughters who preserved their libraries, carried on their businesses, and founded twentieth-century institutions with goals similar to those of the Banneker Institute. Through its efforts to create and support a self-conscious and cohesive black intellectual community, through its internalization of the "need" for bureaucratic institutions, procedures, and disciplines, and through its adaptation of these structures to incorporate an agenda specific to their aspirations of "reflecting great credit," the Banneker Institute has much to tell us about the dreams of an urban black elite to construct a supportive community in a chaotic world. The modernization of the western metropolis came to Philadelphia—and African Americans were in a unique position to use its structures to socialize and inspire its next generation of leaders.

NOTES

1. Minute Book of the Banneker Institute, 1855–1859, April 3, 1856. This document (hereafter, BI Minute Book) is part of a group of records documenting the history of the Banneker Institute. This group of records consists of two minute books (1855–59 and 1865–72), a roll book (1854–72), an order/receipt book, and miscellaneous receipts, broadsides, and ephemera. Preserved among the records of the American Negro Historical Society, they were donated to the Historical Soceity of Pennyslvania (hereafter, HSP) by Leon Gardiner.

2. BI Minute Book, Sept. 9, 1853.

3. Silvio A. Bedini, *The Life of Benjamin Banneker* (New York, 1972).

4. The Annales school has had a profound effect on the way historians have interpreted the interaction of historical phenomena, and a number of scholars have chronicled the events of the nineteenth-century cities within this framework of the interaction of "public" and "private" events. Good examples are the work of Sam Bass Warner, Bruce Laurie, David Grimsted, and Billy G. Smith, but it is Arnold Thackray who comes closest to describing a situation analogous to that of the Banneker Institute: Arnold Thackray, "Natural Knowledge in Cultural Context: The Manchester Model," *American Historical Review* 79 (1974), 672–709. See also, Tamara Hareven, "The Dynamics of Kin in an Industrial Community," in Naomi Gerstel and Harriet Engel Gross, *Families and Work* (Philadelphia, 1987), 55–84; Stuart Blumin, *The Emergence of the Middle Class: Social Experience in the American City, 1760–1900* (New York, 1989); and Peter Burke, *The French Historical Revolution: The Annales School, 1929–1989* (Stanford, 1990).

5. Leon Litwack, *North of Slavery: The Negro in the Free States, 1790–1860* (Chicago 1961), 3–14.

6. Broadside, Box 13G, Leon Gardiner Collection, HSP.

7. Edwin Wolf II, *Philadelphia: Portrait of an American City* (Philadelphia, 1975), 103; [Joseph Willson], *Sketches of the Higher Classes of Colored People in Philadelphia, by a Southerner* (Philadelphia, 1841), 61–68.

8. See, for example, the entries in BI Minute Book, April 3, 1856; Jan. 26, Feb. 23, 1859.

9. Emma Lapsansky, "Since They Got Those Separate Churches: Afroamericans and Racism in Jacksonian Philadelphia," *American Quarterly* 32 (1980), 54–78.

10. Harry Silcox, "Philadelphia Negro Education: Jacob C. White, Jr., 1837–1902," *Pennsylvania Magazine of History and Biography* (hereafter, *PMHB*) 97 (1973), 75–98.

11. Charline Conyers, "A History of the Cheyney State Teachers' College" (Ph.D. diss., New York University, 1960), 100; BI Roll Book.

12. In 1847 the Philadelphia Yearly Meeting of Friends sponsored a "Census of the Colored People of Philadelphia" (hereafter, 1847 Friends Census) that listed names, household size, birthplace and occupation of head of household, value of real and personal property, and more. Of the more than 5,000 households listed in the census, only a few hundred appear to have been in an economic position to sustain membership in the Banneker Institute. See also the discussion of Philadelphia elites in Julie Winch, *Philadelphia's Black Elite: Activism, Accommodation and the Struggle for Autonomy, 1787–1848* (Philadelphia, 1989).

13. BI Roll Book; Harry C. Silcox, "Nineteenth-Century Philadelphia Black Militant: Octavius V. Catto, 1839–1871," *Pennsylvania History* 44 (1977), 53–76; Will no. 458 (1872), will book 75, 105; Administration no. 680 (1871), book U, 36; Archives of the City of Philadelphia.

14. Adger sold these volumes as a unit in 1904 to Mrs. Ella Smith Elbert who later donated them to her alma mater, Wellesley College. For the books and their provenance,

see Wendy Ball and Tony Martin, *Rare Afroameriana: A Reconstruction of the Adger Library* (Boston, 1981), xii.

15. BI Roll Book; BI Minute Books.

16. Philip S. Foner, "The Battle to End Discrimination Against Negroes on Philadelphia Streetcars. Part 1, Background and Beginning of the Battle" *Pennsylvania History* 40 (1973), 261–89.

17. Between 1968 and 1985 the Philadelphia Social History Project compiled a computerized data base of organizations and members from disparate sources (church records, roll and account books, broadsides, censuses, and contemporary local histories). Some of the biographical data used in this study is derived from this compilation, now housed in the University of Pennsylvania's Van Pelt Library (hereafter, PSHP Organization List).

18. BI Roll Book; BI Minute Books.

19. BI Roll Book; BI Minute Books; PSHP Organization List.

20. Silcox, "Nineteenth-Century Black Militant," 69.

21. Willson, "Sketches of the Higher Classes," 102, 109–11.

22. 1847 Friends Census; PSHP Organization List.

23. George Rogers Taylor, "'Philadelphia in Slices' by George G. Foster," *PMHB* 93 (1969), 23–72.

24. BI Order/Receipt Book, 1867–72, Receipt nos. 31, 33.

25. BI Order/Receipt Book, 1867–72, Receipt no. 29, Jan. 14, 1868; BI Minute Book, May 25, 1854.

26. BI Minute Book, Oct. 5, 1854, 42–43; Jan. 4, 1855, 49.

27. Lapsansky, "Since They Got Those Separate Churches," 62–66.

28. William Whipper, "An Address . . . Before the Colored Reading Society of Philadelphia, For Mental Improvement," quoted in Dorothy Porter, *Early Negro Writing, 1760–1837* (Boston, 1971), 105–6.

29. BI Roll Book; PSHP Organization List.

30. BI Roll Book; BI Order/Receipt Book, 1865–69.

31. BI Roll Book.

32. BI Minute Books.

33. Silcox, "Nineteenth-Century Black Militant," 66–67; Emma Lapsansky, "Friends, Wives and Strivings: Networks and Community Values Among Nineteenth-Century Philadelphia Afroamerican Elites," *PMHB* 108 (1984), 3–24.

34. BI Minute Book, 1855–59, 3.

35. Robert C. Toll, *Blacking Up: The Minstrel Show in Nineteenth-Century America* (New York, 1974).

36. Silcox, "Philadelphia Negro Educator," 83.

37. John Runcie, "Hunting the Nigs' in Philadelphia: The Race Riot of August, 1834," *Pennsylvania History* 39 (1972), 187–218.

38. BI Minute Book, Jan. 26, March 23, Feb. 16, Dec. 4, 1859.

39. BI Minute Book, 1855–59, 2–30.

40. Ibid., 3.

41. BI Minute Book, Jan. 4, 1855, 49.

42. BI Minute Book, 1855–59, 45; BI Order/Receipt Book, 1855–68, Aug. 8, 1860; Jan. 18, Nov. 8, 1865; Aug. 10, 1869.

43. BI Minute Book, Feb. 2, 1859; PSHP Organization List.

44. Silcox, "Nineteenth-Century Black Militant," 65–66.

45. Dorothy Sterling, *We Are Your Sisters: Black Women in the Nineteenth Century* (New York, 1984), 164–75; BI Minute Book, Nov. 6, 1855; Oct. 6, Dec. 20, 1859.

46. PSHP Organization List; Benjamin Quarles, *Black Abolitionists* (New York, 1969), 105.

47. BI Minute Book, Jan. 29, 1855; BI Order/Receipt Book, Receipt no. 31, Feb. 1, 1868.

48. BI Minute Book, 1855–59, April 3, 1856.

PART FOUR

RESISTANCE
AND
REPRESENTATION
OF
BLACK
MEN

SIXTEEN

"Fly across the River":
The Easter Slave Conspiracy of 1802

DOUGLAS R. EGERTON

Although it was just dawn, a large crowd had assembled in Petersburg, Virginia, to witness the execution of Peter, the recalcitrant property of William Claiborne and the last slave to face death for his complicity in Gabriel's conspiracy. Blacks, who were allowed—even urged—to attend the hanging as a lesson against such schemes, sang hymns, cried softly, or watched silently, sullenly. The trap fell open and the rope pulled taut. The date was Friday, October 24, 1800.[1]

Virginia authorities hoped that would be the end of it. They were wrong. Even as Peter swung from the Dinwiddie County gallows, other slaves in and below Petersburg, at least one of them a member of Gabriel's conspiracy, began to organize a second one. This essay examines that largely unexplored plot. By tracing the path of the conspiracy as it moved from town to town and from rebel to rebel, it demonstrates that the second conspiracy was born of a single source and was not a number of isolated acts of overt resistance (or number of isolated instances of white paranoia). And by analyzing the occupation and goals of the convicted conspirators, it argues that the conspiracy of 1802 should be understood not as a totally new conspiracy but as a second chapter of the planned insurrection two years earlier.[2]

The intrigues that began sometime in 1801 were whispered by a particular kind of man. The leading conspirators of the previous year had been skilled artisans (Gabriel himself was a blacksmith), and those who began "the business" a second time had an equally important skill: they were watermen. Virtually all early-nineteenth-century southern towns had large numbers of slaves trained to work on the rivers. Ship artisans, pilots, sailmakers, riggers, caulkers, and dock workers could all be found laboring in shipyards in Virginia and the Carolinas. In a region built upon both the export of staple crops, most of which were carried by the river, and human bondage, it was not surprising that slaves were trained to perform a myriad of shipping occupations.[3]

The most mobile, and certainly the most arduous, of those occupations was that of riverman. Rivermen were the slaves who sailed scows and flatboats up and down southern waterways. Both types of boats were capable of transporting nearly eighty hogsheads of tobacco. Moving that cargo safely downriver was tricky work and required years of training. Returning the boats, laden with tools and other goods, back up the rivers required strong backs; rivermen often had to force their reluctant vessels along with oars and poles. The voyage was typically a long one. Slaves pushed into the heart of Virginia on the James and Appomattox rivers. Cargo from the southwestern part of the state was brought down the Roanoke (Staunton) River into the Albemarle Sound.[4]

Many rivermen were slaves for hire, bondmen whose labor was sold by their masters—sometimes even by themselves—to others on a short-term basis. So accepted was the practice in the late eighteenth century that one astonished visitor to Norfolk observed—with only a little exaggeration—that it was "not at all uncommon for a White to keep Blacks to let out as horses are in England." Required to pay their owners a set amount yearly, bond hirelings were free to do as they wished with whatever money they earned above that amount. Cash was therefore introduced into a labor relationship that was supposed to be based upon paternalism, a concept already weakened by the dislocation and upheaval of the Revolutionary era. For a class that owned no means of production, cash was a new and potent symbol of liberty and power.[5]

By necessity, black rivermen were absent from their masters' homes for long periods of time. Both those who hired their time and those who worked only for their owners found it convenient to live away from their masters and to find their own resting places in towns that lined the waterways. Unlike hiring out, living out was illegal, but as the economy demanded it, Virginia authorities fell into the habit of overlooking the practice. In effect, the rivermen lived much as free blacks did. Although still slaves in the eyes of the law, those who lived out were left alone so long as they surrendered most of their annual earnings to a distant owner.[6]

Evidence for the crucial role that rivermen played in the economy of the border South can be seen in the fact that whites made no effort to crack down on their relative freedom, despite the fact that they escaped in unacceptable numbers. Already skilled and partly assimilated to white culture, rivermen were able to peddle their arts in a free-labor market. And with their knowledge of southern geography many hirelings, who often knew large numbers of friendly free blacks along the rivers, simply never returned from a long voyage. One by one and acting as individuals, they disappeared from sight. Between 1736 and 1801, watermen made up 14 percent of all skilled slave runaways.[7]

Whites allowed those practices to exist despite the fact that they feared the rivercraft to be vehicles of discussion, that is, subversion. If plantations fragmented laborers by isolating one group of slaves from another, towns and rivers did just the opposite. News and ideas passed as freely as goods in the cities, where literate black artisans dealt with their less-assimilated brethren on a daily basis. Rivermen, moving from town to town, served as a vital link between urban areas. White fears were so great that in 1784 the Virginia General Assembly passed a law mandating that no more than one third of the crew of any rivercraft could consist of slaves. The law was unenforceable and unenforced.[8]

Perhaps white fears were somewhat assuaged by the knowledge that acculturated, skilled slaves, unlike their African ancestors who had been brought to the Chesapeake region in the early eighteenth century, fought back or escaped as individuals. If so, white Virginians failed to perceive a crucial point. Even as their assimilation to white culture broke down the African tradition of collective resistance, their occupations gave them a new basis for collective rebellion. Skilled hirelings had their own unique demands: not only their freedom but also the right to all their earnings. Gabriel had told his brother Solomon that they had the right to "possess ourselves of [the] property" their labor had secured for others. Skilled slaves conspired to overturn the central class relationship in their society but not that society itself. They were too much a part of it. From their perspective, their demands were simple justice; from that of their owners, the demands were truly radical.[9]

The highly mobile watermen had the means to set a conspiracy afoot. In the fall of 1801 the conspiracy began to take shape in the northern part of Halifax County, Virginia. The extant evidence does not indicate which slave first raised the standard of rebellion, although the likely man was Sancho. His owner, John Booker, lived in Amelia, several counties away, but owned a ferry on the Roanoke River, which formed the border between Halifax and Charlotte counties. In the western portion of those two counties, the latter of which had a black majority, the "plot was most matured." Sancho operated the ferry for his owner, who wrongly believed him to be a loyal slave; the bondman "had tried to induce others to join the insurrection under Gabriel." Most likely, Sancho had been in Amelia and had been a member of the Petersburg wing of the widespread 1800 conspiracy.[10]

During the formative stage of the conspiracy Sancho was careful to contact only other watermen, assimilated hirelings who were already on the edge of freedom and were in the best position to prosper should true independence come. Hailing Bob, a hired slave who operated William Royall's ferry, as "a valuable fellow," Sancho urged him "to join me to raise against the White people." Bob stammered that it "was impossible." Remember "what was done at Richmond," he cautioned, "they all rose there [and] were destroyed." But Sancho only replied that "he reckoned it could be done."[11]

Evidently most of the slaves Sancho approached were less cautious, for by November "about Sixty [men] had inlisted." If Sancho really was a member of the 1800 conspiracy, he had learned a valuable lesson. Instead of trying to enlist as many men as possible, he worked instead to recruit a small, dedicated group of followers who would raise men quickly when the time came. That lessened the chance of a less-courageous slave's hearing of the plot and passing word to his master, a flaw that had destroyed Gabriel's plan. "[W]e shall most certainly Suceed without difficulty if our Schem is not betrayed, beforehand," wrote one conspirator, "as there is but one in a Family to know of it untill the time is but Actually arrived."[12]

That date was a closely guarded secret. Only those at the very vortex of the plan knew that the date was to be either "good fryday" or Easter Monday of 1802. Like Christmas, Easter was "a general holiday" for the slaves, who were typically "disbanded till [the following] Wednesday morning." Thus, whites would not think it unusual to see many slaves moving about or heading for the nearest town. The "sound of a horn, Trumpets, &c" would be the signal for the leaders to begin raising men. Sancho also avoided the risk of trying to make and stockpile arms. Anticipating Nat Turner's plan, the insurgents would instead "be furnished with them" as they went from house to house.[13]

As for the plan itself, it was as simple as Gabriel's was complex. Little is known about Sancho, but even if literate, as a resident of Halifax (and perhaps occasionally Petersburg) he surely lacked the information that had been available to Gabriel, who lived just outside Richmond. In place of careful planning and rational calculation Sancho substituted a flexible frame of mind that was able to rise to meet new situations. Once Sancho's immediate followers had each recruited a handful of men, they were to meet at Daniel Dejarnet's ordinary. Killing of "the White people" would then begin, but how long it would continue was undetermined. Evidently the leaders assumed that the authorities would quickly offer concessions. Only then would the rebels formulate their final demands, which certainly would include their freedom, the right to their earnings, and an equitable distribution of property.[14]

Whatever their differences, both Gabriel and Sancho built their plans upon the assumptions that the fighting would be brief and that they were not precipitating an all-out race war. Gabriel had "expected the poor white people [to] join him." The conspirators of 1802 were not as sanguine in that hope, but they did count upon "the poor [white] sort that has no blacks" at least to remain neutral. The "great Conflagration of Houses fodder Stacks &c," insisted one rebel, "will Strike such a damp on there Spirets that they will be . . . willing to Acknowledge, liberty & Equallity." Such a hope was not completely naive. In southern cities and towns blacks and poor whites lived and labored in close proximity. Urban alleys and grog shops were "distinguished for the equality which reigned." Therefore, it was not irrational for Virginia authorities to believe that some whites were actively "connected in the plot [and would] give aid when the negroes should begin."[15]

A brief composite biography of the insurgents demonstrates the basis for such beliefs. Of the sixteen Virginia slaves found guilty of complicity in the Easter conspiracy, the vast majority (eleven) were probably skilled, for the worth of each was above the market value of $333.33 (£100) the state paid at the time for healthy but unexceptional male slaves executed or transported. All were in almost daily contact with working-class whites and artisans. Many of the slaves were literate and kept in close contact through letters, a notable fact because more than 90 percent of slaves were illiterate. Most hired their time, and half (eight men) were listed as property of deceased owners. That meant they were the property of unsettled estates or were owned by women or children, a tenuous link in a society built upon paternalism. Most were probably married, and hence fathers, for in the settled Chesapeake region slave women settled into stable relationships in their early twenties. In short, if the conspirators were young, strong men with little prejudice against violence, they also had much to live for.[16]

With the conspiracy well under way in Halifax, news of the rising began to ripple down the river arteries that bound the region together. Absalom, a member of the leadership nucleus, told several slaves "that he had been over the [Roanoke] river to the county of Charlotte" in an attempt to enlist a handful of potential leaders. Cautiously contacting only men who could be counted on if not to join then at least to keep silent, the slave cadre kept in close contact through written notes. "[W]e have intellegence from almost all parts," observed one slave, "that our intentions have Successfully Spread with the greatest Secrecy."[17]

That state of affairs could not last for long. Charlotte County touched upon several smaller rivers that fed into the Appomattox, a major route to Petersburg. As Sancho was a hireling, he probably spent some days in late 1801 and early 1802 at his master's home in Amelia, directly on the Appomattox. Even if he did not, the river connected the southwestern portion of the state to Petersburg. One traveler, noting that the "streets of Petersburg were crowded with hogsheads of tobacco," was told that wagons and scows were "coming eighty or a hundred miles from the interior." As cargo passed from hand to hand, so did word of the conspiracy.[18]

The inclusion of Petersburg in the scheme was both a blessing and a burden. Surely the news found fertile ground in the city. Two years before, Gabriel had reached out to the skilled blacks of Petersburg, a "union of plan" that had cost Claiborne's Peter his life. But the larger the Easter conspiracy grew, the more likely it became that word would be passed to a slave who could not be trusted to keep it secret. Indeed, news of the rising became so general that, on Christmas Day of 1801, Grief Green's Ned overheard three unknown slaves in Petersburg speak of the plan. The next day, as he walked back to his home in neighboring Nottoway County, he was approached by yet another slave, who "said he wished to join . . . and help him kill all the White people."[19]

Ned insisted he would have nothing to do with the plot, but bolder men were willing to listen. In Nottoway, a nucleus soon formed around the widow Jones's Joe and John Royall's Bob, who were spreading word of the plot as early as a week prior to Christmas. Their plan, clearly based upon Sancho's scheme, was simple. The rebels would "commence the business" in Nottoway then march on Petersburg, "killing and robbing as they went." There, armed with whatever "they got from the Country Inhabitants," they would move "on to [a] General Rendezvous" with the Halifax slaves.[20]

Had the conspiracy spread no further, perhaps it would have stood a chance of success. But the more it moved down the rivers, the more control over it slipped from the grasp of the Halifax men. Even with their relative freedom of movement and their ability to pass written communications, the conspirators were unable to guide a vast group of rebels, who would have to rise quickly and at nearly the same time. There is good reason to believe, as did white authorities in Halifax, that the conspiracy in their county was connected to the one "in Notoway." If it spread further, however, ties of communication would surely snap.[21]

Snap they did when the word of the conspiracy passed out of the mouth of the Appomattox into the James, washing both upriver toward Richmond and downriver toward Norfolk. In moving north, the conspiracy followed the path of that of two years earlier. Just before Easter, Lewis, a Goochland ferryman known to some of the Nottoway rebels and traveling "under a free pass written by himself," headed out of Petersburg for Richmond. His purpose was to recruit "among the Negroes and to prepare them for a General insurrection." But north of Petersburg he found few takers. Perhaps the brutal lesson administered to the conspirators of 1800 cooled their ardor.[22]

But events were flowing too fast to be dammed by the hesitancy of the Richmond slaves. News of the plan sailed down the James. Surely at least several scows carried the volatile cargo; one of them was "a free negro's vessell." Two years before, a bond skipper who hired out his ship had ferried correspondence between Petersburg and Norfolk, and "about twenty Norfolk slaves had assembled" to await word from Gabriel. Now another black captain was acting as a link between conspirators in Norfolk and "the negroes of the upper country."[23]

News of a second attempt to do "the business" evidently found a receptive audience in Norfolk. The port city was home to roughly 3,000 blacks, the great majority of them slaves; whites numbered just under 4,000. Most slave hires and free blacks crowded into Loyall's Lane, a waterfront area only slightly more ramshackle than the rest of the unsightly wooden town. As word moved along the docks, slaves like Will, a hireling, were given to understand that the time of rising was "on [Easter] Monday Holy day night."

But there is little evidence that most of the slaves who got word of the date understood themselves to be part of a larger conspiracy. The Halifax men had lost control of their own plan.[24]

And yet, it is clear that word of the conspiracy reached slaves strikingly similar to Sancho's group. Will's owners, Mary and William Walke of the neighboring county of Princess Anne, were both deceased. The estate was unsettled, and the Walke heirs continued to allow Will to hire his time around the region. The Norfolk conspirators, whose number was never estimated by either black or white sources, also expected poor whites to join them after the fighting began. A few even believed that several white men "had arms concealed for the purpose," a claim that bore suspicious resemblance to the persistent rumors about two white Frenchmen who had offered support to Gabriel. The second time, however, it was probably nothing more than false hope.[25]

Word of the conspiracy did not stop in Norfolk. Once more it took to the water. Norfolk handled much of the commerce of North Carolina; that is, much of North Carolina's commerce was handled by black Virginians. Numerous black skippers ferried passengers and mail between Norfolk and Elizabeth City. One of them, perhaps the same man who carried word downriver from Petersburg, became the "emissary" to North Carolina. Soon "a correspondence [was] held by [Norfolk] meetings with similar ones in North Carolina."[26]

But that was only one way that word of the rising reached North Carolina. The news also arrived by a second path. At the same time that the secret found its way north out of Halifax to the Appomattox, it was flowing south from Booker's Ferry down the Roanoke to Brunswick County. There the message found a willing recruit in Isaac, a skilled slave of the recently deceased Joseph Wilkes. Isaac told several Brunswick slaves that he in turn had recruited Randolph Hagood's Phill "to raise a company" when the time came. More fearful slaves, like Isaac's own mother, begged him not to join, for the authorities "would raise a company and take him." Isaac merely "nodded his head and replyed he would raise a Company too."[27]

From Isaac's home on the Roanoke, it was but a short distance downriver into North Carolina. Perhaps Isaac worked on the river, and surely he hired his time (he was valued well above the market price), for he told Ephraim Jackson's Ransom "that he had been in No[rth] Carolina a doctering and raising men." When the business began, they would join the insurrection.[28]

Isaac probably ventured no farther than the Roanoke rapids, but his words of rebellion spread much further. South of Brunswick the Roanoke ran through Halifax County, North Carolina, a region in almost daily contact with Virginia. Slaves and free blacks carried much of the upriver "produce" north to Virginia, observed one foreign traveler, "where [farmers found] a beter market than they Could Expect in any part of their own province." As cargo passed back and forth across the state line, so did "letters . . . to, and from" the "lower counties" of Virginia.[29]

Those who joined the conspiracy in North Carolina understood themselves to be part of a much larger group. Levin Bearmas's George "said the negroes were going to rise in Virginia & would carry it on here." One literate rebel, Davy, claimed that "they could get encouragement from Virginia." The "head negroes" live there, he insisted. Even those who had no idea "where the plan originated or how far it extended" agreed that "a negro man somewhere in Virg[ini]a," probably Isaac, "was at work under the ground ... & that when the fight was begun all the negroes were to join those who commenced."[30]

It is evident that at least minimal contact along the Roanoke was kept up throughout the life of the conspiracy, for the plan in North Carolina was very similar to Sancho's scheme. As in Virginia, only those men "as were noted for their ... secrecy, were intrusted with the plot, and not more than one or two in a family." Few knew the actual date of the rising, and those who did would not tell their contacts "until the night before." Neither did the North Carolina slaves make any attempt to gather and store arms. Instead, like the Virginia conspirators, they planned "to furnish themselves with Arms [taken] from those who were first killed."[31]

Clearly too, the men who joined in North Carolina were cut from the same cloth as those farther up the Roanoke. Many were rivermen, and some were hirelings. Several had recently deceased owners. They had tasted just enough independence—physical and economic—to want more. Typical was Salem, who recruited in the "ship yards." He was fighting, he told others, for the right to control "*their* [own] *time*" and reap the full fruits of their labor. United, he boasted, they "could do anything"; they could "fly across the river." Surely "after killing the Whites sufficiently," agreed another, they would be granted "their freedom & live as White People." It says much about the aspirations of these men that they did not plan to flee the state but to live and labor among southern whites, if not their former owners (many of whom would lie dead).[32]

Despite all the similarities and ties to Sancho's plot, however, the North Carolina wing of the conspiracy began to take on a life of its own. Unlike the Norfolk conspirators, the North Carolina slaves always understood that they were a branch of a larger group, but in the end the lower Roanoke, like Norfolk, essentially became a separate conspiracy. Given the distance the conspiracy had traveled, it is surprising the plot remained as cohesive as it did. In any case, when ties to the lower Roanoke wing of the conspiracy also snapped, its own leaders began to rise to the fore. "Captain" King Brown and David Sumner's Frank, two literate slaves, quickly seized control. Ignoring the Easter timetable, the Carolina blacks chose instead the night of Thursday, June 10, as the moment of the rising. That evening was the quarterly meeting of the Kehukee Baptist Association, a time when most whites would be neither armed nor on their guard. The rebels would begin by setting fire to "the Houses in Windsor," a small hamlet north of the Roanoke. By the next day, they hoped, they would "receive considerable reinforcements from up and down the river." Bolstered by those numbers, they would march toward "Virginia and help the blacks there." Slaves "who did not join," Brown warned, "should not live among them [and] they wou'd kill them."[33]

The decision to burn Windsor is revealing. It indicated that the conspiracy had come all the way down the Roanoke to the Albemarle Sound. Windsor was in Bertie, a county that shared the river with Martin. And those two counties had already heard of the insurrection by way of Norfolk. The conspiracy had thus come full circle. By May 6, King Brown told a rebel "that all up the [Roanoke] River were joined & ready." As former Governor Richard Dobbs Spaight later wrote, "I am decidedly of Opinion that it was to have been General through out the State, at least the Sea board part." The conspirators waited for the word.[34]

The word would never come. Even as news of the conspiracy traveled down the James and Roanoke rivers, it was beginning to unravel at its source. It is unnecessary to speculate about whether the revolt, had it taken place, would have been anything other than a bloody failure. More to the point, Sancho's inability to limit the conspiracy geographically meant that it would never reach the point of combustion. As early as December, 1801, hints began to surface around Petersburg that a conspiracy was afoot. Perhaps the insurgents in the neighboring county of Nottoway did not hear of the alarms; perhaps they did but were careless; or perhaps the patrols simply were lucky. But on January 1, "the Patrollers [in Nottoway] caught them in the business." Crashing into the midst of a meeting, the patrol swept up Bob and Joe and several other slaves. News of the arrest was rushed to Petersburg, "whence it was immediately communicated" to Governor James Monroe. With those county leaders in custody, the slave chain of command was all but broken near the source.[35]

Wasting no time, the Nottoway County court of oyer and terminer—a Virginia tribunal reserved for slaves only—sat within the week. The court was composed of five justices. There were no jury and no appeal except to the governor. Unlike in other capital cases brought against slaves, conspiracy and insurrection did not allow for benefit of clergy, the ancient branding and release of the guilty. The legalistic-minded Virginians did, however, assign defense counsel to the slaves, in this case Edward Bland. The counsel entered the requisite plea of not guilty and typically exerted himself little in behalf of his clients.[36]

The recipients of this justice, the widow Jones's Joe and John Royall's Bob, "were brought separately to the bar" on January 7. Several slaves provided roughly the same story against each but made it clear that the two were not the originators of the plot. By dusk, both had been found guilty and sentenced to hang on the morning of January 16. Monroe, who allowed twenty-six slaves to hang two years earlier (another, William Wilson's Jacob, the black skipper, allegedly committed suicide while in custody), "thought [it] proper to let the law have its course" in this case as well. And so on the third Saturday of the new year, Bob and Joe swung together from the Nottoway gallows.[37]

That the executed slaves were not the organizers of the conspiracy bothered area authorities. "We have here been very assiduous," Richard Jones of Nottoway assured the Petersburg mayor, "but find much difficulty in discovering their full design." Patrols increased in size and frequency; slaves were questioned; and, although the extant record is unclear on this point, several fingers evidently were pointed across the border into Brunswick. They pointed at the highly mobile Isaac, the slave of widow Henrietta Wilkes.[38]

In early February Isaac and Randolph Hagood's Phill were arrested. Three slaves, one of them also owned by the late Joseph Wilkes, insisted that Isaac had traveled into North Carolina to recruit men for the plot. Their stories varied enough to indicate they had not been coached by the anxious authorities. Edmund Cooper, the defense counsel for both men, ventured a laconic plea of not guilty. The court thought otherwise. "[B]eing moved & Seduced by the devil" to commit conspiracy and rebellion, Isaac and Phill were found guilty and sentenced to hang on February 12. Once more Monroe declined to intervene and so, like Bob and Joe, the two Brunswick conspirators died together.[39]

Up to that point, Virginia authorities had thought the conspiracy was confined to a few counties. The testimony against Isaac, however, raised the specter of a plot that encompassed two states. Frightened whites began to fear—and with good reason—that word of the rising had reached their towns. "For some weeks past," Norfolk mayor John Cowper confided to Monroe, "it has been rumored that an insurrection of the Negroes was to take place on the Night of [Easter] Monday." The mayor doubted the rumors but urged area whites to be especially vigilant nonetheless.[40]

That vigilance paid off on April 15, the Thursday before Easter, when Walke's Will was picked up outside the city by Caleb Roush and a poor white identified only as Jarvis. Jarvis, who was much "in liquor," knew the Princess Anne hireling and swore he was "of bad character." When Will was unable to show his captors a pass, Jarvis insisted that he was one of the "sons of bitches" involved in the conspiracy and was probably about on the business.[41]

Will was carried to the Norfolk home of John Floyd, who had hired the slave for the year. Floyd told Jarvis that Will had left his home that morning, which contradicted Will's claim that he was coming from Princess Anne. Caught in a lie, Will remained quiet for some time. "[N]o threats [were] made" by either man, but finally Will began to speak. He admitted that he had heard of the plan "to burn Norfolk" on "Monday Holy day night," but he insisted "that he refused to join." He had been contacted several times, he claimed, by the late John Ingram's Ned, John Cornick's Jeremiah, and Ned, a fellow slave of the legally troubled Walke estate. Before allowing Will to sign his statement, Floyd reminded him "that the lives of the persons he had informed against depended upon his evidence." Will insisted that it was all true.[42]

Now convinced of the reality of a conspiracy, Mayor John Cowper wasted no time in sweeping up those named by Will. A "strong patrole of the citizens" scoured the area nightly. Easter night found the city nervous, but, except for a thunderstorm reminiscent of the gale that hampered Gabriel's plan, the town remained quiet. By Tuesday morning "six negroe men [had been] taken up and confined in gaol."[43]

The Norfolk borough court of oyer and terminer made equally quick work of the case. Within a week of their arrest, Walke's Ned and Cornick's Jeremiah were found guilty before "a numerous audience [of] about 300" and sentenced to hang. Will was the only witness against either; he testified that he had encountered both men outside of Norfolk "above the Town Bridge," where they had tried to recruit him for their plan. The court, which included the mayor, set the value of Jeremiah at four hundred dollars, well above market price and an indication of literacy or a marketable skill.[44]

The court's verdict was not acceptable to all area whites, however. George McIntosh, a Norfolk merchant and small planter who had married into the intermingled Walke-Cornick families, hurried evidence to Monroe that suggested that Will had implicated innocent men. McIntosh argued that Ned could not have possibly been at the Town Bridge when Will claimed to have met him there because he was visiting his pregnant wife a half mile away. Several days later conflicting evidence arrived from Cowper and former mayor Thomas Newton, who had been involved in crushing the conspiracy two years earlier. Cowper insisted that both men were guilty and that another slave had provided supporting information—although not testimony. Newton agreed but suggested that Ned was simpleminded and "easily brought to any measure proposed to him." Monroe delayed the sentence until his council could examine the evidence, "unexpected interference" that led to "much discontent" among the uneasy Norfolk whites. And Monroe was never a politician to swim against the tide.[45]

Were Ned and Jeremiah innocent? Perhaps. Will's testimony against Ned was almost a mirror image of that he provided against Jeremiah. Still, questions about their innocence remain. Jarvis accused Will only of being a conspirator; it was Will who provided the date of the uprising. Surely, then, Will had at least heard of the plot; if he was involved, why would he name innocent men? It is interesting to note that the three men Will implicated—Jeremiah and the two Neds—all belonged to recently deceased owners, a situation common to conspirators across the state. Finally, the fact that Will and Ned shared the same owner provides an important link between the two. Perhaps Thomas Newton was right and the foolish Ned had indeed contacted Will, a mobile hired man of his acquaintance.[46]

But if the evidence presented a mixed picture, why did McIntosh fight so hard to prove Will's innocence? Possibly McIntosh's concern was partially economic. The execution of Ned would represent a financial loss to the five

Walke heirs, one of whom was married to McIntosh. But by acting "in defiance at that time of the universal obloquy of [the Norfolk] community," McIntosh was likely to find his business a lonesome venture. Instead, it appears that the young Scotsman, a relative newcomer to the region, simply did not believe that slaves could be rebellious. He based his reading of the evidence, he later told Henry Wise, on "the belief that, the Negro population in this Section of the State are too intelligent to enter into a combination to effect any measure by force."[47]

Either way, the mood of the city demanded a corpse. On Friday, May 28, Jeremiah and Ned were placed in a tumbrel and carried to the gallows. Jeremiah "took leave [of his] wife and two children," shouted a final "declaration of his innocence," and went to his death. To the disappointment of the assembled throng, word arrived at the last moment that Ned was to return to jail.[48]

Evidently the governor could not bring himself to allow the execution of a simpleminded slave, a possibly innocent one at that. Instead, Ned was "removed to the penitentiary for transportation," a sentence that somewhat mollified the anger of Norfolk whites. As a result, only Jeremiah died in Norfolk. The widow Ingram's Ned was tried in June, but only five of six justices found him to be guilty—the oyer and terminer courts required unanimity—and so he was released. The other three slaves who had been arrested had "but hearsay evidence, appearing against them, [and] they [too were] discharged."[49]

During the same week that the Norfolk slaves were swept up, the conspiracy collapsed at its source. Halifax authorities had always assumed a connection between the conspirators in Nottoway and rivermen in neighboring counties. On May 1 Monroe directed that the "plot and parties to it should be traced" upriver. And the plot stopped at John Booker's ferry. A large number of slaves were "taken up." Those seized were questioned "at a considerable distance from each other" so that they could not make up a common story. Without prodding and without beatings, several confessed a "concurrent tale" and, tragically, implicated each other in the process.[50]

Over a period of nearly two weeks thirteen men were put on trial, the largest number in any county in 1802. Among them were the leaders, including Sancho and Absalom. Several slaves testified against each of the two; and, unlike in Norfolk, there was never any doubt among whites as to the guilt of those at the top. Monroe concluded that the five slaves found guilty "shou'd be neither repreived or pardoned." On Saturday morning, May 15, Sancho, Absalom, Martin, and Frank swung together from the Halifax gibbet; all but Martin were valued well above the average market price set by Virginia. The next day Abram was also carried to the gallows.[51]

The last of the Virginia conspirators to be taken was Lewis, the Goochland ferryman who had traveled toward Richmond just before Easter. In late April the literate hireling was picked up in Nottoway, several counties away from the home of his owner, John Brown. Lewis was told to reveal "very fully the whole Scheme." When he did not, he was "repeatedly and severely whipped." Finally Lewis gave the names of the contacts he knew in Petersburg, Arnold and a free black named Jumper. "[T]hreatened with immediate death if he did not disclose [all of] his partizans in the conspiracy," the bleeding Lewis provided the name of a Richmond carpenter—Arthur Farrar—whom he had not seen in years, an apparently false revelation that set off a wave of panic in Henrico and Hanover counties.[52]

The North Carolina conspirators were then on their own. If word was flowing down the Roanoke about the collapse of the Virginia rebellion, it was riding alongside a letter from a former governor of North Carolina to the current chief executive. William R. Davie warned that the upper Roanoke was the source of the conspiracy and that Halifax justices of the peace had reason to believe that it extended downriver into North Carolina. Indeed, at that moment "nightly meetings" were taking place in Bertie. There the leaders stayed in touch by passing letters from hand to hand and waited for June 10.[53]

Given the need to rise rapidly as a group, that the literate rivermen stayed in touch through letters is not surprising. The poor state of communications in the region was the reason the plot had fragmented into three smaller conspiracies. But the use of correspondence, even when it was carried by other slaves, presented dangers as well as opportunities. Should even one letter be captured, authorities would know the names of the cadre so necessary to the scheme. On June 1, Fed encountered several slaves on a road near Colerain in Bertie County. One of them was David Sumner's Frank, who gave Fed a letter to carry to King Brown. Fed obviously knew of the plot, for Frank felt free to remind him that on "the 10th June they were agoing to make a Start & come down to the Ferry [and] then come to Mr. Hunters Store & Break it open & get what powder was there." But when Fed reached the home of Judy (perhaps King's wife) the next morning, he gave the letter to "her little Girl [and] told her to give it to her mother."[54]

In the meantime, Davie's letter of warning had scared the patrollers into action. Since late May they had been searching the cabins of blacks along the rivers for arms but, of course, had found none. Sometime around midday on June 2, they forced their way into Judy's home, where they found not guns but the letter "containing the names of about 14 negro men." The terrified woman confessed that it had been "left with her that morning by Fed," who had promised "to carry [it] to [Joseph] Brown's King."[55]

The capture of Frank's letter destroyed what little remained of the Easter conspiracy. "The negroes named on the paper . . . were apprehended," and word of the plot was rushed to "the adjacent counties" of Hertford and Martin. By June 10, large numbers of slaves had been picked up and confined near Jamestown. A howling mob of whites wanted to shoot them "on the spot," but several justices of the peace urged that a "Committee of Enquiry" be formed "to examine and take down the depositions of the prisoners." The committee separated the slaves and had "the youngest and most foolish lad" brought before them. They told him that his name was on Frank's letter and that if he confessed "he should be forgiven." Like some of the terrified men of Halifax, Virginia, he agreed.[56]

A second young slave was brought forward. Again the "promise of pardon" was made; "the lash" was not necessary. He agreed to "discover the whole plot," and he knew a great deal. As "an officer," he had been involved for some time, although he had not been given the final date of the rising until June 1. Because of the cautious method of recruitment, he could not name every slave involved, only those "belonging to the same company." Over the course of two days nearly thirty more slaves were examined individually. The authorities insisted that they were not coached and that there was no way that they could know "what had been previously declared by others." Most were then whipped or cropped or released. Those who were implicated as leaders were carried to the town of Windsor for trial. Sent with them as evidence were Frank's letter and a missive from Virginia "also found at Colerain."[57]

If anything, the North Carolina authorities were even more legalistic-minded than those in Virginia. Since 1790 a number of changes had been made in the slave code. Unlike in Virginia, slaves in North Carolina were allowed trial by jury and appeal to the state supreme court. Care had been taken, however, to stipulate that the jury must be composed of slaveholders if the case involved a crime "the punishment whereof shall extend to life, limb, or member." In the Bertie trials, "six or seven" slaves testified against "the officers." Nine men, including King Brown, were found guilty and executed on Wednesday, June 16. Two more eventually followed them to the Windsor gallows.[58]

At the same time, trials were held in the neighboring counties. In Hertford, to the north of Bertie, ten slaves were tried. Only Frank, who had been captured as he fled north, was executed. The other nine, "who did not appear equally criminal with Frank and King [Brown], were punished by cropping, whipping, and branding." Two slaves died in Martin, a county that shared the Roanoke with Bertie, and Mrs. Foord's Sam was executed in Halifax County, North Carolina, on June 27. In all, twenty-five men from Virginia and North Carolina paid with their lives for their demand for liberty and the just fruits of their labor.[59]

The Easter conspiracy was over, but the white fear it inspired was not. As in Henrico County, the number and might of the insurgents was wildly overestimated. Published accounts insisted that slaves were "embodied in large companies, armed, in the Great Swamp," or that massive risings were taking place in the North Carolina counties of Perquimans and Hertford. One paper even reported that slaves had captured "the town of Windsor, and had committed great havock." A rider from Winton galloped toward Windsor "to ascertain the truth of the report" but met only a rider coming from that town to find out whether rumors that Winton was under attack were true. It was not until early August that the state settled down to the fact that the alarm was "generally allowed to have been greater that the occasion warranted."[60]

While the corpses were buried in North Carolina, the four Virginia slaves who had been reprieved, including Walke's Ned, awaited word of their fate. (Lewis escaped "from the [Dinwiddie] County Jail, and has not been heard of Since.") A law passed shortly after Gabriel's conspiracy allowed for transportation outside the state in place of execution if the governor saw fit; the question was where. Monroe's mentor Thomas Jefferson suggested the slaves be sent to the British West African colony of Sierra Leone. But slavery was outlawed there; Virginia would have to emancipate the insurgent slaves before transporting them, more a reward than a punishment. Such a solution would hardly deter future rebels. Finally, trader William Fulcher offered to buy the slaves in the penitentiary for $266.40 (£80) each, far below what the state paid their owners. The governor's council was clearly displeased with the offer, but it was "nearly double [the] price offered" by the only other trader to make a bid. "Fulcher's proposition [was] accepted." The four slaves dropped from the sight of history; quite likely they were resold in Havana.[61]

Sancho, a veteran of Gabriel's conspiracy, had thought that "it could be done." Carefully avoiding the mistakes of his 1800 coconspirators, Sancho convinced others like himself, rivermen such as Salem, to risk their lives for their freedom and their earnings, to try once more to "fly across the river." Sancho's courage and resolve to fulfill the vision of Gabriel won him followers in a time when the air was filled with the sound of defeat. The next widespread slave conspiracy along the Virginia and North Carolina border would come after the age of revolution, and it would be the work not of secular rebels determined to fight their way into the political system but of messianic slaves committed to destroying the white world and bringing on the day of jubilee.

NOTES

1. Sentence of Claiborne's Peter, October 20, 1800, Condemned Slaves 1800, Auditor's Item 153, Box 2, Virginia State Library and Archives, Richmond, hereinafter cited as Condemned Slaves 1800; Payment warrant to estate of William Claiborne, January 23, 1801, Condemned Slaves 1800. On the desire of whites to have slaves witness the execution of blacks, see Edward L. Ayers, *Vengeance and Justice: Crime and Punishment in the 19th-Century American South* (New York: Oxford University Press, 1984), 136.

2. Compared to other slave conspiracies, that of 1802 has received surprisingly little attention. Herbert Aptheker, *American Negro Slave Revolts* (New York: International Publishers, fifth edition, 1983), 230, hereinafter cited as Aptheker, *American Negro Slave Revolts*, views the unrest as isolated acts of physical resistance, not as a larger two-state conspiracy. Bertram Wyatt-Brown, *Southern Honor: Ethics and Behavior in the Old South* (New York: Oxford University Press, 1982), chapter 15, hereinafter cited as Wyatt-Brown, *Southern Honor*, denies the existence of a slave conspiracy anywhere in Virginia in 1802 but concentrates on Norfolk and Hanover counties, not Halifax. John Scott Strickland, "The Great Revival and Insurrectionary Fears in North Carolina: An Examination of Antebellum Southern Society and Slave Revolt Panics," in *Class, Conflict, and Consensus: Antebellum Southern Community Studies*, edited by Orville V. Burton and Robert C. McMath, Jr. (Westport, CT: Greenwood Press, 1982), 57–95,

examines white fears of slave plots and implicitly denies the actuality of any conspiracy. Jeffrey J. Crow, "Slave Rebelliousness and Social Conflict in North Carolina, 1775–1802," *William and Mary Quarterly*, XXXVII (January, 1980), 96–101, hereinafter cited as Crow, "Slave Rebelliousness," and *The Black Experience in Revolutionary North Carolina* (Raleigh: Division of Archives and History, Department of Cultural Resources, 1977), 89–91, dissents from that view, but he does not present the North Carolina plot as the wing of a larger network. R. H. Taylor, "Slave Conspiracies in North Carolina," *North Carolina Historical Review*, V (January, 1928), 31, covers the plot in one paragraph.

3. Raymond B. Pinchbeck, *The Virginia Negro Artisan and Tradesman* (Richmond: William Byrd Press, 1926), 31, hereinafter cited as Pinchbeck, *Virginia Negro Artisan*; Tommy L. Bogger, "The Slave and Free Black Community in Norfolk, 1775–1865" (unpublished doctoral dissertation, University of Virginia, 1976), 163, hereinafter cited as Bogger, "Slave and Free Black Community."

4. Charles Christopher Crittenden, "Inland Navigation in North Carolina, 1763–1789," *North Carolina Historical Review*, VIII (April, 1931), 149.

5. Clement Eaton, "Slave-Hiring in the Upper South: A Step toward Freedom," *Mississippi Valley Historical Review*, XLVI (March, 1960), 677–678; Eugene D. Genovese, *Roll, Jordan, Roll: The World the Slaves Made* (New York: Pantheon Books, 1974), 392, hereinafter cited as Genovese, *Roll, Jordan, Roll*; Robert S. Starobin, *Industrial Slavery in the Old South* (New York: Oxford University Press, 1970), 135; Entry of October 18, 1798, David Erskine Copybook, Manuscript Collection, University of Virginia Library, Charlottesville. No hard data exist on the numbers of slaves who were hired out in the late eighteenth century, but the careful analysis of Sara S. Hughes, "Slaves for Hire: The Allocation of Black Labor in Elizabeth City County, Virginia, 1782–1810," *William and Mary Quarterly*, XXXV (April, 1978), 265, suggests that the practice was far more common than it would be in the late antebellum period. For example, Robert Carter, the largest slaveholder in the state, hired out more than two thirds of his 509 slaves in 1791.

6. Richard C. Wade, *Slavery in the Cities: The South, 1820–1860* (New York: Oxford University Press, 1964), 48–51, 66, hereinafter cited as Wade, *Slavery in the Cities*.

7. Marvin L. Michael Kay and Lorin Lee Cary, "Slave Runaways in Colonial North Carolina, 1748–1775," *North Carolina Historical Review*, LXIII (January, 1986), 18–19; Gerald W. (Michael) Mullin, *Flight and Rebellion: Slave Resistance in Eighteenth-Century Virginia* (New York: Oxford University Press, 1972), chapter 2; James B. Farr, *Black Odyssey: The Seafaring Traditions of Afro-Americans* (New York: Peter Lang, 1989), 180–181.

8. Duncan J. MacLeod, "Toward Caste," in *Slavery and Freedom in the Age of the American Revolution*, edited by Ira Berlin and Ronald Hoffman (Urbana: University of Illinois Press, 1986), 227, hereinafter cited as MacLeod, "Toward Caste," volume hereinafter cited as Berlin and Hoffman, *Slavery and Freedom*; Pinchbeck, *Virginia Negro Artisan*, 32. For an excellent discussion of how craftsmen provided a link to the wider world for unskilled laborers in another agrarian society, see Eric Hobsbawm and George Rude, *Captain Swing* (New York: W. W. Norton, 1968), 18.

9. Genovese, *Roll, Jordan, Roll*, 397; MacLeod, "Toward Caste," 228; Confession of Prosser's Solomon, September 15, 1800, Letter Book, Executive Papers, Virginia State Archives, hereinafter cited as Executive Letter Book. As Genovese has written in *From Rebellion to Revolution: Afro-American Slave Revolts in the Making of the Modern World* (Baton Rouge: Louisiana State University Press, 1979), 2, American slave revolts "must be understood primarily as part of the most radical wing of the struggle for a democracy that had not yet lost its bourgeois moorings."

10. John B. Scott to James Monroe, April 21, 1802, Executive Papers, Virginia State Archives, hereinafter cited as Executive Papers; Unidentified newspaper clipping, William Palmer Scrapbook, Virginia Historical Society, Richmond, hereinafter cited as William Palmer Scrapbook.

11. Testimony of Sandifer's Bob at trial of Booker's Sancho, April 23, 1802, Executive

Papers, Pardon Papers, Virginia State Archives, hereinafter cited as Executive Papers, Pardon Papers. This was evidently not the William Royall of Sweet Springs. The author has avoided using the admonitory *sic.*

12. John B. Scott to James Monroe, April 21, 1802, Executive Papers; J. L. C. to unknown correspondent, n.d., Slavery Papers, Miscellaneous Collections, Archives, Division of Archives and History, Raleigh, hereinafter cited as Slavery Papers. This letter was from a Virginia conspirator. For a discussion of the same type of organization in a slightly different context, see Marcus Rediker's "profile" of a ship mutiny in *Between the Devil and the Deep Blue Sea: Merchant Seamen, Pirates, and the Anglo-American Maritime World, 1700–1750* (New York: Cambridge University Press, 1987), 227–229.

13. Testimony of Smith's Abram at trial of Booker's Sancho, April 23, 1802, Executive Papers, Pardon Papers; Testimony of Smith's Robin at trial of Smith's Abram, May 1, 1802, Executive Papers, Pardon Papers; Rhys Isaac, *The Transformation of Virginia, 1740–1790* (Chapel Hill: University of North Carolina Press, 1982), 103.

The choice of Easter as the date of the revolt raises the question of religious motivation among the insurgents. Many historians have argued that the great revivals of the early national period led to collective resistance to slavery. See, for example, Vincent Harding, "Religion and Resistance among Antebellum Negroes, 1800–1860," in *The Making of Black America: Essays in Negro Life and History*, edited by August Meier and Elliott Rudwick (New York: Oxford University Press, 2 volumes, 1969), although Harding does not mention the Easter conspiracy. While it is no doubt true that religious slaves, fired by the words of stump preachers, occasionally decided to carry their egalitarian faith to its logical conclusion and emancipate themselves in this world as well as the next, evidence that the Easter rebels were overtly religious is surprisingly scant. The records for Virginia and North Carolina in 1800 and 1802 rarely mention religion and speak far more often of political and economic goals. The view presented here is that the date simply provided the rebels with an opportune moment. For a discussion of the myth that Gabriel was a messianic figure who wore his locks long in imitation of Samson, or that his brother Martin was a preacher, see the author's "Gabriel Conspiracy and the Election of 1800," *Journal of Southern History*, LVI (May, 1990), 192, note 4, hereinafter cited as Egerton, "Gabriel's Conspiracy."

14. Testimony of Smith's Abram at trial of Booker's Sancho, April 23, 1802, Executive Papers, Pardon Papers; Testimony of Smith's Abram at trial of Robertson's Frank, April 23, 1802, Executive Papers, Pardon Papers. This is very nearly the classic urban mob discussed by Eric Hobsbawm in *Primitive Rebels: Studies in Archaic Forms of Social Movement in the 19th and 20th Centuries* (New York: W. W. Norton, 1959), 111.

15. Testimony of Prosser's Ben at trial of Prosser's Gabriel, October 6, 1800. Executive Papers, Negro Insurrection, Virginia State Archives, hereinafter cited as Executive Papers, Negro Insurrection; J. L. C. to unknown correspondent, n.d., Slavery Papers; Wade, *Slavery in the Cities*, 85; Ira Berlin, *Slaves Without Masters: The Free Negro in the Antebellum South* (New York: Oxford University Press, 1974), 260–61; John Scott to James Monroe, April 23, 1802, Executive Papers.

16. This composite biography, which is admittedly crude, is drawn from the following: Condemned Slaves 1802, Executed, Auditor's Item 153, Box 2, Virginia State Archives, hereinafter cited as Condemned Slaves 1802, Executed; Condemned Slaves 1802, Transported, Auditor's Item 153, Box 2, Virginia State Archives, hereinafter cited as Condemned Slaves 1802, Transported; Executive Papers, Pardon Papers, 1802; and "A List of Slaves Reprieved for Transportation and Sold," March 8, 1806, Executive Papers. Unfortunately, the sparse documentation defies quantitative analysis. Surely far more slaves were involved in Halifax than the thirteen put on trial, and at least one of the sixteen Virginia slaves found guilty around the state, as argued below, was probably innocent. A full portrait would include the North Carolina rebels, many of whom appear to have been rivermen. But as the North Carolina records are even less complete and reliable, the profile is restricted to Virginia.

The discussion of the early national upper-South slave family is taken from Mary Beth Norton, Herbert G. Gutman, and Ira Berlin, "The Afro-American Family in the Age of

Revolution," in Berlin and Hoffman, *Slavery and Freedom*, 178–179; Kenneth M. Stampp, "Rebels and Sambos: The Search for the Negro's Personality in Slavery," *Journal of Southern History*, XXXVII (August, 1971), 367; and Allan Kulikoff, "A 'Prolifick' People: Black Population Growth in the Chesapeake Colonies, 1700–1790," *Southern Studies*, XVI (Winter, 1977), 413–414.

17. Testimony of Ned at trial of Hilliard's Absalom, April 26, 1802, Halifax County Court Order Book, Virginia State Archives, hereinafter cited as Court Order Book, with appropriate county; J. L. C. to unknown correspondent, n.d., Slavery Papers.

18. Sentence of Booker's Sancho, April 23, 1802, Condemned Slaves 1802, Executed; James G. Scott and Edward A. Wyatt, *Petersburg Story: A History* (Petersburg: Titmus Optical Company, 1960), 73, 90.

19. Testimony of Prosser's Ben at trial of Prosser's Gabriel, October 6, 1800, Executive Papers, Negro Insurrection; James McClurg to James Monroe, n.d., [1800], Executive Papers, Negro Insurrection; Testimony of Green's Ned at trial of Royall's Bob, January 7, 1802, Executive Papers.

20. Richard Jones to [Petersburg mayor] William Prentis, January 2, 1802, Executive Papers; Sentence of Jones's Joe, January 7, 1802, Executive Papers; Testimony of Jones's Hampton at trial of Jones's Joe, January 7, 1802, Executive Papers.

21. [Former North Carolina governor] William R. Davie to Benjamin Williams, February 17, 1802, Private Collection, Historical Society of Pennsylvania Papers, PC 244, North Carolina State Archives, hereinafter cited as Historical Society of Pennsylvania Papers, PC 244.

22. Grief Green to Peterson Goodwyn, May 1, 1802, Executive Papers; Grief Green to James Monroe, n.d., Executive Papers; Confession of Lewis, May 5, 1802, Executive Papers.

23. Thomas Newton to James Monroe, May 14, 1802, Executive Papers. On the Petersburg-to-Norfolk link of 1800, see: *Virginia Herald* (Fredericksburg), September 19, 1800, hereinafter cited as *Virginia Herald*; *Virginia Argus* (Richmond), October 10, 1800, hereinafter cited as *Virginia Argus*; William Prentis to James Monroe, n.d., [1800], Executive Papers, Negro Insurrection.

24. Thomas Wertenbaker, *Norfolk: Historic Southern Port* (Durham: Duke University Press, second edition, 1962), 126–127; Office of the Census, *Return of the Whole Number of Persons of the United States, 1800* (Washington: Government Printing Office, 1802), 70; Testimony of Walke's Will at trial of Ingram's Ned, June 20, 1802, Norfolk County Court Order Book; *Virginia Herald*, May 18, 1802.

25. "Families of Lower Norfolk and Princess Anne Counties: Walke Family," *Virginia Magazine of History and Biography*, V (July, 1897), 148–150, hereinafter cited as "Walke Family"; Unidentified newspaper clipping, William Palmer Scrapbook. For a discussion of the existence of the two white Frenchmen, see Egerton, "Gabriel's Conspiracy," 204–207.

26. James H. Broussard, *The Southern Federalists, 1800–1816* (Baton Rouge: Louisiana State University Press, 1978), 5; Bogger, "Slave and Free Black Community," 165; Thomas Mathews to James Monroe, March 10, 1802, Executive Papers.

27. Testimony of Jackson's George at trial of Wilkes's Isaac, February 11, 1802, Executive Papers; Testimony of Jackson's Adam at trial of Isaac, February 11, 1802, Executive Papers; Testimony of Wilkes's Jeffrey at trial of Isaac, February 11, 1802, Executive Papers.

28. Testimony of Jackson's Ransom at trial of Wilkes's Isaac, February 11, 1802, Executive Papers; Unidentified newspaper clipping, William Palmer Scrapbook.

29. "Documents: Journal of a French Traveller in the Colonies, 1765," *American Historical Review*, XXVI (July, 1921), 736–737; *Raleigh Register*, July 27, 1802. As Jeffrey J. Crow has written, "The interconnecting waterways of eastern North Carolina evidently made the transmission of information not only feasible but unstoppable." See Crow, "Slave Rebelliousness," 97.

30. Deposition of Bearmass's George, June, 1802, Slavery Papers; Deposition of Dick Blacksmith, June, 1802, Slavery Papers; Thomas Blount to John Gray Blount, June 28,

1802, in Alice Barnwell Keith, William H. Masterson, and David T. Morgan (eds.), *The John Gray Blount Papers* (Raleigh: Division of Archives and History, Department of Cultural Resources, 4 volumes, 1952–1982), III, 517, hereinafter cited as Keith and others, *Blount Papers*.

31. *Spectator* (New York), August 4, 1802, hereinafter cited as *Spectator*; Testimony of Boston at trial of Salem, Slavery Papers; Deposition of Turner's Isaac, June, 1802, Slavery Papers. Guns and bayonets were found in the homes of slaves in Currituck and other counties, but as discussed in note 59 below, those alleged conspiracies do not appear to be connected to the main conspiracy. On the arms found, see the *Spectator*, August 4, 1802, and the *Virginia Herald*, May 18, 1802.

32. Testimony of Boston at trial of Salem, Slavery Papers; Deposition of Turner's Emanuel, June, 1802, Slavery Papers.

33. Unsigned letter to editor, June 14, 1802, *Times* (Alexandria), June 18, 1802, hereinafter cited as *Times*; Deposition of Turner's Emanuel, June, 1802, Slavery Papers; Deposition of Hunter's Simon, June, 1802, Slavery Papers; *Virginia Herald*, June 19, 1802; *Raleigh Register*, July 27, 1802. The choice of June 10, the date of the quarterly meeting of the Kehukee Baptist Association, like the choice of Easter, is here depicted as having no religious significance but rather as being a moment of weakness for Carolina whites.

34. Richard Dobbs Spaight to John Steele, July 12, 1802, Private Collections, Walter Clark Papers, PC 8, North Carolina State Archives; Deposition of Hunter's Simon, June, 1802, Slavery papers.

35. [Former governor] Richard Jones to William Prentis, January 2, 1802, Executive Papers; William Prentis to James Monroe, January 5, 1802, Executive Papers; Testimony of Willis Pillar at trial of Jones's Joe, January 7, 1802, Executive Papers; James Monroe to General Assembly, January 16, 1802, Executive Letter Book.

36. Daniel J. Flanigan, "Criminal Procedure in Slave Trials in the Antebellum South," *Journal of Southern History*, XL (November, 1974), 544; St. George Tucker, *A Dissertation of Slavery with a Proposal for the Gradual Abolition of It in the State of Virginia* (Philadelphia: Mathew Carey, 1796), 62; Sentence of Jones's Joe, January 7, 1802, Executive Papers. On the creation of the oyer and terminer courts, see Philip J. Schwarz, *Twice Condemned: Slaves and the Criminal Laws of Virginia, 1705–1865* (Baton Rouge: Louisiana State University Press, 1988), 17.

37. James Monroe to General Assembly, January 16, 1802, Executive Letter Book; Sentence of Jones's Joe, January 7, 1802, Condemned Slaves 1802, Executed; Sentence of Royall's Bob, January 7, 1802, Condemned Slaves 1802, Executed; Certification of death for Bob signed by William Canabiss, January 16, 1802, Condemned Slaves 1802, Executed; Certification of death for Joe signed by William Canabiss, January 16, 1802, Condemned Slaves 1802, Executed.

38. Richard Jones to William Prentis, January 2, 1802, Executive Papers.

39. Testimony of Jackson's Adam, Jackson's George, and Wilkes's Jeffrey at trial of Wilkes's Isaac, February 3, 1802, Executive Papers; Council Journal, February 11, 1802, Virginia State Archives, hereinafter cited as Council Journal; Sentence of Wilkes's Isaac, February 3, 1802, Condemned Slaves 1802, Executed; Sentence of Hagood's Phill, February 3, 1802, Condemned Slaves 1802, Executed; Certification of death for Isaac signed by James Rice and John Tucker, September 13, 1802 (misdated 1800), Condemned Slaves 1802, Executed; Certification of death for Phill signed by James Rice and John Tucker, September 13, 1802 (misdated 1800), Condemned Slaves 1802, Executed.

40. *Virginia Herald*, May 18, 1802; *Alexandria Advertiser*, May 18, 1802; John Cowper to James Monroe, April 17, 1802, Executive Papers.

41. *Spectator*, May 22, 1802; *Alexandria Advertiser*, May 18, 1802; *Virginia Herald*, May 18, 1802; Testimony of Caleb Roush at trial of Ingram's Ned, June 20, 1802, Executive Papers; Testimony of Walke's Will at trial of Ingram's Ned, June 20, 1802, Norfolk County Court Order Book.

42. "Walke Family," 149–151; Testimony of Walke's Will at trial of Walke's Ned, April 26, 1802, Executive Papers, Pardon Papers; Testimony of Walke's Will at trial of Ingram's

Ned, June 20, 1802, Norfolk County Court Order Book; Testimony of John Floyd at trial of Ingram's Ned, June 20, 1802, Norfolk County Court Order Book. Wyatt-Brown, *Southern Honor*, 430, argues that Jarvis and Floyd used "threats of torture" on Will. Certainly the possibility of white violence was implicit in such a situation, but, as noted in the text, Floyd testified that no overt threats were made.

43. John Cowper to James Monroe, April 17, 1802, Executive Papers; *Raleigh Register*, May 18, 1802; A. G. Roeber (ed.), "A New England Woman's Perspective on Norfolk, Virginia, 1801–1802; Excerpts from the Diary of Ruth Henshaw Bascom," *Proceedings of the American Antiquarian Society*, LXXXVIII (1978), 307, hereinafter cited as Roeber, "Bascom Diary."

44. Sentence of Walke's Ned, April 26, 1802, Condemned Slaves 1802, Transported; Sentence of Cornick's Jeremiah, April 26, 1802, Executive Papers, Pardon Papers; Thomas Newton to James Monroe, May 7, 1802, Executive Papers, Pardon Papers; Testimony of Walke's Will at trial of Walke's Ned, April 26, 1802, Executive Papers, Pardon Papers.

45. George McIntosh to James Monroe, May 5, 1802, Executive Papers, Pardon Papers; John Cowper to James Monroe, May 18, 1802, Executive Papers, Pardon Papers; Thomas Newton to James Monroe, May 7, 1802, Executive Papers, Pardon Papers; *Spectator*, May 22, May 26, 1802; *Norfolk Herald*, May 18, 1802.

46. Council Journal, May 8, 1802, 227; Sentence of Ingram's Ned, June 20, 1802, Norfolk County Court Order Book.

47. George McIntosh to Henry A. Wise, December 22, 1856, Executive Papers. Wyatt-Brown, *Southern Honor*, 428, writes: "There is no indication that [McIntosh] had any pecuniary interest in Jerry's fate." Perhaps not, but he did in Ned's. The slaves of William and Mary Walke were divided among their five children, one of whom was married to McIntosh. The estate had not been settled.

48. *Virginia Herald*, May 11, 1802; *Norfolk Herald*, May 29, 1802; *Petersburg Intelligencer*, June 4, 1802; Roeber, "Bascom Diary," 316; Certification of death for Cornick's Jeremiah signed by James Boyce, May 28, 1802, Condemned Slaves 1802, Executed.

49. Council Journal, June 5, 1802, 251; Sentence of Ingram's Ned, June 20, 1802, Norfolk County Court Order Book; *Virginia Herald*, May 18, 1802. Daniel Hylton, who incidentally was Thomas H. Prosser's father-in-law, certified that Ned was brought to Richmond for transportation. See his certification as clerk, October 5, 1802, Condemned Slaves 1802, Transported.

50. John Scott to James Monroe, April 30, 1802, Executive Papers; James Monroe to John Scott, May 1, 1802, Executive Letter Book; Richard Dobbs Spaight to John Gray Blount, July 1, 1802, Keith and others, *Blount Papers*, III, 518.

51. Council Journal, May 8, 1802, 225; Halifax County Court Order Book, April 23–May 5, 1802; *Raleigh Register*, June 22, 1802; *Virginia Herald*, June 15, 1802; *Norfolk Herald*, June 10, 1802; *Columbian Centinel* (Boston), June 23, 1802; Certification of death for Bass's Martin signed by John Wimbish, July 6, 1802, Condemned Slaves 1802, Executed; Certification of death for Hilliard's Absalom, June 4, 1802, Condemned Slaves 1802, Executed; Certification of death of Smith's Abram, July 6, 1802, Condemned Slaves 1802, Executed; Certification of death for Robertson's Frank, July 6, 1802, Condemned Slaves 1802, Executed; Certification of death for Booker's Sancho, May 15, 1802, Condemned Slaves 1802, Executed.

52. Grief Green to Peterson Goodwyn, May 1, 1802, Executive Papers; Grief Green to James Monroe, n.d., Executive Papers; Peterson Goodwyn to James Monroe, June 12, 1802, Executive Papers; Arthur Farrar to James Monroe (dictated), June 12, 1802, Executive Papers. Wyatt-Brown, *Southern Honor*, 426, argues convincingly that the story Lewis attributed to Arthur, about an attack on Richmond, "bore suspicious resemblance to the public accounts of the Gabriel plot." But Lewis was doubtless aware of the Nottoway-Dinwiddie wing of the plot. It is unlikely, even impossible, that, as a ferryman on the upper James, he would not have heard of the plan. And the story he told about Jumper mentioned the date of Easter. (Jumper was arrested, but as he was a free black

Lewis's testimony against him was not admissible.) Arthur was found guilty but was not executed, contrary to the account in Joseph C. Carroll's highly unreliable *Slave Insurrections in the United States, 1800–1865* (1938; New York: Negro Universities Press, 1973), 60–61. He was transported. See Council Journal, July 10, 1802, 272.

During the scare, two slaves of the late Paul Thilman, Tom and Glasgow, were also implicated, tried, and found guilty. Here, too, the story bore no resemblance to the larger Easter plan; the two were surely innocent. In the end both were reprieved and transported. See Paul Woolfolk to James Monroe, May 24, 1802, Executive Papers; Reprieve, 1802, Executive Papers; Council Journal, May 22, 1802, 237. Interestingly, three slaves of the recently deceased Thilman were involved in Gabriel's conspiracy. One was executed, one was transported, and the other was pardoned.

53. William R. Davie to Benjamin Williams, February 17, 1802, Historical Society of Pennsylvania Papers, PC 244; Unidentified newspaper clipping, William Palmer Scrapbook; *Virginia Herald*, May 18, 1802; Unsigned letter from Murfreesboro, June 8, 1802, *Times*, June 28, 1802; Deposition of Fitt's Dennis, June 15, 1802, Slavery Papers.

54. *Raleigh Register*, July 6, 1802; Deposition of Fitt's Fred, June, 1802, Slavery Papers.

55. *Raleigh Register*, July 6, 1802; *Virginia Herald*, June 29, 1802.

56. *Raleigh Register*, July 6, July 27, 1802.

57. John Folk to William Williams, June 6, 1802, Slavery Papers; *Raleigh Register*, July 27, 1802.

58. Ernest J. Clark, Jr., "Aspects of the North Carolina Slave Code, 1715–1860," *North Carolina Historical Review*, XXXIX (Spring, 1962), 151; *Spectator*, July 7, 1802; *Raleigh Register*, July 27, 1802; Unsigned letter from Murfreesboro, June 14, 1802, *Times*, June 28, 1802.

59. *Raleigh Register*, July 13, 1802; *Virginia Herald*, June 29, 1802; Unsigned letter from Murfreesboro, June 14, 1802, *Times*, June 28, 1802; *Raleigh Minerva*, June 15, 1802; Crow, "Slave Rebelliousness," 100. Other slaves were hanged in the neighboring counties of Camden, Currituck, and Perquimans, but the evidence connecting them to the Roanoke wing of the conspiracy is weak. Moreover, the alleged conspirators in those counties have not been tied to the June 10 date and so have not been included in the larger Easter conspiracy. Aptheker, *American Negro Slave Revolts*, 230, note 77, does not devote much attention to the 1802 plot but does argue that, in Virginia alone, as many as thirty-seven slaves were executed during that year. He bases that number on owners compensated, and, as shown in note 61 below, many were compensated for slaves who were transported. Moreover, Aptheker's assumption that all slaves who were executed or transported were part of various conspiracies is not supported by trial records. Many were guilty of isolated capital crimes, not insurrection.

60. *Norfolk Herald*, June 15, 1802; *Virginia Herald*, June 15, 1802; *Virginia Argus*, June 23, 1802; *Raleigh Register*, July 6, August 10, 1802.

61. James Monroe to Thomas Jefferson, June 11, 1802, Thomas Jefferson Papers, Library of Congress; William Fulcher to James Monroe, July 3, 1802, Executive Papers; Peterson Goodwyn to James Monroe, October 6, 1802, Executive Papers; Council Journal, July 10, 1802, 271; Thomas Newton to James Monroe, September 8, 1802, Executive Papers. Twenty-five slaves were transported in 1802. Fulcher bought thirteen of them, including the four men convicted of complicity in the Easter conspiracy. See "Memorandum of Negroes Sentenced for Transportation & Sent to the Penitentiary for Safe Keeping," December 2, 1806, Executive Papers, and "A List of Slaves Reprieved for Transportation and Sold," March 8, 1806, Executive Papers. On the removal of convicted slaves, see Philip J. Schwarz, "The Transportation of Slaves from Virginia, 1801–1865," *Slavery and Abolition*, VII (December, 1986), 215–240, especially 223 for data on the 1802 conspirators.

SEVENTEEN

The Rape Myth in the
Old South Reconsidered

DIANE MILLER SOMMERVILLE

In Southampton County, Virginia, the site of Nat Turner's 1831 revolt, another man of color was alleged to have committed an egregious act a few years earlier; in 1826 and 1827 Henry Hunt appeared before superior court accused of raping a white woman named Sydney Jordan. Hunt was a twenty-two-year-old laborer from St. Luke's parish and was described by his jailer as six feet tall, "straight and well made" with "a considerable share of effron-tery." The latter attribute may have been prompted by Hunt's escape from jail. His flight from justice, however, was short-lived, as he was quickly ap-prehended.[1] Hunt's defense rested on his assertion that his relations with Sydney Jordan were entirely consensual. In fact, Hunt claimed to have "long been in the habit of sexual intercourse" with Jordan. Furthermore, Hunt maintained that on the night of the alleged sexual assault not he but another free black man had bedded Jordan.[2]

Hunt's protestations notwithstanding, the jury found him guilty of rape and sentenced him to hang.[3] In an astonishing turn of events, a group of white citizens from Southampton County, including Hunt's jailer, the court clerk, and a member of the jury that had found him guilty, petitioned the governor and the executive council and asked that they extend clemency to the convicted rapist.[4] Sydney Jordan, the petitioners explained, had commit-ted perjury. Hunt averred throughout his defense that his and Jordan's re-lationship was based on mutual consent. Jordan denied this; in fact, she de-nied having met Henry Hunt prior to the night of the alleged assault. The crowning piece of evidence put forth in the petition defending Hunt was the statement that Jordan had given birth to a "black child" over a year after the alleged rape. The birth of a nonwhite child belied Jordan's assertion that she had not maintained intimate relations with black men and thus lent credibility to Hunt's account. Eventually Jordan acknowledged that the child's father was Nicholas Vick, the free black man whom Hunt claimed to have found in bed with Jordan on the night she claimed to have been raped by Hunt. With her lies unsalvageable, Jordan admitted having had "frequent criminal intercourse with . . . Henry Hunt" as well as with Nicholas Vick. The petitioners concluded that Henry Hunt was not guilty of the alleged sexual assault and pleaded that "humanity requires the interposition of the Executive council to rescue him from an undeserved doom."[5] A sympathetic governor granted Hunt a pardon.[6]

Seizing a pen instead of rope and fagot to deal with an accused black rapist seems irreconcilable with the image, largely the product of the postbellum period, of lawless, unrestrained southern lynch mobs bent on vigilante "justice" and retribution. Not only did this black man receive a trial, presumably attendant with certain procedural rights, but he also became the object of white citizens' sympathies and concern.[7] The collective fear and anxiety about black sexual assault that loomed large in postbellum southern society seem conspicuously absent in the case of Henry Hunt.[8] Moreover, his case is not isolated; over 250 cases of sexual assault by black males on white women or girls are reported in the records of twelve southern states from 1800 through 1865.[9] Although this study focuses primarily on Virginia and North Carolina, admittedly two of the northern-most slaveholding states, secondary sources as well as published primary sources, such as appellate decisions, reveal that similar occurrences were turning up throughout the slave South.[10] In Virginia alone there are over 150 cases from 1800 through 1865 of African American men, free and slave, condemned to die for sexually assaulting white women or children.[11] Nearly half of these condemned black rapists escaped their sentences of execution, suggesting that antebellum white southerners felt less compelled to exact death from a black man accused of sexually violating a white female than did postbellum white southerners. The argument here is that the rape trial of Henry Hunt, as well as those of dozens of other black southern males, demonstrates that antebellum white southerners were not nearly as consumed by fears of black men raping white women as their postbellum descendants were. As Eugene Genovese has written, the "titillating and violence-provoking theory of the superpotency of that black superpenis, while whispered about for several centuries, did not become an obsession in the South until after emancipation. . . ."[12] The pervasive sexual and racial anxieties that galvanized scores of lynch mobs after the war failed to manifest themselves before emancipation. Why is it, then, that so much scholarship has perpetuated the notion that such fears were a constant throughout the history of the slaveholding South?

A quick look at the historiography of the subject may shed light on the perpetuation of the "myth" about the "rape myth." Some scholarly works that have documented early white sexual anxiety about black men have led to the belief that white fears of the African American man as a rapist grew out of the slave experience and persisted in the antebellum South. A close examination of the historical literature reveals how this postbellum white anxiety about black male sexuality, which a number of historians have documented, was read backwards into the antebellum period. Significantly, the generation of late-nineteenth-century radical racists who argued against education and enfranchisement of blacks on the grounds that these innovations only exacerbated the "race problem" tended to romanticize the relations between slave and master. Turn-of-the-century writers and editors often denied that slaves of the Old South had posed any sexual threat to white women. Animated by perceived changes in the "New Negro," increases in the black population, and an unprecedented political threat, many authorities of the late nineteenth and early twentieth centuries waxed nostalgic about the cross-racial plantation family.[13] White mistresses did not fear slave men then because of "the natural trust and affection subsisting between the two races."[14] During the antebellum era, these southern apologists argued, illiterate, unschooled blacks rarely raped white women. Even during the Civil War, when white protectors were away from the plantation, women had nothing to fear when left alone with their male slaves. Henry McHatton had grown up on a Louisiana plantation where, he reminisced, "there was no lock between any negro and my mother's bedroom. My father was often absent. During the war, there were thousands of white women on isolated plantations alone under the care of the slaves for months, and even years. Many women made trips through the country day and night alone in charge of negro drivers. If this trust was ever betrayed, I have never heard of it."[15] Myrta Lockett Avary blamed northern interlopers for the change in black demeanor toward white women: "This crime [rape] was a development of a period when the negro was dominated by political, religious and social advisors from the North and by the attitude of the Northern press and pulpit. It was practically unknown in wartime, when negroes were left on plantations as protectors and guardians of white women and children."[16]

In an article published in 1900 a University of Georgia professor and Baptist clergyman, John Roach Straton, posed the rhetorical question, "Will Education Solve the Race Problem?" to which he answered an emphatic and resounding no. Straton drew a rather unscientific correlation between nearly universal illiteracy among slaves and the infrequency of blacks' raping white women in the years before the Civil War. He further observed that, after emancipation, black literacy increased and, concomitantly, so did black crime.[17] Such claims "proved" that education made blacks sexually dangerous and provided the underpinnings for political disfranchisement and social segregation of black southerners in the late nineteenth and early twentieth centuries.

It was not until 1918 that the portrayal of the male slave as sexually non-threatening was disputed. Ulrich B. Phillips, himself a southern apologist for slavery, challenged this portrait of the black male in his classic *American*

Negro Slavery. Phillips documented 105 cases of rape or attempted rape by slaves in Virginia from 1780 through 1864, as well as similar cases in five other southern states. In doing so, Phillips debunked the myth of the eunuch slave, discrediting the "oft-asserted Southern tradition that negroes never violated white women before slavery was abolished."[18] This stance might strike the reader as inimical to Phillips's well-known portrayal of slaves as docile, content with their bondage. Phillips, however, utilized the discussion of slave "crime in abundance" as a means to showcase the benevolence of the southern judicial system as well as the paternalism and humanitarianism of slave owners. Not coincidentally, Phillips documented numerous acquittals of slaves for serious offences, as well as a pattern of lenient punishment. Furthermore, he asserted that the felonies with which slaves were charged were generally viewed as "criminal regardless of the status of the perpetrators." By implication, southern jurisprudence was color-blind and characterized by "considerable impartiality to malefactors of both races and conditions."[19]

In the 1930s and 1940s southern white liberals unleashed their assault on radical racist ideology and their criticism of southern culture, including the characterization of black men as "beasts." What, for U. B. Phillips and other scholars of the early twentieth century, had been evidence of rape, clear and simple, became, for a Freudian generation, a "rape complex." Wilbur J. Cash in his seminal work *The Mind of the South* (1941) denied contemporary racist claims of rampant black sexual assault, laying greater odds that a white woman would be struck by lightning than that she would be raped by a black man. Cash placed the "rape complex," as he termed it, squarely at the doorstep of antebellum slave society, which elevated the white woman to a pedestal and worshipped her as the symbol of virtue, honor, and chastity. Southern white men, he claimed, practiced "gyneolatry," or the deification of their women, which, in effect, purged white women of their sexuality and made them sexually inaccessible. These same men, Cash wrote, turned instead to slave women to satisfy their lust. Over time, white southerners came to identify white womanhood with the South itself. "What Southerners felt, therefore, was that any assertion of any kind on the part of the Negro constituted in a perfectly real manner an attack on the Southern woman."[20]

The relationship between sex and race was at last examined in a major historical work in 1968. Winthrop D. Jordan expanded upon the work of Cash and others by grafting their ideas onto the body of historical treatments of slavery. Cash's ideas on white womanhood, for example, were developed and elaborated upon by Jordan in his exhaustive study of colonial race relations, *White over Black*, which traced the glorification of white women to early English efforts to populate and colonize New World settlements. Jordan wrote that "white women were, quite literally, the repositories of white civilization. White men tended to place them protectively upon a pedestal and then run off to gratify their passions elsewhere." Jordan theorized that guilt-ridden white men who sexually exploited slave women and who were jealous of presumed black male potency in turn projected their own sexual desires onto slave men, in the process creating an irrational fear of black male sexuality. "It is not we, but others, who are guilty. It is not we who lust, but they."[21]

Jordan's conjectures on the ties between sex and race have proven very influential in informing subsequent studies of southern history. Works by Lawrence J. Friedman, Earl E. Thorpe, and Peter H. Wood, to name a few, have accepted the argument put forth by Jordan in *White over Black* and have thus perpetuated the assumption that white fears of black ravishment pervaded southern attitudes during the colonial period and in the years before and during the Civil War.[22] These scholars, looking backward, have projected postbellum assumptions into antebellum southern culture, in the process finding widespread sexual anxiety and hysterical fear where it did not occur.[23] Slaveholders assuredly feared acts of violence by their slaves — arson, poisonings, assault, murder, and, perhaps most of all, armed rebellion.[24] There is no evidence, however, to suggest that white southerners were apprehensive or anxious about their slaves raping white women.

One need only return to the work of U. B. Phillips and to the cases of black men accused of rape or attempted rape in the years before the Civil War to see that neither white judicial institutions nor white communities were sufficiently obsessed with sexual danger posed by black men to deprive accused or even convicted black rapists of due process. In the lower courts, which had original jurisdiction over such cases, white witnesses sometimes testified on behalf of the accused, either to extol the prisoner's industrious character or to malign the integrity of the white female victim. These same courts often scrutinized testimony to ferret out coerced confessions. In the event of a guilty verdict, the convicted rapist could utilize his right to appeal in most southern states. On many occasions southern appellate courts threw out convictions of black rapists on myriad legal technicalities.[25] Finally, if none of these avenues were effective, the condemned black rapist, or white men acting on his behalf, could, and many times did, petition the governor for a reprieve. Black men stood a reasonable chance of acquittal, clemency, or leniency for raping or attempting to rape white women or girls, which belies claims that the rape myth exercised considerable sway in antebellum southern society. Simply put, the image of the menacing black rapist did not become the obsession of the southern white mind until sometime after emancipation.[26] It is hard to imagine, for example, a group of white citizens petitioning the governor of Alabama in 1931 on behalf of the nine black males charged with raping two white women on a freight train near Scottsboro, even in a case in which a great deal of credible evidence cast doubt on the veracity and integrity of the white accusers. In spite of such evidence and rumors that the Scottsboro women might have been prostitutes, a defiant North Carolina newspaper posited that "in the South it has been traditional . . . that its white womanhood shall be held inviolate by an 'inferior race'." Protection applied to every white woman regardless of class — whether she was a "spotless virgin or a 'nymph de pavé'."[27] Clearly Southampton County residents considered Sydney Jordan the latter, and, as such, she ultimately forfeited any privilege of protection, if indeed, it had ever been extended to her.

A quick overview of southern statutes suggests that legislators considered sexual assault a heinous crime whether committed by black or white males. Eight slaveholding states at various times before the Civil War prescribed death for white rapists.[28] Death sentences, however, seem to have been reserved for white rapists of children.[29] The more prevalent punishment for white offenders was imprisonment. Of the southern states and territories that punished white rapists with prison, the terms ran the gamut from Georgia statutes, being the least harsh (from two to twenty years), to Alabama, Louisiana, and Mississippi statutes, which at one time or another sentenced white offenders to life imprisonment.[30] Virginia prison registers reveal that the sentences of white men serving time for rape or attempted rape ranged from three to twenty years, although most averaged between ten and seventeen years.[31]

The trend of rape statutes through the Civil War, nonetheless, was to lessen the punishment for convicted white rapists while retaining capital punishment for African Americans, free and slave.[32] As an example, a Virginia law passed in 1847 called for convicted white rapists to serve from ten to twenty years in prison while prescribing the death penalty for black men.[33] In most southern states by the beginning of the Civil War, racial disparity permeated sexual assault statutes. Rape statutes were equally discriminatory in defining the victims. Females of color, whether free or slave, assaulted by white men found virtually no redress from the judicial system. The widely held belief in the depraved and promiscuous nature of African American women coupled with a female slave's status as the property of a white man shielded rapists, whether black or white, from prosecution.[34]

Though statutes expressly addressed race, issues of class or "respectability" are not mentioned in laws on rape. In applying these statutes to individual cases, judges, jurors, and community members nonetheless took it upon themselves to utilize juridical prerogative and frequently applied such standards to cases of sexual assault, as in the case of Sydney Jordan.[35] Jordan was no doubt one of the Old South's "unruly women" portrayed in Victoria Bynum's recent study of the same name.[36] Jordan, who was white but outside the circle of the genteel, defied rigid race and gender conventions by engaging in illicit sexual behavior with African American men. Because she did so and was caught at it, the protection bestowed upon her, presumably because of her whiteness, was withdrawn. In short, she had not behaved as a proper white woman should and was therefore not to be treated as one.[37] Instead, the overseers of her community, white men who were probably her social betters, accused her of perjury and sought clemency for the black man who she alleged had sexually violated her. Her race failed to shield her from assaults on her moral character.[38]

Like Sydney Jordan twenty years later, Sarah Sands of Henry County, Virginia, claimed to have been raped by an African American man. She accused a slave named Jerry owned by Edward Osborne. Also like Jordan, Sands was reported to have kept company with black men. Jerry was tried in the local court in 1807, found guilty, and sentenced to be hanged. A petition to the governor penned by Jerry's legal counsel, Peachy R. Gilmer, purported to reflect the sentiments of others who attended the trial and argued for a reduction in sentence from execution to transportation.[39] Gilmer based his request on Sands's indiscreet sexual history and cited Sands's "very infamous character" and her status as another man's concubine. And if a questionable character weren't enough to erode Sand's credibility, the petition places in evidence the woman's size. Gilmer portrayed Sands as "large and strong enough to have made considerable resistance if she had been so disposed, yet there was by her own confession no mark of violence upon any part of her."[40]

Undoubtedly Jerry's counsel presented this evidence at the 1807 trial, but the court remained unconvinced and rendered a guilty verdict. A number of the white residents of the community believed that the honor of such a deviant, debased woman was not worth the life of the rapist, and they took their case to the governor, who granted Jerry a reprieve.[41]

A group of Virginians made a similar appeal in 1803 on behalf of Carter, a slave found guilty of raping a poor white woman who, like Jordan and Sands, had a reputation for consorting with African American men:

> Carter did commit the said offense—from the whole of the evidence your subscribers felt themselves bound by law to pass sentence of death upon the said Carter. Yet for reasons, hereinafter mentioned the court aforesaid are of the opinion that the said Carter is a proper object of mercy. . . . [I]t appeared that the said Catherine Brinal was a woman of the worst fame, that her character was that of the most abandoned in as much as she (being a white woman) has three mulatto children, which by her own confession were begotten by different negro men; that the said Catherine has no visible means of support; that from report she had permitted the said Carter to have peaceable intercourse with her, before the time of his forcing her.[42]

According to the petitioners, having previously consented to "peaceable" sexual relations with Carter, Catherine Brinal effectively lost her right to deny him sex at any future time. Brinal, and white women like her who flouted prevailing social conventions about race and sex, risked the embarrassment of the public airing of their social histories. Carter cheated the executioner and was transported out of the state.[43]

Consider also the case of Cato, a Florida slave accused in 1860 of raping Susan Leonard, a white woman whom twelve defense witnesses described as a "common prostitute." Nevertheless, the lower court judge instructed the jury that if they were satisfied that Cato had "carnal knowledge . . . against her will" they must find Cato guilty, which the jury ultimately did. On review, the Florida Supreme Court acknowledged its own role as judicial patriarch and balanced "the fact that a most foul offence" had been perpetrated against the consideration that the "life of a human being" was dependent on the outcome.[44] Mindful of its commitment to oversee justice of accused slaves, the court boasted of the "crowning glory of our 'peculiar institution,' that whenever life is involved, the slave stands upon as safe ground as the master." The court was disturbed by the "abundant proof" that the alleged victim and her friend who testified for the state were "common prostitutes." Lacking corroborative testimony, the court refused to turn its back on Cato. Quoting the seventeenth-century English jurist Lord Chief Justice Matthew Hale, the court sympathized that "rape is an accusation easily to be made and hard to be proved and harder to be defended by the party accused. . . ." The high court vacated the execution decree and ordered a new trial.[45]

Although not all cases led to reprieves or pardons of convicted African American rapists, the defense could be counted on to raise questions about the character of the female accuser. In the 1829 rape case of Lewis, a Virginia slave, two witnesses tarnished the reputation of the accuser, Amy [Amey] Baker, and her housemate, who had been an eyewitness to the assault, with accusations of debauchery and sexual impropriety.[46] Five other witnesses, however, took the stand to defend the reputations of the two women. As Baker, who was forty-five years old, and her live-in companion, "old Mrs. [Drucilla] Kirkland," recounted, in the dark hours before daybreak on May 23 the accused came to Baker's house demanding to be let in. After the women refused to admit Lewis, he broke down the door. They claimed that Lewis brutally raped Amy Baker four times over a two-hour period while Mrs. Kirkland hid under the bed. Soon thereafter the accused dozed off, and the two women fled to the home of a neighbor, Burwell Coleman, whose son, Richard Coleman, returned with them to their house. Coleman groped blindly in the dark and found the intruder still lying on the bed clothed only from the waist up. After a brief struggle Coleman subdued the alleged rapist and demanded to know what had driven the slave to such unthinkable behavior. Lewis replied that he did not know but he reckoned he was drunk.[47]

The court-appointed defense counsel surely faced a difficult task since the accused had been apprehended partially clad at the scene. Lewis's attorney, Alexander G. Knox, appears to have formulated a three-pronged strategy as revealed in the depositions of various witnesses. First, he challenged the women's ability to identify the accused by pointing out that the assault had taken place entirely in the dark. Upon cross-examination Baker flip-flopped a bit, at first claiming that there had been sufficient moonlight to identify the rapist but then contradicting herself somewhat by admitting that as dawn broke the light had not carried to her attacker. Despite the darkness, however, upon seeing the prisoner the next day she was confident that he had been her assailant.[48]

The presence of an eyewitness was rare in a rape case since most rapists targeted unaccompanied females in desolate or distant locations, out of earshot of bystanders. The testimony of Mrs. Kirkland, then, must have been considered crucial in the prosecution's case.[49] Nonetheless, discrediting

Kirkland's testimony was the second prong in Knox's strategy to vindicate Lewis. At first glance, Mrs. Kirkland seems to have made a poor eyewitness to the crime since by her own admission she spent the entire assault hiding beneath a bed, presumably the very bed where the rape took place. She claimed, however, that at some point she emerged from her hiding place and "at the risque of her life" made up a light by which she was able to identify the assailant who was on top of Amy Baker. Knox, no doubt skeptical of this testimony (Baker had not mentioned Kirkland's putting on a light), then took another tack with Kirkland. He inquired about her marital and maternal status, thus insinuating her ignorance of coitus and therefore her unreliability in testifying that sexual intercourse had in fact taken place in her presence. This deft defense maneuvering placed Kirkland in an awkward position. If she admitted to having had intercourse outside of marriage, jurors would in all likelihood dismiss her testimony as unreliable due to the woman's bad character. If she denied having had intercourse, she lent weight to the defense claim that she may not have known intercourse if she saw it. Kirkland appears by her answer to have been piqued by Knox's intimation and replied rather indignantly that indeed she had neither married nor borne children but that she certainly "had seen such acts of [intercourse performed] and knows very well that the prisoner was in the act of enjoying Mrs. Baker."[50]

The third prong of the defense strategy was to impugn the character of Amy Baker and her friend Drucilla Kirkland and, by implication, to question their veracity. One of only two witnesses who testified to Baker's dubious history was William Coleman, who claimed that he "had been to the house of Mrs. Baker for the purpose of unlawful intercourse with females and have known others to do so." Coleman reported that her neighbors were suspicious of Mrs. Baker. He did not consider her to be a "respectable woman" and would not believe her "as soon as he would a respectable woman." Alexander Pritchett, the second defense witness, did not admit to engaging in illicit sexual relations with women at the Baker house as did Coleman, but reported that on two occasions he had observed several Negro men on the premises, who were, by implication, up to no good.[51]

The prosecution summoned five character witnesses to refute the accusations levied by Coleman and Pritchett about Baker and Kirkland. Their testimony variously described Baker as "industrious," "always correct," and of "good character." Samuel Farrar claimed never to have heard anyone speak ill of Amy Baker and discounted allegations that she consorted with black men, reasoning that had Baker "been in the habit of entertaining slaves" he would have heard about it.[52]

Perhaps the sheer number of witnesses who testified to Amy Baker's good character provides a good reason to doubt that she "entertained" slaves— which, even if proven true, obviously does not prove that she lied about being sexually assaulted. But Knox's finding even one witness willing to admit in public to having had sexual intercourse with women at Baker's home is surprising. Given the likelihood of swift admonishment from family and community members, public acknowledgment of illicit sexual relations is astonishing. Such an admission by a white male was indeed aberrant and, in terms of evidence, was probably unnecessary; in most rape cases sufficient proof of a woman's bad character was gleaned from the hearsay testimony of people who had merely heard about the alleged victim's reputation through the neighborhood gossip network.[53]

Quite possibly the most revealing evidence pertaining to Baker's status in the community is her own testimony. Her deposition is striking for its explicit, graphic detail and bawdy language. Typically, depositions contained language that was carefully couched, especially any testimony relating to a sexual act, usually cryptically referred to as "it." Drucilla Kirkland, for instance, testified to the intruder's bellowing that he "was sent there for it and was told that there was a plenty of it there." Amy Baker's testimony defied such conventions. Her deposition reveals a complete lack of inhibition in retelling the details of the crime she alleged. She repeated verbatim what the accused had said upon entering the house. "He came for cunt and cunt he would have, that he had been told that there was a plenty of it there and he would have his satisfaction before he left." Nor did Baker choose to mince words when describing a brutal sexual assault. She testified that the prisoner penetrated her four times and during one instance he threw "her head over the bedstead and forced her legs over the prisoner's shoulders and used such violence in the penetration of the act as almost to have deprived her of her life."[54]

Baker's choice of language in retelling her account of the assault, her decision not to mince words, suggests a conscious effort to forgo any pretense about her status in southern society. Nor did the court transcriber feel compelled to "clean up" her deposition. At the very least the evidence suggests that Baker lived on the margins of respectability in the eyes of this white community. The guilt or innocence of Lewis the slave at times seems to have taken a back seat to the contest over Amy Baker's reputation.

In the end, the court remained unswayed by allegations of Baker's past sexual improprieties and found Lewis guilty of rape. Possibly Lewis's admission that he had been drunk at the time of the alleged assault made the attack seem more plausible to the jury. Or perhaps the well-documented brutality of the assault ruled out Baker's compliance.[55] These factors, combined with Lewis's capture at the scene, no doubt were crucial in the jury's decision to levy a guilty verdict and death sentence with no attendant recommendation for mercy. In contrast to cases cited previously in this study, this case demonstrates that not every incident of an accused black rapist led to reprieve. Considering the weight of the evidence against Lewis, however, what is surprising is not so much his conviction and subsequent hanging as the vigor with which his defense was conducted.[56] And the typical form of an ambitious defense was an attack on the character of the white accuser.

Even white female children who claimed to have been sexually assaulted by African American men found their lives probed for clues of past sexual indiscretion or immoral conduct. Few good things were said by anyone about the character and integrity of Rosanna Green, an eleven-year-old orphan servant girl who lived in Wythe County, Virginia, with the family of Peter Kincer. Neighbors, slaves, and of course Kincer himself rallied in 1829 to defend Gabriel, a slave owned by Kincer, from Rosanna's charge of rape. Another Kincer slave testified to having heard reports that Green had "behaved badly with a black boy in the neighborhood." In addition, Green had a reputation for "telling stories" and "making mischief," which seriously jeopardized the credibility of her testimony. The court found Gabriel guilty, but extenuating circumstances led the court to recommend leniency.[57]

By no means was sympathy for the slave universal. In a letter to the governor one Wythe County resident urged the executive to disregard pleas for leniency. Of Gabriel, the accused rapist, Alexander Smyth wrote: "I think it right to say, that I apprehend him a proper subject to be made an example, and that example is required. It is not many years since a man suffered emasculation for an attempt on his mistress; and a few days since a youth received 120 lashes from his master for an attempt on a girl. This fellow seems to be 40, and is notorious as a thief." With the letter Smyth enclosed a newspaper clipping that conveyed sympathy for the orphan girl. "[H]ad her father been living, or, had she have had any natural protector, who had reaked [sic] the vengeance due to such an offense, in the blood of the perpetrator, we could never have consented to his punishment for the offence."[58] In other words, male kin would have sought personal justice through revenge and not left the girl to be vilified in the local court. Likewise, one can infer that the author of the piece sensed class bias in the adjudication process. Had Rosanna Green not been a servant girl, the outcome might have been substantially different. In the end, Smyth's appeal went unheeded, and Gabriel was sold and transported out of Virginia.[59]

Indeed, nonslaveholding whites at times openly displayed disgust at what some believed to be the blatant economic motives of a master's behavior in trying to exonerate his slave from the charge of rape. This is evident in the 1831 rape case of Dick, a slave belonging to Hamilton Rogers. Dick was charged with attempting to ravish Pleasant Cole, wife of Peter Cole, of Leesburg, Virginia. Mrs. Cole successfully fought off her attacker, struggling with him for about fifteen minutes before a friend, hearing her screams, frightened Dick off. Cole managed to scratch Dick's face, a fact entered as evidence by the prosecution. Cole boasted that she "kept him off by catching [Dick] by his privates."[60]

Throughout the trial witnesses described Cole as a "woman of truth." One witness swore that he made some inquiries of her character "to do justice to the prisoner" and found everyone spoke "in the highest terms of her character."[61] The jury found Dick guilty and ordered his execution. However, as a last resort, Dick's owner, Hamilton Rogers, and his defense counsel quickly fired off letters to the governor requesting a reduced sentence, a request made more difficult because the jury had made no recommendation for leniency. On Dick's behalf, attorney Burr W. Harrison and Hamilton Rogers, Dick's owner, cited mitigating circumstances, including Mrs. Cole's uncertainty about the identity of the perpetrator and discrepancies in the testimony of various prosecution witnesses. Harrison also cited Dick's age (which he did not state) and the fact that "no actual injury . . . [was] sustained by the object of his attempt." No mention is made of Mrs. Cole's character with the exception of a single unexplained reference to her "indiscretion."[62] In addition to Harrison and Rogers, at least one other petitioner, who identified himself as "a member of the court who found him [Dick] guilty," concurred that mitigating circumstances, foremost being the very severe punishment, warranted mercy.[63]

Other members of the community, probably friends of the Coles, got wind of the letter-writing campaign on Dick's behalf and put pen to their own angry grievances. The complaints accused Hamilton Rogers, Dick's master, of cronyism; he reportedly had persuaded a sheriff, a relative of his, to investigate the character of Mrs. Cole. To the delight of the petitioners the inquiry yielded only that she was a woman of "unblemished character." They were appalled at the naked self-interest of the slaveholder. Venting class discord, the petitioners pondered the future safety of the community if Dick were set free, especially for "females in the humble walks of life, who have not thrown around them the protection of wealth and influential friends," an obvious dig at Hamilton Rogers. These folks, who seem to have shared a greater identification with the "more humble walks of life" than with Rogers, observed that in this case the availability of legal protection ran along class lines.[64] Pleasant Cole, decidedly not a member of the slaveholding class, lacked money and powerful friends but did have a good reputation and neighbors who were outraged not only at the greed of a slaveholder more interested in his pocketbook than in justice and community safety but also at the legal system's apparent favoritism to the rich. In an analysis of community, class, and crime in the Old South, Bertram Wyatt-Brown argues that non-elites chafed at the bias they observed in the judicial process. "When decisions seemed flagrantly generous toward those with powerful friends, money, and batteries of legal talent, feelings of class animosity could be aroused."[65] No doubt aware that the case had created a political hornet's nest, which he was not eager to disturb, the governor denied Hamilton Roger's appeal, and the death sentence was allowed to stand. Dick was executed, and his owner had to settle for $400 in compensation from the state, no doubt less than the market value of the slave.[66]

Class chafing is also observed in a letter to Virginia's governor following the 1846 trial of Anthony, a King George County slave. "Suppose for instance that she [the alleged victim] had . . . been of a rich family . . . you know he [the accused rapist] would never have gotten to gaol, but because she was poor she must suffer. . . ." The governor was unmoved by the plea and had Anthony transported out of the state.[67]

The oft-cited 1825 North Carolina case of Jim and his alleged rape of a young white servant also reveals class divisions among southern whites.[68] The numerous documents that this case generated permit a rare glimpse into what quite plausibly had been consensual sex between a poor white servant woman and a slave, which was tolerated until the resulting pregnancy forced the community to confront the "taboo" relationship.

Polly Lane, a white servant about eighteen years old, and Jim, a slave, both worked in the home of Abraham Peppinger, an elderly man. Jim was one of several slaves owned by Peppinger. According to Polly Lane's testimony at Jim's subsequent trial, one morning in mid-August 1825 Jim overtook her, forced her to drink brandy, and then raped her several times. Because Jim had threatened her, she claimed, she did not call out for help until well after dark. Another slave, Dick, after hearing the commotion sneaked to where Polly and Jim were. Dick claimed that he had heard Jim implore Polly to quiet down and then heard Polly say "that if I am left in the fire I am now in I shall surely die." Dick then made himself known to the couple whereupon Polly accused Jim of assaulting her and implored Dick not to tell the Peppingers of the attack. She also confided to Dick that she was "big" and offered him a dollar to "get her something to destroy it." The inference to be made, of course, is that Polly and Jim had been having an affair, she became pregnant, then feigned the rape, perhaps realizing that the only way out of the embarrassing situation was to deny that consensual sexual relations had ever taken place with Jim. Several witnesses challenged her account, however, by testifying that they had seen Polly and Jim together intimately on numerous occasions.[69]

Members of the jury, which convened in October and heard testimony, believed that the evidence weighed more heavily in favor of Polly Lane; they convicted Jim and set the date for his execution later that year, on December 23, despite suspicions that Polly was pregnant at the time of the trial, which she denied.[70] As the execution date neared, Polly Lane was no longer able to conceal her pregnancy, which by this time had caused considerable excitement in the community. Had Jim, not Polly, told the truth? Had Polly been trying to conceal their relationship? Was she desperate to ward off ostracism from family and community, even at the cost of Jim's life? The white community was very divided and contentious in its response to these and other questions.

Six white male petitioners asked the governor to transport Jim out of the state or at least to grant him a reprieve until the birth of Polly Lane's child.[71] Alexander Gray, a juror who had voted for conviction, defended the jury's guilty verdict in the face of weak evidence presented by the defense. While Gray acknowledged that "in that neighborhood a greater intimacy existed between the blacks and whites than is usual or considered decent," Jim's attorney failed to prove that Jim and Polly had an illicit sexual relationship. Though Gray continued to believe the correct verdict had been rendered, he nonetheless wanted to hedge his bets and requested the governor to postpone the execution. A second letter by Gray in March reveals an about-face; by that time Lane's advanced pregnancy had all but unraveled her tale, and Gray expressed outrage that she had knowingly perjured herself by denying consensual sex with Jim before the night of the alleged rape. "If this is the case and she knew it at the time [of the trial], no part of her testimony ought to be believed."[72]

As the birth of Polly Lane's child approached, fewer and fewer of her supporters, such as Gray, remained in her camp. But as late as March 24 Jim's legal counsel, James Martin, feared that "many persons in the county . . . would execute this negro."[73] Martin worried that the birth might be concealed in order to facilitate Jim's hanging. Martin's qualms appear not to have been unfounded, for when local officials attempted to serve bastardy papers on Polly Lane, she could not be located. On advice of those "anxious for the execution" of Jim she had hidden herself.[74]

Polly Lane's mixed-race baby was born on April 7, thus strengthening Jim's claim that she was already pregnant in mid-August when she claimed to have been raped. Alexander Gray concluded his thoughts on the matter by writing the governor that the birth of Polly Lane's baby proved that "she must have knowingly and willingly sworn to a falsehood in saying . . . she was not pregnant [at the time of the trial. The] presumption naturally arises that the rest of it [her testimony] ought not be entitled to credit."[75] Even in the face of strong material evidence, however, some members of the white community stubbornly refused to desert Polly Lane, choosing instead a different tack in arguing for Jim's execution. Doggedly denying that Polly Lane's baby was mulatto, John Smith denounced Jim's character as "one of the worst in my memory." Another letter writer reported that some residents of the county "are anxious for his execution not because they believe the conviction rightful but on account of general bad character." In other words, Jim's execution need not be sanctioned by Polly Lane's claim of sexual assault, which had been proved to be baseless. Jim was a troublemaker pure and simple, reason enough in and of itself to kill him.[76] However, the governor's sympathies clearly rested with those who argued for Jim's release. Instead of being hanged, Jim was transported out of North Carolina.[77]

Whether or not this protracted and bitter dispute among the white residents of Davidson County, North Carolina, was primarily caused by class prejudices is not certain. However, it is clear, because she was employed as a domestic servant, that Polly Lane was from a poor family. The Lane family's claim to honor is evidenced by its defiant attempt to shield Polly from probing community members bent on ascertaining the truth about very private and intimate matters. It is also conceivable that the Lanes saw themselves challenged by a propertied slaveholder, Abraham Peppinger, whose financial stake in saving Jim's life necessarily required that he challenge the integrity of their daughter and hence of the Lane family. Peppinger was wealthy enough to hire two of North Carolina's finest barristers, James Martin and John Motley Morehead, the latter of whom served two terms as

Virginia Slaves Convicted of Rape or Attempted Rape, 1800–1865, and Verifiable Outcomes

	Transported	Executed	Unknown outcome	Total known outcome
1800–1809	7 (39%)	10 (56%)	0	18[1]
1810–1819	0 (0%)	9 (82%)	0	11[1,2]
1820–1829	10 (37%)	17 (63%)	2	27
1830–1839	8 (42%)	11[3](58%)	0	19[3]
1840–1849	14 (54%)	12 (46%)	0	26
1850–1859	16 (55%)	13 (45%)	0	29
1860–1865	7 (70%)	3 (30%)	4[4]	10

SOURCES: Data gathered from an array of sources at the Library of Virginia, including Letters Received in the Virginia Executive Papers, Pardon Papers, Transportation and Execution records from the Auditor of Public Accounts as well as bond documents, county court order and minute books: Philip J. Schwarz, *Twice Condemned: Slaves and the Criminal Laws of Virginia, 1705–1865* ([Baton Rouge], 1988); and James Hugo Johnston, *Race Relations in Virginia and Miscegenation in the South, 1776–1860* (Amherst, Mass., 1970). Percentages are based on the total of known and verifiable outcomes.

[1]Includes one sentence of castration.
[2]Includes one slave who escaped from jail.
[3]Includes one case of rape/murder.
[4]No records of financial compensation can be located among funds dispersed by the Virginia treasury, indicating a strong probability these four were pardoned by the executive.

governor in the 1840s.[78] These two lawyers had developed a greater stake in procuring Jim's pardon because Abraham Peppinger promised to turn Jim over to the two should their efforts prove successful.[79]

Ties of kinship and friendship, inextricably linked to class, also probably shaped the principals' sympathies and their responses to the unfolding events. John Smith, characterized by Bertram Wyatt-Brown as a "semiliterate member of the clan to which Polly Lane belonged," refused to sign a bastardy warrant against Polly Lane, yet magistrate Jesse Hargrave, himself the owner of twenty-eight slaves, did.[80] Other motives vied for attention as well: humanitarianism (Peppinger's attachment to Jim; community members unwilling to see an innocent man, black or white, go to the gallows); financial interests (Peppinger's financial loss if Jim were executed; Jim's attorneys' prospect of acquiring Jim if his life were spared); and perceptions about gender and sexuality (proof of Polly Lane's compliance negated her claims of sexual assault).

As sectional tensions worsened and the political debate over slavery heated up in the years preceding the outbreak of war, one might expect to find a concomitant increase in anxiety about black sexual assault, especially since abolitionists had brought the issue of sexual assault of slave women to the forefront, making it a highly charged subject.[81] By looking at the trends in transportation of convicted slaves out of the state during this time, one can indirectly gauge the pulse of the white community for any fears of black rapists. Governors were in no position to antagonize large pools of voters by pardoning or commuting sentences of convicted African American rapists if concerns over the "black-beast-rapist" were rampant.

In fact, transportation patterns by Virginia executives reveal that, as the Civil War approached, a convicted black sex offender was far more likely to be transported than hanged (see table). Execution was the punishment of choice for slaves convicted of rape or attempted rape in the early part of the century. But as the Civil War approached and tensions heightened, state officials spared the lives of convicted slave rapists in a majority of cases.

The pattern, at least for antebellum Virginia, then, is one of greater leniency as the nineteenth century progressed.[82] The irony here is that although the statutes for rape by black men of white women became harsher, implementation of the harsher penalties did not automatically follow.[83] One can only speculate about the reasons. Perhaps as state executives became more concerned with fiscal savings, they increasingly utilized transportation of slave criminals, an option that allowed them to recover at least some of the compensation costs paid to the slaves' owners. The defensive posture struck by southerners in response to abolitionism may offer another explanation for the tendency to spare the lives of convicted black rapists. By showcasing their humanitarianism, elected officials may have hoped to demonstrate the benevolence and justice of slavery.

Whatever the motivation, the trend documented here appears to have been part of a larger tendency among authorities in Virginia to administer slave justice, even in these most serious cases, without resorting to capital punishment. Philip Schwarz's comprehensive account of slave crime in Virginia reflects similar patterns from the eighteenth century to the mid-nineteenth century. For example, the statistics he marshals on slaves executed or transported for murder from 1785 through 1829 also show a greater utilization of transportation as the decades wore on. Of the twenty-three Virginia slaves who were convicted of murder from 1785 through 1794, all twenty-three were executed. But from 1820 through 1829, a period in which eighty-three slaves were condemned to die for murder, sixty-one (73 percent) were actually hanged while twenty-two (27 percent) were transported out of Virginia. Similarly, Schwarz documents less reliance on execution of slaves convicted of conspiracy and insurrection. Of eleven slaves convicted for this crime from 1790 through 1799, one received corporal punishment and ten were executed. However, during the period 1830 through 1834, a time when the Nat Turner revolt had deeply aroused the Virginia countryside, eighty-nine slaves were tried for insurrection, of whom only forty-five were convicted. Of these, one was pardoned, twenty-one transported, and twenty-three, or just about half, were executed.[84] The trend toward saving convicted slave rapists from the gallows, then, appears to have been part of a larger tendency toward sparing the lives of all convicted slave criminals. Furthermore, there does not seem to have been any special onus attached to slave rapists that mandated special, harsher punishment.

If one accepts for the moment that the financial self-interest of the state, as well as that of the individual slaveholders, was the chief motive in sparing these slaves' lives, what then could have been the motivation for some whites in siding with the free African American men accused of raping white women or girls? Official records yield two cases of attempted rape of young white girls by free black men in Virginia in 1833, only two years after the Nat Turner rebellion. Caleb Watts, a free black, met eleven-year-old Jane Barber one summer day at the local mill, and Watts offered to carry the girl's ground corn at least as far toward her home as he was going. At the place where the two were to part, according to Barber, the assault took place. By his own admission, Watts demanded some sort of compensation for his good deed. Barber replied that she was but a poor girl who had nothing to give but herself. "Give me yourself, then," Watts was said to have demanded. Barber cried out and apparently Watts choked the girl and wielded a knife in order to quiet her during the assault. Watts was indicted and tried for assault upon Jane Barber, and the jury found him guilty.[85] Defense counsel then appealed the conviction on the inventive grounds that the victim was, at the time of the assault, under the age of twelve and thus had not yet attained puberty; therefore, Jane Barber was not a woman under the strict statutory definition of a woman. How then could Watts be guilty of raping a woman, reasoned his appeal. The Virginia high court found no merit in this argument and ordered that the death sentence be passed upon the prisoner.[86]

As a last resort, Watt's attorney Edward Wood launched a feverish correspondence with the governor of Virginia. Wood wrote two letters himself and penned a preachy but emotional petition ostensibly signed by "almost every man of respectability" including one jury member. Although the sexual morality of the girl was never challenged directly, Wood did claim that she and her mother were of the "lowest order in society" and questioned the credibility of "a girl who has been raised with an aunt who has given birth to several bastard children."[87]

The attorney for the Commonwealth, W. Thurman, who prosecuted the case in county court, also wrote to the governor claiming that he himself harbored doubts about the alleged victim and cited discrepancies in the testimony of some witnesses who Thurman claimed possessed "prejudice against the defendant, and eagerness for his condemnation." He questioned the ability of the jury to have arrived at a fair and impartial decision given the "strong popular prejudice and excitement against the prisoner" that prevailed in the community.[88] Although the light-skinned Caleb Watts did not have the unanimous support of the white community, he did seem to have the sympathy of several members of the local elite. Whether or not their patronage was sufficient to win a reprieve for Watts is not known, as no documentation of his ultimate fate has been found.[89] Nonetheless, the case demonstrates that the white community was far from unified. Clearly, the alleged crime excited the community, and some citizens no doubt wished to see Watts hang. Still, others apparently not motivated by economic self-interest as a slaveholder might be displayed great empathy for the free black man and his predicament, a man who "had borne a character of singular respectability for one of his own caste."[90] Presumably his boosters were quite willing to sacrifice the reputation of an eleven-year-old white girl to save Caleb Watts's life.

Free black Tasco Thompson, a blacksmith from Frederick County, Virginia, was also found guilty in 1833 of the attempted rape of an eleven-year-old white girl, Mary Jane Stevens. However, the defense had presented mitigating circumstances that persuaded the jury foreman to recommend leniency. He cited

> the exceedingly disreputable character of the family of the said Stevens. . . . It was notorious that the mother had long entertained negroes, and that all her associations, with one or two exceptions were with blacks. . . . In a word she was below the level of the ordinary grade of free negroes. . . . There is no doubt that he [Thompson] repaired to the house of Mrs. Stevens in the belief that she would cheerfully submit to his embraces, as she doubtless had often done before, but finding her absent he probably supposed his embraces would be equally agreeable to her daughter. . . .[91]

The sins of the mother are the sins of the daughter. Furthermore, the foreman argued, had Mrs. Stevens been colored there would have been no case. The Stevenses "yielded their claims to the protection of the law by their voluntary associations with those whom the law distinguishes as their inferiors." In short, Mrs. Stevens acted "colored" and therefore should be treated as "colored."[92] In the eyes of the foreman of the jury, because of her liaisons with black men, Mrs. Stevens had forfeited the privilege that her white skin might have accorded her, not only for herself but also for her daughter.

As these and numerous other cases demonstrate, judicial vindication for white females who claimed to be victims of sexual assault at the hands of black men in the Old South was neither axiomatic nor unconditional. White women who claimed to have been sexually violated by African American men sometimes actively sough redress from the courts. They may or may not have received it. A court or community's decision to extend support hinged on any number of factors, not the least of which was a white woman's compliance with socially acceptable behavior. Deviant conduct severely undercut a white woman's demand for protection in the Old South. Those white females, or their network of female kin, who failed to obey the established code of race and gender conventions may have found their road to protection strewn with obstacles. Race, then, was far from being the sole determining factor in the outcome of these cases.

As far as can be determined, most of the females claiming to have been sexually assaulted by African American males were not members of the planter class. The records reveal very few instances in which elite women and girls charged rape by a slave or free black man.[93] If female members of the slaveholding class did levy accusations of rape or attempted rape against black men, mob action or plantation justice may have supplanted official authority in an endeavor to spare the women or girls the notoriety of a public trial. Such action, however, would run counter to slave owners' financial interest since masters did not receive compensation for the loss of slaves at the hands of de facto plantation executioners or lynching parties.[94] In cases involving female family members, however, revenge and pride could well have overridden the concern for financial compensation.

Most complainants were poor white women or girls. They frequently lacked a male protector, either father or husband. Some were described by the courts as "weak-minded" or "idiots."[95] Free black men and slaves seem to have assaulted poor white women and sometimes even to have gotten away with it, which indicates how marginal these women were to antebellum southern society.[96] As Victoria Bynum has observed, poverty defeminized and thus further marginalized white women in the Old South.[97] In strictly economic terms, poor white women in southern slave society were less valuable to elites than slaves were. And since slavery defined the status of most southern blacks, white racial solidarity across class lines was not necessary in the antebellum period; it became critical after emancipation, when African Americans, whose place in society was in constant flux, assumed unprecedented political positions and posed a threat to white elites.[98]

Whites in the Old South appear not to have been so blinded by fear and anxiety of black male sexual assault as to deny the accused procedural rights. In confrontations between two marginalized groups in the South, poor white females and African American males, race proved not to be the sole factor shaping the outcome or the responses of white observers. Instead, any of a myriad of motives could have prevailed in the development and denouements of these violent sexual dramas. Masters motivated by economic self-interest repeatedly utilized the judicial system in last-ditch efforts to keep their valuable property from the gallows.[99] In cases such as these, the slave's status as chattel worked effectively to save his life. By protecting their property, however, slaveholders turned their backs on women who shared their race but not their class.

More perplexing, perhaps, are the circumstances of free blacks who represented no such financial interest. Even so, community members, courts, and elected officials at times intervened to save the life of a convicted free black rapist.[100] Motives here are less apparent but could include any combination of humanitarianism, personalism, misogyny, class prejudice, personal grievance, and fear of job competition.[101]

The common denominator in sexual assault cases of both slave and free defendants, however, seems to be that white elites were animated by notions of class and gender that permitted them to hold poor white women and girls in such low regard that they would ally with African American men against the white female accusers.[102] This does not mean that every black man charged with raping a white female could with certainty expect reprieve or pardon. In this context, it is instructive to answer the question, Under what circumstances would whites ever ally with an accused black rapist? And more important, What do such cases reveal about the nature of race and class relations in the Old South? Recently, Nell Irvin Painter issued a challenge to historians of the South to go "beyond lazy characterizations in the singular" and to recognize "the complex and contradictory nature of southern society." "Though southern history must take race very seriously," Painter continued, "southern history must not stop with race."[103] If Professor Painter will permit the addendum, nor must southern historians use race as their starting point, a long-standing practice that has tended to mute the inherent contradictions of antebellum southern society. Was there far greater fluidity in race relations — and less in class relations — than historians heretofore have been willing to recognize?[104] The recent scholarship of Martha Hodes and Victoria Bynum suggests as much. Peculiar cross-racial alliances such as the ones played out in these rape cases underscore the complex web of contested loyalties confronting antebellum southerners. Appreciation of fissures in the mind of white southerners along the fault lines of gender, race, and class may lead to a more complete understanding of how various groups within southern society configured in relation to each other. Simply stated, race represented only one of a number of competing interests and frequently gave way to those other interests, often at the expense of racial allegiances.

In the slave South, then, protection was not bestowed unconditionally upon white women simply because of their race. Evidence suggests that poor white females, especially those who flouted sexual and racial mores, may have been stripped of protection when they claimed to have been sexually violated by a black man — if in fact protection had ever been accorded to them. Sometime after emancipation, however, poor white women began to receive some of the privileges and honor previously the sole domain of their wealthier, well-behaved cousins. As Jacquelyn Dowd Hall has noted, "the connotations of wealth and family background attached to the position of the lady in the antebellum South faded in the twentieth century, but the power of 'ladyhood' as a value construct remained."[105]

At the third trial of the Scottsboro Boys in 1933 the defense attorney attempted to discredit the testimony as well as the credibility of one of the accusers, whom he described as "a 'lewd woman'" and "a 'girl tramp'" "with the vicious quick wit of a wanton."[106] This strategy, which had been successfully used to defend black rapists in the first half of the nineteenth century, severely backfired in 1933. Underscoring how critical race had become in black-on-white rape cases, an outraged courtroom spectator later rebutted that the alleged victim "might be a fallen woman, but by God she is a white woman."[107] The defense attack elicited a more damaging response from the presiding judge, who in his charge to the jury reasoned that: "Where the woman charged to have been raped, as in this case is a white woman there is a very strong presumption under the law that she would not and did not yield voluntarily to intercourse with the defendant, a Negro; and this is true, whatever station in life the prosecutrix may occupy, whether she be the most despised, ignorant and abandoned woman of the community, or the spotless virgin and daughter of a prominent home of luxury and learning."[108]

By the 1930s the definition of interracial rape had evolved substantially from that of the antebellum period. No longer was a white woman's character considered a mitigating factor in the defense of a southern black man on trial for rape or attempted rape. "Interracial rape was not simply the assault on a white woman by a black man; it was sex between a black man and a white woman because most Southerners assumed that a white woman would never yield voluntarily to a black man. . . ."[109] The confluence of race and class relations, which in the Old South had been fluid and malleable, later became rigid and intractable as whites confronted the reconfigured economic, political, and social conditions of the postbellum South and recognized that African Americans were no longer completely under their control. In the process, poor white women, previously marginalized and disparaged by Old South elites, found themselves suddenly hoisted tenuously and precariously onto the pedestal of ladyhood and catapulted to their place in the twentieth-century white supremacist South.

NOTES

1. Box 294 (May 21–July 31, 1826), Letters Received, Virginia Executive Papers (hereinafter LR, VEP) (Library of Virginia, Richmond). The enumeration of this group of boxes is sometimes erratic and confusing, with some boxes labeled several times. Wherever possible I have noted the box number currently intended for use. See also entries for June 12, 1826, and November 20, 1827, pp. 114 and 188 of Southampton County Court Minutes, 1824–1830 (Library of Virginia) (microfilm reel no. 33). The author would like to thank Jan Lewis, Suzanne Lebsock, Thomas P. Slaughter, Deborah Gray White, Philip J. Schwarz, and David R. Goldfield for their valuable comments and encouragement. Funding for this project was made possible in part by research grants awarded by the North Caroliniana Society, the Virginia Historical Society, the American Historical Association, and Rutgers University. An earlier version of this article was presented at the Ninth Berkshire Conference on the History of Women, Vassar College, June 1993. Commentators Jane Turner Censer and Martha Hodes and the several anonymous referees from the *Journal of Southern History* deserve thanks for their thoughtful comments and criticism.

2. June 15, 1827 folder, box 299 (June 1–July 1827), LR, VEP.

3. *Ibid.* and October 22–31 folder, box 334 (August 1–October 31, 1833), LR, VEP. Rape or attempted rape of a white female by a free black male was a capital offense mandating the death sentence. Juries that found such defendants guilty were given no leeway in sentencing and were required to affix the death sentence. Sympathetic jurors finding a black man guilty of rape but with mitigating circumstances, however, could and did recommend pardoning to the governor. This procedure applied to free men of color as well as slaves. Virginia, *Acts* . . . (1824–25), Ch. 23, p. 22.

4. June 15, 1827 folder, box 299, LR, VEP. On the practices of governors and executive councils regarding pardons see Bertram Wyatt-Brown, "Community, Class, and Snopesian Crime: Local Justice in the Old South" in Orville Vernon Burton and Robert C. McMath, Jr., eds., *Class, Conflict, and Consensus: Antebellum Southern Community Studies* (Westport, Conn., and London, 1982), 194–97; Ernest James Clark, Jr.,

"Aspects of the North Carolina Slave Code, 1715–1860," *North Carolina Historical Review*, XXXIX (April 1962), 153; Edward L. Ayers, *Vengeance and Justice: Crime and Punishment in the 19th-Century American South* (New York and Oxford, 1984), 63–64; Philip J. Schwarz, *Twice Condemned: Slaves and the Criminal Laws of Virginia, 1705–1865* ([Baton Rouge], 1988), 23; Ulrich B. Phillips, *American Negro Slavery, A Survey of the Supply, Employment and Control of Negro Labor as Determined by the Plantation Regime* (New York, 1918; first paperback ed., Baton Rouge, 1966), 461–62; and "Slave Crime in Virginia," *American Historical Review*, XX (January 1915), 339; Michael S. Hindus, *Prison and Plantation: Crime, Justice, and Authority in Massachusetts and South Carolina, 1767–1878* (Chapel Hill, 1980), 104, 112–24, 155–56; Daniel J. Flanigan, "Criminal Procedure in Slave Trials in the Antebellum South," *Journal of Southern History*, XL (November 1974), 543–45; Arthur Howington, "The Treatment of Slaves and Free Blacks in the State and Local Courts of Tennessee" (Ph.D. dissertation, Vanderbilt University, 1982), 162; Lawrence M. Friedman, *Crime and Punishment in American History* (New York, 1993), 92; and Arthur P. Scott, *Criminal Law in Colonial Virginia* (Chicago, 1930), 116–21.

5. June 15, 1827 folder, box 299, LR, VEP.

6. Letter dated July 11, 1827, from William I. Everitt, jailer of Southampton County, box 299, LR, VEP.

7. The broader question, hotly debated among historians, of whether blacks, and particularly slaves, generally received fair trials, is beyond the scope of this essay, although a major argument here is that they were indeed afforded certain procedural rights that were routinely denied accused black rapists in the postbellum South. Among those historians who argue that accused slave criminals were treated fairly, at least to a certain degree, are Daniel Flanigan, "Criminal Procedure in Slave Trials," 537–64; A. E. Keir Nash, "Fairness and Formalism in the Trials of Blacks in the State Supreme Court of the Old South," *Virginia Law Review*, LVI (February 1970), 64–100; Nash, "A More Equitable Past? Southern Supreme Courts and the Protection of the Antebellum Negro," *North Carolina Law Review*, XLVIII (1970), 197–242; Nash, "The Texas Supreme Court and Trial Rights of Blacks, 1845–1860," *Journal of American History*, LVIII (December 1971), 622–42; Guion Griffis Johnson, *Ante-bellum North Carolina: A Social History* (Chapel Hill, 1937), 497–510; Clark, "Aspects of the North Carolina Slave Code," 148–64; R. H. Taylor, "Humanizing the Slave Code of North Carolina," *North Carolina Historical Review*, II (July 1925), 323–31; Ayers, *Vengeance and Justice*, 134–37; Royce G. Shingleton, "The Trial and Punishment of Slaves in Baldwin County, Georgia, 1812–1826," *Southern Humanities Review*, VIII (Winter 1974), 67–73; E. Merton Coulter, "Four Slave Trials in Elbert County, Georgia," *Georgia Historical Quarterly*, XLI (September 1957), 237–46; John C. Edwards, "Slave Justice in Four Middle Georgia Counties," *Georgia Historical Quarterly*, LVII (Summer 1973), 265–73; Eugene D. Genovese, *Roll, Jordan, Roll: The World the Slaves Made* (New York, 1974), 25–49; Martha Hodes, "Sex Across the Color Line: White Women and Black Men in the Nineteenth-Century American South" (Ph.D. dissertation, Princeton University, 1991), 77–78; and Patrick S. Brady, "Slavery, Race and the Criminal Law in Antebellum North Carolina: A Reconsideration of the Thomas Ruffin Court," *North Carolina Central Law Journal*, X (Spring 1979), 248–60. Those who draw less sanguine conclusions about "fairness" include Kenneth M. Stampp, *The Peculiar Institution: Slavery in the Ante-bellum South* (New York, 1956), 224–28; Alan D. Watson, "North Carolina Slave Courts, 1715–1785," *North Carolina Historical Review*, LX (January 1983), 24–36; Judith Kelleher Schafer, "The Long Arm of the Law: Slave Criminals and the Supreme Court in Antebellum Louisiana," *Tulane Law Review*, LX (June 1986), 1247–68; Bertram Wyatt-Brown, *Southern Honor: Ethics and Behavior in the Old South* (New York and Oxford, 1982), 387–89; Wyatt-Brown, "Community, Class and Snopesian Crime," 173–206; Michael S. Hindus, "Black Justice Under White Law: Criminal Prosecutions of Blacks in Antebellum South Carolina," *Journal of American History* LXIII (December 1976), 596–99; Friedman, *Crime and Punishment*, 91; and Schwarz, *Twice Condemned*, 23. A. E. Keir Nash dissects some of these important works in an

extensive historiographical analysis. See "Reason of Slavery: Understanding the Judicial Role in the Peculiar Institution," *Vanderbilt Law Review*, XXXII (January 1979), 7–218 and a response by Robert B. Jones, "Comment: Reason of Slavery: Understanding the Judicial Role in the Peculiar Institution," *ibid.*, 219–23.

8. For a discussion of the rape myth in the later nineteenth century see George M. Fredrickson, *The Black Image in the White Mind: The Debate on Afro-American Character and Destiny, 1817–1914* (New York and other cities, 1971), especially Chap. 9, "The Negro as Beast: Southern Negrophobia at the Turn of the Century"; Joel Williamson, *Crucible of Race: Black-White Relations in the American South Since Emancipation* (New York and Oxford, 1984), 111–39, 306–9; and Madelin Joan Olds, "The Rape Complex in the Postbellum South" (D.A. dissertation, Carnegie-Mellon University, 1989). For works dealing with twentieth-century subjects of the rape complex see Gunnar Myrdal, *An American Dilemma: The Negro Problem and Modern Democracy* (New York and London, 1944), 561–62, 587–92, 1355–56n41; Allison Davis, Burleigh B. Gardner, and Mary R. Gardner, *Deep South: A Social Anthropological Study of Caste and Class* (Chicago, 1941), 25–28; Jacquelyn Dowd Hall, *Revolt Against Chivalry: Jessie Daniel Ames and the Women's Campaign Against Lynching* (rev. ed.: New York, 1993); and Nancy MacLean, *Behind the Mask of Chivalry: The Making of the Second Ku Klux Klan* (New York and Oxford, 1994), 128–57. A number of black rape cases in the 1930s received considerable contemporaneous attention and have been the subject of recent analysis. Consult Dan T. Carter, *Scottsboro. A Tragedy of the American South* (Baton Rouge, 1969); James Goodman, "Stories of Scottsboro" (Ph.D. dissertation, Princeton University, 1990); Goodman, *Stories of Scottsboro* (New York, 1994); James R. McGovern, *Anatomy of a Lynching. The Killing of Claude Neal* (Baton Rouge and London, 1982); Charles H. Martin, "Oklahoma's 'Scottsboro' Affair: The Jess Hollins Rape Case, 1931–1936," *South Atlantic Quarterly*, LXXIX (Spring 1980), 175–88; and Beth Crabb, "May 1930: White Man's Justice for a Black Man's Crime," *Journal of Negro History*, LXXV (Winter–Spring 1990), 29–40. For post–World War II cases of black southerners accused of improper sexual advances toward or rape of white women see Stephen J. Whitfield, *A Death in the Delta: The Story of Emmett Till* (New York and London, 1988); Eric W. Rise, "Race, Rape, and Radicalism: The Case of the Martinsville Seven, 1949–1951," *Journal of Southern History*, LVIII (August 1992), 461–90; Charles H. Martin, "The Civil Rights Congress and Southern Black Defendants," *Georgia Historical Quarterly*, LXXI (Spring 1987), 25–52; Steven F. Lawson, David R. Colburn, and Darryl Paulson, "Groveland: Florida's Little Scottsboro," *Florida Historical Quarterly*, LXV (July 1986), 1–26; and Nick Davies, *White Lies: Rape, Murder, and Justice Texas Style* (New York, 1991).

9. With few exceptions, the cases cited here are those in which the defendant was charged officially with rape or attempted rape, sometimes referred to as ravishment. Two cases of murder/rape are included. I have made no attempt to scrutinize assault and battery (also referred to as affray) cases that may have involved females resisting sexual assault. It should also be noted that an overwhelmingly disproportionate number of extant documents dealing with black sexual assault involve those males actually convicted of rape or attempted rape. Transcripts, many of them rich in detail and often accompanied by judges' and juries' opinions, were routinely forwarded to the governor and/or the executive council for review and therefore are filed among state papers. A black man acquitted of rape or attempted rape had no need for his court records to be sent to state officials. The archival result is that a wealth of material exists on this topic and is readily found in state repositories. However, only dogged and systematic research in county court minute and order books will provide the information required to make more reliable generalizations about rape and race.

10. This essay examines cases in all former Confederate states in addition to the border states Maryland, Missouri, and Kentucky, focusing, as stated in the text, more closely on those in Virginia and North Carolina. The primary sources yielding information about accused black rapists include local and appellate court records and documents, petitions and letters to governors, and newspapers. My decision to look at these two states was

shaped by a number of factors—primarily the availability and preservation of large numbers of official documents and the extensive scholarship on these two states for both the antebellum and postbellum periods. For those readers who might take exception with my decision to concentrate on Virginia and North Carolina, citing their geographic proximity to "the North," I would beg two considerations. First, though the notion of "the South" encompasses the extensive diversity and complexities of that region's past, all southern states, including North Carolina and Virginia, shared the institution of forced enslavement of African Americans through the Civil War. Secondly, one need only look to twentieth-century statistics on rape, race, and execution to discern how deeply the "rape complex" was embedded in the cultures of both Virginia and North Carolina. Virginia, for example, was one of only three states in the country that continued to punish attempted rape with death. Furthermore, in the years from 1908 through 1962, fifty-four black Virginians were executed for either rape or attempted rape while not a single white man was sentenced to death for the same crime. This trend is mirrored in North Carolina. From 1801 through 1861, sixty-three blacks were sentenced to die for rape; seven whites and two Indians were sentenced to death for the same crime. In William J. Bowers, *Legal Homicide: Death as Punishment in America, 1864–1982* (Boston, 1974), 514–19, 472–79; and Donald H. Partington, "The Incidence of the Death Penalty for Rape in Virginia," *Washington and Lee Law Review,* XXII (Spring 1965), 43–75. Further research may demonstrate whether findings presented in this study apply to other former slaveholding states.

11. In all cases the alleged victim was a white woman or girl as the sexual assault of a black female slave generally was not a capital offense and was not even a crime in some states. Nonetheless, occasionally black men appeared in court on charges of raping or attempting to rape black females, both enslaved and free. See citations in note 34, Susan Brownmiller, *Against Our Will: Men, Women, and Rape* (New York, 1975), 162; Catherine Clinton, "Bloody Terrain: Freedwomen, Sexuality and Violence During Reconstruction," *Georgia Historical Quarterly,* LXXVI (Summer 1992), 315; and Clinton, "'Southern Dishonor': Flesh, Blood, Race, and Bondage," in Carol Bleser, ed., *In Joy and Sorrow: Women, Family, and Marriage in the Victorian South, 1830–1900* (New York, 1991), 65; Deborah Gray White, *Ar'n't I a Woman? Female Slaves in the Plantation South* (New York and London, 1985), 152; Karen A. Getman, "Sexual Control in the Slaveholding South: The Implementation and Maintenance of a Racial Caste System," *Harvard Women's Law Journal,* VII (Spring 1984), 135; Thomas R. R. Cobb, *An Inquiry Into the Law of Negro Slavery in the United States of America* (New York, 1858; rpt. 1968), 99; and Friedman, *Crime and Punishment,* 93.

12. Genovese, *Roll, Jordan, Roll,* 461–62.

13. Fredrickson, *The Black Image in the White Mind,* 204–9; and Williamson, *Crucible of Race,* especially Chap. 4, "The Rise of the Radicals."

14. Francis A. Shoup, "Uncle Tom's Cabin Forty Years After," *Sewanee Review,* II (November 1893), 96.

15. Henry McHatton, "The Sexual Status of the Negro—Past and Present," *American Journal of Dermatology and Genito-urinary Diseases,* X (January 1906), 8.

16. Myrta Lockett Avary, *Dixie After the War* (New York, 1906), 384.

17. John Roach Straton, "Will Education Solve the Race Problem?" *North American Review,* CLXX (June 1900), 786–87 and 789.

18. Phillips, *American Negro Slavery,* 458–60 (quotation on p. 459).

19. *Ibid.,* 454 (first quoted phrase) and 456 (second and third quotations). Phillips nonetheless cites, as does Kenneth Stampp, instances of mob violence directed at alleged black rapists. See Phillips, *American Negro Slavery,* 461–63; and Stampp, *Peculiar Institution,* 190–91; as well as Clement Eaton, "Mob Violence in the Old South," *Mississippi Valley Historical Review,* XXIX (December 1942), 367; and Paul D. Lack, "Slavery and Vigilantism in Austin, Texas, 1840–1860," *Southwestern Historical Quarterly,* LXXXV (July 1981), 1–20.

20. W. J. Cash, *The Mind of the South* (New York, 1941; page numbers from Vintage paperback ed.), 119 and 89 (quotations), 88–89, 116–20, and 131. Works written at ap-

proximately the same time as Cash's book that analyzed the connection between sex and race relations include John Dollard, *Caste and Class in a Southern Town* (Garden City, N.Y., 1937), especially pages 134 and 135; Lillian Smith, *Killers of a Dream* (New York, 1949; rpt., 1961), especially pages 145, 121–24, and 169; and Davis, Gardner, and Gardner, *Deep South*, 25–28. On the nineteenth-century conception of sexual passionlessness as a womanly ideal see Nancy F. Cott, "Passionlessness: An Interpretation of Victorian Sexual Ideology, 1790–1850," *Signs*, IV (Winter 1978), 219–36; Robert M. Ireland, "The Libertine Must Die: Sexual Dishonor and the Unwritten Law in the Nineteenth-Century United States," *Journal of Social History*, XXIII (Fall 1989), 28–29; Jan Lewis, "The Republican Wife: Virtue and Seduction in the Early Republic," *William and Mary Quarterly*, 3d Ser., XLIV (October 1987), 681–82; and Estelle B. Freedman, "Sexuality in Nineteenth-Century America: Behavior, Ideology, and Politics," *Reviews in American History*, X (December 1982), 199–200, 202, and 208. On the desexualization of southern white women see John D'Emilio and Estelle B. Freedman, *Intimate Matters: A History of Sexuality in America* (New York, 1988), 94–95; Catherine Clinton, *The Plantation Mistress: Woman's World in the Old South* (New York, 1982), 110–11 and 209; Smith, *Killers of the Dream*, 141, 120–21; and Adele Logan Alexander, *Ambiguous Lives: Free Women of Color in Rural Georgia, 1789–1879* (Fayetteville, Ark., 1991), 64. Elizabeth Fox-Genovese questions this characterization and argues that "slaveholding culture emphasized control of female sexuality; it did not deny its existence." *Within the Plantation Household: Black and White Women of the Old South* (Chapel Hill and London, 1988), 235–36 (quotation on p. 236) and 240. Similarly, Steven M. Stowe documents the "culture of romantic love" embraced by southern cities as well as the concern espoused by moral advisors for "the latent power of female passion," Stowe, *Intimacy and Power in the Old South: Ritual in the Lives of the Planters* (Baltimore and London, 1987), 50–121 (first quotation on p. 96; second on p. 54). See also Wyatt-Brown, *Southern Honor*, 293; and Dorothy Ann Gay, "The Tangled Skein of Romanticism and Violence in the Old South: The Southern Response to Abolitionism and Feminism, 1830–1861" (Ph.D. dissertation, University of North Carolina, Chapel Hill, 1975), 105–6.

21. Winthrop D. Jordan, *White Over Black: American Attitudes Toward the Negro, 1550–1812* (Chapel Hill, 1968), 148 (first quotation) and 152 (second quotation).

22. Lawrence J. Friedman, *The White Savage: Racial Fantasies in the Postbellum South* (Englewood Cliffs, N.J., 1970), 11; Earl E. Thorpe, *The Old South: A Psychohistory* (Durham, N.C., 1972), 122; Peter H. Wood, *Black Majority: Negroes in Colonial South Carolina from 1670 through the Stono Rebellion* (New York, 1974), 236–37; and Getman, "Sexual Control in the Slaveholding South," 134. Attesting to the staying power of Jordan's work is the recent article by Peter W. Bardaglio in which he claims that "white southerners, both inside and outside the legal system, widely shared the belief that black men were obsessed with the desire to rape white women." Bardaglio, "Rape and the Law in the Old South: 'Calculated to Excite Indignation in Every Heart'," *Journal of Southern History*, LX (November 1994), 752. A few notable works do, however, dissent; for example, Genovese, *Roll, Jordan, Roll*, 33–34; and Fox-Genovese, *Within the Plantation Household*, 291. Most recently the work by Martha Hodes suggests that white fears of black male sexual threats did not pervade the antebellum or even the war years. In "Wartime Dialogues on Illicit Sex: White Women and Black Men," she writes that "while whites feared slave uprisings during the Civil War, no great tide of sexual alarm engulfed white southerners as white men left white women at home with slave men." Hodes's essay appears in Catherine Clinton and Nina Silber, eds., *Divided Houses: Gender and the Civil War* (New York and Oxford, 1992), 239. See also Hodes, "Sex Across the Color Line," 9–10, 40, and 79. A number of scholars outside the discipline of history have accepted that white fears of black rape originated in the slave South. See, for example, sociological studies on race and sex by Calvin C. Hernton, *Sex and Racism in America* (New York, 1965), 15–19; as well as Coramae Richey Mann and Lance H. Selva, "The Sexualization of Racism: The Black as Rapist and White Justice," *Western Journal of Black Studies*, III (No. 3, 1979), 169–70.

23. This is not to deny the existence of white beliefs about the innate promiscuity and licentiousness of both black men and women that Winthrop Jordan has rooted in the earliest English contacts with Africa (see *White over Black*, 24–40). I do, however, take issue with those who make the leap from assumptions about black men as libidinous to those about black men as rapists. Though related, these two concepts are not one and the same. For a discussion on white perceptions about African American female sexuality in the Old South see White, *Ar'n't I a Woman?* 29–46, 60–61; D'Emilio and Freedman, *Intimate Matters*, 97, 101; Melton A. McLaurin, *Celia: A Slave* (Athens, Ga., and London, 1991), 22–23; Alexander, *Ambiguous Lives*, 64 and 144; Clinton, *Plantation Mistress*, 222; Angela Y. Davis, *Women, Race, and Class* (New York, 1983), 174 and 182; Fox-Genovese, *Within the Plantation Household*, 292 and 325–26; Genovese, *Roll, Jordan, Roll*, 427–28; Joseph T. Glatthaar, *Forged in Battle: The Civil War Alliance of Black Soldiers and White Officers* (New York and London, 1990), 91; Mary Frances Berry and John W. Blassingame, *Long Memory: The Black Experience in America* (New York and Oxford, 1982), 115–16; Hodes, "Sex Across the Color Line," 41; Getman, "Sexual Control in the Slaveholding South," 115–17; Margaret A. Burnham, "An Impossible Marriage: Slave Law and Family Law," *Law and Inequality*, V (July 1987), 189 and 221–22; and Hazel V. Carby, *Reconstructing Womanhood: The Emergence of the Afro-American Woman Novelist* (New York and Oxford, 1987), 20–39.

24. On white fears of slave violence consult Herbert Aptheker, *American Negro Slave Revolts* (New York, 1943); Phillips, *American Negro Slavery*, 473–76 and 481–88; Stampp, *Peculiar Institution*, 127–28 and 136–38; John W. Blassingame, *The Slave Community: Plantation Life in the Antebellum South* (rev. ed.: New York and Oxford, 1979), 230–38; Williamson, *Crucible of Race*, 117; Johnson, *Ante-bellum North Carolina*, 510–21; Jeffrey Crow, *The Black Experience in Revolutionary North Carolina* (Raleigh, 1977), 40, 56–61, and 85–95; and Fredrickson, *Black Image in the White Mind*, 8–9. Fears of slave conspiracy and uprising during the Civil War are explored in Winthrop Jordan, *Tumult and Silence at Second Creek: An Inquiry into a Civil War Slave Conspiracy* (Baton Rouge and London, 1993).

25. Some of the grounds for appellate reversals included the faulty wording of indictments, especially those that failed to state the race of the victim (*Henry v. State of Tennessee*, 4 Humphreys 270 [1843]; *Grandison v. State of Tennessee*, 2 Humphreys 451 [1841]; *Commonwealth v. Mann*, 2 Va. Cas. 210 [1820]; *State v. Charles*, 1 Fla. 298 [1847]); procedural improprieties (*State v. Jesse*, 19 N.C. 297 [1837]); coerced confessions (*State v. Gilbert*, 2 La. Ann. 244 [1847]); failure to allow a slave owner to testify on behalf of his or her slave (*State v. Peter*, 14 La. Ann. 527 [1859]); the absence of force in the sexual assault, namely through the assailant's impersonation of the accuser's husband (*Lewis v. State*, 30 Ala. 54 [1857] and *Wyatt v. State of Tennessee*, 2 Swan 394 [1852]); and the youth of the accused rapist (*State v. Sam*, 60 N.C. 293 [1864]).

26. There is evidence to suggest that even after the Civil War some black men accused of sexually assaulting white women or girls received a sympathetic hearing from certain quarters of various white communities. Laura Edwards recounts that sixty men petitioned Governor William W. Holden of North Carolina for the pardon of William Somerville, convicted in 1869 of the attempted rape of a white woman. See "Sexual Violence, Gender and Reconstruction in Granville County, North Carolina," *North Carolina Historical Review*, LXVIII (July 1991), 250. Edwards also observes that most cases involving black males on trial for the rape or attempted rape of white females during this highly volatile and violent period generally proceeded through the courts with little excitement. And as late as 1881 the trial of Morris Locke, a black sixteen-year-old, resulted in a hung jury. He stood accused of raping an eight-year-old white girl. A subsequent trial found him not guilty of the rape but guilty of assault with intent to commit a rape for which he was sentenced to fifteen years of hard labor at the state penitentiary. In Rowan County Criminal Action Papers, 1846–1883 (1881 and 1882 folders) and Rowen County Superior Court Minute Docket, 1879–1883, pp. 332, 337, 346, 349, 369, 370, 429, and 446 (North Carolina Department of Cultural Resources, Division of Archives and History, Raleigh). These examples are bolstered by the

conclusions of Joel Williamson who writes, "For a generation after the Civil War, Southern whites seemed to have no greater fear of black men as rapists than they had of white men committing the same crime," *Crucible of Race*, 183.

27. Winston-Salem *Journal*, October 15, 1932, quoted in Carter, *Scottsboro*, 105. See also Goodman, *Stories of Scottsboro*, 218–20.

28. Alabama, *Digest of the Laws* . . . (Toulmin, 1823), p. 207; Arkansas, *Acts* . . . (1842–43), p. 19; Florida, *Acts* . . . *of the Territory* . . . (1828), sec. 19, p. 53 and *Acts* . . . *of the Territory* . . . (1832), no. 55, sec 2, p. 63; Louisiana., *Acts* . . . *of the Territory of Orleans* (1806), ch. 29, sec 1, p. 122 and *Acts* . . . (1855), no. 120, sec. 4, p. 130; Mississippi, *Laws* . . . (June 1822), sec. 11, p. 207; North Carolina, *Revised Code* (Moore, Biggs, and Rodman, 1855), ch. 34, sec. 5, p. 203; South Carolina, *Alphabetical Digest of the Public Statute Law* (3 vols; Brevard, 1814), I, title 21, sec. 17, p. 77; and Virginia, *Statutes at Large* (3 vols.; Shepherd, 1835–1836), I, 178 (Act of 1792). On antebellum southern rape statutes and race see Getman, "Sexual Control in the Slaveholding South," 134–36; Jennifer Wriggins, "Rape, Racism, and the Law," *Harvard Women's Law Journal*, VI (Fall 1983), 105–6; and Bardaglio, "Rape and the Law in the Old South," 751–60.

29. *State v. Alfred Goings* (alias Terry), 20 N.C. 289 (1839); *State v. Jesse Farmer*, 26, N.C. 224 (1844); and Bertie County Superior Court Minutes, March 19, 22, 23 and September 16, 1844 (North Carolina Department of Cultural Resources, Division of Archives and History). Death was not the automatic penalty for white rapists of young girls, however. In 1810 William Dick, a white laborer from Monroe County, Virginia, allegedly raped Nancy Maddy, a girl between ten and twelve years old. Dick was sentenced to eighteen years of solitary confinement in the state penitentiary but was pardoned by the governor after fourteen years. See September 11–20, 1810 folder, box 168 (August–September 1810), LR, VEP.

30. Alabama, *Acts* . . . (1840–41), ch. 3, sec. 14, p. 124 (life imprisonment); Arkansas, *Acts* (1838), sec. 4, p. 122 (5 to 21 years); Georgia, *Acts*. . . . (1816), sec. 33, p. 151 (2 to 20 years hard labor); Kentucky, *Acts*. . . . (1801), ch. 67, sec. 7, p. 120 (10 to 21 years); Louisiana, *Acts* . . . *of the Territory of Orleans* (1804), ch. 50, sec. 2, p. 416 (life imprisonment at hard labor); Mississippi, *Laws* (1839), tit. III sec. 22, p. 116 (not less than 10 years); Missouri, *Revised Statutes* . . . (W. C. Jones, 1845), art. II, ch. 47, sec. 26, p. 348 (not less than 5 years); Tennessee, *Acts* . . . (1819), sec. 4, pp. 195–96 (5 to 15 years) and *Acts* (1829), ch. 23, sec 13–14, p. 29 (10 to 21 years); Texas, *A Digest of the General Statute Laws* (Oldham and White, 1859), tit. 17, ch. 6, art. 529, p. 523 (5 to 15 years); Virginia, *Digest of Laws* (Tate, 1823), p. 127 (Act of 1819) (10 to 21 years); and *Code of Virginia* (Patton and Robinson, 1849), tit. 54, ch. 191, sec 15, p. 725 (10 to 20 years).

31. State Penitentiary Prisoner Registers, 1863–1876, Records of the Department of Corrections, Record Group 42 (Library of Virginia).

32. Peter Bardaglio has put forth the racial disparity in the composition of antebellum southern rape statutes as evidence of southern white anxieties about "black sexual aggression." "Rape or attempted rape of a white woman by a bondsman demanded especially fierce retribution because it challenged slavery and the racial order of southern society." Bardaglio, "Rape and the Law in the Old South," 752 and 755. There are limitations, however, on forming societal generalizations on the basis of statutes and/or appellate decisions. William M. Wiecek cautions that "statutes are not evidence of actual social conditions. When a statute prohibits a certain type of behavior . . . it is no more reasonable to infer from the enactment of the statute that such behavior was common than to infer that it was rare. Nor can we assume that the statutes were rigorously enforced by vigilant authorities." Wiecek, "The Statutory Law of Slavery and Race in the Thirteen Mainland Colonies of British America," *William and Mary Quarterly*, 3d. Ser., XXXIV (April 1977), 279. Similarly, G. Edward White outlines what he considers to be the problems of legal historians relying too heavily upon appellate law. White, "The Appellate Opinion as Historical Source Material," *Journal of Interdisciplinary History*, I (Spring 1971), 491–509. See also Friedman, *Crime and Punishment*, 256.

33. Virginia, *Acts* (1847–48), tit. 2, ch. 3, sec. 15, p. 97 (pertaining to whites) and tit.

2, ch. 12, sec. 4, p. 125 (pertaining to slaves). For statutes specifically stating that African Americans who had been convicted of rape or attempted rape of white females were to be sentenced to death, see Alabama, *Acts* (1830–31), sec. 1, p. 13 and *Acts* (1840–41), ch. 15, sec. 3, p. 188; Georgia, *Acts* (1816), sec. 1, p. 15; Kentucky, *Acts* (1802), ch. 53, sec 19, p. 116; Louisiana, *Acts* (1806), ch. 33, sec. 7, p. 198; Mississippi, *Acts* (1813) sec. 6, p. 10; North Carolina, *Acts* . . . (1823), ch. 51, p. 42; South Carolina, *Acts* . . . (1843), no. 2893, p. 258; Tennessee, *Public Acts* (1835–36), ch. 19, sec. 10, p. 92; Texas, *Digest of the Laws* (Hartley, 1850), art. 2539, p. 777; and Virginia, *Acts* (1847–48), tit. 2, ch. 12, sec 4, p. 125 (slaves) and tit. 2, ch. 13, sec. 1, p. 126 (free blacks).

34. On the rape and sexual exploitation of enslaved females see Thelma Jennings, "'Us Colored Women Had to Go Through a Plenty': Sexual Exploitation of African American Slave Women," *Journal of Women's History*, I (Winter 1990), 45–74; Clinton, *Plantation Mistress*, 201–22; Clinton, "'Southern Dishonor,'" 57–58 and 61–68; Clinton, "Bloody Terrain," 315; Darlene Clark Hine, "Rape and the Inner Lives of Black Women in the Midwest: Preliminary Thoughts on Culture of Dissemblance," *Signs: Journal of Women in Culture and Society*, XIV (Summer 1989), 912; Wriggins, "Rape, Racism, and the Law," 118–19; Berry and Blassingame, *Long Memory*, 117–18; Alexander, *Ambiguous Lives*, 64–66; Harriet A. Jacobs, *Incidents in the Life of a Slave Girl, Written by Herself*, edited by Jean Fagan Yellin (Cambridge, Mass., and London, 1987), 27–29; D'Emilio and Freedman, *Intimate Matters*, 100–103; Jacqueline Jones, *Labor of Love, Labor of Sorrow: Black Women, Work, and the Family from Slavery to the Present* (New York, 1985), 149; McLaurin, *Celia*; Genovese, *Roll, Jordan, Roll*, 422–29; White, *Ar'n't I Woman?*, 152–53 and 164–65; Stampp, *Peculiar Institution*, 353–61; Brenda Stevenson, "Distress and Discord in Virginia Slave Families, 1830–1860," in Bleser, ed., *In Joy and Sorrow*, 121–22; Getman, "Sexual Control in the Slaveholding South," 142–51; Burnham, "Impossible Marriage," 199–200; and Steven E. Brown, "Sexuality and the Slave Community," *Phylon*, XLVII (Spring 1981), 7–8. Though rare, there are a few instances of men brought before southern courts charged with sexually assaulting women of color; for instance, in 1797 a Virginian slave was hanged for the rape of a mulatto woman, 1799 folder, Condemned Blacks Executed or Transported, Condemned Slaves (hereinafter CS), Auditor of Public Accounts (hereinafter APA), Record Group 48 (Library of Virginia). Three cases of rape of female slaves by male slaves appeared before the Virginia courts from 1850 through 1858. In 1856 Coleman was found guilty of raping a slave child, Harriet, and was sentenced to transportation out of the county, CS, Transported, 1857 and December 1856 folder, LR, VEP. Charges were brought and subsequently dropped against William, a Loudoun County slave, for raping a female slave in 1858. Schwarz, *Twice Condemned*, 293n21. John was sentenced to transportation for the rape of a slave in Spotsylvania County. Bond dated January 21, 1850, Bonds for Transportation of Condemned Slaves (hereinafter Bonds) 1840–1857 (Library of Virginia); and Schwarz, *Twice Condemned*, 293n21. Several cases of slaves raping free women of color have also been found. Tom, a slave in New Kent County, was sentenced to hang for raping Dolly Boasman, a married free mulatto woman. He was spared and transported instead, CS, Transported, 1810 and January 11–20 folder, box 164 (January–February 20, 1810), LR, VEP. Charles, a Halifax County slave, was sentenced to transportation for the rape of Ann Freeman, Halifax County Court Minute Book, July 1857, p. 341 (Library of Virginia) (microfilm reel no. 73); CS, Transported, 1857; and Bond dated September 18, 1857, Bonds 1840–1857. In December 1864 Henry Robertson, a Wythe County slave, was tried for the rape of Mary Jane Wilson, a twenty-eight-year-old free woman of color, Pardon Papers, January–April 1865, LR, VEP. The Raleigh *Register and North Carolina Gazette* noted on April 12, 1836, that Jones Kiff (no mention is made of his race) was tried and acquitted in the rape of an eighty-year-old free black woman. Only one case of white-on-black sexual assault appears to have resulted in conviction. In 1858 Edward B. Ledbetter of Sussex County, Virginia, was sentenced to ten years in the state penitentiary for the assault and rape of a twenty-four-year-old "free negress." Relying on a jury's recommendation for clemency, however, the governor par-

doned Ledbetter, who was imprisoned three years later for raping another free woman of color, August 1863 folder and document dated December 1861, Pardon Papers, January–June 1862, and July–November 1863, LR, VEP. Despite these instances of African American women bringing charges of rape before officials, their numbers are indeed few. Since most statutes specified the race of the victim in sexual assault as white, females of color found that by and large statutes did not protect them from rape. Such was the judicial logic in 1859 in the case of George v. The State of Mississippi in which a male slave was found guilty of raping a female slave and sentenced to hang. That state's supreme court ruled in favor of the convicted rapist, finding that the statutory definition of rape was race-specific. In fact, one justice reasoned, "The crime of rape does not exist in this State between African slaves." George v. State, 37 Miss. 316 (1859). A Mississippi statute passed in 1859 did, however, outlaw the rape of a negro or mulatto child under the age of twelve. See Mississippi, Laws (1859–60) ch. 62, sec. 1, p. 102.

35. Two noted legal historians have observed that while punishments prescribed in sexual assault statutes grew harsher for men of color, juries at times appeared reticent in administering severe penalties. See A. Leon Higginbotham Jr. and Barbara K. Kopytoff, "Racial Purity and Interracial Sex in the Law of Colonial and Antebellum Virginia," Georgetown Law Journal, LXXVII (August 1989), 2017–18.

36. Victoria E. Bynum, Unruly Women: The Politics of Social and Sexual Control in the Old South (Chapel Hill and London, 1992).

37. For more on white women whose sexual behavior deviated from prescribed antebellum mores and beliefs about those women, see Bynum, Unruly Women, especially Chapter 4, "Punishing Deviant Women: The State as Patriarch"; Hodes, "Sex Across the Color Line," 41–42 and 63; Hodes, "Wartime Dialogues," 235; Clinton, Plantation Mistress, 204 and 210; Clinton "'Southern Dishonor'," 58–60; D'Emilio and Freedman, Intimate Matters, 96 and 103–4; James Hugo Johnston, Race Relations in Virginia and Miscegenation in the South, 1776–1860 (Amherst, Mass., 1970), 253–68. Several works assert that women of the planter class were monitored so closely that they did not have the opportunity to engage in illicit sexual liaisons. See Clinton, Plantation Mistress, 72–74, 102, and 109; Fox-Genovese, Within the Plantation Household, 208 and 241; Wyatt-Brown, Southern Honor, 293–94, 298, and 315–19. Wyatt-Brown further argues that nearly all white women who willingly engaged in sexual relationships with African American men were "women with defective notions of their social position" (p. 315) and were quite probably "mentally retarded or else had a very poor self-image" (p. 316).

38. Of course white women who brought sexual assault charges against white men were also subjected to interrogation about their sexual histories. See Edwards, "Sexual Violence, Gender, and Reconstruction in Granville County," 244. See also the following cases of two white Virginia males: In 1846 eighteen-year-old William B. O. Franklin was found guilty of raping Mrs. Lucinda Dearing, who some petitioners claimed was a lover of Franklin's who cried rape to "appease the jealousy of her husband." December 1846 folder, box 384 (November–December 1846), LR, VEP; and William Ball, a father, husband, and soldier during the Civil War, was convicted of raping a woman described as a "common strumpet" and was sentenced to twelve years in the state penitentiary, October 1863 folder, Pardon Papers, July–November 1863, and January–April 1865, LR, VEP.

39. Six years prior to this case the Virginia legislature passed a law allowing the governor and the executive council to sell condemned slaves to persons who promised to carry them out of the country, never to return to Virginia. This allowed the state to recoup some of the loss that resulted from compensation of slaveowners of condemned slaves. From 1801 through 1864, fifty-four Virginia slaves were transported after their conviction of rape or attempted rape. In Schwarz, Twice Condemned, 27–28, and Schwarz, "The Transportation of Slaves from Virginia, 1801–1865," Slavery and Abolition: A Journal of Comparative Studies, VII (1986), 216–21. Michael Hindus asserts in his study of antebellum South Carolina that high rates of executions of slaves (six per

year in the period 1800–1855) indicate that "[b]anishment was clearly not a complete substitute for execution." Hindus, "Black Execution Under White Law," 596–97.

40. Letter of June 4, 1807, from P. R. Gilmer, June 1–18 folder, box 145 (May–June 1807), VEP. It is worth noting that the same arguments presented in this case by the defense—a woman's past sexual history, no evidence of force—were typically used well into the twentieth century to defend men against the charge of rape. It has only been relatively recently that statutory reforms have been initiated to protect victims of sexual assault and empower prosecutors to disallow such evidence. See Brownmiller, *Against Our Will*, 371–74, and 384–87.

41. June 1–18, 1807 folder, box 145, VEP; and CS, Transported, 1807.

42. May 9, 1803, LR, VEP, as quoted in Johnston, *Race Relations in Virginia*, 260.

43. *Ibid.*; and CS, Transported, 1803. While transportation was certainly preferable to death, one shouldn't underrate the possible harshness of this punishment. Banishment most assuredly meant separation from one's family network. Furthermore, masters frequently threatened their slaves with sale to states in the Deep South. Slaves and masters alike seem to have believed that conditions were far worse there than in the upper tier of slaveholding states. My appreciation to Philip Schwarz for making this point.

44. *Cato v. State*, 9 Fla. 163 (1860), at 165 (first quotation), 166 (second quotation), and 173 (last two quotations). This appellate reasoning was not extraordinary in the sense that a number of southern judges and justices seem to have fancied themselves paternalists of last resort. This tendency for judges to assume the role of judicial patriarch appears to be part of a wider nineteenth-century trend observed by Michael Grossberg in issues of domestic relations. *Governing the Hearth: Law and the Family in Nineteenth-Century America* (Chapel Hill and London, 1985), 291–307.

45. *Cato v. State*, at 174, 165, 181, and 186. On Lord Hale's quote on rape see Brownmiller, *Against Our Will*, 369.

46. Philip J. Schwarz refers to this case also, although he depicts Baker as a free black (*Twice Condemned*, 207). He bases this characterization upon testimony to the court by Baker herself in which she mentions having lost her "register." Neither the 1820 nor 1830 censuses list Baker. The court documents repeatedly refer to her as a "free white woman," so if she was a woman of color, the court did not recognize her as such. Contradictory classifications on the basis of race were not at all out of the ordinary, exemplifying, according to Adele Logan Alexander's recent work on free Georgian women of color, "the shifting, questionable, and amorphous lines of both race and freedom." Alexander, *Ambiguous Lives*, 63.

47. June 1–20, 1829 folder, box 311 (May 1–July 20, 1829), LR, VEP.

48. *Ibid.*

49. Drucilla Kirkland is repeatedly referred to as "Mrs. Kirkland" although she revealed during her deposition that she had never married. More curious is the nature of her relationship with Amy Baker, which was never addressed by court officials or by the two principals themselves. Neither woman appears in the federal decennial censuses of 1820 and 1830.

50. June 1–20, 1829 folder, box 311, LR, VEP. Mrs. Kirkland's insistence at having personally witnessed coitus suggests an extraordinary lack of privacy, similar to that documented in eighteenth-century New England. See Nancy F. Cott, "Eighteenth-Century Family and Social Life as Revealed in Massachusetts Divorce Records," *Journal of Social History*, X (Fall 1976), 20–43.

51. June 1–20, 1829 folder, box 311, LR, VEP.

52. *Ibid.*

53. *Ibid.*

54. *Ibid.*

55. Amy Baker testified that Lewis assaulted her with such "great violence" that after the assault she was "so weak that she could scarcely move her body." Drucilla Kirkland swore that after the assault and while the accused slept she had to bathe Baker's legs and feet and minister to her before Baker could walk. *Ibid.*

56. Lewis was executed July 24, 1829. See CS, Executed, 1829.

57. June 1–20, 1829 folder, box 311, LR, VEP.

58. June 21–30, 1829 folder, *ibid.*

59. 1806–1839 folder, Bonds for Transportation, and August 7, 1829 entry in "A list of slaves and free persons of color received into the penitentiary of Virginia for sale and transportation, June 25, 1816-Feb 1, 1842," both in APA.

60. July 1831 folder, box 320 (July–August 1831), LR, VEP.

61. *Ibid.*

62. Letter from Hamilton Rogers, July 12, 1831, and letter from Burr W. Harrison, July 7, 1831, *ibid.*

63. Letter dated July 9, 1831, Leesburg [author's name illegible], *ibid.*

64. Petition dated July 11, 1831, Leesburg, *ibid.*

65. Wyatt-Brown, "Community, Class, and Snopesian Crime," 189.

66. July 1831 folder, box 320, LR, VEP; and CS, Executed, 1831. In 1840 the Virginia legislature modified its compensation policy to require that the value of the condemned slave be adjusted to market value and the purchaser be told of the slave's offense. Virginia *Acts* (1839–40), ch. 61, sec. 1, p. 51. Compensation rates for executed slaves varied widely over time and from state to state. Georgia, for example, offered slaveowners no compensation whatsoever (Edwards, "Slave Justice in Four Middle Georgia Counties," 266). By most accounts colonial compensation rates appear to have been liberal, but the rates diminished as the nineteenth century advanced, perhaps because payments for compensation grew so costly. For example, the Virginia legislature appropriated $265,500 from 1835 through 1863 as compensation to slaveowners for executed slaves (Virginia, *Acts*, for the years from 1835 through 1863). It seems highly unlikely that slaveholders in the antebellum period would have been fully compensated for executed slaves, and, therefore, they might well have been motivated to salvage the value of their property by seeking criminal penalties short of death, such as sale and transportation. For the colonial and revolutionary periods see Marvin L. Michael Kay and Lorin Lee Cary, "'The Planters Suffer Little or Nothing': North Carolina Compensations for Executed Slaves, 1748–1772," *Science and Society*, XL (Fall 1976), 288–306; Taylor, "Humanizing the Slave Code of North Carolina," 329; Hindus, "Black Justice Under White Law," 595–96; Crow, *Black Experience in Revolutionary North Carolina*, 25–26; Phillips, "Slave Crime in Virginia," 336; Wood, *Black Majority*, 279–281; and Schwarz, *Twice Condemned*, 11, 20, 40, 52–53, and 73. For the antebellum period see Hindus, "Black Justice Under White Law,"; Taylor, "Humanizing the Slave Code of North Carolina," 329; and Phillips, "Slave Crime in Virginia," 336–40. On the economic benefits of transporting condemned slaves to other southern states see Schwarz, "Transportation of Slaves from Virginia," 221–23.

67. An undated letter received December 16, 1846, box dated November–December 1846, LR, VEP; and CS, Transported, 1847; and Bonds, 1840–1857. On class conflicts in southern communities over rape trials of free blacks and slaves see Daniel J. Flanigan, "The Criminal Law of Slavery and Freedom, 1800–1868" (Ph.D. dissertation, Rice University, 1973), 68–69.

68. This case is recounted in Wyatt-Brown, *Southern Honor*, 317–18; Johnson, *Antebellum North Carolina*, 71; John Hope Franklin, *Free Negro in North Carolina* (New York, 1943), 37 and most recently and with far greater detail and analysis by Martha Hodes in "Sex Across the Color Line," Chapter 2, "Fornication: Polly Lane and Jim," 39–83. See also Hodes, *Sex Across the Color Line: White Women and Black Men in the Nineteenth-Century American South* (New Haven, forthcoming), Chap. 3. Facts relating to this case are taken from these secondary sources as well as from the subsequently cited primary sources.

69. Petition dated December 8, 1825, Papers of Governor Hutchins Gordon Burton, Governors' Papers 55 (hereinafter GP 55) (North Carolina Department of Cultural Resources, Division of Archives and History).

70. M. Henderson to Governor Burton, December 5, 1825, and Alexander Gray to Burton, December 8, 1825, and March 24, 1826, GP 55. Considerable debate and

correspondence was devoted to the suspected pregnancy, which as time passed was confirmed. One issue was the date of conception. During the October trial Polly Lane denied that she was pregnant. If Jim's contention that she was one month to six weeks pregnant by the date of the alleged rape, August 16, were true, her pregnancy would have been difficult to conceal but not entirely impossible. As the advanced pregnancy made her lie untenable, Polly Lane changed her story and claimed that she had been impregnated on August 16, the date she claimed that Jim had raped her. That version of the story would have meant a delivery date around May 16, according to those Davidson County residents who were keeping track. When, in late March, the birth appeared imminent, about five weeks before an August 16 conception due date, Polly Lane again adjusted her account to say that if the child born to her was mulatto, it was conceived at the time she claimed Jim had raped her. But if the child was white, it was begotten by a Mr. Palmer, a white man. A second but related concern was whether or not a woman could conceive as the result of a rape. Conventional, as well as medical, wisdom of the time erroneously stated that arousal of the woman was necessary for fertilization. Governor Burton even solicited the opinion of a physician who concluded that "if an absolute rape were to be perpetrated it is not likely she would become pregnant." Letter of March 27, 1826, GP 55.

71. Six petitioners to Burton, December 8, 1825, *ibid.*

72. Alexander Gray to Burton, December 8, 1825, and March 24, 1826, *ibid.*

73. James Martin of Lexington to Burton, March 24, 1826, *ibid.*

74. A.W. Shepperd to Burton, March 24, 1826, *ibid.*

75. Alexander Gray to Burton, May 18, 1826, *ibid.*

76. Letters from John M. Smith to Burton, March 23, 1826, and May 6, 1826 (quotation from Smith) and letter from A. W. Shepard, March 24, 1826, *ibid.*

77. Wyatt-Brown, *Southern Honor*, 318; and Hodes, "Sex Across the Color Line," 59.

78. Hodes, "Sex Across the Color Line," 49n29. It is worth noting that Morehead's political career was not tarnished by his defense of a slave rapist.

79. John M. Smith to Burton, March 23, 1826, and J. M. Morehead to Burton, May 20, 1826, GP 55.

80. Wyatt-Brown, *Southern Honor*, 317; and James Martin to Governor Burton, March 24, 1826, and Jesse Hargrave to Burton, March 24, 1826, GP 55.

81. Ronald G. Walters, "The Erotic South: Civilization and Sexuality in American Abolitionism," *American Quarterly*, XXV (May 1973), 177–201.

82. This trend is corroborated by Schwarz's study of Virginia slave crime, *Twice Condemned*, 292. He writes that "the number of slaves sentenced to death for rape of white women declined steadily while the percentage of slaves transported rather than executed rose steadily."

83. On the passing of rape laws that mandated harsher punishment for African American males see Higginbotham and Kopytoff, "Racial Purity and Interracial Sex in the Law of Colonial and Antebellum Virginia," 2017. For information on the more general trend of stricter slave regulation see Fogel and Engerman, *Time on the Cross*, 37. And on harsher slave laws offset by more lenient treatment of slaves see Julius Yanuck, "Thomas Ruffin and the North Carolina Slave Law," *Journal of Southern History*, XXI (November 1955), 473.

84. Schwarz, *Twice Condemned*, 236 and 248.

85. July 1834 folder, box 267 (April–October 1834), LR, VEP; and Westmoreland County Superior Court Order Book, October 16, 1833, pp. 163–65, and April 23, 1834, p. 183 (Library of Virginia) (microfilm reel no. 77).

86. *Commonwealth of Virginia* v. *Watts*, 4 Leigh 672 (1833).

87. Undated petition and letters by Ed. Wood, June 26, 1834 (second quotation) and July 9, 1834 (first and third quotations), July 1834 folder, box 267, LR, VEP.

88. Thurman to the governor, June 11, 1834, *ibid.*

89. Watts's name does not appear on transportation or execution records, indicating that he may very well have been pardoned.

90. Thurman to the governor, June 11, 1834, July 1834 folder, box 267, LR, VEP.

Such support for free blacks in southern communities was not as rare as we might first suspect. Perhaps we should re-examine U. B. Phillips's claim that southern whites in some localities embraced and respected industrious and productive free African Americans. Phillips, *American Negro Slavery*, 430–37. See also Crow, *Black Experience in Revolutionary North Carolina*, 32; Franklin, *Free Negro in North Carolina*, 45–46; Gary B. Mills, "Miscegenation and the Free Negro in Antebellum 'Anglo' Alabama: A Re-examinaton of Southern Race Relations," *Journal of American History*, LXVIII (June 1981), 16–17, 27, and 31–32; Alexander, *Ambiguous Lives*, 120; John E. Fisher, "The Legal Status of Free Blacks in Texas, 1836–1861," *Texas Southern University Law Review*, [IV] (Summer 1977), 342–62; Thomas E. Buckley, S.J., "Unfixing Race: Class, Power, and Identity in an Interracial Family," *Virginia Magazine of History and Biography*, CII (July 1994), 349–80. For a contrasting view see Michael Hindus, "Black Justice Under White Law," 584. His study of two South Carolina counties documents free blacks prosecuted at a rate six times that of slaves.

91. October 18, 1833, LR, VEP, as quoted in Johnston, *Race Relations in Virginia*, 263. This document could not be located at the Library of Virginia as cited by Johnston. Also, see *Thompson v. Commonwealth of Virginia*, 4 Leigh 652 (1833); and Frederick County Superior Court Order Book, 1831–1835, entries for May 22, 23, June 10, 1833, pp. 208, 210, and 224 (Library of Virginia) (microfilm reel no. 100). On Thompson's occupation refer to Rebecca A. Ebert, "A Window on the Valley: A Study of the Free Black Community of Winchester and Frederick County, Virginia, 1785–1860" (M.A. thesis, University of Maryland, 1986), 48.

92. October 18, 1833, LR, VEP. No documentation that verifies the outcome of Thompson's appeal has been found. However, his name does not appear on lists of blacks executed or transported in the early 1830s.

93. I have found only eleven cases, eight in the nineteenth century before the Civil War, in which it appears that the complainant was a member of the slaveholding class. In most of these cases the victim was a member of the master's family. An Alabama newspaper reported in 1855 that a slave had ravished and murdered his master's fourteen-year-old daughter. See Huntsville *Democrat*, May 24, 1855, as reported in James B. Sellers, *Slavery in Alabama* (University, Ala., 1959, 1964 ed.), 253; and Phillips, *American Negro Slavery*, 462. Phillips reported that the slave was burned alive. In 1844 a Tennessee slave attempted an assault on a pregnant woman who was en route to visit her mother, a slaveowner. *Bill, a Slave v. State of Tennessee*, 5 Humphreys 155 (1844). See also Trial of Tom, September 14, 1775, and Trial of Nat, September 6, 1775, Lancaster County Court Order Book (1778–1783), pp. 8 and 7 (Library of Virginia) (microfilm reel no. 30); Trial of Bob, June 13, 1783, Southampton County Court Order Book (1778–1784), p. 336 (Library of Virginia) (microfilm reel no. 27). Also consult the cases of Dick, who was convicted of raping the four-year-old daughter of his master. Charles Briggs of Southampton County, box 157, LR, VEP, and CS, Executed, 1808; Arche. of Botetourt County, who was found guilty of raping Rosanna Switzer, the wife of his master, CS, Executed, 1805; Beverly, of Halifax County, condemned for raping his owner's wife, CS, Executed, 1843, and April 15, 1843, Halifax County Court Book (1838–1845), pp. 141–44 (Library of Virginia) (microfilm reel no. 71); Stephen, of Fauquier County, who was convicted of raping Lucinda Jeffries (her relationship to owner, Enoch Jeffries, is unknown but most likely a female relative), CS, Executed, 1811; Joshua, of Monongalia County, for raping the daughter-in-law of his owner James Collins, July 1–10, 1827 folder, box 299, LR, VEP; and John, of Rockingham County, convicted for the attempted rape of Mary Sipe, an unmarried female over the age of 16 who lived in the home of John's owner, Jacob Sipe, CS, Transported, 1841. Of these latter six, only John's life was spared.

94. In some southern states, for example South Carolina, slave owners were required by law to present for trial any slave accused of a capital crime. Hindus, "Black Justice," 582. There is no adequate measure of the frequency of slave owners' compliance with this law.

95. *Stephen v. State*, 11 Ga. 225 (1852). Also, see the South Carolina cases, *State v. Harry*, November 5, 1851, and *State v. Daniel*, January 15, 1859, both cited in Hindus, "Black Justice Under White Law," 592. In all three cases the slave defendants were convicted. In 1819 a Cumberland County, Virginia slave, Dennis, was sentenced to hang for the rape of Elizabeth Smith, described in court records as "a very simple weak woman." Dennis broke jail before his scheduled execution. June 24–30, 1819 folder, box 254 (June 1819), LR, VEP; and Virginia, *Acts* (1819), ch. 143, pp. 103–4. A white teenaged girl who could not speak and was regarded by many in the neighborhood as "an idiot" was allegedly raped by a slave who was sentenced to transportation by the jury. January–June 1862, Pardon Papers, VEP; and CS, Transported, 1862.

96. The issue of presumed guilt in this essay is indeed tricky for the historian, especially in light of the many trumped-up charges in the latter part of the nineteenth-century. To assume that all these defendants were guilty seems just as unwarranted as assuming that none of them were guilty. In some cases the evidence is more forthcoming, allowing the researcher to venture an educated guess. Other times, the evidence is stingy, yielding little. And never are we privy to the actual voice of the black accused. Nevertheless, it seems reasonable to concede that sexual assault takes place in all cultural universes. So, too, we must assume that some of these cases did in fact represent unwanted sexual violence against white women and girls. That stated, the use of discretion and caution in assessing culpability is essential in these cases.

97. Bynum, *Unruly Women*, 57.

98. The work of Laura Edwards confirms that, at least for Granville County, North Carolina, in the two decades following the Civil War, sexual violence in all but a few cases was committed against poor white and African American women. "Sexual Violence, Gender, and Reconstruction in Granville County," 237–60.

99. As Kenneth Stampp has asserted, "The slave as property clearly had priority over the slave as a person." *Peculiar Institution*, 204 (quotation) and 227–28. See also Hodes, "Sex Across the Color Line," 77.

100. Other sexual assault cases involving free men of color as defendants include *Thurman v. State*, 18 Ala. 276 (1850); *Commonwealth v. Jerry Mann*, 2 Va. Cas. 210 (1820); *Commonwealth v. Tyree*, 2. Va. Cas., 262 (1821); *Commonwealth of Virginia v. Fields*, 4 Leigh 648 (1832); *Day v. Commonwealth of Virginia*, 2 Grattan 562 (1845) and 3 Grattan 629 (1846); *Smith v. Commonwealth of Virginia*, 10 Grattan 734 (1853). The Richmond *Daily Dispatch* of April 27, 1854, reported that a free black man stood accused of attempting to rape a white woman whose credibility the paper seemed to doubt because of her associations with the "lowest and most debased free negroes in the valley. . . ." Quoted in Hodes, "Sex Across the Color Line," 79. The Raleigh *Register* reported the case of Henry Carroll, a free African American convicted of raping a white woman. His death sentence was stayed, at least for a time, by the governor in response to a petition signed by "respectable portions of our citizens. . . ." Raleigh *Register and North Carolina Gazette*, April 14, 1831, p. 3 and May 12, 1831, p. 3 (quotation); and Governor Montfort Stokes, Letterbook No. 29, May 5, 1831, pp. 22 and 45 (North Carolina Department of Cultural Resources, Division of Archives and History).

101. This last motive explains fissures along class lines in the white community. Working-class and middling whites may have worried about free black men selling their skills and wares cheaply, a factor that would also account for elite patronage of free blacks. Phillips, *American Negro Slavery*, 453.

102. This observation is consistent with Joel Williamson's overarching characterization of southern race relations from 1850 to 1915. In 1850, Williamson writes, the white elite allied with the "black mass," enabling the elite to maintain control over society. But by 1915 the white elite had virtually abandoned their connection with blacks and bonded instead with the "white mass." Williamson, *Crucible of Race*, 512 and 519.

103. Nell Irvin Painter, "Of *Lily*, Linda Brent, and Freud: A Non-Exceptionalist Approach to Race, Class, and Gender in the Slave South," *Georgia Historical Quarterly*, LXXVI (Summer 1992), 259.

104. See, for example, Buckley, "Unfixing Race," 349–80.

105. Jacquelyn Dowd Hall, "'The Mind That Burns in Each Body': Women, Rape, and Racial Violence," in Ann Snitow, Christine Stansell, and Sharon Thompson, eds., *Powers of Desire: The Politics of Sexuality* (New York, 1983), 335–36.

106. Carter, *Scottsboro*, 295.

107. *Ibid.*

108. *Ibid.*, 297; and Goodman, *Stories of Scottsboro*, 227.

109. Goodman, "Stories of Scottsboro," 403.

EIGHTEEN

Invisible Men:
Blacks and the U.S. Army
in the Mexican War

ROBERT E. MAY

Margaret Mitchell's *Gone With the Wind* had its share of interpretive distortions regarding mid-nineteenth-century America, but it also picked up on a few aspects of the historical record that are often overlooked. When the recently widowed Scarlett O'Hara arrives at the Atlanta railroad station early in the Civil War, she encounters Uncle Peter, a servant about whom she had been apprised by her late husband: "He went through all the Mexican campaigns with Father, nursed him when he was wounded—in fact, he saved his life."[1] In alluding to the participation of American blacks in the Mexican War, Mitchell showed her familiarity with something that has not only eluded scholars of black history, but even specialists in the black military experience. While historians have devoted massive amounts of print to blacks in the Revolution, War of 1812, Seminole War, Civil War and even the peacetime pre–Civil War military establishment, they have virtually ignored the presence of blacks in American armies south of the Rio Grande during what Robert W. Johannsen has emphasized as the nation's first foreign war.[2] Recent studies perpetuate the oversight: Bernard C. Nalty's *Strength for the Fight: A History of Black Americans in the Military* lacks even an index entry for the Mexican War, while Martin Binkin and Mark J. Eitelberg's *Blacks and the Military* skips from the War of 1812 to the Civil War without mentioning the war with Mexico. The *Encyclopedia of Black America* parries the issue by suggesting that "[s]ervice by Afro-Americans in the Mexican War was apparently limited to those who served as crews of Navy vessels on duty off the Mexican coast and in California."[3]

The rationale for this gap in black history is that Afro-Americans, prior to the conflict with Mexico, had been excluded from U.S. Army service. Although the navy imposed a five percent quota system on free black enlistments (and prohibited any slaves from being "entered for the naval service or to form a part of the Complement of any Vessel of War of the United States"), the army, by virtue of a February 18, 1820 order and General Regulations issued in 1821, excluded *all* blacks.[4] State militias also refused to admit blacks. Delaware's volunteer militia act, passed on the eve of the Mexican War, limited membership in all prospective branches—artillery, infantry, cavalry, dragoons, riflemen and grenadiers—to "free white male citizens."[5] Since the closest blacks came to soldiering in Mexico was as servants of whites, they could hardly merit attention. After all, they did not affect the course of campaigns or battles, and servant duty in war was something of a universal experience: what was true of one conflict should be true of others. After dwelling on the War of 1812 for four pages in his synthesis of the black American military experience, Jack D. Foner dismissed the Mexican War service in a brief statement: "Blacks served in the Mexican War only as body servants. Pre-Civil-War America saw the black as cowardly and childlike, with little fighting ability."[6]

One can hardly criticize scholars for ignoring participation in a war in which black Americans themselves seemed to take little pride. A leading scholar of the Negro Civil War experience explained that mid-nineteenth-century black Americans, when they urged that Union armies be opened to Negro enlistments, used the Revolution and War of 1812 to illustrate black fighting ability. This slighting of the black experience in Mexico presents problems, and not just because there is evidence that a scattering of American Negroes did participate as soldiers. Rather it leaves those blacks who served in *any* capacity during the Mexican War as erased from the record as Ralph Ellison's unacknowledged "Invisible Man." Akin to black cowboys in Texas and black miners in the California gold rush prior to their discovery by modern scholars, it implies that there is no story worth telling, no social history worth relating, about Negroes in the land campaigns of the Mexican War.[7] This study demonstrates that there is indeed a history to be written about blacks in the Mexican War.

The black experience in the Mexican War derived from the desire of most American army officers to have servants attend to their needs and comforts south of the border. This was true of regulars prior to the actual outbreak of hostilities. Ulysses S. Grant, stationed at the New Orleans barracks in July 1845, wrote his fiancée Julia Dent upon getting orders for the Rio Grande frontier, "I have a black boy to take along as my servant that has been in Mexico. He speaks English, Spanish and French. I think he may be very useful where we are going." Following the large influx of volunteers after the outbreak of war, the selection and procurement of a sufficient number of competent servants constituted one of the most pressing responsibilities of newly commissioned officers prior to departure for the seat of war. Colonel William B. Campbell of the First Tennessee Volunteers wrote to his wife from Nashville on June 3, 1846 that he would "get me a free negro here for a servant," only to hear from his uncle several days later, "I fear in your hurry you have not attended to one very important matter. Have you provided yourself with a good servant? This is all important. You ought to have two, but one will answer, if a good one." Likewise, Captain James Lawson Kemper, commissioned assistant quartermaster, recorded the following in his diary about an interview with Colonel John Francis Hamtrack of the First Virginia Volunteer Regiment: "Was sorry to find Col. so great a stickler for the minutiae of military regulations as to equipments. He thinks it vastly important that I should be looking after spurs, sword, servant, and all that." Several days later Kemper went "over to Pourtsmouth in search of a servant," was unsuccessful, but eventually engaged one named Peter. While the hiring of servants was generally an individual concern, on occasion servants were employed on behalf of whole units. A Kentucky officer in Zachary Taylor's army, for instance, wrote the editor of the Louisville *Morning Courier* in July 1846: "We brought a negro man with us from New Orleans. We pay him $20 a month."[8]

Many officers took several servants with them across the Rio Grande. Colonel Campbell wound up procuring two servants. General Taylor used four, while General William J. Worth employed three. Generals Winfield Scott and William O. Butler each had four servants. Federal statutes established a sliding scale in which one could have extra servants the higher his rank. Captains and lieutenants of infantry and artillery, for instance, were restricted to one servant, colonels and majors two, brigadier generals three, and major generals four. Since the federal government reimbursed officers for servant hire ($7–$8 per month per servant), provided clothing allowances ($2.50 per month per servant) and extra rations for servants, and mandated that company officers could only detail soldiers as private waiters when "hired servants" could not "be obtained," there was every incentive for officers to arrange for a maximum retinue. Few officers failed to meet their servant quotas.[9]

Blacks, therefore, must have been a part of every contingent of American troops bound for the war, from its early stages prior to Congress' declaration of war through its conclusion. Theodore Talbot, who joined John C. Frémont's famous third exploring expedition of 1845, noted that Frémont's mess included "a Negro," while John Kenley, aboard the transport *Alexandria* in July 1847, found himself in a detachment of "eleven officers and one hundred and ninety-eight enlisted men, with some half-dozen servants." Not all Mexican War servants, by any means, were black. William Campbell reassured his uncle that he had hired a "kind & attentive" "Irish servant." Major Philip Barbour found a "Mexican boy" at Matamoros who would "come to me tomorrow at $4.00 a month." Talbot recorded that a Chinook Indian accompanied Frémont. Many whites, such as R. C. Reeder, undoubtedly a relation to his employer Lieutenant Thomas A. Reeder of the Arkansas Cavalry, also turn up in the record. Still, the percentage and total number of black servants is striking. One group of army pay vouchers lists 192 private servants; of these 34 are described as "black," 17 "slave," 59 "dark," 6 "mulatto," 4 "Negro," and 4 "copper." While some servants were undesignated by race, it appears that the great majority, if not two-thirds, of all Mexican War servants were Negroes.[10]

Most Mexican War black servants were male, but a sprinkling of Negro females, such as the mulatto "Blanche" who worked for Lieutenant P. P. Peel of the Second Indiana Volunteers, do turn up in the record. The records show that northerners also used large numbers of black servants. Pay vouchers for officers of the New York volunteers reveal that seven of fifteen servants were Negroes, and not all of them were drawn from the nation's free black community. One pay voucher for example, from A. G. Whiteside, Second Illinois Volunteers, requested a $7 reimbursement for his slave named Samuel, who served with him at Buena Vista.[11]

Some blacks in America's Mexican War army also served as soldiers. At least one mulatto slave defied army regulations and enlisted, using the government's call for volunteers as a cover to cross the color line into temporary freedom. On April 1, 1848, Colonel Henry Wilson, commanding the Department of Vera Cruz, drummed John Taylor of the Voltigeurs out of the service with a dishonorable discharge when it was discovered that the former slave had tricked a U.S. recruiting officer into believing he was white. Dick Green, servant of Charles Bent, the American appointed governor of occupied New Mexico, was allowed to shoulder arms after Bent's assassination, and would later suffer a wound as a member of Colonel Sterling Price's command at the battle of El Embudo.[12]

Countless other blacks, because they were expected to hold the reins of their masters' horses, found themselves risking their lives in battle even though not formally enrolled as soldiers. Lieutenant Dabney Maury, remembering his wound at Cerro Gordo, retained this very image many years later when he recalled how he had appropriated another lieutenant's horse, being held by a Negro named Tom, to reach a surgeon in the rear: "I was a sorry spectacle, covered with blood, pale and faint, one man leading my horse, while Tom . . . glad enough to get off from that field, kept close to me with a flask of brandy. . . ." Even servants well behind the battle lines faced danger. General John A. Quitman learned after the fighting for Monterrey on September 21, 1846, that Harry Nichols, his body servant, had been under heavy enemy fire. "He declares," Quitman wrote home, "while far in the rear of my Brigade, that the Mexicans kept shooting cannon balls at *him*. Sometimes he avoided them by dodging, sometimes by jumping & sometimes by lying flat on the ground." Quitman's daughter wrote back that Colonel Jefferson Davis' servant had returned to Mississippi with similar accounts. "[H]e says, the day of the battle, he was so often *aimed* at, & to avoid the bullet[s] & bombs that were flying about as thick as hail, he was obliged to *dodge so much,* that when night arrived he was so sore & stiff that he could scarcely walk. . . ." War correspondents on occasion posted jocular accounts of servant cowardice, calculated to appeal to the racial stereotypes of their readers. "Truth" in the New York *Spirit of the Times* told about Bill, the "big, two fisted negro" from Louisville who left fellow Kentucky "darkies" boasting of the Mexicans he intended to kill, only to cower behind a Veracruz sand hill the first time he heard a rifle crack. A New Orleans *Daily Delta* reporter recounted how two "niggers" had taken precipitate flight at Buena Vista, one of them seeking refuge in an army bake oven! Whether or not these particular tales were apocryphal, accounts of servant bravery overshadow them. One black servant even seems to have sacrificed his life to save his master. According to a Washington *Union* correspondent, David, the slave of an army captain, threw himself in front of an enemy lance at Huamantla, and died within minutes.[13]

During battles, black body servants fulfilled an important function by bringing their masters the sustenance necessary to keep fighting under exhausting conditions. Lieutenant Raphael Semmes of the navy, who accompanied American ground forces during the Mexico City campaign, observed that General Worth's slave/servant, Abram, would always turn up "near the general, toward the close of an engagement, with a basket of refreshments on his arm." According to one of John Quitman's daughters, after the assault on Mexico City's Belén gate her father felt so obligated to his slave/servant Harry Nichols for providing him a bowl of chicken broth following a day without any food, that he henceforth rewarded Harry with a five-dollar gold piece on the battle's anniversary.[14]

Of course camp duty and other non-combatant assignments accounted for most Afro-American service in the Mexican war. Servants often cooked for their masters, and it would appear they often were hired or taken to Mexico expressly for that purpose. In September 1846 Quitman's daughter recorded: "Cousin Mary wrote to me that you had purchased a cook in New Orleans, . . . I hope that he succeeds better in making biscuit than Harry did." Black cooks also prepared a substantial share of the American army's campaign fare. In addition, servants performed an almost infinite variety of camp functions: they rubbed down horses, scoured Mexican markets for fresh fruit, solicited army physicians for Christmas rum and brandy for the troops, entertained the soldiers with song, and handled the washing and drying of clothing. Perhaps the description of the duties of the Kentucky servant mentioned in the Louisville *Morning Courier* best conveys the rhythm and context of Negro life in the Mexican War army: "His business is to wait on the Company officers . . . to cook for us & c. In short he is our man-of-all-work. We buy our provisions from the Sutler, and our man has his . . . chest in which he keeps them, together with his cooking utensils, table ware, and other small articles." The same chest served as bed for this servant at night.[15]

Their contributions to the military in Mexico extended well beyond routine camp chores. En route to the war theater, blacks assigned to look after officers' baggage battled seasickness. On the march, Negro teamsters drove army wagons. After battle, they indeed established antecedents for the Uncle Peter fictional character by nursing the wounded. Thus Lieutenant Colonel Alexander K. McClung, hit by enemy fire at Monterrey, requested a week later that a private be assigned "to assist my servant in turning me over, and in lifting me out of bed." Second Lieutenant William M. Gardner, after taking a musket ball in the chest a Churubusco, was removed to a "small unoccupied house in San Angel, and left there in charge of Moses, my negro servant. . . ." Occasionally particular skills brought blacks unusual assignments. John C. Frémont took Jacob Dodson, a free black servant, on an 840-mile mission in California in 1847, because he needed Dodson's expertise with the lariat to lasso horses for mount changes. For at least one slave, war service terminated when he was assigned to accompany his dead master's corpse back home.[16]

Service with the American army in Mexico brought Negroes little relief from the prejudices, indignities and violence they suffered back in the states; American troops carried "nigger" jokes and the rest of their racist cultural baggage with them. Major Luther Giddings denigrated black servants with the Ohio Volunteers as the "sable descendants of Ham." Despite such ill treatment black servants *could* win appreciation for loyal service. George T. M. Davis, John Quitman's aide, recalled later how Quitman's body servant Harry Nichols earned his "profound admiration and esteem" for "single-hearted devotion, watchfulness, and obedience to his master. . . . No more true, kind, generous and considerate heart ever beat in the breast of a white man," Davis believed, "than that which throbbed in good old Harry's." But perhaps more revealing than Davis' recollections was the court martial in Los Angeles of Dragoon Private Ed Cuneau for his refusal to take some horses out to pasture on grounds that he "would not be hurried, & drove like a Negro."

It is instructive to contrast the sentence of hanging which a U.S. military commission handed down to a Kentucky officer's free black servant for the rape of a Mexican woman, with the one-year imprisonment imposed on a white American accused of murdering an "American mulatto man." In the first case, an army officer, troubled by whether justice could be achieved for a member of a "degraded and friendless race" surrounded by few "from whom he could expect either compassion or pity," provided defense counsel. The second lieutenant who carried out the actual execution years later expressed guilt about enforcing what may well have been an unjustified sentence and reflected that the incident had "completely destroyed" his appetite for Veracruz garrison duty.

> I am not certain that I did not hang an innocent man, but my office was to obey orders, not to speculate as to the innocence or guilt of my prisoner, who had been convicted by a military court on the charges of having offered violence to a Mexican woman of low order.

Nor was the murder of the American mulatto at Puebla an isolated case. General Persifor F. Smith reported from the headquarters of the Louisiana brigade on July 9, 1846: "On the day after we arrived here . . . 1st Corporal William Winchester . . . shot Mayor Lyon's servant Samuel Venables a free man of color with a pistol & killed him. As the story is related by the witnesses it was an unprovoked murder." Other such incidents may have passed unreported. There is little reason to discredit J. B. Robertson's (First Tennessee Regiment) later reminiscence of the time a Texas Ranger at Camargo called a Negro a "darkie" and knocked him off his saddle into the San Juan River because the servant refused to apologize for spattering water on him. The servant, it turned out, belonged to none other than army commander Zachary Taylor. The Ranger, quick to recount the incident to Taylor before Taylor could say anything to him, boasted that he would have done it to the "darkie" even had "it been Old Zack's negro himself." Taylor, disarmed by the "half compliment to himself," decided not to punish the Ranger.[17]

Everyday hazards incident to military life only compounded the racial hostility blacks encountered. Disease killed several times more regulars and volunteers than did battle wounds. Servants, who received less clothing, shelter, food and medical care, surely suffered a proportionate number of deaths. No statistics about Mexican War mortality for blacks are available, but Mexican War manuscripts mention sick Negroes and Afro-Americans who met a variety of misfortunes. Colonel Ethan Allen Hitchcock, commander of the Third Infantry Regiment under Zachary Taylor at Corpus Christi, Texas, recorded in his diary just prior to the war: "One of the most terrific storms I ever knew. Two valuable colored servants struck by lightning." Private J. W. H. Tipton penned in his journal about the crossing of a river during the Tampico campaign, "there was a Molato Negro driving a wagon; and as he was puling up the Bank the bolt pin broke of[f] of his wagon he dis Mounted from his Saddle Horse and got in the wagon to throw the lode out; there being a loded Pistol liing in the wagon; he picked it up and it went off and shot him through the left hand with three balls." General Quitman wrote home from Monterrey during some cold weather in December 1846, "Poor Harry has been very sick—chill & fever with tendency to inflamation of the brain." Servants suffered scorpion bites at Tampico, and dropped from heatstroke on the march from Camargo to Cerralvo. Should it be any wonder that Captain Robert Buchanan of the Fourth Infantry was instructed to report in his next letter home whether "the Black Boy you took with you from W[ashington] is still with you, as his Parents are anxious"? The separation from loved ones, and the anxieties and homesickness it engendered, no doubt constituted the highest price that many American blacks paid for their contribution to the Mexican War.[18]

Still, for some blacks the Mexican War provided opportunity. The deprivations of military service compelled white soldiers and black servants to mix together at cockfights and other social amusements, and the inevitable result was a temporary democratization of race relations. Private William S.

Johnson, participating in the occupations of Puebla in July 1847, noted how American-run betting operations had sprung up in the city, and that he had seen "Commissioned Officers among Army followers, Teamsters, Soldiers and *Negroes!* All engaged in gambling together. . . ." Black army servants in the Mexican War (like black American soldiers in World War I France) also discovered that foreign women had greater racial tolerance of them than did white females back in the States. In occupied Santa Fe, black servants "took the shine" at their own fandangos and, in the eyes of local inhabitants, outclassed their employers and masters. New York *Herald* correspondent "MEXICANA," reporting on a bash which General Stephen Watts Kearny threw at the Governor's House, commented it was "astonishing" how "Mexican women prefer attending the parties of gentlemen of color, to any others that are given."[19]

Economic opportunities for blacks supplemented social betterment. An American sheet in Mexico City announced that one "Harry," previously a cook for General Worth, was running a restaurant in the capital and guaranteeing "the best Suppers ever given, since the arrival of the American army." Similarly, two black servants with American forces invading California later secured positions as cooks at Sutter's Fort and the Monterey jail.[20]

From the outset of the war, blacks, capitalizing on Mexico's lack of slavery, fled to enemy lines. In a letter dated April 14, 1846, from the army's camp on the Rio Grande opposite Matamoros, *Spirit of the Times* correspondent Captain William S. Henry reported that "three or four of the officers' slaves have run away." Observing the same phenomenon, Captain Philip N. Barbour wondered whether fellow officers might be compelled to switch to white servants if the army remained on the border much longer. Military penetration of Mexico only multiplied escape opportunities. Raphael Semmes mused that William Worth's "faithful fellows" might have departed "without let or hindrance" "at all times" during the Mexico City campaign, and there is scattered evidence of fugitives throughout the war record. In fact, growing publicity about the Mexican escape hatch may have enticed a few slaves who remained in the states. "The steamers Palmetto and Edith arrived at Vera Cruz on the 8th inst . . . ," noted the New Orleans *Daily Picayune* on June 17, 1847. "On the Palmetto a lady is said to have arrived from New Orleans in search of a runaway slave. Her pursuit is represented as successful."[21]

The question becomes not whether army slaves chose to run away, but rather why more of them did not. The fact that references to runaways in reminiscences, letters and war correspondents' reports are scattered indicates that the overwhelming proportion of slaves remained with their masters, a curious pattern in light of the epidemic of fugitive incidents which marked the American Civil War just a decade and a half later. Perhaps slaves were less informed of opportunities in Mexico than in the American North. Maybe the language barrier deterred slave runaways. Officers/masters may have had effective ways of imposing camp control over their slaves. Perhaps slaves shared their masters' cultural biases regarding Mexican civilization; Semmes contended that slaves observed the degraded condition of Mexican peons and concluded that they were better off as gentlemen's servants than consorting as free men with "Indian trash." Mixed reports from fugitives returning to American camps, however, probably had more to do with giving potential runaways pause. Correspondent Henry noted that a major's "boy" returned to Taylor's army with accounts of having been treated with "the most distinguished consideration" behind enemy lines and offered "the first seat at the table, and the best bed in the house," but William M. Gardner reported that his Moses, who took leave in Mexico City, encountered a less open-armed reception. "I never could get much out of him about his period of freedom," Gardner later recalled, "but he certainly looked both hungry and seedy when he returned." For their part, officers may have made subtle adjustments in the master/slave dialogue while in Mexico to offset temptations. "It would amuse you to hear the difference in the *tone* of orders to the slaves, produced by two or three degrees of latitude," Henry related. "It's now, in the *softest* coaxing manner, 'Willis, boy, have you got dinner cooked? Get it as soon as you can'—whereas, away from here, it would be 'why have you not got your dinner ready, you rascal? you had better be on the look out, or you'll catch a little of the d--st licking.'"[22]

Unfortunately, much of the story of blacks in the Mexican War will continue to elude historical disclosure. How useful it would be to know what transpired when free blacks and slaves interacted in American forces south of the border; however it is unlikely that scholars will ever find out. What is missing in particular is the black perspective on the war. The Afro-American history of the conflict must, it appears, continue to be derived from extant white materials. By the 1930s, far too many years had passed for Federal Writers' Project interviewers to find a group of surviving slaves with memories of the Halls of Montezuma. The index to the massive published collection of 1930s ex-slave interviews offers only one mention of the Mexican War, the recollections of Lewis Adams of Copiah County, Mississippi, who merely reported that he had gone off to Mexico as the servant of a volunteer captain. Earlier opportunities to record the black Mexican War experience were simply overlooked. When "James," who served as a slave in the Mexican War, was presented by his former mistress to attendees of a United Confederate Veterans meeting in 1899, the veterans apparently made no inquiries about his service in Mexico.[23]

Scattered evidence does provide some hints about how blacks internalized their own Mexican War experience. Rather than conceptualize their service as involuntary or passive, Negro veterans (along with blacks in all other conflicts this nation waged during the ages of slavery and segregation), focused on the positive aspect of their participation and found cause for pride. General Thomas J. Wood's "man" illustrated their attitude. He stayed with Wood at a New York hotel after the war, and assumed the role of a military authority as he regaled various servants at the hotel with recollections of the war. In 1861, Jacob Dodson, arguing in behalf of fellow black Mexican War veterans that free blacks living in the nation's capital should be allocated a role in the city's defense, recalled to Union Secretary of War Simon Cameron that he had been "three times across the Rocky Mountains in the service of the Country with Fremont." Several years earlier, in fact, he had applied for and won Mexican War service pay from Congress, by claiming that he had technically been mustered into Richard Owens' company of the California Battalion under Frémont. Dodson's congressional advocates, including former Mexican War generals Senator James Shields of Illinois and slaveowning Representative John A. Quitman of Mississippi, blanched not at all at Dodson's pretensions as a U.S. army veteran; rather, Quitman lauded Dodson for joining the army. Both houses of Congress must have agreed with Senator John B. Weller of California that Dodson fully merited just "what he would have received if he had been of a different color—in other words, if he had been a white man." The Dodson relief bill passed without debate.[24]

Most U.S. Army blacks fared less well than Dodson and returned from the Mexican War as invisible men. Amidst the vast literature generated by the conflict no black soldier emerged a war hero. Newspaper lists of officers aboard homeward-bound ships from the seat of war made no mention of attendant chattels and hired servants.[25] But blacks, in a variety of capacities, had nonetheless made a substantial contribution to the American ground effort in Mexico, and the surviving details are worth relating, despite gaps in the historical record. That blacks participated in the war at all reminds us not only that it is impossible to write (or portray in the media) American military history oblivious to its racial dimension, but also of the symbiotic relationship binding American white and black history in general even regarding subjects presumably immune to the connection. The details enrich understanding of legal discriminations confronting antebellum blacks, the reciprocal context of slave/master relations, slave resistance and loyalty, and, indirectly, the desperate economic plight of many antebellum urban free blacks. That large numbers of Afro-American dwellers in both northern and southern cities would agree to endure severe hardship and risk their lives and health for low pay in Manifest Destiny's war—a conflict often depicted in the urban press and discussed on city streets as a strike for slavery's expansion—is a profound statement of their own career prospects. Invisible men, it seems, faced some rather human dilemmas even in the relatively prosperous late 1840s. Service with the American army in Mexico seemed to offer a promising alternative to the marginal existence they forsook back home.

NOTES

1. Margaret Mitchell, *Gone with the Wind* (New York, 1936), 143–44.
2. Robert W. Johannsen, *To the Halls of the Montezumas* (New York, 1985), 12.

3. Bernard C. Nalty, *Strength for the Fight: A History of Black Americans in the Military* (New York, 1986); Martin Binkin and Mark J. Eitelberg, *Blacks and the Military* (Washington, 1982), 13; W. A. Low and Virgil A. Clift, eds., *Encyclopedia of Black America* (New York, 1981), 834; Jack D. Foner, *Blacks and the Military in American History* (New York, 1974), 30. The categories in Lenwood G. Davis and George Hill, eds., *Blacks in the American Armed Forces, 1776–1983: A Bibliography* (Westport, 1985), skip from "Blacks in the War of 1812" to "Blacks in the Civil War," though the heading "Blacks in the American West" does include an article on Jacob Dodson, a black who served in the Mexican War.

4. Harold D. Langley, "The Negro in the Navy and Merchant Service — 1789–1860," *Journal of Negro History* 52 (October 1967): 279–80; Foner, *Blacks and the Military*, 27. See also Abel P. Upshur to John White, 5 August 1842 and J. C. Spencer to White, 5 August 1842, in "The Negro in the Military Service of the United States," Records of the Adjutant General's Office, Record Group [RG] 94, National Archives, M858. These letters show that some slaves served in the navy as personal servants of officers, and that there were hundreds of blacks, primarily slaves, serving in the U.S. army prior to the Mexican War as laborers, dock hands, cooks, coopers, carpenters and in a variety of other capacities.

5. *Laws of the State of Delaware, 1845* (Dover, 1845), 74.

6. Foner, *Blacks and the Military*, 22–25, 30.

7. James M. McPherson, ed., *The Negro's Civil War: How American Negroes Felt and Acted during the War for the Union* (New York, 1965), 162–63; Ralph Ellison, *Invisible Man* (1947; reprint, New York, 1982), 3; Philip Durham and Everett L. Jones, *The Negro Cowboys* (New York, 1965); Rudolph M. Lapp, *Blacks in Gold Rush California* (New Haven, 1977).

8. U. S. Grant to Julia Dent, 6 July 1845, in John Y. Simon, ed., *The Papers of Ulysses S. Grant*, 14 vols. (Carbondale, 1967–1985), 1:49. William B. Campbell to Fanny Campbell, 3 June 1846, and David Campbell to W. Campbell, 12 June 1846, Campbell Family Papers, William R. Perkins Library, Duke University, Durham, N.C.; James Lawson Kemper Diary, 8, 12, and 15 February 1847, in Robert R. Jones, ed., "The Mexican War Diary of James Lawson Kemper," *Virginia Magazine of History and Biography* 74 (October 1966): 417, 419, 425. W. P. F. to Walter N. Haldeman, 26 July 1846, Louisville *Morning Courier*, 21 August 1846. See also Sylvester Churchill Journal, 25 July 1846, Library of Congress [LC].

9. Vouchers of: W. Campbell, 1 November 1846 to 31 March 1847, File Box 1176; Zachary Taylor, 1–20 November 1846, and William J. Worth, 1–31 December 1846, File Box 1175; Winfield Scott, 1 January to 28 February 1847, and William O. Butler, 1 November 1846 to 31 January 1847, File Box 1187, Records of the General Accounting Office, Records of the Paymaster, RG 217. "Pay and allowances to officers in the army, 1812, 1820, 1838, and present time," *Senate Document 246*, 29th Cong., 1st Sess., (Serial 474); John F. Callan, ed., *The Military Laws of the United States* (Philadelphia, 1863), 276; U.S. War Department, *General Regulations for the Army of the United States, 1841* (Washington, 1841), 18. Whether the servant reimbursement rate was $7 or $8 depended on the branch of service, because it was indexed at the pay of privates, which varied by branch. Thomas M. Exley, comp., *A Compendium of the Pay of the Army from 1785 to 1888* (Washington, 1888), 56. Prewar stipulations about servant privileges in the regular army were extended to the volunteers by Congress' initial war act. *U.S. Statutes at Large* 9 (1846): 10.

10. Theodore Talbot to his mother, 25 June 1845, in Robert V. Hine and Savoie Lottinville, eds., *Soldier in the West: Letters of Theodore Talbot During His Services in California, Mexico, and Oregon, 1845–53* (Norman, Okla., 1972), 23. John R. Kenley, *Memoirs of a Maryland Volunteer, War with Mexico, in the Years 1846–7–8* (Philadelphia, 1873), 279. W. Campbell to D. Campbell, 3 July 1846, Campbell Papers; voucher of Thomas A. Reeder, 1 January to 31 March 1847, File Box 1188, RG 217. The National Archives contain twenty-one boxes of paymasters' vouchers for the Mexican War. Civilians connected with the American forces, such as treaty negotiator Nicholas Trist,

also brought black servants to Mexico. And at least one black civilian—a Galveston free mulatto barber, who was later murdered in Matamoros—voluntarily followed the army. Kenneth M. Johnson, "Nicholas Trist: Treaty-Maker," in *The Mexican War: Changing Interpretations*, ed. Odie B. Faulk and Joseph A. Stout Jr. (Chicago, 1973), 189. New Orleans *Daily Picayune*, 24 April 1847.

11. Vouchers of P. P. Peel, 1–30 April 1847, A. G. Whiteside, 1–28 February 1847, File Box 1188, and vouchers of officers of the New York Volunteers, File Box 1175, RG 217. For another northern officer who had a slave servant, see the voucher for Lieutenant S. S. Condon, 1 January to 31 March 1847, File Box 1188, RG 217.

12. Orders No. 125, 1 April 1848, and Orders—Special Orders, Department of Vera Cruz, 1847–1848, RG 94. "Documents from War Department," *SED 1*, 30th Cong., 1st Sess. (Serial 503), 526.

13. Dabney Herndon Maury, *Recollections of a Virginian in the Mexican, Indian, and Civil Wars* (New York, 1894), 36, 38. John A. Quitman to Eliza Quitman, 22 November 1846, and Louisa Quitman to J. Quitman, 29 December 1846, Quitman Family Papers, Southern Historical Collection, University of North Carolina, Chapel Hill. New York *Spirit of the Times*, 17 April 1847; New Orleans *Daily Delta*, 2 June 1847; Washington *Union* correspondent quoted in New York *Hearld*, 23 November 1847. Davis' servant was Jim Green, whose particular job had been horse care at Davis' Brierfield plantation. James T. McIntosh, ed., *The Papers of Jefferson Davis*, 5 vols. (Baton Rouge and London, 1971–1985), 3:95n.

14. Raphael Semmes, *Service Afloat and Ashore During the Mexican War* (Cincinnati, 1851), 316. Rosalie Quitman Duncan, "Life of General John A. Quitman," *Publications of the Mississippi Historical Society* 4 (1901): 421.

15. L. Quitman to J. Quitman, 18 September 1846, and J. Quitman to E. Quitman, 22 November 1846, 3 June 1847, Quitman Family Papers, J. B. Robertson, *Reminiscences of a Campaign in Mexico by a Member of "The Bloody-First"* (Nashville, Tenn., 1849), 96; Philip Gooch Ferguson diary, 13 August 1847, in Ralph P. Bieber, ed., *Marching with The Army of the West, 1846–1848* (Glendale, Calif., 1936), 312–13; Samuel G. French, *Two Wars: An Autobiography of Gen. Samuel G. French* (Nashville, 1901) 69–70. Louisville *Morning Courier*, 21 August 1846.

16. J. Davis to Varina Howell Davis, 10 December 1846 in McIntosh, *Papers of Jefferson Davis* 3:94; George Rutledge Gibson journal, 9 July 1846, in Bieber, ed., *Journal of a Soldier Under Kearny and Doniphan, 1846–1847* (Glendale, Calif., 1935), 140; K. Jack Bauer, *Zachary Taylor: Soldier, Planter, Statesman of the Old Southwest* (Baton Rouge, 1985), 152. J. Quitman to E. Quitman, 14 August 1846, Quitman Family Papers; Alexander K. McClung to J. Quitman, 1 October 1846, J. Quitman Papers, Mississippi State Department of Archives and History, Jackson, Miss.; The Memoirs of Brigadier-General William Montgomery Gardner, United States Military Academy Library, West Point, N.Y., 31–33; G. M. Bergman, "The Negro Who Rode With Frémont in 1847," *Negro History Bulletin* 28 (November 1964): 31–32; James M. Guthrie, *Camp-Fires of the Afro-American* (Philadelphia, 1899), 230. Neal Harlow claims that Frémont only traveled 750 miles, and notes that Dodson gave out on the last day. Neal Harlow, *California Conquered: War and Peace on the Pacific, 1846–1850* (Berkeley, 1982), 255–61.

17. New York *Herald*, 8 March 1847; [Major Luther Giddings], *Sketches of the Campaign in Northern Mexico in Eighteen Hundred Forty-Six and Seven by an Officer of the First Regiment of Ohio Volunteers* (New York, 1853), 110; George T. M. Davis, *Autobiography of the Late Col. Geo. T. M. Davis: Captain and Aide-De-Camp Scott's Army of Invasion (Mexico), From Posthumous Papers* (New York, 1891), 136–37, 294. Gardner Memoirs, 16–17; Orders No. 35, Orders Book, Seventh New York Volunteer Regiment, Jonathan D. Stevenson Papers, New York Historical Society, New York City; General Orders No. 101, 9 April 1847, Headquarters of the Army in Mexico, and General Orders No. 245, 3 August 1847 [copy], Regimental Order, Letter and Casualty Book, First Infantry, New York, RG 94. Robertson, *Reminiscences*, 112–14. Some of the volunteers may have avenged the hanging of the black servant at Veracruz, since he had

been attached to the Tennessee Regiment, by assaulting a couple of Mexican civilians and killing one of them. See Robert Anderson to his wife, 11 April 1847, in Eba Anderson Lawton, comp., *An Artillery Officer in the Mexican War, 1846–1847: Letters of Robert Anderson* (New York, 1911), 128.

18. Bauer, *The Mexican War, 1846–1848* (New York, 1974), 397; Ethan Allen Hitchcock diary, 24 August 1845, in W. A. Croffut, ed., *Fifty Years in Camp and Field: Diary of Major-General Ethan Allen Hitchcock, U.S.A.* (New York, 1909), 197. J. W. H. Tipton journal, 30 December 1846, microfilm edition, Tennessee State Library and Archives, Nashville; J. Quitman to E. Quitman, 10 December 1846, Quitman Family Papers. Kenley, *Memoirs*, 228; [Giddings], *Sketches*, 110. Carolina V. M. Frye to Robert C. Buchanan, 15 September 1846, Robert C. Buchanan Papers, Maryland Historical Society, Baltimore.

19. New Orleans *Daily Picayune*, 31 October 1847. William S. Johnson diary, 17 July 1847, in John Hammond Moore, ed., "Private Johnson Fights the Mexicans, 1847–1848," *South Carolina Historical Magazine* 67 (October 1966): 218; John Taylor Hughes diary, 15 January 1847, in William Elsey Connelley, ed., *Doniphan's Expedition and the Conquest of New Mexico and California* (Topeka, 1907), 92. New York *Herald*, 25 January 1847.

20. Mexico City *Daily American Star*, 24 December 1847. Lapp, *Blacks in Gold Rush California*, 7–8.

21. New York *Spirit of the Times*, 16 May 1846, 10 July 1847; Philip N. Barbour journal, 4 April 1846, in Rhoda van Bibber Tanner Doubleday, ed., *Journals of the Late Brevet Major Philip Norbourne Barbour* (New York, 1936), 28. Semmes, *Service Afloat and Ashore*, 316; New Orleans *Daily Picayune*, 17 June 1847. Llerena Friend, *Sam Houston: The Great Designer* (Austin, 1954), 182–83. A Matamoros paper, on April 11, 1846, put the number of slave runaways from Taylor's army at six; see Bauer, *Mexican War*, 43.

22. Semmes, *Service Afloat and Ashore*, 317; New York *Spirit of the Times*, 16 May 1846. Gardner Memoirs, 36.

23. George P. Rawick, ed., *The American Slave: A Composite Autobiography*, 41 vols., (Westport, 1972–1979), Supplement, Series I, vol. 6, p. 5; Guthrie, *Camp-Fires*, 230.

24. Loren Schweninger, ed., *From Tennessee Slave to St. Louis Entrepreneur: The Autobiography of James Thomas* (Columbia, Mo., 1984), 122–23; Jacob Dodson to Simon Cameron, 23 April 1861, in McPherson, *Negro's Civil War*, 19; *Congressional Globe*, 33d Cong., 2d Sess., 210, 493, and 34th Cong., 1st Sess., 136, 392, 482, 913, 938, 985. The Dodson bill was introduced in the Thirty-Third Congress and passed the Senate. Reintroduced in the Thirty-Fourth Congress, it passed the Senate on February 21, 1856 and the House of Representatives on April 15, 1856. President Franklin Pierce, yet another Mexican War general, signed the bill into law on April 18. The legislation awarded Dodson "all the pay and allowances" of a U.S. army private for service between July 7, 1846 and April 14, 1847, minus $281 which Frémont had already paid him "for his services as a member of the exploring expedition within this period." It should be noted that Congress made this award despite Secretary of War Jefferson Davis' formal opinion that Dodson had never been enrolled in the California Battalion, but rather had served the battalion in a civil capacity. Jefferson Davis' endorsement is found on Richard Burgess to Jefferson Davis, 19 August 1854, summarized in the calendar in Lynda Lasswell Crist, ed., *The Papers of Jefferson Davis*, 5:367.

25. See for example the lists in the New Orleans *Daily Delta*, 24, 28, and 30 November 1847 and 19 January 1848. The best discussion of Mexican War heroes and literature is in Johannsen, *Halls of the Montezumas*, 108–43, 175–203.

PART FIVE

"TAKING FREEDOM": BLACK MEN AS SOLDIER CITIZENS

NINETEEN

"I's a Man Now": Gender and African American Men

JIM CULLEN

At one point in the 1989 film *Glory*, a former slave named Rawlins who has enlisted in the Union army gets angry at a fellow soldier. A runaway South Carolinian private named Trip has just insulted Searles, an educated Bostonian, by telling him he acts like "the white man's dog." Offended by this remark, Rawlins gives Trip a piece of his mind, criticizing him for his insolent attitude toward whites, his fellow soldiers, and the war effort in general. "The time's comin' when we're goin' to have to ante up and kick in like men." Rawlins tells Trip. "Like men!" Trip is not instantly transformed by these remarks, and he will take some of his rebellious skepticism to a sandy grave off the coast of Charleston. But while he later tells his commanding officer that he does not wish to carry the regimental colors, he echoes Rawlins by saying he plans to "ante up and kick in." And on the eve of the battle, he tells his fellow black soldiers that whatever may happen, "we men, ain't we." (They affirm him in unison.)

   Like so much popular culture, these fictionalized characters reveal—and conceal—a good deal about American history and culture. Cast in an unabashedly heroic light where even rebels like Trip ultimately carry the flag, *Glory* obscures the ambivalence, ambiguity, and disillusionment that military experience held for many African American men and women during the Civil War. Indeed, the absence of black women in the film belies their presence in many military encampments as civilians, nurses, or, in the case of Harriet Tubman, crucial strategic combatants. On the other hand, *Glory* does suggest the diversity of black life in the United States in its cast of characters, and does, like many recent popular and academic histories, recognize the role African Americans played in securing their own emancipation.

Glory is also illuminating in the way it deals with gender. As the above example suggests, a concern with becoming and behaving like a man is an important theme of the movie, as indeed it was for many actual black soldiers. In newspaper articles, government affidavits, and letters to officials, families, and each other, manhood surfaces again and again as an aspiration, a concern, or a fact of life. But while it's one thing to note the recurring reference to manhood in such documents, it's another to know exactly what these people meant by it. Is one born (slave or free) with manhood, or must one earn it? Is it derived by virtue of one's sex, or is it the result of acting in a particular way? Did manhood mean the same thing to black people as it did to white people? Since many of these men were semi-literate—or had to depend on others to write for them—they were not inclined to elaborate on their terminology. Even those who were quite literate did not bother to explain what they assumed their readers would understand.

However varied their understanding of the term, what's striking in looking over the records these men left behind is a widely shared sense that the Civil War did indeed mark a watershed for black manhood. As the *material* conditions of their lives changed—as they joined the armed forces, were freed from slavery, or both—so too did their *ideological* conceptions of themselves as men. In some cases these new ideas were expressed explicitly; other times implicitly. As historian Joan Scott has noted, an awareness of sexual difference as fact or metaphor has always been important, though the concept of gender as a separate analytic category is very much a late-twentieth-century invention.[1] This means any exploration of gender in historical contexts should proceed with some caution. But proceed it should, because the attempt, however imperfect, to understand how other people understood themselves can perhaps still teach us something about them—and ourselves.

The outbreak of war in 1861 led men all over the country to volunteer for military service, and African Americans were no exception. In Washington, Pittsburgh, Cleveland, Boston, and many other cities and towns, black men offered their services singly or in groups to recruiting officers. Almost without exception, they were turned down. Ironically, black men had some of their best success in the Confederacy, though they were generally put to work building fortifications or other kinds of tasks requiring heavy labor. In one sense, this is hardly surprising: southern society had been organized for blacks to perform these roles, which were probably accepted during wartime in the hope of being looked upon with favor in the event of Confederate victory. Except in emergencies, southern blacks were not permitted to fight, and organizations like New Orleans's Native Guards (a part of the state militia composed of free African Americans) found offers of their services declined. Rejections varied in tone, but their content often echoed that of a Cincinnati man who said, "We want you damn niggers to keep out of this; this is a white man's war."[2]

Officially, he was right—at first it was a white man's war. The efforts of abolitionists to the contrary, secession, not slavery, was the pretext for the outbreak of hostilities, and the Lincoln administration assiduously courted slaveholding states still in the Union by avoiding any appearance of restructuring existing race relations. President Lincoln personally countermanded the orders of generals like John Fremont and David Hunter who attempted to free slaves in occupied Confederate territory, and resisted Congressional efforts to punish rebellious slaveholders by confiscating their "property."

Under such circumstances, one might wonder why African Americans wanted to fight at all. And in fact, some did question getting involved. "We have nothing to gain, and everything to lose, by entering the lists as combatants," wrote one man from Troy, New York. Wrote another from Colorado: "I have observed with much indignation and shame, their [African Americans'] willingness to take up arms in defence of this unholy, illbegotten would-be Republican government." Many of those opposed to African American involvement were appalled by the prospect of fighting for a country that made no promise of redressing centuries of injustice. "I, as the Captain, in behalf of the company, am resolved never to offer or give service, except be it on equality with all other men," stated a prospective volunteer from Philadelphia.[3]

At the same time, however, many African Americans were eager to join the struggle even before the Emancipation Proclamation was issued, and cast their advocacy in gendered terms. On May 1, 1861, a group of freemen in New York City met and voted down a resolution offering to fight they knew would be rejected. Nevertheless, the *Anglo-African*, a weekly newspaper that circulated in the metropolitan area, urged its readers to remain in a state of readiness. Acknowledging the argument that the conflict was "a white man's war," the paper nevertheless asserted that the northern way of life offered privileges of free labor, education, and freedom from divided families that should be guarded, if not expanded. "Are these rights worth the having?" the *Anglo-African* asked. "If they are then they are worth defending with all our might and at any cost. It is illogical, unpatriotic, nay mean and unmanly in us to shrink from the defence of these rights and privileges." While some men challenged the *Anglo-African's* position in letters to the editor, still others wrote to support it. "The issue is here; let us prepare to meet it with manly spirit," wrote one Philadelphia man in rebuke to another who had argued for a more neutral approach to the war.[4]

In mid-nineteenth-century America, the word "manly" was rich with connotations of an acquired sense of civilization and duty.[5] For participants in the *Anglo-African* debate, the manly thing to do was defend, and perhaps expand, a way of life by fighting, a behavior considered the unique province of males. It also meant having the will to act on one's own behalf. "God will help no one that refuses help himself," the Philadelphia writer said in his letter. "The prejudiced white man North or South never will respect us until they are forced to by deeds of our own."[6]

Yet a willingness to fight, and thus achieve manhood by waging a war for freedom, seemed moot if African Americans were barred from fighting. "Why does Government reject the negro?" asked a frustrated Frederick Douglass in August of 1861. "Is he not a man? Can he not wield a sword, fire a gun, march and countermarch, and obey orders like any other?"[7] For Douglass, of course, the questions were rhetorical. All black men needed was the chance to demonstrate the important truth that they were the white man's equal in war as well as peace.

Actually, some men had been quietly getting the chance from the very beginning. Despite the official federal ban on black recruitment, unofficial African American units were organized in Kansas, South Carolina, and Louisiana, and saw action in the early years of the war (indeed, blacks had been participants in the guerrilla warfare over "Bloody Kansas" for years). Moreover, as readers of Herman Melville's fiction know, the American navy had long been a multiracial institution.[8] Some men also worked as spies. Many others weakened the Confederate war effort with acts of insubordination on plantations or by escaping from them, often finding refuge behind Union lines and working as cooks or laborers.

All these actions made official policy increasingly irrelevant. Meanwhile, intractable rebel resistance, military defeat, and growing difficulties in meeting manpower needs from white volunteers impelled the Lincoln administration to widen its war aims and turn the political screws on the Confederacy. It is in this context that the President issued the preliminary Emancipation Proclamation in September of 1862, which placed the war on new footing and placed the status of African Americans at the very center of national life.

Even as the political tide on slavery was turning in the summer of 1862, so was the U.S. position on arming African Americans. In July, Congress passed a confiscation act enabling the President "to employ as many persons of African descent as he may deem necessary and proper for the suppression of this rebellion." It also repealed a 1792 law that barred blacks from the military. Lincoln himself also made the case for black enlistments that month when discussing emancipation with the Cabinet, and gave the go-ahead even before the proclamation was issued in September or took effect in January of 1863.

Simultaneously, military considerations became even more urgent than political ones. In the spring of 1862, the Confederate-spurned Native Guards of New Orleans offered to join the Union effort after General Benjamin Butler occupied the city. Butler at first refused, but when threatened by a Confederate attack in August, he changed his mind and recruited three black regiments. At the same time, the need to withdraw cavalry forces from captured territory in the South Sea Islands off the coast of South Carolina led to the formation of the "Department of the South," under which freed slaves were permitted to become soldiers.

It was the Emancipation Proclamation, however, that opened the floodgates for black enlistment. Now possessing the means—and promised a wor-

thy end—leaders of the black community enthusiastically joined the recruitment effort. John S. Rock, William Wells Brown, Sojourner Truth, and
many other luminaries from the northern abolitionist community worked as
recruitment agents. The first two northern regiments were formed in Massachusetts, though in fact they were comprised of men from all over the North
and even Canada. Meanwhile, over 20,000 volunteers were raised in the
Mississippi valley between April and December of 1863 alone. By the end of
the war, approximately 180,000 African Americans served in the United
States Armed Forces. Constituting less than 1 percent of the North's population, African American soldiers comprised roughly 10 percent of the army.[9]

One of the most tireless proponents of black enlistment was Frederick
Douglass, whose own sons joined the fabled Massachusetts 54th Volunteer
Infantry. "Let the black man get upon his person the brass letters 'U.S.'; let
him get an eagle on his button, and a musket on his shoulder and bullets in
his pocket, and there is no power on earth which can deny that he has earned
the right to citizenship in the United States," he wrote in one widely quoted
article.[10]

The editor of *Douglass's Monthly* was also fond of drawing on the manly
rhetoric of action. In another piece, he asserted that African Americans were
fighting "for principle, and not from passion," and that the black soldier
secures "manhood and freedom" via civilized warfare. Douglass went on to
make an unfortunate comparison between blacks and Native Americans,
"who go forth as a savage with a tomahawk and scalping knife," but in doing
so he revealed a definition of manhood as less the amoral use of brute force
than the controlled application of power to achieve a just objective.[11]

It wasn't only Douglass—or the black leadership—who drew on the language of manhood. Enlisted soldiers often appeared as featured speakers
during recruitment drives and made such appeals to their audience. The
remarks of one soldier in Nashville in 1863 are highly revealing in this
regard:

> Come boys, let's get some guns from Uncle Sam, and go coon hunting;
> shooting those gray back coons that go poking about the country nowadays
> (Laughter) . . . Don't ask your wife, for if she is worth having she will call you
> a coward for asking her. (Applause and waving of handkerchiefs by the la-
> dies.)[12]

This passage is striking in two ways. First, it draws on the southern white
habit of describing slaves as animals. Here, the blacks are the men and the
rebels are the animals, rendered in a mode of male bravado that is still
common in our own day. Second, these comments also suggest a definition
of manhood derived from gender conventions understood—and endorsed—
by women, of man as fighter who leaves the home in order to protect it.

Unfortunately, the story of the struggle for black enlistment is not an
altogether happy one, and not only because these men fought for the right
to kill and be killed. A variety of factors marred the effort. First among these

was racism, which impeded the project in the North and checked it in the Confederacy until the very end of the war. "If you make [the African American] the instrument by which your victories are won," an Ohio congressman warned, "you must treat him as a victor is entitled to be treated, with all decent and becoming respect." Others supported black enlistment because they would rather have blacks die than whites. "But as for me, upon my soul!/So liberal are we here/I'll let Sambo be murthered instead of myself/On every day of the year" went a popular song attributed to Irish-Americans. Nor were such attitudes limited to the working classes. "When this war is over & we have summed up the entire loss of life it has imposed on the country I shall not have any regrets if it is found that a part of the dead are *niggers* and that *all* are not white men," wrote the Governor of Iowa to the general-in-chief of the army in 1862.[13]

Indeed, white eagerness to have blacks serve in the army reached vicious proportions. Civilians and government officials soon realized that enlisted blacks could be credited toward conscription quotas, and coercion and terror were often the result, as some black men were literally abducted from their homes and forced into the army. Northern states would send agents to enlist "underemployed" men of the occupied South for a fee, and they wandered the countryside in search of recruits, often impeding military operations and demanding food, forage, and transportation from their "hosts." In many cases, these men also bilked enlistees of their bounties.[14]

Even those who entered the army freely and enthusiastically quickly encountered situations making it clear that even if the Union was committed to freedom, it had no intention of offering equality. Once black enlistment became official policy, the government ordered that all black units should have only white commissioned officers, barring advancement to enlisted African Americans. Many blacks who were already officers, especially in New Orleans, were systematically hounded into resigning their commissions. The army did permit the commissioning of chaplains and surgeons, and there were some exceptions made to the rule, most notably Martin Delany, who was promoted to major at the very end of the war. Noncommissioned officers were also allowed, but these had much less prestige.[15]

Another source of frustration was pay. Despite the promise of receiving the same amount of money as whites, black soldiers were paid only about half of what their white counterparts were. Some black units refused their pay in protest, at great personal cost to themselves and their families, and still others threatened to lay down their arms. Some were shot or jailed for their protests. Some 80 percent of U.S. soldiers shot for mutiny were black.[16]

A letter to the Governor of Massachusetts by a commander of black troops suggests how central a place manhood—more specifically, a sense of manhood that insisted upon an equality previously limited to whites—occupied in such disputes.

> They enlisted because *men* were called for, and because the Government
> signified its willingness to accept them as such not because of the money

offered them. They would rather work and fight until they are mustered out of the Service, without any pay than accept from the Government less than it gives to other soldiers from Massachusetts, and by so accepting acknowledge that because they have African blood in their veins, they are less men, than those who have saxon.[17]

When, after much delay, Congress finally acted to correct the situation in June of 1864, it did so by making an invidious distinction between those who had been slaves before the war and those who were free. Such a policy impaired morale within these regiments, and exacerbated tensions between northern and southern blacks, and the previously slave and previously free.[18]

Finally, African Americans were often given a disproportionate amount of fatigue duty. Ordered to dig ditches, build fortifications, clean latrines, or other dirty work, they were often denied the opportunity to drill or perform the more esteemed tasks of soldiering. Such practices not only bred resentment but also contributed to the higher disease rate among blacks, many of whom shouldn't have been in the army in the first place or who were overworked by their officers. Whereas two white soldiers died of disease for every one who died in battle, for blacks the ratio was about ten to one. One in twelve whites in the Union army died of disease in the war; one in five blacks did.[19]

The flagrant abuses suffered by these men led many recruiters, including Douglass, to suspend their efforts, while those oppressed by these injustices sought the aid of sympathetic officers or government officials. Here, too, the language of manhood was used, not so much as an assertion that African Americans were entitled to the same challenges whites were, but as a request for decency for those whose identities could not be reduced to that of a mere worker, as was the case under slavery. "The black men has wives and Sweet harts Jest like the white men," stated an anonymous New Orleans black man in 1863:

> ... it is rettin that a man can not Serve two master   But it Seems that the Collored population has got two a rebel master and a union master   the both want our Servises   one wants us to make Cotton and Sugar and the Sell it and keep the money   the union masters wants us to fight the battles under white officers and the injoy both the money and the union.[20]

"Today the Anglo Saxon Mother, Wife, or Sister are not alone, in tears for departed Sons, Husbands, and Brothers," wrote another man to President Lincoln, describing the apathy and contempt with which blacks were treated, and the deprivations endured by the "needy Wives, and little ones" at home. "We have done a Soldiers Duty," he said. "Why cant we have a soldier's pay?"[21] Implicit in such writings was a belief that manhood meant responsibility not only to the nation or even one's race but to the "Sweet harts" and families whose pride—and, more pointedly, whose livelihoods—depended on those in the service. Indeed, it seems there were times when men affirmed their manhood by preferring family over the army. "I poor man, wid large famerly—my wife Rinah she can't work," said one husband, who had already served in the army, to a recruiter. "Dey took me an' kep me tree mont' an' nebber pay me, not one cent. My wife hav notting to eat— mus' starve."[22]

Despite the multiple setbacks these African American soldiers endured, some did find entrance into the armed forces to be an affirming experience. "Now we sogers are men—for the first time in our lives," a sergeant based in South Carolina told a meeting in Philadelphia. "Now we can look our old masters in de face. They used to sell and whip us, and we did not dare say one word. Now we ain't afraid, it they meet us, to run the bayonet through them." A former slave agreed with this assessment. "This was the biggest thing that ever happened in my life," he said. "I feel like a man with a uniform on and a gun in my hand." Even whites who worked with these men were struck by the transformation. "Put a United States uniform on his back and the *chattel* is a *man*," observed one white soldier. "You can see it in his look. Between the toiling slave and the soldier is nothing but a god could lift him over. He feels it, his looks show it."[23]

Becoming a "man" killed two racist conceptions of African Americans with one stone. In the years before the war, southern whites had defended their peculiar institution by describing blacks as children or animals, depending on which description made their "stewardship" more rhetorically defensible.[24] As armed soldiers, these people were neither. War has always been seen as a place where "boys" become men, but for African American men in the Civil War, this was particularly true, even poignant. Soldiering also endowed these men with a new power to prevent the capricious abuse of those who could no longer be considered property. "The fact is, when colored Soldiers are about they are afraid to kick colored people on the streets as they usually do," black minister Henry Turner told the secretary of war in February of 1866.[25]

Becoming a man also had sexual dimensions. Turner described an experience eight months before, when the men in his regiment stripped their clothes to cross a stream:

> I was much amused to see the secesh women watching with the utmost intensity, thousands of our soldiers, in a state of nudity. I suppose they desired to see whether these audacious Yankees were really men, made like other men, or if they were a set of varmints. So they thronged the windows, porticos, and yards, in the finest attire imaginable. Our brave boys would disrobe themselves, hang their garments upon their bayonets and through the water they would come, walk upon the street, and seem to say to the feminine gazers, "Yes, though naked, we are your masters."[26]

In this striking passage—and, one imagines, widely elsewhere—manhood becomes sexual power. In the antebellum South, intercourse (sexual and otherwise) was either taboo or cast African American men in a subordinate position. Now, however, these men have attained mastery over their bodies which they use for their own purposes, a mastery that compels white southerners to observe it in action. No force is used, no words are exchanged, but the effect of the new sexual order is unmistakable, symbolized by bayonets supporting (Yankee) uniforms.

For many men, black and white, the ultimate test of manhood was combat. As noted, African Americans participated in a number of land and sea battles in the first two years of the war, but three engagements in 1863 went far to validate — and valorize — the contributions of African Americans. The first of these was at Port Hudson in Louisiana, a key Confederate stronghold for the control of the Mississippi River. Black troops participated on an assault on the fort, which failed. But their performance impressed many observers. "It is no longer possible to doubt the bravery and steadiness of the colored race, when rightly led," the New York *Times* reported.[27] There is more than a little paternalism in this statement, as in Thomas Wentworth Higginson's remark that the men under his charge were "growing more like white men — less naive and less grotesque."[28] Yet just as much as the black soldiers it was white observers who were re-evaluating their perceptions in light of new developments.

This is true even of Confederates. Barely ten days after Port Hudson, at the battle of Milliken's Bend, African Americans played a crucial role in resisting a rebel attack designed to weaken the Federal grip around Port Hudson and Vicksburg. Perhaps the best explanation of what followed was offered by a southern general: "The charge was resisted by the negro portion of the enemy's force with considerable obstinacy, while the white or true Yankee portion ran like whipped curs almost as soon as the charge was ordered."[29] Even though "true" Yankees are white, this man allows that it was black soldiers who defeated the Confederates.

The most celebrated battle involving black troops was the struggle for Fort Wagner off the coast of Charleston in July of 1863. (This event forms the backdrop for *Glory*.) In part this stems from the participation of the Massachusetts 54th led by Robert Gould Shaw, the son of the prominent abolitionists, who would die in assault and be lionized for the next century. As in the case of Port Hudson, the assault on Wagner was a failure in military terms, but a resounding political and cultural victory for blacks. "It is not too much to say that if this Massachusetts 54th had faltered when its trial had come, two hundred thousand colored troops from whom it was a pioneer would never have been put into the field," according to the New York *Tribune*.[30] Black troops would later play an important role in the Virginia theater in 1864, and were the first to march into Charleston when the city finally fell in 1865.

As in so many other aspects of black life, these victories came at a price. First among these costs was death. At Milliken's Bend, one Louisiana regiment lost almost 45 percent of its men to death or casualties, one of the highest proportions of any battle in the whole war.[31] There is a cruel irony that black men did so much dying on the battlefield — considered the very zenith of manhood — even as they were still dismissed as less than men.

There was also a persistent concern that African Americans were used as cannon fodder. Seven months after the Fort Wagner attack, an attack all knew would be a bloodbath for the unit that led it, a correspondent from the New York *Tribune* testified before the American Freedmen's Inquiry Commission that a battle planner had said, "Well, I guess we will let [abolitionist general George] Strong lead and put those d----d niggers from Massachusetts in the advance; we may as well get rid of them, one time or another."[32] Ironically, even when white commanders had relatively good intentions, they could backfire. At the last minute, black units trained to lead the attack at the Battle of the Crater in 1864 were held back in favor of white units to avoid charges of treating black life casually. But when white units foundered in the assault, the blacks were sent to assist, got trapped, and the result was disaster for all.

Another problem was the enemy. The Confederacy refused to treat black soldiers as prisoners of war in exchange negotiations, which led the Union to stop exchanges altogether, with particularly tragic results for those in dangerously unhealthy prison camps. Threats to execute all black soldiers were never officially enacted, perhaps in fear of reprisals President Lincoln promised would follow. But rebel hatred for black troops led to widespread reports of brutal massacres, most notably at Fort Pillow, Tennessee, where future Ku Klux Klan founder Nathan Bedford Forrest allegedly allowed black soldiers who had surrendered to be executed and allegedly condoned the burning of a hospital. "Remember Fort Pillow!" became a rallying cry for black soldiers who subsequently fought with even greater ferocity, often flying a black flag that signified that they would not expect—or give—any mercy.

The most sincere form of flattery is imitation, and the Union's success in mobilizing black manpower led to proposals from leading Confederates to arm African Americans. To do so, however, would create difficult ideological contradictions for a would-be nation predicated on white supremacy and slavery, and such proposals were rejected. Still, as one proslavery theorist told Jefferson Davis in 1865, blacks could fight and be granted their freedom, but that's all—no voting, legal protection, or any form of equality. Indeed, such a suggestion seems prescient in suggesting the fate of African Americans before and after Reconstruction.[33] Even more persuasive than the force of such logic was the deteriorating military situation, and the support of General Robert E. Lee in enlisting blacks led the Confederate government to change its mind in the spring. By then, however, it was too late; within weeks, black Union troops would be first to march into Richmond. They would also be among the last to leave the army; the black population of the armed forces went from about one-tenth to over one-third by the fall of 1865, as earlier enlistees were mustered out first and some blacks were sent to remote outposts.[34]

The passage of the Thirteenth Amendment and Union victory in 1865 represented a watershed in African American history, one in which the actions of many blacks, North and South, slave and free, man and woman, had participated. The sense of pride of—and in—army veterans was especially strong, and many went on to become leaders in their communities. Some, like naval hero Robert Smalls and army officer Martin Delany, became important political leaders in state and national politics. For the rest of their lives, black men would relish their contributions. "If we hadn't become sojers, all might have gone back as it was before," former slave and army veteran Thomas Long wrote after the war. "But now tings can neber go back, because we have showed our energy and our courage and our naturally manhood."[35]

Perhaps the most important, and lasting, change freedom and fighting wrought was in African American families. For Long, demonstrating manhood was important not only for what it taught the outside world but also for the authority it would give him at home. "Suppose you had kept your freedom witout enlisting in dis army; your chilen might have grown up free and been well cultivated as to be equal to any business," he speculated. "But it would always have been flung in dere faces—'Your fader never fought for he own freedom'—and what could dey answer? Neber can say that to dis African Race any more."[36]

For some men, military experience provided a sense of empowerment even while they were away during the war. "Don't be uneasy my children I expect to have you," wrote a Missouri soldier to his two enslaved daughters in September 1864. To their master, he wrote, "I want you to understand that mary is my Child and she is a God given rite of my own and you may hold on to hear as long as you can but I want you to remember that the longor you keep my Child from me the longor you will have to burn in hell."[37] (The man was hospitalized on this day with chronic rheumatism and it's not known what happened; one can only hope the girls were recovered—and that father and daughters took solace from a sense of assertiveness that well might have been unimaginable three years before.)

Before the war, the white gender conventions of separate spheres and the cult of true womanhood were at best irrelevant and at worst oppressive to African Americans. Unlike elite white women, for example, black women were expected to work outside the home. Like some whites, black men performed physical labor, but as historian James Horton argues, "slavery demanded that black men forego the intellectual, emotional and temperamental traits of manhood. The ideal slave recognized his inability to control his life." The coming of emancipation then offered black women the possibility of returning to the home, and gave black men a powerful sense of agency over their own lives and responsibility for their families.[38]

In this regard, the war realigned gender conventions in the black community; as a result, they more closely resembled those of whites.[39] Indeed, at this point in their history, many African Americans rejected any attempt to suggest racial difference. Much to his frustration, Martin Delany, often consid-

ered a father of black nationalism, found it "dangerous to go into the country and speak of color in any manner whatever, without the angry rejoiner
'we don't want to hear that; we are all one color now.'"[40] This rejection of
racial difference would not remain in place for all people and all times; by
the end of the century, for example, some black women were finding that
white conceptions of womanhood were still irrelevant or oppressive, and
some white men were arguing that true manhood was predicated on whiteness.[41]

"How extraordinary, and what a tribute to ignorance and religious hypocrisy, is the fact that in the minds of most people, even those of liberals,
only murder makes men," W. E. B. Du Bois would later write. "The slave
pleaded, he was humble; he protected the women of the South, and the
world ignored him. The slave killed white men; and behold, he was a man."[42]
Yet if manhood was often conflated with the power to kill and destroy, the
documents explored here suggest that at least some black men also saw it as
a source of power to preserve and create. The key to that power was a personal
transformation, a fusion of biological fact and social aspiration that allowed
a man to help change his world. "What are you, anyhow," a white man
insultingly asked a South Carolina soldier in the middle of the war. "When
God made me I wasn't much," came the answer, "but I's a man now."[43]

NOTES

1. Joan Scott, *Gender and the Politics of History* (New York, 1988), 41.
2. James McPherson, *The Negro's Civil War: How Americans Felt and Acted During
the War for the Union* (Urbana, 1965), 22.
3. *Ibid.*, 33–34, 29.
4. *Ibid.*, 31.
5. This definition of manly—in contrast to masculine, which has more innate connotations—is developed in Gail Bederman, "Manly Civilization/Primitive Masculinity:
Race, Gender, and Evolutions of Middle-Class American Manhood" (Ph.D. dissertation, Brown University, 1992).
6. *The Negro's Civil War*, 32–33.
7. *Ibid.*, 162.
8. On p. 230 of *The Negro in the Civil War* (Boston, 1969), Benjamin Quarles
estimated one-quarter of naval enlistments were black. More recent calculations show
the figure to be around 9 percent.
9. *Ibid.*, 198; Ira Berlin, Joseph P. Reidy, and Leslie S. Rowland, eds., *Freedom: A
Documentary History of Emancipation 1861–1867, Series II: The Black Military Experience* (New York, 1982), 14.
10. Leon F. Litwack, *Been in the Storm So Long: The Aftermath of Slavery* (New York,
1980), 72.
11. Douglass quoted in *Black Writers and the Civil War*, ed. Richard A. Long
(Secaucus, 1988), 313.
12. *Been in the Storm So Long*, 74.
13. *Ibid.*, 66, 71; *Freedom*, 85.
14. *Freedom*, 77.

15. Joseph Glatthaar, *Forged in Battle: The Civil War Alliance Between Black Soldiers and White Officers* (New York, 1991), 9, 36. For the specific ways black officers were harassed, see documents in *Freedom,* 303–47.

16. *Forged in Battle,* 115.

17. *Freedom,* 387.

18. The inequality of the Union pay structure is well documented, and is discussed in much of the literature on African American soldiers in the Civil War. For one particularly good discussion, see McPherson's *The Negro's Civil War,* 193–204.

19. For documents pertaining to fatigue duty, see *Freedom,* 483–516; for figures on disease and explanations for the disparity between blacks and whites, see 633–37.

20. *Ibid.,* 153.

21. *Ibid.,* 385–86.

22. Willie Lee Rose, *Rehearsal for Reconstruction: The Port Royal Experiment* (New York, 1964), 267.

23. *Been in the Storm So Long,* 64, 101; *Forged in Battle,* 79.

24. For a discussion of such strategies, see William Taylor, *Cavalier and Yankee: The Old South and the American National Character* (New York, 1961).

25. *Freedom,* 757.

26. *Ibid.,* 97.

27. *Forged in Battle,* 130.

28. Thomas Wentworth Higginson, *Black Life in an Army Regiment* (1869; New York, 1984), 224.

29. *The Negro's Civil War,* 186–87; *Forged in Battle,* 133.

30. *The Negro's Civil War,* 191.

31. *Forged in Battle,* 134.

32. *Ibid.,* 137.

33. *Freedom,* 291–95.

34. *Ibid.,* 733.

35. *Been in the Storm So Long,* 102.

36. *Ibid.*

37. *Freedom,* 689–90. The owner of the girls wrote a letter to the commander of the Department of the Missouri asking that the soldier be forced to leave the state. "To be insulted by such a black scoundrel is more than I can stand," he said, claiming he had always been a Unionist, and, as such, his property should be protected (p. 691).

38. James Oliver Horton, "Freedom's Yoke: Gender Conventions Among Antebellum Free Blacks," *Feminist Studies* 12, no. 1 (Spring 1986): 53. For the work strategies of African American women, see Jacqueline Jones, *Labor of Love, Labor of Sorrow: Black Women, Work and the Family from Slavery to Freedom* (New York, 1985).

39. See the discussion of gender roles in *Freedom,* 30–32.

40. Eric Foner, *Reconstruction: America's Unfinished Revolution* (New York, 1988), 288.

41. Hazel Carby, *Reconstructing Womanhood: The Emergence of the Afro-American Novelist* (New York, 1987); Gail Bederman, "Civilization, the Decline of Middle-Class Manliness, and Ida B. Wells's Anti-Lynching Campaign (1892–1894)," *Radical History Review* (Winter 1992).

42. W. E. B. Du Bois, *Black Reconstruction* (New York, 1935), 110.

43. *The Negro in Civil War,* 199.

TWENTY

Raising a Black Regiment in Michigan: Adversity and Triumph

MICHAEL O. SMITH

At Detroit's Michigan Southern Railroad Depot on 28 March 1864, an infantry regiment boarded a train bound for Annapolis, Maryland, and a rendezvous with the Union Army. After bidding a quiet farewell to a few relatives and friends, the regiment left without the music, speeches, and public fanfare usually accorded men marching off to fight in the Civil War. This regiment was unlike the thirty other infantry regiments Michigan provided for the Union Army; eager young black men filled the ranks of the First Michigan Colored Infantry. The response of Detroit's two major newspapers to the regiment's departure reflected its stormy tenure in Detroit. For the Republican *Detroit Advertiser & Tribune* the regiment was a "fine body of men, earnest and loyal at heart," but the Democratic *Detroit Free Press* claimed otherwise: "This regiment left us yesterday, and its departure secures the peace and tranquility of our city. . . . Removed from [the] opportunity of disturbing the peace, and chances to indulge in their favorite pastime of clearing out German republican lager beer saloons, we little doubt that they will fully conform to Mr. Lincoln's idea of Negro troops."[1]

As reflected in the opposing viewpoints of the Detroit press, the First Michigan Colored Infantry was the focal point of heated political controversy. Indeed, federal policy notwithstanding (the government did not fully endorse the enlistment of blacks until it established the Bureau of Colored Troops on 22 May 1863), the regiment was organized only after much public debate and political posturing. Michigan's white citizens were divided over the First Michigan Colored Infantry; for the most part, Republicans supported the organization of the regiment and Democrats opposed it. But to

Michigan's black community, the First Michigan Colored Infantry fulfilled its long-held desire to contribute to the war effort, demonstrate loyalty to the Union, and earn a full measure of equality. To all groups, pro-black and anti-black, the First Michigan Colored Infantry represented, first and foremost, a symbol of black advancement. That it was also a combat unit was almost incidental.

The historiography of the Civil War is, perhaps, the largest concerning any American event, yet only a handful of studies address the role of black soldiers. Most of these writings focus on the federal government's slow progress toward acceptance of black enlistment, the government's subsequent recruitment and administration of black troops in the Union Army, the efforts a few northern states made to raise black units, and the battlefield exploits of notable black regiments. Originally published over thirty years ago, Dudley T. Cornish's *The Sable Arm* remains the single best volume on the subject. Likewise, Benjamin Quarles's *The Negro in the Civil War*, though dated, is still pertinent and highly informative. A few works—the bulk of which are post-war memoirs—describe the experiences of black troops at the regimental level. The most widely-read personal narrative concerning a black regiment is Thomas Wentworth Higginson's published diary, *Army Life in a Black Regiment*. Although his observations are those of a patronizing, albeit benevolent, white commanding officer of a black regiment, they are an invaluable resource. Several monographs, such as Peter Burchard's history of the renowned 54th Massachusetts, *One Gallant Rush: Robert Gould Shaw and his Brave Black Regiment*, focus on the more celebrated black regiments and the lives of their white commanding officers.[2] Overall, the vast majority of these contemporary and modern studies of black regiments concentrate on military life and combat experiences. The struggles to recruit and organize black troops at the local level are rarely explored.

This essay is about the First Michigan Colored Infantry, a not-so-famous black regiment about which little has been written.[3] It is about the political controversy surrounding the recruitment and organization of the regiment, the obstacles blacks faced in their struggle to enlist, and their final triumph. It is about raising a regiment in an often hostile, racist environment. The men of the First Michigan Colored Infantry were not destined for fame; however, they faced hardships that were common to all black soldiers in the Civil War, and a few that were unique to Detroit and Michigan. And, as soldiers, they were standard bearers for African-American freedom and equality.

From the moment the first shell burst upon the walls of Fort Sumter, blacks in Michigan viewed the advent of war as a means of achieving freedom for their southern brethren and equality for themselves. Within a few days, black Detroiters met at the Second Baptist Church[4] to affirm their loyalty to the Union, and resolved to sacrifice their lives and repel any invasion "at all hazards and to the last extremity." The following night, the

Detroit Liberty Guards, a black quasi-military unit, also met and pledged themselves to the same cause. But along with the solemn covenants of both groups, as the Liberty Guards' resolution so succinctly stated, Michigan blacks were "relying on the magnanimity of the American People to render us those rights, privileges, and protections which the Declaration of Independence, the Constitution, and laws of the government extend to, and should be *extended* to all men!" In other words, for their loyalty and possibly their lives, they expected to attain full citizenship.[5]

Although blacks in Michigan were eager to fight, two years and four months would pass before the First Michigan Colored Infantry began organizing. At the outset of the Civil War, Abraham Lincoln and his administration maintained that this was a war to save the Union, not to free the slaves, and took the position that the war should be fought by white men. As the war progressed, however, the Union Army's insatiable demand for soldiers, a changing attitude in the Northern policy toward black troops, and increasing recognition of slavery as the central issue of the conflict allowed the Lincoln administration to slowly take steps toward black enlistment. Finally, soon after the Emancipation Proclamation was decreed on 1 January 1863, the U.S. War Department began to authorize northern states to recruit and organize black troops.

The white public's perception of blacks was the major impediment to the enlistment of black troops. Despite the reputation of Michigan and other Midwestern states as strongholds for Radical Republicans and abolitionists, racism and Radical Republicanism were generally compatible. Many Michiganders and Midwesterners considered slavery a vile institution and sought its eradication, but they did not regard blacks as their equals, racially, politically, or socially.[6] For them, the Civil War was a white man's war and the use of black troops would insult Union soldiers. A number of white soldiers agreed. "The idea of arming the Negroes takes very well among those who want office . . ." wrote the young soldier Christopher Kellar to his parents in Michigan, "but the majority of soldiers do not think much of it . . . excuse me from military honors if I have to go among the niggers to get them." Lieutenant John C. Buchanan of the 8th Michigan Infantry claimed to have "seen none of these Colored Gemmen [*sic*] as yet who would be capable of fighting & will venture the assertion, such is their servility, that fifty of their masters would put to flight a Reg.[iment] of them."[7]

The issue of black enlistment also figured prominently in the partisan rivalries featured in Michigan's Republican and Democratic newspapers. *The Detroit Daily Advertiser* and *The Detroit Daily Tribune*, which merged in 1862 to become *The Detroit Daily Advertiser & Tribune*, championed black rights, the Republican Party platform, and the enlistment of blacks. *The Detroit Free Press*, which supported the Democratic Party and was virulently anti-black, remained resolute in its opinion that the only virtue of organizing a black regiment would be a decrease in the city's black population. Outstate newspapers were equally opinionated. Throughout the war these partisan journals, particularly the *Advertiser & Tribune* and the *Free Press*, debated the issue of black enlistment in their editorials and reports. The *Advertiser & Tribune* filled its pages with stories that argued for the enlistment of blacks, proclaiming complete faith in the ability of blacks to serve the Union in a devoted and courageous manner. "No one doubts the loyalty of the Negro population of Michigan, nor will anybody question their courage and determination to act," the newspaper claimed, and furthermore, "The Greatest eagerness is manifested by them that immediate measures be adopted for [black] enlistment." The *Free Press* had a different perspective. Before the organization of a black regiment was authorized by the federal government, it stated, "Now we wish the [Lincoln] administration to distinctly understand that the Democrats in Michigan are in favor of their taking every negro in the State; and not only that, but they would rejoice to see, in case enough negroes cannot be found to make a full regiment, that the balance should be made up from the ranks of abolitionists, without regard to their age." Once recruitment for the First Michigan Colored Infantry began, the *Free Press* withdrew any limited support for black enlistment it may have had, and denounced all efforts to raise a black regiment.[8]

While many editorials in Detroit's Republican newspapers encouraged black enlistment, they simultaneously reinforced popular racial stereotypes, claiming that blacks possessed great imitative powers, learned drill well, were more susceptible to discipline than white soldiers, and could furnish much of the heavy labor required by the Union Army. Speaking for the *Daily Advertiser*, its correspondent "Wolverine" wrote that "there is much they [blacks] might do to relieve the soldiers. All the cooking, camp cleaning, cutting wood, drawing water, handling heavy supplies, repairing roads, and much more might be done by them." The *Advertiser & Tribune* argued that black troops would create a supply of acclimated troops for duty in the sickly sections of the South. Finally, the *Advertiser & Tribune* appealed to the practical side of the white community: "Every Negro soldier enlisted and sent into the field diminishes by one the number of white men drafted. Therefore a squeamish fellow who objects to having his fighting done by 'a nigger' should at once report himself to the nearest recruiting office and enlist."[9]

The *Advertiser & Tribune*'s promotion of black enlistment went beyond rhetorical support; its editor, Henry Barns, was the primary architect of the First Michigan Colored Infantry. A prominent figure in Detroit and Michigan for many years, Barns began his journalistic career in 1837 as a writer for his future rival, the *Free Press*, and remained on its editorial staff for fourteen years. Along with several other individuals, Barns established the *Detroit Tribune* in 1851. When that journal merged with the *Detroit Advertiser*, he became editor of the *Detroit Advertiser & Tribune*. From this influential position, Barns advocated the organization of black troops, and actively campaigned for the recruitment of a black regiment in Michigan.[10]

In the spring of 1863, Barns asked Michigan's Radical Republican governor, Austin Blair, for permission to organize a black regiment. Although Blair favored raising black troops, and had previously applied to the federal government for authorization to recruit black soldiers, he could not organize a black regiment without the express consent of the U.S. War Department. For this reason, Blair denied Barns's request. Barns then appealed directly to Secretary of War Edwin M. Stanton. In August 1863, Governor Blair finally received orders from Stanton to raise a black regiment. Stanton also suggested that it "would be gratifying if you should give such authority to Mr. Barns."[11] Finally, on 12 August 1863, Michigan Adjutant General John Robertson authorized Barns to raise a black regiment. Barns was commissioned Colonel of the First Michigan Colored Infantry and began to recruit with a passion.[12]

By this time, there had been a dramatic change in the North's attitude toward black soldiers. Mounting casualty lists from two years of war, especially those from the recent battle at Gettysburg, caused many citizens and the government to look favorably upon black enlistment. Northerners were no longer eager to enlist, and the War Department needed to replenish the ranks of its armies. Black troops had also proved their mettle at Fort Wagner and in several other engagements, causing many white soldiers, like Lt. John Buchanan, to change their perceptions of black soldiers: "The raising of negro troops goes on & they do nobly in battle. [They] vie even with the Anglo Saxon."[13]

Predictably, the raising of a black regiment in Michigan, particularly one commanded by the editor of a Republican journal, further stimulated the newspaper war. In an especially vehement attack, the *Free Press* condemned Barns, claiming that while organizing the regiment he had endeavored to "educate Negroes to hate white men." Blacks, the editorial contended, should not have an "obnoxious white man forced upon them as a 'nigger head'. . . . Neither the editor of the *Advertiser & Tribune*, nor the Negro man under him, can be induced to go out of the State into the field for actual war." The *Advertiser & Tribune* denounced the attacks on Barns: "It was not expected that the Editor of the *Free Press* would approve 'the use of negroes in the war' *because* that would injure his 'Southern brethren,'" and that "the *Free Press* would rather have a white man drafted and torn from his family than permit a negro to volunteer in his place. . . ."[14]

Undeterred by the diatribes delivered by the *Free Press* and its supporters, Barns concentrated on recruitment. Although Barns and the black community had long desired a black regiment, initially blacks did not rush to the recruiting stations. Early recruitment efforts were frustrated on several fronts: poor enlistment incentives, competition from out-of-state recruiters, a strong economy desperately short of labor, constant accusations by the *Free Press* against the character and motives of Barns, insufficient supplies, pitiful winter barracks, and finally, an often hostile white public reception.

When the First Michigan Colored Infantry began to organize there were no bounties for black enlistees. The state of Michigan, various cities and towns, and even individual wards in the city of Detroit offered enlistment inducements ranging from fifty to one hundred dollars, but these incentives were exclusively reserved for white soldiers. Black soldiers were not eligible for federal bounties until mid-1864. Because of competition from out-of-state recruiters, the lack of bounties was particularly damaging to recruiting efforts. For example, recruiters for the 54th Massachusetts Infantry, easily the most famous black regiment of the Civil War, had been recruiting in Michigan since the spring of 1863 and offered enlistment bounties of one hundred fifty dollars. (According to one source, over sixty Michigan blacks were on the roster of the 54th Massachusetts.) Furthermore, at the same time that the First Michigan Colored Infantry began to organize, the state's flourishing wartime economy produced numerous civilian employment opportunities.[15]

It should not be construed that blacks volunteered only for the prospect of a financial reward. Nevertheless, economic considerations were extremely important to many black recruits. Besides the absence of enlistment bounties, the Union Army paid black soldiers much less than white soldiers. Many black soldiers also had families to support and were reluctant to accept anything less than the best offer for their services. In other words, once a black man decided to fight for the Union, why would he enlist in Michigan's black regiment when he could receive a substantial bounty by joining another state's regiment, and why should he receive less pay than his white counterparts?[16]

Barns was well aware that blacks enlisting in the First Michigan Colored Infantry deserved a bounty, and he made several efforts to secure bounties for them. Shortly after he began organizing the regiment, Barns requested that the Detroit Board of Aldermen (which was a Democratic stronghold) offer an enlistment bounty of fifty dollars for each recruit. His request was denied. At the same time, Barns also appealed unsuccessfully to the state for bounties for black soldiers. In October he wrote to the Adjutant General of the United States requesting a modest fifteen dollar premium for each recruit. Three months later Barns received a reply denying his request but offering this encouragement: "It is confidently expected that Congress will, at a very early day, by enactment place all who bear arms in the service of the country on the same footing as regards pay, bounties, and premiums." The "early day" would not occur for another six months.[17]

Later in the fall of 1863 several Michigan communities finally began to offer bounties to black recruits. Motivated by the impending draft—as the *Advertiser & Tribune* suggested, each black man enlisted reduced by one the number of white men needed to meet draft quotas—these communities viewed black recruits as a means of filling their draft quotas. The Board of Aldermen finally approved a one hundred dollar bounty for every volunteer, regardless of race, credited to Wayne County's draft quota. This bounty, however, was issued in the form of a bond that could not be cashed until the black soldier's enlistment obligation expired. Soon after the Board of Alder-

men bounty was approved, individual wards in Detroit offered small bounties, and out-state communities, such as Kalamazoo and Ypsilanti, also began offering enlistment incentives for black recruits.[18]

If the frustrations associated with the lack of bounties for enlistees were
not enough to cause recruitment problems, Barns was further hindered by
the personal attacks of the *Free Press*. At the outset of his recruitment operations the newspaper had labeled Barns's efforts to raise a black regiment
an "imposture," but during the fall of 1863 the accusations of the *Free Press*
became increasingly vehement. The most damaging attack concerned the
bonds that were issued as bounties to enlistees in the First Michigan Colored
Infantry. Beginning in October, the *Free Press* accused Barns of forcing
recruits to sign their bonds over to him for a quarter of their value, and
insisted Barns was reaping huge profits for himself. The newspaper also
named as co-conspirators two prominent black citizens, George DeBaptist
and John Richards, who were important recruiters for the regiment. A few
days later, the rampaging journal claimed that Barns was also securing for
himself a two dollar enlistment fee, a twenty dollar ward bond, and any
township or other city bounties that may have been offered to recruits. The
Free Press further charged that Barns was guilty of bullying, abusing, and
generally punishing those recruits who did not sign over their bonds. "Complaints are becoming more numerous every day from members of the colored regiment . . ." claimed the *Free Press*, and furthermore: "They are only
poor, ignorant colored men, and none of the government officials will listen
to their story."[19]

Barns, of course, defended himself through the editorial page of the *Advertiser & Tribune*. He explained that he secured the bonds to protect the
recruits from unscrupulous speculators, and that the regiment was fully
aware of his attempt to protect the full worth of the bonds for their benefit.
He dismissed the accusations against him, declaring: "The libellers of the
Free Press and its correspondents cannot divert me from my purpose."[20]

In this same editorial, Barns also provided his reasons for organizing the
black regiment. First, he had been sought out by influential black Detroiters
and petitioned to lend his name and support to the establishment of a black
regiment. Arguing that blacks in Michigan had long desired the opportunity
to serve in the Union Army and prove themselves, Barns gave two additional
reasons for his participation: to "give the colored people of this section an
opportunity to vindicate their patriotism and bravery," and to "avoid a draft in
this City, County, and State."[21]

Barns did not face this attack alone. The black community endorsed his
actions on several occasions, with prominent black Detroiters such as William Lambert, John D. Richards, William Webb, and George DeBaptist
speaking in support of Barns and the black regiment. On 23 November
1863, for example, black community leaders from Detroit held an important
meeting at the Second Baptist Church. They passed resolutions praising the
work of Barns and denouncing the *Free Press* as their sworn enemy.[22]

Despite the obstacles to recruitment, the ranks of the regiment began to fill. The enlistments came slowly at first, and by the end of October the strength of the regiment stood at three hundred.[23] But after the Detroit Board of Aldermen issued enlistment bounties in November, the pace of enlistment began to increase. During December, due to a grand recruitment tour of southern Michigan, the strength of the regiment doubled.

About 250 members of the First Michigan Colored Infantry, including the newly formed regimental band, began a whirlwind tour of southern Michigan on 8 December, visiting Ypsilanti, Ann Arbor, Jackson, Marshall, Niles, Kalamazoo, and Grand Rapids. They paraded in Ypsilanti and "the ladies and gentlemen thronged the streets to get a glimpse of the colored soldiers." In Jackson, the black soldiers were reviewed by Governor Blair, who declared: "I hope you will be able to fight as to put the country under obligation to you." At the other stops along the way they were cheered and generally well-received. The black soldiers returned to Detroit on 15 December, having enlisted new recruits at each stop, and having demonstrated to a good portion of the state their ability to bear themselves in a military manner.[24]

The First Michigan Colored Infantry reached a full strength of 895 on 17 February 1864 and was mustered into the Union Army.[25] Still, the regiment waited six weeks before it left the state and joined the Union Army. Many of the men had been "soldiering" for over five months by this time, following a dreary routine of drill, fatigue duty, and numerous parades and inspections, and they were becoming restless. Unfortunately, during the last two months the regiment was stationed in Detroit there were a number of desertions from the regiment, and frequent confrontations between its members and white Detroiters.

The extremely harsh physical environment the soldiers endured during this period was one of their toughest opponents. Essentials such as blankets and clothing were always in short supply throughout their sojourn in Detroit, but the most serious problem was their barracks at Camp Ward. Although Camp Ward was constructed as a temporary facility, the regiment was billeted there until it left the state. U.S. Army Surgeon Charles Tripper inspected Camp Ward in December and found appalling conditions: leaky roofs and walls, no flooring, and straw-stuffed bedsacks instead of bunks were but a few of the problems cited. And the winter of 1863–64 was a particularly bitter one, which caused great suffering among the regiment's members. Many men became sick, and twenty-five died. The situation became intolerable for many of the black soldiers, and they decided to abandon the regiment; 122 of the 187 total regimental desertions (65%) were recorded between December 1863 and March 1864.[26]

While the newspapers acknowledged the plight of the soldiers at Camp Ward, most of the public's attention was directed toward inimical encounters between black soldiers and white citizens of Detroit. There were many reports, in both newspapers, of confrontation with local "roughs," saloon brawls, and instances where members of the 1st Michigan Colored Infantry were abused physically or verbally or both. Most irksome to many white Detroiters, especially those in the German section of the city near Camp Ward, were the black soldiers' attempts to enter establishments traditionally for "whites only" and unaccustomed to serving blacks. Their reception in such places was less than friendly. Another example of the indignities suffered by the regiment occurred in March 1864, when the returning 10th Michigan Infantry, upon learning that the 1st Michigan Colored Infantry's band would lead their parade, refused to march behind them.[27]

Predictably, the *Free Press* was the first to declare the 1st Michigan Colored Infantry "unruly." "The practice of allowing members of 'Colonel Barns's' Darkey regiment to parade the streets . . . is fast approaching a stage where it should be declared a nuisance, and abated as such. . . . They enter saloons and restaurants, where it has always been the custom to refuse selling niggers, and if not accommodated, commence preparations for a fight." The *Free Press* surmised that Barns condoned this behavior because he had the audacity to claim that blacks were as good as white men and should be entitled to the same privileges at saloons and eating houses as white men. The *Advertiser & Tribune* reluctantly acknowledged incidents of disorderly conduct and occasions of drunkenness by members of the First Michigan Colored Infantry, but emphasized the outstanding general character of the regiment and recognized the patience displayed thus far.[28]

A few black soldiers of the First Michigan Colored Infantry were indeed involved in several unsavory affairs, but their motives for this behavior were seldom discussed. Some incidents resulted from drunkenness or ill-temper, but others resulted from frustration. When black men donned the uniform of the 1st Michigan Colored Infantry, soon to be the uniform of the Union Army, they felt that some respect was due them. After all, the colonel of the regiment and black community leaders had been telling them that, through military service, they would soon cause whites to recognize their right to the privileges that white men enjoyed. Instead, black soldiers of the 1st Michigan Colored Infantry did not have the same prerogatives as white soldiers, and often faced a hostile white community.

Despite these difficulties and the intense emotions surrounding the First Michigan Colored Infantry, blacks filled the ranks of the regiment, and in March it left to join the Union's Department of the South. But recruitment for the 1st Michigan Colored Infantry did not end with its departure. Michigan was one of the few states that replenished the ranks of its existing infantry regiments after casualties and desertions depleted them; therefore, recruiting for the 1st Michigan Colored Infantry continued until the end of the war. While 895 men were members of the regiment when it first mustered into the Union Army, additional men joined the regiment at later dates, ultimately bringing the total enlistment to 1555.[29]

The continuing recruitment for the regiment reinforced the First Michigan Colored Infantry's primary appeal to the white community, which was related to the Enrollment Act of March 1863 (i.e. the draft); for every black who enlisted in the 1st Michigan Colored Infantry, one white was removed from the state's draft quota. But beyond this simple equation, one specific section of the Enrollment Act directly affected the regiment's relationship to the white community. This was Section 13, which provided for substitution and commutation, and represented the most controversial provision of the draft. Under this section, draftees could pay men to serve in their places, or escape military service completely by paying the federal government a $300 commutation fee. Substitution was legal throughout the four federal drafts, while commutation was in effect for the first two. In theory, substitution enabled any draftee with a civilian station or occupation that was crucial to the war effort to remain at work, but in practice it allowed any citizen with sufficient financial resources to avoid military service.[30]

After the commutation clause was eliminated and blacks began to substitute for whites in the summer of 1864, a significant portion of enlistments in the 1st Michigan Colored Infantry were substitutes. Over 254 blacks enrolled as substitutes, or about 16 percent of the total regimental enlistments. In comparison, for the entire war, an estimated two percent of Michigan troops and three percent of the Union Army as a whole were substitutes.[31]

Substitution had a greater impact upon the 1st Michigan Colored Infantry than the regimental substitution rate indicates. If the initial muster of 895 men and the desertions and deaths before the regiment came under federal authority are eliminated, substitution accounts for 50.7 percent of enlistments after the regiment left the state. During the last two drafts in Michigan, in fall 1864 and spring 1865, when blacks were allowed to substitute for whites, 1022 of 2480 men drafted secured substitutes. Black substitutes represented 24 percent of these state substitutes, and all evidence suggests that the men hiring black substitutes were white.[32]

The primary attraction for blacks who chose to offer their services as substitutes was an economic one. Demand for substitutes was high, and with a shrewd substitute broker—brokers almost completely controlled the supply of men willing to substitute for others—and a little luck, a man could earn a substantial sum in a short period of time. For example, William H. Butler enlisted in the 1st Michigan Colored Infantry as a substitute and received $860 for his services; John Carmel received $1100. Clearly, every substitute did not fare as well as these two; however, almost all of them received more than $300.[33]

One other dimension of substitution in the 1st Michigan Colored Infantry deserves mention. During the Civil War drafts the Union Army never managed to cope with the serious problem of mass substitute desertion. Many men accepted bounties or became substitutes only to desert the moment they received their money. The First Michigan Colored Infantry's experience was the direct opposite of the national one. The overwhelming majority of the substitutes in the regiment fulfilled their military obligations. Of a total of 245 substitutes, only seven deserted.[34] The reasons for this phenomenon are not clear. Perhaps it was a geographical reason. The regiment was stationed in the South, where desertion meant entering Confederate-held territory and the prospect of extremely harsh treatment or death if captured. The practice of withholding a significant portion of a substitute's bounty until his enlistment obligation was fulfilled may also have had an effect. It may have been due to extraordinary dedication to the regiment, and to the "cause." There is no evidence that explains the low substitute desertion rate, but it remains one facet of the 1st Michigan Colored Infantry's splendid service record.

Although its military record was exemplary, the beginning of the 1st Michigan Colored Infantry's tour of duty was hardly auspicious. Upon leaving Detroit in March, the regiment was assigned to the Union Army's Department of the South. It arrived at Hilton Head Island, South Carolina, on 16 April 1864. Soon thereafter the regiment was redesignated the 102nd United States Colored Troops. With the exception of a two-week raid into Florida, the regiment spent the months from April to November, 1864, in drilling, picketing, and constructing fortifications. Indeed, most of the regiment's tour with the Union Army was spent in this manner.[35]

Once attached to the Union Army there was a change in command of the 1st Michigan Colored Infantry. During the organization of the regiment, Henry Barns had admitted a lack of military experience and stated that he would not lead the regiment into battle. True to his word, on 12 April 1864 he resigned his commission and returned to Detroit. Three days later Lt. Colonel Henry L. Chipman was promoted to Colonel, and he commanded the regiment for the remainder of the war. Chipman was a West Point graduate and a career military man. Prior to duty with the 1st Michigan Colored Infantry, he had served with the Second Michigan Infantry and regular army units. Chipman was meritoriously promoted three times during the course of the war, the third time while commanding the 1st Michigan Colored Infantry. Like all other officers of the regiment, he was white. (Almost all officers of black regiments in the Union Army were white.)[36]

The regiment had its first encounter with the enemy in August 1864. Along with Union detachments, the 102nd conducted a one-hundred-mile raid into Florida to destroy railroad tracks. On 11 August it was suddenly attacked by Confederate cavalry. After a brief skirmish, the 102nd easily repulsed the enemy, convincing its officers of the "reliable and gallant fighting qualities of their men."[37]

From November 1864 through April 1865, the 102nd United States Colored Troops fought several pitched battles and numerous skirmishes with Confederate forces, performing with courage on each occasion. The regiment's severest test and greatest achievement came on 30 November 1864, at the battle of Honey Hill, South Carolina. Three hundred officers and men of the 102nd United States Colored Troops were attached to Brigadier-General John Hatch's Coast Division, which was charged with breaking the Charleston and Savannah Railroad. In a hot fight with rebel forces at Honey Hill, the men of the 102nd United States Colored Troops fought bravely and tenaciously. One officer, Lieutenant Orson W. Bennett, won the Congressional Medal of Honor for his actions. (Several months later, Lieutenant Charles Barrell, also of the 102nd United States Colored Troops, won the Medal of Honor at Swift's Creek.) Until the opposing Confederate forces finally surrendered on 21 April 1865, the 102nd United States Colored Troops campaigned in South Carolina, skirmishing with the enemy, demolishing miles of railroad, and burning enemy supplies. Alonzo Reed, one of the members of the 102nd United States Colored Troops, wrote about the regiment's activities from Charleston on 25 February 1865: "We have had pretty hard marching through the state. . . . We have ransacked every plantation on our way and burnt up everything we could not carry away."[38] After a summer of guard duty in the South, the regiment was mustered out of the Union Army on 30 September 1865. Its losses were six killed in action, five dead from battle wounds, and 129 dead from disease. The regiment returned to Detroit within several weeks, and even the *Free Press* acknowledged that the First Michigan Colored Infantry had "fought nobly."[39]

During the two years the First Michigan Colored Infantry existed as an organized military unit, the regiment's primary status was that of a political symbol. To some of its white supporters the regiment was proof that blacks were fully capable of military service, and therefore deserving of civil rights. To others it was merely a means of reducing the burden of the draft. To its detractors the First Michigan Colored Infantry was inherently evil, and represented a threat to the superior position of whites. To the black community in Michigan it was the vehicle by which they could demonstrate their loyalty and courage, and thus hopefully procure equal rights as citizens.

The First Michigan Colored Infantry never received national acclaim for its wartime service. Attached to the Union's Department of the South, it served in a minor theater of the Civil War and never participated in a famous battle. Nevertheless, these black soldiers deserve some recognition. From the time they enlisted until they mustered out of the Union Army they faced numerous obstacles and hardships that white soldiers never encountered, and pursued a dream that white soldiers would never understand.

NOTES

1. *The Detroit Advertiser & Tribune*, 29 March 1864; *The Detroit Free Press*, 29 March 1864.
2. Dudley T. Cornish, *The Sable Arm: Black Troops in the Union Army, 1861–1865* (New York: Longmans, Green and Co., Inc., 1956; reprint, Lawrence, University Press of Kansas, 1987); Benjamin Quarles, *The Negro in the Civil War* (Boston: Little Brown and Company, 1953); Thomas Wentworth Higginson, *Army Life in a Black Regiment* (Boston: Fields and Osgood, 1870; reprint, New York: W. W. Norton and Company,

1984); Peter Burchard, *One Gallant Rush: Robert Gould Shaw and his Brave Black Regiment* (New York: St. Martin's Press, 1965). The most recent general history of black soldiers is Hondon B. Hargrove, *Black Union Soldiers in the Civil War* (Jefferson, NC: McFarland & Company, Inc., 1988). The best single bibliography of writings on black soldiers in the Civil War is Lenwood G. Davis and George Hill, *Blacks in the American Armed Forces, 1776–1983: A Bibliography* (Westport: Greenwood Press, 1985). It should also be noted that *Glory*, an excellent and substantially accurate feature film concerning the 54th Massachusetts Infantry, was released in 1989.

3. Several secondary sources briefly mention the First Michigan Colored Infantry. Willis F. Dunbar and George S. May, *Michigan: A History of the Wolverine State*, rev. ed. (Grand Rapids, MI: William B. Eerdmans Publishing Company, 1980); Silas S. Farmer, *The History of Detroit and Michigan* (Detroit: Silas Farmer & Company, 1884); Charles Lanman, *The Red Book of Michigan: A Civil, Military and Biographical History* (Detroit: E. B. Smith & Company, 1871). The only detailed accounts of the First Michigan Colored Infantry are: Norman McRae, *Negroes in Michigan During the Civil War* (Lansing, MI: Michigan Civil War Centennial Observance Commission, 1966); William Dunn, "A History of the First Michigan Colored Regiment" (Master's Thesis, Central Michigan University, 1967); Michael O. Smith, "The First Michigan Colored Infantry: A Black Regiment in the Civil War" (Master's Thesis, Wayne State University, 1987).

4. The Second Baptist Church was created and so named because the white "First Baptist Church" of Detroit refused to allow blacks into its congregation.

5. *The Detroit Daily Tribune*, 16 April 1861, 26 April 1881, 27 April 1861, 4 May 1861; *The Detroit Daily Advertiser*, 2 May 1861.

6. V. Jacque Voegeli, *Free But Not Equal: The Midwest and the Negro During the Civil War* (New York: Harper and Row, 1977), 1–9, 98–99. This is an excellent study of the Civil War socio-political environment in the North.

7. Christopher H. Kellar to George and Esther Kellar, 8 May 1863, The James Schloff Civil War Letter Collection, The William L. Clements Library, Ann Arbor, Michigan; John Buchanan to his wife, Sophie Buchanan, 29 December 1861; George M. Blackburn, ed., "The Negro Viewed by a Michigan Civil War Soldier: Letter of John C. Buchanan," *Michigan History*, 47 (March 1963), 81.

8. *The Detroit Advertiser & Tribune*, 29 January 1863, 14 April 1863; *The Detroit Free Press*, 22 April 1863. For examples of outstate newspaper opinions on black soldiers, see *The Grand Rapids Eagle*, 19 February 1863; *The Jackson Citizen*, 6 May 1862; *The Niles Republican*, 8 August 1863.

9. *The Detroit Advertiser & Tribune*, 14 April 1863, 2 May 1863, 2 June 1863, 3 June 1863; *The Detroit Daily Advertiser*, 1 May 1862.

10. *Early History of Michigan with Biographies of State Officers, Members of Congress, Judges, Legislators, Published Pursuant to Act 59, 1887* (Lansing, MI: Thorp, Godfrey, State Printers and Binders, 1888), 70–71; Norman McRae, *Negroes in Michigan During the Civil War*, 80–81.

11. Secretary of War Edwin M. Stanton to Governor Austin Blair, in Michigan Adjutant General's Office, *Michigan in the War*, comp. John Robertson, adjutant General, rev. ed. (Lansing, MI: W. S. George and Co., 1882), 488–89.

12. *The Detroit Free Press*, 30 October 1863; Adjutant General of Michigan John Robertson to Henry Barns, Robertson, *Michigan in the War*, 489.

13. Cornish, *The Sable Arm*, 152–156; John C. Buchanan to Sophie Buchanan, 30 July 1863, in Blackburn, "The Negro as Viewed by a Michigan Civil War Soldier," 84.

14. *The Detroit Free Press*, 21 August 1863; *The Detroit Advertiser & Tribune*, 22 August 1863, 25 August 1863.

15. Cornish, *The Sable Arm*, 188; *The Detroit Advertiser & Tribune*, 21 April 1863, 27 June 1863, 16 September 1863; *The Detroit Free Press*, 22 April 1863, 17 September 1863; Luis F. Emilio, *A Brave Black Regiment: History of the 54th Regiment of Massachusetts Infantry, 1863–1865*, 2nd ed. (New York: Arno Press and the *New York Times*, 1969), 327–28.

16. Cornish, *The Sable Arm*, 184–195. For numerous examples of black soldiers' financial problems, see Ira Berlin, ed., *Freedom: A Documentary History of Emancipation, 1861–1867, Series II, The Black Military Experience* (New York: Cambridge University Press, 1982); for an example concerning the 1st Michigan C.I., see George G. Freeman to United States Chief Justice, 25 June 1865, 379.

17. Assistant Adjutant General C. W. Foster to Henry Barns, 14 December 1863, Records of the Michigan Military Establishment, 1828–1941, Regimental Service Records of the First Michigan Colored Infantry, Archives of the State of Michigan, Lansing, MI (cited hereafter as Regimental Service Records); *The Detroit Advertiser & Tribune*, 18 September 1863, 26 October 1863, 26 November 1863; *The Detroit Free Press*, 25 August 1863, 18 November 1863.

18. *The Detroit Advertiser & Tribune*, 25 August 1863, 9 October 1863, 26 November 1863; *The Detroit Free Press*, 29 October 1863, 18 November 1863.

19. *The Detroit Free Press*, 25 August 1863, 21 September 1863, 24 October 1863, 29 October 1863, 18 November 1863, 28 March 1865, 25 February 1866.

20. *The Detroit Advertiser & Tribune*, 30 October 1863; a case concerning the soldiers' bounties was filed against Barns and a trial was held in February 1866. On 20 February 1866 the *Free Press* reported that the suit was decided in his favor.

21. *The Detroit Advertiser & Tribune*, 30 October 1863.

22. *The Detroit Advertiser & Tribune*, 26 November 1863; *The Detroit Free Press*, 24 November 1863.

23. *The Detroit Advertiser & Tribune*, 30 October 1863.

24. *The Detroit Advertiser & Tribune*, 9–15 December 1863.

25. *The Detroit Advertiser & Tribune*, 15 January 1863; Robertson, *Michigan in the War*, 489.

26. *The Detroit Advertiser & Tribune*, 23 December 1863; *The Detroit Free Press*, 28 December 1863; Michigan Adjutant General's Office, *Record of Service of Michigan Volunteers in the Civil War, 1861–1865*, vol. 46; *The First Michigan Colored Infantry* (Kalamazoo, Ihling Bros. and Everhard, 1905).

27. *The Detroit Advertiser & Tribune*, 21 January 1864, 21 February 1864, 7 March 1864, 19 March 1864; *The Detroit Free Press*, 12 March 1864.

28. *The Detroit Advertiser & Tribune*, 7 March 1864; *The Detroit Free Press*, 15 January 1864, 24 February 1864.

29. Michigan Adjutant General, *Service Record* lists 1555 total enlistees. According to the U.S. Provost Marshal, 1387 served in the Union Army. Report of the Provost Marshal General's Bureau, 17 March 1866. Part IV, cited in Morris J. McGregor and Bernard C. Natty, *Blacks in the United States Armed Forces*, vol. II (Wilmington: Scholarly Resources, 1977), 171.

30. Eugene C. Murdock, *One Million Men: The Civil War Draft in the North* (Madison: The State Historical Society of Wisconsin, 1971), 178–80; *The Detroit Free Press*, 10 February 1865.

31. Murdock, *One Million Men*, 356; Robertson, *Michigan and the War*, 69–72; Muster-In Rolls, Regimental Service Records. The discussion of substitution is derived from a more extensive treatment in Smith, "The First Michigan Colored Infantry," 89–98.

32. Murdock, *One Million Men*, 180, 353; Muster-In Rolls, Regimental Service Records; Michigan Adjutant General's Office, *Annual Report of the State of Michigan for the Year 1863* (Lansing, John A. Kerr and Co., 1864), 13. I have not conducted an in-depth analysis of the men hiring substitutes, but those that I have located in the census, Detroit City Directories, and other sources, have been white.

33. Muster-In Rolls, Regimental Service Records; Murdock, *One Million Men*, 259; *The Detroit Free Press*, 22 April 1863, 18 November 1863, 12 August 1864.

34. Ibid.; Smith, "The First Michigan Colored Infantry," 99–102; Ella Lonn, *Desertion During the Civil War* (New York: The American Historical Association and the Century Co., 1928), 138–42; Murdock, *One Million Men*, 184–187, 194.

35. For more extensive treatments of the Regiment's military service, see Smith, "The

First Michigan Colored Infantry," 105–135; and Dunn, "A History of the First Michigan Colored Regiment," 66–126.

36. Monthly returns, April 1864, Service Records of the First Michigan Colored Infantry; Robertson, *Michigan in the War*, 188–189, 204, 796; Smith, "First Michigan Colored Infantry," 109–112.

37. Robertson, *Michigan in the War*, 490.

38. U.S. War Department, *The War of the Rebellion: A Compilation of the Official Records of the Union and Confederate Armies*, 128 vols. (Washington: Government Printing Office, 1880–1902), ser. 1, vol. XLIV, 421–27, 432–34, and ser. 1, vol. XLVII, 1027; Alonzo Reed to his mother, 25 February 1865, The Alonzo Reed Papers, Duke University Library.

39. Robertson, *Michigan in the War*, 493; *The Detroit Free Press*, 18 October 1865.

TWENTY-ONE

"To Come Forward and Aid in Putting Down This Unholy Rebellion": The Officers of Louisiana's Free Black Native Guard during the Civil War Era

MANOJ K. JOSHI AND JOSEPH P. REIDY

The social transformation surrounding slave emancipation profoundly affected Southern free blacks, but none more so than Louisiana's free people of color. The Civil War and Reconstruction at once threatened their privileged position and promised to enlarge their liberty along with that of all blacks. By so doing, wartime and postwar events magnified the forces that had historically pulled free blacks in contradictory directions: toward the world of the white planters and toward the world of the black slaves. Struggling to maintain their balance and, if possible, to enhance their own position as the old order crumbled, the free people wavered between the two worlds. Despite nearly universal white opposition to black equality, the free people developed only a shaky alliance with the former slaves, seemingly natural allies in the battle against prejudice. Differences rooted in the eighteenth century continued to haunt relations between those free before the war and those freed by the war. The free blacks' response to civil war and reconstruction illuminates both their unique past and the new postwar order they helped shape.

From the time of Spanish and French rule in Louisiana, New Orleans free people of color enjoyed privileges far beyond those of black slaves. Openly claiming European as well as African ancestry, many freemen flaunted their cosmopolitan backgrounds and culture. On the eve of the Civil War, New

Orleans freemen owned two million dollars' worth of property, and fully 85 percent worked as artisans, professionals, and proprietors. The most prosperous owned large plantations and hundreds of slaves. Unlike free blacks elsewhere in the South, they could travel without restriction; they could testify against whites; and they did not have to register with the state or acknowledge dependence upon a white guardian. Though they lacked the vote, on several occasions they successfully mobilized white patrons and allies to defeat attempts to limit their liberty. In short, the Louisiana free black community enjoyed economic, social, and cultural privileges scarcely matched by any free black caste in the Western Hemisphere.[1]

Free blacks in New Orleans had long used military service, first on behalf of the French and Spanish and later on behalf of the United States, to protect their privileged position. For their efforts in the War of 1812 and particularly during the fighting at New Orleans in 1814 and 1815, they earned the praise of General Andrew Jackson.[2] Although Louisiana authorities eventually stripped them of their arms, the state paid free colored soldiers pensions and the federal government granted them bounties. Denied the chance to maintain their military organization, the soldiers refused to let die their proud tradition. They formed a benevolent association, the "Association of Colored Veterans of 1814 and 1815," which provided mutual support in the event of death or incapacity to work and celebrated their martial past.[3]

With the outbreak of the Civil War, Confederates viewed the free black community suspiciously, fearing a potentially explosive union between freemen and slaves. Rebel partisans threatened severe reprisals to any free person of color suspected of disloyalty and watched closely for suspicious signs. In the circumstances, many free people of color viewed military service as the surest guarantee of their security.[4] Confederate authorities concurred, and, beginning in November 1861, sponsored mass meetings in New Orleans to promote enlistments in a free black regiment. Under the plan, leading freemen would recruit companies (of one hundred men each), then serve as officers (one captain and two lieutenants) for the companies they raised. Ten companies would form the regiment, which trusted whites would command. In March 1862 Confederate Governor Thomas O. Moore inducted the regiment into the state militia, denominating it the "Native Guard." The regiment received neither clothing nor arms from the state. It did not drill with the white units and never fought for the Confederacy. Expressing little enthusiasm for Confederate service, the men attended regimental musters only irregularly,[5] apparently exerting the least effort necessary to allay Confederate suspicions.

Within weeks of their formal muster into the state militia, the Native Guards resolved the dilemma created by their mobilization on behalf of the rebel cause. In April 1862 Union military and naval forces attacked New Orleans, and the Confederates fled. Unlike their white counterparts, the colored militiamen remained, not to resist but to welcome the federals. Discreetly disbanding, they slipped quickly back into the comparative anonymity of the French Quarter, but soon they desired to serve the Union, hoping thereby to protect and perhaps enhance their privileges.

Filled with a sense of duty "to come forward and aid in putting down this unholy rebellion and save our country from her awful threatened doom," as one later expressed it, the Native Guard officers tendered their services to General Benjamin F. Butler, commander of the newly created Department of the Gulf.[6] Butler admitted being struck by the intelligence and sincerity of the officers, "the darkest of whom was about the color of the late Mr. Wester." Nonetheless, he declined their offer on the grounds that the War Department did not then permit black soldiers, let alone black officers.[7] The officers received a more sympathetic hearing from General John W. Phelps, commander at Camp Parapet, several miles above New Orleans on the Mississippi River. Phelps, a Vermont abolitionist, was anxious to organize an army of slaves to destroy the Confederacy. Service of privileged free blacks in such a force would compromise his vision, to be sure, but Phelps had no objection in principle to such service and recommended the former Native Guard officers to General Butler. While Butler stalled, Phelps pushed. The ensuing struggle between the two over Phelps's proposal to arm slaves provided cover for the free blacks to enter federal service.

Through the summer of 1862 Phelps repeatedly requested authority to enlist slaves. Butler rejected each such request but dutifully submitted it to Secretary of War Edwin M. Stanton asking that President Abraham Lincoln rule on the question. Rather than allow Phelps to arm the slaves who had taken refuge in the camp, in July Butler ordered the abolitionist to employ them as wood choppers. Phelps resigned rather than serve as a "slave-driver."[8] When Confederates reversed the momentum of federal advances, recapturing Baton Rouge later in the summer and threatening to attack New Orleans, Butler had to act. Desperate to enlarge his fighting force, he invited the Native Guard officers to his headquarters. When they assured the general that their men would welcome the chance to serve the Union, Butler authorized their muster. The Confederate Native Guard became the 1st Louisiana Native Guard.

Try as he might, Butler could not recruit enough white Louisianans to fill his growing military needs. Hence, through the fall of 1862 he continued to "call upon Africa," authorizing formation of two more regiments of freemen. As he had done with the first regiment, he permitted free blacks to command the companies they raised. While he also followed the Confederate precedent of placing white colonels in command of the regiments, he appointed Francis E. Dumas, a freeman serving as a captain in the first regiment, major in the second. Dumas, a wealthy slave-owning sugar planter and distant relative of French novelist Alexandre Dumas, thus became the first nonwhite to hold a field office in the United States army.[9] In mid-December 1862, when Butler relinquished command of the Gulf Department of General Nathaniel P. Banks, the 1st Louisiana Native Guard was at full strength and the two additional regiments were well on their way toward completion.

The change of commanders boded ill for the free black officers. Banks had a history of opposition to black soldiers. In 1859, in his capacity as governor of Massachusetts, he vetoed legislation that would have admitted blacks to the state militia on the grounds that it violated the whites-only provision of the 1791 federal Militia Act.[10] Upon assuming command in New Orleans, Banks again resorted to formalities. Considering the freemen unqualified to hold commissions, he intended to remove them from the service, by persuasion if possible, by force if necessary.

He moved first against the officers of the third regiment, summoning them for an interview early in February 1863. Inquiring whether they had any complaints, Banks suggested that those who voiced grievances resign.[11] Within weeks, the eighteen free black officers of the regiment submitted a joint letter of resignation. Their statement affirmed that they "did most certainly expect the Privileges, and respect due to a Solider who had offered his services and his life to his government, ever ready and willing to Share the common dangers of the Battle Field," though they denied any expectation of full social equality. Denouncing the "Scorn and contempt" that whites of all ranks had heaped upon them, they claimed that "This treatment has sunk deep Into our hearts. We did not expect It and therefore It is intolerable. We cannot serve a country In which we have no more rights and Priviledges given us."[12] Without so much as an investigation of the charges, Banks accepted their resignation.

In the eyes of General Banks and the white commanders of the Native Guard regiments, the free colored officers lacked the qualifications required of Union officers. In the words of Banks's adjutant, the officers' presence "led to much ill-feeling among the officers and men of some of the white regiments, resulting often in controversy and on several occasions in violence. By their arrogance and intolerant self-assertion, the officers . . . had conclusively shown that they were not the men to pioneer this experiment, even before they proceeded to demonstrate their hostile and uncompromising spirit by seeking occasions to force their complaints upon the Dep^t. Commander." Although the freemen admitted to a "limited Knoledge of military Disciplin" in their resignation letter, they fully understood that officers in white regiments often had no greater formal military training than they. They considered their ouster a flagrant violation of military etiquette. Having entered federal service with General Butler's full assurance of equal treatment, they refused to have that promised equality abridged.[13]

In the spring of 1863, sensing that Banks would soon oust them, officers in the 2nd Louisiana Native Guard also began to leave federal service. In early March, after consulting among themselves, five officers stationed at Fort Pike, Louisiana, resigned, submitting nearly identical letters of resignation. "When I Joined the united States army," declared Lieutenant Robert H. Isabelle, "I did so with the sole object of laboring for the good of the union supposing that all past prejudice would be suspended for the good of our Country and that all native born americans would unite together to sacrefice their blood for the cause as our fathers did in 1812 & 15 to save our native soil from her threatened doom."[14] Although they expressed disappointment that their performance had not demolished long-standing prejudices, all affirmed that military success required harmony, and they consented to resign in the face of undiminished hostility among whites. When several officers in the second regiment refused to take their cue, Banks delivered a clearer message. He convened a special board to examine their qualifications. The freemen pointedly observed, "the officers detailed to compose said Board are in the Majority of inferior rank (1st Lieutenants of the same Regiment) whose promotion would be Effected by our dismissal." When the composition of the board remained unchanged despite the clear violation of protocol, still other black officers resigned in protest.[15] Undaunted by Banks's threats, several black officers appeared before the board and passed examination, but by the fall of 1863 the last holdouts, Major Dumas and Captain P. B. S. Pinchback, had had enough. They, too, resigned.

The officers of the 1st Native Guard Regiment escaped the frontal attack their counterparts in the second and third regiments endured, but, early in 1864, resenting the constant sniping at their qualifications, they too began to resign. "I respectfully tender my immediate and unconditional resignation," wrote Captain Joseph Follin, "because daily events demonstrate that prejudices are so strong against Colored Officers, that no matter what would be their patriotism and their anxiety to fight for the flag of their native Land, they cannot do it with honor to themselves."[16] The officers of the first regiment, admitted earliest into service, appropriately remained in service the longest, the last until the summer of 1864. Despite their pride in being first and their reluctance to depart, they abandoned the military rather than submit to the disrespect of white comrades.

While General Banks considered black officers an encumbrance, he desperately required black troops to protect the ever-expanding Union-occupied domain. When rebels threatened attack, as they did repeatedly during the spring and summer of 1863, his need increased in proportion to the credibility of threats. Sensing Banks's vulnerability, a group of resigned officers, for the most part from the 3rd Native Guard, requested permission to recruit a black regiment, "to assist in putting down this wicked rebellion, And in restoring peace to our once peaceful country." Once again citing the precedent of their forefathers who fought with Jackson, they reasoned: "The commanding Gen¹ may think that we will have the same difficulties to surmount that we had before resigning. But sir give us A commander who will appreciate us as men and soldiers, And we will be willing to surmount all other difficulties."[17] In the same vein, the secretary of the association of resigned officers expressed to General Daniel Ullmann, commander of black troops in the Gulf Department, his desire to raise a "Company of Cavalry of picked men of full stature who are free Born intelligent men who have been used to the saddle from infancy never having done any thing Else since they were old enough But Catch wild attakapas Cattle and hunt." The officer confidently boasted, "They are men who understand the use of the Lassoe so well that they will wager to Catch a beef at full speed by any one of his feet."[18] Ullmann responded, as he did routinely to such cases, that he lacked the authority to commission blacks as officers though he would gladly issue warrants for noncommissioned offices to those deemed qualified.[19] The freemen declined Ullmann's offer, and Banks held fast to his course.

Flouting Banks's determination to keep the officer corps white, the resigned officers repeatedly sought permission to raise new companies of black soldiers. Robert H. Isabelle, a former Lieutenant in the 2nd Native Guard who had passed the board of examination before resigning, offered the services of more than 1,000 free blacks in New Orleans whose only request, "is the privilege of selecting their own line officers or for you to select from our race such persons as you might find qualified."[20] In midsummer 1863, as rebel threats on New Orleans intensified, Banks capitulated. He authorized the resigned officers to raise and serve as company officers of two regiments, the 6th and 7th Louisiana Infantry, whose term of service would be sixty days. One officer, Charles W. Gibbons, later reported having re-assembled his company in two hours.[21] Jordan W. Noble recruited with similar ease, drawing upon his illustrious military background as a drummer during the war of 1812, the Seminole War, and the Mexican War.[22] Although the Confederates did not attack, the incident demonstrated Banks's continuing dependence upon the resigned officers. While he considered them unqualified to command, he knew that no one could enlist black recruits as quickly as they.

Banks's successor, General Stephen A. Hurlbut, proceeded from scratch in learning the same lesson. In the fall of 1864 declining black enlistments plagued Hurlbut, desperately short of soldiers to guard the ever-extending lines and to protect the freedmen working on government plantations. To complicate Hurlbut's plight, his superior, General Edward R. S. Canby, weary of the constant complaints about recruiters' "excesses," had banned forcible impressment of blacks into the army. To solve his problem, Hurlbut somewhat sheepishly followed Butler's and Banks's precedents and turned to the freemen. Late in October he began organizing new black regiments, authorizing the former Native Guard officers to recruit companies and promising them commissions provided they passed the qualifying examination. On the brink of implementing his plan, Hurlbut changed his mind. Black recruitment languished as a result, but, more important, the free blacks lost another chance to serve as commissioned officers. It proved their last.[23]

From beginning to end, the purge of the black officers of the three Native Guard regiments lasted nearly eighteen months. The earliest fatalities, the officers of the third regiment, for the most part left the service together in February 1863. The last holdouts, officers of the first and second regiments, did not succumb to the pressure until the summer of 1864. Those who remained in service with the odds stacked increasingly against them at times found room in which to preserve their dignity and retain some semblance of respect. Even they eventually gave up in desperation.

Through it all, Banks demonstrated a curious combination of vindictiveness and benevolence. Despite his numerous violations of established protocol in forcing the officers to resign, Banks scrupulously adhered to other guidelines of military decorum in apparent contradiction of his larger strategic aims. For example, in the midst of his purge, he did nothing to block the promotion of two lieutenants, James H. Ingraham and Alfred Bourgeau, found qualified for the rank of captain.[24] Pending the final success of his campaign to oust the officers, Banks supported their demand for equal pay. When General Butler first enlisted the Native Guard regiments, he promised pay, bounties, and other emoluments equal to those received by whites, and it appears that the freemen drew at least one pay on those terms.[25] In a celebrated decision of July 1863, the War Department ruled that all blacks, regardless of rank, should receive a mere $10 per month.[26] The Native Guard officers protested the new policy to Secretary of War Stanton, describing it as an affront both to their dignity and to Butler's promise of equal pay, and Banks endorsed their petition affirmatively.[27] Even while Banks maneuvered to eliminate the freemen from the officer corps, he apparently considered them entitled to the full benefits of Union officers.

As Banks quietly purged the free black officers, they and their men won unexpected national attention. In May 1863 volunteers from the first and third regiments took part in the ill-conceived assault on Port Hudson, Louisiana, which resulted in the virtual massacre of the Native Guards who spearheaded the attack. One of the colored officers, Captain Andrew Cailloux, died in the fighting, and commanders up to General Banks himself praised the gallantry of both officers and men. In the same month, at East Pascagoula, Florida, and Ship Island, Mississippi, officers and men of the second regiment also won the praise of their superiors, with Major Francis E. Dumas achieving special distinction.[28] Black officers hoped that battlefield heroics would demolish all opposition to the service and assure full acceptance into the officer corps. Resigned officers of the third regiment, seeking readmission to the service, posited precisely such a connection when they requested to "be allowed to share the dangers of the battle field and not be Kept for men who will not fight. If the world doubts our fighting give us A chance and we will show them what we can do."[29] Nonetheless, as black soldiers later recruited from among former slaves would find out, valor provided no guarantee of honorable treatment, either within military ranks or among whites in general.

While their struggle for equality in the Union army ground slowly to a halt, the resigned officers broadened their campaign, at first aiming to capture for themselves the privileges of full citizenship previously denied them, and ultimately incorporating the freedmen into the struggle for equal rights. Segregated public transportation facilities offered a clear target. While still in federal uniform, the black officers were repeatedly denied first-class railroad accommodations. The officers resisted such discriminatory treatment and on occasion used their pistols to back their arguments.[30] When expulsion from the army removed the cloak of authority represented by their uniforms and shoulder straps, they helped organize a public campaign against the long-despised, segregated "star cars" and petitioned military authorities to put an end to that hallmark of inferiority. After the war, the agitation spread and eventually succeeded in integrating the New Orleans streetcars for the rest of the nineteenth century.[31] The campaign to integrate the cars represented one prong on the all-out assault on the vestiges of slavery.

Perhaps the most important prong of that attack centered upon the extension of voting privileges to blacks. From antebellum times, free people of color had desired the suffrage, but the particular turn of wartime events gave them an unprecedented opportunity to press their case. In light of the Emancipation Proclamation and the service of blacks in the Union army, the political reorganization of Louisiana in 1863 and 1864 set the stage for broadened political participation. Freemen pressed for the suffrage in mass meetings and in the columns of their newspapers, L'Union and the Tribune, and persuaded sympathetic white Unionists to support suffrage extension. During months of agitation, they refused to be rebuffed by the cool indifference of General Banks, Lincoln's point man in Louisiana. On the eve of the 1864 state constitutional convention, they circulated a petition demanding that intelligent, free-born blacks have the right to vote. They dispatched two emissaries, John B. Roudanez, brother of the Tribune's owner, and Arnold Bertonneau, a former Native-Guard Captain, to Washington. After consulting with Congressional Radicals, the two men included in the petition the demand for universal black suffrage, a clear signal that freemen had begun to view their own political future as inseparable from that of the soon-to-be-liberated slaves. When the delegation returned to New Orleans, the implications of that realization grew.[32]

In January 1865, in the aftermath of the National Convention of Colored Men held in Syracuse the previous October, New Orleans freemen sponsored a state equal rights convention. True to form, the resigned Native Guard officers played a prominent role. Of the eight former officers—all captains—among the hundred-odd delegates, three particularly distinguished themselves. James H. Ingraham, Jordan B. Noble, and Ernest C. Morphy constituted the organizing committee, and each subsequently served as a convention officer. The three-part program for economic, political, and social change called for the removal of all federal restrictions upon the labor contracting process, unrestricted manhood suffrage regardless of color, and an end to all civil distinctions based upon color. The convention marked the first organized bid by blacks who had long enjoyed freedom to join hands in struggle with blacks who had just gained freedom but the subsequent implementation of the program exposed differences which threatened to keep them apart.[33]

Significant divisions, rooted in different relationships to productive property, provided the most serious obstacle to unity between freemen and freedmen. Whereas freemen had for years owned land, buildings, tools, merchandise, animals, and even slaves, freedmen had until recently been property and now owned little of productive worth. Property ownership in turn conferred upon the freemen a measure of economic independence denied to many whites as well as to former slaves. In abolishing slavery and nationalizing the free market in labor, the Civil War enabled the freemen to exercise their entrepreneurial talents without the restraints put upon them by the bondage of blacks. At the same time, while the war liberated the slaves, it consigned them to continuing economic dependence as wage laborers or share croppers. These material differences between the free and the freed blacks gave rise to profound social and cultural distinctions that the mere sharing of African ancestry could not bridge.

In some ways the forces unleashed by the Civil War helped to narrow the gap between free and freed blacks. For instance, the service of several companies of Native Guards in the plantation districts supervising the transition from slavery to freedom forced free colored officers and enlisted men to scrutinize their own biases. Socially, the free black officers frequently had more in common with the loyal planters and plantation lessees than with the freed people working on the plantations. The officers dined at the big houses and, in turn, entertained the leading figures of plantation society. They listened sympathetically as employers described insolence and insubordination on the part of plantation hands and exhorted the freedmen to labor faithfully and industriously. That notwithstanding, black officers saw disturbing signs that the old order had not completely died, and they waged all-out war on whipping and all similar vestiges of slavery. In turn, employers charged the officers with prompting unrest among their hands and demanded removal of the Native Guard from the countryside.[34] The officers strove to supervise the new plantation system with strict impartiality, protecting the rights of both employers and employees, but with the balance of experience and force on the side of the former, the officers often had to take sides openly with the latter. They and the larger free black community faced similar choices in the years that followed, as their African ancestry and their social position drew them in apparently opposite directions.

Just as material circumstances differentiated free and freed blacks, the two groups had different ideological perceptions of federal policies toward the liberated slaves. Most free people viewed the economic problems of the freed people through lenses tinted by their own privileged position before the war. Whereas most freed blacks welcomed federal supervision of plantation labor, the free blacks opposed government interference. To an extent matched by few of their contemporaries in the North or the South, Louisiana's free people of color adhered to the tenets of economic laissez-faire. They felt that unrestrained market forces would mediate the transition from slavery to freedom more efficiently than the contrived plans of civil or military officials possibly could. Hence, they sternly criticized the tightly circumscribed and closely supervised labor system devised by General Banks. At a mass meeting held in New Orleans in March 1865, co-chaired by former Captain James H. Ingraham, the freemen stated their case. The key resolution argued "That the right of the employee to freely agree and contract according to his best judgment, with his employer, for the term of labor is the unquestionable attribute of every freeman." Other resolutions called for the removal of all restrictions upon mobility and for the abolition of the army's Bureau of Free Labor, established to safeguard the interests of the former slaves. In response to the resolutions, General Stephen A. Hurlbut stressed the "bitterness of feeling" between those born free and those freed by the war: "You are striving for social equality, they for personal freedom." Hurlbut vigorously defended the army's plan; without it, he argued, freed people would be entirely at the mercy of their former owners.[35]

Hurlbut's characterization served to demonstrate how the economic and social differences dividing the free and the freed black communities had given rise to strong prejudices on both sides. Inasmuch as the free people did not shy away from making their feelings known publicly, even Hurlbut's unsophisticated eye could quickly comprehend the situation. More than once, free blacks attempted to magnify the social distance separating them from slaves in an apparent attempt to close the gap between themselves and whites. Late in 1864, for instance, freemen in Baton Rouge, led by former Native Guard Captain Samuel W. Ringgold, vehemently protested being rounded up and "placed on an equality with contrabands" during a military impressment of laborers to work on the levee. Claiming a respected position on the "social scale" by virtue of their education, their property ownership, and their payment of taxes, they demanded to be "treated as freemen."[36] Throughout the war and after, certain freemen preferred to use freedmen as mudsills upon which to erect their own rights rather than as allies in a common struggle for mutual rights.

Countering the forces pulling the two groups apart, a few stalwart free blacks worked to strengthen the alliance between the freeborn and the slaveborn that had tentatively emerged during the closing months of the war. The Bureau of Industry, established by the 1865 Louisiana Equal Rights Convention, investigated conditions on the plantations in an effort to increase freedom of contract and mobility, but it apparently accomplished little. Louis C. Roudanez, influential owner of the *Tribune*, continued to advocate the unity of economic and political interests between free people and freed people throughout Reconstruction, but he fought an uphill battle with steadily decreasing numbers of free black allies.[37] Profoundly different economic interests and circumstances daunted the alliance; the two found common ground in struggling first for the extension of and then for the protection of political and civil rights.

Black manhood suffrage became a reality under the Reconstruction Acts of March 1867, and in the following months Louisiana blacks registered and voted for the first time. As earlier, the former Native Guard officers stepped to the fore, moving quickly into leadership of the fledgling Republican party. In the state's first gubernatorial contest after passage of the Reconstruction Acts, former Major Francis E. Dumas ran for the Republican nomination against Henry Clay Warmoth but lost. In 1872 Dumas ran for secretary of state on the Liberal Republican ticket and again lost. Undaunted by Dumas's setbacks, approximately twenty former Native Guard officers won public office in Louisiana during Reconstruction. The most prominent, P. B. S. Pinchback, served as lieutenant governor and for a short time as acting governor.[38]

In the hothouse atmosphere that characterized Radical Reconstruction, social differences within the free black community eventually assumed political form. The main fault line there fell between free people of Gallic-American and those of Anglo-American ancestry. For the most part, the latter remained faithful to the regular Republican party, where they sought first public office and later party patronage in their quest for economic security. The freemen of French descent, however, displayed less fealty to the regulars and had to live without the crumbs of patronage as a result. Instead, they pursued economic and social security within the French Quarter and cultivated a fierce pride in their Gallic past.[39] In the postwar era, differences in social background crippled the efforts of black Louisianans to establish a unified political movement, dividing free people from former slaves and fragmenting the free community within itself.

As successive Republican administrations, beginning with that of Rutherford B. Hayes, abrogated responsibility for protecting the rights of Southern black voters, the long struggle of New Orleans freemen for equality took on renewed significance. In 1871, for instance, P. B. S. Pinchback threatened to sue the Pullman porter company for denying sleeping berths to blacks who held first-class passenger tickets. In practice, such rights meant little to plantation freedmen who could not afford first-class fares in any event; but in principle, the fight for equal accommodations kept alive the larger struggle for equality. Throughout the rest of Reconstruction, the former free people fought for educational privileges and equal public accommodations and challenged all efforts to curtail the advances they had won.[40] In the post-Reconstruction years, when Democrats assaulted the advances in civil and political rights, Louisiana blacks tried to resist the onslaught, but in the face of new political realities, most of the earlier fire was gone.

In 1890 Louisiana legislators enacted bills to deprive blacks of equal accommodations on railroads and other public conveyances, and the fateful final episode in the freemen's struggle for equal rights began. Sparked by the new laws, the handful of surviving former officers organized immediate opposition. Pinchback and James Lewis, joined by blacks from around the country and a handful of whites like the renowned carpetbagger Albion W. Tourgée, organized the American Citizens' Equal Rights Association. In conjunction with the ad hoc Citizens' Committee to Test the Constitutionality of the Separate Car Law, the association sponsored a series of lawsuits against the railroads, which eventually led to the landmark 1896 Supreme Court case of *Plessy v. Ferguson.*[41] The court's adverse decision marked the end of the Civil War era and the beginning of the era of segregation. And it paralyzed the free black community. In 1906 the star cars reappeared.

The free blacks of New Orleans attempted to use military service to gain full admission into free society. When that effort failed, they shifted tactics, pressing for full citizenship rights in society at large and joining forces with the newly emancipated slaves in a common struggle for economic, political, and civil rights. The alliance of groups with such vastly different social backgrounds and historical experiences proved fragile, and the partners quickly drifted apart. While freed people fought for the economic and political fruits of freedom, free people concentrated on civil equality. During the early postwar years, when both groups enjoyed some success, the partnership held hope of lasting. When Reconstruction ended, and many of freedom's achievements fell victim to Democratic assault, the allies separated again. Freed people on the plantations struggled to free themselves from share cropping's close confines, and the former free people struggled to maintain equal public services and accommodations. By the end of the nineteenth century, neither struggle held much promise of success.

Most of the Native Guard officers did not live to see Reconstruction's denouement in the Plessy case. Perhaps it is just as well. Some of the veterans may well have contemplated a return to arms rather than wait indefinitely for Congress to complete the unfinished business of the Civil War era.

NOTES

1. Ira Berlin, *Slaves Without Masters: The Free Negro in the Antebellum South* (New York, 1974), 108–30; H. E. Sterkx, *The Free Negro in Ante-Bellum Louisiana* (Rutherford, N.J., 1972); John W. Blassingame, *Black New Orleans 1860–1880* (Chicago, 1973); Laura Foner, "The Free People of Color in Louisiana and St. Domingue: A Comparative Portrait of Two Three-Caste Slave Societies," *Journal of Social History* 3 (Summer 1970): 406–30; David C. Rankin, "The Origins of Black Leadership in New Orleans During Reconstruction," *Journal of Southern History* 40 (August 1974): 417–40; Rankin, "The Impact of the Civil War on the Free Colored Community of New Orleans," *Perspectives in American History* 11 (1977–78): 379–416, esp. 382–83. See also David W. Cohen and Jack P. Greene, eds., *Neither Slave Nor Free: The Freedman of African Descent in the Slave Societies of the New World* (Baltimore, 1972).

2. George W. Williams, *A History of the Negro Troops in the War of the Rebellion 1861–1865* (New York, 1888; rep. 1969), 55–57; Joseph T. Wilson, *The Black Phalanx: A History of the Negro Soldiers of the United States in the Wars of 1775–1812, 1861–65* (New York, 1890, rep. 1968), 72–88; Roland C. McConnell, *Negro Troops of Antebellum Louisiana: A History of the Battalion of Free Men of Color* (Baton Rouge, 1968); and Mary F. Berry, "Negro Troops in Blue and Gray: The Louisiana Native Guards, 1861–63," *Louisiana History* 8 (Spring 1967): 165–90. The service of free blacks with General Jackson generated a legacy that blacks throughout the country drew upon during the antebellum years. See especially the references in the proceedings of various state

conventions of blacks. Philip S. Foner and George E. Walker, *Proceedings of the Antebellum Black State Conventions*, 2 vols. (Philadelphia, 1979), I: 41, 192, 271, 301–2, 324.

3. McConnell, *Negro Troops*, pp. 108–11; see also Antoine Remy, Barthelemy Populus and P. Monette to Major General Butler [1862], P-1 1862, Letters Received, Dept. of the Gulf, Records of U.S. Army Continental Commands, Record Group (RG) 393 Pt. 1, National Archives, Washington, D.C. (hereafter all record group citations will be to documents in the National Archives); and Ml. Moreau et al. to the Senate and House of Representatives of the State of Louisiana [undated], printed copy filed with Letters Received, Bureau of Civil Affairs, Dept. of the Gulf, RG 393 Pt. 1.

4. General Butler's free black translator later explained why freemen chose to serve the Confederacy: "If we had not volunteered, they would have forced us into the ranks, and we should have been suspected. We have property and rights here, and there is every reason why we should take care of ourselves." Quoted in testimony of Benjamin F. Butler before the American Freedmen's Inquiry Commission, 1 May 1863, filed with 0–328 1863 Letters Received, Records of the Adjutant General's Office, RG 94. A Native Guard officer reported that Confederates threatened injury and even death to anyone who refused to cooperate. Testimony of Charles W. Gibbons, *New Orleans Riots*, U.S. Congress, House, Report No. 16, 39th Cong., 2nd Sess., pp. 124–26.

5. Muster rolls, 1st Louisiana Native Guards, Regimental Records, War Department Collection of Confederate Records, RG 109. Rodolphe Lucien Desdunes, *Our People and Our History*, ed. and tr., Sister Dorothea Olga McCants (Baton Rouge, 1973), pp. 120–21.

6. R. H. Isabelle to Brig. Genl. Ullman, 12 June 1863, Isabelle's compiled service record, 74th U.S. Colored Infantry (hereafter USCI), RG 94.

7. U.S. War Department, *The War of the Rebellion: A Compilation of the Official Records of the Union and Confederate Armies*, 128 vols. (Washington, 1880–1901), ser. 1, vol. 15, p. 442; testimony of Butler, 1 May 1863, filed with 0–328 1863, Letters Received, RG 94; Desdunes, *Our People*, pp. 119–20.

8. *Official Records*, ser. 1, vol. 15, p. 535.

9. No other black achieved the field rank of major until the closing months of the war, when Martin R. Delany was appointed major of the 104th USCI, U.S. Adjutant General's Office, *Official Army Register of the Volunteer Force of the United States Army* . . . (Washington, 1865), pt. 8, p. 285.

10. See "The Negro in the Military Service of the United States, 1639–1886," pp. 946–50, Colored Troops Division, RG 94.

11. Joseph G. Parker to E. M. Stanton, 30 May 1863, P-26 1863, Letters Received, Colored Troops Division, RG 94.

12. J. A. Gla et al. to Maj. Gen. N. P. Banks, 19 February 1863, compiled service record of Leon G. Forstall, 75th USCI, RG 94.

13. For hostile views of superior officers, see, for example, the endorsements of Colonel John A. Nelson, commander of the 3rd Native Guard Regiment, upon the resignations of two officers in his regiment, characterizing each as "of no use to the Service And entirely unfit for [command] having no military Knowledge or any Controle over His command." (Capt. Samuel Laurence to Maj. Gen. Nathaniel P. Banks, 4 February 1863, compiled service record of Samuel Lawrence, 75th USCI, RG 94; Et. Longpre, Jr., to Maj. Gen. N. P. Banks, 5 February 1863, compiled service record of Ernest Longpre, Jr., 75th USCI, RG 94.) For Banks's view, see the endorsement of his adjutant, Richd. B. Irwin, 25 November 1863, on Joseph G. Parker to E. M. Stanton, 30 May 1863, P-26 1863, Letters Received, Colored Troops Division, RG 94. The officers' complaints are neatly summarized in Capt. P. B. S. Pinchback et al. to Major Genl. N. P. Banks, 2 March 1863, Letters Received, 6th USCI, Regimental Records U.S. Colored Troops (USCT), RG 94.

14. R. H. Isabelle to Wickham Hoffman, 3 March 1863, compiled service record of Robert H. Isabelle, 74th USCI, RG 94; see also resignations of Arnold Bertonneau to

Wickham Hoffman, 2 March 1863, Ernest Morphy to Hoffman, 3 March 1863, and Octave Rey to Hoffman, 2 March 1863, in their respective compiled service records, 74th USCI, RG 94.

15. S. W. Ringgold to Maj. Genl. N. P. Banks, 7 July 1863, and Samuel J. Wilkinson to Banks, 6 July 1863, in their respective compiled service records, 74th USCI, RG 94. The officers protested the composition of the board in Capt. P. B. S. Pinchback et al. to Maj. Genl. N. P. Banks, 3? March 1863, Letters Received, 6th USCI, Regimental Records USCT, RG 94.

16. Joseph Follin to George B. Drake, 18 February 1864, compiled service record, RG 94.

17. Adolph J. Gla et al. to Majr. Genl. Banks, 7 April 1863, G-35 1863, Letters Received, Civil Affairs, Dept. of the Gulf, RG 393 Pt. 1.

18. Joseph G. Parker, Jr., to Brig. Gen. Daniel Ullman, 22 May 1863, compiled service record, RG 94. Later Banks authorized Pinchback to recruit a company of cavalry but subsequently revoked the approval. William J. Simmons, *Men of Mark: Eminent, Progressive and Rising* (New York, 1887; rep. 1968), pp. 759–81; James Haskins, *Pinckney Benton Stewart Pinchback* (New York, 1973), 27–29.

19. Unlike other high ranking officers in the Department of the Gulf, Ullman seems to have only reluctantly cooperated with Banks's purge of the free black officers. As a rule, he forwarded letters of resignation without comment while other commanders, including General George L. Andrews, vigorously approved the resignations. Cf. the comments of General George Andrews on the resignation of Joseph Follin, cited in n. 17.

20. R. H. Isabelle to Brig. Genl. Ullman, 12 June 1863, Isabelle's compiled service record, 74th USCI, RG 94.

21. *Official Army Register*, pt. 8, pp. 317–18. Gibbons's testimony, "New Orleans Riots," p. 125.

22. Pension file of Jordan B. Noble, RG 15; McConnell, *Negro Troops*, pp. 114–15.

23. Capt. Sheldon Sturgeon to Maj. Geo. B. Drake, 18 November 1864, enclosing Major Geo. B. Drake to Mr. James Lewis, 1 and 16 November 1864, service record of James Lewis, 73d USCI, RG 94. The letter from Sturgeon to Lewis of 1 November is a printed authorization to recruit with Lewis's name inserted in manuscript. A list of names of all the black officers who served in the Louisiana Native Guard appears in Ira Berlin, Joseph P. Reidy, and Leslie S. Rowland, eds., *Freedom: A Documentary History of Emancipation, 1861–1867. Series II: The Black Military Experience* (New York, 1982), p. 310n. That volume also contains transcripts of many of the documents cited in this essay. The names of black officers who served in the two sixty-day regiments raised during the summer of 1863 appear in Adjutant General's Office, *Official Army Register*, pt. 8, pp. 317–18.

24. Lt. Col. C. J. Bassett to Capt. G. B. Halsted, 8 October 1863, Applications for Commissions, Records of Boards of Examination for Commission, Dept. of the Gulf, RG 393 Pt. 1.

25. *Official Records*, ser. 1, vol. 15, pp. 556–57.

26. Herman Belz, "Law, Politics, and Race in the Struggle for Equal Pay During the Civil War," *Civil War History* 22 (September 1976): 197–222; James M. McPherson, *The Negro's Civil War: How American Negroes Thought and Acted during the War for the Union* (New York, 1965), pp. 193–203.

27. Capt. P. B. S. Pinchback et al. to Maj. Genl. Banks, 3 March 1863, Letters Received, 6th USCI, Regimental Books & Papers, USCT, RG 94; Capt. P. B. S. Pinchback et al. to Edwin M Stanton [October 1863], G-104 1863, Letters Received, Colored Troops Division, RG 94. See also Addl. Paymaster H. O. Brigham to Col. T. P. Andrews, 14 July 1863, #632/20, Letters Received, Records of the Paymaster General of the Army, RG 99, for Banks's earlier determination to pay blacks and whites equally.

28. Williams, *History of the Negro Troops*, pp. 214–23; Wilson, *Black Phalanx*, pp. 207–11 and chap. 5 in general. See also the remarks of P. B. S. Pinchback in undated fragments of speeches, "The Negro as a Soldier," and "The Negro in the Civil

War," Pinchback Papers, Moorland-Spingarn Collection, Howard University, Washington, D.C.

29. Adolph J. Gla et al. to Majr. Genl. Banks, 7 April 1863, G-35 1863, Letters Received, ser. 1920, Civil Affairs, Dept. of the Gulf, RG 393 Pt. 1.

30. Rich. J. Evans to Brig. Gen. Bowen, 21 July 1863, Letters Received, Provost Marshal, Dept. of the Gulf, RG 393 Pt. 1.

31. Roger A. Fischer, "A Pioneer Protest: The New Orleans Street-Car Controversy of 1867," *Journal of Negro History* 53 (January 1968): 219–33.

32. J. B. Roudanez and Arnold Bertonneau to A. Lincoln, the Senate and the House of Representatives of the United States, 5 January 1864, HR38A-G25.6, Petitions & Memorials, 38th Cong., Records of the House of Representatives, RG 233; Donald E. Everett, "Demands of the New Orleans Free Colored Population for Political Equality, 1862–1865," *Louisiana Historical Quarterly* 38 (April 1955): 43–64; C. Peter Ripley, *Slaves and Freedmen in Civil War Louisiana* (Baton Rouge, 1974), chap. 9; Peyton McCrary, *Abraham Lincoln and Reconstruction* (Princeton, 1979), chaps. 6–9; William P. O'Connor, "Reconstruction Rebels: The *New Orleans Tribune* in Post-War Louisiana," *Louisiana History* 21 (Spring 1980): 159–81; LaWanda Cox, *Lincoln and Black Freedom: A Study in Presidential Leadership* (Columbia, S.C., 1981), passim; Haskins, *Pinchback*, pp. 26–27.

33. Proceedings of the Louisiana State Equal Rights Convention, New Orleans *Tribune*, 10–15 January 1865. At the convention, the former officers put in another bid to regain their commissions. Ingraham had attended the Syracuse convention. "Proceedings of the National Convention of Colored Men . . . 1864," p. 5, in Howard H. Bell, ed., *Minutes of the Proceedings of the National Negro Conventions 1830–1864* (New York, 1969).

34. Capt. Hannibal Carter to Col. N. W. Daniels, 8 February 1863, filed with J. A. Pickens to Major General Banks, 5 January 1863, Letters Received, 6th USCI, Regimental Books & Papers USCT, RG 94.

35. James H. Ingraham and Dr. A. W. Lewis to Major General S. A. Hurlbut, 21 March 1865, I-5 1865, Letters Received, Civil Affairs, and M.G. S. A. Hurlbut to Ingraham and Lewis, 23 March 1865, vol. 9, pp. 327–30. Letters Sent, Dept. of the Gulf, RG 393 Pt. 1.

36. S. W. Ringgold et al. to the Generals Commanding the District and Department of the Gulf [December 1864], filed with Capt. Geo. E. Smith to Major Geo. W. Durgin, Jr., 2 January 1865, S-1 1865, Letters Received, ser. 760, Dist. of Baton Rouge & Port Hudson, RG 393 Pt. 2 No. 13.

37. Rankin, "The Impact of the Civil War."

38. Rankin, "Origins of Black Leadership," 417–20; Joe Gray Taylor, *Louisiana Reconstructed, 1863–1877* (Baton Rogue, 1974), passim; Charles Vincent, *Black Legislators in Louisiana during Reconstruction* (Baton Rouge, 1976), passim; Haskins, *Pinchback*, chaps. 4–9.

39. Desdunes's *Our People* represents this trend quintessentially.

40. See especially, Louis R. Harlan, "Desegregation in New Orleans Public Schools During Reconstruction," *American Historical Review* 67 (April 1962): 663–75, and Roger A. Fischer, *The Segregation Struggle in Louisiana, 1862–77* (Urbana, Ill., 1974).

41. Otto H. Olsen, *The Thin Disguise: Turning Point in Negro History, Plessy v. Ferguson, A Documentary Presentation, 1864–1896* (New York, 1967); Haskins, *Pinchback*, pp. 253–55; and Desdunes, *Our People*, chap. 12; Fischer, *Segregation Struggle*, pp. 151–54. One of Desdunes's sons, Daniel, filed the first suit that resulted in the Plessy decision.

TWENTY-TWO

Black Troops in the Army of the James, 1863–65

EDWARD G. LONGACRE

Among all the Civil War armies, the Union Army of the James was unique in several related respects. It was the largest field command to be led by a nonprofessional soldier—who happened to be an active if unannounced candidate for President. It contained the lowest percentage of West Point–trained general officers and the highest percentage of generals who had been office-holders or political workers in civil life. It was the only army to have as its primary goal the capture of an objective whose political symbolism was as great as its military value: the Confederate capital at Richmond. That goal was not attained until after the city's evacuation on 3 April 1865—perhaps because the army spent almost as much time fighting among itself, its generals maneuvering for political power, as it did confronting its enemy. In brief, the Army of the James was the most highly politicized fighting force in American history.

The politics of race, which influenced greatly this army's role in the war, provided it with another unique characteristic. The Army of the James contained the largest percentage of USCTs (United States Colored Troops) of any Civil War command—as much as 40 percent of its maximum strength of 40,000 officers and men. In recognition of the fact, the army revamped its organization in December 1864 to form the first and only American army corps composed entirely of black units.[1]

All of this did not come about merely in response to orders out of Washington. In a war in which black soldiers were generally regarded as second-class citizens—both their human and military potential considered inferior—the Army of the James went out of its way to obtain them and to make them feel integral parts of the command. Other armies accepted them reluctantly; relegated them to work as pickets and supply train guards or reduced them to laborers and servants; furnished them substandard equipment, weapons, and rations; discouraged their enlistment in cavalry and artillery units, which called for highly specialized training; and attempted to shift them well to the rear or to another theater of operations. In contrast, the Army of the James used its "sable arm" in the most responsible positions, to spearhead assaults and to secure footholds in enemy territory; provided it with the best rations and material; maintained regiments of black cavalry and sought to recruit black cannoneers despite War Department disapproval;[2] and even traded white regiments to another army in exchange for an equal number of blacks. Moreover, the army constantly sought to bolster the morale of its USCTs, from designing medals honoring their bravery in combat to providing sustenance to their dependents through its Office of Negro Affairs. With just pride, its commanding general could proclaim to the War Office, "I have a fancy that colored troops thrive as well under me as anybody."[3]

That commander was Major General Benjamin Franklin Butler, the best-known political general in the Union ranks. A Boston attorney of wide renown, later a Massachusetts congressman, he had become by the outbreak of the war a power in all factions of the Democratic party (at the 1860 national convention in Charleston, he had cast 57 ballots to nominate Jefferson Davis for the presidency). Aged 45, squat, obese, with a pudgy, ravaged face and one "lop-eye," he resembled a dissipated toad. Beneath, were diverse qualities: a shrewd and subtle intellect, an intense craving for power and high office, a Yankee's love of experimentation, the vision of a romantic, an unswerving devotion to the Union, a remarkable sensitivity to political breezes, and a tendency to line up with the underdog. All coalesced in his wartime decision to champion the cause of ex-slaves in uniform. Although he had entered the conflict suspicious of blacks' military capacity, he experimented successfully with Colored Troops while in command of the Department of the Gulf, in 1862. In 1863 he studied accounts of the creditable battle performances of blacks at Port Hudson, Louisiana; Fort Wagner, South Carolina; and elsewhere.[4] That same year he applauded Abraham Lincoln's resolution to make the war a crusade for emancipation. Despite maintaining his Democratic affiliation, he came to view the Republicans as the statesmen of the future and (doubtless for political as well as humane considerations) to share their desire to allow the black man to help win his freedom.[5] His public utterances to these effects, and his considerable influence with important members of the opposition party, influenced Lincoln to select him that Autumn to head the Department of Virginia and North Carolina, headquartered at Fort Monroe, where the Army of the James would take shape.[6] That stretch of the Virginia peninsula teemed with refugees from Tidewater and Carolina plantations. There, it was assumed, Butler would find a wealth of manpower to complement the 30,000 white troops with whom he would operate against Richmond during the 1864 campaign.

Before Butler's arrival on the peninsula, local blacks, including the families of garrison troops, led a squalid existence. Most were inhabitants of "Slabtown," "Sabletown," and other contraband camps that had materialized on the outskirts of towns such as Norfolk, Yorktown, Hampton, Gloucester Point, Portsmouth, Newport News, and Williamsburg, all of which had been captured and garrisoned during George B. McClellan's invasion campaign of 1862. Ramshackle, cramped, and unsanitary, these ghettoes—where people lay about "without any order under any ragged shelter they could get, in every stage of filth, poverty, disease and death"—offered a life less desirable than the worst of the slave estates their residents had fled. Although the government provided rations to the contrabands, the bulk of the relief effort was carried on by clerical and lay missionaries, some of whom, according to one of Butler's new subordinates, were "cranks" and "scamps" out to exploit rather than to aid. Moreover, the army officers who supervised government relief were likely to be drunken incompetents.[7]

A gifted administrator who embraced a challenge, Butler applied himself to the Slabtown problem within days of his arrival at Fort Monroe on 10 November 1863. He razed the worst hovels, cleaned the others, built sturdy cabins, and relocated some blacks on the farms of local Unionists and upon estates confiscated from secessionists who had gone to war or had fled the area. He also transferred the incompetents and put the "scamps" to flight.

The results were dramatic. By the Spring of 1864 a visitor noted that the compound outside Yorktown was still somewhat crowded but that "absolute neatness surrounds the cabins" and that the inhabitants led "prosperous" and "firm" lives. Those cabins built in the outskirts of Williamsburg were described as "well-built, of uniform size, not crowded . . . [with] nothing unclean to be seen either in front or in the rear." Near Hampton, new dwellings "had sprung up like mushrooms," and even a non-admirer of Butler conceded that they appeared "generally comfortable."[8]

Of course, Butler's primary duty was a military one—to recruit local blacks, as many as the government could feed, clothe, equip, and arm. This he did among the mature, able-bodied contrabands throughout the winter of 1863–64. During this period he also sent forces into the interior of Virginia and North Carolina to free and enroll slaves. So successful were these expeditions that as early as January 1864 the rebuilt Slabtowns had more than 2,000 new residents. Limited housing expansion proved needed, for several hundred of the newcomers became members of Brigadier General Edward A. Wild's "African Brigade," the first command recruited under Butler's auspices.[9]

By April, slave recruiting and training had been in operation for three months and Butler thought it time to mass his new troops. On 23 April,

Wild's three-regiment brigade was combined with three regiments of blacks under Colonel Samuel A. Duncan to form a division (later known as the 3rd division, XVIII Army Corps) led by Brigadier General Edward W. Hinks.[10] A New England acquaintance of Butler, Hinks was a civilian-soldier who had accumulated a distinguished war record and who shared his superior's belief in the military equality of the races. A week later, Butler formed a two-regiment brigade of USC Cavalry and placed it under another officer of tested merit, Colonel Robert M. West (later still, the 5th Massachusetts Cavalry, composed of black enlisted men, would join Butler's ranks).[11] Also attached to the army was a battery of black artillerymen. By the first week in May, when two divisions of white troops on the peninsula completed the formation of the XVIII Corps and three white divisions of the X Army Corps came up from South Carolina, the Army of the James consisted of some 35,000 troops, including 8,000 freedmen or fugitive slaves.[12]

The Army of the Potomac, the larger Union command in Virginia—that entrusted with shoving Robert E. Lee's Confederates back upon Richmond from above—received the vast majority of the white reinforcements sent from Washington during the 1864 campaign. This did not upset Butler, who concentrated on obtaining as many black additions as available. That June he unsuccessfully petitioned the War Department to send him up to 15,000 Colored Troops from his old bailiwick, the Department of the Gulf. In early Fall he was able to secure the transfer of six regiments of blacks from the Department of Kentucky. Other black regiments, including several organized in Maryland, Florida, and the Carolinas, were sent to him at odd intervals.[13]

Not content with these, Butler in August asked for the Army of the Potomac's entire complement of black infantry, its 3rd Division, IX Corps. Noting that the unit had been decimated and demoralized during the recent Crater Mine fiasco outside Petersburg, Butler expressed to General-in-Chief Ulysses Grant a desire to rehabilitate it. He proved his sincerity by giving the Army of the Potomac several large regiments of white troops in return. Given the superior combat experience of the blacks, and Butler's talents at reviving debilitated outfits, the Army of the James got much the better of the bargain.[14]

Soon after absorbing his new division, Butler asked Grant's permission to concentrate his USCTs into a single corps some 16,000 strong. The commanding general agreed, viewing the move (as did Butler) as a means of increasing the blacks' morale and of honoring the service they had rendered the army. The plan came to fruition on 3 December 1864 with the birth of the XXV Corps, commanded by Major General Godfrey Weitzel—Butler's 24,000 white troops forming the XXIV Corps, under Major General Edward O. C. Ord.[15] Though most of the white soldiers would be mustered out of the service within a few months of Appomattox, the XXV Corps would serve on Reconstruction duty in the Southwest until 1866. By then, a total of 35 regiments of blacks would have served in the Army of the James, 27 of them additions to the army's original complement—most secured through the personal efforts of the sable arm's highest-ranking ally.

Butler's dedication to the cause of the Colored Troops went far beyond a willingness to employ them. From departmental funds he paid a small but much appreciated bounty to every local enlistee, even though the federal government seemed chary about awarding bonuses to non-whites. He crusaded for the equalization of pay between the races, insisting that "the colored man fills an equal space in ranks while he lives, and an equal grave when he falls." Not till early in the final year of the war, however, did the government pay each USCT the $13 a month long given to whites. Butler publicly vowed that "every enlisted colored man shall have the same uniform, clothing, arms, equipments, camp equipage, rations, medical and hospital treatment, as are furnished to the United States soldiers of a like arm of the service. . . ." And he established a system by which blacks' grievances could be recorded and injustices against them rectified.[16]

Butler was careful to secure the best officers (white officers, as regulations stipulated) for his Colored Troops. For example, noncommissioned officers in white regiments who exhibited superior leadership qualities were urged to accept positions in black outfits.[17] Meanwhile, incompetent, intemperate, or lax officers in USCT units were speedily discarded. Butler came down especially hard on those who imbibed too freely, proclaiming that "drunken officers are the curse of our Colored soldiers and I will reform it in this Department, if I can, in spite of . . . the Devil." In his eyes, only a cruel or malicious officer was more reprehensible. To all such he meted out severe punishment; most he cashiered. Officers in any outfit who spread slander or ridicule against black soldiers he tongue-lashed and sometimes barred from promotion. And to counter the prejudice which officers and men in black regiments still experienced at the hands of some superiors, Butler decreed that the former could be tried only when a majority of the military court were USCT officers.[18]

Butler was preoccupied with the physical, intellectual, and moral welfare of his blacks. He kept fast to his pledge to provide them with medical and surgical care on a par with that furnished white troops, and he made certain that inspectors-general and regimental commanders scrutinized sanitary conditions in their camps. A welfare worker who in mid-1864 visited the Balfour Military Hospital at Portsmouth exclaimed about the "*excellent* care the colored soldiers received. . . . I have seen in no hospital such *genuine*, direct, and gracious courtesy as the hired nurses in the Balfour show to their colored patients."[19] Much of this seems due to the efforts of Clara Barton, Superintendent of Nurses of the Army of the James, and to her dedicated staff of hospital attendants. At this same time, Butler wrote Grant that "the negro soldiers in this department are by far the healthiest troops I have. With the exception of casualties in battle, the sick are not one & a half per cent."

Particularly for black troops, habitually given the poorest medical care, this was a remarkably low figure.[20]

Realizing that ignorance and illiteracy are barriers to military proficiency, Butler cooperated with missionaries and relief workers to educate the ex-slaves in uniform. With his material and moral support, the United States Christian Commission set up schools among the camps of black troops for the benefit of all who wished in off-duty hours to better their lot.[21] By early 1865 every USCT regiment in the army had a schoolhouse of its own, and the work going on inside was producing gratifying results. One regimental officer remarked after the war:

> The men came to us ignorant of books, ignorant in manners, and with little knowledge of and less interest in anything outside their own little plantation world. Few could read—none scarcely could write their names. When the regiment was disbanded nearly all could read; a large percentage could write fairly, and many had acquired considerable knowledge. . . . What was of even greater importance, they had learned self-reliance and self-respect, and went back to their homes with views enlarged, sympathies quickened, and their interest in the outside world thoroughly awakened."[22]

The great majority of those who schooled the blacks were dedicated to their work. A typical comment was "I could devote my whole time in giving them spelling and reading lessons." Applauding their selfless commitment, Butler furnished rations to the teachers and gave them *carte blanche* to requisition materials and laborers to erect their schoolhouses.[23] He also made available facilities for transporting primers, writing materials, blackboards, and other educational supplies.

The primary purpose of the Christian Commission and of the army's own clergymen—to give religious instruction to the troops—also received Butler's approval. Along with many of his subordinates, he considered the black man innately religious and responsive to the evangelicalism of the day. At least one officer of black infantry found confirmation of this belief, observing that in his regiment religious services were well attended, often to overflowing, with ministers and missionaries crowded out of their chapels by a zealous congregation. To care properly for so large and eager a flock, Butler took pains to ensure that responsible, energetic chaplains were appointed to black outfits. Those who shirked their duties or otherwise gave dissatisfaction were sternly admonished—sometimes in orders disseminated throughout the army. These orders were worded to make clear that men of God in the Army of the James had to answer to more than one higher authority.[24]

Butler worked to ensure the well-being not only of those troops within reach of his authority. From 1862 on, USCTs captured by the enemy had been threatened with a return to bondage, and sometimes with death. Late in 1863 and early in 1864, when some black prisoners were hanged by North Carolina troops, Butler upheld General Wild's announced intent to retaliate on captured Confederates if other blacks were killed, and to execute even the wives of two North Carolina officers. The latter threat was so drastic as to enrage Confederate officials—but it also precipitated an exchange of prisoners.[25]

As the commissioner for the exchange of prisoners in Virginia, Butler labored to persuade Confederate authorities to treat black POWs on a par with captured whites. His most celebrated action in this regard was his October 1864 retaliation for the enemy's decision to put captured USCTs to work upon fortifications within range of Union artillery at Petersburg. Hours after confirming reports of the prisoners' plight, Butler put an equal number of Confederate captives to work on the Dutch Gap Canal, an ill-starred excavation project then in progress on a peninsula above the James River and under daily bombardment by Rebel batteries. Infuriated by this development, the War Department in Richmond vowed to escalate the feud, but finally agreed to release the blacks from labor if Butler removed his prisoners from Dutch Gap. He complied, satisfied that no casualties had occurred on either side—and that he had compelled the Confederacy, at least tacitly, to concede the equality of military captives, no matter their race.[26]

Butler's programs to benefit the blacks in his realm extended beyond those in uniform. To keep high the morale of his troops, he sought at an early date to provide for their families. He thought this only just: "I am very anxious to fulfill my part of the contract to the negroes who by their readiness to enlist are fully up on their side. . . ."[27] His first efforts had been the urban renewal and resettlement projects in Slabtown. In published orders he also called on his white troops to do all possible to assist fugitive slaves in reaching the army's lines and finding a place therein to live. Any soldier who obstructed, abused, or insulted the fugitives would be punished. Then, too, Butler furnished subsistence to a soldier's dependents for the man's full term of service. He prohibited agents recruiting for other armies from taking enlistees out of his department without providing for the economic security of wives and children to be left behind. He asked business acquaintances in New England to provide factory jobs for indigent contrabands, informing one industrialist, "Although darker skinned they are quite as intelligent as the green Irish help which you take into your mills." In August 1864 he provided the means to send 160 widows and orphans of USCTs to New York, Philadelphia, and Boston, where benevolent societies would find jobs for the women and foster homes for the children.[28] Though ever anxious to recruit, Butler furnished employment to civilian freedmen in his department as well as transportation to bring others up from the Deep South. To the most highly skilled workmen required for army projects, he paid $3 a month more than the average pay for private soldiers, plus one ration per day. He refused, however, to countenance idleness among the civilian community declaring that "no subsistence will be permitted to any negro or his family, with whom he lives, who is able to work and does not. . . . Any negro who refuses to work when able; and neglects his family, will be arrested, and reported to these headquarters . . . where he will be made to work." At the same time, he forbade the continuance of a popular practice whereby officers and white enlisted personnel had impressed contrabands for personal, non-military labor.[29]

Black civilians enjoyed many of the same educational facilities available to blacks in the ranks. At Butler's urging the Freemen's Aid Society, the Christian Commission, and other welfare agencies established or expanded upon school-construction programs throughout the department. Here too Butler sought to persuade Northern friends to help out. He even requested the Lowell, Massachusetts school system to send him discarded classroom benches, blackboards, and other items.[30]

Perhaps Butler's most ambitious project to aid Colored Troops directly benefited their families as well. Late in 1864 he established at Norfolk a freedmen's savings bank, in which bounties and wages might be invested. Administered by an experienced financier from Butler's home town, the bank proved an unqualified success. One black infantry regiment alone, by war's close, had contributed $90,000 to its assets. Though some critics charged the institution with financial irregularities, even some political foes of Butler, who audited its accounts, confessed to finding "all its transactions systematic and honest."[31]

Finally, Butler's Office of Negro Affairs, headed by his aide, Lieutenant Colonel J. Burnham Kinsman, oversaw the feeding, clothing, and housing of thousands of soldiers' dependents and other contrabands; provided the able-bodied with appropriate employment at fair wages; regulated contracts between them and white employers; allocated government land to tenants who paid one quarter of their harvest as rent; audited blacks' accounts against the government; and in general furthered a paternalistic system of unprecedented dimensions.[32]

Ben Butler received an honest return on his investment, for all fair-minded critics came to admit that his black soldiers more than carried their share of the burden in camp, in the trenches, and on the battlefield. At the outset, few of the army's white troops predicted this outcome; many thought it folly to entrust former slaves with responsibilities upon which white men's lives might depend. One area of criticism was their dearth of schooling. Late in 1863 a New Hampshire soldier remarked that the USCTs under Butler "are all escaped slaves and a poor miserable ignorant set. They are far inferior to the nigger of the North in intelligence." Other critics decried the effects of Butler's undeniable favoritism toward blacks. Wrote a disgusted officer from the commanding general's home state, "The 'nigger' in this dept is supreme & it is policy for those who desire to bask in the smiles of official favor to be its very devout worshippers. . . . The attempt to mix [the blacks] up with white soldiers & people is productive of mischief, they are very arrogant & insolent presuming altogether too much on their social position." Other whites simply could not regard social inferiors as fighting men. One of Butler's senior brigadiers dismissed Hinks's men as "dressed up like soldiers and euphemistically styled 'Colored Troops' . . . an interesting popular and Government pet and plaything . . . not good to tie to in battle." Others agreed, claiming to know that in combat USCTs "will charge when highly excited, but will not hold what they take."[33]

Some adverse comments came from the blacks' own officers. A certain amount had basis in fact, including references to the soldiers' educational limitations. The commander of the army's single battery of black artillerists observed that "it has been found upon experiment and in actual Service impossible to [teach] the gunners how to point a piece with even tolerable correctness, or to obtain a man who can cut fuzes or fit them correctly, as those who can count must do so, so slowly as to be too often incorrect."[34] Other strictures reveal more about the accusers than the accused. A colonel of black cavalry opined that his men "lack the pride, spirit and intellectual energy of the whites," and that an ex-slave "cannot stand up against adversity. A sick nigger, for instance, at once gives up and lies down to die, the personification of humanity reduced to a wet rag. He cannot fight for life like a white man." Some officers viewed their troops as inherently rowdy and undisciplined, and lacking in respect for authority. Still others felt that Blacks deserved less consideration than white soldiers. A division commander in the XXV Corps confessed, at the outset of the 1865 campaign, that "I shall feel less regret over the slain than if my troops were white. . . . If I must fall myself I should prefer to *die* with my own [kind]. . . ."[35]

Such officers appear to have been in the minority. Most of those who led the blacks seem to have had an abiding faith in the capacity of the rank and file. By late 1863 they were aware that USCTs had served well in other theaters of operations; there seemed no reason to suspect that the Army of the James' material would prove inferior.

In fact, the average officer found that his men learned the rhythm of military movements with relative ease, imitated the characteristics of experienced soldiers till tolerably proficient themselves, and adapted well to roughing it.[36] They displayed other praiseworthy traits. Colonel James Shaw, Jr., commander of the 7th USCT, was impressed by their blameless personal conduct. He claimed to have seen none of his soldiers drunk during over two years of service, to have heard only a few use profanity, and to have witnessed but one fight among them. Furthermore, "In drill I never saw their equal. They took pride in their work and their sense of [timing] is perfect." His colleagues spoke of the "admirable discipline" of black soldiers, of their "ability to handle a musket with good effect," of their "devotion to duty and country" and of "their eagerness to learn their duties." Even the officer who had criticized them as insolent added that they "make good soldiers enough," while the colonel who had maligned their stamina felt that "properly officered, [they] would I believe be as effective as any [infantry] in the world."[37]

Few questioned the depth of the spirit that motivated Butler's blacks to serve. The sergeant-major of the 4th USCT put it simply: "A double purpose induced me and most others to enlist, to assist in abolishing slavery and to save the country from ruin." Another noncommissioned officer, when asked if he had received a bounty when joining the 36th USCT, shook his head indignantly: "I wouldn't 'list for bounty. . . . I wouldn't fight for money; my wages is enough. . . . Them big-bounty men don't make good soldiers. . . . Dey comes in for money; dar's no Country 'bout it, an' dey hasn't no stomach for fightin' and diggin' an' knockin' roun', like soldiers has to." A black enlisted man in the Balfour Hospital was heard to say of his amputated arm: "Oh I *should* like to *have* it, but I don't begrudge it." Exclaimed a second black amputee: "Well . . . 'twas [lost] in a glorious cause, and if I'd lost my life I should have been satisfied. I knew what I was fighting for."[38]

Many of their commanders were similarly idealistic. It would seem that only a commitment to the cause of racial equality could have nerved them against what Butler termed the "stupid, unreasoning, and quite vengeful prejudice" they were liable to encounter in discharging their duties. As General Wild stated shortly after Appomattox, "I was one of the very earliest to start the raising of negro troops; and for more than two years I have been identified with their cause. On this account I have had nothing but prejudice, jealousy, misrepresentation, persecution and treachery, to contend against. . . ."[39]

Still, they served—some, to be sure, from opportunism, for purely selfish reasons of rank and power; but many from a sincere desire to advance libertarian ideals. Brigadier General William Birney, son of a famous abolitionist, expressed his desire to fight "the preconceived idea on the part of many that a negro has no rights whatever, and that he and his family can subsist on nothing." A lieutenant in the 2nd USC Cavalry voiced his determination to "finish my career . . . in such a service in which I now have the honor to hold a Commission, and where the cause for which I am fighting, is such a glorious and ennobling one." And a subaltern in the 5th USCT wrote in his diary: "I did not enter this service from any mercenary motive but to assist in removing the unreasonable prejudice against the colored race; and to contribute a share however small toward making the negro an effective instrument in crushing out this unholy rebellion."[40]

The latter wish, at least, would be fulfilled. As soon as the Army of the James began active campaigning, most of its blacks gave unsparingly of their energy and devotion to the cause. Early in May 1864 Butler transported his two corps from Fort Monroe to Bermuda Hundred, City Point, and other strategic sites near the confluence of the James and Appomattox Rivers, about a dozen miles southeast of Richmond. The first units to land on this unknown stretch of enemy territory were Colored Troops, who seized and garrisoned points along the army's line of communications. Butler gave them so heavy a responsibility because "I knew that they would fight more desperately than any white troops, in order to prevent capture . . . [and being] returned into slavery."[41] His theory was upheld during the latter part of the month, when a number of the garrisons found themselves surrounded by several times as many Confederates. After refusing surrender demands (the

enemy commander warning that he "would not be answerable for consequences" if the works were carried by storm), the blacks withstood assaults
from all sides and repulsed each, inflicting more than twice the casualties
they absorbed. Afterward army headquarters, newspaper editors, political
spokesmen—and more than a few officers previously doubtful about the
blacks' fortitude—praised them for passing their first test of battle in Virginia.[42]

The initial attempt by the Army of the James to capture Richmond, known
as the Bermuda Hundred Campaign, proved a miserable failure, with Butler
and his ranking subordinates sharing the blame. During this period, however, Butler recognized the strategic importance of Petersburg, the supply
center 22 miles below the Confederate capital, and twice attempted to
capture it with troops from Hinks's division. The first effort, on 9 May, was
absorbed at Grant's insistence that the Army of the James move, instead,
against Richmond.[43] The second attempt, exactly one month later, was
partially successful but ended when one of Butler's corps leaders lost the
nerve to assault the city's weakly held defense line. Immediately afterward
General Hinks offered to try again in the same sector, but was turned down
for obscure reasons.[44]

When Grant turned his attention to Petersburg, nevertheless, Hinks's was
the first infantry to be sent against the city. On 15 June the black troops
smashed through defenses on the northern and eastern outskirts and came
away with several cannon as trophies. Their performance went to waste in
the end, when still another of Butler's subordinates failed to act decisively
at a crucial hour and when Grant and Meade botched the Army of the Potomac's advance on the city. Such errors gave General Lee time to stock
Petersburg's works with enough Confederates to force a ten-month siege.[45]

Throughout that siege, Butler's USCTs shared with his and Meade's white
troops the hardships of life in the rifle-pits, losing dozens of men daily to
sniper fire, enemy sorties, and disease. When given the chance to mount
offensives, they served with notable gallantry, even in defeat. During a 28–
30 September movement which Grant ordered Butler to make against the
outer works of Richmond, the latter's ordnance chief, who had recently
refused a commission in a black outfit,

> witnessed an attack by a line of colored infantry on a field breast-work, having
> a well-constructed parapet, [a] ditch in front and strong abbatis [sic] . . . the
> darkies rushed across the open space fronting the work, under a fire which
> caused them loss, into the abatis . . . down into the ditch with ladders, up and
> over the parapet with flying flags, and down among, and on top of, the as-
> tonished enemy, who left in utmost haste. . . . Then and there I decided that
> "The black man would fight" for his freedom, and that I had made a mistake
> in not commanding them. . . .[46]

Despite initial success, this offensive against enemy works along New
Market Heights was doomed to fail. Lack of support, the formidable character of the defenses, and overwhelming opposition from artillery and sharp-

shooters combined to cause mass carnage among the blacks. But they refused to concede defeat, leaping into the ditches before Fort Gilmer, where cut down at close to point-blank range. As earlier, survivors crawled up to the parapet of the fort—but this time were bayoneted and flung back into the ditch, while defenders rained hand grenades on them. The fighting ended with a Union withdrawal, but not before one brigade of blacks had suffered over 50 percent casualties.[47]

After the smoke cleared, Ben Butler crossed a portion of the littered field and wrote his wife: "The man who says the negro will not fight is a coward. . . . His soul is blacker than the dead faces of these dead negroes, upturned to heaven in solemn protest against him and his prejudices." Of 37 Congressional Medals of Honor awarded to participants in the offensive, 14 went to blacks. Considering this gesture inadequate, Butler designed and struck a medal that resembled the Victoria Cross and through the remainder of the war awarded it to all who fit its inscription: "U.S. Colored Troops . . . Distinguished for Courage, Campaign Before Richmond."[48]

Although they never again saw fighting in Virginia on such a scale as they had at New Market Heights, the blacks of the army served just as faithfully through the Petersburg Campaign and during the closing operations about Richmond and Appomattox Court House. And in December 1864 and January 1865 almost 4,000 members of the XXV Corps joined 6,000 white comrades on two expeditions—the first, under Butler, a failure; the second a success under Brevet Major General Alfred H. Terry—against defenses that guarded the entrance to the Confederacy's last open port, Wilmington, North Carolina. On 13–15 January they built a line of works above Fort Fisher and held it against the pressure of enemy reinforcements. In so doing they protected the rear of the white troops and enabled them to capture the fort, closing off Wilmington to the outside world.[49]

That same month the USCTs of the Army of the James lost their most powerful supporter when Grant relieved Butler from command for a combination of military and political reasons. The new commander, General Ord, maintained most of the social programs instituted by his predecessor. Some of his officers, however, declared him a bigot. "He has expressed the meanest opinions [of], and done the meanest things to, and for, the negroes," claimed General Wild; while General Birney noted that even in public, Ord always "spelt 'negro' with two g's."[50]

During the army's final campaign, Ord kept half of his black units near Richmond—deliberately depriving them, some subordinates felt, of the opportunity to share in the glory of Lee's capture. The rest of his command —two-thirds of it white troops—he led southwest of Petersburg and thence, in cooperation with the Army of the Potomac, toward Appomattox on Lee's heels. Even those blacks he brought with him were left behind to guard supply depots while Ord pursued the enemy with the XXIV Corps. The USCTs were finally relieved by a new rear guard and by some of the hardest marching of the war managed to rejoin the army before Lee had been brought to earth. Thereupon Ord relieved their commander, Birney, and attached his troops to the rear of the white's columns.[51]

Meanwhile, the blacks on the Richmond front, under General Weitzel, had to race another white division in the Army of the James for the honor of being the first to enter the evacuated capital. Though they won the contest, the USCTs were held on the outskirts until the white soldiers had taken possession of the city. Only then were they permitted to march through the streets, en route to camps in the suburbs of Richmond.[52]

Upon reaching the Rebel capital after Lee's surrender, Ord refused to allow the Colored Troops to remain anywhere in the vicinity. Upon meeting General Wild, he exclaimed, "You must get these damned niggers of yours out of Richmond as fast as you can!" He relegated them to Petersburg-area campsites recently occupied by white units and now littered, cramped, unsanitary and lacking in good water.[53]

In subsequent weeks the blacks were returned to their old bailiwick, City Point. From there, in May and June, the reunited XXV Corps was shipped to Texas and Louisiana, where it served on provost duty and displayed the flag for benefit of the French in Mexico. The last of its troops were not sent back to Virginia for muster-out until November 1866, ten months after its corps organization had been disbanded.[54]

Thus, the blacks of the Army of the James remained in uniform to serve the Union long after they had helped win the war to preserve it. In the end, they could take satisfaction from knowing that they had made an impressive effort toward lowering 350-year-old barriers of prejudice and discrimination, especially in the military realm. Contemplating the fact years later, one of the colonels vocalized their feelings when he wrote, "To have contributed in ever so small a degree to this glorious result should be a source of pride and pleasure beyond price."[55]

NOTES

1. *War of the Rebellion: A Compilation of the Official Records of the Union and Confederate Armies*, 4 series, 70 vols. in 128 (Washington, D.C., 1880–1901) [hereafter cited as OR], Series I, Vol. 42, Part 3, p. 791; Dudley T. Cornish, *The Sable Arm: Negro Troops in the Union Army, 1861–1865* (New York, 1956), 266, 281.

2. Asst. Adjutant Gen. W. A. Nichols to Major Ge. Benjamin F. Butler (1 March 1864), Dept. of Virginia and North Carolina: Letters Sent and Received, 1863–65 [hereafter cited as DVa&NC], RG 393, Entry 5063, Vol. 5, National Archives, Washington, D.C.

3. OR, I, 42, pt. 2, p. 779.

4. Cornish, 5, 10, 24, 63–67; Hans L. Trefousse, *Ben Butler: The South Called Him BEAST!* (New York, 1957), 131–32; Bell Irwin Wiley, *The Life of Billy Yank: The Common Soldier of the Union* (Indianapolis, 1952), 313.

5. Benjamin F. Butler, *Character and Results of the War: How to Prosecute and How*

to End It (Philadelphia, 1863), 18–19; James Parton, *General Butler in New Orleans: History of the Administration of the Department of the Gulf in the Year 1862* (Boston, 1866), 616–17.

6. OR, I, 29, pt. 2, pp. 397, 447; *Autobiography and Personal Reminiscences of Major-General Benj. F. Butler: Butler's Book* (Boston, 1892), 12; Butler to anon. (8 Jan. 1879), Butler Papers, Library of Congress, Washington, D.C.; Richard S. West, Jr., *Lincoln's Scapegoat General: A Life of Benjamin F. Butler, 1818–1893* (Boston, 1965), 216–19.

7. Brigadier Gen. Isaac J. Wistar to Butler (27 March 1864), Butler Papers; *Autobiography of Isaac Jones Wistar, 1827–1905: Half a Century in War and Peace* (Philadelphia, 1937), 417–19, 438–39.

8. Henry L. Swint, ed., *"Dear Ones at Home": Letters from Contraband Camps* (Nashville, Tenn., 1966), 100, 107, 110; George H. Gordon, *A War Diary of Events in the War of the Great Rebellion, 1863–1865* (Boston, 1882), 360–61.

9. Frederick H. Dyer, *A Compendium of the War of the Rebellion* (Des Moines, 1980), 391; *Address of Martin P. Kennard on Presentation to the Town* [of Brookline, Massachusetts] *of a Memorial Portrait of the Late Brig.-Gen'l Edward Augustus Wild* (Brookline, 1894), 13; West, 222–25; *Butler's Book*, 618.

10. OR, I, 33, pp. 957, 1055, Dyer, 392.

11. OR, I, 33, p. 1057; 51, pt. 1, p. 1160; Butler to Sec. of War Edwin M. Stanton (21 April 1864), DVa&NC, RG-393, E-5046, Vol. 4.

12. OR, I, 36, pt. 3, p. 427; "The Opposing Forces at the Beginning of Grant's Campaign Against Richmond," *Battles and Leaders of the Civil War*, ed. Robert Underwood Johnson and Clarence Clough Buel, 4 vols. (New York, 1887–88), IV, 181–82.

13. OR, I, 40, pt. 2, p. 387; Jessie Ames Marshall, comp., *Private and Official Correspondence of Gen. Benjamin F. Butler during the Period of the Civil War*, 6 vols. (Norwood, Mass., 1917), IV, 428–29; OR, I, 42, pt. 3, pp. 65, 267; Marshall, V, 267–68; *Record of the Services of the Seventh Regiment, U.S. Colored Troops* (Providence, 1878), 60–63; Captain Austin Wiswall (9th USCT) to His Mother (9 Aug. 1864), Wiswall Papers, Southwest Collection, Texas Tech University Library, Lubbock, Tex.; Wiswall Diary (7–8 Aug. 1864), *ibid.*

14. Butler to Lt. Gen. U.S. Grant (19 Aug. 1864), DVa&NC, RG-393, E-5046, Vol. 4; Marshall, V, 355–56; OR, I, 42, pt. 3, pp. 323, 652, 669–70, 685, 702, 709, 716–18; 51, pt. 1, pp. 1191–92.

15. Butler to Brig. Gen. John A. Rawlins (30 Nov. 1864), DVa&NC, RG-393, E-5046, Vol. 4; OR, I, 42, pt. 3, pp. 761, 791.

16. OR, III, 3, pp. 1139–44; "Government of the Contrabands: General Butler's Order," *The Rebellion Record*, ed. Frank Moore, 12 vols. (New York, 1861–68), VIII, 261–64; *The New Regime: Official Journal of the Department* [of Virginia and North Carolina], 2 March 1864.

17. "A Visit to General Butler and the Army of the James," *Fraser's Magazine*, LXXI (1865), 443–44.

18. Butler to Sen. Henry Wilson (4 March 1864), DVa&NC, RG-393, E-5046, Vol. 4; Butler to Stanton (31 July 1864), *ibid*; *History of the Eleventh Pennsylvania Volunteer Cavalry* (Pittsburgh, 1910), 181–82; OR, III, 3, p. 1144; "Government of the Contrabands," 264; Brig. Gen. Edward A. Wild to Major Robert S. Davis (29 June 1864), Wild's Generals' Papers, RG-94, E-159, National Archives; Wild's Generals' Reports of Service, War of the Rebellion, RG-94, E-160, Vol. 10, pp. 390–91, *ibid.*

19. Swint, 122–23.

20. Marshall, IV, 428.

21. Edward P. Smith, *Incidents of the United States Christian Commission* (Philadelphia, 1871), 358; Andrew B. Cross to Edward F. Williams (Field Agent, U.S. Christian Commission, Army of the James) (6 Dec. 1864), Williams Papers, Amistad Research Center, Dillard University, New Orleans, La.; Chaplain G. A. Rockwood (8th USCT) to Williams (19 Dec. 1864), *ibid.*; Chaplains Rockwood and J.T. Leach (19th USCT) to Williams (19 Dec. 1864), *ibid.*; Chaplain Francis A. Boyd (109th USCT) to Williams

(20 Dec. 1864), *ibid.*; Chaplain David Stevens (36th USCT) to Williams (27 Dec. 1864), *ibid.*; Williams Diary (31 Dec. 1864), *ibid.*

22. *Seventh Regiment USCT*, 86–87.

23. Smith, 357–58.

24. *OR*, III, 3, p. 1144; "Government of the Contrabands," 264; John McMurray (6th USCT), *Recollections of a Colored Troop* (n.p., 1916), 63; E. Henry Powell (10th USCT), *The Colored Soldier in the War of the Rebellion: War Paper No. 3, Vermont Commandery of the* [Military Order of the] *Loyal Legion* [of the United States] (Burlington, 1893), 6.

25. Butler to Col. James M. Hinton (27 Jan. 1864), DVa&NC, RG-393, E-5046, Vol. 4; Butler to Lt. William J. Munden and Mr. Pender Weeks (26 Jan. 1864), Edward A. Wild Papers, Massachusetts Commandery, Military Order of the Loyal Legion of the United States Collection [hereafter cited as Mass. MOLLUS], U.S. Army Military History Institute, Carlisle Barracks, Pa.; Wild to Lt. George H. Willis (3rd North Carolina [Colored] Infantry) (14 Jan. 1864), Willis Papers, Mugar Memorial Library, Boston University; *OR*, I, 29, pt. 2, pp. 595–96; II, 6, pp. 776–77, 847, 877–78, 1128.

26. Marshall, V, 97–98; Trefousse, 140–45; *OR*, I, 42, pt. 3, pp. 216–17, 285–86; Copy of General Orders 126, Dept. of Virginia and North Carolina (13 Oct. 1864), John M. Spear Papers, Mass. Historical Society, Boston; Marshall, V, 263–64, 271; *Daily Richmond Examiner* (20, 28 Oct. 1864); *New York Times* (23 Oct. 1864); *New York Herald* (23 Oct. 1864); Howard Swiggett, ed., *A Rebel War Clerk's Diary at the Confederate States Capital*, 2 vols. (New York, 1935), II, 308–09; Richard J. Sommers, "The Dutch Gap Affair: Military Atrocities and Rights of Negro Soldiers," *Civil War History*, 21 (1975), 51–64.

27. Butler to John M. Forbes (18 Dec. 1863), DVa&NC, RG-393, E-5046, Vol. 3.

28. *OR*, III, 3, pp. 1139–44; "Government of the Contrabands," 261–64; *Joint Committee on the Conduct of the War*, 3 vols. in 8 (Washington, D.C., 1863–68), 1865 Vol., pt. 2, p. 47; Butler to John Wright (25 April 1864), DVa&NC, RG-393, E-5046, Vol. 4; *New York Herald* (4 Aug. 1864).

29. *OR*, I, 42, pt. 2, pp. 411, 600, 610–11; III, 3 pp. 1139–41; "Government of the Contrabands," 262; *New York Times* (13 Sept. 1864).

30. Marshall, V, 345–46; Butler to William P. Webster (12 March 1864), DVa&NC, RG-393, E-5046, Vol. 4; Harold B. Raymond, "Ben Butler: A Reappraisal," *Colby Library Quarterly*, VI (1964), 466.

31. *Seventh Regiment USCT*, 87–89; James Shaw, Jr., *Our Last Campaign and Subsequent Service in Texas: Personal Narratives of Events in the War of the Rebellion: Being Papers Read Before the Rhode Island Soldiers and Sailors Historical Society* (Providence, 1905) [hereafter cited as *Narratives*], 33; [Lt. Col. John Coughlin, Superintendent of Negro Affairs, Department of Virginia and North Carolina] to Major Gen. Edward O. C. Ord (13 Feb. 1865), Ord Papers, Bancroft Library, University of California at Berkeley.

32. *OR*, III, 3, pp. 1142–44; "Government of the Contrabands," 263–64; Gordon, 360–61; Butler to Wistar (27 Nov. 1863), DVa&NC, RG-393, E-5046, Vol. 3.

33. Pvt. John H. Burrill to His Parents (7 Nov. 1863), Burrill Papers, USAMHI; Capt. William A. Walker to "Dear Jas." (16 Jan. 1864), James Perkins Walkers Papers, Firestone Library, Princeton University; *Autobiography of Wistar*, 446; Sgt. Washington Vosburgh to "Ella" (18, 22 Aug. 1864), TSS, in Nina Ness Collection, Bentley Historical Library, University of Michigan, Ann Arbor.

34. Capt. Francis C. Choate (Battery B, 2nd USC Artillery) to Major Gen. William Farrar Smith (27 June 1864), Smith Papers, Vermont Historical Society, Montpelier.

35. Worthington Chauncey Ford, ed., *A Cycle of Adams Letters, 1861–1865*, 2 vols. (Boston, 1920), II, 195, 216–17; "War Letters of Charles P. Bowditch [5th Mass. (Colored) Cavalry]," *Massachusetts Historical Society Proceedings*, LVII (1924), 474; Brevet Major Gen. August V. Kautz to "My Dear Mrs. Savage" (12 Feb. 1865), Kautz Papers, Illinois State Historical Library, Springfield.

36. George E. Sutherland (13th USC Artillery), "The Negro in the Late War," *War*

Papers: Read Before the Commandery of the State of Wisconsin, Military Order of the Loyal Legion of the United States, 3 vols. (Milwaukee, 1891–1903), I, 175, 180.

37. *Seventh Regiment USCT*, 89; Shaw, 33; Capt. G. W. Kelley to Smith (2 July 1898), Smith Papers; Lt. Charles A. Currier Memoirs, 148–49, Mass. MOLLUS Collection; Sutherland, 183; *Seventh Regiment USCT*, 86; Walker to "Dear Jas." (16 January 1864), Walker Papers; *Adams Letters*, II, 216.

38. Sgt. Christian A. Fleetwood (4th USCT) to Dr. James Hall (8 June 1865), Carter Woodson Collection, LC; Smith, 364; Swint, 123.

39. *Butler's Book*, 672; Wild to Major Gen. Godfrey Weitzel (8 May 1865), Wild Papers, Mass. MOLLUS Collection.

40. Brig. Gen. William Birney to Sec. of Treasury Salmon P. Chase (25 April 1864), Chase Papers, Historical Society of Pennsylvania, Philadelphia; Lt. Henry T. Knox (2nd USC Cavalry) to Major Atherton H. Stevens (4th Mass. [Colored] Cavalry) (18 Dec. 1864), Stevens Papers, Mass. Historical Society; Lt. Joseph J. Scroggs (5th USCT) Diary (30 March 1864), TS. in USAMHI.

41. OR, I, 36, pt. 2, pp. 21–22, 165, 430; *Official Records of the Union and Confederate Navies in the War of the Rebellion*, 30 vols. (Washington, D.C., 1894–1922) [hereafter cited as OR-N], I, 10, pp. 4–5; Marshall, IV, 163–64; Scroggs Diary (5–7 May 1864), USAMHI; Sgt. Christian A. Fleetwood (4th USCT) Diary (5 May 1864), Fleetwood Papers, LC. *New York Times* (8 May 1864); Thomas L. Livermore (Staff Officer, Hinks's Division), *Days and Events, 1860–1866* (Boston, 1920), 334–37; McMurray, 28; A.H. Stein, *History of the Thirty-Seventh Regt. U.S.C. Infantry* (Philadelphia, 1866), 15; Edward Simonton (1st USCT), "The Campaign up the James River to Petersburg," *Glimpses of the Nation's Struggle: Minnesota MOLLUS*, 6 vols. (Saint Paul 1887–1909), V, 481–82; Sylvester B. Partridge, "With the Signal Corps from Fortress Monroe to Richmond, May, 1864–April, 1865" *War Papers: Maine MOLLUS*, 3 vols. (Portland, 1898–1908), III, 85–86; *Butler's Book*, 670.

42. OR, I, 36, pt. 2, pp. 24, 269–72; pt. 3, pp. 180–82, 204; OR-N, I, 10, pp. 88–92; Marshall, IV, 262, 264, 267; *Butler's Book*, 669–70; *Memorial of Adjt. M. W. Smith* [1st USCT]: *A Tribute to a Beloved Son and Brother* (Newark, N.J., 1864), 41–42; Simonton, 482–83; Solon A. Carter (Staff Officer, Hinks's Division), "Fourteen Months' Service with Colored Troops," *Civil War Papers: Massachusetts MOLLUS*, 2 vols. (Boston, 1900), I, 161; Partridge, 87; William B. Avery, *Gun-Boat Service on the James River: Narratives, RISSHS* (Providence, 1884), 19–23; "The Attack on Fort Powhatan," *Rebellion Record*, XI, 504; *Memorial of Gen'l Wild*, 14, 26–27.

43. OR, I, 36, pt. 2, pp. 22–23, 590, 593–94; Marshall, IV, 182–86; *Butler's Book*, 645–48; Butler to Hinks (8–9 May 1864), Hinks Papers, Mugar Memorial Library, Boston University; Fleetwood Diary (9 May 1864), Fleetwood Papers; Butler to "W.P. Darby [Derby]" (26 June 1882), Butler Papers, LC., Livermore, 338–42; Alfred P. Rockwell, "The Tenth Army Corps in Virginia, May 1864," *Papers of the Military Historical Society of Massachusetts*, 14 vols. (Boston, 1895–1918), IX, 280–83.

44. OR, I, 36, pt. 2, pp. 273–319; pt. 3, pp. 705–09, 718–20; Lt. Col. Edward W. Smith to Major Gen. Quincy A. Gillmore (16 June 1864), Gillmore's General's Papers, RG-94, E-159, National Archives; Hinks to Gillmore (18 June 1864), *ibid.*; Gillmore to Hinks (18 June 1864), Hinks Papers; Marshall, IV, 324–35, 338–41, 343–54; *Butler's Book*, 672–79; Livermore, 353–55; Simonton, 489–90; Carter, 162–63; *Memorial of Adjt. M. W. Smith*, 42.

45. OR, I, 40, pt. 1, pp. 705, 720–25; pt. 2, pp. 75, 83; 51, pt. 1, pp. 263–67; Smith Memoirs, 13–19, Smith Papers; Col. Samuel A. Duncan (4th USCT) to Smith (17 April 1866), *ibid.*; Brig. Gen. William T.H. Brooks to Smith (3 March 1866), *ibid.*; Lt. Nicholas Bowen Diary (15 June 1864), *ibid.*, Marshall, IV, 376–77, 381–83; Fleetwood Diary (15 June 1864), Fleetwood Papers; Livermore, 356–63; McMurray; 35–36; "Letters of Charles Bowditch," 481–82; Carter, 163–69; *Memorial of Adjt. M. W. Smith*, 42–43; Christian A. Fleetwood (4th USCT), *The Negro as a Soldier* (Washington, D.C., 1895), 14–15; George Washington Williams, *A History of the Negro Troops in the War of the Rebellion, 1861–65* (New York, 1888), 236–37; James M. McPherson, *The Negro's*

Civil War: How American Negroes Felt and Acted during the War for the Union (New York, 1965), 224–25; Joseph T. Wilson, *The Black Phalanx: A History of the Negro Soldiers of the United States* (Hartford, Conn., 1890), 398–405.

46. *Memoirs of Brigadier General John Alexander Kress* (n.p., 1925), 32.

47. OR, I, 42, pt. 1, pp. 772–75, 780–81, 817–20; Lt. James H. Wickes (4th USCT) to His Father (2, 4, 16, Oct. 1864), Wickes Papers, Boston Public Library, Boston; Scroggs Diary (29 Sept. 1864); Fleetwood Diary (29 Sept. 1864); Capt. Solon A. Carter (Staff Officer, Hinks's Division) to Hinks (3 Oct. 1864), Hinks Papers; *New York Times* (3 Oct. 1864); *Philadelphia Press* (13 Oct., 15 Nov. 1864); Brevet Brig. Gen. Edward H. Ripley, "Memories: The Battle of Fort Harrison or Chapin's Farm," 1–13, TS. in Douglas Southall Freeman Collection, Alderman Library, University of Virginia, Charlottesville; Brig. Gen. Charles J. Paine's Generals' Reports of Service, War of the Rebellion, RG-94, E-160, Vol. 10, pp. 503–04, National Archives; *Butler's Book*, 721–37; McMurray, 51–58; George R. Sherman (7th USCT), *Assault on Fort Gilmer and Reminiscences of Prison Life: Narratives*, RISSHS (Providence, 1897), 5–63; *General William Birney's Answer to Libels Clandestinely Circulated by James Shaw, Jr.* (Washington, D.C., 1878), 14–23; J.H. Goulding (6th USCT), "The Colored Troops in the War of the Rebellion," *Proceedings of the Reunion Society of Vermont Officers*, II (1885), 149–51; Carter, 170–74; M.L. Richardson, *A Sermon Preached at the Funeral of Lieut. Eber C. Pratt* [6th USCT], (Southbridge, Mass., 1865), 8–9; Williams, 252–54; Wilson, 435–43.

48. Marshall, V, 192; *Butler's Book*, 742–43; Cornish, 266.

49. OR, I, 42, pt. 1, pp. 964–88; 46, pt. 1, pp. 394–425 (especially pp. 423–25); OR-N, I, 11, pp. 207–75, 356–59, 404–05, 430–45; Brevet Major Gen. Alfred H. Terry to Rawlins (27 Jan., 8 Feb. 1865), Terry Family Papers, Connecticut Historical Society, Hartford; Terry to Lt. Col. T.S. Bowers (3 Feb. 1865), *ibid.*; Capt. Adrian Terry to His Wife (24 Jan. 1865), Terry Family Papers, Sterling Memorial Library, Yale University, New Haven; Scroggs Diary (9–31 Dec. 1864, 5–15 Jan. 1865); Fleetwood Diary (13–27 Dec. 1864); Fleetwood to His Father (21 Jan. 1865), *ibid.*; Marshall, V, 431–74; *Conduct of the War*, 1865 vol., pt. 2, pp. 3–104; *Butler's Book*, 774–824; Paine's Generals' Report of Service, War of the Rebellion, RG-94, E-160, Vol. 10, pp. 504–05, National Archives; Adelbert Ames, "The Capture of Fort Fisher," *Civil War Papers: Mass. MOLLUS*, I, 271–95; John Ames, "Fort Fisher," *Overland Monthly*, IV (1870), 489–96; IX (1872), 323–32; Joseph Becker, "Fort Fisher and Wilmington," *Frank Leslie's Popular Monthly* 38 (1894), 230–39; N. Martin Curtis, "The Capture of Fort Fisher," *Civil War Papers: Mass. MOLLUS*, I, 299–327; Edson J. Harkness, "The Expeditions against Fort Fisher and Wilmington," *Military Essays and Recollections: Illinois MOLLUS*, 4 vols. (Chicago, 1891–1907), II, 145–88; H.C. Lockwood, "The Capture of Fort Fisher," *Atlantic Monthly*, 27 (1871), 622–36, 684–90; James Parker, "The Navy in the Battles and Capture of Fort Fisher," *Personal Recollections of the War of the Rebellion: New York MOLLUS*, ed. A. Noel Blackman, 4 vols. (New York, 1891–1912), II, 104–17; Charles E. Pearce, "The Expeditions against Fort Fisher," *War Papers and Personal Reminiscences, 1861–1865: Missouri MOLLUS* (St. Louis, 1892), 354–81; Thomas O. Selfridge, "The Navy at Fort Fisher," *Battles and Leaders of the Civil War*, IV, 655–61; George F. Towle, "Terry's Fort Fisher Expedition," *Our Living and Our Dead*, III (1875), 464–72, 592–604; Daniel A. Ammen, *Our Second Bombardment of Fort Fisher: District of Columbia MOLLUS War Paper 4* (Washington, D.C., 1887), 1–25.

50. Copy of General Orders 1, Adjutant Generals' Office (7 Jan. 1865), Butler's General's Papers, RG-94, E-159; Copy of Special Orders 5, Headquarters, Armies of the United States (7 Jan. 1865), Butler Papers; OR, I, 46, pt. 2, pp. 60–61, 186; Marshall, V, 471–73, 475–76; *Butler's Book*, 827–57; Wild to Sen. Wilson (10 May 1865), Wild Papers; *General Birney's Answer to Libels*, 5, 8.

51. OR, I, 46, pt. 1, pp. 1160–1243; Birney to Ord (4 April 1865), Ord Papers; Shaw, 13–25; *Seventh Regiment USCT*, 66–70; William B. Arnold, *The Fourth Massachusetts* [Colored] *Cavalry in the Closing Scenes of the War* (Boston, n.d.), 1–20; *New York Herald* (14 April 1865).

52. OR, I, 46, pt. 1, pp. 1211, 1227–28; Brevet Major Gen. August V. Kautz Diary (31

March–3 April 1865), LC.; Kautz to "My Dear Mrs. Savage" (29 March, 3 April 1865), Kautz Papers; Kautz Memoirs, pp. 103–05, TS. in Kautz Papers, USAMHI; Major Gen. Godfrey Weitzel, "Entry of United States Forces into Richmond, Virginia, April 3, 1865," pp. 1–9, TS. in Cincinnati Historical Society, Cincinnati; George A. Bruce, *The Capture and Occupation of Richmond* (Boston, 1918), 9–17; *Memorial Address by Hon. George A. Bruce, May 30, 1878* (Somerville, Mass., 1878), 5–9; Arnold, 27–30; Thomas Thatcher Graves (Staff Officer, XXV Corps), "The Fall of Richmond: II. The Occupation," *Battles and Leaders of the Civil War*, IV, 726–28; Abel E. Leavenworth, "Vermont at Richmond," *Proceedings of the Rutland County Historical Society*, II (1891), 27–29; Silas Adams, "Capture of Richmond, Virginia, April 3, 1865," *War Papers: Maine MOLLUS*, III, 253–58; Rembert W. Patrick, *The Fall of Richmond* (Baton Rouge, La., 1960), 65–75; Dallas D. Irvine, "The Fall of Richmond," *Journal of the American Military Institute*, 3 (1939), 76–79; Cornish, 281–83.

53. Wild to Sen. Wilson (10 May 1865), Wild Papers; OR, I, 46, pt. 3, pp. 725, 739, 761, 797–98, 816, 867, 1005–06, 1062, 1148, 1160–61; Copy of Special Orders 99, Headquarters, XXV Corps (12 April 1865), Stevens Papers; Kautz's Generals' Reports of Service, War of the Rebellion, RG-94, E-160, Vol. 10, p. 207, National Archives; Wild's Generals' Report of Service, War of the Rebellion, RG-94, E-160, Vol. 10, pp. 395–96, *ibid.*; Kautz's Memoirs, pp. 107–08, USAMHI; James E. Sefton, *The United States Army and Reconstruction, 1865–1877* (Baton Rouge, LA, 1967), 51–52.

54. OR, I, 46, pt. 3, pp. 1169, 1172, 1198–99, 1201–02, 1206–07, 1262, 1295; *Army and Navy Journal* (10, 24 June, 22 July 1865); *New York Times* (3, 11, 16 June 1865); *New York Herald* (10, 16, 17, 20, 24 June 1865); *Personal Memoirs of U.S. Grant*, 2 vols. (New York, 1885–86), II, 545–46; *Personal Memoirs of P.H. Sheridan*, 2 vols. (New York, 1888), II, 207–28; Frederick W. Browne, *My Service in the [1st] U.S. Colored Cavalry* (Cincinnati, 1908), 11–13; Shaw, 37; Wilson, 461–62; Mark M. Boatner III, *The Civil War Dictionary* (New York, 1959), 201; Dyer, 403.

55. Shaw, 27.

TWENTY-THREE

Nashville's Fort Negley:
A Symbol of Blacks' Involvement
with the Union Army

BOBBY L. LOVETT

To tell the history of Fort Negley, the historian must relate the story of the Union Army's occupation of Nashville, the building of numerous fortifications and the involvement of local blacks in the building of forts and filling of vital positions in the Union Army. Soon after the fall of forts Donelson and Henry, the Confederate Army of Tennessee retreated to Nashville. Upon the advice of engineers, however, the Confederate Army command and Governor Isham G. Harris gave orders to abandon Nashville. On February 22, 1862, the Army of Tennessee retreated southeastward to Murfreesboro. Confusion set in as citizens rushed to evacuate their belongings before the Yankees arrived in Nashville. The town's Negroes hid in order to avoid being forced to load and drive supply wagons; however, a few unlucky black residents were discovered in their hiding places and taken to Murfreesboro.[1]

During the earlier stages of the Civil War, the Confederate Army of Tennessee had attempted to use Negro labor from Kentucky and Middle Tennessee. But slave masters generally resisted the efforts to impress their expensive slaves for dangerous military duty. In June 1862, the Tennessee General Assembly tried to obtain military laborers by passing an Act to Draft Free Negroes as laborers; but Tennessee only had 7,300 free blacks, most of whom were too old, crippled, too young, or too unwilling to serve the Confederate military. Chief Engineer for the Army of Tennessee, J.F. Gilmer, attempted to "procure Negroes from their [Kentucky] masters to work on the entrenchments for defending the city of Nashville against land approach . . . ," but failed.[2]

At last, General Ulysses S. Grant's Union Army of the Ohio began to occupy Nashville on February 23, when the gunboat *Diana* docked at the foot of Broad Street. On February 25, the Sixth Ohio Volunteers' regimental band paraded down Broad playing *Hail Columbia*, as slaves and Unionist residents danced in the street. In March, 1862, President Abraham Lincoln appointed Senator Andrew Johnson of Tennessee as the Military Governor of occupied Tennessee. Johnson, a former tailor and East Tennessee slave master, assumed the rank of Brigadier General for Tennessee Volunteer Forces. Elias Polk, a free Negro, went with a delegation of pro-Union citizens to Murfreesboro in order to accompany Johnson on the train to Nashville. Upon the Military Governor's arrival, crowds of Negroes, Unionists, and Federal soldiers cheered and lined the streets as Johnson led a parade in his honor. Those pro-Confederate citizens who had not fled the city watched in utter disgust as Yankees and runaway slaves took over their town.[3]

Governor Johnson was nervous and quite apprehensive of being kidnapped and hanged as a southern traitor. He began to pressure the Union Army and Secretary of War, Edward Stanton, to fortify the town heavily with an enclosure of forts. Unlike their enemy predecessors, the Union Army engineers believed that Nashville could be defended against great odds with a ring of forts and a garrison of at least 6,000 men. The city was undulating, rocky, with beautiful picturesque scenery, and surrounded, lying like a vast amphitheater, by a range of hills. It occupied six square miles, three miles long by two miles wide.[4] During the late summer of 1862, General Don Carols Buell took his army out of Nashville in pursuit of the Confederate Army into Kentucky, leaving 6,000 troops under General James S. Negley to hold Nashville.[5] Johnson now began to demand immediate erection of fortifications for the city. He tried to convince Lincoln and Stanton that he was better able to command and position Nashville's troops than was General Negley. However, neither Buell nor any other Federal official was about to risk the charge of a Union Army garrison in Johnson's hands. Yet, General Buell did respond to the Governor's sense of urgency and also realized that the Confederate Army could double back and take the city. To make matters worse, indeed, it was rumored that Confederate cavalry units under Nathan Bedford Forrest might attack the city during the late summer of 1862. Buell ordered Captain James Sinclair Morton, a West Point graduate of 1851, from Philadelphia, to take a detachment of men and go to Nashville to help Negley fortify the city. Buell told Morton: "We should be in the edge of the city to command the principal thoroughfares and other prominent points"; Buell also sought to quiet Johnson's fears by ordering Morton to "devise some defenses also around the capitol building."[6]

Captain Morton was born in 1829, the son of Dr. Samuel G. Morton of Philadelphia. He was among the best of Civil War military engineers and was later promoted to Brigadier General. His command was called the Pioneer Brigade, which was equipped with its own arms, ammunition, clothing, axes, hatches, saws, files, spades, shovels, picks, hammers, augers, nails, spikes, rope, wagons, mules, and whatever was needed to go in advance of the army in order to prepare or repair bridges, fortifications, railroads, and roads.[7]

After forcing the Confederate Army to retreat from Kentucky toward Murfreesboro, Buell wired the Nashville command on August 6, 1862, and ordered them to call upon local slave masters for hands to be employed in Morton's Fort Negley project. With the Confederate Army less than 100 miles to the east, Morton assured General Buell that the planned fort would be secure "against any attack except regular approaches and investments."[8] Of course, the Union Army under General Buell was supposed to catch the Confederate Army before it could attack Nashville. But the Confederate Army commanders were masters of deception and well-schooled in the tactics of evading the clutches of the numerically superior Union Army.[9]

For this reason, among others, the completion of Nashville's military fortifications was rushed ahead with all deliberate speed. Morton wired Buell: "I lost 48 hours trying to get Negroes, teams, tools, cooking utensils, and provisions. Only 150 Negroes so far, no tools, teams, etc. I wanted to employ 825 Negroes by the 11th." But Morton found that he needed about 2,000 blacks, including local free Negroes, to complete Fort Negley. On August 12, Colonel John F. Miller, Post Commander, ordered the Nashville *Daily Union* and the Nashville *Dispatch* newspapers to print notices that rebel slaveholders of Davidson County were to supply 1,000 slaves with "daily subsistence and axes, spades or picks with terms of payment to be made known by Certificates of Labor, which will be furnished after the service shall have been performed."[10] Part of Morton's problem was that he had no money to pay the local blacks who wanted to be paid by the day; whereas, ironically, they had worked for nothing as slaves. In order to pay the laborers and keep them on the project, General Negley issued *Special Orders No. 17* (October 17, 1862), which ordered "a known contributor to the rebel cause to be required to advance the money to Captain Morton."[11] Unionist citizens, a minority in Nashville, cheered the Negley decision and hoped that all rebel sympathizers would be similarly punished.

It was known, indeed, that local slave masters tried every trick in the book to keep slaves from coming into contact with the Union Army. The slaves were told that the Yankees were cannibals who would eat them alive. Until blacks learned better, Yankee cavalry often had to run some rural slaves down and force them to walk to the Nashville labor camps.[12]

Notwithstanding, Nashville was an ideal place to find skilled blacksmiths, carpenters, coopers, shoemakers, stone masons, and wagonmakers. In spite of slavery, local blacks resided in the center of town, mostly integrated amongst their masters and patrons. A small concentration of prosperous free blacks resided east of Spruce Street (8th Avenue), between Crawford and

Cedar (Charlotte) streets. Nashville had the largest free black population of any Tennessee town and three semi-independent black church congregations including First Colored Baptist Church which was pastored by a free black named Nelson Merry.

Meanwhile, Morton designed some temporary defenses for the city. General Negley positioned some regiments of cavalry, which were sent to the city for that purpose, around the town along with several batteries of artillery. Siege guns and rifle pits occupied South Nashville, and the fires of Federal camps lit up the night sky in every direction. To feed the growing number of Negro laborers and soldiers, Negley took his army south to Franklin, Tennessee, and foraged 18,000 bushels of corn, as well as bacon, cattle, flour, hams, and horses. It took twenty railroad cars to transport the loot.[13]

Morton forged ahead with the construction of Fort Negley, designed to be the pivot point of Nashville's defenses. On November 7, the 1st Michigan Engineer Corps made their way into the city to build three bridges over Mill Creek in order to reopen the Nashville-Chattanooga Railroad, allowing additional supplies to flow into the city. Nashville now had 11,000 troops in town, enough to provide detachments of cavalry to round up more black laborers and to guard them against Confederate raiders. The Union cavalry surrounded the Colored Baptist Church during its services and marched the able-bodied members of the congregation off to the Fort Negley construction site on St. Cloud Hill.[14] Julius Casey, a former slave, recalled that the Federals took two of his older brothers and one sister. Another former slave, Francis Batson, remembered that the Union Army's constant raiding and labor impressment caused the young black children to become frightened and to run when they saw the "blue mans" (Union soldiers) coming.[15]

During the course of construction, long, impressive lines of wagons went back and forth carrying away felled trees and blasted rock. The blacks chopped St. Cloud Hill completely bare of trees in order to give the fort's guns an unimpaired view of the surrounding terrain and to provide no places for the enemy to hide. Children fourteen to fifteen years old, women, and men were camped on the St. Cloud Hill, some living in tents and others sleeping out in the open. Women and young adults pushed wheelbarrows, cooked the food for the laborers, washed clothes, and frequently served as teamsters for wagons. Black stone masons blasted the rock, fashioned the stone, laid the walls, and dug the underground magazines.[16] Curious citizens could clearly see the construction site from a point near the Murfreesboro Pike.

Although the blacks were often forced to labor without adequate food, warm clothing, shelter, or pay, they were willing to defend their creation with their lives. On November 5, 1862, before the fort was completed, General Nathan Bedford Forrest ordered the city to surrender. With approximately 3,000 men, he attacked the city near the Lebanon and Murfreesboro pikes, east of Fort Negley. The Negro laborers sent a delegation to the officer of the day and asked to be armed for the protection of themselves and the fort.

Their request for guns was denied; but the Army allowed them to make a symbolical stand armed with axes, shovels, and spades.[17]

The Federals, nevertheless, had sufficient forces to defeat the Confederates. Rachel Carter, a pro-Confederate resident, wrote in her diary on November 5, 1862, that one of the artillery shells from the fight "struck Mrs. Trimble's smokehouse."[18] In fact, Mrs. Trimble's smokehouse was east of the guns of Fort Negley and in the general vicinity of today's Cameron-Trimble Bottom, Nashville's oldest black neighborhood. As night came and a drizzling rain fell on November 5, Forrest's cavalry fled to the east, leaving the city in the hands of the Union Army and its black allies. Some 23 Confederate soldiers were captured, and the Union Army suffered 26 men wounded and 19 men missing.[19]

At the least, this demonstration convinced the Union Army's Nashville command that black labor was vital for the release of white soldiers from time-consuming labor chores. By using Negro laborers, the Army could put more white soldiers *Au fort du combat*. Before, the Army allowed slave masters to search the camps and reclaim their runaway slaves. As late as August 7, 1862, for example, the Nashville *Daily Union*, a pro-Union newspaper, published a notice for two twenty-three-year-old runaways named Foster and Edmund who belonged to Dr. John L. Cheatham and his brother, William S. Cheatham. Slaves were yet worth $300 to $1,300 apiece. A short time earlier, Davidson County Sheriff Jim Hinton ran an advertisement in the local papers that read as follows:

> July 18, 1862. A Negro man, who says his name is Henry and belongs to Matt Scruggs, Bedford County, Tennessee, age about 28, 5 feet 7 inches high, weighs 155 pounds, color black. The owner is requested to come forward, prove property and pay charges as the law requires.[20]

On February 27, 1863, the Nashville Union Army command issued an order prohibiting the return of fugitive slaves to their masters. Further, the Nashville Provost Marshall threatened to arrest any law officer caught arresting Negroes to be sold or transported to masters.[21]

Nearly a year later, on February 4, 1864, the Union Army ordered Captain Ralph Hunt of the 1st Kentucky Volunteers to establish a contraband camp in the area of the Chattanooga-Nashville Railroad Depot.[22] A larger contraband camp was built on the east side of the Cumberland River, north of Edgefield and near the Louisville-Nashville Railroad tracks; it initially held over 2,000 Negroes. A third contraband camp was located south of Broad Street, between Front and Cherry streets; it was called "Black Bottom." A former slave, Joseph Fowley, recalled that "they had contraband camps, and men, women and children had to be guarded to keep the rebels from carrying them back to the white folks."[23]

After a short time, the Federal government investigated the notoriously inhuman conditions of Nashville's contraband camps. Although camp superintendent Ralph Hunt was accused of stealing supplies meant for the blacks and selling them in his downtown store, nothing ever came of the charges. Attempts were made to "colonize surplus Negroes" on locally abandoned farms. This colonization effort was similar to the Freedmen's Bureau's 1865 relocation program in Memphis which was designed to force thousands of unemployed blacks to leave the urban camps and relocate in the countryside where the cotton crop was suffering from lack of pickers. Undoubtedly, such a relocation effort accounted, in part, for Nashville's Negro population not rising above 10,000 during the war years.

At any rate, the contraband camps and the influx of black laborers into town served the Union Army's purposes by 1865 and at little cost to the government. Between August 1862 and April 1863, for example, the Army paid black workers only $13,648.00 of the $85,858.50 that was owed to them. One author, Peter Maslowski, who has studied Union military occupation of Nashville, estimates that between 600 and 800 blacks died working on fortifications in the Nashville area during the whole occupation period.[24]

By December 7, 1862,[25] Fort Negley was completed. Captain Morton's report included praise for the blacks:

> To the credit of the colored population be it said, they worked manfully and cheerfully, with hardly any exception, and yet lay out upon the works at night under armed guard, without blankets and eating only army rations. They worked in squads, each gang choosing their own officers; one was often amused to hear the Negro captains call out: "You boys over there, let them picks fall easy, or they might hurt somebody."[26]

The creation of the Negro laborers and the Union Army engineers was impressive. The topmost structure was constructed of twelve-foot erect timbers. On the parapet surrounding the outside of the stockade, the artillery rested on carriages which rolled about on smooth planked flooring. This flat area for the artillery operations was protected by three-foot-high ramparts, nine-foot-thick embankments of earth walled with stone. The ramparts on the east and west side of the stockade had projected redans. Below the east and west ramparts and parapets were scarps, steep slopes, which were in turn protected by a glacis, a smooth, gentle slope. At the bottom of these hills on the left and right side of the south section of the fort were two groups of four blockhouses, which were really bombproofs topped with railroad iron, timbers and dirt. Each blockhouse had embrasures or openings for riflemen's guns. The bastioned blockhouses were protected by a salient system that projected out from the fortification. Above the bastion was a stoned scarp, protecting the first two blockhouses, an entrenchment connecting the two parallel blockhouses, another stoned scarp rising above the entrenchment, and the other two blockhouses rising above the scarp, with a passageway between the blockhouses. The fort's entrance was on the north side with a gentle slope; visitors passed a sharp salient, a gateway, a timber-structured guardhouse, and a loop-holed bomb-proof flanking the gate. And on top of each corner of the wooden stockade were rounded gun turrets.

Adapted to the local situation, Fort Negley was a copy of an old European architectural system, a repeat of the Castillo de San Marcos, built by the Spaniards of St. Augustine, Florida. San Marcos used a bastion system which was developed by sixteenth century European military engineers. The fort was polygonal. Eight lower salients, four on the east and west sides, projected from the fort; each of these salients had broad parapets apparently for infantrymen, stone scarps, and glacis. Again, each set of four blockhouses had a salient; thus the fort resembled a many-sided star. There was no "dead" space in the design, and every inch of ground could be covered by defenders. The enemy had to climb the bastions, scale the glacis, jump over the ramparts, cross the parapets, climb another glacis, scale a scarp, jump over another rampart and fight the defenders behind the main parapets and ramparts, before setting siege to the troops and horses behind the stockade. But if the enemy chose to come in from the south side, he had to face the murderous rifle fire from the blockhouses as well.

The entire fort consumed a staggering 62,500 cubic feet of stone and 18,000 cubic yards of dirt. It occupied a space of 600 by 300 feet and claimed 51 acres of St. Cloud Hill. It was 620 feet above sea level, some 150 feet above the surrounding terrain, and two miles south of the city limits.[27] A typical garrison for Fort Negley was described in 1864 as the "12th Indiana Battery and Battery C of the 1st Tennessee Light Artillery Volunteers." Occasionally, various infantry regiments camped on the lower part of the hill, including the 105th Illinois Volunteers and the 33rd Indiana Volunteers.[28]

Fort Negley's first major military role was in the Battle of Nashville, December 15–17, 1864. After taking Atlanta, General William T. Sherman sent General George H. Thomas and 20,000 troops hurrying back to Tennessee to set up a defense against the Confederate Army of Tennessee which was moving across Northern Georgia and Northern Alabama. Inevitably it was headed for Nashville, in hopes of drawing Sherman back from his intended march through Georgia. Fort Negley became the pivot point of Thomas's defense at Nashville. Thousands of soldiers from Wisconsin, Illinois, Indiana, Ohio, and other northern states camped near St. Cloud Hill while dining on boiled beef, beans, baker's bread, coffee, and occasionally some rabbits, squirrels, turkeys, and other wild game. Some of the soldiers thought that Nashville was "quite a nice place for the South."[29] Thomas collected nearly 50,000 troops by obtaining reinforcements from Chattanooga, Missouri, and some 13,000 black troops.

Thomas made heavy use of local blacks as forced laborers. He used the labor organization techniques that had been perfected by the building of Fort Negley and the building of the Northwestern Military Railroad. Between August 1863 and March 1864, Governor Johnson and the Union Army impressed thousands of blacks into labor battalions of 98 persons each—with white officers, a cavalry escort, and Negro labor captains—to build a railroad from Nashville seventy-five miles to Johnsonville on the east bank of the Tennessee River. Fully 20 percent of the black laborers were women, and the ages of the black laborers ranged from 14 to 55. The completion of the Northwestern Railroad made it logistically possible for Sherman to launch his famous march through Georgia. Union steamers brought supplies to Johnsonville, where they were shipped on cars to Nashville warehouses, and on to Sherman's staging area at Chattanooga. Thomas sought to resurrect this system in order to expand Nashville's fortifications. One former slave remembered being captured by the Federals as he made his escape from a Murfreesboro plantation. He recalled that General Thomas seldom was able to provide the black laborers with sufficient rations, and he added:

> We would kill a beef, cut off the head, take out the insides, skin it, and cut the meat into big chunks. Then we would put our meat on a long-forked pole, one end buried in the ground and the other slanting up and pointing towards the fire. It would make me awful sick at times, and I would throw up a lot.[30]

General Thomas's engineers had a problem in recruiting an adequate supply of black labor. For instance, many of Middle Tennessee's black males between the ages of eighteen and forty-five were mustered into the military, leaving few able-bodied Negroes for labor duties. On September 10, 1863, a Bureau for the Recruitment of United States Colored Troops was established at 38 Cedar Street (Charlotte Street). Similarly, recruitment stations were established at Clarksville, Columbia, Lynneville, Murfreesboro, Pulaski, Shelbyville, Tullahoma, and Wartrace. Even the black laborers who had completed the Northwestern Railroad project were marched to their camps, sworn into Federal service, armed, and trained as soldiers. Consequently, the Davidson County area contributed to the filling of five infantry and two artillery units, including the 2nd U.S. Colored Light Artillery Battery A and the 9th U.S. Colored Heavy Artillery Battalion, which used 380 free black Ohioans to complete the organization. Additionally, two infantry regiments were organized at the Clarksville contraband camps; the units relied heavily on recruiting runaway slaves from Kentucky. The 14th U.S. Colored Infantry Regiment was organized at the Gallatin contraband camp and recruited slaves from Robertson, Sumner, and Wilson counties. Four infantry regiments were organized at Pulaski's contraband camps and consisted of so many runaways from Northern Alabama that the regiments were at first named the 1st, 2nd, 3rd, and 4th Alabama Infantry Regiments of African Descent; but they were later renamed the 101st, 106th, 110th, and 111th regiments of the United States Colored Troops.[31]

Equally important, after finding the local agricultural economy to be devastated because of the scarcity of black labor and pro-Union citizens lustily protesting their financial ruin, on November 10, 1863, the army command at Nashville issued orders to prevent this growing economic-political disaster by directing Union officers to take no more than "one-half of any loyal master's slaves."[32] For even Sherman took two Middle Tennessee black regiments and black laborers to be used as supply troops and teamsters during his long march through Georgia. Therefore, Thomas's engineers found few black laborers for impressment. As a result, on November 1, 1864, General Thomas issued orders to recall black soldiers and white garrisons from their Middle Tennessee posts. These troops, along with available black laborers, worked on the fortifications.[33]

Thomas's job was made easier because of the existing fortifications that had been built by Captain Morton in 1862. These fortifications included the capitol building which had been fortified and named Fort Johnson, Fort Casino which overlooked Fort Negley, and Fort Morton which in turn protected Fort Casino. In contrast to Fort Negley, these forts were smaller and consisted of earth parapets, timber-reinforced blockhouses, crushed stone glacis, and dozens of light artillery pieces. Nevertheless, the area these forts would help to defend was very important to the Union. The District of Nashville included the defense of the Nashville-Chattanooga Railroad as far as the Duck River, the Nashville-Decatur Railroad as far south as Columbia, the Northwestern Railroad southwest to the Tennessee River, the Louisville-Nashville Railroad to the Kentucky state line, and the posts of McMinnville, Clarksville, Fort Donelson, and Nashville—the apex of the iron quadrangle.

From November 1 to December 1, 1864, the black workers and the Union Army soldiers struggled through heavy rains to complete the ring of forts. Fort Morton, situated on Curry's Hill near Granny White Pike and Jackson Street, was reinforced. Next in line to the north, Fort Houston was built near Belmont and Broad streets, and named after Russell Houston, a strong Union supporter, who allowed his home to be blown up to make way for the fort. Fort Houston was designed to hold over 35 guns and to protect the Charlotte Pike. A small fort was built on Hill 210 by the 182nd Ohio Volunteers in an octagon-shape, with blockhouses and underground magazines to protect the Northwestern Railroad and warehouses in West Nashville. Fort Dan McCook was built just east of Fort Negley; it held 26 guns for the cover of the main fort and the Nashville-Decatur Railroad. On the present site of Fisk University's Jubilee Hall, Fort Gillem was constructed (later named Fort Sill). Fort Gillem was built by a native of Jackson County, Tennessee, General Alvin Gillem, and the 10th Tennessee Volunteer Regiment. Fort Gillem was about 120 feet square with narrow ditches, walled with stone, 6 feet high, with emplacements for 8 artillery pieces. North of Fort Gillem was Fort W.D. Whipple (Redoubt Donaldson); between Forts Gillem and Whipple was Hyde's Ferry Fort (Fort Garesche) on the south bank of the Cumberland River, and built by the 82nd Ohio Volunteers in November 1864. The 15th Illinois Volunteer Regiment built a small redoubt on the north side of the Cumberland River in order to cover the Louisville-Nashville Railroad. Fort Negley was expanded at a cost of $20,000 by adding the interior double-cased blockhouses and entrenchments. The inspector of fortifications, General Z.B. Tower, wrote to Thomas with this request: "If I can secure a black regiment, some 200 men, which have been promised, it will be a great gain."[34] By November 30, over 10,000 black troops were working on the fortifications and carrying out reconnaissance patrols on alternate days beginning December 1 and ending December 13. The entire fortifications project cost an estimated $300,000 and $130,000 for Fort Negley. The city of Nashville was enclosed within a ring of twenty-three forts, redoubts, and fortified bridges.[35]

From September to October 1864, Hood's army encountered much resistance from the black and white Union garrisons at Decatur and Sulphur Trestle, Alabama, and Pulaski and Johnsonville, Tennessee. Many black soldiers lost their lives and hundreds more were shipped as prisoners to Mobile, Alabama. Further, Hood's army of 36,000 caught General John Schofield's Union Army of 23,000 at Franklin and forced it to fight. Although the federals lost 2,000 men, the Confederates lost 6,000 men and 6 of their best generals; moreover, while the enemy slept on that night of November 30, 1864, Schofield abandoned his dead and wounded and sneaked across the Harpeth River and arrived safely in Nashville, thirty miles away, on December 1. After receiving Schofield's reinforcements, General Thomas had nearly twice Hood's troop strength.

And yet, General Hood unwisely turned his battered army toward Nashville instead of retreating into the deep South. Hood could not turn back because he had slept on too many dreams and had made a personal pledge to President Jefferson Davis to carry out a successful campaign. As the Army of Tennessee approached Nashville on December 2, they saw a formidable fortress gleaming with new forts, behind which more than 50,000 Union troops waited. The gods cursed the Confederates by blasting the Nashville area with a winter storm that left glistening ice. A Maury County Confederate soldier said: "being in range of the guns of Fort Negley, we were not allowed to have fires at night." During the day, however, an unspoken truce allowed both sides to gather firewood.[36]

On the cold, foggy morning of December 15, 1864, the ice melted and the guns of Fort Negley came alive to signal the start of the Battle of Nashville. Out of the mist came the dark, shining faces of seven regiments of Colored Troops, who advanced on the enemy's right flank near Brown's Creek—east of the guns of Fort Negley. Patsy Hyde, a former slave, recalled the moment: "When dey wuz fighting at Fort Negley, de cannons would jar our house. The soldiers' band played on Capitol Hill: 'Rally round the flag boys, rally round the flag'." Another slave remembered "when the Yankees on Capitol Hill gave the signal—God bless your soul—it sounded like the cannons would tear the world to pieces. I could hear the big shells humming as they came; they cut off trees like a man cutting weeds with a scythe."[37]

Two days later, the Confederate Army was in mass retreat. They left behind 10,000 prisoners and 68 pieces of artillery. One Negro soldier, Joseph Fowley [Farley], who joined the Union Army along with his father at the Clarksville contraband camp, recalled the Confederate soldiers were captured just as bare-footed "as they could be." He said: "I brought my gun from Nashville right here to Clarksville and kept it for 25 years."[38] The Negro troops took part in the pursuit of Hood's army as far south as central Alabama. Nashville's 17th Colored Troops Regiment won personal recognition for bravery from General Thomas and the New York *Times* (December 19, 1864). The Battle of Nashville was one of the last major military actions of a dying Confederacy that surrendered in April 1865.

What some men create, other men let weather and die. In short, Fort Negley and its sister forts were not monuments that a defeated South wanted to preserve. The forts were gradually forgotten and allowed to go into ruins. In 1865, Fort Negley was renamed Fort Harker; and in 1867, the Union Army abandoned the fort. Fort Harker became the secret meeting place for the Nashville Den of the Ku Klux Klan, which was active until 1869. In that year the Nashville Klan defied a government ban against public demonstrations and marched through the streets to Fort Negley where they burned their robes and officially disbanded.[39] Until the late 1890s, citizens took wagons and streetcars out to the fort at Chestnut and Ridley streets and held Sunday picnics just as in prewar days.

Years later, during the Great Depression, Fort Negley was restored and opened to the public. The Works Progress Administration provided funds to put Davidson County's unemployed to work in a restoration project. According to the Nashville *Tennessean* (January 31, 1936), the Fort Negley restoration project became one of the top WPA programs in the state. When the WPA workers finished the project in 1937, they left a crudely chiseled stone at the entrance, which read: "Fort Negley, Restored by the WPA, 1936." The Tennessee WPA Federal Writers' Project, which was designed to put unemployed writers to work, compiled histories of the state's forts, including a two-page overview of the history of Fort Negley.[40] The restored fort was a city park until 1941, with a "museum." The WPA workers attempted also to restore the subterranean magazines; they built some stone walkways to make the fort and the "museum" more accessible to visitors. A drainage ditch, covered with natural stone, encircled the bottom of the hill. Air photographs that were taken in 1941 and preserved by the Tennessee Department of Conservation revealed a road of rough gravel and a parking lot on the north side near the entrance of the fort.[41]

With the coming of World War II the fort was forgotten and allowed to be overgrown by weeds and other vegetation. Not until the Civil War Centennial celebration of 1964 did the Nashville Committee for the Civil War Centennial include a tour of the old fort, and local college professors came out to speak on the history of the fort. In 1975, the Metro Historical Commission made application to have the fort placed on the National Historic Register.[42] On May 14, 1979, according to the Nashville *Tennessean*, the Metro Historical Commission and the Council on Abandoned Military Posts jointly suggested that the city restore the fort. In August 1980, a feasibility study was completed for the Metro Historical Commission with the recommendation that the fort be made into a recreational historic park at a projected cost of $145,521.38.[43]

Though covered with vines and trees, and hidden from easy view, Fort Negley continued to serve as a monument to local Afro-American and Civil War history. The fortress and its sister forts served as symbols of the uneasy alliance between the Union Army and local blacks in their successful campaign to preserve the Union and destroy slavery. Consequently, much history was hidden beneath Fort Negley and its sister fortifications, including the lost histories of thousands of black laborers, the contributions of 13,000 black Union soldiers, and the blood and tears of thousands of black women.

In brief, the Fort Negley project was the Union Army's first heavy use of local black labor. It set the precedent for using black laborers on all large Middle Tennessee Union military projects. Such use, one might reflect, made the Union officers realize the utility value of maintaining contraband camps—ready sources of black laborers and Negro soldiers. Indeed, the Union Army fully utilized both in winning the war. Hence, the influx of Negroes into Nashville doubled the black population between 1862 and 1865.

Finally, one might argue that the Union Army's labor system, which was first induced by the need to build Fort Negley, the Northwestern Railroad, and other military projects, acted as a catalyst for the development of black Nashville communities. Ironically, the Union Army's efforts to control the local Negro population for military purposes caused a disintegration of antebellum controls over slaves and free blacks. Freed at last from the legal restraints of black codes and slave codes, the free blacks and the former slaves built communities in Nashville and Edgefield that were complete with economic, political, and social institutions including a black-owned drugstore, a black-edited newspaper (the *Colored Tennessean*, 1865–1866), and a branch of the Freedmen's Savings and Trust Company bank. In 1865 the Union Army and the Freedmen's Bureau attempted to force thousands of Negroes to relocate on rural farms; however, the black migration into Nashville continued into the twentieth century. On the whole, although the Union Army occupied Nashville in 1862 without any intention of becoming involved in the social and political questions of slavery and Negro affairs, the Union Army and its agencies served as grudging agents for social change in Nashville and paradoxically were responsible for the genesis of ghettoizing blacks due to segregating and concentrating them into local contraband camps.

NOTES

1. Stanley F. Horn, "Nashville During the Civil War," *Tennessee Historical Quarterly*, IV (1945), 3–22.

2. J.F. Gilmer to Lt. Colonel W.W. Mackall, Bowling Green, Kentucky, December 7, 1861, *The War of the Rebellion: A Compilation of the Official Records of the Union and Confederate Armies*, series I, vol. 52, part II (Washington, 1898), 233.

3. H.W. Crew (ed.), *History of Nashville* (Nashville, 1890), 101–02.

4. Doug King (ed.), *Nashville City Directory 1865* (Nashville, 1865), 1, 10.

5. Stanley F. Horn, *The Army of Tennessee: A Military History* (Indianapolis, Indiana, 1941, 1952), 394–411.

6. *War of the Rebellion*, series I, vol. 26, part II, 268; Mark M. Boatner, *The Civil War Dictionary* (New York, 1959), 571; Morton authored several books on fortifications; Paul M. Angle (ed.), *Three Years in the Army of the Cumberland: The Letters and Diary of Major James A. Connolly* (Bloomington, Indiana, 1959), 37–39; Thomas Jordan and J.P. Pryor, *The Campaigns of Lieut.-Gen. N.D. Forrest* (Dayton, Ohio, 1973), 179.

7. *Annals of the Army of the Cumberland* (Philadelphia, 1864), 181–91; Mead Holmes, *A Soldier of the Cumberland: Memoirs of Mead Holmes, Jr., Sergeant for Company K, 21st Regiment, Wisconsin Volunteers* (Boston, 1952); Fred A. Shannon, *The Organization and Administration of the Union Army, 1861–1865*, 2 vols. (Cleveland, Ohio, 1928); Thomas Van Horne, *History of the Army of the Cumberland: Its Organization, Campaigns, and Battles* (Cincinnati, Ohio, 1875). Note: the Corps of Engineers and the Corps of Topographical Engineers merged as the Corps of Engineers. The Engineering Department and the Pioneer Corps made heavy use of hired and impressed black labor.

8. Buell to Morton, Kentucky, August 6, 1862, and Morton to Col. J. B. Fry, Nashville, August 13, 1862, *War of the Rebellion*, series I, vol. 26, part II, 326–27.

9. Jordan, *The Campaigns of Lieut.-Gen. N.B. Forrest*; Frederick A. Dyer (ed.), *A Compendium of the War of the Rebellion: Numbers and Organization of the Armies of the United States*, 3 vols. (New York, 1959).

10. Nashville *Dispatch*, and Nashville *Daily Union*, August 13, 1862.

11. Nashville *Daily Union*, October 18, 1862.

12. Buell to Morton, Kentucky, August 20, 29, 1862, *War of the Rebellion*, series I, vol. 26, part II, 408.

13. "Yanks in Nashville," in the Chattanooga *Rebel*, October 12, 1862, quoted by the *Daily Union*, October 18, 1862. The Union Army recognized the claims of area citizens for properties destroyed by the Federal Army—see Report on Nashville Defenses, *War of the Rebellion*, series I, vol. 49, part III, 197.

14. *Annals of the Army of the Cumberland*, 194, includes a sketch of the Negroes leaping from the church windows; *The Official Atlas of the Civil War* (New York, 1958), plate CXXXIV contains an illustration of blacks working on Fort Negley, as reported in the *War of the Rebellion*, series I, vol. 49, part III, October 15, 1862.

15. Slave Testimony, George P. Radwick (ed.), *The American Slave: A Composite Autobiography, God Struck Me Dead: Religious Conversion Experiences of Ex-Slaves*, vol. 18 by Fisk University's Social Sciences Division (Westport, Ct., 1941, 1975), 121–25; Mechal Sobel, "'They Can Never Both Prosper Together': Black and White Baptists in Antebellum Nashville, Tennessee," *Tennessee Historical Quarterly*, XXXVIII (1979), 296–307; Federal Writers' Project, Works Progress Administration, Tennessee Slave Narratives in Radwick (ed.), *The American Slave*, vol. 16, pp. 3, 68.

16. *War of the Rebellion*, series I, vol. 49, part III, 196–98. The October 15, 1862, report by Chief Inspector of Fortifications, General Z.B. Tower, does not mention a secret tunnel; however, local rumor has it that Fort Negley had a secret tunnel that permitted Union soldiers to emerge from the Old City Cemetery just east of the fort. A recent (1980) engineering report did not confirm the existence of a tunnel but did not rule it out; archaeologists will have to have the final word.

17. *The Photographic History of the Civil War*, 10 vols. (New York, 1957), vol. 3, 266–70 and 248–58 contain illustrations and actual photos of Fort Negley in 1864 and just prior to the Battle of Nashville.

18. Louise Davis, "Box Seat on the Civil War: Rachel Carter's Diary," *The Tennessean Magazine*, Nashville, April 1979, 6–11.

19. "Box Seat on the Civil War," 6–11; Nashville *Banner*, December 16, 1961; Juanita Gaston and Samuel Shannon, *Cameron-Trimble Neighborhood Project: A Pictorial Guide* (Nashville, 1979), 1–10.

20. Nashville *Daily Union*, August 10, 1862.

21. Nashville *Dispatch*, February 27, 1863.

22. This camp was between Church and Demonbreum streets. Benjamin "Pap" Singelton held his organizational meetings for the Black Exodus to Kansas in the former Edgefield contraband camp between 1877 and 1879. A housing project and interstate highways occupy the Edgefield site. Urban renewal also cleaned the blacks out of "Black Bottom," the Crawford Street area and the Church/Demonbreum area. Some moved into the Napier and Taylor housing projects.

23. Slave testimony, Radwick (ed.), *The American Slave*, vol. 19, *Unwritten History of Slavery*, by Fisk University, pp. 128–29.

24. Peter Maslowski, *Treason Made Odious: Military Occupations and Wartime Reconstruction in Nashville, 1861–1865* (Milwood, Illinois, 1978), 100–12; Porter Nimrod Diary and Notebook, 1861–1898, Southern Historical Collection, University of North Carolina, Tennessee State Library and Archives, Manuscripts Division, Nashville.

25. *Banner*, December 16, 1862.

26. *Annals of the Army of the Cumberland*, 620–33.

27. Metro Historical Commission, Application to the National Historic Register, February 21, 1975, Nashville; *Fort Negley: A Study for the Metropolitan Historical Commission* (Nashville, 1980), A-1.

28. *Three Years in the Army of the Cumberland*, 37–39; Frank L. Byrne (ed.), *The View From Headquarters: Civil War Letters of Harvey Reid* (Madison, Wisconsin, 1965), 121–26; *Photographic History of the Civil War*, 248, has a photo of a battery manning the fort; *Southern Battlefields: On and Near the Lines of the Nashville, Chattanooga and St. Louis Railroad* (Nashville, 1956); Federal Writers' Project, WPA, *Tennessee Forts and Fortresses*, Della Yoe, "Fort Negley," (Nashville, 1940), TSLA, MD; Bruce Grant, *American Forts Yesterday and Today* (New York, 1965), 58; Federal Writers' Project, WPA, *Tennessee, A Guide to the State* (New York, 1939); Harold L. Peterson, *Forts in America* (New York, 1964), 1–25.

29. *The View From Headquarters*, 121–26; Susan K. Parman, "The Battle of Nashville," M.A. thesis, George Peabody College for Teachers, 1932.

30. Slave testimony, *God Struck Me Dead*, 116. It is likely that nearly 2,000 blacks served in the Confederate Army of Tennessee as laborers and personal servants to officers. Some of the black Confederates received state pensions as a result of the 1906 Confederate Pension Act being amended in 1921 to include former black servants. Nearly 300 Colored Men's Pension Applications are filed at the TSLA, Nashville. However, Thomas's Union Army of the Cumberland used thousands of black laborers as part of his Quartermaster Corps, Engineering Corps, Pioneer Corps, Medical Department, and Subsistence Department. For this reason, Thomas was able to place a huge number of soldiers in the battle itself. It is likely that Union blacks and Confederate blacks made some abrasive contact during the Battle of Nashville.

31. *The Negro in the Military Service of the U.S.*, 1630–1866, NARS, Washington; Compiled Service Records of Military Units in Union Organizations; U.S. Colored Troops, Tennessee, part of Record Group 94, NARS; Bobby L. Lovett, "The Negro's Civil War in Tennessee, 1861–1865," *Journal of Negro History*, 59 (1976), 31–50; Dudley T. Cornish, *The Sable Arm: The Negro in the Union Army, 1861–1865* (New York, 1956), 248–49; George Washington Williams, *A History of the Negro Troops in the War of the Rebellion, 1861–65* (New York, 1888, 1968), 273–90.

32. *Special Orders No. 301*, Department of the Cumberland, Nashville, November 10, 1863, Adjutant General's Office, RG 21, TSLA; *War of the Rebellion*, series I, vol. 31, part III (Washington, 1890).

33. *General Orders No. 43*, Department of the Cumberland, Nashville, November 1, 1864, Adjutant General's Office, RG 21; "The Negro's Civil War in Tennessee," 31–50.

34. Tower to Thomas, Nashville, November 1, 1864, *War of the Rebellion*, series I, vol. 49, part III, 755–81; William Waller, *Nashville in the 1890s* (Nashville, 1970) contains a map showing the approximate positions of the old forts; Thomas to Gen. Rousseau, Chattanooga, January 31, 1864, *War of the Rebellion*, series I, vol. 33, part III (Washington, 1891), 203.

35. Tower's 1865 Report, *War of the Rebellion*, vol. 49.

36. Samuel R. Watkins, *Maury County Grays: First Tennessee Regiment, C.S.A.* (Nashville, 1882), 225; J.F.C. Fuller, *Decisive Battles of the U.S.A.* (New York, 1942), 292–323; *The Army of Tennessee*, 394–411; S.F. Horn, *The Decisive Battle of Nashville* (Baton Rouge, 1956); William J. McMurray, *History of the Twentieth Tennessee Regiment Volunteer Infantry, C.S.A.* (Nashville, 1904), 329; *History of Nashville*, 198–201.

37. Slave testimony, *God Stuck Me Dead*, 116.

38. Slave testimony, *Unwritten History of Slavery*, 121; *Battles of the Civil War: A Pictorial Presentation, 1861–1865* (New York, 1960), includes a color illustration of Thomas's black troops attacking the Confederate positions on Overton Hill (Peach Orchard Hill), December 16, 1864, where the blacks suffered greatly; however, the Negro troops took the hill. A Metro Historical Commission marker designates the site near the corner of Harding Place and Franklin Road.

39. "Fort Negley," 1–2, by Yoe is brief but informative.

40. "Fort Negley," 1–2; see also: Directory of WPA Manuscripts, TSLA.

41. Photos of Fort Negley Restoration, Department of Conservation Photographs, TSLA.

42. Application, Metro Historical Commission.

43. *Fort Negley: A Study*, Metro Historical Commission, 1980.

SOURCES

Becker, William H. "The Black Church: Manhood and Mission." *Journal of the American Academy of Religion* 40.3 (1972): 316–333.

Bedini, Silvio. "Peter Hill, the First African American Clockmaker." *Prospects* 17 (1993): 135–175.

Bolster, W. Jeffrey. "'To Feel Like a Man': Black Seamen in the Northern States, 1800–1860." *Journal of American History* 76.4 (1990): 1173–1199.

Cimbala, Paul A. "Black Musicians from Slavery to Freedom: An Exploration of an African-American Folk Elite and Cultural Continuity in the Nineteenth-Century Rural South." *Journal of Negro History* 80.1 (1995): 15–29.

Cullen, Jim. "'I's a Man Now': Gender and African American Men." In *Divided Houses: Gender and the Civil War*, 76–96. New York: Oxford University Press, 1992.

Desrochers, Robert E., Jr. "'Not Fade Away': The Narrative of Venture Smith, an African American in the Early Republic." *Journal of American History* 84.1 (1997): 40–66.

Dew, Charles B. "Disciplining Slave Ironworkers in the Antebellum South: Coercion, Conciliation, and Accommodation." *American Historical Review* 79.2 (1974): 393–418.

Egerton, Douglas R. "'Fly across the River': The Easter Slave Conspiracy of 1802." *North Carolina Historical Review* 68.2 (1991): 87–110.

Gilje, Paul A., and Howard B. Rock. "'Sweep O! Sweep O!': African-American Chimney Sweeps and Citizenship in the New Nation." *William and Mary Quarterly* 51.3 (1994): 506–538.

Horton, James Oliver, and Lois E. Horton. "Violence, Protest, and Identity: Black Manhood in Antebellum America." In *Free People of Color: Inside the African American Community*, 80–97. Washington, D.C.: Smithsonian Institution Press, 1993.

Joshi, Manoj K., and Joseph P. Reidy. "'To Come Forward and Aid in Putting Down This Unholy Rebellion': The Officers of Louisiana's Free Black Native Guard during the Civil War Era." *Southern Studies* 21.3 (1982): 326–342.

Kaplan, Sidney, and Emma Nogrady Kaplan. "Bearers of Arms: Patriot and Tory." In *The Black Presence in the Era of the American Revolution*, ed. Sidney and Emma Nogrady Kaplan, 32–89. Boston: University of Massachusetts Press, 1989.

Kay, Marvin L. Michael, and Lorin Lee Cary. "Slave Runaways in Colonial North Carolina, 1748–1775." *North Carolina Historical Review* 63.1 (1986): 1–39.

Landers, Jane. "Gracia Real de Santa Teresa de Mose: A Free Black Town in Spanish Colonial Florida." *American Historical Review* 95.1 (1990): 9–30.

Lapsansky, Emma Jones. "'Discipline to the Mind': Philadelphia's Banneker Institute, 1842–1872." *Pennsylvania Magazine* 117.1/2 (1993): 83–102.

Longacre, Edward G. "Black Troops in the Army of the James, 1863–65." *Military Affairs* 45.1 (February 1981): 1–8.

Lovett, Bobby L. "Nashville's Fort Negley: A Symbol of Blacks' Involvement with the Union Army." *Tennessee Historical Quarterly* 41.1 (1982): 3–22.

Marks, Bayly E. "Skilled Blacks in Antebellum St. Mary's County, Maryland." *Journal of Southern History* 53.4 (1987): 537–564.

May, Robert E. "Invisible Men: Blacks and the U.S. Army in the Mexican War." *Historian* 49.4 (1987): 463–477.

Schweninger, Loren. "The Free-Slave Phenomenon: James P. Thomas and the Black Community in Ante-Bellum Nashville." *Civil War History* 22.4 (1976): 293–307.

Smith, Michael O. "Raising a Black Regiment in Michigan: Adversity and Triumph." *Michigan Historical Review* 16.2 (1990): 22–41.

Sommerville, Diane Miller. "The Rape Myth in the Old South Reconsidered." *Journal of Southern History* 61.3 (1995): 480–517.

Thornton, John K. "African Dimensions of the Stono Rebellion." *American Historical Review* 96.4 (1991): 1101–1113.

SELECTED BIBLIOGRAPHY

Abbott, Richard H. "Massachusetts and the Recruitment of Southern Negroes." *Civil War History* 14.3 (1968): 197–210.

Adeleke, Tunde. "Black Biography in the Service of a Revolution: Martin R. Delany in Afro-American Historiography." *Biography: An Interdisciplinary Quarterly* 17.3 (1994): 248–267.

Akpan, M. B. "Alexander Crummell and His African 'Race-Work': An Assessment of His Contributions in Liberia to Africa's 'Redemption,' 1853–1873." *Historical Magazine of the Protestant Episcopal Church* 45.2 (1976): 177–200.

Allen, Ray. "African-American Sacred Quartet Singing in New York City." *New York Folklore* 14.3–4 (1988): 7–22.

Anderson, Jervis. "Black Heavies." *American Scholar* 47 (1978): 387–395.

Andrews, David. "The Fact(s) of Michael Jordan's Blackness: Excavating a Floating Racial Signifier." *Sociology of Sport Journal* 13.2 (1996): 125–158.

Bailey, Anne J. "A Texas Cavalry Raid: Reaction to Black Soldiers and Contrabands." *Civil War History* 35.2 (1989): 138–152.

Bailey, Ben E. "Music in the Life of a Free Black Man of Natchez." *Black Perspective in Music* 13.1 (1992): 3–12.

Banat, Gabriel. "Le Chevalier de Saint-Georges, Man of Music and Gentleman-at-Arms: The Life and Times of an Eighteenth-Century Prodigy." *Black Music Research Journal* 10.2 (1990): 177–212.

Barbour, George. "Early Black Flyers of Western Pennsylvania, 1906–1945." *Western Pennsylvania Historical Magazine* 69.2 (1986): 95–119.

Barr, Alwyn. "Black Legislators of Reconstruction Texas." *Civil War History* 32.4 (1986): 340–352.

Bartlett, Andrew. "Cecil Taylor, Identity Energy, and the Avant-Garde African American Body." *Perspectives of New Music* 33 (Summer 1995): 275–293.

Beaver, Harold. "Run, Nigger, Run: Adventures of Huckleberry Finn as a Fugitive Slave Narrative." *Journal of American Studies* 8.3 (1974): 339–361.

Belz, Herman. "Law, Politics, and Race in the Struggle for Equal Pay during the Civil War." *Civil War History* 22.3 (1976): 197–213.

Benedetto, Robert. "The Presbyterian Mission Press in Central Africa, 1890–1922." *Presbyterian History* 68.1 (1990): 55–69.

Berenson, William, Kirk Elifson, and Tandy Tollerson. "Preachers in Politics: A Study of Political Activism among the Black Ministry." *Journal of Black Studies* 6.4 (1976): 373–392.

Bergeron, Arthur W., Jr. "Free Men of Color in Grey." *Civil War History* 32.3 (1986): 247–255.

Bigsby, C. "The Divided Mind of James Baldwin." *Journal of American Studies* 13.3 (1979): 325–342.

Biles, Roger. "Robert R. Church, Jr. of Memphis: Black Republican Leader in the

Age of Democratic Ascendency, 1928–1940." *Tennessee Historical Quarterly* 42.4 (1983): 362–382.

Bisher, Catherine. "Black Builders in Antebellum North Carolina." *North Carolina Historical Review* 6.4 (1984): 423–461.

Blackett, Richard. "Fugitive Slaves in Britain: The Odyssey of William and Ellen Craft." *Journal of American Studies* 12.1 (1978): 41–62.

——. "William G. Allen: The Forgotten Professor." *Civil War History* 24.1 (1980): 39–52.

Blankenship, Kim. "Bringing Gender and Race In: U.S. Employment Discrimination Policy." *Gender and Society* 7.2 (1993): 205–226.

Bogle, Lorie. "On Our Way to the Promised Land: Black Migration from Arkansas to Oklahoma, 1889–1893." *Chronicles of Oklahoma* 72.2 (1994): 160–177.

Boyd, Richard. "Violence and Sacrificial Displacement in Harriet Beecher Stowe's *Dred*." *Arizona Quarterly* 50.2 (1994): 51–72.

Boyer, Horace Clarence. "Charles Albert Tindley: Progenitor of Black-American Gospel Music." *Black Perspective in Music* 11.2 (1983): 103–132.

Bruce, Dickson D., Jr. "Ancient Africa and the Early Black American Historians, 1883–1915." *American Quarterly* 36.5 (1984): 684–699.

——. "National Identity and African-American Colonization, 1773–1817." *Historian* 58.1 (1995): 15–28.

Bynum, Marjorie. "Thomas Washington Talley: A Pathmaker in African-American Folklore." *Tennessee Folklore Society Bulletin* 57.4 (1996): 154–165.

——. "Violence, Revolution, and the Cost of Freedom: John Brown and W.E.B. DuBois." *Boundary 2* 17.1 (1990): 304–330.

Campbell, Finley C. "Prophet of the Storm: Richard Wright and the Radical Tradition." *Phylon* 38.1 (1977): 9–23.

Campbell, Randolph B. "The Burden of Local Black Leadership during Reconstruction: A Research Note." *Civil War History* 39.2 (1993): 148–153.

Captain, Gwendolyn. "Enter Ladies and Gentlemen of Color: Gender, Sport, and the Ideal of African American Manhood and Womanhood during the Late Nineteenth and Early Twentieth Centuries." *Journal of Sport History* 18.1 (1991): 81–102.

Carney, Judith. "From Hands to Tutors: African Expertise in the South Carolina Rice Economy." *Agricultural History* 67.3 (1993): 1–30.

Carter, Marva Griffin. "In Retrospect: Roland Hayes—Expressor of the Soul in Song (1887–1977)." *Black Perspective in Music* 5.2 (1977): 188–220.

Cartwright, Joseph. "Black Legislators in Tennessee in the 1880's: A Case Study in Black Political Leadership." *Tennessee Historical Quarterly* 32.3 (1973): 265–284.

Cato, John David. "James Herman Robinson: Crossroads Africa and American Idealism, 1958–1972." *American Presbyterians* 68.2 (1990): 99–108.

Cecelski, David. "The Hidden World of Mullet Camps: African-American Architecture on the North Carolina Coast." *North Carolina Historical Review* 70.1 (1993): 1–13.

——. "The Shores of Freedom: The Maritime Underground Railroad in North Carolina, 1800–1861." *North Carolina Historical Review* 71.2 (1994): 175–206.

Cheatham, Wallace McClain. "Black Male Singers at the Metropolitan Opera." *Black Perspective in Music* 16.1 (1988): 4–19.

Cheek, William F. "John Mercer Langston: Black Protest Leader and Abolitionist." *Civil War History* 16.2 (1970): 101–120.

Chenier, Robert. "Moses Fleetwood Walker: Ohio's Own 'Jackie Robinson.'" *Northwest Ohio Quarterly* 65.1 (1993–94): 34–49.

Chenoweth, Lawrence. "The Rhetoric of Hope and Despair: A Study of the Jimi Hendrix Experience and the Jefferson Airplane." *American Quarterly* 23.1 (1971): 25–45.

Childs, John. "Concepts of Culture in Afro-Political Thought, 1890–1920." *Social Text* 2.1 (1981): 28–34.

Christian, Garna. "The Ordeal and the Prize: The 24th Infantry and Camp MacArthur." *Military Affairs* 50.2 (1986): 65–70.

Cimbala, Paul A. "Fortunate Bondsmen: Black 'Musicians' and Their Role as an Antebellum Southern Plantation Slave Elite." *Southern Studies* 18.3 (1979): 291–303.

Cimprich, John, and Robert C. Mainfort, Jr., eds. "Fort Pillow Revisited: New Evidence about an Old Controversy." *Civil War History* 28.4 (1982): 293–306.

Clark, James. "Civil Rights Leader Harry T. Moore and the Ku Klux Klan in Florida." *Florida Historical Quarterly* 73.2 (1994): 164–183.

Clegg, Claude. "'A Splendid Type of Colored American': Charles Young and the Reorganization of the Liberian Frontier Force." *International Journal of African Historical Studies* 29.1 (1996): 47–70.

Clifton, James. "The Rice Driver: His Role in Slave Management." *South Carolina Historical Magazine* 82.4 (1981): 331–353.

Cooper, Arnold. "Booker T. Washington and William J. Edwards of Snow Hill Institute, 1893–1915." *Alabama Review* 40.2 (1987): 111–132.

Cosgrove, Stuart. "The Zoot-Suit and Style Warfare." *History Workshop* 18 (1984): 77–91.

Cripps, Thomas, and David Culbert. "The Negro Soldier (1944): Film Propaganda in Black and White." *American Quarterly* 31.5 (1979): 616–640.

Cummins, Roger. "'Lily-White' Juries on Trial: The Civil Rights Defense of Jesse Hollins." *Chronicles of Oklahoma* 63.2 (1985): 166–185.

Dailey, Maceo C. "Booker T. Washington and the Afro-American Realty Company." *Review of Black Political Economy* 8.2 (1978): 202–210.

Dalfiume, Richard. "The 'Forgotten Years' of the Negro Revolution." *Journal of American History* 55.1 (1968): 90–106.

Dann, Martin. "Black Populism: A Study of the Colored Farmers' Alliance through 1891." *Journal of Ethnic Studies* 2.3 (1974): 58–75.

De Genova, Nick. "Gangster Rap and Nihilism in Black: Some Questions of Life and Death." *Social Text* 43 (1995): 89–132.

Dennis, Ruth E. "Social Stress and Mortality among Nonwhite Males." *Phylon* 38.3 (1977): 315–328.

Dibble, Ernest F. "Slave Rentals to the Military: Pensacola and the Gulf Coast." *Civil War History* 23.2 (1977): 101–113.

Dole, Carol. "The Return of the Father in Spielberg's *The Color Purple*." *Literature/Film Quarterly* 24.1 (1996): 12–16.

Douglas, Robert. "Black Males and Television: New Images versus Old Stereotypes." *Western Journal of Black Studies* 11.2 (1987): 69–73.

———. "From Blues to Protest/Assertiveness: The Art of Romaire Bearden and John Coltrane." *International Review of African American Art* 8.2 (1988): 28–43.

Early, Gerald. "The Black Intellectual and the Sport of Prizefighting." *Kenyon Review* 10.3 (1988): 102–117.

Eberhart, George M. "Stack Lee: The Man, the Music, and the Myth." *Popular Music and Society* 20.1 (1996): 1–69.

Erenberg, Lewis. "News from the Great Wide World: Duke Ellington, Count Basie, and Black Popular Music, 1927–1943." *Prospects* 18 (1993): 483–506.

Evans, Robert, and Helen Evans. "Coping: Stressors and Depression among Middle Class African American Men." *Western Journal of Black Studies* 19.3 (1995): 211–217.

Farley, Foster. "The South Carolina Negro in the American Revolution, 1775–1783." *South Carolina Historical Magazine* 79.2 (1978): 75–86.

Faust, Drew. "'Trying to Do a Man's Business': Slavery, Violence and Gender in the American Civil War." *Gender and History* 4.2 (1992): 197–214.

Feldman, Glenn. "Lynching in Alabama, 1889–1921." *Alabama Review* 48.2 (1995): 114–141.

Fenn, Elizabeth. "'A Perfect Equality Seemed to Reign': Slave Society and Jonkonnu." *North Carolina Historical Review* 65.2 (1988): 127–153.

Filene, Benjamin. "'Our Singing Country': John and Alan Lomax, Leadbelly, and the Construction of an American Past." *American Quarterly* 43.4 (1991): 602–624.

Finkle, Lee. "The Conservative Aims of Militant Rhetoric: Black Protest during World War II." *Journal of American History* 60.3 (1973): 693–713.

Fletcher, Marvin E. "The Black Bicycle Corps." *Arizona and the West* 16.3 (1974): 219–232.

———. "The Black Volunteers in the Spanish-American War." *Military Affairs* 38.2 (1974): 48–53.

Flusche, Michael. "On the Color Line: Charles Waddell Chesnutt." *North Carolina Historical Review* 53.1 (1976): 1–24.

Franklin, Clyde W. "Black Male–White Male Perceptual Conflict." *Western Journal of Black Studies* 6.1 (1982): 2–9.

———. "Conceptual and Logical Issues in Theory and Research Related to Black Masculinity." *Western Journal of Black Studies* 10.4 (1986): 161–166.

Freeman, Richard B. "The Relation of Criminal Activity to Black Youth Employment." *Review of Black Political Economy* 16.1/2 (1987): 99–108.

Fryer, Paul H. "Brown-Eyed Handsome Man: Chuck Berry and the Blues Tradition." *Phylon* 42.1 (1981): 60–72.

Gabbard, Krin. "Signifyin(g) the Phallus: *Mo' Better Blues* and the Representations of the Jazz Trumpet." *Cinema Journal* 32.1 (1992): 43–62.

Gaines, Kevin. "Assimilationist Minstrelsy as Racial Uplift Ideology: James D. Corrother's Literary Quest for Black Leadership." *American Quarterly* 45.3 (1993): 341–369.

Gaston, John C. "The Destruction of the Young Black Male: The Impact of Popular Culture and Organized Sports." *Journal of Black Studies* 16.4 (1986): 369–384.

Gatewood, Willard B., Jr. "Black Americans and the Boer War, 1899–1902." *South Atlantic Quarterly* 75.2 (1976): 226–244.

———. "John Francis Cook, Antebellum Black Presbyterian." *American Presbyterians* 67.3 (1989): 221–230.

———. "'To Be Truly Free': Louis Sheridan and the Colonization of Liberia." *Civil War History* 29.4 (1983): 332–348.

Geary, Lynette G. "Jules Bledsoe: The Original 'Ol' Man River.'" *Black Perspective in Music* 17.1–2 (1989): 27–54.

Genovese, Eugene D. "Black Plantation Preachers in the Slave South." *Southern Studies* 2.3/4 (1991): 203–229.

Gibson, Donald B. "Strategies and Revisions of Self Representation in Booker T. Washington's Autobiographies." *American Quarterly* 45.3 (1993): 370–393.

Gill, Glenda E. "Careerist and Casualty: The Rise and Fall of Canada Lee." *Freedomways* 21.1 (1981): 15–27.

Gilman, Stuart. "Black Rebellion in the 1960's: Between Non-violence and Black Power." *Ethnicity* 8.4 (1981): 452–475.

Gilmore, Al-Tony. "The Myth, Legend, and Folklore of Joe Louis: The Impression of Sport on Society." *South Atlantic Quarterly* 82.3 (1983): 257–268.

Gleijeses, Piero. "African Americans and the War against Spain." *North Carolina Historical Review* 73.2 (1996): 184–214.

Gough, Robert. "Black Men and the Early New Jersey Militia." *New Jersey History* 88.4 (1970): 227–238.

Gower, Calvin W. "Edgar G. Brown, a Civil Rights Advocate in Franklin D. Roosevelt's 'Black Cabinet.'" *Western Journal of Black Studies* 8.2 (1984): 111–119.

Griffin, Joseph. "Calling, Naming, and Coming of Age in Ernest Gaines' 'A Gathering of Old Men.'" *Names* 40.2 (1992): 89–98.

Grim, Valerie. "Black Participation in the Farmers Home Administration and Agricultural Stabilization and Conservation Service, 1964–1990." *Agricultural History* 70.2 (1996): 320–336.

Gross, Seymour. "History, Politics and Literature: The Myth of Nat Turner." *American Quarterly* 23.4 (1971): 487–518.

Grothaus, Larry. "'The Inevitable Mr. Gaines': The Long Struggle to Desegregate the University of Missouri, 1936–1950." *Arizona and the West* 26 (1984): 21–42.

Haller, Mark. "Policy Gambling, Entertainment, and the Emergence of Black Politics: Chicago from 1900–1940." *Journal of Social History* 24.4 (1991): 719–739.

Hardin, John A. "Green Pinckney Russell of Kentucky Normal and Industrial Institute for Colored Persons." *Journal of Black Studies* 25.5 (1995): 610–621.

Hardwick, Kevin. "'Your Old Father Abe Lincoln is Dead and Damned': Black Soldiers and the Memphis Race Riot of 1886." *Journal of Social History* 27.1 (1993): 109–128.

Harris, Robert, Jr. "Charleston's Free Afro-American Elite: The Brown Fellowship Society and the Humane Brotherhood." *South Carolina Historical Magazine* 82.4 (1981): 289–310.

Hartnett, Stephen. "Cultural Postmodernism and Bobby McFerrin: A Case Study of Musical Production as the Composition of Spectacle." *Cultural Critique* 16 (1990): 61–85.

Hay, Fred. "The Sacred/Profane Dialectic in Delta Blues: The Life and Lyrics of Sonny Boy Williamson." *Phylon* 48.4 (1987): 317–327.

Hayles, Robert, and Ronald Perry. "Racial Equality in the American Naval Justice System: An Analysis of Incarceration Differentials." *Ethnic and Racial Studies* 4.1 (1981): 44–55.

Hine, Darlene Clark. "Carter G. Woodson, White Philanthropy and Negro Historiography." *History Teacher* 19.3 (1986): 405–425.

Hine, William C. "Black Politicians in Reconstruction Charleston, South Carolina: A Collective Study." *Journal of Southern History* 49.4 (1983): 555–584.

Hodes, Martha. "The Sexualization of Reconstruction Politics: White Women and Black Men in the South after the Civil War." *Journal of the History of Sexuality* 3.3 (1993): 402–417.

Holland, Antonio F. "Education over Politics: Nathan B. Young at Florida A&M College, 1901–1923." *Agricultural History* 65.2 (1991): 131–148.

Holmlund, Christine. "Visible Difference and Flex Appeal: The Body, Sex, Sexuality, and Race in the Pumping Iron Films." *Cinema Journal* 28.4 (1989): 39–51.

Horton, James. "Freedom's Yoke: Gender Conventions among Antebellum Free Blacks." *Feminist Studies* 12.1 (1986): 50–76.

Horton, James Oliver, and Lois E. Horton. "Race and Class." *American Quarterly* 35.1–2 (1983): 155–168.

Howard, Vicki. "The Courtship Letters of an African American Couple: Race, Gender, Class, and the Cult of True Womanhood." *Southwestern Historical Quarterly* 100.1 (1996): 64–80.

Howland, Jacob. "Black Boy: A Story of Soul-Making and a Quest for the Real." *Phylon* 47.2 (1986): 117–127.

Hunter, Andrea, and James Davis. "Constructing Gender: An Exploration of Afro-American Men's Conceptions of Manhood." *Gender and Society* 6.3 (1992): 464–479.

Hyatt, Marshall. "'The Political Ned Negro': Neval Thomas, Civil Rights Ideologue." *Western Journal of Black Studies* 13.2 (1989): 92–102.

Inscoe, John. "Generation and Gender as Reflected in Carolina Slave Naming Practices: A Challenge to the Gutman Thesis." *South Carolina Historical Magazine* 94.4 (1993): 252–263.

Jackson, Kathryn. "LeRoi Jones and the New Black Writers of the Sixties." *Freedomways* 9.3 (1969): 232–247.

Jackson, Walter. "Between Socialism and Nationalism: The Young E. Franklin Frazier." *Reconstruction* 1.3 (1991): 124–134.

James, Portia. "Hubert H. Harrison and the New Negro Movement." *Western Journal of Black Studies* 13.2 (1989): 82–91.

Janken, Kenneth. "African-American Intellectuals Confront the 'Silent South': The *What the Negro Wants* Controversy." *North Carolina Historical Review* 70.2 (1993): 153–179.

JanMohamed, Abdul R. "Negating the Negation as a Form of Affirmation in Minority Discourse: The Construction of Richard Wright as Subject." *Cultural Critique: The Nature and Context of Minority Discourse* 2.7 (1987): 245–267.

Japtok, Martin. "Between 'Race' as Construct and 'Race' as Essence: The Autobiography of an Ex-Coloured Man." *Southern Literary Journal* 28.2 (1996): 33–47.

Jezierski, John. "Photographing the Lumber Boom: The Goodridge Brothers of Saginaw, Michigan (1863–1922)." *Michigan History* 64.6 (1980): 28–33.

Johnson, Charles. "The Army, the Negro and the Civilian Conservation Corps, 1933–1942." *Military Affairs* 36.3 (1972): 82–88.

Johnson, Victoria. "Polyphony and Cultural Expression: Interpreting Musical Traditions in *Do the Right Thing*." *Film Quarterly* 47.2 (1993–94): 18–29.

Jones, George. "The Black Hessians: Negroes Recruited by the Hessians in South Carolina and Other Colonies." *South Carolina Historical Magazine* 83.4 (1982): 287–302.

Jordan, William. "'The Damnable Dilemma': African-American Accommodation and Protest during World War I." *Journal of American History* 81.4 (1995): 1562–1590.

Judy, R. A. T. "On the Question of Nigga Authenticity." *Boundary* 2 21.3 (1994): 211–230.

Kahn, Robert M. "The Political Ideology of Martin Delany." *Journal of Black Studies* 14.4 (1984): 415–440.

Kelley, Robin D. G. "'Comrades, Praise Gawd for Lenin and Them!': Ideology and Culture among Black Communists in Alabama, 1930–1935." *Science and Society* 52.1 (1988): 58–82.

King, Samantha. "The Politics of the Body and the Body Politic: Magic Johnson and the Ideology of Aids." *Sociology of Sport Journal* 10.3 (1993): 270–285.

Kremer, Gary R. "For Justice and a Fee: James Milton Turner and the Cherokee Freedmen." *Chronicles of Oklahoma* 58.41 (1980–81): 376–391.

Kuyk, Betty M. "The African Derivation of Black Fraternal Orders in the United States." *Comparative Studies in Society and History* 25.4 (1943): 559–592.

Lacey, Barbara E. "Visual Images of Blacks in Early American Imprints." *William and Mary Quarterly* 53.1 (1996): 137–180.

Lanning, Michael Lee. "Reconstruction and the Indian Wars." In Lanning, *The African-American Soldier: From Crispus Attucks to Colin Powell*, 62–81, 295–296. New Jersey: Carol Publishing Group, 1997.

Larson, Tom. "The Effect of Discrimination and Segregation on Black Male Migration." *Review of Black Political Economy* 20.3 (1992): 53–74.

Lehman, Cynthia. "The Social and Political Views of Charles Chesnutt: Reflections on His Major Works." *Journal of Black Studies* 26.3 (1996): 275–286.

Levesque, George A. "Boston's Black Brahmin: Dr. John S. Rock." *Civil War History* 26.4 (1980): 326–346.

Lewis, Ronald. "Race and the United Mine Workers' Union in Tennessee: Selected Letters of William R. Riley, 1842–1845." *Tennessee Historical Quarterly* 36.4 (1977): 524–536.

Lichtenstein, Alex. "'A Constant Struggle between Interest and Humanity': Convict Labor in the Coal Mines of the New South." *Labor's Heritage* 7.2 (1995): 64–77.

Lindfors, Bernth. "'Nothing extenuate, nor set down aught in malice': New Biographical Information on Ira Aldridge." *African American Review* 28.3 (1994): 457–472.

Lindroth, Colette. "Spike Lee and the American Tradition." *Literature/Film Quarterly* 24.1 (1996): 26–30.

Littlefield, Daniel F., and Patricia Washington McGraw. "The Arkansas Freeman, 1869–1870: Birth of the Black Press in Arkansas." *Phylon* 40.1 (1979): 75–85.

Lively, Adam. "Continuity and Radicalism in American Black Nationalist Thought, 1914–1929." *Journal of American Studies* 18.2 (1984): 207–236.

Logan, Frenise. "Black and Republican: Vicissitudes of a Minority Twice Over in the North Carolina House Of Representatives, 1876–1877." *North Carolina Historical Review* 61.3 (1984): 310–346.

MacMaster, Richard. "Henry Highland Garnet and the African Civilization Society." *Journal of Presbyterian History* 48.1 (1970): 95–112.

Mahiri, Jabari. "African American Males and Learning: What Discourse in Sports Offers Schooling." *Anthropology and Education* 25.3 (1994): 364–375.

Maloney, Thomas. "Degrees of Inequality: The Advance of Black Male Workers in the Northern Meat Packing and Steel Industries before World War II." *Social Science History* 19.1 (1995): 30–62.

Marable, Manning. "The Politics of Black Land Tenure." *Agricultural History* 53.1 (1979): 142–152.

Massood, Paula. "Mapping the Hood: The Genealogy of City Space in *Boyz n the Hood* and *Menace to Society*." *Cinema Journal* 35.2 (1996): 85–97.

Matthews, John M. "Jefferson Franklin Long: The Public Career of Georgia's First Black Congressman." *Phylon* 42.2 (1981): 145–156.

Mayberry, B. D. "The Tuskegee Movable School: A Unique Contribution to National and International Agriculture and Rural Development." *Agricultural History* 65.2 (1991): 85–104.

McCallum, Brenda. "Songs of Work and Songs of Worship: Sanctifying Black Unionism in the Southern City of Steel." *New York Folklore* 14.1–2 (1988): 9–33.

McGuire, Philip. "Judge William H. Hastie and Army Recruitment, 1940–1942." *Military Affairs* 42.2 (1978): 75–79.

McLean-Meyinese, Patricia, and Adell Brown, Jr. "Survival Strategies of Successful Black Farmers." *Review of Black Political Economy* 22.4 (1994): 73–82.

McMillen, Neil. "Perry W. Howard, Boss of Black-and-Tan Republicanism in Mississippi, 1924–1960." *Journal of Southern History* 48.2 (1982): 205–224.

McTighe, Michael. "Jesse Jackson and the Dilemmas of a Prophet in Politics." *Journal of Church and State* 32.3 (1989): 585–607.

Meier, August. "Benjamin Quarles and the Historiography of Black America." *Civil War History* 26.2 (1980): 101–116.

Miller, Ivor. "Night Train: The Power That Man Made." *New York Folklore* 17.1–2 (1991): 21–43.

Miller, Laura, and Charles Moskos. "Humanitarians or Warriors? Race, Gender, and Combat Status in Operation Restore Hope." *Armed Forces and Society* 21.4 (1995): 615–637.

Moore, Moses N. "Righteousness Exalts a Nation: Black Clergymen, Reform, and New School Presbyterianism." *American Presbyterians* 70.4 (1992): 222–238.

Mootry, Maria K. "J. Saunders Redding: A Case Study of the Black Intellectual." *Western Journal of Black Studies* 7.2 (1983): 62–67.

Mormino, Gary. "GI Joe Meets Jim Crow: Racial Violence and Reform in World War II Florida." *Florida Historical Quarterly* 73.1 (1994): 23–42.

Moses, Wilson. "Where Honor Is Due: Frederick Douglass as Representative Black Man." *Prospects* 17 (1993): 177–189.

Moses, Yolanda T. "Laurence Foster, a Black Anthropologist: His Life and Work." *Western Journal of Black Studies* 7.1 (1983): 36–42.

Nadell, James. "*Boyz n the Hood*: A Colonial Analysis." *Journal of Black Studies* 25.4 (1995): 447–463.

Naison, Mark. "Black Agrarian Radicalism in the Great Depression: The Threads of a Lost Tradition." *Journal of Ethnic Studies* (1973): 47–65.

Nelson, Bruce. "Organized Labor and the Struggle for Black Equality in Mobile during World War II." *Journal of American History* 80.3 (1993): 952–988.

Newton, Merlin Owen. "Rosco Jones and the Alabama Judicial Establishment." *Alabama Review* 48.2 (1995): 83–95.

Oja, Carol J. "'New Music' and the 'New Negro': The Background of William Grant Still's Afro-American Symphony." *Black Music Research Journal* 12.2 (1992): 145–170.

Oldfield, J. R. "A High and Honorable Calling: Black Lawyers in South Carolina, 1868–1915." *Journal of American Studies* 23.3 (1989): 395–406.

Outland, Robert. "Slavery, Work, and the Geography of the North Carolina Naval Stores Industry, 1835–1860." *Journal of Southern History* 62.1 (1996): 27–56.

Palmer, Annette. "The Politics of Race and War: Black American Soldiers in the Caribbean Theatre during the Second World War." *Military Affairs* 47.2 (1983): 59–62.

Park, Marlene. "Lynching and Antilynching: Art and Politics in the 1930's." *Prospects* 18 (1993): 311–365.

Patrick-Stamp, Leslie. "Numbers That Are Not New: African Americans in the Country's First Prison." *Pennsylvania Magazine* 119.1/2 (1995): 95–128.

Philips, Paul. "The Interracial Impact of Marshall Keeble, Black Evangelist, 1878–1968." *Tennessee Historical Quarterly* 36.1 (1977): 62–74.

Piliawsky, Monte. "The Impact of Black Mayors on the Black Community: The Case of New Orleans' Earnest Morial." *Review of Black Political Economy* 13.4 (1985): 5–24.

Pitre, Mergione. "The Economic Philosophy of Martin L. King, Jr." *Review of Black Political Economy* 9.2 (1979): 191–198.

Poe, William. "Lott Cary: Man of Purchased Freedom." *Church History* 39.1 (1970): 49–61.

Porter, Kenneth W. "Negro Labor in the Western Cattle Industry, 1866–1900." *Labor History* 10.3 (1969): 345–374.

Price, Hollis F., Jr. "The Cost of Male Subemployment in the Black Community." *Review of Black Political Economy* 6.2 (1976): 213–224.

Raboteau, Albert J. "Fire in the Bones: African-American Christianity and Autobiographical Reflection." *America* 170.18 (1994): 4–9.

Rachleff, Marshall, ed. "Economic Self Interest versus Racial Control: Mobile's Protest against the Jailing of Black Seamen." *Civil War History* 25.1 (1979): 84–88.

Ransby, Barbara, and Tracye Matthews. "Black Popular Culture and the Transcendence of Patriarchal Illusions." *Race and Class* 35.1 (1993): 57–68.

Redkey, Edwin S. "Black Chaplains in the Union Army." *Civil War History* 33.4 (1987): 331–350.

Reed, Merl. "The FEPC, the Black Worker, and the Southern Shipyards." *South Atlantic Quarterly* 74.4 (1975): 446–467.

Reich, Steven. "Soldiers of Democracy: Black Texans and the Fight for Citizenship, 1917–1921." *Journal of American History* 82.4 (1996): 1478–1485.

Richardson, Joe M. "'Labor Is Rest to Me Here in This the Lord's Vineyard': Hardy Mobley, Black Missionary during Reconstruction." *Southern Studies* 22.1 (1983): 5–20.

Riggs, Gayle D., and Lynn Dwyer. "Salary Discrimination by Black Males? Evidence from an Historically Black University." *American Journal of Economics and Sociology* 54.2 (1995): 231–238.

Riis, Thomas L. "Bob Cole: His Life and Legacy to Black Musical Theatre." *Black Perspective in Music* 13.2 (1985): 135–150.

Riss, Arthur. "Racial Essentialism and Family Values in *Uncle Tom's Cabin*." *American Quarterly* 46.4 (1994): 513–544.

Roberts, Randy. "Galveston's Jack Johnson: Flourishing in the Dark." *Southwestern Historical Quarterly* 87.1 (1983): 36–56.

Roberts, Rita. "Patriotism and Political Criticism: The Evolution of Political Consciousness in the Mind of a Black Revolutionary Soldier." *Eighteenth-Century Studies* 27.4 (1994): 569–614.

Rousey, Dennis C. "Black Policemen in New Orleans during Reconstruction." *Historian* 49.2 (1987): 223–243.

———. "Yellow Fever and Black Policemen in Memphis: A Post-Reconstruction Anomaly." *Journal of Southern History* 51.3 (1985): 357–374.

Rout, Leslie. "Some Post-war Developments in Jazz." *Midcontinent American Studies Journal* 9.2 (1968): 27–50.

Rubin, Anne Sarah. "Reflections on the Death of Emmett Till." *Southern Cultures* 2.1 (1996): 45–66.

Rushdy, Ashraf. "The Properties of Desire: Forms of Slave Identity in Charles Johnson's *Middle Passage*." *Arizona Quarterly* 50.2 (1994): 72–108.

Saillant, John. "The Black Body Erotic and the Republican Body Politic, 1790–1820." *Journal of the History of Sexuality* 5.3 (1995): 403–428.

Savitt, Todd L. "Entering a White Profession: Black Physicians in the New South, 1880–1920." *Bulletin of the History of Medicine* 61.4 (1987): 507–540.

Schubert, Frank. "The Suggs Affray: The Black Cavalry in the Johnson County War." *Western Historical Quarterly* 4.1 (1973): 57–68.

Schweninger, Loren. "James Rapier and the Negro Labor Movement, 1869–1872." *Alabama Review* 28.3 (1975): 185–201.

———. "John Carruthers Stanly and the Anomaly of Black Slaveholding." *North Carolina Historical Review* 67.2 (1990): 159–192.

———. "A Vanishing Breed: Black Farm Owners in the South, 1651–1982." *Agricultural History* 63.3 (1989): 41–61.

Shelden, Randall. "From Slave to Caste Society: Penal Changes in Tennessee, 1830–1915." *Tennessee Historical Quarterly* 38.4 (1979): 463–478.

Shepperson, George. "The Afro-American Contribution to African Studies." *Journal of American Studies* 8.3 (December 1974): 281–301.

Sherer, Robert G., Jr. "John William Beverly: Alabama's First Negro Historian." *Alabama Review* 26.3 (July 1973): 194–208.

Sitkoff, Harvard. "Racial Militancy and Interracial Violence in the Second World War." *Journal of American History* 58.3 (1971): 661–681.

Skinner, Robert. "The Black Man in the Literature of Labor." *Labor's Heritage* 1.3 (1989): 51–66.

Skotnes, Andor. "'Buy Where You Can Work': Boycotting for Jobs in African-American Baltimore, 1933–1934." *Journal of Social History* 27.4 (1994): 734–761.

Slotkin, Richard. "Narratives of Negro Crime in New England, 1675–1800." *American Quarterly* 25.1 (1973): 3–31.

Slovenz, Madeline. "'Rock the House': The Aesthetic Dimensions of Rap Music in New York City." *New York Folklore* 14.3–4 (1988): 151–163.

Smith, David. "Amiri Baraka and the Black Arts of Black Art." *Boundary 2* 15.1–2 (1986–87): 235–254.

Smith, Eric. "'Asking for Justice and Fair Play': African American State Legislators and Civil Rights in Early Twentieth-Century Pennsylvania." *Pennsylvania History* 63.2 (1996): 169–203.

Smith, Ronald. "The Paul Robeson–Jackie Robinson Saga and a Political Collision." *Journal of Sport History* 6.2 (1979): 5–27.

Smith, Thomas G. "Outside the Pale: The Exclusion of Blacks from the National Football League, 1934–1946." *Journal of Sport History* 15.3 (1988): 255–281.

Smith, Timothy. "Slavery and Theology: The Emergence of Black Christian Consciousness in Nineteenth-Century America." *Church History* 41.4 (December 1972): 497–512.

Sommers, Richard J. "The Dutch Gap Affair: Military Atrocities and Rights of Negro Soldiers." *Civil War History* 21.1 (1975): 51–64.

Southern, Eileen. "In Retrospect: Letters from W. C. Handy to William Grant Still." *Black Perspective in Music* 7.2 (1979): 197–235.

———. "In Retrospect: Letters from W. C. Handy to William Grant Still. Part 2." *Black Perspective in Music* 8.1 (1980): 63–119.

Spillers, Hortense. "The Crisis of the Negro Intellectual." *Boundary* 2 21.3 (1994): 64–116.

Staples, Robert. "Black Manhood in the 1970's: A Critical Look Back." *Black Scholar* 12.3 (1981): 2–9.

Stone, Albert E. "After *Black Boy* and *Dusk of Dawn*: Patterns in Recent Black Autobiography." *Phylon* 39.1 (1978): 18–34.

———. "The Return of Nat Turner in Sixties America." *Prospects* 12 (1987): 223–253.

Storhoff, Gary. "Reflections of Identity in *A Soldier's Story*." *Literature/Film Quarterly* 19.1 (1991): 21–26.

Swift, David E. "Black Presbyterian Attacks on Racism: Samuel Cornish, Theodore Wright and Their Contemporaries." *Presbyterian History* 51.4 (1973): 433–470.

Tausky, Curt, and William J. Wilson. "Work Attachment among Black Men." *Phylon* 32.1 (1971): 23–30.

TeSelle, Eugene. "The Nashville Institute and Roger Williams University: Benevolence, Paternalism, and Black Consciousness, 1867–1910." *Tennessee Historical Quarterly* 41.4 (1982): 360–379.

Thorp, Daniel. "Chattel with a Soul: The Autobiography of a Moravian Slave." *Pennsylvania Magazine* 112.3 (1988): 433–451.

Trotman, C. James. "Matthew Anderson: Black Pastor, Churchman, and Social Reformer." *American Presbyterians* 66.1 (1988): 11–21.

Tyler, Bruce. "Black Jive and White Repression." *Journal of Ethnic Studies* 16.4 (1989): 31–66.

Vandeburg, William. "Elite Slave Behaviour during the Civil War: Black Drivers and Foremen in Historiographical Perspective." *Southern Studies* 16.3 (1977): 253–269.

"'A Very Stern Discipline': An Interview with Ralph Ellison." *Harper's* (March 1967): 76–95.

Wade-Lewis, Margaret. "Lorenzo Dow Turner: Pioneer African-American Linguist." *Black Scholar* 21.4 (1991): 10–24.

Watson, Charles. "Portrayals of the Black and the Idea of Progress: Simms and Douglass." *Southern Studies* 20.4 (1981): 339–350.

Weeks, Louis. "Racism, World War I and the Christian Life: Francis J. Grimke in the Nation's Capital." *Journal of Presbyterian History* 51.4 (1973): 471–488.

Westwood, Howard C. "Captive Black Union Soldiers in Charleston—What to Do?" *Civil War History* 28.1 (1982): 28–44.

———. "The Cause and Consequence of a Union Black Soldier's Mutiny and Execution." *Civil War History* 31.3 (1985): 222–236.

———. "Mr. Smalls: A Slave No More." *Times* 25.3 (1986): 20–23, 28–31.

Whatley, Warren. "African-American Strikebreaking from the Civil War to the New Deal." *Social Science History* 17.4 (1993).

White, Frances. "Africa on My Mind: Gender, Counter Discourse and African-American Nationalism." *Journal of Women's History* 2.1 (1990): 73–97.

Whitman, Stephen. "Industrial Slavery at the Margin: The Maryland Chemical Works." *Journal of Southern History* 59.1 (1993): 31–62.

Wiegman, Robyn. "The Anatomy of Lynching." *Journal of the History of Sexuality* 3.3 (1993): 445–467.

Wiggins, David K. "'The Future of College Athletics Is at Stake': Black Athletes and Racial Turmoil on Three Predominantly White University Campuses, 1968–1972." *Journal of Sport History* 15.3 (1988): 204–333.

——. "'Great Speed but Little Stamina': The Historical Debate over Black Athletic Superiority." *Journal of Sport History* 16.2 (1989): 158–185.

——. "Peter Jackson and the Elusive Heavyweight Championship: A Black Athlete's Struggle against the Late Nineteenth Century Color-Line." *Journal of Sport History* 12.2 (1985): 143–168.

——. "Wendell Smith, the Pittsburgh *Courier-Journal* and the Campaign to Include Blacks in Organized Baseball, 1933–1945." *Journal of Sport History* 10.2 (1983): 5–29.

Williams, Brett. "The Heroic Appeal of John Henry." In *John Henry: A Bibliography*, 110–126. Connecticut: Greenwood Press, 1983.

Williams, Donald R. "Job Characteristics and the Labor Force Participation Behavior of Black and White Male Youth." *Review of Black Political Economy* 18.2 (1989): 5–24.

Williams, Nudie. "The African Lion: George Napier Perkins, Lawyer, Politician, Editor." *Chronicles of Oklahoma* 70.4 (1992–93): 450–465.

——. "Black Men Who Wore the Star." *Chronicles of Oklahoma* 59.1 (1981): 83–90.

——. "The Black Press in Oklahoma: The Formative Years, 1889–1907." *Chronicles of Oklahoma* 61.3 (1983): 308–319.

——. "United States vs. Bass Reeves: Black Lawman on Trial." *Chronicles of Oklahoma* 68.2 (1990): 154–167.

Wilson, Dale. "Recipe for Failure: Major General Edward M. Almond and Preparation of the U.S. 2d Infantry Division for Combat in World War II." *Journal of Military History* 56.3 (1992): 473–479.

Wright, Beverly. "Ideological Change and Black Identity during Civil Rights Movements." *Western Journal of Black Studies* 5.3 (1981): 186–198.

Wright, George C. "The Billy Club and the Ballot: Police Intimidation of Blacks in Louisville, Kentucky, 1880–1930." *Southern Studies* 23.1 (1984): 20–41.

Wright, W. D. "The Thought and Leadership of Kelly Miller." *Phylon* 39.2 (1978): 180–191.

Wyatt-Brown, Bertram. "The Mask of Obedience: Male Slave Psychology in the Old South." *American Historical Review* 93 (1988): 1228–1252.

Wynes, Charles. "William Henry Heard: Politician, Diplomat, A.M.E. Churchman." *Southern Studies* 20.4 (1981): 384–393.

INDEX

DARLENE CLARK HINE is John A. Hannah Professor of History at Michigan State University. She is co-editor of *More Than Chattel: Black Women and Slavery in the Americas*, co-author of *A Shining Thread of Hope: The History of Black Women in America*, and author of *Hine Sight: Black Women and the Reconstruction of American History*.

EARNESTINE JENKINS is Assistant Professor of Art History in African and African American Art in the Department of Art at the University of Memphis. She has published articles that have appeared in numerous books and journals, including *Milestones in Black American History* and *Aspects of Ethiopian Art*.